ATTITUDES AND OPINIONS

STUART OSKAMP

Claremont Graduate School

In collaboration with:

Catherine Cameron *LaVerne College*
Mark W. Lipsey *Claremont Graduate School*
Burton Mindick *Claremont Graduate School*
Theodore Weissbach *Pomona College*

PRENTICE-HALL, INC.
Englewood Cliffs, New Jersey 07632

Library of Congress Cataloging in Publication Data

OSKAMP, STUART.
    Attitudes and opinions.

    Bibliography: p.
    Includes index.
    1. Public opinion.   2. Attitude (Psychology)
3. Public opinion polls.   I. Title.
HM261.075 1977   301.15'4   76-52999
ISBN 0-13-050393-2

Clinical and Social Psychology Series, RICHARD LAZARUS, editor

Printed in the United States of America

10 9 8 7 6 5 4 3 2 1

Prentice-Hall International, Inc., *London*
Prentice-Hall of Australia Pty. Limited, *Sydney*
Prentice-Hall of Canada, Ltd., *Toronto*
Prentice-Hall of India Private Limited, *New Delhi*
Prentice-Hall of Japan, Inc., *Tokyo*
Prentice-Hall of Southeast Asia Pte. Ltd., *Singapore*
Whitehall Books Limited, *Wellington, New Zealand*

To Cathy, help-mate, lover, and colleague,
And to David and Karen, my joy and occasional sadness,
who I hope will become my friends.

Contents

Preface

Writing a book is not just another task to be completed. For me, as for many authors, it has become a major slice in my life, continuing for many years from concept through planning, to writing, revisions, and the final profusion of details to be checked and rechecked. Having invested years of energy and hopefulness, drudgery and sleepless nights in this volume, what can I tell you, the reader, about it that will be useful in providing perspective?

First, attitudes and opinions are crucial in people's daily lives and in the affairs of groups, organizations, and nations. We all show our recognition of this fact by the frequency and stress with which we refer to people's attitudes and related concepts such as beliefs, values, and intentions. The famous psychologist Gordon Allport went so far as to state that attitude was the most indispensable concept in the field of social psychology. Yet surprisingly, texts by psychologists generally give attitudes a skimpy and narrowly-focused treatment, at best.

Second, the area of attitudes and opinions is not just the province of psychologists and laymen. Among other disciplines, sociologists and political scientists have a long-standing commitment to this area of study, and even historians and philosophers have closely related interests. If we divide social scientists according to their methodological approaches, which cut across disciplinary boundaries, at least five different groups have strong vested interests in the topic of attitudes and opinions: descriptive researchers, measurement specialists, public opinion pollers, theorists, and experimenters. Consequently, this book on attitudes and opinions makes a strong attempt to bridge the gaps between these methodological approaches and between the various behavioral science disciplines. Wherever possible, it brings together experimental data, field observations, and survey findings as well as theories and measurement principles, and it considers them from an interdisciplinary perspective.

Breadth of coverage is one over-riding goal of this volume. The aim is a balanced and thorough treatment of the field, avoiding the one-sided emphasis of so many texts in this area. Many other textbooks have concentrated exclusively on one or two aspects of the field, such as (a) attitude theories, (b) attitude change, or (c) attitude measurement. These topics are given due attention here, but in addition major sections of the book are devoted to (d) conceptual questions, (e) the structure and function of attitudes, (f) the nature of public opinion, (g) public opinion polling, (h) attitude formation, (i) communication of attitudes and opinions, (j) problems and prospects in the field, and (k) the content of public opinion on a number of socially-important topics.

Relevance is the second major goal of this book. It focuses strongly on meaningful and important research, attempting to show its connection with issues and concerns which are salient and recurrent in people's lives. In particular, Part II of the book, on the content of public opinion, covers many social issues of current importance. These topics include political attitudes and voting behavior, international attitudes, racism and prejudice, sexism, attitudes on pollution and the environment, and attitudes toward population issues.

This book is intended primarily for upper-division or graduate students in courses on Attitudes, on Survey Research, on Public Opinion, or on other related topics. Such courses, which presuppose at least a basic introduction to the principles of social science research, may be offered in departments of Psychology, Sociology, and/or Political Science.

I have tried to keep constantly in mind the needs and interests of potential readers. In keeping with the emphasis on relevance, the writing style aims at readability and interest, but without talking down to the reader. As learning aids, each chapter features an introductory outline, a thorough summary, and annotated suggestions for further reading. For students with limited backgrounds in research-oriented courses, Chapter 2 contains a brief section to help clarify the ways in which research findings are presented. On the other end of the continuum, I have tried to serve the needs of advanced students for a scholarly reference work by including a very large number of citations to the research literature (from two to ten times as many as other texts in this area). Thus the book aims to be rigorous in approach, but also interesting both in content and style.

I hope you will find that these goals have been met, at least to a substantial degree, and that the book will satisfy your expectations and hopes.

THANKS

Like most authors, I owe more intellectual and personal debts for this book's form and content than I can acknowledge or am even still aware of. Foremost among my expressions of thanks I must mention Claremont Graduate School, my professional home for 17 years, which has provided me with a congenial atmosphere, precious freedom in structuring my professional activities, and the opportunity to earn a salary for learning things that interest me and doing things I (mostly) enjoy. My faculty colleagues and graduate students have supported and stimulated me far more than I can express or repay, and many colleagues elsewhere have also encouraged my professional development and evolving interests.

My four collaborators on this book deserve thanks for their careful and thorough work, as well as for promptness and efficiency which allowed the book to be published on schedule. I also want to acknowledge the reviewers whose suggestions and criticisms helped to make this a better book. They are Robert Abelson, Yale University; Clive Davis, Syracuse University; Kay Deaux, Purdue University; John McConahay, Duke University; Norman Miller, University of Southern California; William Samuel, California State University at Sacramento; Joy Stapp, University of Texas at Austin; and Stephen Thayer, City College of the City University of New York.

I am also grateful to Barbara Stewart for drawing the art work and to Linda Stevens, Georgine Pion, and Jane Gray, who have rendered yeoman service at the typewriter. Finally, my wife and children have provided inspiration in ways they never realized—just by being themselves and helping to make my life happy and rewarding. To them I lovingly dedicate this work.

STUART OSKAMP

ATTITUDES
AND
OPINIONS

part I

Approaches to Studying Attitudes and Opinions

In this section the most important aspects of attitude and opinion research are discussed. Chapter 1 introduces the history and concepts of the field. Chapters 2 and 3 discuss the measurement of attitudes and their structure and functions while Chapters 4 and 5 cover the procedures of public opinion polling and the structure of public opinion. Next, a chapter on how attitudes and opinions are formed is followed by one on how they are communicated. Chapters 8 and 9, on attitude change, present both theories and research findings, as well as methodological issues. The final chapter in this part, Chapter 10, takes up problems and prospects in order to put the field of attitudes and opinions into some perspective.

Part II of the book deals with the content of public opinion. It focuses on several classical areas and a number of current important topics. Included in Part II are: political attitudes and voting, international attitudes, racism and prejudice, sexism and women's roles, attitudes toward pollution and ecology, and attitudes toward population problems.

chapter 1

Background:
History and Concepts

The concept of attitude is probably the most distinctive and indispensable concept in contemporary American social psychology.—Gordon W. Allport.

The development of sociology as a natural science has been hindered by . . . too much attention to subjective factors, such as . . . attitudes.—Read Bain.

Opinion has caused more trouble on this little earth than plagues or earthquakes.—Voltaire.

These varied statements suggest some of the conflict that has occurred over the years concerning the topic of attitudes and opinions. The positions of eminent and reputable social scientists have ranged from espousing ''attitude'' as an indispensable concept to damning it as an unscientific notion not worthy of study. In short, attitudes about ''attitude'' have varied widely. This book will try to clarify these controversies and to provide its readers with a factual foundation for an informed opinion on the topic of attitudes—as well as a balanced attitude on the topic of opinions!

WHY STUDY ATTITUDES?

In 1935, when social psychology was still in its formative stages as an area of study, Gordon Allport stressed the central importance of attitudes, writing: ''This useful, one might almost say peaceful, concept has been so widely adopted that it has virtually established itself as the keystone in the edifice of American social psychology'' (Allport, 1935, p. 798).

In 1969, following several decades of burgeoning laboratory and field research in social psychology, McGuire's monumental review of the attitude literature

Photograph courtesy of Harvard
University News Office. Reprinted by
permission.

Box 1-1 GORDON ALLPORT, *Champion of Attitudes*

Gordon Allport (1897–1967) was one of the most famous and beloved social psychologists of his day. He received his B.A., M.A., and Ph.D. from Harvard and taught there continuously since 1930. He has served as chairman of Harvard's psychology department, president of the American Psychological Association, editor of the major journal in social psychology for 12 years, and member of numerous national and international committees.

Allport's interests within social psychology were broad. He wrote several major text-books on personality, as well as The Psychology of Rumor, The Nature of Prejudice, The Psychology of Radio, *books on religion, expressive movement, and research methods, and also over 200 articles. An authority on attitudes, he wrote classic chapters covering that topic in three successive editions of the* Handbook of Social Psychology *(1935, 1954, and 1968).*

echoed Allport's conclusion: "Attitude research has in the past decade returned to the dominant status within social psychology that it had 30 years ago, after passing through an era in the 1950s when it was overshadowed by work in the group-dynamics area" (McGuire, 1969, p. 136). Even more recently, Kelman (1974, p. 310) has concurred: "In the years since publication of Allport's paper, attitudes have, if anything, become even more central in social psychology." Laymen, as well as scientists, frequently use the concept of attitude in their descriptions and explanations of human behavior. For instance, "She has a very good attitude toward her work." Or, "His suspicious attitude made me want to avoid him." In everyday conversation we often speak of a person's attitude as the cause of his actions toward another person or an object; e.g., "Her hostile attitude was shown in everything she did." Similarly, in his 1935 review, Allport concluded that the concept of attitudes was "bearing most of the descriptive and explanatory burdens of social psychology" (Allport, 1935, p. 804).

Why is attitude such a popular and useful concept? We can point to several reasons:

(1) "Attitude" is a *shorthand* term. A single attitude (e.g., love for one's family) can summarize many different behaviors (spending time with them, kissing them, comforting them, agreeing with them, doing things for them).

(2) An attitude can be considered the *cause* of a person's behavior toward another person or an object.

(3) The concept of attitude helps to explain the *consistency* of a person's behavior, since a single attitude may underlie many different actions. (In turn, Allport says, the consistency of individual behavior helps to explain the stability of society.)

(4) Attitudes are *important in their own right,* regardless of their relation to a person's behavior. Your attitudes toward various individuals, institutions, and social issues (e.g., a political party, the church, capital punishment, the President of the United States) reflect the way you perceive the world around you, and they are worth studying for their own sake.

(5) The concept of attitude includes the idea of *unconscious determinants* of behavior and the dynamic interplay of conflicting motives, whose importance has been stressed by Freud and other psychoanalysts.

(6) The concept of attitude *bridges the controversy between heredity and environment* as factors influencing behavior, for both instinct and learning can be involved in the formation of attitudes.

(7) Within psychology, the concept of attitude provides a *common topic of interest* for schools of thought as diverse as phenomenology and behaviorism.

(8) Within the field of sociology, some authors have viewed attitudes as the most central concept and the *basis of all social behavior,* since they provide the mechanism by which cultural patterns influence individual behavior.

(9) Within political science, the concept *public opinion* is essential as a sum-

mary of the shared attitudes of the members of a society, i.e., attitudes that are important and highly standardized within the society.

Yet, in spite of the popularity and apparent utility of the concept of attitude to laymen and scientists alike, some scientists have challenged the value of the concept. Some of the crucial issues in this debate are analyzed in later chapters. In particular, the relation of attitudes to behavior and the influence of public opinion on public policy are discussed in Chapter 10.

Five Ways of Studying Attitudes

Five different ways of studying attitudes and opinions have typified most of the research studies in the area. Surprisingly, there has been very little overlap or interaction between the adherents of these five approaches, so that in most cases their work has been carried on with little cross-fertilization from the methods or findings of the other groups of researchers. This compartmentalization has undoubtedly served to hold back scientific progress to some extent, and it is hoped that the interdisciplinary character of this book will help to remove this obstacle. The five different approaches are:

Description. Attitude describers typically study the views held by a single interesting group of people (for instance, unwed mothers, or state legislators). Or they may compare the opinions of two or more groups (for example, the attitudes of white-collar workers versus those of blue-collar workers on the topic of labor unions). To some extent they may overlap with the next two groups of researchers (the measurers and the pollers), but the describers are usually less concerned with sophisticated quantification than are the measurers and less concerned with representative sampling than are the pollers.

Measurement. Attitude measurers have developed many highly sophisticated methods for quantifying and scaling attitudes. The best-known methods of building attitude scales are those of Bogardus, Thurstone, Likert, Guttman, and Osgood, which will be discussed in Chapter 2. It is surprising, but true, that public opinion pollers and attitude experimenters have made very little use of these sophisticated measurement methods, and attitude describers have made only a little more use of them.

Polls. Public opinion pollers are generally concerned with the attitudes on important social issues held by very large groups of people (for instance, the voting intentions of all registered voters of a state, or the opinions concerning drug abuse and drug laws held by all adult citizens). The procedures and problems of public opinion polling are discussed in Chapter 4. Some of the best-known polling organizations are those headed by George Gallup, Elmo Roper, and Louis Harris. At their best, polls are careful to *sample* systematically or randomly (rather than haphazardly) from the total population so that their results will be *representative* of the opinions of the total population.

Theories. Attitude theorists are primarily concerned with describing the basic nature of attitudes, how attitudes are formed, and how they can be changed. In most cases they have not been concerned with the precise measurement of attitudes nor with their content, socially important or not. However, since they need to demonstrate the correctness of their theories through experimental evidence, there has been more overlap and interaction between the theorists and the experimenters than between any of the other groups. Chapters 8 and 9 will discuss both theories and research on attitude change.

Experiments. By definition, experiments involve manipulating a situation so as to create two or more different levels of the independent variable (for instance, two different kinds of persuasive message) and observing their effect on the dependent variable. Attitude experimenters have concentrated on investigating the factors that can produce attitude *change* and on testing the hypotheses of the attitude theorists. They have usually been relatively unconcerned with sophisticated measurement methods, and they have usually chosen to experiment on attitude topics of little importance or relevance to their subjects, since such attitudes can more easily be changed in a short-term laboratory situation. However, there have also been a number of experiments done on topics of greater social importance, such as basic personal values, racial attitudes, or health-care practices.

DEFINITIONS OF "ATTITUDE"

So far we have been using the term "attitude" without defining it. Since it is a common term in the English language, every reader will probably have a notion of its meaning. Unfortunately, however, there may be little overlap between the notions of different readers. Indeed, there has sometimes been little overlap between the definitions of "attitude" suggested by different social scientists.

Originally the term "attitude" referred to a person's bodily position or posture, and it is still sometimes used in this way—for example, "He sat slumped in an attitude of dejection."

In social science, however, the term has come to mean a "posture of the mind," rather than of the body. In his careful review, Allport cited many definitions with varying emphases and concluded with a comprehensive definition of his own which has been widely adopted. The aspects stressed in the various definitions include attitude as a mental set or disposition, attitude as a readiness to respond, the physiological basis of attitudes, their permanence, their learned nature, and their evaluative character. Sample definitions illustrating each of these points are presented in Box 1-2, together with Allport's comprehensive definition. Though Allport's definition may seem unduly complex, careful thought will show that each of its phrases makes a specific and important contribution to understanding the concept. Interested readers might want to consult

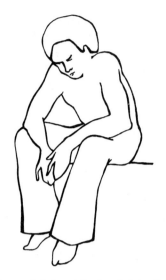

Figure 1-1 An attitude of dejection.

McGuire's chapter for a detailed presentation of the implications of every aspect of the definition (McGuire, 1969, pp. 142–149).

The central feature of all these definitions of attitude, according to Allport, is the idea of **readiness for response**. That is, an attitude is not behavior, not something that a person does; rather it is a preparation for behavior, a predisposition to respond in a particular way to the attitude object. The term **attitude object** is used to include things, people, places, ideas, or situations, either singular or plural. For instance, it could be a group of people (e.g., teenagers), or an inanimate object (e.g., the city park), or an abstract concept (e.g., equality), or an idea linking several concepts (e.g., equal rights of teenagers to drink beer in the city park).

Another point to note is the **motivating** or driving force of attitudes. That is, attitudes are not just a passive result of past experience; instead they impel behavior and guide its form and manner. Allport suggests this motivating force by describing an attitude as "exerting a directive or dynamic influence."

The **relatively enduring** nature of attitudes is also important. This stability has been illustrated in a recent study by Thistlethwaite (1974). Three successive yearly measures of many different attitudes of men enrolled at 25 American universities showed that even the tremendous impact of the 1970 campus protests of the U.S. Cambodian incursion and the Kent State and Jackson State student shootings had a relatively small average effect on relevant social attitudes of these students. The most striking finding of the study was the stability of individuals' attitude scores over the three-year period. Newcomb has also provided evidence for the relative stability of attitudes of his former Bennington College students over a period of *25 years*. For instance, he showed that their political

---

Box 1-2 *Differing Definitions of "Attitude"*

Many different aspects of the concept of "attitude" have been stressed in definitions offered by different authors:*

SET—[An attitude] denotes the general set of the organism as a whole toward an object or situation which calls for adjustment. (Lundberg, 1929)

READINESS TO ACT—Attitude . . . a condition of readiness for a certain type of activity. (Warren, 1934)

PHYSIOLOGICAL BASIS—The attitude, or preparation in advance of the actual response, constitutes an important determinant of the ensuing social behavior. Such neural settings, with their accompanying consciousness, are numerous and significant in social life. (F.H. Allport, 1924)

PERMANENCE— . . . a more or less permanently enduring state of readiness of mental organization which predisposes an individual to react in a characteristic way to any object or situation with which it is related. (Cantril, 1934)

LEARNED NATURE—An attitude, roughly, is a residuum of experience, by which further activity is conditioned and controlled. . . . We may think of attitudes as acquired tendencies to act in specific ways toward objects. (Krueger & Reckless, 1931)

EVALUATIVE NATURE—An attitude is a tendency to act toward or against something in the environment, which becomes thereby a positive or negative value. (Bogardus, 1931)

COMPREHENSIVE DEFINITION—An attitude is a mental or neural state of readiness, organized through experience, exerting a directive or dynamic influence upon the individual's response to all objects and situations with which it is related. (G.W. Allport, 1935)

*The sources of all these definitions are fully referenced in Allport (1935).

Source: Extracts from pages 804, 805, and 810 of Allport, G. W., Attitudes. In C. Murchison (Ed.), *A Handbook of Social Psychology*. Worcester, Mass.: Clark University Press, 1935.

---

and economic attitudes, measured when they were in college in the early 1930s, were significantly related to their voting patterns in the 1960 presidential election between Kennedy and Nixon (Newcomb, Koenig, Flacks, & Warwick, 1967).

In recent years the **evaluative** aspect of attitudes has been increasingly stressed. That is, an attitude is now generally seen as a disposition to respond *in a favorable or unfavorable manner* to given objects. For example, in many studies the evaluative dimension of Osgood's Semantic Differential (Osgood, Suci, & Tannenbaum, 1957) is used *alone*, without other dimensions, as the sole measure of attitudes. This emphasis is clearly shown in Bem's simple definition: "Attitudes are likes and dislikes" (1970, p. 14). Though this statement is an oversimplification, it emphasizes the central importance of the evaluative aspect of attitudes.

Since all of these aspects of attitudes are important, a comprehensive definition of the concept will be used in this book. Another useful example of such a comprehensive definition of attitude is offered by Fishbein and Ajzen (1975, p. 6): "a learned predisposition to respond in a consistently favorable or unfavorable manner with respect to a given object."

COMPONENTS OF ATTITUDES

One common view of attitudes is that they have three components:

(1) A **cognitive** component, consisting of the ideas and beliefs which the attitude-holder has about the attitude object. For example, let us take Martians as an attitude object (you can substitute any other group if you wish). Examples of the cognitive component of an attitude would be:

"Martians look strange—they have green skins and antennae coming out of their foreheads, you know."

"Martians can read your thoughts."

(2) An **affective (emotional)** component. This refers to the feelings and emotions one has toward the object. For instance:

"Martians make me feel uncomfortable—I feel queasy to think of them reading my mind."

"I don't like Martians."

(3) A **behavioral** component, consisting of one's action tendencies toward the object. For example:

"If I saw a Martian, I'd run away as fast as I could."

"I certainly wouldn't let one into my club or allow my daughter to marry one."

This conceptual distinction between thoughts, feelings, and actions as separate but interrelated parts of an attitude has a long history in philosophy. Though the term "attitude" was first used by Herbert Spencer in 1862 (Allport, 1935, p. 799), the thought-emotion-behavior distinction is essentially identical with one made by Plato, who used the terminology of cognition, affection, and conation.

However, honored as this tripartite division is in tradition, and clear as it seems conceptually, there is still an important question about its *empirical* validity and usefulness. It is conceivable that one or more of the components are really unimportant and do not have any relationship to events in the real world. Or, it is also possible that the three components are so closely interrelated as to be indistinguishable when we attempt to measure them carefully. McGuire (1969) suggests that this latter possibility is supported by most of the available research evidence and consequently "that theorists who insist on distinguishing them should bear the burden of proving that the distinction is worthwhile" (p. 157). We will take up this unresolved question at length in Chapter 3.

Distinction Between Beliefs, Attitudes, and Behavioral Intentions

A theoretical approach that maintains a somewhat different distinction between the three components has been proposed by Fishbein and Ajzen (1972). They suggest that the term "attitude" be reserved solely for the affective dimension, indicating evaluation or favorability toward an object. The cognitive dimension they label as "beliefs," which they define as indicating a person's subjective probability that an object has a particular characteristic (for example, how sure the person feels that "This book is interesting," or that "Smoking marijuana is no more dangerous than drinking alcohol"). The behavioral dimension they refer to as "behavioral intentions," defined as indicating a person's subjective probability that (s)he will perform a particular behavior toward an object (e.g., "I intend to read this book," or "I am going to write my congressman asking him to vote for legalization of marijuana").

Fishbein and Ajzen point out that a person usually has various beliefs about the same object and that these beliefs are not necessarily related. For instance, if someone believes "This book is interesting," that person may or may not also believe that "This book is attractively printed" or that "This book is inexpensive." The same situation also holds true for behavioral intentions. "I intend to read this book" does not imply "I am going to buy this book" nor even "I am going to study this book carefully." By contrast, these authors say, all measures of a person's *affect* toward a particular object should be highly related. "I like this book" *does* imply "I enjoy reading it," and such responses should be quite consistent with the same person's answers to an attitude scale evaluating the book.

A final point about Fishbein and Ajzen's view of attitudes is that there is no necessary congruence between beliefs, attitudes, and behavioral intentions, though some writers would consider them components of the same attitude. For Fishbein and Ajzen, "I like this book" (attitude) does *not* necessarily imply "This book is inexpensive" (belief), nor does it imply "I am going to buy this book" (behavioral intention). Thus these distinctions provide a justification for treating the three concepts as entirely separate entities. As we will see later, this viewpoint seems to have both theoretical and empirical advantages over the older tripartite view of attitude components.

RELATED CONCEPTS

At this point we will present brief definitions of several other terms which are related to the concept of attitude, or are sometimes even used synonymously with it. Again, keep in mind that each of these terms has been used and defined in various ways, and that there would not be complete agreement with the definitions offered here. However, these definitions will help to clarify the distinction between these terms and the concept of attitude.

Belief

We have seen that Fishbein and Ajzen (1972) define **beliefs** as statements indicating a person's subjective probability that an object has a particular characteristic. Another way of putting this is that they assert the truth or falsity of propositions about the object, or that they state a relationship between the object and some characteristic. For instance: "This book is informative," "Einstein's theory of relativity is important," "My boss is easygoing." This viewpoint is advantageous in that it distinguishes clearly between beliefs and attitudes: beliefs are cognitive—thoughts and ideas; whereas attitudes are affective—feelings and emotions.

This raises a question, however, about how to treat an intermediate category which we may call **evaluative beliefs:** that is, beliefs which state a value judgment about an object. For instance: "My boss is a nice guy," or "Freedom of the press is a good thing." Clearly, evaluative beliefs are closely linked to attitudes of liking or disliking, and sometimes they are almost indistinguishable from them. For instance: "My boss is a nice guy" (evaluative belief), and "I like my boss" (attitude). The best approach seems to be to consider a person's attitude toward an object as *a summary of all of his evaluative beliefs about the object.*

An alternative approach is to consider beliefs, both evaluative and nonevaluative, as the cognitive component of attitudes (cf. Krech, Crutchfield, & Ballachey, 1962, p. 178). However, this approach may produce problems because it implies a necessary consistency between the three components of attitudes. As mentioned in the previous section, often beliefs and attitudes are not completely consistent, and sometimes they are not even closely related. Thus, this approach is less desirable than drawing a clear distinction between beliefs and attitudes.

Opinion

As the title of this book indicates, **opinion** is an important concept and one closely related to the concept of attitude. Oftentimes the two terms have been used synonymously, leading McGuire (1969, p. 152) to characterize the situation as "names in search of a distinction, rather than a distinction in search of a terminology." When distinctions between attitude and opinion have been drawn, they have been of several general types.

One viewpoint, and the one that we prefer, *equates opinions with beliefs;* that is, they are generally narrower in content or scope than the broad evaluative orientation which we call an attitude, and they are primarily cognitive rather than emotion-laden. Another way of putting this is that opinions involve a person's judgments about the likelihood of events or relationships, whereas attitudes involve a person's wishes and desires about events or relationships (McGuire, 1960). Thus, according to this viewpoint, "I think this book is interesting" is an opinion; "I want to buy this book" is an attitude.

Another viewpoint distinguishes between attitude and opinion in terms of verifiability: opinions deal with matters which are factual (that is, at least potentially verifiable., whereas attitudes deal with unverifiable matters involving personal taste or preference (Osgood, Suci, & Tannenbaum, 1957). A major disadvantage of this view is that it uses the term "opinion" in a way contrary to the common-sense layman's view that opinions deal with matters of judgment rather than of fact.

Another proposed distinction is based on overtness versus covertness: the ultimate extension of this view is to regard an opinion as merely the overt verbal or written expression of an underlying, covert attitude (e.g., Childs, 1965). However, if that is the only distinction, there is no need for two different terms, since one can just as easily use the term "attitude statement" instead of opinion. Also, this distinction is undesirable because it is contrary to the common-sense notions that a person can hold an opinion even if he doesn't express it, and that a person can state an attitude in words.

McGuire (1969) warns about definitional distinctions such as the ones we have been considering, emphasizing that in order to be useful they must have clearcut empirical consequences. He suggests that we should

> allow distinctions between sets of beliefs called "opinions" and others called "attitudes" only insofar as it has been demonstrated that one set behaves differently from the other in an experimental situation. If, for example, order effects in persuasion are shown to be different for [the two sets], then the distinction should be maintained (p. 153).

Though McGuire doubts the value of this distinction, we shall see in Chapter 3 that there seem to be sound theoretical and empirical reasons for maintaining it.

Value

There is more general agreement about the relationship of values to attitudes than about the previous terms. The most common view is that a **value** is an important life-goal or standard of behavior for a person—a standard toward which the individual has a strong positive attitude. For instance, a person may value happiness, freedom, service to others, self-actualization, or even the acquisition of money as a major goal in life. Values are the most important and central elements in a person's system of attitudes and beliefs. They are ends rather than means; they are the goals a person strives for and which help to determine many of his (her) other attitudes and beliefs.

Habit

Habits can also be easily distinguished from attitudes. They are frequently-repeated patterns of behavior, whereas attitudes are not behavior. Habits are usually quite automatic and standardized in their manner of performance, but they require the presence of the appropriate stimulus object in order to occur (e.g., saying "sir" to a superior officer in the armed forces). By contrast, attitudes may be expressed in many different ways, and even in the absence of the stimulus object (e.g., I like to watch snow falling even though, as a Southern Californian, I haven't seen any close-up in several years). Like attitudes, habits are learned through experience, but unlike them, they are frequently nonevaluative in nature. For instance, a habit of scratching one's head or of saying "you know" frequently in conversation does not necessarily imply a favorable attitude toward these activities. However, some habits are evaluative; for instance a habit of voting Democratic probably would imply a favorable attitude toward the Democratic Party (Allport, 1935).

ATTITUDES ARE INFERRED

We have defined attitudes as constituting a readiness for response, but we stated that they are not behavior per se. Thus, it follows that they cannot be directly observed, as habits or other responses can be. How then can we reach conclusions about them? Only through a process of inference, based on the study of responses which *are* observable. Allport (1935) phrased the situation clearly:

> how does one know that [attitudes] exist at all? Only by necessary inference. There *must* be something to account for the consistency of conduct. It is the meaningful resemblances between activities and their congruence with one another that leads the psychologist inescapably to postulate some such generalized forms of readiness as the term "attitude" denotes (p. 836).

More recently, Campbell (1963) has agreed: "A social attitude is (or is evidenced by) consistency in response to social objects" (p. 96).

Thus an attitude has the status of an **intervening variable:** that is, an attitude is a theoretical construct which is not observable in itself, but which mediates or helps to explain the relationship between certain observable stimulus events (the environmental situation) and certain behavioral responses. For instance, as McGuire (1969) suggests, the concept that a man has a prejudiced attitude can help to explain the relationship between such an antecedent event as his being seated next to a black person and such responses as an increase in his galvanic skin response (GSR) measure, or his getting up and moving to a different chair. Similarly, a person's political attitudes can help to explain why he would go to hear and cheer a speech by one political candidate, but turn off the TV when a different candidate was on the air.

A diagram of this view of attitudes is shown in Figure 1-2. It indicates that a person's attitudes are the result of his past experiences (both vicarious and actual), and that they combine with the present stimulus situation to determine his responses.

Latent Process Viewpoint.   This definition of attitude as an unobservable intervening variable has also been termed the "latent process" viewpoint (De-

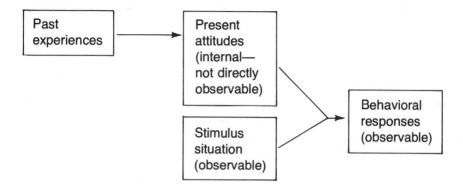

Figure 1-2 Attitudes are unobservable intervening variables which influence the relationship between stimulus events and behavioral responses.

Fleur & Westie, 1963). That is, this viewpoint postulates a hidden process occurring within the individual, which we call his attitude; and it uses his attitude as an explanation of the relationship between stimulus events and the individual's responses.

Probability Viewpoint. Another viewpoint on the nature of attitudes is the behavioristic, or positivistic, one (for others see McGuire, 1969, pp. 144–147). This viewpoint avoids all intervening variables and insists on direct operational measures of all concepts used. In this framework "attitude" would be defined as a particular type of response, rather than as a readiness to respond. For instance, a person's attitude might be operationally defined as his response to a specific question, or to a set of questions about his likes and dislikes, or as an increase in his GSR measure, or as his willingness to be photographed in a social situation with a Negro* of the opposite sex. DeFleur and Westie (1963) have called this the "probability" definition of attitude—defining it in terms of the probability of occurrence of a particular response or type of response.

There are a number of difficulties presented by the probability position. First, a habit is a typical response or behavior pattern of an individual, and its probability of occurrence can be determined. But, as mentioned in the previous section, many habits are nonevaluative in nature and hence cannot be considered as attitudes. Thus the occurrence of such kinds of habitual responses could not be used as an indication of a person's attitude, and the same thing is true of many isolated nonhabitual responses: As Fishbein and Ajzen (1972) have pointed out:

---

*Throughout this book the words "black" and "Negro" are used interchangeably, generally depending on the usage of the original research reports which are referred to. Similarly, though we will try to combat grammatical sexism by frequent use of "(s)he" and "his (her)," when repetition makes that awkward, we will sometimes fall back on the use of the generalized "he" and "his."

"if a single belief or intention is to be used as an index of attitude, evidence has to be provided for a high correlation between responses to that item and some standard measure of attitude" (p. 496). On a different point, McGuire (1969) has raised the objection that the behavioristic viewpoint is inefficient, since it requires that the relationship between each antecedent measure and each response measure must be separately established, instead of linking each antecedent measure to just one intervening variable (the attitude) and then in turn linking the single attitude to the various response measures. Further, Campbell (1963) has pointed out that in actual practice the behaviorists follow the same procedure as other investigators by *inferring* attitudes from a pattern of responses:

> even those whose behavioristic orientation leads to a rejection of such mentalistic definitions as Allport's . . . in research practice do not equate *isolated* responses with attitudes; but on the contrary, look for the appearance of *response consistencies* (p. 96).

As mentioned earlier, the issue of the degree of consistency between beliefs, attitudes, and behavioral responses is still an open question, and an important one. We will take up two different aspects of this question at length in Chapter 3 and Chapter 10.

WHAT IS PUBLIC OPINION?

You are undoubtedly familiar with public opinion polls such as those of George Gallup and Louis Harris, and you know that they involve asking questions of large groups of people. However, you might be surprised to learn that the term "public opinion" is one which has led to just as many difficulties in definition as the term "attitude."

In general, **"public opinion"** refers to the shared opinions of large groups of people (sometimes called "publics"), who have particular characteristics in common, such as all adult male citizens of the state of Connecticut. However, there are some aspects of more complete definitions which have provoked debate for 200 years or more. Childs (1965) has reviewed these controversies in detail and concluded that it is unwisely restrictive to include additional specifications in defining "public opinion," such as the particular public involved, the subject matter of the opinions, or the extent of consensus, etc. Box 1-3 contains a sample of specific definitions of "public opinion," presented both for their quaintness and their historical interest. The list concludes with Child's general definition, which is recommended as the most useful one for our purposes because of its breadth and lack of restrictions.

Historically, public opinion polls were used to get indications of the strength of political candidates as early as 1824. In that year newspapers reported two

---

Box 1-3 *Differing Definitions of "Public Opinion"*

Many quaint definitions of the concept of "public opinion" have been suggested by different authors over the years, emphasizing the following specific aspects:*

RATIONALLY FORMED—Public opinion is the social judgment of a self-conscious community on a question of general import after rational public discussion. (Young, 1923)

WELL-INFORMED (ELITE GROUP)—Public opinion may be said to be that sentiment on any given subject which is entertained by the best informed, most intelligent, and most moral persons in the community. (MacKinnon, 1828)

HELD BY SECONDARY GROUP—When the group involved is a public or secondary group, rather than a primary, face-to-face group, we have public opinion (Folsom, 1931). What the members of any indirect contact group or public think or feel about anything and everything. (Bernard, 1926)

IMPORTANT TOPIC—The attitudes, feelings, or ideas of the large body of the people about important public issues. (Minar, 1960)

EXTENT OF AGREEMENT— . . . a majority is not enough, and unanimity is not required, but the opinion must be such that while the majority may not share it, they feel bound, by conviction, not by fear, to accept it. (Lowell, 1913)

INTENSITY— . . . public opinion is more than a matter of numbers. The intensity of the opinions is quite as important. Public opinion is a composite of numbers and intensity. (Munro, 1931)

MODE OF RESPONSE—Public opinion consists of people's reactions to definitely worded statements and questions under interview conditions. (Warner, 1939)

EFFECTIVE INFLUENCE—Public opinion in this discussion may simply be taken to mean those opinions held by private persons which governments find it prudent to heed. (Key, 1961)

GENERAL DEFINITION—The study of public opinion is, therefore, the study of collections of individual opinions wherever they may be found. (Childs, 1965)

*The sources of all these definitions are fully referenced in Childs (1965).

Source: Extracts from pp. 13–24 of *Public Opinion: Nature, Formation, and Role* by H. L. Childs. © 1965 by Litton Educational Publishing, Inc. Reprinted by permission of Van Nostrand Reinhold Co.

---

straw votes, one in Delaware and one in North Carolina, where a select group of citizens were asked who they preferred for President. Interestingly enough, Andrew Jackson won both of these "polls," though it was not until 1828 that he gained wide enough support to be elected President (Roll & Cantril, 1972).

APPROACHES TO ATTITUDE AND OPINION RESEARCH

The several disciplines which have been interested in attitudes and opinions have typically approached their study in rather different ways. The three major disciplines which treat attitudes and opinions as part of their subject matter are sociology, political science, and psychology. In each field there have been many scientists who have done excellent, highly-regarded work on attitudes and opinions, utilizing a variety of approaches. Though it is dangerous to overgeneralize, some of the five ways of studying attitudes mentioned early in this chapter are more common in each field than are others.

Photograph courtesy of Princeton University Archives. Reprinted by permission.

Box 1-4 HARWOOD CHILDS, *Authority on Public Opinion*

Harwood Childs (1898–1972) was a pioneer in the public opinion field. After receiving his B.A. and M.A. from Dartmouth, he taught briefly at two colleges before earning his Ph.D. in political science at the University of Chicago. Following three years' teaching at Bucknell, he joined the Princeton University faculty, remaining there until his retirement as Professor of Politics in 1966.

In 1936, Childs was founding editor of the Public Opinion Quarterly, *which became the most important journal in its field, and he again served as its editor in the 1960s. As the result of two research periods spent in Germany, he was one of the first Americans to recognize the evils of Nazism. He translated* The Nazi Primer, *edited* Propaganda and Dictatorship, *helped establish the U.S. foreign propaganda monitoring system before World War II, and wrote* Propaganda by Short Wave. *His three books on the nature of public opinion are considered classics in that area.*

In sociology, the most frequently used method of attitude research has been *description* of various social groups. Quite often the choice of groups to study has been based on variables such as social class or position in an organization (e.g. supervisors). To a lesser extent such research usually also involves some attitude *measurement*.

In political science, the most common approach has been *polling*, though again some workers have used other methods, particularly *description*. A predominant interest in political science has been the study of public opinion, and the most common way of determining public opinion is to use a face-to-face interview, asking many detailed questions of a large sample of people from the relevant classification (e.g., voters, PTA members, or business executives).

In psychology, the most common way of studying attitudes has been *experimentation*, though each of the other approaches has had its adherents. Usually the focus of experiments has been on attempts to change an attitude by manipulating one or more situational factors and/or measuring individual differences (such as personality dimensions) which are related to attitude change. Very often the attitude chosen for changing is one that is unimportant or even completely new to the subjects, so that it can be influenced more easily, and usually only immediate or short-term attitude change is studied. There are two favored settings for such research—the classroom and the laboratory—and McGuire (1969) has sketched out some of the typical differences between the types of research done in the two settings, as follows.

Classroom research, which may be typified by the work of Carl Hovland, generally studies large groups of subjects, involves relatively weak manipulations of the independent variable (usually a persuasive communication), uses statistical methods of controlling the effects of other variables, and concentrates on careful measurement of the dependent variable. In contrast, laboratory research, exemplified by the work of Leon Festinger, usually gives an individual experimental treatment to a smaller number of subjects, striving for a powerful manipulation of the independent variable (usually a theoretical concept), using careful experimental controls of other variables, but paying less attention to sophisticated measurement of the dependent variable.

We will see many of these research features and the approaches typical of each discipline illustrated in the ensuing chapters.

SUMMARY

The concept of attitude was a very important one in social psychology's formative years and still remains so today. Though many conflicting definitions have been offered, in general, an attitude can be defined as a readiness to respond in a favorable or unfavorable manner to a particular class of objects. Attitudes have been studied using five relatively-independent approaches: description, measurement, polls, theories, and experiments. A common view of attitudes is that they have three components: cognitive, affective, and behavioral. However, there is still disagreement about whether such a breakdown is either necessary or useful. An alternative approach is to consider these three aspects as separate and distinct dimensions, calling them beliefs, attitudes, and behavioral intentions.

Beliefs, opinions, values, and habits are concepts which are related to the concept of attitude, but are not synonymous with it. Whereas an attitude is a broad evaluative orientation toward an object, a belief or an opinion is narrower and more cognitive in nature. Public opinion refers to the shared opinions of large groups of people.

It is universally agreed that attitudes and opinions are inferred from behavioral responses, but there are conflicting views as to whether they should be considered theoretically as unobservable intervening variables (the viewpoint recommended in this text) or merely as summaries of observed response consistency.

Sociologists, political scientists, and psychologists have typically used different approaches to study attitudes and opinions, but all three disciplines have given a central place to these concepts. This book aims to clarify some of the conflicts concerning attitudes and opinions and to provide a basis for an informed opinion about attitudes (or vice versa).

Suggested Readings

Allport, G. W. The historical background of modern social psychology. In G. Lindzey & E. Aronson (Eds.), *The Handbook of Social Psychology* (2nd ed.), Vol. 1. Reading, Mass.: Addison-Wesley, 1968.—Pages 59–64 contain a brief history of the attitude concept in social science.

DeFleur, M. L. & Westie, F. R. Attitude as a scientific concept. *Social Forces*, 1963, 42, 17–31.—Contains a well-researched historical overview, a clear theoretical section, and a partisan advocacy of the probability conception of attitude in preference to the latent process conception.

Fishbein, M. & Ajzen, I. Attitudes and opinions. *Annual Review of Psychology*, 1972, 23, 487–544.—Pages 487–496 have a highly-critical bird's-eye view of recent attitude research and the authors' suggestions for resolving some of the confusion by more precise definitions of terms.

McGuire, W. J. The nature of attitudes and attitude change. In G. Lindzey & E. Aronson (Eds.), *The Handbook of Social Psychology* (2nd ed.). Vol. 3. Reading, Mass.: Addison-Wesley, 1969.—Pages 136–149 hold a brief historical review of attitude research and a detailed treatment of the definition and theoretical status of attitude.

chapter **2**

Measurement
of Attitudes

Man, I dig the Stones the most.

Businessmen are just out to make as much money as possible, and they don't give a damn about the poor consumer.

I wanted the President to win that election so badly I would have done anything to help him.

I just don't like Jews. They make me feel uncomfortable.

These are all expressions of attitudes. They describe a person's feelings toward another person, a group, or a situation. Attitudes can be expressed in many ways—with different words, different tonal inflections, and different degrees of intensity. Some of the color and richness of the ways in which attitudes and opinions are often expressed is captured in the quotations from actual public opinion interviews shown in Box 2-1.

How can statements like these be studied scientifically? In order to compare them in any systematic way, they have to be at least **classified** into two or more categories (e.g., pro-Negro vs. anti-Negro) or, preferably, **measured** on a quantitative scale (e.g., indicating *degree* of favorability or unfavorability). Furthermore, the classification or measurement must be **reliable**, that is, consistent. Reliability means (a) that two different raters agree on their classification of the statements most of the time, and also (b) that on two different occasions the respondents' statements are generally consistent.

Box 2-1 *Examples of Opinion Interview Responses*

The following responses are selected quotations from public opinion interviews conducted in 1968 by the Survey Research Center at the University of Michigan on the subject of white attitudes toward Negroes, and particularly toward the urban riots of the preceding year.

Just for fun, you might try to guess the sex, social class, and educational background of these two respondents. (Answers are printed at the end of the box.) Here are some quotes from the first respondent:

Q. What do you think was the main cause of these disturbances?

A. Nigger agitators. Martin Luther King and Rap Brown and that black bastard Carmichael.

Q. Have the disturbances helped or hurt the cause of Negro rights?

A. Hurt. Whites are starting to wise up what a danger these people can be. They are going to be tough from now on. People are fed up with giving in and giving them everything their little black hearts want.

Q. What do you think the city government could do to keep a disturbance from breaking out here?

A. Ship them all back to Africa. Lock up all the agitators and show them we mean business.

Q. Would you go along with a program of spending more money for jobs, schooling and housing for Negroes . . . or would you oppose it?

A. I'd oppose it. They're getting too much already. If they want something they can damn well work for it. The government would just waste the money anyway. . . .

Q. That finished the interview. Is there anything you would like to add to any of the subjects we've discussed?

A. I just want to say that I don't have anything against Negroes as long as they don't get pushy and stay in their place. One of my best buddies is a nigger so I don't have anything against them.

By contrast, here are some answers from a second respondent:

Q. What do you think was the main cause of these disturbances?

A. Dissatisfaction. They are dissatisfied with the way they live, the way they are treated and their place in the social structure of America.

Q. Have the disturbances helped or hurt the cause of Negro rights?

A. They have helped because they have forced white people to pay attention and have brought the subject out into the open and you can't ignore it anymore. They haven't helped yet but overall it will help. . . .

Q. What do you think the city government could do to help a disturbance from breaking out here?

A. Not only promise but actually improve conditions, education, housing, jobs, and social treatment . . .

(Answers: The first respondent was a 31-year-old single man with two years of college education, employed as a traveling salesman in California, but the son of a tobacco share-cropper in North Carolina. The second respondent was a young woman college graduate in Philadelphia.)

Source: Campbell, A. *White Attitudes toward Black People*. Ann Arbor, Mich.: Institute for Social Research, University of Michigan, Copyright © August 1971. Pp. 2–4.

TYPES OF ATTITUDE QUESTIONS

There are two basic types of questions which are used to obtain statements of attitudes and opinions. Some of the interview questions quoted in Box 2-1 are **open-end** questions, ones which give the respondent a free choice of how to answer and what to mention (e.g., "What do you think was the main cause of these disturbances?"). Other questions are **closed-end**, that is, ones which present two or more alternative answers for the respondent to choose between (e.g., "Have the disturbances helped or hurt the cause of Negro rights?"). Often an interview will use both types of questions because they have complementary advantages and disadvantages.

Open-end questions have the advantages of eliciting the full range, depth, and complexity of the respondent's own views, with minimal distortion, in his or her own words. They reduce the likelihood of overlooking important possible viewpoints which the investigator has not thought of or not included in the questionnaire. For these reasons they are often used as introductory questions to open up a topic, which will subsequently be probed more deeply and intensively with closed-end questions. (This is the **funnel sequence** of questioning.) The chief disadvantages of open-end questions are the difficulty and frequently the unreliability of scoring or **coding** them. That is, trying to decide how the response should be classified or what quantitative point on a scale it best represents can be difficult and time-consuming, and sometimes it cannot be done with adequate agreement between raters. For instance, how would you score the second respondent's answer in Box 2-1 that the disturbances "have helped. . . . They haven't helped yet but overall it will help. . . ."?

For these reasons closed-end questions are likely to make up a large majority of the items on most interviews and questionnaires. They have the advantages of being easy to score and relatively **objective**. That is, independent observers or scorers can reach a high percentage of agreement on which response was given or on what score should be assigned to the response. Of course, unlike open-end questions, they have the possible disadvantage that they may force the respondent to use the concepts, terms, and alternative answers preferred by the investigator, rather than expressing his own ideas and preferences (Lazarsfeld, 1944).

Closed-end questions have to be very carefully written so as not to lead to biased answers. Without such care in item construction, the results will be far less reliable, and sometimes they may be so slanted that they are seriously misleading. For instance, here is an item which was sent out on a questionnaire by U.S. Congressman John Dowdy of Texas (Wilcox, 1966, p. 390).

> . . . A drive has recently been announced to destroy the independence of the Congress by purging Congressmen who refuse to be rubber stamps for the executive arm of government. Would you want your Representative in Congress to surrender to the purge threat and become a rubber-stamped Congressman?
> YES_____ NO_____

Obviously, the question as it is worded pulls strongly for a "No" answer. Consequently, the reported response percentage undoubtedly greatly overestimated the number of Texas citizens who were really concerned about the issue.

Before proceeding to consider specific ways to measure attitudes and opinions, let us briefly review some of the ways in which attitude research results are typically presented and how they may be interpreted.

WAYS OF PRESENTING RESEARCH FINDINGS

The simplest way of reporting a group's opinions is to give **item response** percentages separately for each item (e.g., 30% say they are Republicans, 45% Democrats, and 25% Independents). Several items on the same general topic can be combined to form a **scale**, with a single score for the group of items computed for each respondent (e.g., a scale of political liberalism vs. conservatism). Scales give us a broader range of scores than a single item, and including more items increases the reliability of the overall score. **Frequency distributions** of all the scores for a group of respondents can be shown in tabular form or in graphs such as frequency polygons, histograms (bar graphs), or pie-charts. Comparison of a group's responses on two different items or scales is often presented in **crosstabulations**, such as this hypothetical breakdown of political party members:

	Democrats	Republicans
Liberal	40%	15%
Middle-of-the-road	40	45
Conservative	20	40
	100%	100%

Often it is useful to have a single number, such as the mean or median, which simply and precisely describes the scores of a whole group. Using such a number for each of two or more groups, we can perform a test of **statistical significance**, to see if the difference between the groups is large enough to be dependable —that is, not just a chance finding, but one which would be repeated in another similar study. For our present purposes, the precise mathematical formulas for significance tests are unimportant. It is only necessary to know that any such test ends by computing a probability (p) that the given result could have occurred by chance alone. If the p value is small enough (usually less than .05), we can conclude that the obtained difference between groups is a real one rather than a chance occurrence. We should also keep in mind that statistical significance is *not* synonymous with the importance of a finding, for a very small and unimportant difference can sometimes be significant. *Statistical significance is necessary but not sufficient* for a finding to be considered important.

Research results are often stated in terms of **correlations**, which indicate the amount of relationship between two variables or two attitude items (e.g., between age and political conservatism). The product-moment correlation coefficient (r) is defined in such a way that a value of $+1.00$ represents a perfect positive relationship between two variables, while a value of -1.00 represents a perfect negative (inverse) relationship, and 0.00 means a completely random (chance) relationship. The farther the value of r is from zero, the better is our ability to predict one variable by knowing the other one. The square of the correlation coefficient is equal to the proportion of variance which is accounted for by the relationship between the two variables. Thus an $r = .70$ accounts for 49% of the variance, but an $r = .50$ for only 25%.

A final statistical technique which needs some general understanding is **factor analysis**. It is based on the correlations between variables, and its goal is to find a few underlying "factors" which can summarize the pattern of correlations among a large number of variables. The computational procedures are very complex, but the basic principle involved is simple. Variables (or items) which are highly correlated are apt to "load on," or represent, the same "factor" or underlying dimension; while items having low intercorrelations will probably be found to load on different factors. After the basic factors are determined statistically, they are named and interpreted in terms of the variables which load most highly on each factor. Some further details on applications of factor analysis are given later in this chapter in the sections on Osgood's Semantic Differential and on Triandis' work with social distance measures.

Now let us consider the major types of scales that have been developed to measure attitudes.

ATTITUDE SCALING METHODS

During the late 1920s and early 1930s a number of attitude scaling methods were developed which are still in common use today. More recently a few additional methods have been developed which are also met in research reports. Each of the major attitude scaling techniques will be discussed below rather briefly, primarily to clarify their major characteristics and points of difference. This will not prepare you to use these methods yourself to build an attitude scale, but it will provide you with enough information to understand references to such methods later in this book or in the research literature.

In 1925 Bogardus was one of the first individuals to use quantitative measurement methods in the field of social psychology. Thus, surprisingly, the quantitative study of attitudes is just over 50 years old, even though quantitative research in psychology goes back about 100 years to the founding of Wundt's laboratory in 1879, though the term "attitude" has been used in the psychological sense for over a century, and though cognition, affect, and conation have been discussed by philosophers ever since the time of Plato. It is no wonder, considering this short history of quantitative research on attitudes and opinions, that many questions remain to be answered.

Bogardus' Social-Distance Scale

Bogardus (1925) proposed a scale of **social distance** that could be used to determine attitudes toward various racial or nationality groups, many of which at that time were relatively recent immigrants to the United States. For instance, people's attitudes toward Englishmen, Germans, and Turks could be compared by obtaining their judgments according to the following instructions:

> According to my first feeling reactions, I would willingly admit members of each race (as a class, and not the best I have known, nor the worst members) to one or more of the classifications under which I have placed a cross.
>
> 1. To close kinship by marriage
> 2. To my club as personal chums
> 3. To my street as neighbors
> 4. To employment in my occupation in my country
> 5. To citizenship in my country
> 6. As visitors only to my country
> 7. Would exclude from my country

As can be seen, the scale points progress systematically from acceptance of members of the racial or national group into the most intimate family relationships, down to complete exclusion of the group. The respondent's attitude score toward that group is taken as the closest degree of relationship which he is willing to accept. By computing a mean score for a group of respondents (for instance, farmers), their attitudes can be compared with those of another group, such as assembly-line workers.

More recent variations of this technique have allowed measurement of attitudes toward any social group, not just racial or nationality groups, and have also broadened the range of response options. Triandis (1964) has done extensive work in this area. Using factor analysis, he has found five relatively-independent dimensions of attitudes toward social classifications of people, and he has developed a scale having several items to measure each dimension. The five dimensions are listed below, together with a sample item for each (Triandis, 1971, p. 53):

1. Respect—admire the ideas of this person.
2. Marital Acceptance—fall in love with this person.
3. Friendship Acceptance—eat with this person.
4. Social Distance—exclude this person from my neighborhood.
5. Superordination—command this person.

This scale represents a considerable advance over the original social-distance measures, since it reflects some of the complexity of human social behavior. For instance, a person may feel very differently about relations with members of another race in intimate areas such as friendship and marriage than in more formal areas such as working together. (As one example, see Minard's [1952] data on the social relations of white and Negro coal miners in Chap. 10, Box 10-1.)

Thurstone's Method of Equal-Appearing Intervals

Thurstone (1928) proposed the next attitude scaling method. In contrast to the Bogardus scale, where the seven points were not necessarily considered as equidistant, Thurstone attempted to develop a method which would indicate rather precisely *the amount* of difference between one respondent's attitude and another's. The method that he developed is rather complex.

First, the investigator collects or constructs a large number (100 or so) of opinion statements representing favorable, neutral, and unfavorable views about the topic of interest (for instance, Thurstone studied attitudes toward the church, Negroes, capital punishment, birth control, etc.). Then the investigator must obtain a large group of people to serve as judges and rate each statement's favorability or unfavorability toward the topic. Each judge sorts the statements into eleven equally-spaced categories, disregarding his (her) own attitude toward the topic, and considering only how *favorable* or *unfavorable* the statement is toward the attitude object. Statements about which different judges show substantial disagreement are discarded as ambiguous; and other items may be discarded as irrelevant to the topic. The remaining statements are assigned **scale values** based on the median favorability rating of the judges. From these statements a final scale of about 20 items (or sometimes more) is selected, using two criteria. The aim is to choose items having (a) scale values at approximately **equal intervals** along the 11-point scale of favorability, and (b) high agreement among the judges' ratings (that is, low spread or variability of their ratings).

After the items for the final scale have been chosen, they are randomly arranged on the questionnaire form without any indication of their scale values. Respondents check only the items they agree with and leave the others blank. A person's attitude toward the topic can then be defined as the mean (or the median, since both methods have been used) of the scale values of the items which he has checked.

An example of a Thurstone scale is shown in Box 2-2.

Box 2-2 *A Thurstone Scale of Attitudes Toward the Church*

A selection of some items from one of Thurstone's original scales is shown below. Although the items are arranged here in the order of their scale values, on the actual questionnaire form they would be arranged in random order, and the scale values would not be shown.

Scale value	Item no.	Item
0.2	31.	I believe the church is the greatest institution in America today.
1.2	44.	I believe the church is a powerful agency for promoting both individual and social righteousness.
2.2	45.	I like to go to church for I get something worth while to think about and it keeps my mind filled with right thoughts.
3.3	29.	I enjoy my church because there is a spirit of friendliness there.
4.5	6.	I believe in what the church teaches but with mental reservations.
5.6	15.	Sometimes I feel that the church and religion are necessary and sometimes I doubt it.
6.7	32.	I believe in sincerity and goodness without any church ceremonies.
7.5	19.	I think too much money is being spent on the church for the benefit that is being derived.
8.3	1.	I think the teaching of the church is altogether too superficial to have much social significance.
9.2	41.	I think the church seeks to impose a lot of worn-out dogmas and medieval superstitions.
10.4	40.	The church represents shallowness, hypocrisy, and prejudice.
11.0	17.	I think the church is a parasite on society.

Source: Thurstone, L. L., & Chave, E. J. *The Measurement of Attitude*. Chicago: University of Chicago Press. Copyright 1929 by the University of Chicago. Pp. 61–63, 78–79.

Thurstone's method makes the important assumption that the opinions of the judges do not affect the scale values of the items obtained from their judgments. This assumption has been shown to be reasonably correct when the judges do not have extreme views on the topic. However, if many of the judges have extreme views or are highly ego-involved in the topic, the obtained scale values of the items will be affected (Hovland & Sherif, 1952). Specifically, judges who are highly favorable to a topic rate only a few of the most extreme statements as favorable, and they displace their ratings of most of the statements toward the unfavorable end of the judgment scale. The opposite is true for judges who are highly unfavorable toward a topic.

The other major drawback of Thurstone's method is that it is time-consuming and tedious to apply. For that reason it is used much less extensively than the method described next.

Likert's Method of Summated Ratings

Shortly after Thurstone's work, Likert (1932) proposed a simpler method of attitude scale construction which does not require the use of judges to rate the items' favorability. Better still, the reliability of Likert scales has been shown to be at least as high as that of the more difficult-to-construct Thurstone scales (Murphy & Likert, 1938; McNemar, 1946; Poppleton & Pilkington, 1964).

Likert's method was the first approach which measured the *extent* of the respondent's agreement with each item, rather than simply obtaining a "yes-no" response. In this method, again, a large number of opinion statements on a given topic are collected, but each one is phrased in such a way that it can be answered on a 5-point rating scale. For instance, here is an example from Likert's original scale of internationalism (Likert, 1932)—it is interesting to note how many of these attitude items still have an up-to-date ring:

> We should be willing to fight for our country whether it is in the right or in the wrong.
> ———— Strongly approve
> ———— Approve
> ———— Undecided
> ———— Disapprove
> ———— Strongly disapprove

Respondents check one of the five choices, which are scored 1, 2, 3, 4, and 5 respectively. (Of course, items on the opposite end of the continuum—ones expressing a favorable attitude toward internationalism—would be scored in reverse: 5, 4, 3, 2, and 1 respectively.) This method uses only items that are clearly positive or negative toward the attitude object, whereas Thurstone's method also requires some relatively neutral items.

As the name "summated ratings" indicates, a respondent's attitude score is determined by adding his ratings for all of the items. This procedure is based on the assumption that all of the items are measuring the same underlying attitude. As a consequence of this assumption it follows that all the items should be positively correlated, in contrast to the Thurstone method, which does not impose this requirement. Though the correlations between items are not usually high, since each item is measuring its own unique content as well as the general underlying attitude, the assumption can be, and should be, checked. The usual way to do this is to correlate the score on each item with the total score for the whole pool of items combined; any items with correlations near zero are discarded since they are not measuring the common factor shared by other items.

Photograph courtesy of Rensis Likert.
Reprinted by permission.

Box 2-3 RENSIS LIKERT, *Attitude Measurement Pioneer*

Rensis Likert's distinguished career has included pace-setting work in four major areas: attitude measurement, survey research methodology, research on organizational management, and applications of social science to important social problems. Beginning with an interest in engineering at the University of Michigan, he shifted to a Ph.D. in psychology at Columbia. His dissertation research, published in 1932, developed the attitude measurement technique which bears his name. After teaching briefly at New York University, he moved to full-time research on organizational management. In 1939, as founding Director of the Division of Program Surveys for the U.S. Department of Agriculture, he began making major contributions to methods of survey interviewing, probability sampling, and wartime public opinion research.

Following World War II, Likert founded the University of Michigan's Institute for Social Research, and under his leadership it became the largest university-based social science research agency in the U.S. Retiring in 1970, he started a consultation and research firm on organizational management. Author of 100 articles and six books, including New Patterns of Management *and* The Human Organization, *he has also been elected President of the American Statistical Association, a director of the American Psychological Association, and received the highest honor of the American Association for Public Opinion Research.*

A great strength of the Likert method is its use of **item analysis** techniques to "purify" the scale by keeping only the best items from the initial item pool. A common way of accomplishing this is to compare the groups of respondents scoring highest on the total pool of items (say, the top 25%) with the group scoring lowest (the bottom 25%), thus eliminating the middle group whose attitudes may be less clear, less consistent, less strongly-held, and less well-informed. If a particular item does not **discriminate** significantly between these groups—that is, does not have significantly different mean scores for the top and bottom groups—it is clear that it is measuring some other dimension than the general attitude involved in the scale. For example, in a scale of internationalist attitudes, a nondiscriminating item might be concerned with a hope for world peace, for high scorers (internationalists) and low scorers (isolationists) might both share this hope.

The Likert method of attitude scale construction quickly became and remains the most popular method, and a number of variations of it have also gained wide usage. One variation is to eliminate the "Undecided" or "Neutral" category, thus forcing respondents to choose between favorable and unfavorable stances. For instance, an item from the California F Scale, for measuring authoritarian or "fascist" attitudes, is scored as follows (Adorno, Frenkel-Brunswik, Levinson, & Sanford, 1950):

> An insult to our honor should always be punished.
> +1: slight support, agreement   −1: slight opposition, disagreement
> +2: moderate support, agreement   −2: moderate opposition, disagreement
> +3: strong support, agreement   −3: strong opposition, disagreement

A more important, and unfortunate, departure from Likert's procedure is the frequent omission of an item analysis. When this occurs, there is no empirical evidence that the items are all measuring the same underlying attitude, nor that they are useful, discriminating items. This situation is often signaled by use of the term "Likert-type" scale, which is apt to be an indication of hasty, slipshod research, quite out of keeping with Likert's own procedures.

Guttman's Scalogram Analysis

One of the limitations of both the Thurstone and Likert techniques is that the respondent's attitude score does not have a unique meaning. That is, any given score can be obtained in many different ways. On a Likert scale, for instance, a mid-range score can be obtained by giving mostly "undecided" responses, or by giving many "Strongly approve" responses balanced by many "Strongly disapprove" responses, or by both "Approve" and "Disapprove" responses, etc.

Guttman (1944) proposed a method in which scores would have unique meanings. This was to be accomplished by insuring that response patterns were

cumulative. That is, in the Guttman method, a respondent who is moderately favorable to the attitude object should answer ''yes'' to all of the items accepted by a mildly favorable respondent *plus* one or more additional items. Similarly, a strongly favorable respondent should endorse all the items accepted by moderately favorable respondents *plus* additional one(s).

This reasoning can be clarified by some examples. Actually, the top five steps on the Bogardus Social Distance Scale approximately fit these requirements, as can be seen on page 26. A respondent who was very unfavorable toward Negroes might be willing to accept them to citizenship in the country but not to the higher categories. Another person might agree to citizenship and also to equal employment. A favorable respondent might accept both of these items and also endorse accepting blacks into his neighborhood and his social club; and so on, up to respondents who agreed with all the items.

Guttman suggests that if a scale displays the cumulative pattern just described, we can be sure that it is **unidimensional**—i.e., that it is measuring just one underlying attitude. By contrast, Thurstone and Likert scales may be measuring two or more underlying dimensions, and Triandis' (1964) expansion of the social distance scale illustrates the possibility of several related but different dimensions in one measure (see page 27).

Guttman has proposed a stringent criterion for determining the unidimensionality of a scale, and as a consequence Guttman scales are apt to be quite short (perhaps 4–10 items) and restricted to a narrow topic. Box 2-4 presents an example of a Guttman scale constructed to measure attitudes toward racial integration (the ''attitude object''). Notice that all the items are on a rather narrow topic, concerning various aspects and examples of racial integration, while many other aspects of racial prejudice and discrimination are not represented. However, they could be included in other Guttman scales measuring other aspects of prejudice, such as stereotyped beliefs about blacks.

In order to develop a unidimensional scale by Guttman's procedure, an initial pool of items is given to a large group of respondents, each item being stated in a ''yes-no'' or ''agree-disagree'' format. Next, the items are arranged according to the number of respondents agreeing with them. In this procedure, by definition, the item agreed to by the fewest respondents is the item most favorable toward the attitude object (e.g., racial integration in the scale shown in Box 2-4); that is, it is the most-difficult-to-accept item. Each respondent's score is then determined very simply: it is merely the rank-number of the most favorable item which he endorsed (answered in the scored direction). The answers of each respondent are examined separately (usually by computer nowadays). This is done in order to discover all instances of inconsistent response patterns: that is, cases where a respondent endorses an item and fails to endorse one of the less-favorable items. According to the theory of measurement underlying this scaling method, each such instance is considered a response error, and no more than 10% of inconsistent responses are allowed if a scale is to be considered unidimensional. (Guttman refers to this as an **index of reproducibility** of .90 or higher). Items which

Box 2-4 *An Example of a Guttman Scale*

Attitudes toward racial integration were measured in a survey conducted in 1963 by the National Opinion Research Center. Responses to interview questions were obtained from a representative national sample of 1230 white adults.

The eight-item Guttman scale which was constructed from the survey responses is shown below. Items were scored in the pro-integration direction, and the scored responses are shown in parentheses. The mean scale score for the whole sample was 4.3, and some evidence of the scale's validity is furnished by the fact that the mean score for Southerners was 2.6, while for non-Southerners it was 5.0.

The index of reproducibility *of the scale was .93 (only 7% inconsistent responses), and the cumulative structure of the items was equally strong for Southern men, Southern women, non-Southern men, and non-Southern women. This scale is a Guttman scale because of the decreasing percentages of pro-integration answers on the successive questions,* and *the fact that most respondents who were scored on any given item also received points on* all *of the lower-numbered items.*

Items (in rank order, not in their order on the scale)	*% of pro-integration responses*
1. Do you think Negroes should have as good a chance as white people to get any kind of job, or do you think white people should have the first chance at any kind of job? (As good a chance.)	82
2. Generally speaking, do you think there should be separate sections for Negroes in streetcars and buses? (No.)	77
3. Do you think Negroes should have the right to use the same parks, restaurants, and hotels as white people? (Yes.)	71
4. Do you think white students and Negro students should go to the same schools, or to separate schools? (Same schools.)	63
5. How strongly would you object if a member of your family wanted to bring a Negro friend home to dinner? (Not at all.)	49
6. White people have a right to keep Negroes out of their neighborhoods if they want to, and Negroes should respect that right. (Disagree slightly or Disagree strongly.)	44
7. Do you think there should be laws against marriages between Negroes and whites? (No.)	36
8. Negroes shouldn't push themselves where they're not wanted. (Disagree slightly or Disagree strongly.)	27

Source: Treiman, D. J. Status discrepancy and prejudice. *American Journal of Sociology*, 71, (1966), 656. Copyright 1966 by the University of Chicago. Reprinted by permission of University of Chicago Press.

have many inconsistent responses are probably measuring a different underlying dimension, and accordingly they are deleted from the pool of items. After a number of rounds of computation and discarding of items, a short scale may be developed which meets Guttman's criteria for unidimensionality. However, recent analyses by Robinson (1973) have demonstrated that even more procedural safeguards than those recommended by Guttman are necessary in order to be sure that a truly unidimensional scale has been developed.

Osgood's Semantic Differential

In contrast to the above methods of constructing attitude scales, Osgood's Semantic Differential is actually a scale in itself. But it is a scale of such a general sort that it can be applied to any concept at all. This has the great advantage that one does not have to construct and try out a new scale every time one wants to study a new topic. No doubt this convenience is a major reason for the sustained popularity of the Semantic Differential since it was introduced (Osgood, Suci, & Tannenbaum, 1957).

The reason for the name "Semantic Differential" is that the technique attempts to measure the **connotative meaning** of the concept or object being rated: that is, its implied meaning, or differential connotations to the respondent. In contrast with the other major attitude scaling methods, the Semantic Differential does not consist of opinion statements about the attitude object. Instead it uses a series of 7-point scales with two opposing adjectives (e.g., "good" and "bad") at the ends of each scale. Respondents check the point on each scale which corresponds to their impressions of or feelings about the object or concept being rated. An abbreviated example of the instructions and the rating form is shown in Box 2-5.

Osgood, Suci, and Tannenbaum (1957) have reported a great deal of research on the application of this Semantic Differential approach to the measurement of a wide variety of concepts, and more recent work has applied it in many different cultures (Osgood, 1965). Using the method of factor analysis, Osgood and his colleagues have studied the underlying dimensions in connotative meaning, and time after time they have come up with generally-similar results. They have concluded that there are three basic dimensions on which people make semantic judgments, and these are applicable quite universally to varied concepts, varied adjectival rating scales, and various cultures. The three dimensions are as follows: (a) the **evaluative** dimension, involving adjectives like good-bad, beautiful-ugly, kind-cruel, pleasant-unpleasant, and fair-unfair; (b) the **potency** dimension, marked by adjectives like strong-weak, large-small, and heavy-light; (c) the **activity** dimension, identified by adjectives like active-passive, hot-cold, and fast-slow.

Of these dimensions, the one most heavily weighted in people's judgments is evaluation. Osgood (1965) has recommended using it as the prime indicator of attitude toward the object. Clearly it is an affective dimension whereas the other two seem more cognitive in nature. Normally each dimension can be measured reliably by the use of only three or four adjective scales, so use of the Semantic Differential is simple and convenient for the investigator and relatively easy for respondents as well.

Box 2-5 *An Example of a Semantic Differential Rating Task*

Both the instructions and the rating form are substantially shortened in this demonstration example. Ordinarily many concepts to be rated would be presented to each respondent in a stapled booklet, one concept on each page; and more adjective scales might also be used for each concept. Note that the end of the scale representing the positive pole on the dimension is systematically varied between left and right.

INSTRUCTIONS: *The purpose of this study is to measure* meanings *of certain things to various people by having them judge them against a series of descriptive scales. In taking this test, please make your judgments on the basis of what these things mean to you.*

Here is how you are to use these scales: If you feel that the concept at the top of the page is very closely related *to one end of the scale (for instance, very fair), you should place your check mark as follows:*

fair__X__:___:___:___:___:___:___unfair

If you feel that the concept is only slightly related *to one or the other end of the scale (for instance, slightly strong), you should place your check mark as follows:*

weak___:___:___:___:__X__:___:___strong

The direction toward which you check, of course, depends on which of the two ends of the scale seem most characteristic of the thing you're judging.

If you consider the concept to be neutral *on the scale, both sides of the scale equally associated* with the concept, *or if the scale is* completely irrelevant, unrelated to the concept, *then you should place your check-mark in the middle space.*

Rate the concept on each of these scales in order, and do not omit any. Please do not look back and forth *through the items. Do not try to remember how you checked similar items earlier in the test.* Make each item a separate and independent judgment. *Work at fairly high speed throughout this test. Do not worry or puzzle over individual items. It is your first impressions, the immediate "feelings" about the items, that we want. On the other hand, please do not be careless, because we want your true impressions.*

SEPARATION OF CHURCH AND STATE

	(Dimension)*
good___:___:___:___:___:___:___bad	(evaluative)
weak___:___:___:___:___:___:___strong	(potency)
active___:___:___:___:___:___:___passive	(activity)
large___:___:___:___:___:___:___small	(potency)
slow___:___:___:___:___:___:___fast	(activity)
unfair___:___:___:___:___:___:___fair	(evaluative)

*Of course, the dimensions are not shown on the respondents' forms.

Source: Adapted from Osgood, C. E., Suci, G. J., & Tannenbaum, P. H. *The Measurement of Meaning*. Urbana, Ill.: University of Illinois Press, 1957. Pp. 36–38, 82–84.

A modification of the Semantic Differential which has gained some attention is the Behavioral Differential (Triandis, 1964). This is a way of analyzing the behavioral component of attitudes, or behavioral intentions. It illustrates the great flexibility of the Semantic Differential in allowing modifications for various specific purposes. In it, the respondent is presented with a brief description of a category of persons (e.g., a black male street cleaner, a 50-year-old Jewish physician, etc.), and he is asked to rate the probability of his engaging in a long list of behaviors with that type of person. For instance:

A 50-year-old Jewish physician

would___:___:___:___:___:___:___:___:___would not
 have a cocktail with this person

would___:___:___:___:___:___:___:___:___would not
 vote for this person

As mentioned earlier, by using this approach Triandis has demonstrated that there are at least five basic factors involved in behavioral intentions toward other people.

Final Comments on Attitude Scales

This work by Triandis illustrates the possibility of multidimensional scaling of attitudes. Though most attitude scales have concentrated on measuring the **magnitude** of attitudes—that is, their degree of favorability or unfavorability (also sometimes called their **valence**)—several other dimensions of attitudes have been suggested as worthy of study. In particular, these dimensions include the **complexity** or elaboration of attitudes, their **centrality** or importance to the person who holds them, and their **salience** (closeness to awareness, or readiness for expression). The structure of attitudes will be considered in more detail in Chapter 3; also see Scott (1968, pp. 204–208) for a further discussion of attitude dimensions.

It should also be emphasized here, as was mentioned in Chapter 1, that carefully constructed attitude scales have been very little used by researchers and only occasionally utilized by attitude pollers for practical assessment. Instead, their major contribution has been to provide theoretical understanding of specific domains of attitudes.

A number of other attitude scaling methods have been proposed (e.g., Edwards & Kilpatrick, 1948; Coombs, 1950). However, no methods other than the "big five" described above appear at all frequently in the attitude and opinion research literature. Though these scaling methods are different in structure, they generally yield scores which are quite highly correlated with the other methods —Fishbein and Ajzen (1974) reported typical intercorrelations of around $+.7$, though Tittle and Hill (1967) found lower figures averaging around $+.5$. Both studies showed the Likert scale to be most highly correlated with the various other attitude measures.

A common limitation shared by all attitude measurement methods is that the scales which they produce are **ordinal** scales rather than equal-interval scales. This means that respondents can successfully be placed in their *rank order* on the attitude dimension, but we cannot be sure that the actual attitudinal distance between two values on the scale is equal to the distance between two other values. For instance, on a Likert scale, is the distance between "Undecided" and "Approve" (3 and 4) the same as the distance between "Approve" and "Strongly approve" (4 and 5)? The two distances are numerically equal, but they may not be psychologically equal. Even though Thurstone's method strives to achieve "equal-appearing intervals," it is nevertheless an ordinal scale rather than an interval scale.

Technically, ordinal scales require the use of nonparametric, distribution-free statistical techniques involving measures such as the median. For this reason it is statistically improper to add or multiply scores together, compute mean scores, use *t*-tests, analysis of variance, etc. However, these restrictions are almost universally disregarded, largely because statistical research has shown that in most instances violations of the assumptions underlying the use of parametric techniques do not lead to serious distortions of their results. Thus, scores are customarily added, means computed, and *t*-tests and *F* tests used on attitude scale results. It is well to keep in mind, however, that occasionally, when distributions are markedly skewed or variances are grossly different, use of parametric techniques may produce misleading conclusions.

PROBLEMS AFFECTING THE VALIDITY
OF ATTITUDE SCALES

In addition to attitude scales, there are a number of other ways to measure attitudes. However, before describing them, we should discuss in some detail the problems inherent in the use of attitude scales.

The wording of attitude questions is one of the main factors affecting the validity of attitude scales. However, since principles regarding the wording of attitude questions are also applicable to the wording of public opinion interviews, they are discussed in detail in Chapter 4.

The major problem to be discussed here is the ways in which **response sets** can invalidate attitude questionnaire answers. Response sets are systematic ways of answering which are not directly related to the question content, but which represent typical behavioral characteristics of the respondents. Several types of response sets are mentioned below and some possible solutions to them discussed.*

---

*This section draws on material from the author's chapter on research methods in *Social Psychology in the Seventies* (Wrightsman, 1972).

Carelessness

When respondents are unmotivated or careless, their answers will be variable and inconsistent from moment to moment or from one testing session to another. Such a situation will reduce the questionnaire's **reliability** (consistency of measurement), and unreliable questionnaires are necessarily low in **validity** (accuracy or correctness of measurement). They are like an elastic tape measure which stretches a different amount each time it is used; obviously, the resulting "measurements" would seldom be correct.

Some carelessness and low motivation can be minimized by building good rapport, stressing the importance of the task, and engaging the respondent's interest in it. However, despite such precautions, some respondents may still answer carelessly or fail to follow directions through misunderstanding or poor comprehension. Therefore, the response sheets are usually scanned visually, and the data are either discarded or analyzed separately for respondents who (a) omit answers to many items, (b) answer almost all items in the same way, or (c) show systematic patterns of responding (for example: a, b, c, d, a, b, c, d).

Social Desirability

The social desirability response set is the tendency to give the most socially acceptable answer to a question, or to "fake good." It operates both in attitude scales and public opinion interviews. For example, people will rarely describe themselves as dishonest, even though almost everyone occasionally fudges on the truth or cheats a little bit (by glancing at an opponent's cards, etc.). In extensive studies on this topic Edwards (1964) has shown that personality characteristics which are considered as desirable in our culture are also ones which are claimed by most respondents as applying to themselves, and vice versa. In one study of 140 items, the correlation was $+.87$, an almost-perfect relationship. Edwards (1964) has developed a personality scale which indicates the degree of an individual's tendency to give socially desirable answers about himself, and Crowne and Marlowe (1964) have done a great deal of research on a similar scale that they have constructed.

To control for social desirability responding, Edwards has advocated the use of **forced-choice** items. In this technique of scale construction two items of approximately equal social desirability, but indicating, for instance, two different social needs, are paired together; the respondent has to pick the one which is most true of himself. This was a creative proposal, but unfortunately the evidence of its success in solving the problem of social desirability responding is disappointing (Barron, 1959, p. 116; Scott, 1968, p. 241). Consequently, only a few scales have been built in this way, the best-known of which is Rotter's (1966) scale of internal versus external locus of control.

None of the available methods for combatting social desirability responding is entirely satisfactory. The techniques which are most often used are: (a) selecting innocuous items, where social desirability seems not to be an issue, (b) providing anonymity for the respondents, (c) stating that there are no right or wrong answers since the items cover matters of opinion rather than fact, (d) urging respondents to answer honestly and stressing that it is their own opinions which are desired, (e) use of the forced-choice technique of item construction, discussed above, and (f) auxiliary use of personality scales to identify respondents who are particularly high or low in social desirability responding.

Extremity of Response

An extremity response set can only occur on items where there are more than two alternative answers. For example, on a Likert-type scale having responses scored from +3 to −3, an extremity response set would be demonstrated by a respondent who picked mostly +3 and/or −3 answers. Its opposite, a mid-range response set, would be shown by a large number of +1 and/or −1 answers.

There has been little study of the effects of extremity response sets or mid-range response sets on questionnaire validity. Their effects can be reduced if equal numbers of items on a scale are keyed in the positive and negative directions, for then the +3 answers of an extreme responder will tend to counterbalance his −3 answers (and similarly for the +1 and −1 answers of a mid-range responder). Another possible remedy is to eliminate extremity response set altogether by using only items with two alternatives (Yes-No, or Agree-Disagree).

Acquiescence (Yea-Saying)

Acquiescence response set has two relatively-independent dimensions. The more fully studied one is **agreement** response set, or yea-saying, defined as a tendency to agree with any questionnaire item regardless of its content. It has been studied extensively in the California F Scale measure of authoritarianism (Adorno et al., 1950), but it also is an issue in many other attitude and personality scales, particularly in the Minnesota Multiphasic Personality Inventory (MMPI). An example of agreement responding might be a person who answered "Yes" to both of the following items: "I am basically a happy-go-lucky person" and "I often feel grouchy and out-of-sorts."

The fact that acquiescence is a problem on the California F Scale is the result of a poor decision regarding the construction of the scale. All 28 items were worded in such a way that agreement indicated authoritarianism and disagreement indicated lack of authoritarianism; that is, all items were keyed in the positive direction. At the time that the authoritarianism studies were being formulated, this was not recognized as a major issue in scale construction, but it has since become so.

It is relatively easy to rid a scale of agreement response bias effects during its construction stages by reversing the wording and the keying of half of the items from that of the other half. The result is called a **balanced scale**—that is, one having half of the items on the scale scored if the answer is "true," and half keyed "false." If the two groups of items are equally good, are positively intercorrelated, and have an equal spread of responses, this procedure will cause any agreement response effect to cancel out on the two groups of items.

However, this was not done on the California F Scale, and debates raged for years about the resulting problems. One group of authors (e.g., Bass, 1955; Campbell, Converse, Miller, & Stokes, 1960) claimed that the scale was more a measure of acquiescence than of authoritarianism. Another group, using different statistical methods, concluded that there was little relationship between authoritarianism and acquiescence (Couch & Keniston, 1960). A third group (e.g., Christie, Havel, & Seidenberg, 1958) found that there was some admixture of acquiescence in F Scale scores, but argued that there *should* be because agreeing with an authoritatively-worded statement is really one aspect of being an authoritarian.

For investigators who want to eliminate agreement response set from their studies, there is a relatively simple solution: use a balanced scale. For those who want to study agreement responding, alone and unconfounded, Couch and Keniston (1960) have developed a relatively pure scale of "agreeing response set." Thus this problem has been largely resolved, though other well-known attitude scales are still being built without balanced scoring (e.g., Rokeach's Dogmatism Scale, 1960), and Rokeach (1967) has argued that there are some circumstances under which balanced scales may not be desirable.

A nay-saying or disagreement response set—i.e., a tendency to disagree with any item regardless of its content—is the other end of the agreement dimension. It is relatively rare and has been little investigated. One study found the disagreement response set more common among Republicans than among Democrats (Milbrath, 1962).

The second, separate dimension of acquiescence is **acceptance** response set. Defined as the tendency to accept positively worded items and reject negatively worded ones, it has only recently been demonstrated (Bentler, Jackson, & Messick, 1971). It is still little understood by attitude researchers, but it appears less common in attitude measurement than in personality measurement. Fortunately, the use of a balanced scale, as defined above, will also remove acceptance response set, provided that the items are all worded positively rather than reversed by adding "not" or other negative wording. Since negatively worded items are usually avoided due to the confusion which they produce when answered negatively, it seems that acceptance response set is not likely to pose major problems in attitude measurement.

Conclusions

In summary, it seems clear that response sets do affect the answers of some respondents on attitude scales, particularly when the items are ambiguous in meaning or unimportant to the respondent. We have also seen that there are ways in which each kind of response set can be at least partially controlled or overcome.

Another important approach to improving attitude measurement has been suggested by Cook and Selltiz (1964) in a review of all of the varied techniques which have been utilized to study attitudes. They strongly recommend that in any study some of these experimental and admittedly-imperfect methods should be used in conjunction with verbal attitude scales, in order to develop a broader and more valid picture of people's attitudes that can be yielded by any one measurement method alone.

One of the most promising ways of supplementing attitude scale scores is the use of **unobtrusive measures** of behavior (observations made without attracting the attention of the people being studied), as suggested in a fascinating paperback book by Webb, Campbell, Schwartz, and Sechrest (1966). An excellent example of this approach was contained in a study by Wrightsman (1969) which used bumper stickers on cars as an unobtrusive measure of the owners' political attitudes, and showed that these attitudes were related to a measure of law-abidingness. (Despite George Wallace's campaign appeals for "law and order," his supporters were significantly less law-abiding than Nixon's or Humphrey's.) Further use of such imaginative approaches could help to solve the problems inherent in interpreting the results of attitude-scale and opinion-interview research.

OTHER WAYS OF MEASURING ATTITUDES

Following the above survey of the major attitude scaling methods and the problems which are common to them, we now turn to a brief description of some other approaches to measuring attitudes. In general, most of these approaches have been used only experimentally rather than in any large-scale measurement program. Some of them have limited areas of applicability, and others are based on questionable or unestablished assumptions. In comparison to the well-known attitude scaling methods considered above, most of these approaches have yet to prove their usefulness, and their reliability and/or validity is often unknown. Nevertheless, they can be very helpful when used in conjunction with verbal attitude scales, because multiple measurements through different methods can add greatly to the depth and richness of our understanding of attitude patterns and variations.

A classification scheme listing five broad categories or types of attitude measures has been suggested by Cook and Selltiz (1964), and other recent writers have reviewed a wide range of indirect methods of attitude measurement (Kidder & Campbell, 1970; Fishbein & Ajzen, 1975, pp. 89–95). The five categories presented by Cook and Selltiz will provide the framework for our following discussion:

Photograph courtesy of Donald
Campbell. Reprinted by permission.

Box 2-6 DONALD CAMPBELL, *Methodologist and Attitude Researcher*

Donald Campbell has received nearly every major honor which psychology has to offer—notably election to the National Academy of Sciences, the presidency of the American Psychological Association (APA), and the Distinguished Scientific Contribution Award of the APA. He has been honored as a methodologist and a philosopher, a field researcher and a laboratory experimenter, and for work in anthropology, political science, and sociology as well as psychology.

Born in 1916, Campbell took his B.A. and Ph.D. at the University of California at Berkeley, where his dissertation was a noteworthy study of the consistency of racial attitudes. After short periods of teaching at Ohio State and the University of Chicago, he settled in 1953 at Northwestern, where he is now professor of psychology.

Campbell is widely known as coauthor of books on unobtrusive measures and on quasi-experimental research methods. Among his 130 articles, one on indirect methods of measurement is particularly relevant to the topic of this chapter. Chapter 3 cites his research on attitude consistency; and in Chapter 10 his critique of attitude-behavior pseudo-inconsistency is described, and his call for planned experimentation on social and governmental programs is seconded.

1. Measures utilizing self-reports of beliefs, feelings, or behavior.
2. Measures involving observation of behavior toward the attitude object.
3. Measures of reactions to or interpretations of relevant partially-structured stimuli.
4. Measures involving performance on relevant objective tasks.
5. Measures of physiological reactions to the attitude object.

In using measures from any of these categories, it should again be emphasized that the researcher's conclusions about people's attitudes is an inference from the particular measures taken. This is true even where the measure used is the individual's self-report of his own attitude, for the researcher still has to decide whether the respondent truly is aware of his own attitudes and is reporting them accurately.

Self-Report Measures

This category contains all of the attitude scaling methods described above. Since they have already been discussed at some length, only one additional type of self-report measure will be mentioned.

Taylor and Parker (1964) have suggested use of an "attitude report question." This is merely a single general question such as, "In general, how do you feel about Jews?" combined with a graphic rating scale (a line with words at each end such as "Very favorable" and "Very unfavorable," and numbers below it indicating its units) where the respondent marks his (her) degree of favorability. Surprisingly, for such a simple technique, it has been found to be as reliable as 5- or 6-item Guttman scales. Of course, even more than most self-report measures, responses to it can be easily faked. Its virtues are its directness and simplicity, but a resulting drawback is the the impossibility of measuring different aspects or dimensions of the general attitude with this technique. For some types of attitudes and some people, an overall global attitude measure may be quite sufficient because there is little differentiation of nuances and details; but for other attitudes and/or other people, **multidimensional** attitude scaling may demonstrate a much more complex pattern of attitudes.

Observations of Behavior

Compared with verbal self-report measures, behavioral measures of attitudes have been very little used and consequently are poorly-developed and crude in their methodology. In large part this is because they are difficult, time-consuming, and expensive to utilize.

Cook and Selltiz (1964) have described three different types of behavioral measures: (a) apparently unstaged standardized situations in which a subject's behavior can be observed, (b) staged role-playing situations in which the subject is asked either to respond as he would in real life, or to take the part of a particular other person, (c) use of sociometric choices which the subject believes will have real-life consequences (e.g., his choice of one or a few members of a group to work with on a joint task). In all three of these approaches, of course, the situation chosen is one in which the attitude object (e.g., narcotics addicts) is presented in some way. However, surprisingly, Cook and Selltiz recommend having the attitude object only *represented symbolically* (in words, pictures, etc.), rather than present in person. Alert readers may note that this really entails study of the subject's behavioral intentions (what he *says* he would do) rather than his actual behavior toward the object. Thus, it is still relying on the subject's self-report. Cook and Selltiz acknowledge this fact but stress that the difference in this type of measure is that *the subject is convinced that there will be real-life consequences* flowing from his response.

Since Fishbein and Ajzen (1972) have reported very high correlations between behavioral intentions and behavior, the use of behavioral-intention measures may be justifiable here. Cook and Selltiz have defended it on the grounds that it is less subject than real-life behavior to a variety of extraneous influences. However, we should emphasize that it is sometimes possible to observe actual behavior in situations where extraneous influences are relatively inoperative. For instance, in a small-group discussion situation, choice of a seat next to a crippled person rather than one farther away could indicate a person's attitude toward cripples. Since Wicker (1969) and others have shown that there is often little relationship between verbal self-report attitude measures and behavior, the use of actual behavior measures here may be preferable to behavioral intention measures.

A few examples may illustrate the types of behavioral intention measures which have been used. DeFleur and Westie (1958) have developed a method in which white subjects, after seeing some relevant slides, are asked whether they would be willing to be photographed with a Negro of the opposite sex. The subjects are also requested to sign a "standard photograph release agreement" indicating which of a variety of purposes they would be willing to have such a photograph used for—from showings solely to professional sociologists for research purposes, to a nationwide publicity campaign in favor of racial integration. A role-playing approach was used by Stanton, Back, and Litwak (1956) to determine the favorable and unfavorable feelings held by slum residents in Puerto Rico about public housing projects. Finally, sociometric choice techniques have been used by Mann (1959) to study the effects of interracial contact among graduate students.

Reactions to Partially-Structured Stimuli

This measurement approach involves the use of **projective techniques**. The stimuli are not clearly structured, i.e., they do not provide sufficient information to determine a person's response. Therefore, the subject must draw on his own needs and dispositions in interpreting or describing the characteristics of the attitude object. For instance, a picture of the head of a black girl may be presented, and the subject be asked to describe her characteristics or to make up a story about her. The task is usually presented as a test of imagination or social sensitivity or some similar concept, rather than as a measure of the subject's attitudes.

Obviously, in a sense this approach uses the subject's verbal self-report, and so is similar to that measurement approach. The primary differences are the use of the somewhat ambiguous stimulus instead of an explicitly-named attitude object, and the disguised goal of the measurement (e.g., as a test of ability to judge people's characteristics rather than an attitude measure). It is assumed that these aspects of the technique decrease the likelihood of subjects distorting their true feelings in an attempt to present themselves in a favorable light to the investigator. However, the literature on projective techniques is full of critiques questioning the validity of their results (e.g., Suinn & Oskamp, 1969; Molish,

1972). It is clear that projective responses may reflect an individual's attitude; but they may also merely indicate a person's awareness of the common cultural patterns of response, such as unequal treatment of various minority groups.

As a result of these limitations, systematic use of projective techniques in the study of attitudes and opinions has been rare. One successful example was the study by Riddleberger and Motz (1957) which found that relatively prejudiced and unprejudiced subjects (as measured by a self-report instrument) differed in their interpretations of a pictured interracial group. Partially-structured projective pictures can also be used as stimulus materials to obtain responses on typical attitude scales such as the Semantic Differential, as was done in a study by Perlman and Oskamp (1971).

Performance on Objective Tasks

This measurement approach has been used somewhat more widely than the previous ones. Cook and Selltiz (1964) describe it as follows:

> Approaches in this category present the respondent with specific tasks to be performed; they are presented as tests of information or ability, or simply as jobs that need to be done. The assumption common to all of them is that performance may be influenced by attitude, and that a systematic bias in performance reflects the influence of attitude (p. 50).

Thus, in a sense this approach is similar to observations of behavior. It differs in that the task is structured for the subject, and that the relevance of his performance to measurement of his attitudes is usually quite thoroughly disguised.

Some examples may clarify how this can be done. Horowitz and Horowitz (1938) asked children to show which pictures, from a set including individuals of different races and sexes, "belong together;" and they inferred the children's attitudes from their groupings of the pictures. Hammond (1948) devised an "information" test with alternative answers that were equally far on either side of the correct response (which was not provided as an alternative). He showed that the subject's choice of erroneous responses was generally consistent with his own attitudes. For instance, a prounion subject would generally choose an answer which overestimated labor unions' membership size, rather than an answer which underestimated it, while the opposite would usually be true for an antiunion subject. Hovland and Sherif (1952) showed that subjects' attitudes, if they were extreme, systematically influenced their judgments of the favorableness of items which they rated in the process of construction of a Thurstone scale. Similarly, Brigham and Cook (1970) had subjects judge the plausibility of pro-integration and anti-integration arguments, and the judgments were treated as indicators of the subjects' own attitudes toward racial integration.

Two problems are present in interpreting measures of this sort. If a subject shows a consistent bias in performance, it seems safe to infer that the subject's attitudes are responsible. However, if a consistent bias is not shown, it may not be safe to infer that the subject's attitude is a weak one, for we do not know how sensitive such measures are. Second, a particular bias in response might reflect either the subject's wishes or fears; "a member of the Communist party may overestimate the number of Communists in the United States, but so may a member of the John Birch Society" (Cook & Selltiz, 1964, p. 51). Thus additional information may be needed to determine the direction of the subject's attitude from a biased performance.

Physiological Reactions

A fairly wide variety of physiological reactions have been used as indicators of attitudes: galvanic skin response (GSR), blood vessel constriction, heart rate, dilation of the pupil of the eye, and even the conditioned response of salivation in humans. As examples, Rankin and Campbell (1955) compared GSRs obtained from subjects who were placed in close physical contact with a Negro experimenter and a white experimenter. Westie and DeFleur (1959) showed subjects pictures of whites and Negroes in social situations and found a relationship between GSR, blood vessel constriction, and a verbal measure of attitudes. Hess (1965), using careful eye photograph techniques, reported pupillary dilation in response to interesting or pleasing stimuli and pupillary constriction as a response to unpleasant stimuli. Though some later studies have not been able to replicate these findings (Collins, Ellsworth, & Helmreich, 1967; Woodmansee, 1970), other results have suggested that their failure was due to methodological deficiencies (Hicks & LePage, 1976). Undoubtedly the most familiar physiological measure of emotional reactions is the polygraph machine or "lie-detector," the validity of which has been analyzed by Lykken (1975). A variety of other applications of physiological measures to social behavior are presented in a volume by Leiderman and Shapiro (1964).

In these techniques it is assumed that the amount of the physiological reaction indicates the extent of the subject's arousal, the intensity of his feelings, and hence the extremity of his attitudes. However, with the possible exception of pupil dilation, physiological measures are generally **nondirectional** in nature; that is, they do not indicate whether the feeling involved is a pleasant or unpleasant one. Thus additional information is usually necessary in order to interpret them adequately.

The purpose of the physiological measurement may or may not be disguised. It usually makes little difference to the results, for normally these physiological reactions are not under the conscious control of subjects. Thus, even if they knew the purpose of the study and wanted to present a particular impression of themselves, they probably could not modify their responses accordingly. However, unfortunately, physiological responses are sensitive to many other variables, such as stimulus characteristics and environmental factors, in addition to the subjects' attitudes. Therefore particularly careful control of the measurement situation is needed, and this generally restricts the use of these measures to experimental laboratory studies.

SUMMARY

Attitudes and opinions may be expressed in many colorful ways, but for purposes of scientific study, they must be classified into categories or measured on a quantitative scale. Research studies usually compare the mean or median score of two or more groups by using a test of statistical significance. Several attitude scores or other measures for a single group of respondents may be compared by using correlation methods, and the complex statistical technique called factor analysis can be used to determine the basic psychological dimensions underlying responses on a collection of attitude items or attitude scales.

The development of attitude scaling methods in the 1920s was the first major application of quantitative measurement in the field of social psychology. In terms of the frequency of their use, the "big five" of attitude scaling methods are Bogardus' scale of social distance toward various ethnic groups, Thurstone's method of equal-appearing intervals, Likert's method of summated ratings (the most popular of all), Guttman's Scalogram Analysis method of constructing a unidimensional scale, and Osgood's scale of connotative meaning, the Semantic Differential. All of these methods produce scales which are ordinal in nature, and therefore some caution must be exercised if parametric statistics are used in analyzing their results.

Problems which affect the validity of attitude scales include the response sets of carelessness, social desirability, extremity, and acquiescence (yea-saying). With due care in constructing and interpreting attitude scales, all of these problems can be at least partially overcome.

In conjunction with attitude scales, it is recommended that other less-common methods of studying attitudes also be more widely used in research, in order to provide a broader multidimensional measurement approach. These additional methods include other self-report measures, observations of behavior (particularly unobtrusive observations), reactions to partially-structured stimuli such as projective techniques, measures of performance on objective tasks in attitude-relevant situations, and physiological reactions to attitudinal stimuli.

Suggested Readings

Scott, W. A. Attitude measurement. In G. Lindzey & E. Aronson (Eds.), *The Handbook of Social Psychology* (2nd ed.). Vol. 2. Reading, Mass.: Addison-Wesley, 1968. Pp.

204–273.—A definitive but technical presentation of methods of attitude measurement and factors affecting the reliability and validity of measurement.

Shaw, M. E., & Wright, J. M. *Scales for the Measurement of Attitudes.* New York: McGraw-Hill, 1967—An interesting and thorough collection of the available information on published scales which have been used to measure attitudes on topics ranging from international affairs to self-acceptance.

Webb, E. J., Campbell, D. T., Schwartz, R. D., & Sechrest, L. *Unobtrusive Measures: Nonreactive Research in the Social Sciences.* Chicago: Rand McNally, 1966. (Paperback)—An intriguing description of indirect ways to study social attitudes and behavior without directly asking questions of the people being studied.

chapter 3

Structure and Functions of Attitudes and Beliefs

My attitude is my greatest asset. As long as a person has a positive attitude, he can always make it.—Glenn Turner, millionaire super salesman.

If a man would register all his opinions upon love, politics, religion, and learning, what a bundle of inconsistencies and contradictions would appear at last.—Jonathan Swift.

Belief in the general credibility of our senses is the most central belief of all; nearly all of our other beliefs rest upon it, and to lose our faith in it is to lose our sanity.—Daryl J. Bem.

What do attitudes and opinions do for the person who holds them? Some people feel that their favorite football team is the best in the country; others are so anti-Negro that much of their identity is based upon their prejudiced attitudes. Do the attitudes that you hold help you to live your daily life, to fulfill your psychological needs, and to get along effectively in your world? Social scientists have traditionally answered these questions with a resounding "Yes." Though your attitudes and opinions may not make you wealthy, they can at least help to make you healthy and wise. Let us take a closer look at the functions of attitudes, which have been most clearly stated by Daniel Katz (1960).

FUNCTIONS OF ATTITUDES

Katz has suggested that there are four major functions which attitudes perform, as defined below. Examples are given of each function in order to clarify their similarities and differences.

1. *Understanding.* Many attitudes help us to understand our world and to make sense of occurrences around us. They provide consistency and clarity in our explanation and interpretation of events. This has also been called the **knowledge** function of attitudes, but that term does not imply that attitudes provide a factually truthful picture of the world—merely one that is meaningful and understandable to the particular individual who holds them. For one person, the unfolding story of the Watergate cover-up might be understood in reference to an attitude that "Republicans are no damn good." Another person might relate the same facts to the belief that "Power tends to corrupt." In each case the person's beliefs or attitudes provide a context for the new information, aiding in its interpretation and assimilation into the person's belief system.

2. *Need Satisfaction.* Many attitudes are formed as a result of our past rewards and punishments for saying or doing particular things. Once formed, these attitudes usually continue to be useful in helping us to satisfy our needs or to reach our goals. These attitudes have also been termed **adjustive** in the sense of helping us to adjust to life situations, or **utilitarian** in the sense that they are useful in reaching our goals. Examples would include the attitudes of a worker who favors a political party because he believes it will "do more for the working man," or the pupil who comes to like math classes because he has done well in them in the past and been rewarded by the teacher's praise and his own feeling of competence.

3. *Ego Defense.* Attitudes can also help to enhance our self-esteem and to defend us against the "thousand slings and arrows" of life. All people use defense mechanisms to some extent, but they are used much more by individuals who are insecure or feel inferior or who have deep internal conflicts. Prejudiced attitudes are often used as a crutch to bolster the self-esteem of the holder, a phenomenon which has been called the "scapegoat view of prejudice." Simi-

larly, the employee who shrugs off criticism from the boss by saying "The boss is just always bad-tempered" may be using an unrealistic ego-defensive attitude to avoid thinking about his (her) own failings.

4. *Value Expression.* A value-expressive attitude is one which helps to establish a person's self-identity, which portrays the sort of person he is, which says in effect "This is the way I am." Examples include the motorcyclist's liking for his black leather jacket, and the teenage girl's preference for her favorite color in most of her clothes. More important attitudes often express an individual's basic values, as with the conscientious objector's aversion to all aspects of warfare and violence.

These four types of needs which attitudes can serve for a person are useful in classifying and understanding attitudes. But they also have other uses. As Katz pointed out, they can also help to explain the types of situations in which different attitudes will be aroused, and the types of influences which will be effective in changing different attitudes.

Attitude Arousal

Each of us has hundreds of attitudes toward hundreds of different attitude objects, but they are not all active at the same time. Most of the time most of our attitudes are lying dormant while only a few are in the focus of our conscious attention or directly influencing our behavior. It requires the onset of a particular psychological need or a relevant environmental cue to **arouse** into an active state a particular attitude which we hold. And, importantly, the question of what type of internal need or external cue will arouse a particular attitude is largely determined by the function which that attitude serves for the individual concerned.

To illustrate this relationship, let us take a common attitude, that of racial prejudice, which involves negative feelings toward blacks. This attitude could serve any of the functions mentioned above, but Katz has emphasized that the conditions necessary to arouse the attitude would be different for the different functions. Let us look at each of the functions in turn.

A prejudiced attitude could serve the *understanding* function if it helped the holder to form an explanation as to why most Negroes (s)he had met were poorly educated and held menial jobs. For instance, the person might conclude that all blacks were inferior and stupid. In such a case the attitude would be aroused by raising a question or problem which that attitude would help to solve. Example: should we build a new school in the Negro section of town? With a negative attitude now aroused, the person might answer, "No, they're too dumb to benefit from a better school."

A prejudiced attitude could serve the *need-satisfaction* function if it helped to satisfy the holder's social needs, such as helping him (her) to gain approval or friendship. Such an attitude might have been formed through being rewarded by approval and praise from other prejudiced people (family, friends, etc.) when

Photograph courtesy of Daniel Katz.
Reprinted by permission.

Box 3-1 DANIEL KATZ, *Attitude Theorist and Researcher*

Widely respected and honored as a social psychologist, Daniel Katz is Professor Emeritus at the University of Michigan. His B.A. was earned at the University of Buffalo and his M.A. and Ph.D. at Syracuse. Before moving to Michigan he taught at Princeton, was chairman of the psychology department at Brooklyn College, and served in the Office of War Information in World War II.

In this chapter, Katz's theory of the functions of attitudes is prominently mentioned. He has also been influential as a researcher in many different attitude areas and as editor of the outstanding journal in social psychology from 1962 to 1967. He has been elected president of three different divisions of the American Psychological Association and served on its Board of Directors. His early research on racial stereotypes is mentioned in Chapter 14, and he has also done cross-national research in Norway, Denmark, Greece, and Yugoslavia.

stating or acting on negative feelings toward blacks. In this type of situation the attitude would be likely to be aroused by the recurrence of the relevant social need. For instance, a prejudiced person who is feeling lonely or wanting approval may joke or tell unflattering stories about Negroes as a way of gaining attention and approval.

A prejudiced attitude could serve the *ego-defense* function in people who feel inferior, insecure, and low in self-esteem. For instance, a poor, illiterate, unhappy "redneck" might easily accept the belief that Negroes are inferior since it reassures him (her) that there are people lower on the totem pole than (s)he is. Such ego-defensive attitudes will be aroused particularly when the individual's tenuous security is threatened or when appeals to hate feelings and other repressed impulses are received. Demagogues use these techniques to get many people's negative attitudes aroused to the point where they will take strong action on them.

A prejudiced attitude could serve the *value-expressive* function if it was linked to some of the holder's most important values or to his(her) self-concept. For example, an individual who was brought up believing that the finest flowering of American culture was the plantation society of the pre-Civil-War South might develop a value of white supremacy, which would be supported by negative feelings toward and beliefs about Negroes. These attitudes could be aroused by the occurrence of cues related to the value (e.g., from viewing a movie like *Gone with the Wind*) or by appeals to the person's self-image as a Southern gentleman in order to get him to take some action like joining a White Citizens' Organization.

Thus we have seen that the same attitude may be aroused in several different ways, depending on what function it serves for the individual. Attitudes serving the understanding function are apt to be aroused by a cognitive problem while attitudes serving the adjustment function may be prompted by a social need. Ego-defensive attitudes can be aroused by threats to the holder's security or by appeals to hate feelings, whereas value-expressive attitudes may be aroused by appeals to a person's ideals or self-image.

Many attitudes serve more than one of the types of functions discussed above, and consequently they can be aroused in several different ways. For instance, one attitude may serve both an understanding and a need-satisfaction function for a person. Still, it is important to know which functions the attitude is serving for the individual in order to know what external cues or internal needs will arouse the attitude into an active state.

Attitude Change

As with attitude arousal, it takes different forces and pressures to **change** attitudes that are serving different functions. For example, the conditions that might lead to changing a person's understanding-oriented attitude may be quite different than the conditions necessary for changing an ego-defensive attitude.

Understanding-oriented attitudes are most likely to change in situations which have become ambiguous for the attitude holder due to new information or a changed environment. For example, prejudiced individuals may learn about the achievements of black doctors, scientists, statesmen, or authors. If the prejudiced attitudes had been serving the understanding function, they would probably then be changed in order to establish a more consistent, complete, and logical cognitive structure.

Need-oriented attitudes, on the other hand, are likely to change only if the holder's goals or needs have changed or if the person's needs are no longer being satisfied by the attitude in question. An example would be the prejudiced merchant who realizes that the hiring of black employees and the serving of black customers can increase profits. If the merchant's attitudes toward blacks were utilitarian in nature, they would be very likely to change.

Ego-defensive attitudes are unlikely to be changed by the procedures which work with other types of attitudes, such as providing new information or offering positive incentives for change. Since ego defenses are erected to protect the person from threats and conflicts, it is necessary first to remove the threat or conflict before attitude change can occur. This can sometimes be done by establishing a supportive atmosphere, as in a long-term therapy situation; or individuals may gradually outgrow the emotional conflicts which underlie their prejudices, or they may acquire insight into their defense mechanisms.

Value-expressive attitudes are also usually difficult to change because people's values are apt to be very important and central parts of their cognitive structure. White supremacists whose prejudiced attitudes express some of their most strongly-held values are unlikely to change those attitudes. However, change could occur if they were to become seriously dissatisfied with their self-concept or former values, as for instance if they underwent a religious conversion. A more common way in which value-expressive attitudes may change is by the holders becoming aware that the attitudes don't really fit with their values. For example, Rokeach (1971) found that experimental subjects' prejudiced attitudes and behavior were changed following a dramatic demonstration that they were really inconsistent with one of the subjects' basic values, the idea of equality for all.

For a more extended discussion of the conditions of attitude arousal and change as related to the functions which attitudes serve, you might want to read the interesting article by Katz (1960). The topic of attitude change will be taken up at length in Chapters 8 and 9 of this book.

THE STRUCTURE OF BELIEFS

We will turn now from the topic of function to that of structure—from the question of how attitudes work to how they are built. In doing this, we will consider first the structure of beliefs and belief systems, drawing upon the thinking of Rokeach (1968) and of Jones and Gerard (1967).

Centrality and Intensity of Beliefs

What factors determine how important a belief is in the belief system of the person who holds it? The concept of a *belief system* may help to answer this question. A system is a set of interconnected parts which function in relationship to each other. Just so, beliefs and attitudes do not exist in isolated separateness, but they are connected with many other beliefs in an organized system.

The **centrality** of a belief, that is, its importance in the person's belief system, may be defined in terms of its degree of connectedness with other beliefs—the number of ''implications and consequences it has for other beliefs'' (Rokeach,

1968, p. 5). Rokeach has suggested four principles which help to spell out the concept of centrality in more detail:

1. Beliefs about one's *self*, one's existence and identity, are much more central than other beliefs.
2. **Shared** beliefs about one's existence and self-identity are more central than unshared beliefs (ones held only by oneself).
3. Beliefs which are **derived** from other beliefs (rather than from contact with the object of belief) are *less* central than underived beliefs.
4. Beliefs concerning *matters of taste* are *less* central than other beliefs. They are usually seen by the holder to be arbitrary in nature, and thus they are relatively inconsequential in their impact on other beliefs.

The **intensity** of a belief refers to how strongly the belief is held, or how sure the person is about it. Central beliefs are usually intensely held, but the opposite does not follow. Beliefs concerning matters of taste may be intensely held even though they are not central. I may like pistachio ice cream with a passion (intensely), but that fact probably does not affect my attitude toward people who prefer vanilla or my beliefs about the nutritive value of pistachio nuts. My belief in the tastiness of pistachio ice cream is not central in my belief system because it does not influence other beliefs, and if it were to change, there would be few consequences for my other beliefs.

Primitive Beliefs

Rokeach (1968, p. 6) has suggested the term **primitive beliefs** for ones which are very central and which "have an axiomatic, taken-for-granted character." They are formed through direct contact with the object of belief (that is, they are not derived beliefs), and they are "psychologically incontrovertible because they are rarely, if ever, experienced as subjects of controversy." Such beliefs are the person's "basic truths" about the world, about other people, and about one's self. Examples would be: "My name is_____." and "Water is wet." However, they do not have to be shared beliefs. They can be based solely on one's own experience, and thus they can include pathological beliefs such as phobias, delusions, and hallucinations. Examples of unshared primitive beliefs would be: "No matter what others may believe, I know that my mother doesn't really love me." and "I believe I am Jesus Christ returned to earth."

The importance of primitive beliefs to the individual holding them can be demonstrated by challenging them and observing the person's response. An effective challenge may produce astonishment, disbelief in the challenge, anger, intense anxiety, or even pathological symptoms of withdrawal and confusion if continued long enough. The humor in the television show *Candid Camera* often came from seeing the astonishment of persons whose primitive beliefs were being challenged, for instance by seeing water apparently running uphill or an inanimate object apparently moving under its own power. Rokeach has observed that when a parent unexpectedly calls a young child by a name which isn't his own, the child will first enjoy it as a new game; but if the parent continues, the child will soon ask for reassurance that it really is a game, and before long intense anxiety will result, with tears, panic, and desperate attempts to get the parent to stop.

Daryl Bem (1970) has described several types and sources of primitive beliefs in an entertaining selection which is reprinted in Box 3-2.

Box 3-2 *Types of Primitive Beliefs*

Many beliefs are the product of direct experience. If you ask your friends why they believe oranges are round, they will most likely reply that they have seen oranges, felt oranges, and that oranges are, indeed, round. And that would seem to end the matter. You could, of course, ask them why they trust their senses, but that would be impolite.

Consider a more complicated belief. If you ask your friends why they believe the asteroids are round (that is, spherical), the more sophisticated among them might be able to show how such a conclusion is derived from physical principles and astronomical observations. You could press them further by asking them to justify their belief in physical principles and astronomical observations: Whence comes their knowledge of such things? When they answer that question—perhaps by citing the New York Times—*you can contine to probe: Why do they believe everything they read in the* Times? *If they then refer to previous experience with the accuracy of the* Times *or recall that their teachers always had kind words for its journalistic integrity, challenge the validity of their previous experience or the credibility of their teachers.*

What you will discover by such questioning—besides a noticeable decline in the number of your friends—is that every belief can be pushed back until it is seen to rest ultimately upon a basic belief in the credibility of one's own sensory experience or upon a basic belief in the credibility of some external authority. Other beliefs may derive from these basic beliefs, but the basic beliefs themselves are accepted as givens. Accordingly, we shall call them "primitive beliefs."

Zero-Order Beliefs

Our most fundamental primitive beliefs are so taken for granted that we are apt not to notice that we hold them at all; we remain unaware of them until they are called to our attention or are brought into question by some bizarre circumstance in which they appear to be violated. For example, we believe that an object continues to exist even when we are not looking at it; we believe that objects remain the same size and shape as we move away from them even though their visual images change; and, more generally, we believe that our perceptual and conceptual worlds have a degree of orderliness and stability over time. Our faith in the validity of our sensory experience is the most important primitive belief of all.

These are among the first beliefs that a child learns as he interacts with his environment, and in a psychological sense, they are continuously validated by experience. As a result, we are usually unaware of the fact that alternatives to these beliefs could exist, and it is precisely for this reason that we remain unaware of the beliefs themselves. Only a very unparochial and intellectual fish is aware that his environment is wet. What else could it be? We shall call primitive beliefs of this fundamental kind "zero-order" beliefs. They are the unconscious axioms upon which our other beliefs are built.

First-Order Beliefs

Because we implicitly hold these zero-order beliefs about the trustworthiness of our senses, particular beliefs that are based upon direct sensory experience seem to carry their own justification. When a man justifies his belief in the roundness of oranges by citing his experiences with oranges, that in fact usually does end the matter. He does not run through a syllogistic argument of the form:

> *1st Premise:*   *My senses tell me that oranges are round.*
> *2nd Premise:*   *My senses tell me true.*
> *Conclusion:*   *Therefore, oranges are round.*

There is no such inferential process involved in going from the first premise to the conclusion, as far as the individual himself is concerned, because he takes the second premise for granted: it is a zero-order belief. Accordingly, the first premise ("My senses tell me that oranges are round") is psychologically synonymous with the conclusion ("Oranges are round"). We shall call such conclusions "first-order" beliefs. Unlike zero-order beliefs, an individual is usually aware of his first-order beliefs because he can readily imagine alternatives to them (oranges could be square), but he is usually not aware of any inferential process by which they derive from zero-order beliefs. Like zero-order beliefs, then, first-order beliefs are still appropriately called primitive beliefs—that is, beliefs which demand no independent formal or empirical confirmation and which require no justification beyond a brief citation of direct experience.

Primitive Beliefs Based on External Authority

We not only experience our world directly, we are told about it as well. It is in this way that notions about such intangibles as God, absent grandmothers, and threatened tooth decay first enter a child's system of beliefs. And to the child, such beliefs may seem as direct, as palpable, and as assuredly valid as any beliefs based on direct sensory encounter. When mommy says that not brushing after every meal causes tooth decay, that is synonymous with the fact that not brushing after every meal causes tooth decay. Such a belief is a primitive first-order belief for the child because the intervening premise, "Mommy says only true things," is nonconscious; the possibility that mommy sometimes says false things is not a conceivable alternative. First-order beliefs based upon a zero-order belief in the credibility of an external authority, then, are functionally no different from first-order beliefs based upon an axiomatic belief in the credibility of our senses. As sources of information, mommy and our senses are equally reliable. Our implicit faith in them are zero-order beliefs.

This emphasis upon the innocence of childhood should not obscure the fact that we all hold primitive beliefs. It is an epistemological and psychological necessity, not a flaw of intellect or a surplus of naiveté. We all share the fundamental zero-order beliefs about our senses, and most of us hold similar sorts of first-order beliefs. For example, we rarely question beliefs such as "This woman is my mother" and "I am a human being." Most of us even treat arbitrary social-linguistic conventions like "This is my left hand" and "Today is Tuesday" as if they were physical bits of knowledge handed down by some authority who "really knows." Finally, most religious and quasi-religious beliefs are first-order beliefs based upon an unquestioned zero-order faith in some internal or external source of knowledge. The child who sings "Jesus loves me—this I know, / For the Bible tells me so" is actually being less evasive about the metaphysical—and hence nonconfirmable—nature of his belief than our founding fathers were when they presumed to interpret reality for King George III: "We hold these truths to be self-evident . . ."

Source: From *Beliefs, Attitudes, and Human Affairs*, by Daryl J. Bem, pages 5–7. Copyright © 1970 by Wadsworth Publishing Co., Inc. Reprinted by permission of the publisher, Brooks/Cole Publishing Co., Monterey, Calif.

Empirical evidence that there really is a difference between the various types of beliefs discussed above has been presented by Rokeach (1968). He showed that primitive beliefs which are shared with other individuals were most resistant to change, followed by primitive beliefs which are not widely shared. Next in resistance to change came beliefs about authority, such as "The Pope is infallible in matters of faith and morals" or "The philosophy of Karl Marx is basically a sound one, and I am all for it." Next came derived beliefs, such as "Birth control is morally wrong" or "The Russians were justified in putting down the Hungarian revolt in 1956." Finally, easiest to change were inconsequential beliefs concerning matters of taste, like "I think summertime is a much more enjoyable time of the year than winter" or "There is no doubt in my mind that Elizabeth Taylor is more beautiful than Dinah Shore."

Syllogistic Structure of Beliefs

We have seen that nonprimitive beliefs such as the ones just quoted can be derived from other beliefs which we hold. Beliefs exist in interconnected networks, and a useful way of thinking about their connections is to use the syllogistic model proposed by Jones and Gerard (1967) and earlier by McGuire (1960). As you may remember from studying logic, a syllogism is a set of three statements, two of which (the first and second premises) lead logically to the third (the conclusion). For example:

> 1st Premise: Using birth control protects a woman from getting pregnant.
> 2nd Premise: I want to be protected from getting pregnant.
> Conclusion: Therefore, I should use birth control.

The conclusion is a derived belief, and in this case both premises are also derived from other beliefs. Let us trace a possible chain of derivations for this conclusion back to a primitive belief. The next step back might be:

> My doctor says that using birth control protects a woman from getting pregnant.
> My doctor is an authority about medical matters.
> Therefore, using birth control protects a woman from getting pregnant.

Here the second premise is a belief about authority, and for many people this step in reasoning might end the matter. They trust their doctor as a reliable source of facts about medical matters, though of course they wouldn't necessarily accept him as an authority in other fields such as car repair or politics. If this is the end of a person's chain of reasoning, then we have arrived at one of his primitive beliefs, an idea so self-evident to him that he takes it for granted: "My doctor knows about medical matters."

The Vertical Structure of Beliefs. Another person, however, might have a longer, more elaborate chain of reasoning, one with more links between the ultimate conclusion and the underlying primitive belief. This characteristic of the belief system has been called its **vertical structure**. Tracing the chain of reasoning back several more steps, this person might have beliefs about the doctor's candor and about his source of information:

My doctor believes that using birth control protects a woman from getting pregnant.
My doctor says what he really believes.
Therefore, my doctor says that using birth control protects a woman from getting pregnant.

Scientific studies show that using birth control protects a woman from getting pregnant.
My doctor believes scientific studies.
Therefore, my doctor believes that using birth control protects a woman from getting pregnant.

The journal *Science* has reported scientific studies showing that using birth control protects a woman from getting pregnant.
Science is an authoritative source of accurate information.
Therefore, it is true that scientific studies show that using birth control protects a woman from getting pregnant.

Again we have reached a primitive belief about authority as the underlying premise in this chain of reasoning. No matter how wise or well-informed we are, many of our beliefs ultimately rest on our faith in some authority: the Bible, the *New York Times, Time* magazine, the encyclopedia, the President, William Buckley, or some other source of information which we trust.

The Horizontal Structure of Beliefs. Fortunately, most of our beliefs do not rest on just one line of reasoning nor stem from just one authority. There are usually several different routes to the same conclusion. The breadth of support for a given belief has been called its **horizontal structure**. For instance, there may be several other chains of reasoning leading to the same conclusion about personal use of birth control. One might be:

> World overpopulation leads to famine.
> Famine is bad.
> Therefore, world overpopulation is bad.
>
> World overpopulation is bad.
> Birth control programs can reduce world overpopulation.
> Therefore, birth control programs are good for the world.
>
> Birth control programs are good for the world.
> I should take part in programs which are good for the world.
> Therefore, I should use birth control.

Another part of the horizontal structure might be:

> Using birth control produces a more enjoyable sex life.
> I want an enjoyable sex life.
> Therefore, I should use birth control.

Of course, these supporting chains of beliefs are not necessarily in the person's awareness at any given time, and the person may not even be able to verbalize them without extensive self-searching and introspection. Also, a person's beliefs are rarely all consistent in leading to the same conclusions. There are usually some contradictory beliefs also present, such as:

> Using birth control has some medical hazards.
> I don't like to run the risk of medical hazards.
> Therefore, I shouldn't use birth control.

The question of the amount and importance of consistency in a person's belief systems is one which has been widely debated by attitude theorists, as we will see in Chapter 9.

"Psycho-Logic" in Belief Systems. It is important to realize that, though we have used logical syllogisms to indicate the structure of belief systems, a person's beliefs are not usually completely logical or rational. In fact, some of the syllogisms quoted above would not meet the rigorous specifications of a logician. The following reasoning is no more illogical than the first syllogism supporting birth control above, but it would probably be much less acceptable to most women:

> Never associating with men can prevent a woman from getting pregnant.
> I don't want to get pregnant.
> Therefore, I should never associate with men.

Not only may the basic reasoning process be faulty, but even if the reasoning is correct, false premises may lead to incorrect conclusions. Also, as Bem (1970,

p. 13) has pointed out, "there are often inconsistencies between different higher-order beliefs even though the internal reasoning behind each separate belief is consistent within its own vertical structure. That is, one line of reasoning leads to one conclusion: a second line leads to a contradictory conclusion."

Thus, the typical state of people's belief systems is a kind of rough, partial consistency rather than complete logical rationality. If we look closely, there are usually many gaps, overlaps, and conflicts among the beliefs which we hold. Abelson and Rosenberg (1958) have coined the term **psycho-logic** to describe the way in which people's beliefs are based on ideas and concepts which seem to "go together" comfortably from their subjective viewpoints rather than being derived by strict deductive logic. If there are inconsistencies or contradictions, they can often be avoided by denial, or by redefining concepts, or by other cognitive mechanisms, or simply by refusing to think about the conflict.

Finally, there is evidence that people often choose their beliefs in order to support their feelings about a topic. McGuire (1960) called this process "wishful thinking" in his extensive experimental study which clearly demonstrated the prevalence of such nonlogical thinking side by side with more logical reasoning processes. Other studies have suggested that people may selectively search for information supporting their feelings or selectively avoid contrary information, rather than rationally considering all the evidence. This common phenomenon of beliefs supporting feelings leads us to our next topic, the question of the relationship between the cognitive (thinking), emotional (feeling), and behavioral aspects of attitudes.

THE STRUCTURE OF ATTITUDES

Moving now from discussion of the structure of beliefs to the structure of attitudes, we need to consider two important dimensions: the valence and complexity of attitudes.

Valence and Complexity of Attitudes

Attitudes are, by many definitions, intrinsically evaluative; that is, they involve positive and/or negative feelings toward the attitude object. The **valence** of an attitude is the degree of favorability or unfavorability of the person's feelings toward the object. An example would be how favorable or unfavorable one feels toward the Democratic Party. It is this evaluative dimension of attitudes which is usually measured by the type of scales which we discussed in Chapter 2.

Another, less-commonly-measured characteristic of attitudes is their **complexity**, that is, the number of elements which they contain. This dimension has also been referred to as **multiplexity** (Krech, Crutchfield, & Ballachey, 1962). Each of the three aspects or components of an attitude can range from being very simple to very complex. For instance, in the area of political attitudes, the cognitive component of active members of a political party is likely to be highly differentiated (complex)—i.e., composed of many different beliefs. In the United States a party member is apt to have information and beliefs about several potential candidates for President, about many issues important to the party's platform, about a number of Senators, Congressmen, and other party figures, about important events in the party's history, etc. By contrast, many Americans probably have very simple belief systems regarding Britain's Labour Party, perhaps even just a single dim impression that it is connected somehow to the labor union movement, or that its leader was Harold Wilson.

Similarly, the affective component of attitudes can range from simple liking or disliking for a distant acquaintance to a very complex set of feelings toward someone we know well. Close associates of a political leader might hold a complex mixture of feelings toward him, possibly including admiration, supportiveness, envy, resentment, amusement, and occasional anger. Likewise, the third component of attitudes, behavioral tendencies toward such a public figure, might range from simply intending to vote for him, to the other end of the scale, where one might be ready to carry out a complex set of actions such as advising him, helping to write his speeches, soliciting public support from his colleagues, running errands, and even taking the blame for his political mistakes.

Theoretical Views Regarding Attitude Components

As mentioned in Chapter 1, the view of attitudes as having separate cognitive, affective, and behavioral components raises the question of consistency between these components. This view requires a relatively high (but not perfect) degree of consistency. If there is little or no consistency among them, there is no reason to consider the three components as aspects of the same concept (attitude); instead they would have to be viewed as entirely independent entities. On the other hand, if they are perfectly correlated, they cannot be separate components; in this case they would merely be different names for the same thing.

McGuire (1969, p. 157) concluded, after surveying the literature, that the three components have proven to be so highly intercorrelated that it is probably not worthwhile to maintain distinctions between them. However, an opposite conclusion has been reached by Krech, Crutchfield, and Ballachey (1962), who favor the tripartite view. On the basis of their review of the literature, they stated that there is only a "moderately high" relationship between the three components (typically, a correlation coefficient of about $+.5$); and they even cited evidence from one study showing a relationship as low as $r = +.2$ or $+.3$ between the cognitive and behavioral components.

These conflicting findings suggest that Fishbein and Ajzen's (1972) viewpoint concerning beliefs, attitudes, and behavioral intentions is preferable, since it does not require a necessary connection between these concepts, but it does allow

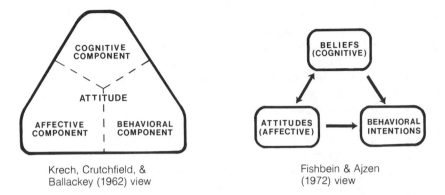

Krech, Crutchfield, &
Ballackey (1962) view

Fishbein & Ajzen
(1972) view

Figure 3-1 Two viewpoints on components of attitudes.

for a strong relationship under certain specified conditions (see Fig. 3-1). They point out that most attitude scales are made up of several items stating various beliefs and/or intentions about the attitude object. However, many beliefs or intentions will not make satisfactory items for such a scale. Examples include beliefs which are so widely agreed upon that they are not held differentially by people with different attitudes ("President Nixon was a Republican"); or statements whose evaluative significance is ambiguous (e.g., "As a national leader, President Nixon's performance was about average"—disagreement here might indicate either a high or a low evaluation of Nixon). Thus, it is only when an "attitude scale" has been carefully constructed from several well-chosen belief or intention items that we should expect it to correlate highly with other standard attitude measures. And in any case there will always be many belief and intention items which will not correlate highly with such a scale (Fishbein & Ajzen, 1972, pp. 495–496).

A further question related to the topic of attitude structure is whether attitudes and **behavior** (that is, overt responses) are consistent. Considerable attention has been directed to this question in recent years, and we will consider it at length in Chapter 10.

Research Findings Regarding Attitude Components

In this section we will briefly describe three successive waves of research on attitude components. The first wave was part of the great burst of empirical research in social psychology which followed World War II. It was marked primarily by **correlational** studies, that is, ones which measured the *naturally occurring* covariation in two or more variables. (The term "correlational" is not limited solely to studies which use correlation coefficients as their statistical procedure.) The second wave consisted of **experimental** studies, that is, ones which *manipulated* one or more independent variables and observed their effects on one or more dependent variables. Typically these were studies of attitude change in which one component of an attitude was influenced by an experimental procedure and the resulting effects on another component of the attitude were observed. The third, recent wave of research investigated less-global, more-detailed questions; it focused on the *conditions* under which the several attitude components would be similar and the conditions under which they would be different. We will mention only a few studies from each wave as representatives of that type of research and its findings.

The first wave of correlational research on attitude components was typified by a study by Donald T. Campbell (1947). He studied attitudes toward five different ethnic minority groups (Negroes, Jews, Japanese, etc.) among non-minority-group college students and high school students. He measured the behavioral component of attitudes with a social distance scale, indicating tendencies to avoid contact with members of each minority group. The affective component was measured by feelings of liking or disliking for each group, and the cognitive component was measured by three scales indicating beliefs in each group's competence, morality, and degree of blame for social problems. In general, the several dimensions for each group were found to correlate around +.5, showing a substantial positive relationship, but not a complete identity.

A study by Rosenberg (1956) related two dimensions of the cognitive component to the affective component of subjects' attitudes on two issues: "whether members of the Communist Party should be allowed to address the public," and "allowing Negroes to move into white neighborhoods." The two cognitive dimensions involved subjects' ratings of the **importance** to them of each of 35 possible values (e.g., "Being well-informed about current affairs." "People being strongly patriotic"), and the **perceived instrumentality** of the attitude object for each value (i.e., to what extent would "allowing members of the Communist Party to address the public" either aid or block the attainment of the value). The results were analyzed using a statistical technique called Chi square instead of correlation coefficients, but the findings were very similar to the previously-cited study. The results were identical for both the Communist-speaker issue and the Negroes-in-white-neighborhoods issue. Both of the cognitive dimensions, value importance and perceived instrumentality, were found to be very significantly and positively related to subjects' overall affective reaction to the issue.

The second wave, consisting of experimental, attitude-change studies, began in the 1950s. One example was Carlson's (1956) study which, like the Rosenberg study described above, hypothesized that the affective component of a person's attitude might best be predicted by using the product of the two cognitive dimensions, value importance and perceived instrumentality. In this study the primary attitude issue was Negro housing segregation, and the attitude-change procedure was directed at modifying perceived instrumentality. It consisted of both experimenter-initiated and subject-volunteered arguments showing that "allowing Negroes to move into white neighborhoods" would help to accomplish certain important goals, such as improving American prestige abroad and providing equality of opportunity. As a result of this manipulation of a cognitive dimension of attitude, the affective dimension was significantly changed in the same direction, as predicted. In addition, it was shown that the attitude change was only significant for subjects with moderate initial attitudes and not for extremely prejudiced or extremely nonprejudiced subjects.

The high-water-mark of experimental studies on attitude components occurred in a volume produced by the Yale University research group headed by Carl Hovland (Rosenberg, Hovland, McGuire, Abelson, & Brehm, 1960). It contained several studies showing the influence of one attitude component on other components. Rosenberg (1960) reported a study using hypnotic suggestion to change the *affective* component of feelings toward issues such as U. S. foreign economic aid; he found resulting parallel changes in the cognitive components of value importance and perceived instrumentality. These changes were also shown to remain stable for a full week, until the hypnotic suggestion was removed, at which time they rapidly reverted but did not immediately return all the way to their original level of extremity. Brehm (1960) showed, consistent with hypotheses from dissonance theory, that changes in the *behavioral* component of attitude (achieved by inducing teenage children to agree to eat a vegetable they disliked) produced parallel changes in the subjects' beliefs about the vegetable's beneficial vitamin content.

Another study in this same volume (McGuire, 1960) assessed subjects' beliefs in many different propositions, which included subgroups of statements having a clearcut logical relationship to each other. McGuire found a high degree of consistency in beliefs about these cognitive elements, but the consistency was far from perfect because of tendencies toward "wishful thinking" and toward cognitive isolation of inconsistent opinions in "logic-tight compartments." One part of the study showed that the Socratic method of inquiry (merely asking subjects to state their beliefs) was sufficient to produce greater cognitive consistency on a retest one week later. Another portion of the study provided evidence for both *wishful thinking* (a conclusion's desirability influencing belief in its probability) and, on the other hand, for *rationalization* (a conclusion's probability influencing belief in its desirability).

The third wave of studies on attitude components has focused on some of the conditions which lead to similarity or dissimilarity between the components. We have already seen one example in Carlson's (1956) finding that attempts at cognitive change led to significant affective change only for subjects who had moderate initial attitudes, and not for extremely prejudiced or extremely nonprejudiced subjects. A more recent study was done by D. Smith (1968) concerning college students' attitudes (the affective component—called "opinions" by the author) and their factual knowledge and beliefs (the cognitive component) on the issue of Federal aid to Catholic elementary and secondary schools. The general finding was that, as predicted, there was a strong relationship between the subjects' beliefs and their feelings on this issue. But Smith analyzed the data further and showed that this relationship was stronger (a) for those subjects whose feelings were extreme than for subjects with more moderate feelings, and (b) for those subjects who perceived important other people (parents, friends, etc.) as agreeing with their own feelings than for subjects who perceived others as disagreeing with them. For instance, most subjects believed more facts which were consistent with their feelings on the issue than ones which were in opposition to their feelings, but subjects whose friends and/or parents disagreed with their feelings were quite likely to believe just as many or more uncongenial facts as facts which favored their own affective position.

Another study comparing cognitive and affective components was done by A. Smith and Clark (1973), focusing on high school and college students' attitudes toward Negroes. The study utilized Fishbein's (1963) model, which had shown that a person's attitudes could be very successfully predicted by a formula combining his beliefs in the attitude object's characteristics with his evaluation of those characteristics. However, these authors analyzed the separate contribution to the overall attitude provided by each of 11 characteristics which subjects might believe to be typical of Negroes (e.g., dark skin, lazy, musical, friendly). They found some characteristics (e.g., dark skin) where the evaluative (affective) reaction to the characteristic was crucial in predicting subjects' overall attitudes, several characteristics where the cognitive component was crucial (e.g., the strength of belief that Negroes were hard workers), and several characteristics which did not contribute appreciably to attitudes at all (e.g., athletic, musical).

From this brief review of research on the components of attitudes, it should be clear that, though there is general consistency between the three components, nevertheless many situations have been found where there are meaningful distinctions and differences among them. McGuire (1969) seems to be in a distinct minority in questioning the utility of these distinctions—an especially paradoxical situation since some of his earlier research (McGuire, 1960) helped to establish evidence of cognitive-affective differences.

Katz and Stotland (1959) have suggested that some attitudes have mostly cognitive elements, others mostly affective elements, and others mostly behavioral elements. This viewpoint can also be linked to the question of attitude functions with which this chapter began, for understanding-oriented attitudes might be more likely to be largely cognitive, while value-expressive attitudes might be largely behavioral, etc. Finally, it may be speculated that ego-defensive attitudes are most likely to have components which are not consistent, whereas other types of attitudes are more likely to have consistent components (Katz & Stotland, 1959).

A DIFFERENT APPROACH—ATTITUDE LATITUDES

A rather different approach to the structure of attitudes has been taken by Muzafer Sherif and his colleagues (Sherif, 1960; Sherif & Hovland, 1961;

Photograph courtesy of Muzafer Sherif.
Reprinted by permission.

Box 3-3 MUZAFER SHERIF, *Proponent of Attitude Latitudes*

Born in Turkey in 1906, Muzafer Sherif did graduate work at the University of Istanbul, Harvard, the University of Berlin, and received his Ph.D. from Columbia in 1935. His dissertation research, published as The Psychology of Social Norms, *achieved fame as a pioneering experimental study in social psychology. Returning to Turkey, he taught at Ankara University, conducted research on social judgment and on adolescence, and translated many American psychological works into Turkish.*

Following World War II, Sherif held research fellowships with Hadley Cantril at Princeton and Carl Hovland at Yale. Each of these collaborations resulted in a well-known book. From 1949 to 1966 he was professor of psychology at the University of Oklahoma, and subsequently professor of sociology at Pennsylvania State University. His 100 publications include over 20 books which he has written, coauthored or edited; and in 1968 he received the American Psychological Association's highest honor, the Distinguished Scientific Contribution Award. His major recent research has concentrated on intergroup conflict and cooperation, and on processes of social perception and judgment. His social judgment theory of attitude change is discussed in Chapter 9, and his contributions to attitude measurement are pointed out in this chapter.

Sherif, Sherif, & Nebergall, 1965). Sherif has called his viewpoint a social judgment approach, emphasizing that the process by which a person makes judgments about social objects (other people, objects, events, issues, etc.) is both affective and cognitive at the same time. That is, it involves both evaluation of the objects and categorization of them as similar to or different from other objects. Thus he stresses that the "cognitive" and "affective" aspects of attitudes are inextricably intertwined.

Sherif's major contribution to attitude theory and measurement is the concept of **latitude**, that is, a range of attitudinal positions which a person may accept or reject concerning a given issue. Sherif stresses that a single score cannot give us sufficient information about a person's attitude.

Even if two individuals have the same position on an issue—say, both favor segregation—they may differ with respect to the other stands each is willing to consider or tolerate and to the range of viewpoints each consigns to definitely objectionable categories. Such differences, even among persons espousing similar positions, should be considered in predicting how these individuals will react to a specific event bearing on their attitude, to a discussion of the pros and cons of the issue, as well as to a communication aimed at persuading people to change (Sherif et al., 1965, pp. 7–8).

Thus, since most attitude-measurement techniques yield a single score for each respondent, Sherif feels that they are inadequate to the job of fully understanding attitudes. Though they may be

> . . . useful for locating individuals who take a stand on one or the other side of a controversial issue, [they] tell us very little about the person who adopts a moderate or neutral position. They tell us little about the subject's possible susceptibility to change, the direction in which change is most likely, how tolerant the individual is of other positions, or how committed he is to his own stand (Sherif et al., 1965, p. 21).

How does Sherif propose to determine all this? First, by measuring the individual's latitudes of acceptance, rejection, and noncommitment, and second, by developing an indicator of his **ego-involvement**, that is, his personal commitment to his own stand on the issue. The **latitude of acceptance** is the set of positions on an issue (or toward a person or object) which a person finds acceptable. The **latitude of rejection** is the set of positions which the person finds objectionable. The **latitude of noncommitment** is any other positions on the issue, which the person neither accepts nor rejects. Research findings have led Sherif to the conclusion that the best measure of ego-involvement is the breadth of the person's latitude of rejection. (Highly ego-involved people reject more positions as personally unacceptable than do uninvolved individuals.)

The procedure for measuring the three latitudes requires subjects to make judgments about the acceptability and then the unacceptability of a fairly large number of attitude positions. In a typical study concerning the 1960 presidential election, Sherif et al. (1965) used nine positions ranging from strongly pro-Republican positions, through milder ones, to neutrality, and on to strongly pro-Democratic positions. As examples, here are positions number 1, 3, and 5 in the sequence of 9:

1. The election of the Republican presidential and vice-presidential candidates in November is absolutely essential from all angles in the country's interests.
3. It seems that the country's interests would be better served if the presidential and vice-presidential candidates of the Republican party were elected this November.
5. From the point of view of the country's interests, it is hard to decide whether it is preferable to vote for presidential and vice-presidential

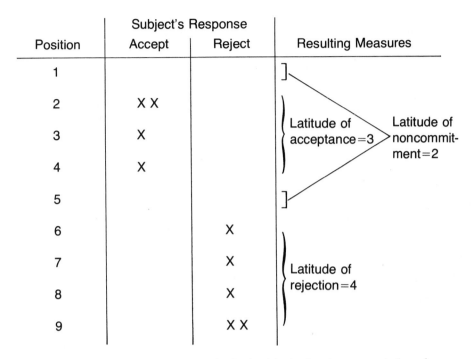

Figure 3-2 Responses of a hypothetical subject, showing computation of attitude latitudes.

candidates of the Republican party or the Democratic party in November.

A typical subject might check position number 2 as most acceptable and numbers 3 and 4 as also acceptable, check positions 6, 7, 8, and 9 as unacceptable, and leave positions 1 and 5 unchecked. Thus, according to Sherif's definitions, this person would have a latitude of acceptance of three positions, a latitude of rejection of four positions, and a latitude of noncommitment of two positions (see Figure 3-2).

Research Findings on Attitude Latitudes

What would you guess about the relative size of the three latitudes? Would you expect people to accept more positions than they rejected, or vice versa? And what kind of people reject the most positions? Results from extensive studies using the latitude concept, summarized by Sherif et al. (1965), may surprise you. They found, first of all, that no matter what the person's own position on the issue was, the average size of the latitude of *acceptance* was about the same (approximately three positions). Second, the latitude of *rejection* was the largest of the three latitudes and, as predicted, its size was greater for subjects holding extreme positions than for more moderate or neutral subjects. Third, as predicted, the latitude of *noncommitment* was largest for individuals holding a neutral viewpoint and considerably smaller for ones with extreme positions. Thus extreme Republicans and extreme Democrats were found to be nearly identical in their attitude structure (the number of positions which they accepted, rejected, and were noncommittal about) despite their opposition in attitude content. Also, the extreme party supporters on both sides were markedly different in attitude structure from the more moderate supporters of the same party.

These interesting results are graphically displayed in Figure 3-3. Very similar results have been found for some other issues such as right-to-work legislation and federal farm policy questions.

These findings suggest that moderates on any issue typically accept about the same number of positions that they reject. However, people with extreme viewpoints ("far out" on either fringe) typically reject substantially more positions than the number that they accept. There are also usually a few individuals with roughly neutral positions who nevertheless hold to their positions very strongly; for instance, in the political arena such individuals would be dedicated independents. Unlike other neutral or "undecided" respondents, they typically reject nearly as many positions as do the extreme partisans. Sherif et al. (1965, p. 59)

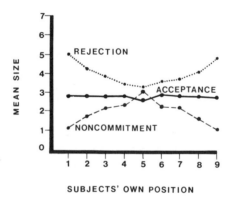

SUBJECTS' OWN POSITION

Figure 3-3 Average size (number of positions) of latitudes of acceptance, rejection, and noncommitment for persons endorsing different positions as most acceptable in the 1960 presidential election. Positions along base line range from 1 (most extreme Republican) through 5 (nonpartisan) to 9 (most extreme Democrat).

Source: Adapted from Sherif, C. W., Sherif, M. and Nebergall, R. E. *Attitude and Attitude Change: The Social Judgment-Involvement Approach*. Philadelphia: Saunders, 1965, p. 52.

concluded that " . . . attitude research has concentrated too exclusively on the subject's agreements or acceptances and far too little on what he rejects."

Sherif's conclusions have not gone unchallenged, and some critics of his theorizing have reinterpreted findings regarding the latitudes of acceptance and rejection in terms of perceptual distortions and the properties of subjective scales (e.g., Dawes—see Triandis, 1971, p. 88). We will return to Sherif's social judgment theory in Chapter 9 and examine its performance in the area of attitude change research.

SUMMARY

In this chapter we have seen that attitudes and beliefs can perform several different functions for the person who holds them. They aid in *understanding* of situations and events; they provide *satisfaction of needs* by helping their holder to adjust to his environment; they form a bulwark of *ego defense* against threats to the person's self-esteem; and they provide a channel for *expression of values* which are important to him. A particular attitude may serve one or several of these functions. The function(s) which it serves will largely determine the particular circumstances which will *arouse* the attitude so that it enters the person's conscious awareness or directly influences his behavior. Similarly, different forces and pressures are necessary in order to *change* attitudes which serve different functions.

The *centrality* of a belief is its importance in the person's belief system, while a belief's *intensity* is how strongly it is held. *Primitive beliefs* are, by definition, very central in the person's belief system, and they are so much taken for granted that the holder hardly ever has reason to question them. Primitive beliefs are formed either through direct contact with the object of belief or through accepting the statement of an unquestioned external authority such as Mommy or the Bible. Derived beliefs, on the other hand, can be built up from basic underlying beliefs in a syllogistic type of structure. They may have a short or a long, multistep vertical structure, and a broad or a narrow horizontal structure of alternative underlying beliefs. Despite their syllogistic structure, beliefs are not usually completely logical or rational. They are built up of elements which "go to-gether" comfortably in the person's belief system, in accordance with a principle of "psycho-logic" or rough consistency, rather than following the rules of strict deductive logic.

The *valence* of an attitude is its degree of favorability or unfavorability toward the attitude object, and its *complexity* is the number of elements which it contains. The common tripartite view of attitudes as having cognitive, affective, and behavioral components requires that there be a high, but not perfect, degree of consistency among the three components. Three waves of research on attitude components have shown that there is very often a general consistency between the components, but there are also many situations where there are meaningful distinctions and differences among them.

A different viewpoint on the structure of attitudes rejects the notion that a person's attitude can be adequately represented by a single point on a scale. Sherif and his colleagues have emphasized the concept of *latitude:* the range of positions which a person accepts or rejects on a given issue. Research has shown that the width of a person's latitude of rejection on an issue is a good measure of his *ego-involvement* in the issue. Extremists typically reject more positions than they accept.

Suggested Readings

Katz, D. The functional approach to the study of attitudes. *Public Opinion Quarterly*, 1960, 24, 163–204.—A definitive description of the functions which attitudes can serve, and the resulting implications for attitude arousal and attitude change.

Rokeach, M. *Beliefs, Attitudes, and Values: A Theory of Organization and Change.* San Francisco: Jossey-Bass, 1968.—Chapter 1, pages 1–21, gives a more complete discussion of the centrality of beliefs, together with some relevant research results.

Rosenberg, M. J.; Hovland, C. I.; McGuire, W. J.; Abelson, R. P.; & Brehm, J. W. *Attitude Organization and Change: An Analysis of Consistency among Attitude Components.* New Haven, Conn.: Yale University Press, 1960.—The most complete collection of experimental research studies on this topic.

Sherif, C. W.; Sherif, M.; & Nebergall, R. E. *Attitude and Attitude Change: The Social Judgment-Involvement Approach.* Philadelphia: Saunders, 1965.—Chapter 2, pages 18–59, describes the measurement of latitudes of acceptance, rejection, and noncommitment and presents empirical results from studies of the 1960 presidential election.

Public Opinion Polling

I don't think the polls are here to stay.—Vice-Presidential candidate Henry Cabot Lodge, 1960.

Look at these poll results.—President Lyndon Johnson, 1966.

Polls interfere with our elective processes.—Senator Albert Gore.

Polls can help make government more efficient and responsive; . . . they can make this a truer democracy.—Pollster George Gallup.

In this chapter and the following one we turn to a consideration of public opinion polling—first its procedures and problems, and then its findings about the structure of public opinion.

Public opinion polling is certainly the aspect of psychological measurement with which the general public is most familiar. The major commercial polls, such as Gallup's and Harris', appear every week or so in hundreds of newspapers throughout the country. Particularly at national election times, there are almost daily reports about the voting intentions of some part of the public, and many aspiring politicians hire private polling firms to help determine their "name recognition" and attractiveness to voters.

Other groups of pollers are located in academic research institutions, the best-known of which are the Survey Research Center at the University of Michigan and the National Opinion Research Center (NORC) at the University of Chicago. They tend to do large-scale and carefully-designed research studies that have less pressing deadlines than those under which the commercial polling firms must operate.

How valid are the results of public opinion polls? The answer to this question depends on several factors, which are discussed in the following sections. Certainly some politicians have concluded that they are not valid. For instance, in 1960 vice-presidential candidate Henry Cabot Lodge said in a campaign speech: "people are going to look back on these polls as one of the hallucinations which the American people have been subjected to. . . . I don't think the polls are here to stay" (Hennessy, 1970b, p. 83). On the other hand, President Lyndon Johnson often pulled the latest poll out of his pocket to show visitors his popularity rating (when it was favorable). It appears that most politicians, whether they complain about the polls or praise them, nevertheless still pay close attention to poll results.

Despite the wide circulation of opinion-poll information, there are still many widespread misconceptions about the methods, results, and uses of polls. There is even a California state legislator who has been trying to ban opinion polls as being undemocratic! (*Los Angeles Times*, 1973). The following section will try to dispel some of the common misconceptions about polls and polling.

CHARACTERISTICS OF OPINION POLLS

Opinion poll results are sometimes obtained on street corners or over the telephone, but most often they are derived from face-to-face interviews held in the respondent's home. The interview usually contains a number of questions and may take as long as an hour or more to complete, depending on the topic and type of interview. Commercial pollers usually use shorter interviews than do academic researchers, but both groups typically find that respondents are glad to spend time talking about their opinions, once any initial resistance or suspicion which they may have is dissipated.

The content of interviews may be highly varied. There are usually questions about attitudes and opinions on important public issues, of course, and questions about demographic characteristics such as the respondent's age, occupation, and voter registration status. Other kinds of information which may be sought include the respondent's extent of knowledge on a given topic, his typical behavior patterns, his personal experiences, and his life circumstances. Thus, many factors may be examined together as possible causes or effects of the respondent's attitudes and opinions. Rather than being merely descriptive, in-depth surveys usually study a variety of possibly-causal factors by means of correlation techniques or by cross-tabulation of one factor against another. Examples of typical opinion interview questions have already been given in Box 2-1.

The **population** (or **public**) in which the poller is interested is usually a very large one. It might be the registered voters of a given state, or all citizens over age 18, or a particular class of citizens such as medical doctors. When such a large population is concerned, it is usually neither necessary nor desirable to contact every member—(the national census is probably the only major exception). Instead, a **sample** of respondents is chosen, whose interview responses will be used as an estimate of the views of the whole population. Therefore, the essential characteristic of any sample is **representativeness**, that is, the degree to which it is similar to the whole population.

A sample does not have to be extremely large in order to be representative, but it does have to be very carefully chosen. Of course, there is always some degree of error in any estimate, and the use of a sample necessarily entails some **sampling error** in estimating the population's views. However, in a careful probability sample, the degree of error of the estimate can be computed beforehand by means of a statistical formula, and the sample can be chosen in such a way as to yield any desired degree of precision. Contrary to common impressions, the factor determining the degree of precision is the size of the sample, *not* the size of the population. This means that just as large a sample is needed to represent a small population as a large population. Thus, a sample of 1500 respondents will estimate the views of the whole nation just as accurately as it will estimate the views of a single city's residents. How successfully? Well, a properly chosen sample of 1500 cases should not miss the true population value by more than 2½% in either direction. For example, if 55% of such a sample say they favor establishing full diplomatic relations with mainland China, the true percentage in the overall population is almost surely between 52.5% and 57.5%.

A sample size of about 1500 cases is typical for most of the national polls. The decision about sample size is necessarily a compromise between the cost (in time, effort, and money) and the degree of precision desired in the final data. More important usually than the size of the sample is the care with which it is chosen, and this is a place where many surveys go astray. Some of the major considerations in choosing the sample are discussed next.

Sampling Procedures*

There are many different types of sampling procedures. We will distinguish four main types here: haphazard sampling, systematically biased sampling, quota sampling, and probability sampling.

Haphazard sampling is an unsystematic, capricious choice of respondents, selected according to the interviewer's whim, or according to who happens to be available. It is the approach customarily used by "inquiring reporters," who often post themselves on a street corner and ask questions of convenient passers-by. It is, most emphatically, *not* identical with random sampling, though "haphazard" and "random" are sometimes used as synonyms in everyday speech. Because of its unsystematic nature, haphazard sampling is not representative of any population, and it therefore has no scientific value.

Systematically biased sampling is also an approach to be avoided. As the name implies, it involves systematic errors in a sample that was intended to be representative. Examples of biased samples would be ones which included too many old people, too many college graduates, too few minority group members, etc. The classic example of this kind of error was made in the 1936 presidential election poll conducted by the magazine *Literary Digest*. The magazine sent over eighteen million postcard ballots to citizens all over the country, and it received more than two million replies. Since the replies favored the Republican candidate, Alfred Landon, the magazine predicted his election. Instead, however, Franklin D. Roosevelt won re-election in a landslide, carrying all but two states. The source of bias in the sample was that the respondents' names were taken from automobile registration lists and telephone books; and in the depression year of 1936, people who could afford to own cars or even have telephones were systematically different in their presidential voting preferences from their poorer neighbors. Interestingly, this bias had been less marked in 1932 and previous elections, when similar sampling methods had correctly predicted the winners (Shively, 1971). After the 1936 fiasco, confidence in the *Literary Digest* was so badly shaken that the magazine died two years later. One clear lesson from this affair is that a large sample is not necessarily a good sample!

Quota sampling is the basic method used by many commercial polls. It achieved sudden prominence in the 1936 election, when several young pollers (George Gallup, Archibald Crossley, and Elmo Roper) all used it to predict Roosevelt's re-election, in dramatic contrast to the *Literary Digest* poll's failure. Many refinements have been added since 1936, but the basic principle is unchanged. This approach tries to achieve a representative sample by choosing respondents whose characteristics correspond to those of the national population on several important dimensions. For instance, the dimensions chosen might be geographic region of the country, urban versus rural residence, sex, age, and

*This section and the following two major sections of this chapter draw heavily from material in the author's chapter on research methods in *Social Psychology in the Seventies* (Wrightsman, 1972).

race. Then an interviewer in Chicago (Midwestern region, urban location) might be assigned a quota of respondents with the following characteristics: 10 respondents, all local residents, 5 women and 5 men, 1 of the women to be black and the other 9 respondents white, 1 woman and 1 man to be in each age decade between 20 and 70. The interviewer may be given a free hand as to how and where she finds these respondents, or in some cases there may be further restrictions on where she goes and whom she chooses to interview. (The word "she" is used here because a very large proportion of poll interviewers are women, employed only part-time. This imbalance in the sex of interviewers may, unfortunately, be a source of bias in their results.)

The quota method of sampling avoids the most obvious sources of systematic bias in the sample, and therefore it is much more likely to yield accurate results

---

Photograph courtesy of George Gallup.
Reprinted by permission.

Box 4-1 GEORGE GALLUP, *Public Opinion Poller*

The best-known figure in public opinion polling, George Gallup was born in Iowa in 1901 and took his B.A. and Ph.D. at the University of Iowa. Before entering the polling field, he taught journalism and psychology at Iowa, Northwestern, and Columbia. He then began doing commercial research on reader interest in newspapers and magazines and audience interest in radio and motion pictures.

In 1935, Gallup founded the American Institute of Public Opinion, of which he is still chairman, to measure public attitudes on social, political, and economic issues. Using the quota system of sampling, he and several other early pollers became famous by predicting President Roosevelt's surprising landslide in the 1936 election, and he also correctly predicted how far wrong the prestigious Literary Digest *poll would be. Since then he has pioneered many new trends and improvements in survey research, including use of some aspects of probability sampling, and regular research by The Gallup Poll has spread to 32 foreign countries.*

Gallup has published many articles and seven books on public opinion. Among his many honorary degrees and awards are election as president of the American Association for Public Opinion Research and receipt of its award for distinguished achievement.

than either haphazard sampling or systematically biased sampling. However, it does not avoid more subtle forms of systematic bias which may be inherent in the interviewer's choice of respondents within the limitations of her assigned quota. For instance, it is common and understandable that interviewers avoid the "seedy" areas of town, choose to interview only at certain times of the day, and bypass individuals whose looks or behavior they find offensive. Unfortunately, however, by doing so they also may be systematically excluding as respondents poor people, night-shift workers, young "hippies," or other classes of citizens. As a result, the accuracy of the poll's results is diminished.

Probability sampling avoids all of these problems. By definition, it requires that every individual in the population must have a known probability (usually an equal probability) of being chosen as a respondent. This in turn requires that there be a complete list of the population or a breakdown of the total population by cities and counties such as is provided in the national census. With this breakdown as the starting point, the investigator can choose his sample in such a way that equal weight is given to all segments of the population (e.g., different sections of the country, different sizes of cities, various racial groups, etc.).

There are several ways of obtaining a probability sample. The simplest is **systematic sampling**, choosing every *n*th name from a list, such as a college student directory. Next easiest is **random sampling**, drawing from a container whose contents have been thoroughly mixed (as in a properly-run Bingo game), or from a table of random numbers. Both of these methods require a complete list of the members of the population, which is not feasible for any population larger than a small city.

For polls of a larger city, a state, or of the whole nation, the method usually used is **area sampling** (which is one type of **stratified random sampling**). In this method the total population is broken down into small homogeneous units, such as counties (the first stratum), and a relatively few counties are chosen randomly to be in the sample. In this way the sample includes a group of counties which are typical of the whole country in characteristics such as income and educational level, racial makeup, degree of urbanization, etc. The chosen counties are then broken down into smaller units such as precincts or census tracts (the second stratum), and again a few tracts from each chosen county are randomly selected to be in the sample. A similar random procedure may be used to select a few blocks or other geographic areas from each chosen tract. For each of these final areas chosen to be in the sample, a field worker called an enumerator is sent out to list every dwelling unit in the area (including apartments over stores, cottages behind main houses, and all divided-up residences). With this list in hand, the sampling staff randomly chooses a few dwelling units from each sample area, and interviewers are sent to those specific dwellings. Finally, the interviewers are instructed to interview a specific person in each unit (e.g., an adult male—if there are two or more adult males living at the address, a final random choice will determine which one is interviewed). If the designated person is not at home, interviewers are instructed to come back, several times if necessary, in order to contact him. Thus, a stratified random sample uses random selection procedures within each stratum (level) of the sampling process.

This description suggests how difficult, time-consuming, and expensive a probability sample is. As a result, this method in its entirety is not used by commercial polls, but only by academic survey researchers. The great advantage of this method is that the expected amount of sampling error in the results can be stated exactly; it is an inverse function of the size of the sample (more precisely, of the square root of the sample size). As mentioned in the previous section, the expected error for a sample of 1500 cases would be no more than plus or minus 2½%. By comparison, for a sample of 500 cases, the expected error would be plus or minus 4½%; for a sample of 5000 cases, it would be plus or minus 1½%.

Probability sampling has the smallest amount of sampling error of any sampling method. Moreover, it is the only method where the expected amount of sampling error can be specified. With the sampling methods used by commercial pollsters such as Gallup, Roper, and Harris, one can only guess at the likely amount of error in their results. Thus, though area sampling is expensive and slow, it is the only way to insure that a sample is really representative of a large population.

Following their incorrect predictions in the 1948 Presidential election, several of the major commercial polling firms adopted some aspects of probability sampling in their procedures for selecting areas within which to interview (Perry, 1960). These changes have undoubtedly improved the representativeness of their samples, but they generally still allow the interviewer some discretion in choosing respondents, as in the quota method of sampling.

PROBLEMS IN PUBLIC OPINION POLLING

Famous Polling Failures

In 1948 President Truman was running for re-election against Governor Dewey of New York, and all the major polls picked Dewey as the probable winner. Partly for that reason, most people in the country seemed to expect Truman to lose, and the *Chicago Tribune* even hit the streets with a postelection headline proclaiming "Dewey Defeats Truman." Yet when the votes were all counted, Truman won. Whereas the Gallup poll, for instance, had predicted that Truman would receive only 44.5% of the vote, he actually won 49.5% of the vote in a four-party race.

Similarly, in the 1970 British elections the Labour Party led by Prime Minister Harold Wilson was widely expected to win. All except one of the major British polling organizations predicted a Labour win with a vote margin of anywhere from 2% to 9%. Yet on election day the Conservative Party led by Edward Heath scored a smashing upset, winning by a margin of nearly 5%.

These two instances represent the most-dramatic failures of scientific polling methods since the prescientific era of 1936 when the *Literary Digest* poll failed so ignominiously. How can these more recent failures be explained? Both elections have resulted in much scrutiny of the polls, and some of the lessons that have been learned are reported later in this chapter. Before trying to explain these failures, we will discuss some of the basic factors which produce problems in constructing polls and in obtaining valid results. The most important of these factors are: sampling, question wording, respondents' lapses of memory and motivated inaccuracy in reporting, nonanonymity of responses, interviewer effects on responses, and other practical problems.

Sampling Problems

Many of the problems in quota sampling procedures have been touched on in the previous section. The most important result of these problems is that the commercial polls, due to their sampling methods, cannot specify the expected amount of sampling error in their data.

In really close elections, such as the 1960 race between Kennedy and Nixon, the margin between the two candidates' popular vote totals is clearly less than the expected sampling error of the polls, and consequently the pollsters have had to admit that their data are not precise enough to be sure of picking the winner. That is a lesson which they learned from their fiasco in 1948 when, to their subsequent sorrow, they failed to exercise an equal degree of caution.

Also, it should be kept in mind that the commercial polls indicate the expected percentage of people voting for a presidential candidate nation-wide (the **popular vote**). By contrast the **electoral college vote**, which determines the winner, is based on the popular vote winner in each state separately. Thus it is conceivable in a close election that the polls could correctly predict the popular vote totals but fail to pick the winning candidate.

Nevertheless, despite the few famous polling failures described above, the general record of the commercial polls in predicting election results has been good. For instance, in the 1950–1970 period, the Gallup Poll's average error in predicting eleven congressional and presidential elections was only 1.6% (Gallup, 1972, p. 2341). Hennessy and Hennessy (1961) have presented an interesting comparison of the predictive success of the commercial polls, less sophisticated newspaper polls, and partisanly sponsored polls in the close election of 1960. Recent findings on the 1968 and 1972 elections show that careful statewide polls have had a good prediction record, even in the volatile, multiple-candidate presidential primary contests, and that polls taken just before the elections have spotted last-minute trends quite well (Felson & Sudman, 1975).

Question Wording

Planning and constructing a public opinion interview is a very large and complex task, about which whole books have been written. As early as 1932,

Wang had presented a comprehensive list of recommendations on the construction and wording of attitude and opinion questionnaires. Due to space limitations, our presentation here can only briefly list the most prominent considerations in wording interview questions. A full treatment can be found in the excellent book by Payne (1951), *The Art of Asking Questions*, and other interesting points are mentioned by Roll and Cantril (1972).

1. *Rapport.* The interview usually should begin with an explanation of its purpose and sponsorship and then some comments intended to put the respondent at ease as much as possible. The first questions are usually rather simple and factual ones which will be easy for respondents to answer and which will not threaten them in any way.

2. *Format of Questions.* They may be either multiple choice or open-ended ones which respondents answer in their own words. Both kinds have important and legitimate uses, and many interviews use some of each.

3. *Order of Questions.* Considerable thought must be given to having the questions in a logical order and to avoiding any influence of earlier questions on later answers. A common method which aims toward these goals is the **funnel sequence** of questions: asking broad, open-ended questions first, followed by somewhat more limited ones, and finally focusing very specifically on narrow aspects of the topic.

4. *Vocabulary Used.* When interviewing a representative sample of citizens, it must be remembered that many respondents will have little education, limited vocabularies, and rather poor understanding of technical terms. In addition to wording the questions carefully, it is essential to **pretest** them in order to determine how they are interpreted by respondents. An amusing example of this was a question about stock ownership on an early Gallup Poll, which found an unusually high level of ownership in the Southwest. It developed that many respondents there were thinking of livestock instead of stocks and bonds, so the question had to be reworded (Roll & Cantril, 1972).

5. *Clarity.* Ambiguity can be avoided in the following ways (adapted from Wang, 1932):

   a. Keep the questions short, simple, clear and direct.
   b. Avoid the use of negatives and especially of double negatives.
   c. Avoid use of the passive voice.
   d. Avoid questions that may be interpreted in more than one way.
   e. Avoid "double-barreled" questions (e.g., Do you favor stronger efforts to eliminate smog and water pollution?—The respondent may have different views on the two topics.)
   f. Avoid having so many alternative answers that the question is confusing.
   g. Avoid having so few alternative answers that the list is incomplete.

6. *Biased Questions.* The question should be as neutral as possible. If the question states one side of an argument and not the other, the usual tendency is

for most respondents to agree with the side stated (an example of acquiescence response set). Notice the responses to these two questions from Cantril (1944):

    a. Because every man is entitled to safe and healthy working conditions, labor (in defense industries) should be allowed to strike for them.—45% agreed, 45% disagreed.
    b. Because working conditions in this country are the best in the world, labor (in defense industries) should not be allowed to strike about them.—74% agreed, 17% disagreed.

Other question-biasing techniques to be avoided are the use of emotionally-laden words or phrases (e.g., "communist agitators," "police brutality") and the use of prestige names or symbols in the question. For instance, if an idea is attributed to a well-known and respected person (e.g., "President Ford's policy"), more people will generally agree with the idea than if the prestige name is omitted from the question.

7. *Incomplete Specification.* It has been said that people will answer what they think you mean rather than what you actually say. In a large part, this is a problem of interviewer and respondent having different frames of reference, and it can often be counteracted by asking supplementary questions. (The question "Why?" is often particularly valuable in determining the frames of reference or reasons behind a respondent's attitudes.)

A classic example of the frame of reference problem was provided by Bancroft and Welch (1946) from results of Bureau of the Census interviews designed to determine the number of employed persons in the U.S. The original question used was, "Did you do any work for pay or profit last week?", and it consistently underestimated the employed population. Apparently this occurred because many people such as housewives or students answered it in terms of their main occupation, overlooking the explicit term "any work." The solution adopted was to ask two questions: the first about the respondent's major activity, and a second one (for persons giving "nonworker" responses) as to whether they did any work for pay in addition to their major activity. As a result of this simple change, the official estimate of employment was raised by more than a million persons.

Memory Errors

We know that human memory is fallible, and many studies have been done to investigate the degree of interviewing errors due to faulty memory. In general they show that less important facts are forgotten more quickly than more important facts, and that memory becomes less accurate as the time interval from the event becomes longer. Even important past information is apt to be distorted by later events: Withey (1952) found reports of past years' income were often distorted in the direction of the respondent's current income.

A number of means can be used to increase the respondent's motivation to remember events accurately and to assist him in his efforts. These include: asking him to consult available records (diaries, income tax forms, birth certificates, etc.), providing contextual information in the question which will help the respondent locate an event in time or space, alerting him to the problem of bias in memory so that he can intentionally combat it in his response, and wording questions so that they require recognition rather than unaided recall. For instance, a list of possible responses (such as illnesses which he might have suffered) can be presented to the respondent, who is then asked to indicate which ones are applicable to him (Cannell & Kahn, 1968, p. 562).

Social Desirability Needs of Respondents

Interview questions are often worded with the implied assumption that the respondent knows something about the topic: "How do you feel about the government's farm policy?" Wanting to be obliging, and not wanting to show their ignorance, many respondents are inclined to fake a knowledge and interest that isn't real: "I think it's pretty good." Studies have shown that such answers from uninformed or uninterested respondents are almost useless, for they have very low reliability (Converse, 1964). Clearly, a needed safeguard is to learn the degree of a respondent's interest in a topic before asking him detailed questions about it.

However, social desirability bias is much more pervasive than just the nuisance of over-obliging respondents. On any topic where society's norms point to one answer as more socially desirable than another, we can expect an over-reporting of the "good" behaviors and an under-reporting of the "bad" ones. Some examples of social desirability bias in interview responses are shown in Box 4-2.

Several different methods can be used to combat social desirability response bias in interviews. First, there are many helpful techniques in wording the questions: using neutral (unbiased) wording, presenting two opposing alternatives for the respondent to choose between, stating that the question is a matter of opinion with no right or wrong answer, etc. Also, the interviewer should establish good rapport, reassuring the respondent by his supportive manner that any type of response will be perfectly acceptable in the interviewing situation. Detailed **probes** following a more general question may often turn up inconsistencies and avoid some over-reporting. Finally, where the researcher knows that bias is likely, as with retrospective voting reports, he can make appropriate statistical corrections to his obtained data.

Nonanonymity of Responses

A study comparing a "secret ballot" technique with the usual direct questioning interview method was carried out by Edwards during an election campaign in

---

Box 4-2 *Examples of Social Desirability Bias in Interview Responses*

1. Of a group of 920 Denver adults interviewed in 1949, at least 34% who claimed to have donated money to the community chest had not actually done so according to official records (Parry & Crossley, 1950).

2. Of the same group, about 22% falsely claimed to have voted in a particular recent election (the figure ranged from 13% to 28% for six different elections), whereas only 2% on the average incorrectly reported that they had not voted.

3. Of the same group, 10% incorrectly claimed to have a driver's license, whereas only 2% falsely reported that they did not possess one.

4. In a World War II study, Hyman (1944) found that 17% of his respondents falsely denied having cashed in any U.S. war bonds, and among upper-income groups, 43% refused to admit it.

5. Periods of hospitalization are often not reported, especially ones involving socially-threatening kinds of ailments (such as hemorrhoids, cancer, or mental illness). Cannell, Fisher, and Bakker (1961) found less than 10% under-reporting of hospitalizations which had occurred in the most recent 5 months, but as much as 56% under-reporting of hospitalizations for threatening illnesses which had occurred only 10–12 months previously.

6. Similarly, with the passage of time, there is an increasing tendency for respondents to report that they voted for the winning candidate in past elections, no matter how they actually voted. An extreme instance is that, by 1964, 64% of respondents reported having voted for Kennedy in 1960 instead of the 50% who actually did so (Mueller, 1973).

Source: Adapted from Oskamp (1972b, p. 55).

Seattle. The issue was a proposed state bill providing cash bonuses to war veterans. Interestingly, the "secret ballot" technique produced many more unfavorable responses (apparently opposition to veterans' bonuses was socially undesirable behavior). A public referendum vote a few weeks later validated the findings, since the actual vote was much closer to the "secret ballot" poll than to the direct interview results (Edwards, 1957, p. 4). A number of commercial polling organizations have adopted this "secret-ballot" technique to increase the validity of their presidential vote predictions (Perry, 1960).

However, several studies suggest that the importance of anonymity may have been overemphasized. At least among adolescents, anonymity is not necessary in order to obtain full reporting of socially undesirable behavior such as delinquent acts or drug usage (Kulik, Stein, & Sarbin, 1966; Josephson, Haberman, & Zanes, 1971).

Interviewer Effects on Responses

A vast body of scientific studies shows that the interviewer's behavior and personal characteristics can affect a respondent's answers. Some of the most interesting and most pervasive factors producing interviewer effects are listed briefly on the next page:

1. *Lack of Personal Sensitivity and* lack of ability to build rapport with respondents. There is unanimous agreement that such interviewer characteristics would lead to invalid responses (in fact, often to no responses at all).

2. *Inadequate Training.* Great improvement in interviewing performance can be produced by careful training in field research methods (Richardson, 1954).

3. *Variations in Putting Questions.* Even carefully trained interviewers have been found to vary in minor ways in their reading of questions. Unfortunately, such variation in questions often produces variation in answers. Furthermore, the rules for using additional follow-up questions **(probes)** can never be completely structured, so additional variability in interviewers' behavior occurs here.

4. *Variations in Reacting to Respondents' Answers.* For instance, an interviewer's reinforcement of answers by frequently saying ''good'' can systematically influence a respondent's later answers (Hildum & Brown, 1956).

5. *Interviewers' Expectations.* One common expectation is that a respondent's answers to related questions will be consistent, and so interviewers often fail to notice inconsistencies which are present (Smith & Hyman, 1950). Other expectations also undoubtedly decrease validity.

6. *Interviewers' Attitudes.* Numerous studies show that interviewers tend to get (or hear) an excess of responses which are similar to their own attitudes and opinions. Thus the results obtained by interviewers with opposing opinions often vary noticeably (Cannell & Kahn, 1968, p. 549; Phillips & Clancy, 1972).

7. *Interviewers' Social Class.* Interviewers from working-class backgrounds tend to get more radical opinions from respondents on some questions than do middle-class interviewers (for instance, a 47% vs. 32% endorsement of our government owning the nation's banks—Katz, 1942).

8. *Interviewers' Age.* This factor may influence the information obtained, particularly across the ''generation gap.'' For instance, when interviewing adolescent girls, older interviewers obtained fewer reports of behavior considered undesirable by middle-class adult standards (Erlich & Riesman, 1961).

9. *Interviewers' Race.* Many studies agree that Negro respondents tend to give different answers to white interviewers than to Negro interviewers. The differences are usually a matter of ''telling whitey what he wants to hear'' whenever the topic is a stressful or controversial one. Black interviewers typically obtain from black respondents more indications of resentment over discrimination and distrust of whites than do white interviewers (Hyman et al., 1954; Sattler, 1970; Schuman & Hatchett, 1974). Recent findings show that white respondents also avoid offending black interviewers (Hatchett & Schuman, 1975), and similar results have been found for Jewish interviewers asking respondents about their attitudes toward Jews (Robinson & Rohde, 1946).

Finding solutions to these problems of interviewer effects is not easy. Sensitive and well-trained interviewers are a first requirement, but one that many polling organizations fail to meet. Training can at least reduce variability in reading questions, in the use of probes, and in the amount of verbal reinforcement used by interviewers. To some extent training can also help interviewers to avoid expectational "halo effects." The effects of interviewers' attitudes, social class, sex, and age can be handled by the principle of "balanced bias," that is, by attempting to get approximately equal numbers of interviewers from each class, age group, etc. Unfortunately, however, this is rarely done, and the great majority of opinion poll interviewers are middle-aged, middle-class women. The problem of respondents' race, and often of their age and social class, can best be met by using interviewers who have the same race, age, and/or social class as the respondents. Encouragingly, this procedure is being followed increasingly in recent years, especially with race; and the consequence is much more valid survey results.

Other Practical Problems

Public opinion polling is a very complex business, whether done by commercial firms or academic research institutions. Between the time of choosing the initial topic for study and the distribution of the final report of findings, there are many phases of the polling operation, each of which can pose its own problems and difficulties. One way of considering these difficulties is in terms of the skilled workers who are needed at the different phases. In addition to the field interviewers, whose characteristics, training, and behavior were discussed in the preceding section, many other talents are needed. First there is the planning staff who develop the interview schedule and specify how and where the sample of respondents will be obtained. Then there are field supervisors who oversee the work of the interviewers. Next, coders in the main office transform the interview responses into quantitative scores on dozens or hundreds of items, and keypunchers transfer these scores onto IBM cards. Then computer experts are needed to process the data, and finally analysts and writers make a coherent picture out of the computer output and prepare a written report of their conclusions.

Another major problem is the cost of polling research. Just the interviewing costs alone for contacting one respondent and completing an interview may run from $10 to $30 or more, and inflation is driving these figures up rapidly. Interviewing costs depend partly on the length of the interview as well as on the location to which the interviewer must travel. When call-backs are required in the survey design, to find previously not-at-home individuals, interviewing costs may double. Consequently methods have been developed to weight more heavily the viewpoints of less-frequently-at-home individuals who were successfully interviewed, as a substitute for the more expensive call-back procedure. Telephone surveys may cost only half as much as face-to-face interviewing, but over 10% of U.S. households don't have telephones, and people are reluctant to give critical or controversial responses over the phone (Roll & Cantril, 1972).

Because of the high costs of survey research and the skilled manpower which it requires, very careful advance planning and specification of detailed research goals is essential. A very helpful book which stresses the how-to-do-it aspects is *Survey Design and Analysis* by Herbert Hyman (1955). Hyman (1972) has also written a volume on principles and procedures for **secondary analysis** of survey data which were originally collected by someone else for a different purpose—a very economical procedure compared to fresh data collection. Also, Sudman (1967) has described numerous methods which have been used by the National Opinion Research Center to hold down survey costs.

REASONS FOR FAMOUS POLLING FAILURES

Some of the major reasons why opinion polls have sometimes failed to predict election results correctly are last-minute changes in voting intentions, the undecided vote, people who are not at home when the interviewer calls, the effects of the polls themselves on voter behavior, and differential voter turnout.

Last-minute changes in voting intentions were apparently the main factor causing the incorrect predictions in the 1948 election when Truman defeated Dewey (Mosteller et al., 1949). In that year, as in previous elections, some polls stopped interviewing several weeks before the election date. Since that fiasco, the major commercial polls have extended their interviewing as late as possible, and many have adopted a "last-minute" telegraphic poll taken on the weekend before the election. Thus, by keeping their staffs up all night, they can make the Monday papers with their final predictions on the day before the election. Even then, a late surge in one candidate's strength could catch them flat-footed, as very nearly happened in Humphrey's uphill fight against Nixon in 1968.

The undecided vote was also an important factor in the 1948 election, for an unusually-high 19% of the voters were still undecided one month before the election (Campbell, Gurin, & Miller, 1954). The usual assumption made is that undecided respondents will divide their votes in the same proportion as those who have already decided, but in 1948 most of those votes apparently went for Truman.

Potential respondents who are not at home are always a headache for the polls. In a careful study, Hilgard and Payne (1944) showed that "not-at-homes" who could not be interviewed until the second, third, or fourth visit had significantly different characteristics than respondents who were home on the interviewer's first visit. The not-at-homes were more likely to be young adults, employed outside the home, with smaller families, and renters rather than homeowners. The moral is clear: in order to get an adequate sample, it is essential to use **call-backs** or some other procedure which gives fair representation to respondents who are less often at home.

The effects of the polls themselves on voters have not been thoroughly studied, but they are widely believed to have an effect on voter turnout and on the undecided vote. For instance, in the 1970 British election a disgruntled Labour Party worker complained: "They should ban the polls. They lost it for us. Our people just stayed at home, resting on the polls' prediction that it was in the bag" (*Newsweek*, 1970). An even more striking example occurs regularly in the United States because of the differential in time zones between the east and west coasts. In the last few elections, the national television networks have predicted the winning party on the basis of east coast votes well before the close of voting on the west coast. The potential impact of this procedure is so great that legislation has been suggested to prevent its future occurrence. Several studies of the influence of such telecasts on west coast voting have not shown any noticeable effects (Weiss, 1969; Mendelsohn & Crespi, 1970; Tuchman & Coffin, 1971), but early returns did influence voting in one study of a less emotionally involving nonpartisan referendum on a single issue (Mann, Rosenthal, & Abeles, 1971).

Differential turnout seems to have been a major reason for the polls' incorrect predictions in the 1970 British election (Abrams, 1970; Hollander, 1971), though another factor was the lack of last-minute telegraphic samples to pick up late shifts in voting intentions. Whether a given respondent will actually vote when the election occurs is always a difficult prediction to make. Useful methods for predicting voter turnout have been developed (Kinsolving, 1971; Perry, 1971), but unfortunately they were not utilized in the 1970 British election. The only polling firm which correctly picked the Conservative Party to win did so because of its observation that the Labourite voters' traditionally-lower degree of enthusiasm for their preferred candidate was even lower than usual in 1970. So, as the head of the polling firm put it, "We took the calculated risk—we adjusted more than usual for the turnout factor" (*Newsweek*, 1970).

Apparently taking risks sometimes leads to better prediction in the polling business. But, as indicated in the previous section, there are many ways of substantially reducing every possible source of invalidity in opinion poll results. As in other fields, "eternal vigilance" is the price of polling validity.

IMPACT OF POLLS IN POLITICS

Since about 1960, most politicians have come to consider poll information as essential in their election campaigns. Privately commissioned polls have become commonplace in races for major state and national offices. One study showed 90% of U.S. senators and governors using private polls, and up to 80% of newly elected congressmen (King & Schnitzer, 1968). In the 1968 election about 200 different polling firms were engaged in conducting these private polls, and about $6 million was spent on them by candidates for office at all levels. Just the Presidential candidates alone spent $1.5 million for private polls (Roll & Cantril, 1972).

Obviously, political polling has become big business. But the question remains: Is it good for the country? Oftentimes excessive public relations zeal can lead to merchandising political candidates in the same way that toothpaste is advertised. A political consultant in Los Angeles advertises: "You can be elected state senator; leading public relations firm with top flight experience in statewide campaigns wants a senator candidate." This firm's approach is to choose a catchy campaign slogan, give it saturation exposure, and keep the candidate from making speeches or personal appearances. Unfortunately, this approach works all too often (Bogart, 1972a, p. 8).

However, such excesses cannot all be blamed on public opinion polling. And when criticisms of polls are made, it is important to distinguish between several types of polling organizations. The major commercial polls, such as Gallup, Harris, Roper, and a number of statewide polls, use large samples and established scientific methods, and they do not sell their services to individual candidates. By contrast, the 200 or so firms that do private political and market polling vary widely in the carefulness and scientific adequacy of their procedures, and some unfortunately have been known to succumb to pressures for slanted reports or other unethical procedures. A third group of polls are those conducted by newspapers, radio or TV stations, which again vary greatly in the scientific adequacy of their sampling, interviewing, and reporting. For interesting data on the predictive success of various types of polls, see Hennessy and Hennessy (1961), Gallup (1972, p. 2341), and Felson and Sudman (1975).

In the following sections we will consider, first, the major criticisms, and second, some of the arguments in favor of modern public opinion polling. We will concentrate our discussion mainly on evaluation of the major commercial polls, but with some attention to the merits and abuses of private political polling.

Criticisms of Political Polling

As mentioned earlier in this chapter, opinion polls have been accused of influencing the preferences and the turnout of voters. They have also been criticized as "undemocratic" and elitist, since they report the views of only a small and not-wholly-representative sample of citizens. On the opposite flank, polls have been accused of destroying the courage and independence of political leaders and enshrining the conventional and unconsidered opinions of the poorly-informed "average man." This reduction of political opinion to the lowest common denominator, it is alleged, may keep good men and women from running for office or prevent incumbent politicians from telling the public unpleasant truths or from adopting unpopular positions. On still another front, polls have been criticized for making little contribution to the essential democratic processes of discussion and reconciliation of opposing viewpoints, because they often emphasize divergency in opinions and thus may discourage compromise or consensus. Obviously, these are all controversial viewpoints, with persuasive arguments on both sides.

Some of these arguments were made in the early years of polling by Ranney

(1946) and Rogers (1949), and a more recent summary is presented by Bogart (1972a). In 1960, Senator Albert Gore of Tennessee gave a speech to the Senate containing a detailed critique of political polls. His most serious concern was about the effects of such polls on the processes of democratic government. Pertinent extracts from that speech are presented in Box 4-3. Though his concerns are legitimate ones, it may help in understanding the strength of Senator Gore's sentiments to know that his speech was made in the midst of a fiercely-contested election, following reports that his party's candidate, John F. Kennedy, was running behind his opponent, Richard Nixon.

Though Senator Gore's speech was written some time ago, the same issues are still being actively debated (Nedzi, 1971; *Los Angeles Times*, 1973). Gore also

---

Box 4-3 *Senator Gore Criticizes the Polls*

"I am concerned with the significance which a considerable number of people attach to political polls. It is because so many people think they are important that they have become an unduly significant factor in our national politics. . . .

Incidentally, Dr. Gallup has a remarkable record of inaccurate prediction. . . . Then, there is 1948, when all the polls elected the wrong man. . . . some pollsters have learned one lesson. They crowd the center near election day and use fuzzy language to avoid being stuck with gross mispredictions. . . .

This is a publicity guessing game . . . at a time when world tension and national and international affairs compete for space on the printed pages to inform our people, large areas of printed space on the front pages of our daily newspapers are devoted to this worthlessness. . . .

Such polls interfere with our elective processes. Not only do they exercise an influence upon the voters, but we observe events such as occurred recently in connection with Governor Rockefeller of New York. . . . When it comes to pass that the Governor of the largest State in our Union can base a major political decision as to whether he will seek the Presidency of the United States upon political polls, then I think it is time for the Senate . . . to take a look at political polls. . . .

Polls may have a very great influence months ahead of a political campaign. They may discourage campaign contributors. They may affect morale of campaign workers. They may influence local political leaders who wish to be with the winner to make an alinement [sic], which they may maintain through the campaign. . . .

There is reason to believe that, especially in the case of early polls, when the minds of many voters have not been made up, published results of polls do exert an influence. Even if such an influence amounts to only 1 percent, the damage to our election processes has been done. That might be the margin between victory and defeat of a good man.

The danger is that polls will be used to influence public opinion rather than reflect it. To the extent that the public considers the polls seriously meaningful, this danger is magnified. . . . From my study, I have concluded that polls do, in fact, have an influence which is entirely unjustified."

Source: Extracts from speech by Senator Albert Gore on political public opinion polls. *Congressional Record*, Aug. 22, 1960, 106, pp. 16958–16965.

raised a number of problems of a more technical nature about political polls. In addition to questions about the size and representativeness of samples and the possible effects of interviewers on responses (topics discussed earlier in this chapter), he mentioned the following problem areas: (a) determining which possible candidates should be listed on the polling ballot, (b) discounting undue effects of respondents' familiarity with a famous name (e.g., Adlai Stevenson III), (c) establishing whether respondents really intend to vote, (d) handling the responses of people who say they are undecided, and (e) correcting poll results for the expected turnout of each party's voters. Senator Gore also raised another commonly-heard criticism of the polls about which there is much misunderstanding—the question of how large their samples need to be:

> As a layman, I would question that a straw poll of less than 1 percent of the people could under any reasonable circumstances be regarded as a fair and meaningful cross section test. This would be something more than 500 times as large a sample as Dr. Gallup takes (Gore, 1960, p. 16962).

For a country like the United States with a population of 200 million, such a procedure would require a sample of well over one million adult respondents, which would be impossibly costly in time, effort, and money. By contrast, we have pointed out in an earlier section that a carefully-chosen probability sample of 1500 cases will produce results with an expected error of only ±2½%. Thus a sample of 1000 or more cases can be used to predict the total national vote. However, if it is desired to predict the vote *in each state separately*, 50 separate samples each containing 1000 or more cases would be needed. Since the electoral college vote, which determines the winner in presidential elections, is based on the plurality of votes in each state separately, the interest of politicians in having large samples has some justification. However, they have often failed to understand that predicting electoral college returns would require not just one large sample, but a separate large sample for each of the 50 states. Instead of attempting this overwhelming task, Gallup and the other political pollers have limited themselves to predicting the candidates' percentages of the total national vote.

A final accusation which has very often been made against the commercial opinion polls is that early poll results start "band-wagon" movements toward the leading candidate. It is amazing that this criticism still persists, for it has no basis in fact. Truman's underdog win in 1948 and Humphrey's comeback near-win in 1968 are dramatic illustrations disputing the band-wagon myth, and there is an abundance of other research evidence against it as well (Columbia Broadcasting System, 1964; Mendelsohn & Crespi, 1970; Roll & Cantril, 1972).

Some of the unfortunate uses and ethical abuses of private political polls have been described by Roll and Cantril (1972, pp. 12–38). For instance, it is not unheard of for some firms to slant their "findings" in a direction favorable to their customer, and it is common for findings to be "leaked" in attempts to gain political advantage. Early poll results on popularity or "name-recognition" (which are likely to change greatly with time and active campaigning) have nevertheless often discouraged well-qualified candidates from running—a particularly dramatic example was Governor George Romney's withdrawal from the 1968 Republican Presidential nomination race two weeks *before* the first state primary election. Early poll results have often set unrealistic goals for a candidate to reach a certain percentage of the vote in the "numbers game" of Presidential primary elections; and they are also apt to turn on or off the sluice gates of supporters' financial backing and of media attention. Thus there well may be a band-wagon effect among financial contributors and political reporters, if not among voters themselves (Field, 1971). As pollster Samuel Lubell has written:

> Events, not polls, affect people. Polls influence politicians most of all, and, secondly, they influence political writers, and last of all—if at all—they affect the people (quoted in Roll & Cantril, 1972, p. 28).

Defenses of Political Polling

In response to these criticisms of polling, many supporting arguments have been raised. Roll and Cantril (1972, pp. 39–64) have cited many ways in which private polls can be genuinely useful to political candidates. They can inform candidates about the public's concerns and indicate which arguments on an issue will probably be best received. They can demonstrate trends in public support or recognition and help to show where campaign efforts will be most effective. Further, they can pinpoint aspects of the candidate's own public image, the opponent's weaknesses, and the likely effects of other candidates and issues.

Early defenders of commercial political polls (e.g., Gallup, 1948; Bendiner, 1953), though readily admitting that polling methods and results were not perfect, were quick to take issue with many criticisms. Some of their major arguments are stated in George Gallup's vigorous defense of the polls, summarized in Box 4-4. Another major contribution of public opinion polls is an educational one: they encourage both respondents and readers of the results to think about the issues raised. Polls have opened up formerly hush-hush topics, such as birth-control and mental illness, for public discussion. The main limitation of polling is due to the nature of people's opinions, which are often inconsistent and/or shifting, based on their varied roles and conflicting loyalties—a mixture of desires and fears, prejudices and ideals. If this limitation is kept in mind, the polls can perform a very useful public service.

Box 4-4 *George Gallup Defends the Polls*

"Students of government have noted many contributions to our democratic process made by polls. . . .

1. Public opinion polls have provided political leaders with a more accurate gauge of public opinion than they had prior to 1935.

    No responsible person in the field of public opinion research would assert that polling methods are perfect. On the other hand, . . . the indices which were relied upon most in the past—letters, newspaper editorials, self-appointed experts, and the like—have been found to be highly inaccurate as guides to public opinion.

2. Public opinion polls have speeded up the processes of democracy by providing not only accurate, but swift, reports of public opinion. . . .

    In fact in many situations—particularly those in which a substantial portion of the population fails to take the trouble to vote—the poll results might be even more accurate as a measure of public sentiment than the official returns.

3. Public opinion polls have shown that the common people do make good decisions. . . .

4. Public opinion polls have helped to focus attention on major issues of the day. . . .

5. Public opinion polls have uncovered many 'areas of ignorance.' . . .

6. Public opinion polls have helped administrators of government departments make wiser decisions. . . . based upon accurate knowledge of public attitudes. . . .

7. Public opinion polls have made it more difficult for political bosses to pick presidential candidates 'in smoke-filled rooms.' . . .

8. Public opinion polls have shown that the people are not motivated, in their voting, solely by the factor of self-interest, as many politicians have presumed. . . .

9. Public opinion polls constitute almost the only present check on the growing power of pressure groups. . . .

    Poll results show that pressure-group spokesmen often represent only a minority of those within their own groups, and prove baseless their threats of political reprisal if legislators do not bow to their wishes. . . . more important, [polls] can reveal the will of the inarticulate and unorganized majority of the citizens. . . .

10. Public opinion polls help define the 'mandate' of the people in national elections. . . .

    At the same time that the views of voters are obtained on candidates, the views of these same voters can be recorded on issues. In this way, election results can be interpreted much more accurately than in the past. . . .

A true statesman will never change his ideals or his principles to make them conform to the opinions of any group, be it large or small. Rather, such a leader will try to persuade the public to accept his views and his goals. In fact, his success as a leader will in large part be measured by his success in making converts to his way of thinking. . . .

Leaders who do not know what the public thinks, or the state of the public's knowledge on any issue, are likely to be ineffective and unsuccessful leaders, and eventually to lose their opportunity to lead. . . .

Great leaders will seek information from every reliable source about the people whom they wish to lead. . . . The public opinion poll will be a useful tool in enabling them to reach the highest level of their effectiveness as leaders.''

Source: *A Guide to Public Opinion Polls* (rev. ed.). Selections from George Gallup. Copyright 1948 by Princeton University Press, pp. ix-xii, 5, 8. Reprinted by permission of Princeton University Press.

Pollers naturally tend to agree that their findings provide a great service to the nation. George Gallup is fond of pointing out that the people's attitudes on controversial issues are often ahead of their elected leaders' views. Both Gallup and Roper agree that the information which they provide about public opinion on various issues is much more important than their more-highly-publicized attempts to forecast election results. However, they point out, in defense of their prediction record, that election returns are not a perfect indication of the accuracy of opinion poll results, since factors like bad weather on election day, ballot-box stuffing, and energetic turn-out-the-vote campaigns can distort election results.

Recent additions to the code of professional ethics and practices which is followed by most reputable polling organizations have made published poll results easier to interpret. These new standards for reporting poll results specify the inclusion of information on the poll's sponsor, wording of questions, method and time of interviewing, the population sampled, sample size, likely sampling error, and other details (Field, 1971).

As a final point in favor of polls, George Gallup has argued:

> that legislators do not follow poll results, and that we would have appreciably better government if they did. As Bryce pointed out, the people are better fitted to determine ends than to select means. The task of the leader is to decide how best to achieve the goals set by the people. . . . In the last thirty years [polls] have tried out hundreds of proposals, many of which are widely approved but may have to wait for years until Congress catches up with the people (Gallup, 1965, p. 463).

SUMMARY

Public opinion polling is the type of psychological measurement which is most familiar to the general public. The accuracy of poll results depends on many factors, but most importantly on the representativeness of the sample of respondents chosen. The commercial polling organizations generally use various modifications of the quota sampling procedure, which is faster and less expensive but also less accurate than probability sampling. However, despite occasional failures the major polls have a very good overall record in predicting election results.

In addition to sampling procedures, another problem in public opinion polling involves the wording of questions, which is extremely important to the validity of both interview and questionnaire results. Memory errors and social desirability needs of respondents can also distort poll results, as can nonanonymity of responses and variations in interviewers' behavior or characteristics. The many complex phases of scientific polling demand many types of skilled workers and lead to very high research costs. With proper procedures, there are ways of reducing all of the potential sources of error in poll results.

The main reasons why political polls have sometimes failed to predict election results correctly are last-minute changes in voting intentions, the undecided vote, failure to interview "not-at-homes," the possible effects of the polls themselves on the final vote, and differential voter turnout on election day.

Although political polling has become a pervasive part of the American scene, questions remain about its desirable or undesirable consequences. Political opinion polls have been criticized for being "undemocratic," for unduly influencing voters, for paralyzing political leadership, and for emphasizing conflict and controversy. Many other criticisms of a technical nature have been met by improved polling procedures and reporting standards. Though a band-wagon effect of polls on voters has not been demonstrated, one of the most serious concerns about polls is that they may unduly influence financial contributors and media coverage in election campaigns.

The defenders of polls have responded to criticisms against them by pointing out many valuable contributions which polls have made to the processes of democratic government. They have an important educational function, both for the public at large and for legislators who need to be informed about public viewpoints. Poll information also has many important uses for political candidates, though safeguards are needed to prevent its improper use.

Suggested Readings

Cannell, C. F., & Kahn, R. L. Interviewing. In G. Lindzey & E. Aronson (Eds.), *The Handbook of Social Psychology* (2nd ed.). Vol. 2. Reading, Mass.: Addison-Wesley, 1968. Pp. 526–595.—A sophisticated treatment of empirical findings concerning the effectiveness of research interviews and interviewing procedures.

Oskamp, S. Methods of studying human behavior. Chapter 2 in L. S. Wrightsman, *Social Psychology in the Seventies*. Monterey, Calif.: Brooks/Cole, 1972. Pp. 30–67.—An introduction to the goals and methods of social psychological research, including discussion of research problems with polls, interviews, and questionnaires.

Payne, S. L. *The Art of Asking Questions*. Princeton, N. J.: Princeton University Press, 1951.—An excellent how-to-do-it book on planning and carrying out interview research.

Roll, C. W., Jr., & Cantril, A. H. *Polls: Their Use and Misuse in Politics*. New York: Basic Books, 1972.—Written for the lay reader by polling experts, this short book contains many fascinating tidbits and a thoughtful discussion of the promise and problems of political polling.

The Structure
of Public Opinion

Q. *What do you believe is the most important problem facing the country right now?* (early 1960s)

A. *Cuba.*

Q. *Why do you think Cuba is the most important problem . . . ?*

A. *We should blast Cuba off the map. I don't care why. Just do it. It should be obvious why.*

Q. *What do you think the government should do about this situation?*

A. *It's hard to say really. I am really not one to say like my husband was. We should stop sending all our money to the Commies. And we should make all the draft dodgers and those Commies at (state university) fight on the front lines some day. My ex-husband was a retired Army man, you know. . . .*—John H. Kessel (1965, pp. 378, 381).

The above responses (which were actually given by a survey respondent) are not conspicuous for their informational content nor their logical consistency. Yet they were fairly typical of about 25% of an upper-middle-class sample living near a major state university.

According to the theory of democratic government, an informed populace is the bulwark of freedom. It is the citizen's duty to form an opinion about public affairs and to express it at the ballot-box. And democratic governments are expected to be responsive to public opinion on important issues.

But are the average citizen's attitudes on major public issues well-informed? Are they internally consistent? Are they responsive to new information and new situations? And do they have an effect on public policy? The answers to these questions bear on some of the most central assumptions underlying the democratic form of government.

Many authorities have concluded that the populace is ignorant rather than informed. As far back as 1947, Hyman and Sheatsley concluded (p. 412): "There exists a hard core of chronic 'know-nothing's'" in the American population; and more recently Converse (1964, p. 245) wrote, "large portions of an electorate do not have meaningful beliefs. . . ." Yet there are arguments and evidence supporting the opposite viewpoint as well, so this issue is by no means a simple one to settle. In this chapter we will examine first the extent of public information on current affairs, next the evidence for the elitist view of public opinion, and finally the evidence for the mass participation view of public opinion.

THE EXTENT OF PUBLIC INFORMATION

As a college student, learning is a part of your life. You are used to taking in information every day, discussing it, and (we may hope) using it in your regular activities. Most of your friends are probably also students, or at least educated individuals with an interest in current affairs. From such a position in life, it is often very hard to remember that you are not a typical member of society. Even in this age of mass education, only slightly more than half of the population ever attends college, and only 15% graduate from college. Of the total adult population, less than one quarter have had any college education at all (U.S. Bureau of the Census, 1973).

These facts are important because one's level of education is a very strong determinant of how much one knows. Of course there are "self-educated" men and women but, in general, college-educated individuals have a much larger store of factual knowledge than persons with less education. To take only one example, a national poll in 1955 asked respondents to identify ten famous men ranging from Columbus (the best known with 90% correct identification) through Shakespeare, Napoleon, Karl Marx, Leo Tolstoy, to Freud (known by only 22%). The average score for the ten famous men was 47% correct, and the figures for different levels of education were dramatic: college-educated respondents were 77% correct, high school-educated ones 51% correct, and grade school-educated ones only 26% correct (Erskine, 1963a).

So you are not a typical member of society in your level of information. How much does the "average citizen" know, and on what topics is (s)he likely to be well-informed or poorly informed? Findings from many different national polls have been compiled by Hazel Erskine (1962, 1963a, 1963b, 1963c) in several interesting articles in the *Public Opinion Quarterly*. Though these data are fairly old, they are undoubtedly still quite typical of the American population, and they comprise the most complete data available on the level of public information.

First, let us look at the area of general information. Some items of knowledge are very widespread, but most are not. In a 1954 poll on religious knowledge, 95% of the population could name Jesus' mother and 64% knew his birthplace; but only 49% knew the first book of the Bible, and only 21% could name an Old Testament prophet.

Many information items which you might expect to be almost universally known are not. For instance, the best-known of many famous statements in the mid-1950s was "Hi Yo, Silver!", but only 71% of the population knew who said it (the Lone Ranger). Bugs Bunny's greeting, "What's up, Doc?", was identified by only 40%. The authors of the following famous quotations, which are often taught to school children, were correctly named by only about 30% of the population: "Speak softly and carry a big stick," "With malice toward none; with charity for all," and "There's a sucker born every minute." Do you know their authors? (They are, respectively, Theodore Roosevelt, Abraham Lincoln, and P. T. Barnum.) Similarly only 40% of the population knew who wrote *Huckleberry Finn* (Mark Twain), and only 22% knew who wrote *A Tale of Two Cities* (Charles Dickens).

However, there are some items of information which are known to most Americans. We may call these **salient** items, meaning that they are in the focus of people's attention. In 1950, 94% of the population had heard or read of flying saucers, and in 1957, 92% knew about the worldwide epidemic of "Asian flu" which was then occurring. Roughly 90% of Americans had heard about the Salk polio vaccine a year or so after it was introduced for nationwide use, and in 1957 about 80% of the population had heard of the recent American Cancer Society report which first clearly linked cancer to cigarette smoking. Similarly about 80% had heard about the hydrogen bomb a few years after its development. Over 90% of Americans knew about the dramatic increase in the length of women's skirts which occurred shortly following World War II, and when "universal military training" was in the current news, 75% of respondents could explain what it meant.

What do these items of widely-known information have in common? First, they are topics which have been very prominently *in the news*—in many news broadcasts, on the first page of newspapers, and therefore in the conversation of

Figure 5-1 Hardly anyone other than a hermit could avoid hearing about flying saucers.

many people. Some, like the polio vaccine and longer skirts, have also been the subject of nationwide *action* which might affect almost every family. Second, each of these topics are quite *unique*, one-of-a-kind items which stand out in the news because there is nothing else like them with which they can be confused. Third, most of these topics have *continued* to be in the news day after day and month after month so that it would be almost impossible for anyone except a hospitalized person or a hermit to escape contact with them.

Knowledge about Public Affairs

Let us compare these data on general information with evidence on citizens' knowledge about public affairs—the facts on which public opinion and political attitudes should be based.

Here again we find there are a few facts which are known to almost everyone. One kind of information which is widely held is **exposure** to terms and issues, as contrasted with knowledge about them. In answering questions of this type respondents merely have to say, ''Yes, I've heard of that,'' rather than giving correct information about the topic. Consequently, percentages of people ''knowing'' about the topic are usually much higher than for questions which require correct information in the answer. In 1960, 96% of the population said they had heard of the American U-2 plane being forced down by the Russians, and in 1961, 89% had heard about the Berlin crisis. Also 88% had heard about the American POWs who stayed with the Communists after the Korean War and later returned to the United States. About 70% of Americans were familiar with the Peace Corps in 1962, and a similar percentage had heard of the United Nations in 1951. These highly-familiar events and organizations share the same characteristics mentioned above as causes of perceptual salience—they are unique, and they have been in the news prominently and repeatedly. By contrast, the European Common Market clearly had not achieved that degree of public exposure in 1961 (only 22% of Americans had heard of it), probably in large part because it was seen as a foreign issue which did not directly affect Americans.

Turning to items of substantive **knowledge**, rather than merely exposure to terms or issues, one category of information which is widely known is the names of the very top level of national leaders. In 1947, two years after the end of World War II, 95% or more of Americans could correctly identify President Truman, General MacArthur, and General Eisenhower. However, no other political figures were this well known; the better-known Senators and Cabinet members received only 50–60% correct identification. When Richard Nixon was the Republican Vice-Presidential candidate in August, 1952, only 45% of respondents could remember his name. Billy Graham is one of those unique individuals whose name is recognized by almost everyone (85% of the population in 1957), but only 56% could name General Franco's country, and only 43% could identify Marshall Tito. Most less-illustrious mortals are recognized by only a tiny fraction of the public; for instance, the U.S. ambassador to the United Nations was known by only 11% of Americans in 1947. (Do you know who the current U.S. ambassador is?)

Only a very few other items of information are widely shared by the U.S. population. About three-quarters of Americans can name our national anthem or identify the meaning of the initials "F.B.I." About four-fifths can correctly point out California or Texas on the map, but only three other states (Pennsylvania, New York, and Illinois) were correctly pointed out by as many as half of the respondents. Similarly, only 65% of people could point out England on a map of Europe, and only 60% could show Brazil's position in South America, while most other countries were located correctly by less than one-third of the respondents.

When we turn to public **issues** about which one might expect citizens to be well-informed, that expectation is rudely shattered. There is rarely ever an issue about which even half of the populace is correctly informed even at the most elementary level. In the midst of the "cold war" between the U.S. and Russia, barely over half of Americans could state the meaning of that term in a reasonably correct fashion. Civics teachers would shudder still more to learn that less than one-quarter of our population can correctly describe any of the contents of the Bill of Rights. Other fascinating examples of the level of general knowledge or ignorance on public issues are given in Box 5-1.

Box 5-1 *The Informed (?) Populace*

The following items from national public opinion polls indicate typical degrees of citizen knowledge on currently-important public issues. The number after each item is the percentage of respondents who were reasonably correct.

Will you tell me what the term "cold war" means?	55%
Can you tell me what the term "filibuster" in Congress means to you?	54
Just in your own words, will you tell me what is meant by the term "farm price supports"?	54
How many U.S. Senators are there from your state?	49
When you hear or read about the Fifth Amendment, what does it mean to you?	42
What does the expression "welfare state" mean or refer to, as you understand it?	36
What is meant by the electoral college?	35
Will you tell me what the North Atlantic Treaty Organization is?	35
What are the first 10 amendments in the Constitution called?	33
Can you recall the names of your Senators?	31
When you hear or read about the term "bipartisan foreign policy," what does that mean to you?	26
What do you know about the Bill of Rights? Do you know anything it says?	21
What are the three branches of the Federal Government called?	19

Source: Erskine (1962, 1963a).

These examples of the low level of public information provide the factual background for our next topic, the **elitist** viewpoint concerning public opinion. This view maintains that coherent systems of political beliefs and attitudes are held by only a small minority of citizens, an "elite" group.

THE ELITIST VIEW OF PUBLIC OPINION

A definitive statement of this viewpoint has been given by Philip Converse (1964) in an influential chapter which provides much of the source material for this section. More recently Bogart (1972a) has echoed many of the same conclusions. After describing the typical low level of citizens' information about public affairs, Converse points out the resulting consequences for individuals' political belief systems. His major thesis is that, as one moves down the information scale from the best-informed "elites," individuals' *understanding* of public affairs fades out very rapidly. Also, the *objects of belief* which are central in the individuals' belief system shift from the remote, generic, and abstract to the increasingly simple, concrete, or "close to home." Where potential political objects (of belief) are concerned, this progression tends to be from abstract, "ideological" principles to the more obviously recognizable social groupings or charismatic leaders and finally to such objects of immediate experience as family, job, and immediate associates (Converse, 1964, p. 213).

Furthermore, these differences in belief systems seem crucial in understanding different individuals' political behavior.

What evidence does Converse have for these conclusions? Most of it comes from a series of major research studies concerning U.S. national elections conducted every two years by the Survey Research Center at the University of Michigan. These studies polled national samples of 1000 to 1800 citizens and were reported in a very important volume called *The American Voter* (Campbell et al., 1960). Converse stresses several different types of findings from these studies.

Use of Ideological Concepts

The first finding concerned the degree of usage of ideological dimensions in understanding public affairs. By **ideological dimension** Converse means a basic principle (such as conservatism or internationalism or socialism) that underlies and helps to determine an individual's beliefs on many different political issues. The respondents in the Survey Research Center studies were asked open-ended interview questions which allowed them to evaluate current political issues and candidates in their own words, showing what evaluative dimensions they used spontaneously. Almost the only ideological dimension used was the *liberal-conservative* one, and only 2½% of the population used any such dimension in a clear and consistent way. A second group of respondents (about 9%) mentioned such an ideological dimension but used it very little or were unclear in their use and understanding of the term. A third group of respondents (the largest one—42%) evaluated political candidates and parties in terms of their expected favorability toward particular subgroups within the nation (e.g., "A Republican victory will be better for farmers"). An interesting example which was classified in this category was a man who declared that he was a Socialist because Socialists were for the working man. This could have been classified as an ideological response if it had been consistently extended to other topics, but instead the man showed his lack of understanding of the ideological dimension by advocating private business control over electric utilities and other clearly non-Socialist ideas.

A fourth group of respondents with even less concern for broad considerations of political policy were those (about 24%) who emphasized only a single narrow issue, such as social security, war vs. peace, or past associations of one of the political parties with national prosperity or depression. Finally, a fifth group of respondents (22½%) entirely ignored policy issues in making political evalua-tions. They might mention personal qualities of the candidates (e.g., "honest," or "handsome"), or favor a party without showing any knowledge of its pro-gram, or be completely uninterested in politics. The distribution of these groups in the national population is depicted in Table 5-1, which also shows that the more ideological groups were more likely to have voted in the previous presidential election. The dramatic conclusion from this table is that no more than 10-15% of the population, at most, thinks about political questions in terms of broad public policy principles or ideological dimensions which underlie many different specific issues.

Converse goes on to present evidence that the level of education declines quite regularly from the first to the fifth category. More important for our purposes, the level of political activity also declines dramatically in the same direction. On the average, the first category of respondents had over three acts of political partici-pation (e.g., party membership, campaign contributions, attendance at political rallies, etc.) in addition to voting, while the fifth category of respondents had less than one such act.

Relationships between Beliefs about Specific Issues

A second major finding in Converse's chapter concerned what he called **constraints** among respondents' beliefs on various political issues. That is, are beliefs interconnected ("constrained") in logically or psycho-logically meaning-ful patterns? Or, on the contrary, are an individual's beliefs on different political issues ioslated into separate clusters—even "logic-tight compartments"—such that beliefs about one issue do not affect beliefs on another issue, even where they may be logically contradictory? This latter viewpoint is the one which

TABLE 5-1 Use of Ideological Concepts Among Total National Sample and Among Voters in Last Presidential Election

Ideological category	Total sample	Voters
1. Used ideological dimension clearly	2½%	3½%
2. Mentioned ideological dimension (unclear)	9	12
3. Stressed interests of a particular group	42	45
4. Emphasized a single narrow issue	24	22
5. Ignored policy issues completely	22½	17½
	100%	100%

Source: Adapted and reprinted with permission of Macmillan Publishing Co., Inc. from Converse, P.E. "The Nature of belief systems in mass publics," in D. Apter (Ed.), *Ideology and Discontent*, p. 218. Copyright © 1964 by The Free Press of Glencoe, a Division of The Macmillan Co.

Converse holds, and it is very similar to Abelson's (1968) theory of isolated "opinion molecules" about a given topic which are not logically interconnected to opinion molecules on other topics.

To support this viewpoint, Converse cites correlational data relating beliefs about seven different political issues in (a) a national cross-section sample, and (b) an elite sample made up of Congressional candidates in the 1958 election. There were four domestic issues and three foreign-affairs issues, as follows:

1. Federal programs for full employment
2. Federal aid to education
3. Federal funds for public housing and electric power
4. Federal F.E.P.C. to prevent discrimination
5. Foreign economic aid
6. Foreign military aid
7. Isolationism vs. commitments abroad

In addition, the respondents' party preferences were obtained. Scores on these eight variables were interrelated using a statistic called tau-gamma, which yields results similar to but somewhat smaller than conventional correlation coefficients. A summary of the results is shown in Table 5-2.

In interpreting these results, it is important to remember that the cross-section sample contained its fair share (about 10%) of "ideologues" and "near-ideologues," the first two categories of people in Table 5-1, and the structure of their political belief systems might be much more like that of the elite sample than that of the remainder of the cross-section sample. Thus, the difference between the two samples was undoubtedly diminished by the inclusion of some "elites" in the cross-section sample. In spite of that, the difference between the samples was marked. The elite sample showed a much greater degree of structure, that is, of relationship between beliefs about different issues. The elite sample also showed a markedly higher relationship between party preference and beliefs on the seven issues than did the cross-section sample.

TABLE 5-2 Average Relationships ("Constraints") between Beliefs on Various Political Issues and Party Preference in Two Samples

Sample	Among domestic issues	Between domestic and foreign issues	Among foreign issues	Between 7 issues and party preference
Elite	.53	.25	.37	.39
Cross-section	.23	.11	.23	.11

Note.—Coefficients are tau-gammas.

Source: Adapted and reprinted with permission of Macmillan Publishing Co., Inc. from Converse, P.E. "The Nature of belief systems in mass publics," in D. Apter (Ed.), *Ideology and Discontent*, p. 229. Copyright © 1964 by The Free Press of Glencoe, a division of The Macmillan Co.

In sum, this finding and many similar ones have led Converse to conclude that elites do have a meaningful structure for their political belief systems, but that the "common man" generally does not. Other experts on political behavior have agreed with this point of view (e.g., McClosky, 1964). Hennessy (1970a) has gone so far as to argue that

> political attitudes are an elite phenomenon. Most people do not have political attitudes. Even in modern high-energy societies most people do not have political attitudes (p. 463).

Importance of Groups in Political Belief Systems

If it is true that the common man generally doesn't have clearly-structured political attitudes, does he have any substitute for them? Or is he completely without political belief systems? Converse would not be willing to carry his argument that far, primarily because of the importance of **reference groups** (either positive or negative) in the belief systems of many people.

Take the case of a lathe operator who works in a large factory, has several children to educate, a large mortgage on the family home, and has occasionally been laid off from work for several months when the company was having financial troubles. This person is apt to organize many beliefs around "what is good for the working man" (just as the boss may organize many beliefs around "what is good for industry"). Thus, if asked, the lathe operator might favor reducing taxes, but might also favor increasing unemployment benefits, since both of these measures would be good for workers, his(her) reference group. That would be logical from this person's standpoint, and it would demonstrate at least a rudimentary type of political belief system. But note a discrepancy here: the worker's two answers fall on opposite sides of the major ideological dimension underlying American political positions, liberalism-conservatism (reducing taxes is a "conservative" position, while welfare measures like unemployment benefits are "liberal" programs). Thus, on Converse's scale, this worker would not be classified in the top two ideological categories, but in category 3, the group-benefit category (along with 40% of the total population—see Table 5-1).

Converse proposes that below the well-informed and ideologically oriented top 10% of the population, the major organizing principle underlying individuals' political beliefs is their attitudes toward major societal groups. That is, whatever political beliefs such individuals have are apt to be organized around their concept of the interests of their own most important reference group, be it a social class, an ethnic or nationality group, a religious group, a regional group (e.g., Easterners), or an occupation (e.g., farmers). This third major conclusion of Converse's paper is sketched diagrammatically in Figure 5-2, which shows the sharp decline in political information below the top 10% of the population and the corresponding increase in reliance on groups as the focus of political beliefs.

One additional feature of this diagram should be pointed out. Below the top

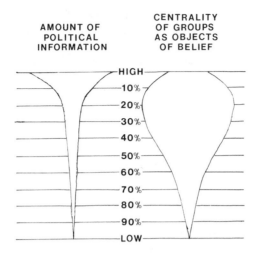

Figure 5-2 Amount of political information and the centrality of groups as factors in political belief systems.

Source: Adapted and reprinted with permission of Macmillan Publishing Co., Inc. from P.E. Converse, "The Nature of belief systems in mass publics," in D. Apter (Ed.), *Ideology and Discontent.* Copyright © 1964 by The Free Press of Glencoe, a Division of The Macmillan Co.

50% or so of the population, the importance of groups in determining individuals' political beliefs drops off quite rapidly. Converse suggests that this finding is due to the very low level of political information held by these individuals. They literally know so little about most political issues that they can't determine how the issue would affect their own group, even when they are aware of being a member of a group which has common interests. As an example, many Americans who know that they are members of the working class have so little information about the political party platforms and policies that they cannot tell whether a Democratic or a Republican victory would benefit them. As a result they form their political opinions on the basis of isolated issues, such as which party will lower taxes (these individuals fall in category 4 of Table 5-1), or on the basis of such factors as the candidate's attractiveness (these people fall in category 5).

Stability of Beliefs over Time

A fourth major finding which supports the elitist theory of public opinion concerns the stability of particular political beliefs over time. Saying that a person has a "belief system" implies that most of his beliefs will be relatively stable and unchanging over a few-year period, rather than fluctuating markedly from time to time. This question was studied by a longitudinal design in which the same panel of respondents was reinterviewed several times about two years apart. They were questioned about political issues such as those listed on page 104. The results were dramatic:

> Faced with the typical item of this kind, only about thirteen people out of twenty manage to locate themselves even on the same *side* of the controversy in successive interrogations, when ten out of twenty could have done so by chance alone (Converse, 1964, p. 239).

By contrast, Converse has deduced from repeated Congressional roll-call votes on comparable bills that an elite sample would show stable opinions over time for about eighteen out of twenty respondents. Thus, you can see that there is a marked difference in the temporal stability of political beliefs, with elites being highly stable in beliefs and mass samples being quite changeable over time.

A further question may be raised as to which beliefs are most stable and which most changeable. Of all the items reported, one was by far the most stable—party preference, with a tau-beta reliability coefficient of more than $+.7$. This stability of people's party identification was one of the major findings of *The American Voter*. By contrast, all of the seven issues listed on page 104 had tau-beta reliability coefficients close to $+.3$ or $+.4$, indicating some continuing temporal stability but also a great deal of change over the two-year-period. The issue which had the highest stability (close to $+.5$) was an item about federal action to promote school desegregation, and the next highest in stability were the items concerning a federal F.E.P.C. and federal programs for full employment. Converse concluded that

> stability declines as the referents of the attitude items become increasingly remote, from jobs, which are significant objects to all, and Negroes, who are attitude objects for most, to items involving ways and means of handling foreign policy (1964, p. 241).

When a third interview was held with the respondents, four years after the first interview, another fascinating finding emerged. Studying the "turnover correlations" between the same beliefs at three different points in time, it was found that these correlations remained very nearly the same from one time to the next. This meant that a person's opinions at time 3 could be predicted just as well from his opinions at time 1 as from his opinions at time 2. This was a surprising finding because test-retest correlations usually tend to decrease with longer time intervals between the original test and the retest, as one would expect if opinion change is a relatively steady or continuous process.

Analyzing the obtained pattern of turnover correlations further with complex statistical techniques, Converse found that they could be explained quite well by an "all or none" model of stability. That is, the model postulated that some respondents had clearcut opinions which were perfectly stable over time, while others (a much larger group) had no opinion in any meaningful sense and were just as likely to change their response randomly upon reinterviewing as to give the same response a second time. The "all or none" model fit the obtained pattern of turnover correlations on one issue perfectly, and it came close to a perfect fit on the other issues as well. Converse suggests that it needs only a slight modification, adding the postulate of a *small* third group of genuine converts, to make it fit the data for all the issues measured.

This is a very important finding, for it indicates once again in a new way that on any given issue the public can be meaningfully divided into a small elite group of the well-informed and a large mass of politically-naive individuals. Moreover, this finding goes a step further and says that most of the latter group have *no meaningful opinions at all* since the changes in their responses over time were completely random in nature. As Converse summarizes the conclusion,

> large portions of an electorate do not have meaningful beliefs, even on issues that have formed the basis for intense political controversy among elites for substantial periods of time (1964, p. 245).

Photograph courtesy of Philip Converse.
Reprinted by permission.

Box 5-2 PHILIP CONVERSE, *Analyst of Political Attitudes*

Widely known for his research on political behavior, Philip Converse is Professor of Sociology and Political Science at the University of Michigan, and Program Director at its Survey Research Center. Born in 1928 in New Hampshire, he earned a B.A. at Denison University and an M.A. and Ph.D. at the University of Michigan. In the following 18 years he published over 40 articles and 7 books, and was elected to the National Academy of Sciences (an especially rare honor for a social scientist).

Converse is most famous for his books written with Campbell, Miller and Stokes: The American Voter, *and* Elections and the Political Order, *which are cited in Chapters 11 and 12 and elsewhere in this book. He has also coauthored a social psychology test with Newcomb and Turner, and written pivotal papers on the structure of public opinion which are described in this chapter. Most recently, he has collaborated on* The Quality of American Life, *cited in Chapter 11.*

Every Issue Has Its Own Public

This leads to the final major conclusion of Converse's paper: that there is not just one political elite group, but there are different **issue publics** for different topics. This means that each important political issue has its own group of interested citizens, partially unique and partially overlapping other issue publics. These issue publics vary in size from about 20% to about 40% of the total population. A small group of people were found to be members of all eight issue publics which Converse studied, and many individuals were not concerned nor informed about any of the issues. Most people were members of only a few of the issue publics; for instance they might be concerned about racial issues, but not about economic ones nor about foreign affairs.

The contrast between elite and mass opinion and the concept of issue publics, who are selectively oriented to some political issues but not to others, are beautifully illustrated in the issue of domestic Communism which was raised by Senator Joseph McCarthy in the early 1950s. Though this controversy was long-continued and heavily emphasized by the news media and political leaders, there is evidence that it was much less salient to the mass public than other political issues of that period such as "corruption" in Washington or the Korean War. Converse concludes:

> The controversy over internal communism provides a classic example of a mortal struggle among elites that passed almost unwitnessed by an astonishing portion of the mass public (1964, p. 251).

THE MASS PARTICIPATION VIEW
OF PUBLIC OPINION

Having discussed the major research findings supporting the elitist view of public opinion, we turn now to its antithesis, which we will call the **mass participation** viewpoint. Here one of the best known contributions has been Robert Lane's (1962) book, *Political Ideology*. Lane believes that common men and women do have political ideologies, though they may not be expressed as easily and articulately as the elites'. However, as he himself recognizes, his method of intensive depth interviews with a few individuals can only provide suggestive evidence but not prove his case (p. 4). Other researchers have found support for the same theoretical viewpoint with empirical work in several areas.

In general, adherents of the mass participation view do not dispute the kind of evidence concerning political belief systems which we have summarized above. Rather, they interpret its meaning differently and add additional evidence which tends to throw a different light on the question.

A Search for Other Ideological Dimensions

Perhaps the smallest departure from the elitist viewpoint has been to search for alternative ideological dimensions, other than the liberal-conservative one, around which individuals' political beliefs might be organized. Since only 10% or so of the population is even reasonably articulate about their ideological viewpoints, as Converse has shown, this search has usually taken the form of examining empirical correlations between different political beliefs in a large population, rather than asking people directly about their ideologies.

An increasingly widespread methodological approach used in many such studies is **secondary analysis** of data already collected and analyzed in other ways by another investigator. The huge repository of successive national sample survey data collected by the Survey Research Center (SRC) at the University of Michigan, which formed the basis for *The American Voter* (Campbell et al., 1960) and other later books, has generously been made available to many other researchers for secondary analysis, as have data from many of the commercial polls of Elmo Roper and of George Gallup. Of course, analysis of such data is limited by the particular questions which were included in the interview schedules and the particular wording of those questions; different questions or choices of wording might provide a better test of many possible hypotheses. Hyman (1972) has recently published a thorough and helpful guide to the principles and procedures of secondary analysis.

A good example of a secondary-analysis study which focused on ideological dimensions was conducted by Axelrod (1967), using SRC data from the 1956 election. In that survey a national sample of nearly 1800 persons had been asked, among many other questions, about their beliefs on 16 political issues, including the seven listed previously in this chapter. Campbell et al. (1960) had reported the results in terms of two clusters of issues, a welfare scale and a foreign policy scale, both of which had rather weak interrelationships among their several items (the average r between items within each cluster was less than $+.3$). Moreover, there was no relationship at all between these two scales (average r very close to 0.0). This finding had demonstrated once again that there was no clear liberal-conservative dimension underlying most people's political views, since a liberal on welfare issues was no more likely to be liberal on foreign-policy issues than he was to be conservative on them.

In his reanalysis of these same 16 political issues, Axelrod found a single cluster of interrelated items which he termed a **populism** cluster because of its similarity to the principles of the American Populist political movement of the 1890s. This cluster included more issues (six), and the issues had slightly stronger intercorrelations than either of the clusters analyzed by Campbell et al. The American Populist movement was concerned with domestic social reform but was opposed to foreigners and to U.S. foreign involvement. Similarly, Axelrod's populist cluster of items favored federal programs for full employment, aid to education, and medical care, but also favored tax cuts and the firing of suspected Communists, and opposed U.S. foreign involvement. Perhaps most surprisingly, this cluster of issues had its strongest intercorrelations for the sub-sample of *nonvoters* in the total sample. The cluster was less coherent for more politically active and informed individuals, and it had the lowest intercorrelations for the college graduate subsample.

Axelrod emphasizes that for a large segment of the American public, "domestic liberalism is not correlated with internationalism," and his evidence for the populism dimension of political attitudes shows that "much of the public views policy questions as they were seen in the 1890s and not the 1930s" (1967, p. 59). Many political commentators have suggested that Governor George Wallace's appeal to this populist sentiment in the less-educated part of the electorate was the primary sources of his attraction for many voters.

Consistency within Single Individuals

A methodological objection to the evidence for the elitist viewpoint has been offered by Bennett (1975), following the conceptual approach of Lane (1973). Both authors stress that various individuals may organize their political attitudes in different ways—that is, using different dimensions, not just liberalism-conservatism or populism. Also, for each person, some topics may represent "non-issues"—questions that the individual hasn't thought about and has no opinion about. This individualistic conception of belief organization suggests the need for a different research methodology to investigate it. Whereas Converse studied the consistency of attitudes on *each separate issue* across a large number of people, Bennett advocated studying the consistency of attitudes *within each person* on a large number of political issues. The difference in results for these two methods is dramatic. Using 20 specific political issues including Converse's familiar seven, Bennett found test-retest stability figures *across people* which were very similar to Converse's (1964) findings—correlations ranging from about +.1 to +.4, even though the respondents were college students and the retest was only three weeks after initial testing. However, looking at the stability of attitudes *within individuals*, the average test-retest correlation was an impressively high +.74. Bennett concludes that "not all people make sense of politics in the same way, but most people make sense of politics in some way" (p. 25).

Down with Issues, Up with Parties

A third line of attack on the elitist viewpoint has been to downgrade the importance of policy issues as major aspects of political attitudes. For instance, Wilker and Milbrath (1970) have argued that since mass political behaviors such as voting patterns show high stability from one election to the next, it is unreasonable to claim that the mass public does not have any stable political belief systems. They accept the evidence that public attitudes on policy issues are apt to be chaotic and poorly informed, but they argue that stands on political policies are not the only basis for belief systems. Instead of being oriented around policies or issues, the mass public's belief systems are more rudimentary, less detailed, and less differentiated. They are apt to be organized around the individual's **party identification** (Democratic or Republican) or his loyalty to one or another group (unions, farmers, Catholics, blacks, etc.) whose perceived interests influence his vote and his political attitudes.

Furthermore, Wilker and Milbrath present data indicating that for many people political activity serves expressive needs rather than being instrumental or goal-oriented. That is, such people's political beliefs and attitudes are attempts to assert their values as to what is good and bad in the world (e.g., "law and order" is good; "using drugs" is bad). This kind of political behavior is largely symbolic and ritualistic rather than being aimed at the accomplishment of specific policy goals, such as passage of a bill or reaching a treaty agreement. To quote Edelman (1964),

> They [election campaigns] give people a chance to express discontents and enthusiasms, to enjoy a sense of involvement. This is participation in a ritual act, however; only in a minor degree is it participation in policy formation (p. 3).

The importance of a person's party identification for his political belief systems has also been stressed by Kirkpatrick (1970a, 1970b). Reanalyzing data from SRC election surveys, he developed a measure of an individual's "total partisan affect" (the number of things which he liked better about one party and its presidential candidate than about the other party and candidate). Then, following a balance theory model, he showed that there was a high degree of consistency between an individual's party identification, his total partisan affect, and the candidate for whom he intended to vote. In a sample of more than 1500, 86% of individuals were consistent and only 14% were inconsistent (for instance, one inconsistent pattern would have been Republican party identification, but partisan affect favoring the Democratic side, and an intention to vote for Johnson rather than Goldwater in 1964).

Thus, Kirkpatrick has shown that when party identification is considered instead of specific policy issues, an overwhelming majority of the population have consistent political attitudes. A similar conclusion was reached by Key and Cummings (1966) in a reanalysis of Gallup Poll data for the 1960 election. They compared individuals' shifts in 1960 voting intentions from their 1956 vote with their answers to the question: "Looking ahead for the next few years, which political party—the Republican or the Democratic—do you think will be best for people like yourself?" They found a very strong tendency for this belief about the parties to be consistent with individuals' voting intentions.

> Those whose opinion on the question and previous vote were congruent remained in high degree with the party they had supported previously. There were very few

1956 Democratic voters who in 1960 felt the Republican party would be better for people like themselves, but among those who did hold this view, the shift to the Republican party was strong (83%). On the other hand, there was a sizable group of 1956 Eisenhower voters—about an eighth of all those holding a preference—who in 1960 felt that the Democratic party would be better for people like themselves. Of them, seven in ten shifted to Mr. Kennedy. The voting decisions of new voters also demonstrated a strong relation to their response to the question (1966, p. 124).

Kirkpatrick (1970a) carried the emphasis on parties as a source of attitude consistency a step farther by relating (a) individuals' *issue* positions to (b) their party identification, and (c) their beliefs about the parties' stands on the same issues. Reanalyzing SRC election survey data for four of the domestic issues discussed earlier in this chapter, he studied consistency among the above three belief elements at one point in time, and *changes* in consistency from one election to the next (1956 to 1958). Because of the measures he used, Kirkpatrick was dealing here with "issue publics," relatively small subsets of the total population who had an interest in one or another of these issues. Within these select groups, he found that consistency among the three belief elements ranged from 83% to 90% for different issues. Moreover, individuals who were consistent in 1956 tended very strongly to remain consistent in 1958 (88% to 99% for different issues), while the few individuals who were inconsistent in 1956 tended to become consistent in 1958 (58% to 76% for different issues).

From the above studies the conclusion seems clear that party preference forms the foundation for consistent political attitudes in a large majority of the population, regardless of whether or not these individuals have information or beliefs about specific issues. In Chapters 11 and 12 we will consider further data from recent studies comparing party identification, policy issues, and candidate images as influences on individual voting decisions.

Local Issues Can Be Important

A fourth objection to the elitist viewpoint stresses that the average citizen may be a good deal more interested in local issues than he is in national or international ones. For instance, Luttbeg (1968) studied attitudes toward ten issues such as urban renewal, bringing in new industry, annexation of suburbs, creation of a metropolitan park along the major river in the area, etc. He sampled over 1200 representative citizens in two Oregon cities and 117 community leaders from the same two cities, who were selected by a reputational technique. Using the technique of factor analysis, he found that five different conceptual dimensions were needed in order to explain the structure of attitudes on these ten issues. These five factors did explain a large amount of the variance (74%) in the attitudes of community leaders, but they also explained nearly as much (65%) of the variance in the citizens' attitudes. Luttbeg concluded, contrary to the elitist viewpoint, that community leaders' attitudes on these local issues were complex rather than unidimensional (e.g., on a liberal-conservative continuum), and second that average citizens' attitudes on local issues were very nearly as highly structured as the leaders' attitudes.

In a later article, Luttbeg (1970) did report some differences between the leaders' and citizens' attitudes on these issues, but not differences in degree of structure. He found that the community leaders tended to be more liberal than the overall population and to support these local programs more strongly than did the average citizen.

Salient Issues—A Better Mousetrap

A final objection to the elitist viewpoint is that most studies have not allowed respondents to specify issues which were important (salient) to them (Litwak, Hooyman, & Warren, 1973). In 1960 the SRC election surveys rectified this situation by adding to their previous closed-ended (multiple-choice) questions a new set of open-ended questions. These questions asked respondents to describe in their own words any "problems you think the government in Washington should do something about," how worried they were about these problems, and which party they thought would be most likely to do what they wanted done about the problems. The subjects' free responses were coded into about 25 different categories, and the results for the 1960 and 1964 elections have been studied by RePass (1971).

RePass analyzed primarily the high-salience issues, that is, ones which respondents were very worried about. He did this because he found that below this level of salience there was a lower level of information about the issue and a poorer perception of party differences concerning it. Thus he was essentially dealing solely with a concerned "issue public" on each issue, and one that had volunteered its concern without any prior cues from the interviewer. It is interesting to note the content of these high-salience problems. In 1960, 62% of them were in the area of foreign affairs and defense (largely problems in relation to Communism), whereas in 1964, 60% concerned domestic issues (most prominently, racial problems).

Concerning the structure of the issues mentioned, RePass found that 14% of respondents could not think of a single problem facing their government; these are the real "know-nothing's" of our time. However, 23% of the total sample mentioned four or more problems even though the interviewers did not encourage them to mention more than three. The average number of problems mentioned was 2.5. Interestingly, Republicans mentioned by far the most problems, Independents next, and Democrats the fewest; and this finding held true for all levels of education. Of the 1016 respondents who mentioned more than one problem, only 10% said that different parties would be best able to handle the different problems they mentioned.

TABLE 5-3 Relation of Party Identification to Perception of Party's "Issue
Advantage" in 1964 Election

Party having perceived "issue advantage"	Party identification				
	Strong Dem. (N=332)	*Weak Dem. (N=308)*	*Indep. (N=272)*	*Weak Repub. (N=175)*	*Strong Repub. (N=150)*
Democratic	78%	53%	39%	26%	7%
No perceived difference	14	26	26	27	11
Republican	8	21	35	47	82
	100%	100%	100%	100%	100%

Source: Adapted from RePass, 1971, p. 399.

In general these issue publics perceived differences in the party positions
concerning the issues which they mentioned, and they showed a fairly accurate
perception of these party differences despite some tendency toward distorted
perception favoring their own preferred party. As shown in Table 5-3, there was
a very strong relationship between their party identification and their perception
of which party could handle their salient issues better; however, a minority of
individuals from each party perceived the other party as better on the issues than
their own party. It is interesting to note that among respondents for whom this
"issue advantage" strongly favored the other party, over 90% ended up voting
against their own party. In other words, when issues are important to individuals,
and when they can see a clear difference between party positions on these issues,
they do tend very strongly to vote in accordance with their issue beliefs.

The overall relationship between these individuals' perception of a party's
"issue advantage" and their presidential vote was +.57 (tau-beta). By way of
comparison, the relationship between their vote and their overall attitude toward
the candidates was almost identical (tau-beta = +.60); and this was in 1964,
when attitudes toward the candidates were unusually salient (Kessel, 1968).
When final voting choice was predicted using multiple correlation techniques and
including party identification as one of the predictor variables, the strongest
weight (.39) was obtained for the candidate image variable, party identification
was next (.27), and party "issue advantage" was close behind (.23). RePass
concludes his study:

> When we allow voters to define their own issue space, they are able to sort out the
> differences between parties with a fair degree of accuracy. . . . we have shown that

the public is in large measure concerned about specific issues, and that these cognitions have a considerable impact on electoral choice (1971, p. 400).

Very similar conclusions have been reached in an entirely different study by Litwak et al. (1973).

RESOLUTION OF THE CONTROVERSY

It is not impossible to resolve this controversy between the elitist and mass-participation viewpoints. Converse himself has pointed out that he is *not* claiming that

> poorly educated people have no systems of beliefs about politics. . . . We do not disclaim the existence of entities that might best be called "folk ideologies," nor do we deny for a moment that strong differentiations in a variety of narrower values may be found within subcultures of less educated people (1964, pp. 255-256).

Rather, he holds that, below the elite 10% or so of the population:

> Instead of a few wide-ranging belief systems that organize large amounts of specific information, one would expect to find a proliferation of clusters of ideas among which little constraint is felt, even, quite often, in instances of sheer logical constraint (p. 213).

What can supporters of the mass-participation view add to this conclusion? First, they would agree strongly that the average man does have beliefs, values, and ideas about some aspects of public affairs. Second, they would probably agree that on national and international issues of government policy, the average man's attitudes are less clear and consistent than the elite's, and less likely to be organized along a liberal-conservative dimension. Third, they would point to the presence of a populist ideology among many members of the mass public, and to the importance of political parties and other reference groups as central elements around which many average citizens organize a consistent set of political attitudes. Fourth, they would point to local issues, and issues which are highly salient to the individual, as areas where the mass public's political attitudes are apt to be very nearly as well-organized and coherent as the elite's. Fifth, some recent studies have pointed out that the elections since 1964 have had a much more ideological, issue-oriented character than the elections of the 1950s, which provided much of the evidence for the elitist viewpoint (Field & Anderson, 1969; A. Miller, W. Miller, Raine, & Brown, 1973—see Chapter 11 for more details).

Finally, a resolution between the elitist view and the mass-participation view of public opinion might point out that in our complex modern world no one can be well-informed in all the areas which touch on his daily life, so a large degree of ignorance is inevitable for everyone. In this situation, it makes sense to concentrate on the knowledge and opinions which are important in one's own job and to largely turn over responsibility for other areas of life to people who are seen as experts in those areas (doctors in health questions, legislators in politics, community leaders in local issues, etc.). It is simply not functional for most people to develop an integrated system of political information and attitudes concerning issues which do not closely affect their everyday lives. This viewpoint has been stressed by Lane (1973) and is also supported by Litwak et al. (1973), who give the following example of the unmanageable complexity of modern life:

> To deal with the problems of water supply in a city like New York, knowledge of at least five major bureaucracies is necessary. If someone had no water, he would contact the health department; if not enough water—the department of water supply; if no hot water or water leaks—the buildings department; if these were major water leaks—the department of water supply; if water was overflowing from the apartment above—the police department; if there was water sewage in the cellar —the sanitation department (p. 330).

Tying the above points back to our discussion of attitude structure and functions in Chapter 3, we can conclude that attitudes serve the same general functions for members of the mass public as for political elites. However, it is much less likely (and less necessary) for political beliefs and attitudes to be central and salient in the belief systems of the average citizen than in those of the highly educated, community leaders, and people who are employed in politics or active in political affairs.

SUMMARY

Though the "informed citizen" is often claimed to be a necessary ingredient of democratic government, most citizens in our society are not very well-informed. A few items of knowledge are very widespread, but most are not. The *salient* bits of information which are known to almost everyone are ones which have been very prominently in the news, which are unique and different from other events, and which have continued to receive public attention over long periods of time.

In the field of public affairs, *exposure* to terms and events (such as the Watergate scandal) is much more widespread than factual knowledge about them. The names of the very top level of national leaders are apt to be known to nearly everyone, but knowledge about public issues and policies is almost always confined to a minority of the population, and often a very small minority.

The *elitist* view of public opinion holds that only the "elite," top 10% or so of the public, has political attitudes and belief systems which provide a broad and coherent basis for understanding public affairs. Only these elites use ideological concepts (such as liberalism-conservatism) in discussing public affairs, and only they show a clear and meaningful pattern of relationships between their beliefs about various political issues and policies. Below this elite level, attitudes toward major societal groups (e.g., farmers, blacks, the working class) provide a major focus for organizing whatever political attitudes are present. Furthermore, non-elite individuals' attitudes on political policy issues are extremely unstable over time, exhibiting so little reliability that the changes appear to be completely random in nature. Finally, each important political issue has its own "issue public" of informed and concerned citizens, always a minority of the total population, and only partially overlapping the issue publics who are interested in each other major issue.

The *mass participation* view of public opinion generally does not dispute the facts cited by the elitist proponents, but does interpret them differently and add other sorts of evidence. Methodological studies have shown high consistency in political attitudes within individuals, though different individuals may differ widely in the dimensions they use to judge political issues. Secondary analysis of some of the earlier Survey Research Center data showed an ideological dimension of populist beliefs among many members of the mass public, particularly those inclined to be nonvoters—beliefs favoring domestic social and economic improvements, but opposing high taxes and U.S. foreign involvement. Also it has been demonstrated that political party preference is a very important factor which forms the foundation for consistent political attitudes in a large majority of the population, many of whom are not concerned about specific policy issues. Finally, evidence shows that for local community issues, and for issues which are highly salient to the individuals concerned, the mass public's attitudes are apt to be very nearly as well-organized as are the elite's. These types of findings have largely resolved the controversy over the political attitudes of the elite versus those of the average citizen.

Suggested Readings

Converse, P. E. The nature of belief systems in mass publics. In D. Apter (Ed.), *Ideology and Discontent*. New York: Free Press, 1964. Pp. 206–261.—A thorough and detailed presentation of the elitist view of public opinion, combining empirical evidence with wide-ranging theory and application.

Erskine, H. G. The polls: The informed public. *Public Opinion Quarterly*, 1962, 26, 669–677.—An entertaining collection of many poll results showing public information and ignorance. This is the first of a series of four such articles on related topics.

RePass, D. E. Issue salience and party choice. *American Political Science Review*, 1971, 65, 389–400.—An interesting secondary analysis of Survey Research Center data on issues which were highly salient to individual respondents in the 1964 election, showing support for the mass participation view of public opinion.

Formation of Attitudes and Opinions

The greatest part of mankind have no other reason for their opinions than that they are in fashion.—Samuel Johnson.

A man is born into his political party just as he is born into probable future membership in the church of his parents.—James West.

Opinions should be formed with great caution and changed with greater.—Josh Billings.

Attitudes and opinions are learned—that much is agreed upon by all authorities. But how are they learned? The processes of attitude formation, and the factors which are most important in the development of attitudes, are still subjects of dispute. Some authorities stress family influences in the child's early years, others underline the importance of the educational system or of peer-group pressures, while still others emphasize the mass media of communication, particularly television. Undoubtedly all of these factors play a part in attitude formation, and the research summarized in this chapter has begun the task of classifying and understanding the processes and the determining factors involved.

Before looking at the research findings regarding attitude formation, one clarification will be helpful. Attitude formation and attitude change are often hard to distinguish from each other and are therefore frequently spoken of together, as if they were synonymous. Undoubtedly many of the same processes and influences are at work when attitudes and opinions are being changed as when they were originally formed. However, the research literature on attitude change, which is voluminous in scope, is rather different in its approach and methods from the work on attitude formation. Since the topic of attitude change will be taken up in two subsequent chapters, we will try in this chapter to focus primarily on attitude formation. However, in some cases where the amount of available research evidence is scanty, we will occasionally cite studies of attitude change in this chapter as well.

The term **attitude formation** refers to the initial change from having *no* attitude toward a given object to having *some* attitude toward it, either positive, negative, or in-between. But what is it like to have no attitude toward an object? For an infant, the situation was described by William James as a world of "blooming, buzzing confusion" where all stimuli are new and strange. For adults to have no attitude may mean that they have never had any experience, either direct or vicarious, with the object (for instance, your attitude toward "Cromelians," a group of people you have never heard of), or simply that they have never thought evaluatively about it (an example might be your attitude toward the planet Jupiter).

Starting from this zero point, what determining factors can cause a person to acquire an attitude toward Cromelians or toward Jupiter? In answering that question we will consider several different factors, starting with internal and personal determinants and moving toward external influences. Then in the latter part of the chapter we will briefly examine the various *processes of learning* by which a new attitude or opinion may be acquired.

GENETIC AND PHYSIOLOGICAL FACTORS

The first type of factor which we will consider is a surprising one because it is rarely mentioned in discussions of attitude formation. Since attitudes are gener-

Box 6-1 WILLIAM McGUIRE, *Systematizer and Gadfly*

Still in his early fifties, William McGuire has made a multiple reputation in social psychology as an experimentalist, theorist, systematizer, editor, and administrator. Born in New York in 1925, he served in the Army in World War II, and then received his B.A. and M.A. from Fordham. Moving to Yale for his Ph.D., he was one of the fruitful group of scholars who worked with Carl Hovland in experimental research on communication and attitude change. Following brief periods of teaching at Yale and Illinois, he spent longer periods on the faculty of Columbia and the University of California at San Diego before returning to Yale as chairman of the psychology department in 1971.

McGuire was influential as editor of the major journal in social psychology from 1968 through 1970. He has already been cited in Chapters 1 and 3 as author of a monumental handbook chapter on attitudes and attitude change, and in later chapters of this book his theoretical contributions to consistency approaches, personality research, and resistance to attitude change will be mentioned. Finally, Chapter 10 describes his role as a gadfly and prophet for the field.

ally agreed to be learned, citing genetic or physiological factors in their formation may sound like support for the fallacious viewpoint that acquired characteristics can be inherited (the discredited theory of the Russian geneticist Lysenko). However, McGuire (1969) has pointed out that it is often wise to question any universally accepted principle—at the very least, it may have some exceptions which have been overlooked.

In the case of genetic factors in attitude formation, the most plausible way they might operate would be in establishing a *predisposition* for the development of particular attitudes. For instance, there is good evidence for genetic factors determining an organism's general level of aggressiveness, as in Scott and Fuller's (1965) studies of different breeds of dogs. In humans, the person's level of aggressiveness might very well help to determine his or her attitudes of hostility to outgroup members, which could be seen in prejudice against other groups (for instance, Jews or foreigners or teenagers). Such intergroup hostility may once have had survival value, though it appears counterproductive in our nuclear age. Another example of possible genetic influences is in determination of individuals' general level of persuasibility, which in turn can influence the attitudes they develop. It is important to realize, as McGuire (1969) points out, that the notion of genetic determinants of some attitudes does not imply that those attitudes could not be changed under the right environmental conditions, though it may make the change process more difficult.

Physiological factors in attitude formation can be seen particularly in such conditions as aging, illnesses, and the effects of various drugs. For instance, the general conservatism often found in old age is likely to affect new attitudes, such as the person's feelings toward a new political candidate. Certain illnesses are reputed to be associated with predispositions to particular attitude states: encephalitis often increases general aggressiveness, while tuberculosis paradoxically seems to increase optimistic attitudes. Such effects are more understandable in light of the attitudinal effects of certain drugs which are clearly physiological in nature. The euphoria produced by marijuana and the opiate drugs is well-known, as are the calming and anxiety-reducing effects of tranquilizers. Thus it is clear that physiological states can influence people's general levels of aggressiveness and persuasibility and their readiness to adopt certain attitudes.

DIRECT PERSONAL EXPERIENCE

The earliest and most fundamental way in which people form attitudes is through direct personal experience with the attitude object. For example, an infant who is given orange juice to drink for the first time is apt to like it because it is sweet, flavorful, pleasantly cool, and filling. Following that experience, the infant has an attitude toward orange juice which is likely to be confirmed and strengthened with further experience. We will consider three aspects of personal experience in the formation of attitudes: salient incidents, repeated exposure, and the development of stereotypes.

Salient Incidents

Many authors have stressed the importance of salient incidents, particularly traumatic or frightening ones, in the development of attitudes. Psychoanalysts and clinical psychologists have described many phobias which originated in a single traumatic experience, for instance with a runaway horse or a fierce dog. Other examples of single incidents markedly affecting attitudes can be seen in religious conversion experiences (written about by William James as long ago as 1902) and in the clinical descriptions of war neuroses (e.g., Sargant, 1957). A typical case is that of a naval pilot who crashed in flames on an aircraft-carrier's deck, was rescued with relatively minor injuries, but was never able to approach a plane again because of extreme, uncontrollable fear and trembling.

It is easy to understand the importance of traumatic incidents, either as an example of powerful negative conditioning (Staats, 1968), or in terms of an information-processing model (Fishbein & Ajzen, 1975). The latter authors suggest that a person's attitude toward an object at any given time is based upon a few (perhaps 5–10) salient beliefs that he or she holds about the object. Obviously, a belief like "It almost killed me" is likely to remain very salient and very powerful in determining the person's attitude for a long time.

In the attitude-change literature, a number of studies have shown marked changes in public opinion stemming from a single dramatic event such as the border war between India and China or the assassination of Martin Luther King (e.g., Hofstetter, 1969). However, in a study of changes in public opinion over a period of time following the crisis of a political kidnapping and assassination in Canada, Sorrentino and Vidmar (1974) concluded that the first strong reaction (in this case, support for the government) is apt to be followed by an eventual return of attitudes to their precrisis levels. Thus, even the effects of dramatic or traumatic incidents are often counterbalanced by the cumulative effect of other events.

Repeated Exposure

Another way in which attitudes are often formed is through repeated exposure to an object (or person or idea) over time. The research literature on this topic has been thoroughly summarized by Zajonc (1968a), who has also done a series of experimental studies with his coworkers to clarify how this effect occurs. Zajonc has emphasized that mere exposure to a stimulus object without any associated reinforcement or tension-reduction is sufficient to enhance a person's attitude toward the object. This effect operates most strongly during the first few exposures, but attitudes continue to increase in favorability at a gradually slower rate over any number of exposures (see Figure 6-1).

The attitude-enhancing effect of repeated exposure is not confined to the research laboratory. It has been found also in field studies, such as in a campus election where number of campaign posters was highly correlated with the

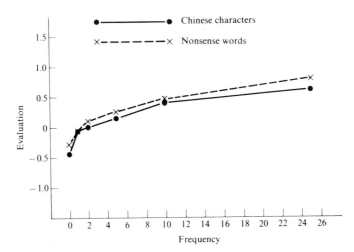

Figure 6-1 Relationship between frequency of mere exposure of an object and attitude toward it. (Data from Zajonc, 1968a; figure reprinted from Fishbein & Ajzen, 1975, p. 282. Reprinted by permission of Addison-Wesley Publishing Co.)

candidate's final vote (Schaffner & Wandersman, 1974). Indeed, this principle seems to underlie much commercial advertising and political campaigning. A rather-frightening corollary of this principle is that a harmful product or a political demagogue can become more popular just by getting more public exposure, despite their injurious nature. An article by Zajonc in 1970 suggested that this corollary applied to then- Vice-President Spiro Agnew, a politician known for his attacks on the press and on "effete intellectual snobs":

> [A]fter repeated exposure, almost anything grows on you—even Spiro Agnew (p. 3).

However, this alarming prospect has since been shown to be unlikely, for several studies have demonstrated that the attitude enhancement effect holds only for positive and neutral stimuli, and it may even be reversed for repeated exposure to stimuli which were originally negative in their impact on the individual (e.g., Perlman & Oskamp, 1971). In addition, it should be remembered that the mere exposure effect is only one of many influences on attitude formation, and it would not be expected to be as strong as many others, for instance the effect of reward or punishment associated with exposure to the stimulus. Thus, if the voice of a particular politician always grates on your ears, or you dislike his insincere manner, you are very likely to become less fond of him with repeated exposure, rather than more fond of him.

Another area where repeated exposure has been studied is in the effect of interracial or international contact on attitude change (Amir, 1969; Harding, Proshansky, Kutner, & Chein, 1969). In this area also, repeated contact can lead to more favorable or less favorable attitudes, depending on the presence or absence of several crucial factors. A number of authors have emphasized that interracial contact is more likely to lead to greater friendliness if it has most or all of the following characteristics: if it is (a) continued over a long period, (b) in cooperative activities, between individuals having (c) equal status, (d) common goals, and (e) similar belief systems, and in situations which are (f) approved of by authorities or by social custom (e.g., Pettigrew, 1969).

Development of Stereotypes

In the formation of attitudes, an important early stage is the development of cognitive categories which classify objects in the surrounding world. For instance, a two-year-old child may classify all four-legged animals as "doggie," but a year later (s)he may have learned the category of "animals" and the subclasses of "dogs," "cats," and "horses." The need to classify our experiences is just as strong in adulthood as it is in infancy, and it is the reason that we develop stereotypes of groups of people. A **stereotype** may be defined simply as an image or set of beliefs which a person holds about most members of a particular social group. Of necessity such beliefs are highly simplified, and they may be highly evaluative and rigidly resistant to change (e.g., "most dogs are vicious," "women are irrational"). Note that this definition does not specify that stereotypes must be inaccurate, as some authors do. The reason for this omission will become clear in the following paragraphs. Note also that the definition does not specify that stereotypes must be shared beliefs—an individual can have his or her own idiosyncratic stereotype of another group of people (e.g., "women are highly logical"), though when we speak of *social* stereotypes, we mean ones which are shared by many individuals.

Stereotypes develop because they are useful. They reduce the tremendous complexity of the world around us into a few simple guidelines which we can use in our everyday thought and decisions. If we "know" that "all politicians are crooked," we can dismiss government scandals without having to think very hard about what should be done to prevent or control them. Similarly, if we believe that "women are irrational," we won't hire one to be our lawyer. Unfortunately, however, the simpler and more convenient the stereotype, the more likely it is to be inaccurate, at least in part.

The inaccuracy of stereotypes has been much emphasized, particularly in the field of racial attitudes, where the terms "stereotype" and "prejudice" have taken on derogatory connotations. In one classic study the stereotype shared by citizens of Fresno, California about the local Armenian minority group was shown not only to be false, but to be opposite to reality on many characteristics—e.g., Armenians were actually more law-abiding rather than less so (LaPiere, 1936). However, several authors have recently pointed out that many stereotypes (though not necessarily all) have a *kernel of truth* in them (e.g., Brigham, 1971). Campbell (1967) has convincingly presented the reasons for a possible kernel of truth, stressing that the traits which are most important to a group and the traits on which it differs most from another group will be likely to enter into its stereotype of the other group. Thus, a stereotype is *determined largely by the nature of the perceiving group*, but also partly by the nature of the group perceived.

It should also be stressed that a person's stereotypes are often not the product of his or her personal experience with the group in question. They may also derive largely, or entirely, from what the person has read or heard from family and friends. That point brings us to the next major factor in attitude formation, the direct teaching and indirect influence of parents. (Both Chapters 14 and 15 contain more information about the specific details of racial stereotypes and sex-role stereotypes.)

PARENTAL INFLUENCE

The amount of parental influence over a young child's behavior and attitudes is so great that McGuire (1969) has referred to childhood as a "total institution,"

Figure 6-2 Parental influence, though usually benevolent, exerts just as much control as a concentration camp.

comparable in its degree of control to confinement in a penal institution or a concentration camp. Parents have almost total control over the young child's informational input, the behaviors demanded of the child, and the rewards and punishments meted out. Thus they have great power to shape the child's attitudes, particularly because the infant has no preexisting attitudes which would be contrary to the parental influence.

A child's attitudes are largely shaped by its own experience with the world, but this is usually accomplished by explicit teaching and implicit modeling of parental attitudes ("Nice kitty. Kitty won't hurt you. Pet the kitty gently."). Thus many childhood attitudes are probably a combination of the child's own experience and what (s)he has heard parents say or seen them do. However, there are many other areas where the average child has no direct experience at all, and in these areas parental influence on the child's attitudes may be very great. Examples include attitudes toward war, toward foreigners, toward other countries, toward political parties and candidates, and toward abstract concepts like freedom and justice.

Prejudice and racial attitudes were prominent areas where parental influence has been studied. A long series of studies shows that in general children's level of prejudice is related to their parents' prejudice and that, at least in part, they take over that prejudice directly (e.g., Bird, Monachesi, & Burdick, 1952; Epstein & Komorita, 1966). In addition, it is quite possible for children to learn from parental behavior indirectly and without any intentional teaching (Trager & Yarrow, 1952). Once learned, prejudiced attitudes tend to be generalized to many outgroups, so there are high positive correlations among the levels of prejudice toward various different minority groups such as blacks, Chicanos, Jews, Japanese, etc. (Frenkel-Brunswik & Havel, 1953). However, as children grow older, there are many other influences on their attitudes in addition to their parents, and by adolescence the degree of parent-child similarity is only a low positive one (Bird et al., 1952; Frenkel-Brunswik & Havel, 1953).

Many studies have attempted to trace children's development of prejudice to the child-rearing methods used by their parents. There is general agreement that emotionally cold, status-oriented parents who stress obedience, discipline, and physical punishment are likely to have highly prejudiced and authoritarian children (Adorno et al., 1950; Triandis & Triandis, 1962). The latter study found that this relationship held in Greece as well as in the United States. However, research has not yet clarified whether this effect occurs indirectly, through the psychodynamic mechanisms posited in *The Authoritarian Personality*—i.e., that harsh child-rearing produces children with low tolerance for frustration and high repressed hostility, which later generate prejudiced ethnic attitudes. A plausible alternative view is that these children learn their prejudice directly by identifying with and copying their parents' attitudes and behavior. Readers interested in a fuller discussion of this topic can find it in an extensive chapter on prejudice and ethnic relations by Harding et al. (1969).

Development of Political Attitudes

The area where children's attitudes and parental influence have been most extensively studied is in the development of political attitudes. Because of the large amount of research in this area, we will take time to survey some of the most interesting empirical findings. Interested readers may want to consult more extensive reviews of political socialization by Sears (1969, pp. 370–399) and Niemi (1973).

The first major finding is the early age at which political attitudes begin to develop. To quote Lane and Sears (1964, p. 17): "Political life, like sexual life, starts much earlier than we had thought." As early as age six or seven many children have developed strong emotional and cognitive associations about their nation, its leaders, and national symbols such as the flag (Lambert & Klineberg, 1967; Easton & Dennis, 1969).

Youthful Chauvinism and Trustfulness. A second finding is the very high degree of chauvinism displayed by young children. For instance, in Hess and

Torney's (1967) large nationwide sample of white children from grades two through eight, over 95% of the children at every grade level agreed that "the American flag is the best flag in the world," and that "America is the best country in the world."

Third, this positive view of the nation extends to nearly-as-positive attitudes toward the government and toward specific leaders. For instance, 77% of fourth-graders in another study agreed that "the government usually knows what is best for people" (Easton & Dennis, 1965). Idealization of the President occurs not only in the United States, but also in Puerto Rico, Australia, Chile, and Japan (Hess, 1963). Among U.S. second-graders 75% agreed that "the President cares a lot what you think if you write to him" (Hess & Torney, 1967). Though the President is rated highest, other politicians are also favorably evaluated by children, being seen as less selfish than most people, more honest, and almost always keeping their promises. However, by the eighth grade, children become somewhat more cynical and doubting of politicians though they are still reluctant to evaluate government leaders unfavorably (Greenstein, 1965; Hess & Torney, 1967). These generally positive views of government are the typical norm, but there are exceptions which we will examine later.

A fourth typical conclusion has been that the parents' role in determining children's political attitudes is large, and that there is a high level of parent-child agreement in political attitudes (Hyman, 1959). The average parental opinion on various political questions tends to be very close to the average opinion of their children. Furthermore, Hyman surveyed a dozen studies and concluded that the typical degree of agreement between parent-child pairs on political matters was a correlation of about +.5. However, this conclusion has had to be markedly modified in recent years due to the availability of new evidence.

Recent Findings—Low Parent-Child Correspondence. All of the studies cited by Hyman were based on "samples of convenience," usually small samples, and unrepresentative of any larger population because of biases in selection, low response rate, and other problems. Nevertheless, in the better-controlled of such studies, the correspondence in attitudes between matched parent-child pairs from the same family was relatively low (around +.2), even though the *group average* of parents' attitudes was very similar to the group average for children (Connell, 1972). A dramatically improved methodology has been used by Jennings and Niemi (1968), who independently interviewed a representative national sample of over 1600 high school seniors and their parents. Their findings conclusively showed rather low positive correlations (between 0.0 and +.4) for parent-child pairs on about 15 measures of political attitudes (political cynicism, attitudes on specific issues and toward various groups, etc.). However, there was one measure with a notably higher relationship, which is discussed next.

Party Identification. The single high relationship in the political area found by Jennings and Niemi was between parents' party identification and their child's party identification—a product-moment correlation coefficient of about +.6. This finding is quite consistent with Converse's (1964) finding, described in the previous chapter, of singularly high stability over time for the party identification measure. In addition to being stable, party identification is a highly salient attitude in the American political system. As a result, it turns out to be the only political attitude transmitted very effectively from parents to their children, though even here there are many cases of noncorrespondence. The limits on even this small degree of parental attitude transmission are shown in findings from France, where voter loyalty to the many and shifting party groupings is much lower than in the U.S. two-party system (Converse & Dupeux, 1962).

The prominence of party identification as an attitude transmitted by parents is paralleled by findings from the area of religious attitudes. There parent-child correspondence in denominational preference was found to be quite high (about 74%, yielding a contingency coefficient of +.88, the highest relationship reported by Jennings & Niemi, 1968). However, just as in the political arena, parent-child agreement on other religious questions dropped to a very modest positive relationship. Thus, we may conclude that transmission of parental values is only apt to be noticeably successful when they deal with simple and highly visible questions of group membership.

> That specific opinions generally come with mother's milk is—for America, 1944–1968—rather decisively disproved (Connell, 1972, p. 330).

Disaffection Toward Government. Another exception to the general findings mentioned earlier in this section is the fact that some groups of children have been found to be far less favorable toward the government and political leaders than the great mass of American youth. For instance, a study of poor school children in Appalachia found high degrees of political cynicism and a view of government leaders as "malevolent" (Jaros, Hirsch, & Fleron, 1968). Other studies have shown differences in political attitudes between black and white children, though many black children are still surprisingly supportive of the government despite the presence of discrimination and poor living conditions (Greenberg, 1970). Abramson (1972) has summarized a number of studies showing greater feelings of political powerlessness among black children and a marked decrease in their political trust following the summer of 1967.

Have these beachheads of disaffection toward government increased and spread among children as a result of the controversy over the Vietnam War and the scandals of the Nixon administration? There is some evidence that they have. In a longitudinal follow-up of their former high school seniors, Jennings and Niemi (1973) found that both they and their parents had increased considerably in political cynicism. Though some studies have still found idealization of the government and its leaders similar to the earlier general findings, increasing reports of disaffection have been appearing (e.g., Tolley, 1973). For instance, upper-class children near Boston were found to be quite hostile to political authority (Arterton, 1974), and lower and middle class San Diego children were markedly less idealistic in their views of the President than earlier studies (Griffith, 1975). It now appears that, to a greater extent than formerly thought, children's attitudes toward political institutions are shaped by the events of the times rather than being invariably positive and idealistic.

GROUP DETERMINANTS OF ATTITUDES

Another important influence on the formation of attitudes is the pressure of various groups. We will touch briefly on four kinds of group pressure: school indoctrination, peer groups, conformity pressures in general, and reference groups.

Schools

Second only to parental influences in determining children's attitudes are school teaching and indoctrination. This has become especially clear in the area of political attitudes, where several recent studies have emphasized the importance of school influence (Almond & Verba, 1963; Hess & Torney, 1967; Tolley, 1973). The highly-favorable attitudes mentioned above which children develop toward government and their idealization of the President and other leaders (even down to the local policeman) are undoubtedly largely due to schoolroom teaching.

We have all experienced this kind of indoctrination, but it is easy to forget or overlook how hard the schools work to instill patriotism. For example, Hess and Torney found that teachers, especially in the lower grades, consciously tried to "emphasize the positive" and to avoid discussion of conflict within the country. They reported that 99% of their sample of teachers displayed the American flag prominently, over 85% at each grade level required the Pledge of Allegiance to be said daily, and in the lower grades most classrooms spent some time every day singing patriotic songs. Though children may not always understand the words ("one nation, invisible"), it is no wonder that they get the message clearly— "my country, right or wrong."

Peer Groups

Following family and school, the next major determinant of attitudes, both chronologically and in relative importance, is the child's peer group. From the end of grade school onward, peer-group contacts become increasingly important and time-consuming. During high school years there is a marked increase in the discussion of politics with friends (Hyman, 1959), and friends' attitudes and

Figure 6-3 The schools instill pro-system attitudes.

voting intentions have been found to influence one's own attitudes and behavior (Coleman, 1961).

The many "generation gap" differences in attitudes between youth and the older generation are undoubtedly due in part to youthful peer-group influences. Some typical examples of research findings concerning generation differences are young people's greater political liberality, toleration of nonconformity, advocacy of civil liberties, and racial tolerance (e.g., Jennings & Niemi, 1968). That such generational differences are related to peer-group influences was shown in an interesting study of moral attitudes in Israeli *kibbutzim*. There the age-group system of child-rearing produced greater differences in attitudes between parents and children than were found with more traditional family living arrangements (Rettig, 1966).

Conformity Pressures

Not only peer groups, but a variety of other conformity pressures can lead to attitude formation and change. We will mention just a few examples. The overall cultural context within which we live can provide a set of assumptions and salient "facts" which determine the attitudes we will develop, without our even being aware of any influence. For example, Pettigrew (1971) has estimated that about three-fourths of Americans who are racially prejudiced are simply reflecting the assumptions and norms of their culture. Moreover, "pluralistic ignorance" tends to cause everyone to believe that others are more prejudiced than oneself, thus creating resistance to change in attitudes or behavior (Breed & Ktsanes, 1961).

However, intergroup contact under the right conditions can ameliorate such prejudice, especially when cooperative efforts toward common goals are required by the circumstances. Such beneficial effects of intergroup contact have been demonstrated in preschool children (Crooks, 1970) and in boys' summer camp groups when conditions conducive to cooperation rather than competition were established (Sherif, Harvey, White, Hood, & Sherif, 1961). Changes in social roles can often exert powerful influences on attitudes, such as when a pro-union worker is promoted to the management job of foreman (Lieberman, 1956). Even more far-reaching changes in attitudes and behavior can be induced when there is relatively complete control over the social environment, rewards, and punishments, as in Marine Corps basic training or in brainwashing of political prisoners (Lifton, 1963).

Reference Groups

A milder form of influence on attitudes, and one which is often unintentional, is seen in **reference groups**. These are groups whose standards and beliefs an individual accepts and measures himself against, regardless of whether he himself is a member of the group. For many teenagers, movie stars or rock musicians serve this function, while for others the "in crowd" at school serves as a reference group.

The point which is central here is that reference groups often influence people's attitudes, even without any overt attempts to do so. In various studies this effect has been found for racial and religious issues, for economic and political attitudes, and for authoritarian attitudes as influenced by college dormitory preference (e.g., Siegel & Siegel, 1957). One of the most important studies of reference groups was the famous Bennington College study by Newcomb (1943). Bennington began as a very liberal college during the depression years, but its incoming students were mostly from upper-class highly conservative families. Thus there was a conflict between the college community's standards and those of the new students. Though some students retained their family as their reference group, most of the students resolved this conflict by adopting the faculty and advanced students as their reference group and gradually changing their own attitudes in a more liberal direction throughout their stay in college. A typical student comment describes this process:

> It's very simple, I was so anxious to be accepted that I accepted the political complexion of the community here. I just couldn't stand out against the crowd unless I had made many friends and had strong support (Newcomb, 1943, p. 132).

MASS MEDIA

The final factor in attitude formation which we will discuss is effects of the mass media—newspapers, magazines, movies, radio, and television. There is no doubt that these media have had enormous impact on our society and on other societies where they have been introduced. Just try to imagine what your life would be like if there were no TV or radio, for instance! Yet there is much less hard evidence on their precise effects than we would like.

We know that American children typically spend from two to three hours per day watching television, and that by the time they finish high school they will have spent as many hours in front of the TV set as in the school classroom. Thus the *informational* impact of TV, and to a lesser extent of the other media, is very great. By age 10, TV and school have replaced the family as the most frequently mentioned sources of children's information (Lambert & Klineberg, 1967). A major British study of the impact of TV reported that the carefully planned BBC programs broadened children's views of other nations and peoples, making them more objective and less evaluative. The programs also had their greatest effect on children who were not already familiar with their subject matter (Himmelweit, Oppenheim, & Vince, 1958).

These findings are relevant to attitude formation, since people's information and beliefs are important factors in their attitudes. However, the media do not simply transmit information. By selecting, emphasizing, and interpreting particular events, and by publicizing people's reactions to those events, they help to structure the nature of "reality" and to define the crucial issues of the day, which in turn impels the public to form attitudes on these new issues (Lang & Lang, 1959). Mass communication is particularly likely to be effective in creating opinions and attitudes on new issues where there are no existing predispositions to be changed (Klapper, 1963).

The topic of media effectiveness will recur again at greater length in the following chapter on attitude communication. However, in the meantime we will consider the various learning processes by which attitudes can be formed.

LEARNING PROCESSES IN ATTITUDE FORMATION

This section briefly examines seven different learning processes which can be involved in attitude formation. A concrete example is given to clarify the nature of each process, and research studies done using each paradigm are cited as a resource for readers who want to study these approaches more thoroughly.

Classical Conditioning

Classical conditioning is the process investigated by Pavlov, who presented meat powder and the sound of a bell to dogs and observed that later the bell alone would cause the dogs to salivate. The paradigm uses a stimulus, called the unconditioned stimulus, which automatically elicits a response from the organism. Another stimulus which does not automatically elicit that response is presented simultaneously with or just before the unconditioned stimulus on several trials. To test the presence of learning, the unconditioned stimulus is then omitted. If the response is given to the other stimulus alone, we say that the response has been conditioned to that stimulus, which is termed the conditioned stimulus.

Applying this paradigm to attitude formation, we might consider a parental spanking as the unconditioned stimulus, which would automatically produce negative, unhappy feelings in a child. If a spanking is applied every time that the child reaches for or touches a valuable vase, the vase will soon become a conditioned stimulus which will by itself produce negative feelings (an attitude). Of course, positive attitudes can be produced in the same way by using unconditioned stimuli, like food or a hug, which make the child feel good. This paradigm is most relevant to formation of the evaluative or feeling aspect of attitudes.

The classical conditioning paradigm has been used in attitude research by many investigators (e.g., Weiss, 1968; Zanna, Kiesler, & Pilkonis, 1970). The major question in its use is whether subjects are *aware* of the S-R connection which the investigator is trying to establish. If so, the subjects' learning may be of an instrumental sort (trying to do what will gain the investigator's approval), or alternatively it may be of a cognitive, information-processing sort, rather than being classical conditioning (Kiesler, Collins, & Miller, 1969).

Stimulus Generalization

Generalization is a process which occurs after an S-R connection has been established by conditioning. It is usually found that the conditioned response can be elicited, not just by the conditioned stimulus, but by other similar stimuli (for instance, a bell of a different pitch in Pavlov's experiments). An example in attitude formation might be the establishment of a negative reaction to one particular black man, an attitude which would then generalize to other men and women having similar skin color or appearance. Moreover, through the use of language, humans can display **semantic generalization** to other stimuli having similar *meanings*. So, for instance, a negative attitude might further generalize to the words "Negro" and "black" and to other words or objects which had a similar meaning. This process has been described in more detail by Bem (1970).

Instrumental Conditioning

This process, sometimes called **operant conditioning**, is the kind of learning so much stressed by Skinner and his followers. It is called *operant* because the organism is allowed to operate freely on its environment instead of being constrained to make one particular response to one particular stimulus. It is *instrumental* in the sense that the organism's behavior is instrumental; that is, the behavior is the means by which reward or punishment is achieved. The researcher does not usually know or care what the original stimulus was for the organism's behavior. Instead, he waits until the organism makes a desired response (say, scratching its ear) and then immediately *reinforces* the response by presenting a food pellet or a piece of candy.

In human attitude formation, the reinforcer is apt to be verbal—either praise or criticism—or nonverbal signs of approval or disapproval. For instance, a child might say "dirty communists" and be rewarded by an approving smile from the parent. As a result, the child would not only be likely to say "dirty communists" more often in the future, but also to form a negative attitude toward communists. Attitude research using this paradigm has been done by Weiss (1968), Staats (1968), and many others. A critique of the methodology and results of some of this research may be found in Kiesler, Collins, and Miller (1969, pp. 101–103, 118–128).

Selective Learning

An extension of instrumental conditioning called **selective learning** has also been studied experimentally by Weiss (1968). In this situation the organism has several alternative responses, and they are differentially reinforced by using different degrees of reward or punishment. As a result, the more-reinforced responses increase in their likelihood of being emitted. An example in the attitude area might be a youthful baseball fan who has expressed liking for several different teams on different occasions. If one attitude ("I like the Dodgers") was reinforced more quickly, more strongly, or more frequently than his statements favorable to other teams, his favorable attitude toward the Dodgers would gradually be selected as his dominant attitude on the topic of baseball teams. Like instrumental conditioning, this paradigm is most directly relevant to formation of the behavioral aspect of attitudes.

Imitation or Modeling

A common type of learning that can occur without any external reinforcement is **imitation** of the behavior of another person who serves as a model. Parents are

Figure 6-4 Classical conditioning (top) pairs a new stimulus object (the pill) with one which already produces a response from the person, and eventually the new object will produce the same response. Instrumental conditioning (bottom) applies a reinforcer (such as a reward) after the person has made a particular response, and as a result the person's tendency to make that response is strengthened.

often disconcerted to find that their children imitate not only their admirable behavior (e.g., helping to feed the baby) but also their antisocial acts (e.g., swearing at the disliked neighbors). In many such modeled actions, the behavioral aspect of attitudes begins to be formed without any explicit instruction or reinforcement by the parent. Much research has shown the effectiveness of models in shaping attitudes and behavior, both in the area of aggression (Bandura, 1965; Scientific Advisory Committee on Television and Social Behavior, 1972) and in the area of helping behavior (London, 1970; Berkowitz, 1972).

Persuasion

Persuasive communication is probably the most common way of trying to change a person's attitude, and it will be taken up at length in Chapters 8 and 9. It can also be used to form attitudes for the first time, as when a friend tells you the good or bad points about a local political candidate of whom you knew nothing before. The typical contents of such a persuasive message include one or more suggested conclusions or recommendations for action, usually together with some supporting facts or arguments (e.g., "He's a good candidate because he's honest and won't make any political deals to get elected"). The format of persuasive messages can be infinitely varied: long or short, logical or emotional, organized or disorganized, etc. They are apt to influence the cognitive aspect of attitudes most directly, and sometimes also the behavioral aspect. Some of the most influential work in this area has been done by the group of researchers who gathered around Carl Hovland at Yale (Hovland, Janis, & Kelley, 1953; Hovland et al., 1957; Janis et al., 1959; and Rosenberg et al., 1960).

Information Integration

The final type of attitude formation process to be discussed here, **information integration**, is emphasized by many cognitive theorists and researchers. They stress that a person's attitude toward an object is based on the beliefs that (s)he holds about it, some of which may be favorable and others unfavorable. In forming their attitudes, people must integrate the beliefs about the object which are salient to them into an overall impression. For instance, your friend may tell you that an unfamiliar political candidate is honest, unwilling to make any deals to get elected, but not a good speaker. To form an attitude toward the candidate, you then have to combine those beliefs (and perhaps also your opinion of your friend's political judgment) in some way. Of course, the evidence on political attitudes cited in Chapter 5 indicates that many people are relatively inattentive and/or inconsistent in their reaction to political information. However, theorists have constructed many different models suggesting ways in which such sets of beliefs are typically combined: additive models, averaging models, weighted-averages, and expectancy-value models. The latter type combines the degree of belief in the attitude object's characteristics with an evaluation of those characteristics, in a way similar to the research of Rosenberg (1956) cited in Chapter 3. Major contributors to research on information integration have been Anderson (1971) and Fishbein and Ajzen (1975).

It should be stressed that the seven learning processes which we have just described are not antagonistic, mutually-exclusive theories of attitude formation. Several or all of these processes may take place in the acquisition of various attitudes, depending on the stimulus situations which a person is exposed to.

SUMMARY

Attitude formation, the step from no attitude to some attitude toward a given object, is similar but not identical to attitude change. It is agreed that attitudes are learned, but many different factors can operate in the acquisition process. Genetic and physiological factors, though seldom mentioned in this connection, may establish a predisposition for the development of particular attitudes.

Direct personal experience, either in salient incidents or in repeated exposure over time, is the most fundamental factor in attitude formation. Because of our need to simplify the tremendous complexity of our personal experience, we develop cognitive categories for classifying events and objects around us. One example of such categories is a *stereotype*, an image or set of beliefs which a person holds about most members of a particular social group. Stereotypes are highly simplified, frequently highly evaluative and rigidly resistant to change, and therefore often inaccurate; however, they are apt to contain at least a small "kernel of truth."

Parental influence is very great in forming the child's early attitudes. This has been shown in extensive studies of prejudice and of political attitudes. However, more recent research has found that by high school age the parent-child similarity is only a low positive one, except on measures of party identification and religious denomination preference, where it remains high. Most children display high chauvinism, with very positive attitudes toward the government and idealization of national leaders, but some recent studies showing greater disaffection have cast doubt on the generality of these tendencies.

The schools are very important in instilling attitudes favorable to the political system. Other group determinants—peer groups, conformity pressures in general, and reference groups—become more important as the child grows older. Finally, the mass media not only provide much of our information, but also help to form our attitudes by highlighting particular events and interpreting the nature of "reality" to us. The influence of mass communication is particularly strong in creating attitudes and opinions on new issues where there were none before.

There are many different learning processes by which attitude formation may occur. Classical conditioning, stimulus generalization, instrumental conditioning, and selective learning are processes which all rely on the effects of reinforcement—reward or punishment. Imitation or modeling of attitudes, on the other hand, often occurs without any reinforcement nor any explicit instruction. Explicit persuasion attempts are one of the commonest methods of attitude change, but they are equally applicable to attitude formation. Information integration is a cognitive process of combining one's salient beliefs into an overall attitude toward an object.

Suggested Readings

Karlins, M., Coffman, T. L., & Walters, G. On the fading of social stereotypes: Studies in three generations of college students. *Journal of Personality and Social Psychology*, 1969, 13, 1–16.—An interesting example of the way ethnic stereotypes have been studied empirically and how they have changed over four decades.

Kiesler, C. A., Collins, B. E., & Miller, N. *Attitude Change: A Critical Analysis of Theoretical Approaches.* New York: Wiley, 1969—Chapter 3 contains a thorough and critical review of stimulus-response learning theories as they bear on attitude formation and attitude change.

Lane, R. E., & Sears, D. O. *Public Opinion.* Englewood Cliffs, N. J.: Prentice-Hall, 1964.—An interestingly written paperback volume covering many aspects of political attitudes. Chapters 3 and 4 concern parental influences and group influences on attitudes.

Newcomb, T. M. *Personality and Social Change.* New York: Dryden, 1943.—The classic study of girls enrolled at Bennington College, showing the strong effect of reference groups on their political and social attitudes.

chapter 7

Communication of
Attitudes and Opinions

Every new opinion, at its starting, is precisely in a minority of one.—Thomas Carlyle.

In the United States, the majority undertakes to supply a multitude of ready-made opinions for the use of individuals, who are thus relieved from the necessity of forming opinions of their own.—Alexis de Tocqueville.

All effective propaganda must be limited to a very few points and must harp on these in slogans until the last member of the public understands what you want him to understand.—Adolf Hitler.

In the United States, both communication and advertising campaigns through the mass media cost about $20 billion per year (McGuire, 1969). That's about $100 for every man, woman, and child in the country, spent to persuade them to change their attitudes and actions—more than the total per capita income of many developing countries!

What do the advertisers get for all their expenditures? Do mass media campaigns successfully sell products or attract voters? Do people rely on the media for information and advice, or do they turn to their families, friends, and neighbors? What are the communication processes by which mass information, propaganda, and advertising efforts are spread and transformed into individual beliefs, attitudes, and actions?

This chapter will consider these questions regarding the communication of attitudes. But first we will begin with a very brief sketch of the history of communication research.

EARLY STUDIES OF COMMUNICATION AND PROPAGANDA

Much of the early research on communication was motivated by deep concern over the effects on society of political propaganda. By the 1930s numerous demagogues had attained political power, in part through the clever use of propaganda techniques: Hitler and Goebbels in Germany, Mussolini in Italy, Huey Long in the United States. The widespread ownership of radios made possible a mass audience of millions for propagandists like Father Coughlin, and there was deep fear that democracy could not withstand this onslaught. The propaganda analysts of that era assumed that millions were listening to demagogic broadcasts, an easily-swayed, captive, and gullible audience. It was also assumed "that propaganda could be made almost irresistible with sufficiently clever use of propagandistic gimmicks in the content of the communication" (Sears & Whitney, 1973, p. 2). As analysis of Father Coughlin's radio speeches made by the Institute for Propaganda Analysis (Lee & Lee, 1939) ascribed his persuasiveness to tricks like name-calling, use of "glittering generalities," a "plain folks" approach, and "card-stacking" techniques of argument. Other fascinating analyses were made of the principles involved in Goebbels' propaganda campaigns (Doob, 1950) and of the successes and failures with the use of Allied propaganda leaflets in World War II (Herz, 1949).

Gradually it became apparent that these propaganda efforts were not nearly so successful as had first been thought. For instance, careful experimental studies of army orientation films showed that they failed to achieve many of the attitude and motivational changes which are intended (Hovland, Lumsdaine, & Sheffield, 1949). Similarly, the first major field study of American voting behavior showed amazingly small effects traceable to the large amount of media exposure during the political campaign (Lazarsfeld, Berelson, & Gaudet, 1948). Also, in commercial advertising it has become clear that, instead of a captive, easily persuaded, and gullible audience, the communicator is faced by an inattentive, difficult-to-persuade, "obstinate audience" (Bauer, 1964).

Two major changes in the orientation of research occurred as a result of these findings. First, attention largely shifted from mass communication to face-to-face interpersonal communication, which was felt to be considerably more influential in affecting people's attitudes and behavior. Second, attention shifted from the content of the communication to other factors in the communication process, such as the source and the audience. In order to understand these trends in research, we need to describe briefly the various factors in the persuasive communication process.

FACTORS IN PERSUASIVE COMMUNICATION

There are two sets of factors to be considered here: independent variables and dependent variables. Independent variables are the elements of the persuasion situation which can be varied or manipulated in some way. The dependent variables are the various aspects of the persuasion process which may occur in response to the communication, that is, the effects of communication.

Independent Variables.   The process of communication can be analyzed in terms of who says what to whom, how, and with what effect. The final item, "with what effect," summarizes all of the dependent variables, while the other four items constitute the major independent variables in communication. More frequently used terms for the major independent variables are **source, message, medium,** and **audience** variables.

Source variables are characteristics of the source of the message, such as its expertness, credibility, etc. Message variables include both the content and structure of the message, how it is organized, its use of emotional appeals, etc. Media variables include the printed word, radio, television, and face-to-face interpersonal transmission. Audience variables are characteristics of the people who are receiving the message, their personalities, interests, involvement in the communication process, etc. McGuire (1969) has analyzed the research findings on all of these variables at length in a monumental summary.

In this chapter we will confine our attention primarily to *media* factors, particularly stressing mass communication media versus personal face-to-face persuasion. Chapters 8 and 9, on attitude change, will present considerable detail on source, message, and audience variables.

Dependent Variables.   In the process of persuasion there are at least five distinguishable steps which must occur in sequence, each one involving a greater degree of persuasive effect. In his summary of persuasive communication ef-

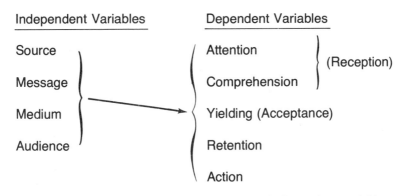

Figure 7-1 The major independent variables and dependent variables which are involved in the study of persuasive communication.

fects, McGuire (1969) has termed these steps **attention, comprehension, yielding, retention,** and **action**. Other authors have used other terms, for instance **reception** to include both attention and comprehension, and **acceptance** instead of yielding (Sears & Whitney, 1973).

Whatever terms are used, it is important to be clear about which stage is being studied in any given research. For instance, media exposure or readership studies are dealing with the first stage: attention to the persuasive communication. Many advertising studies have used the second stage, recall of ads, as their dependent variable because it can be much more easily and precisely measured than other variables at the later stages. Most experiments on persuasive communication or attitude change measure the third stage: yielding, or acceptance of the message. Experiments with delayed post-tests can study the fourth stage: retention of the information or the attitude change. Finally, voting research or studies using advertising sales data are dealing with the fifth stage: action.

Importance of Specifying Variables.   These distinctions are quite clear conceptually but are often forgotten when authors make generalizations about the effectiveness of persuasive communication. A message may be quite effective at one of the early stages but ineffective at some of the later stages. Success at each stage is necessary but not sufficient for effectiveness at each following stage. Hence it is essential to specify, for any given study, what the dependent variables were and which ones showed significant effects.

To illustrate these points, think of a persuasive message in a television commercial. Among the thousands of viewers of that TV program, many will not pay attention to the commercial. Of those who do, some will not understand it for one reason or another. Many of those who understand the message will not agree with it nor yield to its suggestions. Further, those who are persuaded may not remember the suggestions for more than a short time. And finally, even those who are persuaded and remember the message may not act on it. An important point to notice in this example is that different variables may help to determine which viewers will pass from one stage to the next in the persuasion process. For instance, distraction may prevent attention to the message, while low intelligence may decrease comprehension. On the other hand, high intelligence or a high level of knowledge about the topic may reduce yielding to the message. Interference from other messages and activities may decrease retention of the message, while lack of opportunity or lack of money may prevent acting on the suggestion. Thus the effects of persuasive communication are the complex result of many different variables working in interaction with each other.

With these distinctions and cautions in mind, let us examine some of the research on mass communication, and on personal communication, and see what effects they have on the various stages of persuasion.

PERSUASIVE EFFECTS OF THE MASS MEDIA

What is the effect of the mass media on public opinion? In the early days of opinion research this was viewed as a simple question with a simple answer, but now we know that it is a very complex question with many different answers, depending on the circumstances.

In the first place, mass communication rarely serves as a necessary and sufficient cause of persuasive effects. Instead it operates in conjunction with other variables in the audience and the situation to produce combined or interaction effects (Klapper, 1960). Second, the five different types of dependent variables in communication studies can produce five different answers to the question of media influence. Third, the different types of media can have markedly different effects.

Though this latter point has not been subjected to much careful scientific study, there is widespread agreement that the various media have differing advantages and disadvantages (Klapper, 1960). **Print** media (books, magazines, and newspapers) allow readers to determine the time and pace of their exposure and also permit easy reexposure if desired. Research suggests that print media produce better comprehension and retention of *complex* material than other media, but that this advantage does not hold for simple material. The **broadcasting** media (radio and television) now reach nearly everyone in the industrialized nations, including groups such as the aged, young children, and people with low education, who are not easily reached by other media and who may be more persuasible. The **visual** media (television and films) are considered to be uniquely effective because of the "you are there" immediacy conferred by their visual nature. As a result, they typically receive more complete attention than other media, particularly from children. However, research findings are mixed as to whether they also produce more yielding and retention.

We will now look at each of the communication dependent variables in turn and report a few of the studies which have found results relevant to each.

Studies of Attention

The mass media command a great deal of attention in the United States. In the average home the television set is turned on several hours every day, and about 80% of adults read a newspaper on a typical weekday (Robinson & Swinehart, 1968). National surveys have shown that television is now the medium most depended on for political and election information, but newspapers and magazines are used more as sources of information about science and health topics (Wade & Schramm, 1969). In many foreign countries, movies (particularly American movies) provide much of the information about life and conditions in other nations (Weiss, 1969).

In the United States most news events are first learned about through the mass media. A summary study of several major events showed that about 35% of people first heard of them on TV compared with about 25% each for radio and the print media (Ostlund, 1973). However, sensational events such as the shooting of President Kennedy or Governor Wallace or the start of a ghetto riot showed a different pattern—about half of the population first learned of them through word-of-mouth contact with another person, and then most people turned to the media for further information (e.g., Sheatsley & Feldman, 1965). In such calamities news travels very fast—virtually 100% of the U.S. adult population knew of the two assassination attempts within six hours of their occurrence.

In contrast to the breadth of public attention to the mass media, the quality of attention generally leaves much to be desired. Though most people "read" a newspaper, the average reader looks at no more than one-quarter of the stories, and less than half of the readers even examine the front-page stories (Lazarsfeld, 1940; Cutlip, 1954). The most popular sections of the paper are the comics, news pictures, and human interest articles. Similarly with television, entertainment generally takes precedence over information. Only 25% of American adults watch a national network news program on any given evening, and over half of the population doesn't see even one such program in a two-week period (Robinson, 1971).

These figures demonstrate that about 20% of the population are regular, almost-daily viewers of network TV news, while the rest are very sporadic or complete nonviewers. Considerable overlap occurs between interested audiences for the various media. Political information, for instance, tends to be received by the same minority of the population from several different media sources, both in the United States (Berelson, Lazarsfeld, & McPhee, 1954) and in Great Britain

---

Box 7-1 PAUL LAZARSFELD, *Pioneer Communication Researcher*

Probably the most famous figure in the field of communication research, Paul Lazarsfeld was founder and director of the Bureau of Applied Social Research at Columbia University, and Professor of Sociology there since 1940. Born in Austria in 1901, he took his Ph.D. at the University of Vienna, and taught and published sociological research there before coming to the U.S. in the 1930s. Before moving to Columbia, he taught briefly at the University of Newark and Princeton University.

Lazarsfeld was known for many research volumes on the mass media such as Radio and the Printed Page, Radio Research, *and* Communications Research. *He pioneered many new approaches to interviewing, attitude measurement, and survey research, including the panel technique of repeated surveys. His research on personal influence and opinion leadership is cited later in this chapter. Chapter 12 describes his famous work as the originator of large-scale voting studies, reported in* The People's Choice *and* Voting. *Among his many honors were the first distinguished achievement award of the American Association for Public Opinion Research (AAPOR), presidency of AAPOR and the American Sociological Association, and election to the National Academy of Sciences. Following retirement, he continued a vigorous research career until his death in 1976.*

(Trenaman & McQuail, 1961). There is a circular relationship involving attention to the media; attention leads to more knowledge and interest in the topic, but also high levels of knowledge and interest stimulate further attention to the media (Atkin, Galloway, & Nayman, 1973).

In the area of advertising, it has been found that frequency of presentation of ads *per se* does not lead to higher levels of attention, but the quality of the ads does. Ads are better attended to if they are entertaining, usefully informative, humorous, professional in appearance, or feature novel or "catchy" elements (Atkin, Bowen, Nayman, & Sheinkopf, 1973). In a landmark study called *Advertising in America: The Consumer View*, Bauer and Greyser (1968) found that the average consumer only notices about 75 ads each day out of the countless number that impinge on his eyes, ears, and nose. Out of the number that are noticed, only one-sixth are important enough to be classified as enjoyable, informative, annoying, or offensive. These authors also found that advertising which offends or annoys some people entertains or informs others, so that the effects of ads are rarely if ever consistent across all members of the mass audience.

These findings of audience indifference to most persuasive messages and varied reactions to any given message help to explain the fact that mass information and persuasion campaigns so often fail, as pointed out by Hyman and Sheatsley (1947). However, Mendelsohn (1973) has demonstrated that, despite general public disinterest, information campaigns can be relatively successful if they carefully consider specific target audiences and their life-styles, value systems, and media habits. Though only a small proportion of the total population may be reached by such campaigns, that audience may still comprise a great many people in a major metropolitan area such as Los Angeles or New York.

Studies of Comprehension

Comprehension of mass communication has been less studied than attention. Some studies (e.g., Mendelsohn, 1973) have shown successful communication of knowledge, for instance through television special programs such as "The National Drivers Test." However, numerous studies have also documented extensive miscomprehension of communication (e.g., Swanson, Jenkins, & Jones, 1950).

It has often been shown that public comprehension is increased when the conclusion or moral of a communication is explicitly stated rather than left implicit or subtly suggested (Weiss, 1969). Lang and Lang (1968) similarly found that interpretive comments in TV news coverage of a political convention influenced audience perceptions of the events.

A common finding concerning mass communication of political information has been that amount of exposure to relevant messages is either unrelated to knowledge gained or has only a low positive relationship to it (Trenaman & McQuail, 1961; Atkin, Bowen, et al., 1973). However, *attention* to messages is rather closely related to knowledge gain (Atkin, Galloway, & Nayman, 1973). Patterson and McClure (1973) found that televised political ads had marked effects on voters' beliefs (that is, they were well comprehended), but they had practically no effects on voters' attitudes (they did not produce yielding).

Other variables can interact with media variables to produce comprehension of messages. Tichenor, Donohue, and Olien (1970) showed that highly educated individuals grasped new information presented by the media more quickly than did less educated individuals. Furthermore, people who use the print media in preference to television attain greater and deeper knowledge, at least on public affairs, science, and health topics (Wade & Schramm, 1969).

Studies of Yielding

Yielding, or acceptance of the persuasive message, is the dependent variable studied most extensively in the voluminous research on attitude change and conformity. Though yielding cannot occur without reception of the message (that is, attention and comprehension, the two variables previously discussed), the amount of yielding is not necessarily positively related to the amount of reception. Indeed, the most common finding is a lack of any clear relationship between reception and attitude change (Fishbein & Ajzen, 1972).

McGuire (1968a) has developed a theory which may help to account for this lack of relationship by using the target person's personality characteristics, for example self-esteem, as an intervening variable. In general, the theory states that "any personality characteristic which has a positive relationship to reception, tends to be negatively related to yielding, and vice versa" (p. 182). Thus, yielding should be negatively related to self-esteem while reception should be positively related to self-esteem, at least in the medium range of message difficulty. McGuire (1968a) has reported some experimental research results which generally tend to support this theory.

Types of Yielding. An important distinction has been made by Kelman (1958), who described three types of attitude change which have different underlying bases: compliance, identification, and internalization. **Compliance** is public yielding to an influence attempt without private acceptance; its basis is the expectation of gaining rewards or avoiding punishment. **Identification** is yielding to influence in an attempt to emulate an individual or group; its basis is satisfaction in being like the admired other(s). **Internalization** is yielding to influence in situations where the new attitude is intrinsically rewarding, useful, or consistent with one's value system; its basis is the intrinsic value of the new attitude to oneself. Different characteristics of the source of the influence attempt will help to determine which of these types of yielding will occur. A powerful source (and one who has continuing surveillance over one's activities) will be likely to produce compliance. An attractive source will be more likely to produce identification, and a credible source to produce internalization. Experimental results supporting this theory have been reported by Kelman (1958) and by Mills and Harvey (1972).

Importance of the Social Setting. Research on attitude change has most often been done in an experimental laboratory situation, using audiences of selected individuals, compulsory exposure situations, and single communications. These conditions are desirable for their control of experimental variables, but they are far different from the typical situation in which an individual is exposed to mass communication in everyday life. There the audience is mostly self-selected, the message can easily be turned off or avoided, and communications are frequently repeated. In this chapter we are focusing mostly on factors affecting the typical mass communication situation, whereas the following two chapters will deal more with experimental attitude change research findings. Even in the real-world mass communication situation, there can be considerable control of the communication conditions if the media content is highly standardized, as is frequently the case in totalitarian nations. In that case the influence of the mass media on individual attitudes can be very great, though even in oppressive dictatorships there are usually underground and foreign sources of competing information and attitudes. However, in nations with relatively free mass communication systems, there will be many conflicting viewpoints expressed in the media on almost any topic. Consequently the influence of the media on yielding is apt to be much smaller there than in totalitarian societies.

Box 7-2 *Five General Principles Concerning the Influence of Mass Media*

1. *The influence of mass communication is mediated by factors such as personal predispositions, personal selective processes, group memberships, etc.*
2. *Because of these factors, mass communication usually serves to reinforce existing attitudes and opinions, though occasionally it may serve as an agent of change.*
3. *When mass communication does produce attitude change, minor change in the extremity or intensity of the attitude is much more common than is "conversion" from one side of an issue to the other side.*
4. *Mass communication can be quite effective in changing attitudes in areas where people's existing opinions are weak, as in much of commercial advertising.*
5. *Mass communication can be quite effective in creating opinions on new issues where there are no existing predispositions to reinforce.*

Source: Adapted from Klapper (1960, p. 15; 1963, pp. 70, 76).

In an extensive summary of the effects of mass communication, Klapper (1960) has stated a number of general principles about the media's effects on attitudes (see Box 7-2 above).

The fifth principle, concerning creation of opinions on new issues, has been dealt with in the preceding chapter. The other four principles may be illustrated by citing the results of a few representative research studies.

1. Other Factors Mediate Mass Communication Effects. In a classic study, Peterson and Thurstone (1933) found that the famous pro-Klan film *Birth of a Nation* had its strongest effects on children who had had little or no contact with Negroes. More recently, similar findings occurred in the 1960 election debates between Kennedy and Nixon: the first debate led to a definitely improved public image for Kennedy, but the effect was mostly limited to the previously undecided voters (Lang & Lang, 1962).

2. Mass Communication Usually Reinforces Existing Attitudes. An example can be seen in British research on television. When competing programs of different cultural levels were available, viewers clung to the ones representative of their own level of interests or tastes, rather than seeking out new cultural experiences (Himmelweit et al., 1958).

3. Mass Communication Can Produce Minor Changes in Attitudes. However, it rarely produces "conversion" to an opposite viewpoint. Examples of minor change can be found in many studies of political attitudes, starting with the pioneering study of Lazarsfeld et al. (1948). More recently, a large-scale panel study of television's influence in British elections showed again that attitude changes of most voters were either small or absent altogether. Only about 10% of voters changed their intended vote from one party to another during the campaign (Blumler & McQuail, 1969). Even such a major political upheaval as the Watergate scandal, with its massive media coverage, caused relatively small changes in political attitudes among the American public (Robinson, 1974).

4. *Mass Communication Is Most Effective Where Attitudes Are Weak.* This principle applies particularly to advertising, where most people's product preferences are weakly held, but also to politics and many other opinion areas. In politics, Blumler and McQuail (1969) confirmed many past findings that the least involved voters are most apt to change opinions and also showed that they are more likely to be influenced by TV campaigning. In advertising, research as well as common parental experience indicates that children can be more strongly influenced by TV commercials than adults usually are (Goldberg & Gorn, 1974).

Studies of Retention

Retention has been and still is the least-studied dependent variable in attitude change research (Klapper, 1960). Much of the research which does exist was done in classroom experimental settings. There is a particular need for research on the continuing, cumulative impact of the media over a prolonged period of time.

Two types of retention are of interest: retention of message content, and retention of attitude change. In general, these two variables usually show a low-to-moderate positive correlation ($r = +.2$ to $+.5$), though sometimes they have been found to be uncorrelated (McGuire, 1969, p. 257). As with any learned information, retention of message content tends to drop off rather sharply in the first hours and days after exposure, and then gradually to level off. After a period of four to six weeks, retention of newly-learned material may range from a low of about 10% (Watts & McGuire, 1964) to a high of about 75% (Fitzsimmons & Osburn, 1968)—the wide range being due partly to differences in messages (printed selections vs. TV) and partly to differences in methodological procedures for measuring recall or recognition. Some studies have shown substantial amounts of information retention for periods as long as six months.

Retention of attitude change tends to follow a rather similar declining pattern. After four to six weeks, the amount of attitude change retained may be from one-third to two-thirds of the original change (Watts & McGuire, 1964). In their study of five different TV documentaries shown to college students, Fitzsimmons and Osburn (1968) found that only one retained a significant attitudinal effect after four weeks. Many experiments have found attitude changes lasting as long as six months (McGuire, 1969, p. 253), and a very impressive classroom study by Rokeach (1971) showed significant attitude changes lasting well over one year. Keep in mind that all of these findings stem from studies where the persuasive message was delivered only once.

Research has shown that delayed reexposure to a persuasive message will strengthen and prolong the prior opinion change (Cook & Insko, 1968). A dramatic example of this principle may be seen in the 25-year follow-up of

Newcomb's Bennington College students whose attitudes had been changed in a liberal direction by their college experiences (Newcomb et al., 1967). The authors found that many of these women had chosen a supportive postcollege environment of husbands and associates, and as a result they retained much of the attitude change which had been created 25 years before.

Studies of Action

The final dependent variable to be considered in studies of mass communication is behavioral—taking overt action as a result of the persuasive message. The relationship between attitudes and behavior may range from zero to very strongly positive, and we will consider the nature of this relationship between attitudes and behavior at length in Chapter 10. In this section we will describe some of the typical behavioral effects of the mass media.

We know that occasionally the mass media can have very dramatic effects on people's behavior. Perhaps the most famous example is Orson Welles' 1938 radio broadcast dramatizing an invasion of Earth by Martians, a broadcast so realistic and compelling that over a million people were driven to panic and many fled their homes (Cantril, 1940). However, what are the more typical behavioral effects of the media?

Allocation of Time. Weiss (1969) has summarized studies of the amount of time that people spend with the mass media, particularly television. American children, from the age of three onward, spend about one-sixth of their waking hours watching television. However, despite claims to the contrary, Himmelweit, Oppenheim, and Vince's (1958) study in England found that TV had little effect in diminishing children's outdoor play, hobbies, or social activities. Both children and adults often find time for media attention by coordinating viewing or listening with other household activities such as cooking, cleaning, and meals.

Alleged Passivity. A number of authors have claimed that availability of TV, and earlier of radio, has increased the passivity of their audiences, perhaps even creating "half a nation of robots." Klapper (1960) has reviewed research evidence on this question and concluded that there is no evidence of any such effect. Himmelweit et al.'s (1958) elaborate study found no evidence that children's TV viewing produced any of the five different sorts of passivity which concerned school teachers. In fact, viewing in the early years may give children a faster start in school due to a larger vocabulary and a broader set of experiences (Schramm, Lyle, & Parker, 1961).

Social Behavior. Many recent studies have linked watching media violence with the possibility of increases in aggressive behavior (National Commission on the Causes and Prevention of Violence, 1969; Scientific Advisory Committee on Television and Social Behavior, 1972). In view of these data, it is encouraging to

Figure 7-2 Television viewing is often combined with other household activities.

know that television can also stimulate prosocial behavior and behavioral intentions (Fitzsimmons & Osburn, 1968). Viewing programs such as Sesame Street and Mister Rogers' Neighborhood has been shown to encourage children's sharing, cooperation, and self-control (Friedrich & Stein, 1975).

Political Behavior. The major effects of the mass media which are evident during election campaigns are *reinforcement* of voters' current attitudes, and *activation* of any latent motivational predispositions (such as party loyalty or strong issue commitments) which would lead people to vote in the desired direction. There is also some suggestive evidence that media exposure can help to increase voter turnout (Weiss, 1969).

Though most authors have not given the media much credit for ability to change voting intentions from one party to another, Kraus (1972) has argued that television plays a much greater role than usually recognized in the political socialization of children and their subsequent voting patterns. Similarly, contrary to the customary viewpoint, Robinson has presented evidence that endorsements by the nation's newspapers (80% for Nixon in 1968, 90% in 1972) may have decisively influenced the election outcome in 1968 and noticeably affected the vote in 1972 (Robinson, 1972; Institute for Social Research, 1974).

In Chapter 12 we shall return to a more extensive discussion of factors affecting political behavior and voting.

Advertising.　　In developing countries, where mass media availability is new and information about products and fashions is not widespread, advertising in the media may be very effective (Schramm, 1964). However, in the United States and other media-saturated countries, much advertising is directed at maintaining the share of the market already held by a particular toothpaste, automobile, or detergent (that is, it is aimed at reinforcing existing preferences). Paradoxically, though an advertising campaign may cost millions of dollars, it does not have to influence large percentages of people in order to be successful. Bauer (1964) has pointed out that a highly successful sales campaign may increase a brand's share of the market by only one per cent, and it may even alienate more people (not current buyers) than it wins over as new buyers. Thus small percentage effects may have a great dollar value, and yet the advertiser may not care at all what you or I think of his "pitch" or his product, as long as somebody likes them.

PERSUASIVE EFFECTS OF PERSONAL COMMUNICATION

There is general agreement that personal communication usually has a stronger influence on people's attitudes and behavior than does mass communication. Initial evidence for this conclusion came from studies of face-to-face speeches vs. radio vs. printed messages (Cantril & Allport, 1935), and similar conclusions were reached in the early election surveys which had expected to find strong mass media effects (Lazarsfeld et al., 1948; Berelson et al., 1954). Stemming from their findings of greater exposure to personal political conversation than to the mass media, the authors proposed the hypothesis that communication follows a **two-step flow**: from media to "opinion leaders" to other citizens. We will discuss this two-step flow concept in more detail later in this section.

Critics have pointed out that the early data only suggested but did not prove that personal communication had a stronger influence on voting than did the media (Pool, 1959). However, Katz and Lazarsfeld (1955) showed that personal contacts were more effective than the media in influencing women's decisions about marketing, fashion, and movie-going. Similarly, there is very convincing evidence that personal contact increases voter turnout, though it does not seem generally successful in changing people's voting choice (Kramer, 1970; Kraut & McConahay, 1973).

Many reasons can be given to explain the apparent superiority of personal communication. Because it is a face-to-face situation, attention is likely to be higher than with the media, and the message can be given at an appropriate moment and planned to be relevant to the recipient's motives and attitudes. Because such communication is two-way, feedback from the recipient can be used to increase comprehension, counter any objections, and select particularly effective arguments. The communicator will probably have many traits and interests in common with the recipient, and he can repeat his message, if necessary. The personal relationship may cause the recipient to relax any defenses against being influenced, and it may encourage yielding (compliance) in the interests of maintaining smooth social relations. Finally, if the recipient is also participating actively in the conversation, (s)he may occasionally make a public commitment by expressing an agreeing opinion aloud (McGuire, 1969).

Studies of Personal Communication

Though all of these advantages do seem to be available, personal communication rather seldom makes use of them. Any political or buying influence which does take place is apt to be just part of an ordinary everyday conversation rather than a planned influence attempt. Though research studies usually focus on *changes* in opinion or behavior, personal conversations are much more apt to *reinforce* currently held views (Klapper, 1960). Berelson et al. (1954) found about 30% of political conversations did not involve voting preferences (they concerned predictions of who would win, exchange of information, etc.), and over 60% involved reinforcing comments about mutual views on the candidates or the issues. That left only 6% of political conversations which involved any argument or attempt to change opinions!

There have been three major methods used to determine which citizens are **opinion leaders** in personal communication with others. The original method used was *self-designation* as an advice-giver in response to questions like "Have you recently tried to convince anyone of your political ideas?" Many later studies used one or the other of two nomination approaches. In the *sociometric* method, all members of a group (for instance, all local doctors) are asked to list the group members who are most influential in giving information and advice (for instance, about the merits of new drugs). In the *key informant* approach, a limited number of knowledgeable individuals are asked to list the group members who are most influential concerning a given topic, such as choice of fashions. In some studies these "influentials" have also been interviewed to determine who or what had influenced them.

Using any one of these methods, about 20% to 25% of a group are typically found to be opinion leaders on any given topic. Though there are some differences in the individuals identified as leaders by the several methods, there does appear to be substantial consistency in the methods' results (Jacoby, 1974). Another methodological question which is largely unanswered is due to the correlational methodology used in most studies: Is it possible that some, or even many, personal influence attempts are the *result* of a change in product choice or voting intentions rather than a causal factor in that change? That is, do people yield to influence attempts, or do they make influence attempts after they have changed their preferences? Probably both sequences occur, but their relative frequency is still unknown.

What are the characteristics of opinion leaders which have been found in research? First of all, they are very like those people whom they influence —usually from the same social class, though perhaps with a bit more status, and a bit more contact with the media (Katz, 1957). The finding that opinion leaders are more likely than others to split their vote suggests that they may be unusually independent and self-reliant in making up their own mind on political questions (Kingdon, 1970). The breadth of their leadership across different areas of decision making is somewhat at issue. Early studies found no generalization of opinion leadership across different areas such as public affairs and fashion (Katz & Lazarsfeld, 1955), but recent studies have shown considerable overlap of leadership, particularly across somewhat similar product categories such as clothing and cosmetics (Jacoby, 1974).

There are a number of sequential steps in the process by which a person adopts an innovation such as a new farming method or cosmetic product. First, awareness of the innovation must occur, and next, interest must be developed and information obtained. Third, this information must be evaluated for its usefulness, and fourth, the person may try out the innovation in his own situation. If this proves successful, full-scale and continuing adoption may follow. In general it has been found that mass media sources are most important in the early stages of the adoption process (awareness and perhaps also information gathering), while personal sources are more important in the later stages, particularly in evaluation and final decision (Rogers, 1962).

This finding returns us to our earlier question about the direction of flow of communication in the influence process.

The Flow of Communication

Two-Step? Katz (1957) has summarized the evidence from several early studies of the communication process. He concluded that the original ''two-step flow'' hypothesis was largely corroborated. However, additional evidence cited by Katz and other authors makes the picture much more complicated.

Multi-Step? A multi-step theory posits that information flows from the media to opinion leaders and then down through several levels of individuals having decreasing amounts of interest and knowledge concerning the topic. For instance, Katz and Lazarsfeld (1955) proposed that opinion leaders were most interested in the topic, but the people they talked with were moderately interested rather than completely uninterested. More recent studies have shown quite definitively that opinion-givers are also opinion-receivers. For instance, Troldahl and Van Dam (1965) found that 30% of their respondents had asked someone for their opinion on a major news topic in the previous two weeks, and two-thirds of those individuals had also been asked for such an opinion. From these data it appears clear that opinion leaders are also listeners, but that generally no one talks to or listens to the majority of citizens (63% in this study had not discussed any major news topic).

Another complication for the two-step theory is the fact that many "opinion leaders" do not actively try to persuade others of their point of view (Weiss, 1969, p. 154; Kingdon, 1970). The passive leaders, who only give advice when asked, differ significantly from the more active leaders on many dimensions. Again, this suggests that the two-step theory is overly simple.

Circular Flow. Probably the most accurate view of persuasive communication is that its flow is circular, involving much alternation between media sources and personal sources. For instance, we have described above the important finding that different sources are important at different stages of the innovation adoption process. In addition, even though one source may be predominant at a given stage, other sources are usually involved (Rogers, 1962). Examples of how both personal and impersonal sources can alternate in importance may be seen in the studies of two political events. In calamities such as the assassination of President Kennedy, diffusion of the news is largely achieved by word-of-mouth (over two-thirds of the population learned of it within half an hour), but then people turn to the media for confirmation and further details (Greenberg, 1964). Following the opposite sequence, news of Senator McGovern's decision to drop Senator Eagleton from the 1972 Democratic ticket was overwhelmingly learned from media sources (85%), but personal communication occurred very extensively in reaction to this event, with nearly half of the population trying to convince others of their opinion on some aspect of the situation (Ostlund, 1973).

Klapper (1960) has summed up the circular flow of communication very well:

> Personal influence may be more effective than persuasive mass communication, but at present mass communication seems the most effective means of stimulating personal influence (p. 72).

Combining Media and Personal Influence. As a result of research findings about the mutual importance of both methods of communication, a number of attempts have been made to combine them in order to achieve greater persuasive effect. An approach which proved effective for developing community action programs in rural areas was to bring groups of citizens together for a media presentation, immediately followed by a group discussion and consideration of possible action (UNESCO, 1960). With children, following up a TV episode from Mister Rogers' Neighborhood with a discussion by the teacher which focused on the same message about helpfulness proved successful in increasing cooperative behavior (Friedrich & Stein, 1975). These studies illustrate the potential practical importance of some of the research on persuasive communication.

Figure 7-3 Combining media presentation and personal communication on the same topic can have a stronger effect than either alone.

SOME POSSIBLE EXPLANATIONS OF COMMUNICATION EFFECTIVENESS

We will look at four different ideas that have been proposed in attempts to explain the relative effectiveness of the media and of personal communication in influencing attitude. The first of these is **selective exposure**, the notion that people actively avoid information that is inconsistent with or threatening to their beliefs and attitudes, and that they seek supportive information.

Is There Selective Exposure to Communications?

The hypothesis of selective exposure has had an honored history. Hyman and Sheatsley (1947) were among the first public opinion researchers to stress the concept in their explanation of "Some reasons why information campaigns fail." It was invoked as a major explanatory concept in the first major voting study (Lazarsfeld et al., 1948) and in Klapper's (1960) widely cited review of the effects of mass communication, and it assumed an important place in Festinger's (1957) influential theory of cognitive dissonance, as we will see in Chapter 9.

With this unanimity of opinion from many famous attitude researchers, is there any point in asking further questions? Well, yes; there is. This is a good example of the maxim that a universally accepted belief is very unlikely to be completely true and is therefore most in need of critical scrutiny. Following this advice, Sears and Freedman (1967) have made a careful summary of the research evidence concerning selective exposure and have reached some surprising conclusions.

First of all, Sears and Freedman distinguish two different aspects of the concept: **de facto** selectivity, and **motivated** selective exposure. *De facto* selectivity means a greater than chance agreement of opinion between an audience and a communication directed to that audience. For instance, it is mostly Republicans who take the trouble to go to Republican campaign rallies. Similarly, readers of *National Review* are likely to be people who already agree with the editor's conservative viewpoint while most readers of *Ramparts* are apt to be liberal in their political and social attitudes. However, for actions as easy to perform as reading a newspaper editorial favoring one candidate or listening to the President speak on TV, there is probably much less of a tendency for the audience to be biased in favor of the communicator's position.

These examples are consistent with the conclusions reached by Sears and Freedman. In many situations and for many people, *de facto* selectivity of communication audiences is an established fact, though this tendency is not nearly as general a phenomenon as had earlier been thought. Also, some cases of apparent *de facto* selectivity may really be due to other audience characteristics rather than the attitudes they share with the communicator. For instance, Irish-Americans are most likely to go to a speech by an Irish-American politician ("one of our own"), and since in many areas of the United States the Irish also tend strongly toward the Democratic Party, there may be an appearance of selective attitudinal similarity. In any case, though, there is much evidence that *de facto* selectivity in exposure to communications does often occur.

By contrast, there is almost no firm evidence of the *motivated* seeking of supportive information or avoidance of opposing information. This is the kind of selectivity which most previous writers have postulated, perhaps partly because it fits so well into a Freudian defense-mechanism perspective. Despite that fit, selective exposure was not at all verified by Sears and Freedman's review of the evidence. For example, in a study on smoking and lung cancer, Feather (1962) found that neither smokers nor nonsmokers showed a significant preference for reading either of two articles, one of which argued that smoking causes lung cancer and the other of which claimed that it does not. Further, when smokers were divided according to whether they believed that the evidence linking cancer and smoking was convincing or not convincing, both groups preferred the article which *opposed* their own viewpoint—a surprising preference for nonsupportive information by these ego-involved subjects.

Other recent studies of public opinion which cast grave doubt on the hypothesis of motivated selective exposure include Trenaman and McQuail's (1961) British election study, and research on TV political ads in the United States (Atkin et al., 1973). In explaining these findings, several other determinants of exposure to information have been stressed: (1) As mentioned earlier, supportive information is much more extensively available than nonsupportive information in most people's normal environments. (2) *Refutability* of information may be a factor, weak opposing information being desired but strong opposing arguments being avoided. (3) Even more important, the *usefulness* of information will make it desired, whether it is supportive or not (as in obtaining knowledge about a potentially dangerous defect in one's new car). (4) Past exposure history is important because people who are aware of having received one-sided information generally will seek exposure to the other side (as in many simulated jury studies). (5) Educational level is a very powerful predictor of increased exposure to all kinds of information, both supportive and nonsupportive.

Though the question of audience selectivity is a very complicated one, we can be encouraged that research does not show any evidence for a head-in-the-sand avoidance of information which challenges one's presuppositions or attitudes. At the same time, we must realize that most people most of the time are surrounded by a higher proportion of supportive information than of opposing information.

The Media Define "Reality"

Though the mass media have not been found to be very effective in changing public attitudes, they have other effects which are important to consider. The first of these has been termed the creation of "second-hand reality"—that is, the definition of what is really happening in the world beyond one's own first-hand experience. Each one of us has a very limited range of experiences which we have actually participated in first-hand. Beyond that range, all of our knowledge, beliefs, and attitudes come from others, and the great majority probably come from some mass communication medium (ranging from books to billboards to radio and television).

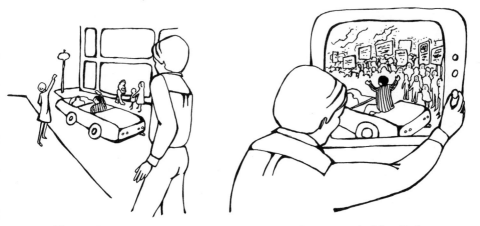

Figure 7-4 First-hand experience and the media portrayal of "reality" can be dramatically different.

If you have ever participated in an event which was written up in the press or described in broadcasts, you have probably discovered how different the media's "second-hand reality" is from what you have experienced first-hand. Inevitably the media select certain details to mention and omit many others. In this process they highlight and emphasize some aspects of the event and obscure others. Often this results in distortion and misleading reports even when there is no intention to mislead the public at all. When the personal beliefs, values, and motives of the newsmen or of the editorial staff enter into the reporting process, as they often do, the resulting picture can be far from an objective, complete, and unbiased account.

The ways in which media selectivity occurs in the reporting process have been described in a number of studies. Bauer and Bauer (1960) have pointed out that an increase in the number of crime stories can give the public the impression that a major crime wave is underway. Cutlip (1954) has demonstrated that only about 10% of the news copy stemming from national news agencies ends up in small-town daily newspapers, so obviously the editors' biases and interests play a very strong part in determining what is available to the public to read. Even large-city dailies have limited numbers of reporters, especially in distant areas, so for many stories they have to rely on the news items selected by the national agencies' staffs. The three major weekly news magazines, *Time, Newsweek,* and *U.S. News & World Report,* have been strongly criticized for the amount of bias and slanted editorial opinion which creeps into their news reporting (Bagdikian, 1962).

Television news broadcasts are particularly prone to creation of their own "reality" because of limitations on what is possible and easy to put on the air and what will attract audience attention (Epstein, 1973). The TV network camera crews are located in six or eight major U.S. cities and three or four foreign capitals. Except in rare instances, the network "news" is confined to events which happen in those cities and which happen early enough so that filming can be arranged and the film flown to New York in time for the evening broadcasts. The only common inputs from other locations are human interest stories or continuing events such as strikes and warfare. Political news is limited, due to the F.C.C.'s fairness doctrine, to stories which can be presented as having two sides, and the networks thus emphasize controversy more than consensus. The result, as Lang and Lang (1968) have pointed out in numerous research examples, is that the picture on the TV tube is often much different than the reality on the streets of the city or the battlefield overseas. Particularly clear examples of this TV creation of reality occurred in the heavy stress on rioting during the 1968 Democratic national convention in Chicago, and in Vietnamese war reporting (Pool, 1969).

However, this creation of second-hand reality by TV should not be confused with polemical slanting of the news. Despite the claims of antiadministration bias in TV reporting of the Vietnam War, Russo's (1971) careful content analysis study concluded that, on the average, network newscasts of the war did not present any noticeable bias against administration policies. Efron's (1971) book, *The News Twisters*, showed that the network TV news programs were more friendly to Humphrey than to Nixon in the 1968 election (opposite to the strong newspaper support for Nixon demonstrated by Robinson, 1972). However, Efron's claim that this was due to a "liberal ideological monopoly" of TV news (p. 206) is based primarily on her partisan definition of what viewpoints are "liberal," and is disputed by some of her own data on the differences between the three TV networks.

The Media Determine the Public Agenda

Probably the most important effect of the mass media is their agenda-setting function (McCombs & Shaw, 1972). There is clear evidence that people attend to, are interested in, and talk about the information and ideas that they receive through the media. Since the media do not reflect reality completely and faithfully, it follows that their selectivity has a marked effect on what most people learn about and respond to.

The selectivity shown by the media in determining the public agenda has been demonstrated in several studies. Funkhouser (1973) has shown that coverage of major public issues in the three major U.S. news magazines from 1960 to 1970 did not show a close correspondence to the occurrence of important actual events. For instance, coverage of the Vietnam War reached its peak and began to decline before the war itself reached a peak. However, media coverage showed a close relationship to, and probably largely determined, people's responses to poll questions about the most important national problem. In political news, Graber (1971) has shown that the media emphasized the personal qualities of Presidential candidates and largely avoided coverage of their political philosophies or executive abilities. The Social Science Research Council has become so concerned about these trends that it set up several research groups to study closely the role of the mass media during the 1976 Presidential election, concentrating on how the media agenda is established and how it affects the public (*Behavior Today*, 1975a).

It appears clear that all of the mass media fulfill the agenda-setting function described by Cohen (1963), who concluded that the press "may not be successful much of the time in telling people what to think, but it is stunningly successful in telling its readers what to think *about*" (p. 13).

The Media Confer Prestige

A final major effect of the media is that, by their very mention of people, events, and issues, they confer importance upon them in the public eye (Lazarsfeld & Merton, 1948; Weiss, 1969, p. 91). Some media celebrities, such as Kate

Smith, Arthur Godfrey, and Johnny Carson, have become so famous that they have been widely credited with personal persuasive power in selling products or ideas. But even formerly obscure nonentities whose actions or thoughts are picked out for coverage by TV or in print are suddenly invested with a seeming importance out of all proportion to their status in life. As a result, the media audience will pay attention to them and their ideas. Dramatic examples of this process have occurred in recent years with attempted Presidential assassins who were featured on the covers of news magazines. As Lazarsfeld and Merton (1948, p. 102) put it:

> The audiences of mass media apparently subscribe to the circular belief: "If you really matter, you will be at the focus of mass attention and, if you *are* at the focus of mass attention, then surely you must really matter."

SUMMARY

Early studies of communication and propaganda were motivated by the fear that demagogues could easily sway the gullible audience. Since then, research has shown that persuasive communication is much less successful and much more complicated in its effects than had first been thought.

The main *independent* variables in persuasive communication are factors related to the source, the message, the medium (the topic of this chapter), and the audience. The main *dependent* variables involve the sequential steps of audience attention, comprehension, yielding, retention, and action. Each of these stages may yield different findings about communication effects because different independent variables may be important at each stage.

Studies of *attention* have shown that the media provide people's first information about most events, though news of great calamities is quickly spread by word-of-mouth. The quality of attention to the media is often weak and sporadic. Though *comprehension* has been little studied, there is ample evidence of audience misunderstanding of communications. Exposure to messages may be quite unrelated to comprehension, but attention is usually much more closely related. However, there is often no relationship between these variables and the next stage of the persuasion process, yielding.

Yielding can include public compliance, private identification with the views of admired others, or internalization of intrinsically rewarding attitudes. Though the mass media sometimes produce "conversions" from one viewpoint to an opposing one, reinforcement of current opinions, minor opinion changes, and the creation of opinions on new issues are much more common effects. Personal and situational factors are important mediators of all of these kinds of communication effects.

Retention is the least-studied dependent variable. Both retention of message content and retention of attitude change drop off rather rapidly after the exposure period, but both may still be significant weeks or even months after exposure to a single message. *Action* resulting from persuasive communication may be closely related to the amount of attitude change, or the relationship may be low or even nonexistent. In politics and in advertising, the mass media usually produce reinforcement of current behavioral tendencies, but occasionally they can have decisive effects in changing behavior.

Personal communication is generally agreed to have stronger effects than mass communication. However, most personal communication is reinforcing or informative rather than persuasive in nature. Influential *opinion leaders* on any given topic tend to be similar to the followers, though perhaps a bit higher in status; and different topics usually have different opinion leaders unless the topics are closely related.

The *two-step flow* of communication (from mass media to opinion leaders to other citizens) was proposed by early studies to help account for the low direct effectiveness of the media. However, research shows that opinion-givers are also usually opinion-receivers, and that most citizens rarely discuss major news topics with anyone. Thus it appears that communication flow tends to be circular, alternating between media sources and personal sources.

Selective exposure to communications has frequently been proposed as a mechanism by which people avoid persuasion. However, research shows little evidence of *motivated* selectivity in seeking or avoiding information, though there is usually considerable *de facto* selectivity in a person's normal environment.

Though the mass media are generally not very effective in changing public attitudes, they define "reality" for us in areas beyond the limited range of our first-hand personal experience. Also, by their selection of events to cover, the mass media determine the public agenda, and they confer prestige and apparent importance on the people, events, and issues which they decide to cover.

Suggested Readings

Epstein, E. J. *News from Nowhere: Television and the News.* New York: Random House, 1973.—A popularly written but thoroughly researched account of how TV news is gathered, edited, and presented to the public. Highly recommended.

Katz, E. The two-step flow of communication: An up-to-date report on an hypothesis. *Public Opinion Quarterly,* 1957, 21, 61–78.—An interesting account of the early studies investigating the two-step flow notion.

Lang, K., & Lang, G. E. *Politics and Television.* Chicago: Quadrangle Books, 1968.—A very readable summary of the Langs' highly regarded research on television over the years, demonstrating the gap between the TV image and objective reality.

Weiss, W. Effects of the mass media of communication. In G. Lindzey & E. Aronson (Eds.), *The Handbook of Social Psychology* (2nd ed.). Vol. 5. Reading, Mass.: Addison-Wesley, 1969. Pp. 77–195.—A detailed scholarly review of research findings on mass communication, including information on personal communication as well as the mass media.

chapter 8

Attitude Change Theories and Research:
methodological problems and learning approaches

We are incredibly heedless in the formation of our beliefs, but find ourselves filled with an illicit passion for them when anyone proposes to rob us of their companionship.—James Harvey Robinson.

Some praise at morning what they blame at night
But always think the last opinion right.—Alexander Pope.

If you give me any normal human being and a couple of weeks . . . I can change his behavior from what it is now to whatever you want it to be, if it's physically possible.—James McConnell.

These three statements about attitudinal and behavioral change illustrate the widely discrepant viewpoints that different authors have held on this subject. The topic of attitude *change* has probably occupied the attention of psychologists more than all the other aspects of attitudes put together. One reason for this is the great importance of attitude changes in human affairs—for example, in events such as religious conversions, political persuasion, commercial advertising campaigns, and changes in personal prejudices. Another major reason for interest in attitude change was expressed by Kurt Lewin: to really understand something, such as the concept *attitude*, one must study it as it changes—not while it remains stable. For instance, in studying gravity, it is not enough to know that all objects fall toward the earth; to learn more we must study situations where the amount of gravitational force differs. Similarly, studying prejudiced attitudes per se is less illuminating than studying factors that can increase or decrease prejudice.

Photograph courtesy of M.I.T. Historical Collections. Reprinted by permission.

Box 8-1 KURT LEWIN, *Theorist, Researcher, and Founding Father*

The most influential single figure in shaping modern social psychology, Kurt Lewin was born in Prussia in 1890. After studying in Freiburg and Munich and receiving his Ph.D. at Berlin in 1914, he served in the German Army in World War I. As professor of philosophy and psychology at the University of Berlin, he was a member of its influential group of Gestalt psychologists until he left Germany in 1932 to escape Nazism. After teaching briefly at Stanford and Cornell, he settled at the University of Iowa. In 1944 he founded the Research Center for Group Dynamics at M.I.T., where he died suddenly in 1947.

As a theorist, Lewin is known for his development of psychological field theory. As a researcher, he introduced methods which allowed scientific study of groups in real-life situations. He was famous for studies of democratic and autocratic group leadership methods and group discussion and decision processes. Advocating "action research," he pioneered in practical projects to lessen prejudice, reduce wartime attitude problems, and introduce group participation methods in industrial management. He helped found the National Training Laboratories, where his group dynamic principles were put to work in "T-groups" designed to improve social adjustment and group effectiveness.

This chapter and the following one will summarize the major theories about attitude change and some selected portions of the huge body of research evidence in this field. We will organize our discussion primarily around five broad theoretical orientations toward attitude change—functional, learning, consistency, dissonance, and perceptual approaches. However, before beginning those topics, we will devote some attention to the various kinds of attitude change research and to the methodological problems involved in doing research in this area.

TYPES OF ATTITUDE CHANGE RESEARCH

As mentioned briefly in Chapter 1, there are two common settings for attitude change research, the classroom and the laboratory, and research done in these settings is apt to differ in many respects (McGuire, 1969).

Classroom research, which may be typified by the work of Carl Hovland, usually uses a large number of subjects who are run in groups. For instance, several classes of students might be given several different versions of a persuasive appeal in order to study how different arguments affect the amount of attitude change. This type of research is generally planned by beginning with a *dependent* variable of interest (such as the effects of persuasive messages) and searching for independent variables to manipulate (such as the trustworthiness of the message source) which will influence the dependent variable. Thus it concentrates more on careful measurement of the dependent variable and less on sophisticated procedures to control or manipulate other variables. Normally many variables are manipulated or measured, and complex statistical designs are necessary to analyze the data, which often show complicated interactions between variables. Because of less-complete controls and weak manipulations of independent variables, there is apt to be much error variance, which in turn necessitates large groups of subjects to obtain significance.

By contrast, laboratory research, typified by the work of Leon Festinger, usually uses a relatively small number of subjects who are run individually. For instance, half of the subjects may undergo a failure experience which temporarily lowers their self-esteem, and the effects of this experience on their acceptance of a persuasive message may be compared with other subjects who did not have a failure experience. This type of research is generally planned by beginning with an *independent* variable of some theoretical interest (such as cognitive dissonance) and searching for many different situations where it can be applied (such as self-exposure to new information, or the results of taking actions which are inconsistent with one's attitudes). Thus it concentrates on manipulation of one independent variable and control of other variables, but much less on measurement techniques for the dependent variable. The manipulation procedures are apt to be complicated and precise, with careful checks on their success, so that a relatively large effect may be found. Since other contaminating variables have been controlled experimentally, a simple statistical design is sufficient, and significance may be obtained even with small groups of subjects. Both types of research have their advantages and their liabilities, and we will see many examples of each in the topics to follow.

Classes of Variables Studied

Another way of categorizing attitude change research is by the types of variables studied. In these two chapters we will be focusing primarily on three major classes of variables involved in the process of communication—namely, *source, message,* and *audience* variables. (The fourth type of variable, the *medium* of communication, was discussed in Chapter 7.) A further presentation of research findings concerning attitude change in an area of great social importance can be found in Chapter 14, on racial attitudes and prejudice. Though most research studies have focused on ways to produce attitude change, a few authors have discussed various methods of increasing *resistance* to change (e.g., McGuire, 1964).

A multitude of topics has been studied in research on attitude change. To assist in orienting ourselves to the major substantive areas within the field, Table 8-1 is included, showing topics important enough to have been discussed by one or more of five major recent reviews of research. The first review listed is the volume by Insko (1967), which contains a very thorough coverage of theories and research on attitude change over a period of several decades. The other four reviews are chapters from the *Annual Review of Psychology*, each covering the immediately preceding three-year period of research. With close scrutiny, some major trends can be spotted in Table 8-1—for instance, the relative decline of Hovland-type communication research and of concentration on dissonance-related variables, and the recent burgeoning interest in attribution processes and variables. The next two chapters will discuss many of the variables listed in the table, particularly those which have had the greatest amount of research attention. Interested readers may also wish to consult the original reviews for further detailed information.

METHODOLOGICAL PROBLEMS

Now we turn to a brief description of some of the most important methodological problems in attitude change research. It should be noted that these problems are not unique to the area of attitude change, being frequently found in most experimental and quasi–experimental research in social psychology.

TABLE 8-1 Recent Trends in Substantive Variables Being Emphasized in Attitude Change Research

Variables emphasized	Recent reviews of research				
	Insko (1967)	*McGuire (1966)*	*Sears & Abeles (1969)*	*Fishbein & Ajzen (1972)*	*Kiesler & Munson (1975)*
Source variables					
Prestige	x			x	
Credibility	x		x	x	x
Similarity to audience (race vs. belief)	x	x	x	x	
Intent to persuade vs. objectivity (forewarning vs. distraction effects)		x	x	x	x
Attraction				x	x
Message variables					
Fear appeals	x	x	x	x	
Size of discrepancy (from audience attitude)	x	x	x		
Order effects (primacy vs. recency; forgetting; set)	x	x			
Informative vs. interpretive messages	x				
Immunization against persuasion	x	x			
Types of defensive arguments included	x				
Wording effects			x		
Victim's degree of responsibility for own injury				x	x
Effects of mere exposure				x	x
Stimulus incongruity					x
Medium variables					
Resolution of controversy in natural groups		x			
Interpersonal contact				x	
Audience variables					
Ego-involvement	x	x	x	x	x
Latitudes of acceptance & rejection	x				
Post-decision processes	x			x	
Forced compliance (counterattitudinal advocacy; insufficient justification; effects of effort; effects of threats)	x	x	x	x	x

Variables emphasized	Recent reviews of research				
	Insko (1967)	*McGuire (1966)*	*Sears & Abeles (1969)*	*Fishbein & Ajzen (1972)*	*Kiesler & Munson (1975)*
Audience variables (cont.)					
Active vs. passive participation	x	x	x		
Social support	x				
Commitment & choice	x		x		x
Personality & persuasibility	x	x	x	x	x
Syllogistic reasoning	x			x	
Consistency in inferences	x		x	x	x
Judgment processes (use of cues; adding vs. averaging information)	x		x	x	
Disconfirmation of expectancies		x			
Selective exposure			x		
Multiple modes of attitude change			x		x
Actor vs. observer (self vs. other attribution)				x	x
Previous salience of attitude					x
Illusion of uniqueness of attitude					x
Arousal & motivation					x
Perceived freedom					x
Self-awareness					x

Research Design

The choice of a research design which will yield valid conclusions is always an important step in research. The problem is greater when attitude change studies move from the laboratory to more natural settings, as is often the case in research on marketing, political attitudes, media exposure, racism, and other important social issues. In such cases, investigators usually can't manipulate all the crucial variables, but they can control the conditions under which the dependent variables are measured. Campbell and Stanley (1966) have presented a thorough and helpful description of many different "quasi-experimental" designs for use in such situations.

A danger to be aware of in pretest-posttest designs is that the pretest may either sensitize subjects to the issue and promote attitude change, or alternatively it may commit them to their initial viewpoints and deter attitude change (Rosnow & Suls, 1970). Fortunately this kind of experimental artifact does not seem to occur frequently (McGuire, 1966). See Insko (1967, pp. 3–6) for more details. Another procedure requiring great caution is the use of change scores in pretest-posttest designs (Cronbach & Furby, 1970). Both of these problems can be circumvented by using posttest-only designs, in which subjects are randomly assigned to treatment and control groups and are not given pretests before the experimental manipulation, or by other more complex research designs.

Measurement Methods

The most common way of measuring attitudes, verbal self-report, has many limitations, particularly if subjects have any reason not to report accurately (e.g., laziness, defensiveness, saving face, etc.). Though seldom used, many other measurement approaches have been proposed, as we have discussed in Chapter 2. Some of these methods are indirect or disguised verbal techniques which actually assess attitudes but appear to measure, for instance, the subjects' factual knowledge or their judgments of the plausibility of persuasive arguments. Others are unobtrusive, nonreactive methods of observation, which are particularly useful in nonlaboratory studies. In these methods, subjects are not aware of being studied; examples include observation of political bumper stickers, or of racial seating patterns in a classroom. Physiological and biochemical measures of attitudes have also been proposed, as have methods which use bogus electronic instruments as a means of reducing subjects' tendencies to give socially desirable responses (Jones & Sigall, 1971). At present, little is known about the comparability of these many differing methods of measurement, and the confusion of noncomparable dependent variable measures may account for many of the conflicting findings in the attitude research literature (Fishbein & Ajzen, 1972).

Demand Characteristics

This term, coined by Orne, refers to perceptual cues which indicate what is expected of people in any given situation (Orne, 1969). Such cues may be explicit or implicit, and they are present in all situations, though it is in laboratory experiments where they are most apt to present a problem in the interpretation of the results. Orne and others have shown that subjects in experimental situations may try to ''cooperate'' with the experimenter and thus respond in ways which will support the experimental hypothesis. To take an extreme example, subjects who learn or are told the experimental hypothesis more often perform in ways that will support it than do other subjects (Weber & Cook, 1972). However, in addition to the ''good subject'' set, several other response sets have been mentioned as being common among experimental subjects (see next section).

Demand characteristic effects on research data can be minimized in several ways. Probably the most important way is through replication of studies in different laboratories and by experimenters with differing theoretical viewpoints. Also important are greater use of nonartificial settings, and detailed postexperimental inquiries about subject suspicions. Careful development of experimental procedures and ''cover stories'' can also help, as can avoidance of designs using pretests which may alert subjects to the focus of study. Fortunately, there is some evidence that subjects are quite conscientious in following experimental instructions even if they are suspicious about the procedures (T. Cook, Bean, Calder, Frey, Krovetz, & Reisman, 1970).

Subject Effects

In addition to the set to be a cooperative "good subject," there are several other sets which experimental participants can adopt. Weber and Cook (1972) have discussed the uncooperative, "negativistic subject"; the "faithful subject" who scrupulously follows task instructions and avoids acting on any suspicions which (s)he may have; and the "apprehensive subject" who is worried about how his(her) behavior may be evaluated. Weber and Cook's extensive review of the research literature concluded that there is much evidence for the operation of **evaluation apprehension**—that is, attempts by subjects to act in socially desirable ways (e.g., Rosenberg, 1969; Rosnow, Goodstadt, Suls, & Gitter, 1973). However, there is little or no clear-cut evidence for operation of the other three subject roles except in certain very restricted situations. Nonetheless, careful researchers will try to minimize the possibility that subject roles are influencing their findings. Appropriate precautions include carefully disguising the experimental hypothesis, doing research in natural settings where subjects are unaware that their behavior is being studied, and/or reducing evaluation apprehension by avoiding anxiety-arousing instructions and maintaining subject anonymity.

Another possible subject effect which has been studied stems from the frequent use of *volunteers* as experimental subjects. Many studies have found that volunteer subjects differ in various ways from nonvolunteers, and these differences may affect their experimental performance. For instance, volunteers are apt to be more intelligent and less authoritarian but higher in need for approval (Rosenthal & Rosnow, 1969b). Because of these possible effects, it is wise to avoid use of volunteer subjects whenever that is feasible. However, in a thorough review, Kruglanski (1975) has concluded that volunteer effects are not a consistent or pervasive source of bias in experiments.

Experimenter Effects

Distortions of research results produced by biases of the experimenter have been extensively studied by Rosenthal (1966, 1969—see Oskamp, 1972b for a brief summary). These biases can lead to errors in observation, recording of data, or computation of results, but the most-studied type of experimenter bias is **expectancies** which affect the subjects' behavior. The experimenter's expectancies are apparently transmitted to subjects by subtle cues of voice tone, gestures, and facial expressions. Though there have been vigorous criticisms of some of Rosenthal's research conclusions (e.g., Barber & Silver, 1968), there is widespread agreement that experimenter effects can occur under some conditions (Insko, 1967; Fishbein & Ajzen, 1972). Thus, attempts to eliminate or minimize them are desirable. Some of the best ways to do so include cutting down on experimenter-subject contact by mechanizing as much of the procedure as possible, using several different experimenters and testing for differences in their results, insuring that the experimenter cannot reinforce subjects' behavior differentially, keeping experimenters "blind" to the research hypothesis, and using extra control groups which differ only in the expectancies given to their members about the research hypothesis.

Deception and Suspicion

Because of the many extraneous variables, such as those discussed above, which can affect the results of attitude change studies, investigators in this area have often felt it necessary or desirable to deceive subjects during the course of experiments (Stricker, 1967; Seeman, 1969). However, deception itself, and the subjects' suspicion which may result, can become additional confounding variables which sometimes bias research results (Stricker, Messick, & Jackson, 1969; Rubin & Moore, 1971). On the other hand, an equal number of studies have shown that prior deception and/or current suspiciousness do not necessarily bias subjects' responses (Fillenbaum & Frey, 1970; Holmes & Bennett, 1974). Thus, situational differences and the carefulness of the researcher are apt to determine whether use of deception poses a threat to valid conclusions.

One approach which has been suggested instead of deception is the **simulated experiment** (sometimes also called an interpersonal replication, or passive role-playing), in which a written or tape-recorded description of the experimental situation is given to observer-subjects instead of actually placing them in the situation (Bem, 1967; Kelman, 1967). However, extensive criticisms of simulated experiments or role-playing studies have indicated that they may create more problems in the interpretation of research results than they solve (R. A. Jones, Linder, Kiesler, Zanna, & Brehm, 1968; A. Miller, 1972—see also the evidence on actor-observer differences cited in the next chapter in the section on critiques of dissonance theory).

Another reason which has been stressed for avoiding experimental deception wherever possible involves questions of ethical propriety (Kelman, 1967). Psychologists and other attitude-change researchers have been very attentive to ethical issues over the years, and these issues will be discussed further in Chapter 10.

Having discussed research methods and methodological problems, we shall turn now to theories of attitude change, beginning in this chapter with functional theories and learning theories. In the following chapter we will discuss cognitive and perceptual theories, including approaches centering on cognitive consistency, dissonance, social judgment, and attribution processes.

WHY HAVE THEORIES?

In considering theories of attitude change, we should first ask: What good are theories? Why do we have them? A number of answers have been given to this question. First, **theories** provide a path to guide our steps in research; they suggest factors that are important to study, ones that we might not think of otherwise. Second, theories help us to understand research findings by putting them into a context; they explain the meaning of the facts which have been discovered—how and why they fit together. Third, theories allow us to predict what will happen under various conditions in the future. In turn, correct prediction of events provides a stringent test of the adequacy of any theory. As Deutsch and Krauss (1965) have put it: "Theory is the net man weaves to catch the world of observation—to explain, predict, and influence it" (p. vii).

Another point which should be stressed is that theories are never proven. They can be disproven at crucial points by negative evidence, but an accumulation of positive evidence merely adds support to a theory rather than proving it in any final sense. These supportive data may also be compatible with another, different theory. When a theoretical relationship between two variables has been confirmed so many times that all authorities agree on its correctness, it is usually called a **law** (such as the gas laws, which describe the relationship between the temperature, pressure, and volume of gas in a closed container). Even with scientific laws, there are often exceptions and limits to the breadth of their applicability (for instance, the gas laws are less accurate at extremely low temperatures). In the social sciences there are very few relationships which have been so thoroughly established that we would call them laws. Consequently, our theories are held tentatively rather than with certainty. They are more like road maps, which display some of the connections between major points, than like detailed topographic maps, which show every feature of the landscape.

There are also different types or levels of theories which vary in their scope or range of applicability. At the narrowest end are miniature theories which deal with very limited subareas within the field of attitude change (for instance, McGuire's (1964) theory of inoculation against persuasion). At the other extreme are broad, general orientations toward ways of thinking about and explaining attitude change (for example, learning theory approaches, and consistency theory approaches). In between are numerous mid-range theories with varying degrees of scope.

There is no classification of attitude theories which is generally agreed upon. Insko (1967) discusses 12 different theoretical approaches, while Ostrom (1968) has listed 34 specific theoretical contributions involving emphasis on different psychological processes. It is important to realize that these theoretical approaches, though stressing different processes, can only rarely be pitted against each other in opposing predictions. Different theories sometimes make similar predictions, and often they stress different independent variables and different areas of applicability. As McGuire (1969, p. 271) put it:

> these broad theories are complementary rather than contentious (though the theorists who have advocated them are often contentious rather than complimentary).

Or to use a more-critical simile, these theories are often like ships that pass in the night, without making contact with each other (Suedfeld, 1971).

FUNCTIONAL APPROACHES TO ATTITUDE CHANGE

We will begin here with functional theories because they are already somewhat familiar from our discussion of the functions of attitudes in Chapter 3, and so we can cover them quickly here.

The key feature of **functional theories** of attitudes is their stress on the functions which attitudes serve in satisfying the personality needs or motivations of the individual. Functional theories hold that attitudes cannot be adequately understood without considering the needs that they serve for a particular individual. This seems to be a valuable viewpoint which has important practical and theoretical consequences.

However, functional approaches to attitude change have not been widely accepted nor frequently studied by researchers. They have been proposed by two main groups of writers: Katz (1960) and his associates, and Smith, Bruner, and White (1956). The latter group conducted a study that was unusual within the field of social psychology in that it used a detailed clinical-assessment, case-study approach to probe the personality characteristics and salient attitudes of ten men. The attitudes on which they focused most strongly were nationalistic and internationalistic viewpoints concerning the United States and Russia— viewpoints which often seemed to reflect the holder's personality needs, values, and defenses.

Both sets of authors have proposed several different kinds of needs which attitudes may serve, and the two lists are quite similar. A crucial feature of the theory is that the different types of attitudes will be *aroused* by different situations and will be *changed* by different types of influences. For instance, the conditions which would lead a person to change an understanding-oriented attitude (e.g., the presentation of new information) should be quite different from the conditions necessary for changing an ego-defensive attitude (e.g., the removal of anxiety or threat). It should also be kept in mind that a given attitude may serve several different functions, and when this is the case it would be harder to change than if it served only one. Katz has summarized the attitude-arousal and attitude-change conditions in a table which is reprinted here with minor changes (see Table 8-2).

Objective evaluation of functional theories is difficult. On one hand, the theoretical stance seems very plausible, and it is consistent with the speculations and findings of many authors (McGuire, 1969, pp. 157–160). On the other hand, very little research has been done specifically to test hypotheses from the theory, and the theory has a number of serious problems (Kiesler et al., 1969, pp. 326–330). It is a broad compendium of ideas from many past thinkers and

TABLE 8-2   Determinants of Attitude Formation, Arousal, and Change in Relation to the Type of Function Served by the Attitude. (Adapted from Katz, 1960, p. 192.)

Function	Origin and dynamics	Arousal conditions	Change conditions
Understanding	Need for understanding, for meaningful cognitive organization, for consistency and clarity	1. Reinstatement of cues associated with old problem or of old problem itself	1. Ambiguity created by new information or change in environment 2. More meaningful information about problems
Need satisfaction	Utility of attitudinal object in need satisfaction. Maximizing external rewards and minimizing punishments	1. Activation of needs 2. Salience of cues associated with need satisfaction	1. Need deprivation 2. Creation of new needs and new levels of aspiration 3. Shifting rewards and punishments 4. Emphasis on new and better paths for need satisfaction
Ego defense	Protecting against internal conflicts and external dangers	1. Posing of threats 2. Appeals to hatred and repressed impulses 3. Rise in frustrations 4. Use of authoritarian suggestion	1. Removal of threats 2. Catharsis 3. Development of self-insight
Value expression	Maintaining self identity; enhancing favorable self-image; self-expression and self-determination	1. Salience of cues associated with values 2. Appeals to individual to reassert self-image 3. Ambiguities which threaten self-concept	1. Some degree of dissatisfaction with self 2. Greater appropriateness of new attitude for the self 3. Control of all environmental supports to undermine old values

researchers (for instance, the ego defensive function comes directly from psychoanalytic theory), but as a result many of the theory's concepts are ill-defined and its hypotheses therefore not clearly testable. Perhaps the greatest problem is in measuring what functions an attitude serves for its holder; until that obstacle is overcome the theory will have only suggestive value rather than predictive power or practical usefulness.

LEARNING APPROACHES TO ATTITUDE CHANGE

Unlike functional theories, learning approaches to attitudes have been the subject of much research. We have presented a summary of some of this research in Chapter 6, which dealt with the formation of attitudes. There we described seven learning processes (e.g., instrumental conditioning) which can be involved in initial attitude formation. Here we should note that any of these processes can also be involved in attitude change.

The key feature of **learning approaches** to attitude change is their stress that learning processes are responsible for attitude change. Though this may seem obvious, it has several less-obvious corollaries. First, since all learning theories are based on the principles of *reinforcement* and/or temporal *contiguity* as being responsible for learning, there is much stress on reinforcement and, to a lesser extent, on association through contiguity in explaining attitude change. Second, because learning theories emphasize *stimulus-response* connections, their application in the field of attitude change has focused much attention on the characteristics of the persuasive stimulus—particularly on the source of the message and on its content. Third, researchers with a learning orientation have tended to emphasize the learning part of the communication process (that is, attention and comprehension) more than other researchers and to be less concerned with the yielding stage of the process (McGuire, 1969, p. 266). Fourth, since much of learning theory has been established through research with animals, a good deal of extension and translation of concepts and procedures was often needed to make them applicable to humans and to the kind of intangible intervening variable which we call an attitude. The gap between animal learning and human attitudes has led to many questions about what extensions and translations were reasonable and proper and what conclusions could be drawn if previously-supported findings with animals failed to be duplicated with humans. In a word, was it the original theories or their translations and applications which were at fault?

A final consequence of applying learning theory to human attitudes has been the profusion of approaches. There are several major competing theories of learning, and there are even more ways of translating and applying them to new situations. As a result, many different attitude researchers claim a "learning theory" orientation, but the details of their approaches often have little in common other than the underlying concern with learning, reinforcement, and S-R associations.

Out of this profusion of approaches we can describe and illustrate only a few of the most influential ones. If you would like to read further in this area, more detailed treatments can be found in Insko (1967), Greenwald, Brock, and Ostrom (1968), and Kiesler, Collins, and Miller (1969).

Conditioning Theories of Attitude Change

One of the first authors to propose the application of conditioning and learning principles to the attitude area was Doob (1947). His approach was derived from Hullian learning theory and suggested that attitudes are a type of implicit (nonobservable) response and are learned and modified through reinforcement just like all other responses. Other researchers who have investigated attitudes within a framework of classical conditioning and/or instrumental conditioning have described their approaches in the volume by Greenwald et al. (1968). These writers' views as they pertain to attitude *formation* have been presented in Chapter 6. Here we will give two examples of conditioning effects on attitude *change*.

Reward for Advocating a Position.   Scott (1959) studied this subject in a debate context, where some college students were assigned to take the side opposite to their own attitudes ("counterattitudinal advocacy"), while others argued for a position less distant from their own, and still others supported their own real viewpoint in the debate. "Winners" and "losers" were randomly determined by the experimenter, though the debaters thought the decision reflected their classmates' votes. In all conditions, the reward of winning produced attitude change toward the position which the student had advocated, while the losers showed no change in attitude as a result of participating in the debate.

Verbal Reinforcement of Opinions.   Students' existing opinions were directly reinforced in an experiment by Insko (1965). Undergraduates in a psychology course were telephoned at home by student interviewers and reinforced with comments like "good," half being rewarded for stating opinions favorable to a possible new campus festival, and half for unfavorable opinions. A week later in class the students participated in an apparently unconnected activity, filling out a long questionnaire, one item of which asked for opinions on the creation of the same proposed festival, thus providing a delayed test of attitude change in a completely different setting from the experimental manipulation. Results showed that the telephone verbal reinforcement had a significant effect on the students' attitudes. Many other studies have provided ample evidence that reinforcement can have a strong effect in modifying attitudes and opinions.

Bem's Behavioral Theory

Daryl Bem (1965) has suggested another learning approach to attitude change, stemming from Skinnerian behavioristic principles. Though he uses cognitive concepts such as beliefs, attitudes, and self-awareness, he attempts to give them rigorously objective definitions. Furthermore, he proposes that the way that people know about their own internal processes, such as attitudes, is the same way they learn about other people's attitudes and feelings—that is, through observation. In the beginning, Bem says, every child learns about his external environment through discrimination training by the adults and other children around him. By verbal labeling and corroboration or correction, children learn to distinguish between dogs and cats, for instance, and between anger and happiness in other people. In the same way, says Bem, through *self-perception* we also learn to label our own inner feelings of hunger, anger, anxiety, or liking. To use his favorite example, we decide that we like brown bread by observing the fact that we eat a lot of it. Bem's major theoretical premise is that a person's cues for self-perception are primarily the same publicly-observable responses by which (s)he perceives and evaluates the feelings and attitudes of other people.

Concerning attitude change, Bem posits that it occurs in reaction to self-observed behaviors *combined with* observation of external cues which indicate whether or not the behavior is apt to be valid or truthful. For instance, if a model in a TV commercial says "I like Busy Bakers' brown bread," but we know that he was paid to make the commercial, we may doubt whether that is his true attitude. On the other hand, if a person is subtly induced to say something contrary to his former opinion under conditions which suggest truthfulness, he is apt to decide that he really believes the statement which he has made.

These examples illustrate another basic principle of Bem's theory, that attitude change often follows from behavior change, rather than the opposite sequence, which most other theories suggest. As a real-life instance of this process, Bem (1970) has asserted that police-station interrogation conditions constitute a truth-telling situation for most people, and that in such situations certain wily interrogation procedures can induce prisoners to make *and to believe in* false confessions about crimes which they have not really committed. This is a particularly surprising and dramatic example of attitude change, and Bem has backed up his claims with clear-cut evidence from a laboratory experiment which showed exactly this process at work. However, it should be noted that other investigators have had difficulty in replicating these results (Kiesler & Munson, 1975, p. 431).

Another aspect of Bem's self-perception theory is its dispute with the principles of dissonance theory, which Bem (1967) has sharply criticized. This dispute will be described when we discuss dissonance theory in Chapter 9. In the meantime we can conclude that Bem has provided some clever and surprising experimental evidence in favor of his behavioristic conception of attitude change.

Hovland's Communication Research Program

At Yale University after World War II, Carl Hovland gathered a gifted and productive group of researchers, whose work dominated the attitude area in the 1950s and continues to be highly influential to this day. This group published

Photograph courtesy of Carl Hovland.
Reprinted by permission.

Box 8-2 CARL HOVLAND, *Leading Persuasion Researcher*

One of the most outstanding researchers on attitude change, Carl Hovland was born in Chicago in 1912 and died an untimely death in 1961. Following a B.A. and M.A. at Northwestern, he took his Ph.D. at Yale in 1936 and joined the Yale faculty, where he remained for the rest of his life. For many years he was chairman of the psychology department and Director of the Yale Communication Research Program.

During World War II, Hovland directed the Research Branch of the U.S. War Department's Information and Education Division. There he studied the effectiveness of Army training films and morale problems. His many years of communication research led to volumes on Experiments on Mass Communication, Communication and Persuasion, The Order of Presentation in Persuasion, Personality and Persuasibility, Attitude Organization and Change, *and* Social Judgment. *He was honored by election to the National Academy of Sciences, and in 1957 he was one of the first recipients of the American Psychological Association's highest honor, the Distinguished Scientific Contribution Award.*

many volumes of research findings, the most important of which in outlining their conceptual approach was *Communication and Persuasion* (Hovland, Janis, & Kelley, 1953).

Hovland and his coworkers were very explicit in stating that they were not presenting a systematic theory, but rather an initial framework of working assumptions about factors affecting attitude change. However, it is clear that their working assumptions derived primarily from a learning and reinforcement point of view. They likened the process of attitude change to the learning of a habit or skill. Just as with learning, they postulated, attitude change will only occur if there is (a) practice ("mental rehearsal" or thinking about the new attitude), and (b) an incentive (a reward or reinforcement) for accepting it. Also they stressed the sequential process described in Chapter 7: attention to the persuasive stimulus is necessary before there can be comprehension, and comprehension is necessary before there can be acceptance of the new attitude.

Because of their stimulus-response viewpoint, Hovland et al.'s (1953) research concentrated heavily on variables in the stimulus situation which might help to determine the amount of attitude change (the response). In particular, they studied aspects of the source of the message, many elements of the content of the message, and some characteristics of the audience. Here we will briefly mention a few of the specific variables which they investigated and their key findings, while in the following sections three of the most important of these research topics will be described in more detail.

Source Variables. The credibility of the communicator was the major source variable studied, and it was found to be positively related to degree of acceptance of the message, though not very closely related to attention, comprehension, or later retention of the message. Other studies analyzed credibility into two separate aspects: the source's expertness (degree of knowledge), and its trustworthiness (lack of intention to deceive or manipulate the audience).

Message Variables. The content of the message was quite extensively studied by Hovland et al. One variable which has stirred continuing interest, the presence of fear-inducing arguments in the message, is discussed below. Other message content factors studied by the Hovland group included where to place the strongest argument in a persuasive communication, and whether to use only arguments on one side of the issue or to include and refute a few of the opposing arguments. In general, this "two-sided" presentation was found to be more effective, especially with intelligent audiences or subsequent contrary messages. Related studies showed that drawing conclusions explicitly was more effective than leaving them implicit.

Several other aspects of order effects within a single persuasive message have been reviewed by McGuire (1969): for instance, whether to present one's conclusions before or after the arguments supporting them; whether to present good news first and bitter pills later, or to reverse the order and "leave them laughing"; whether to present one's strongest arguments first or to save them for later; whether to refute opposing arguments before or after giving one's own arguments. Such questions are of great practical interest to politicians, debaters, lawyers, and commercial advertisers, but they have received relatively little research attention.

By contrast, a great deal of work has been done on the question of whether the first side of a controversy to be presented, or the most recent side, has a persuasive advantage. This **primacy-recency** question involves two opposing messages. Early research results appeared to support a universal "law of primacy," both in debate-type situations (Lund, 1925) and in forming first impressions of other people on the basis of a few bits of information (Asch, 1946). However, Hovland's work and other related research effectively challenged this conclusion and showed that recency effects were regularly obtained under some conditions (Hovland, Mandell, et al., 1957; Luchins, 1957; Anderson, 1959). Thus, as in so many other areas, interest has shifted to the question of *what specific conditions* produce primacy or recency effects.

Subsequent research on order effects has shown that recency effects are more likely as the time interval between the two opposing messages is increased

(Miller & Campbell, 1959; Insko, 1964; Wilson & Miller, 1968). Though these results were predicted from a learning framework, they do not seem to depend heavily on forgetting of the first message during the following time interval. In general, research on order effects has found many variables which interact with each other to determine whether primacy effects or recency effects or neither will occur (Rosnow, 1966; Insko, 1967; Luchins & Luchins, 1970). We can safely conclude that there is no universal law of primacy nor of recency in persuasion.

Audience Variables. Personality factors which are related to persuasibility were extensively studied by Hovland et al. (1953) and by Janis, Hovland, et al. (1959). Another important audience variable which they studied is active participation in stating or making up arguments for a persuasive message. Personality and persuasibility is discussed later in this chapter, while research on active participation is summarized in Chapter 9 in the section on dissonance theory research.

In summary, though Hovland and his colleagues did not present a systematic theory, their approach was very influential in expanding the interest in attitude research among U.S. psychologists. Their research was prolific and well-done, and they opened up many productive areas of inquiry. Their concepts of attention, comprehension, and acceptance have provided a fertile way of analyzing attitude-change effects, even though the interrelationships of these concepts are still not fully understood.

In the next three sections of this chapter we will summarize some of the research evidence concerning three topics which have been studied mainly within a learning framework: source credibility, fear appeals in messages, and audience personality and persuasibility.

Research on Source Credibility

Variables concerning the communication source have most often been studied by presenting a given message to several groups of subjects and telling each group that the message comes from a different source (for instance, Thomas Jefferson or Karl Marx; a Nobel Prize-winning physiologist or the director of the local Y.M.C.A.). Characteristics of the source which have been studied in attitude change research include the source's *similarity* to the audience, its *power* over the audience, its *attractiveness*, and its **credibility**, which has been further subdivided into *expertness* and *objectivity*. Of these characteristics, power has been less extensively studied in relation to attitude change, while source credibility defined as expertness has often been found to be more clearly related to attitude change than are the source's objectivity, attractiveness, or similarity (McGuire, 1969; Simons, Berkowitz, & Moyer, 1970). Therefore we will confine ourselves here to discussion of the expertness aspect of credibility. In experiments, expertness is usually manipulated by ascribing to the source a high degree of knowledge, intelligence, age, prestige or social status, or a relevant professional or occupational background.

A large body of research indicates that a message from a highly credible source will produce more attitude change than one from a low-credibility source (Hovland et al., 1953; Insko, 1967). However, this greater acceptance of the message is not due to greater reception, for the arguments of low-credibility sources are remembered as well as those of highly credible sources.

Though in general an expert source produces more opinion change, there are a number of interesting exceptions and special conditions limiting this conclusion. The expertise usually must be relevant to the topic being addressed (not, for instance, an eminent physiologist giving advice on dressmaking). However, sometimes high status can increase a source's persuasiveness even in irrelevant areas (Aronson & Golden, 1962). In order for the source's expertise to be effective, it must be known to the audience before the message is delivered—a good reason for the practice of introductions which describe the speaker's qualifications (Mills & Harvey, 1972).

Research findings suggest that people often use source credibility as a basis for accepting or rejecting message conclusions without paying much attention to the supporting arguments. If the message does not contain evidence to support the conclusion, the source's credibility is apt to have a greater effect than when adequate evidence is presented (McCroskey, 1970). On the other hand, if there is no credibility information available, then people are forced to pay more attention to the arguments that are presented (McGuire, 1969).

When subjects are highly involved in the issue, the credibility of the source may not increase persuasion (Johnson & Scileppi, 1969). However, communicators are seen as more credible and have a greater persuasive effect when they advocate a position contrary to their own personal interests (such as a sales clerk recommending the cheaper of two products—Walster, Aronson, & Abrahams, 1966).

A final topic here concerns the interaction of source credibility and time passage, which provides the basis for the so-called **sleeper effect**. This term refers to delayed attitude change in the direction advocated by a noncredible communicator (such as a convict arguing for lighter court sentences). Early studies (e.g., Kelman & Hovland, 1953) found that amount of attitude change produced by a credible source decreased over a period of several weeks, but that attitude change produced by the same message from a noncredible source *increased* and eventually reached the same level as that for the credible source. This effect was found to be due, not to the subjects' forgetting the source per se, but apparently to their ceasing to connect the source with the message content. These "sleeper effect" findings were fascinating because they were originally unexpected and yet seemed plausible on further consideration. Unfortunately, however, later studies have found it almost impossible to replicate the "sleeper effect," and it now seems clear that it appears, if at all, only in certain highly unusual situations. Though a gradual decrease in attitude change produced by a credible source is common, a delayed *increase* in attitude change produced by a noncredible source is very rare (Gillig & Greenwald, 1974). Most textbooks have not caught up with these findings and still describe the "sleeper effect" as if it were a well-established reality.

Research on Fear Appeals

One of the most provocative early studies on message content was Janis and Feshbach's (1953) experiment in which they varied the extent of fear-arousing information about tooth decay in persuasive messages about proper dental care. With three levels of fear-arousal, they found that a very weak fear appeal produced the most reported change in toothbrushing practices a week later, whereas the least change was produced by the strongest fear appeal (containing gruesome pictures and personalized threatening information). Their interpretation of this finding stressed that arousal of negative emotions can produce avoidance and defensive reactions to a communication.

Despite this early evidence, Madison Avenue advertising copy writers have continued to use fear appeals in abundance (avoid body odor, watch out for tattle-tale gray, beware of flaky dandruff, etc. (See Figure 8-1.) And in this case, subsequent research has shown that their approach could be effective in producing the desired attitude change. In fact, the bulk of the recent evidence shows strong fear appeals producing more attitude change than weak ones (Higbee, 1969; McGuire, 1969; Leventhal, 1970). Many of these studies have dealt with important real-life issues such as cutting down on smoking, using seat belts, getting chest X-rays, or taking tetanus inoculations.

To explain the conflicting findings of an occasional negative relationship between fear appeals and attitude change and the more commonly-found positive relationship, **curvilinear** theories have been proposed (e.g., McGuire, 1968b). According to this viewpoint, there is an inverted U-shaped relation between amount of fear arousal and attitude change, with the greatest attitude change at moderate fear levels. Accordingly, a positive relationship to attitude change might be found for conditions low on the fear continuum, but a negative relationship for higher fear conditions. McGuire's theory relates this curvilinear pattern to the intermediate processes of reception of and yielding to the persuasive message. Thus, at very low fear levels, audience interest and reception will be low. At higher fear levels, interest and reception will be good, and credible fear appeals will also increase yielding. However, at very high fear levels, both reception and yielding will be diminished by defensive avoidance and discounting mechanisms, so attitude change will be rather sharply decreased. In order to test such a theory, an independent method of scaling degrees of fear-arousal is vitally needed, but such a method has not yet been developed.

A curvilinear theory of fear-arousal effects also implies a number of interactions with other variables. One example of an interaction which has received some empirical support is that a higher level of fear arousal is optimal when highly specific and detailed recommendations are made concerning actions to be taken to reduce the fear—for instance, directions about where to go and what to do to get a tetanus inoculation (Leventhal, 1970).

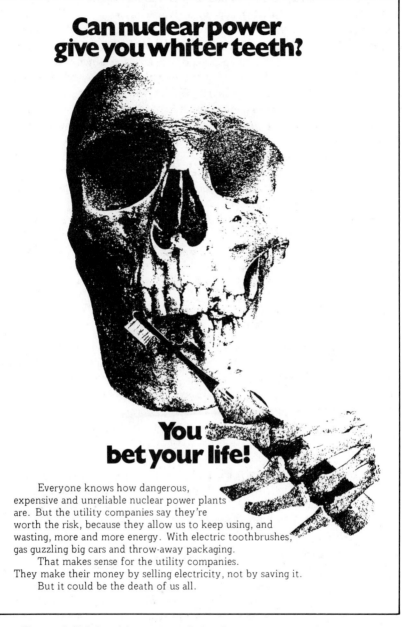

Figure 8-1 Advertising copy writers often use scare techniques.

Photograph courtesy of Public Media Center, San Francisco. Reprinted by permission.

Another fascinating finding in this area is that fear appeals fairly often have differential effects on different dependent variables, such as beliefs, attitudes, behavioral intentions, and actual behavior (Evans, Rozelle, Lasater, Dembroski, & Allen, 1970; Leventhal, 1970). For instance, in two studies by Leventhal and his colleagues, the level of fear appeal markedly affected attitudes and behavioral intentions (to stop smoking, or to get a tetanus shot) but did not have any differential effect on the actual behavior. On the other hand, specific instructions on how to perform the recommended act did not affect subjects' intentions to do so, but did markedly increase the number of people who actually followed through on the recommendation.

In a critique of fear-arousal research, Fishbein and Ajzen (1975) point to these differential results for different dependent variables as one problem and to the confounding of fear levels with the specific content of messages as a problem on the independent variable side. They recommend an attitude-change approach which focuses on raising behavioral intentions to perform a specific, immediate action (e.g., signing up for appointments at an Alcoholic Treatment Unit, rather than completely ceasing to drink). A combination of immediately relevant fear appeals with specific behavioral instructions had the strongest positive effects on both attitudes and actual behavior in a study by McArdle (1972).

Research on Personality and Persuasibility

The final research topic in this chapter concerns audience personality characteristics which are related to susceptibility to persuasion. Early work by Hovland and his colleagues sought to determine to what extent persuasibility is a general personality trait which holds across various topics and situations (Hovland et al., 1953; Janis, Hovland, et al., 1959). Their hypothesis, and the general tenor of their findings, was that there is a significant but small degree of general persuasibility which is topic-free.

Early studies of persuasibility searched for linear relationships between attitude change and personality traits such as self-esteem (Janis & Field, 1959). More recently, McGuire (1968b) has proposed a more complex theory involving two processes which mediate between personality and attitude change: reception (including both attention and comprehension), and yielding (acceptance). We have referred to this theory briefly above, and in Chapter 7 in discussing these mediating processes as some of the dependent variables of communication studies. The complexity of the theory stems from the fact that any personality characteristic (such as intelligence or self-esteem) which is positively related to reception is expected to be negatively related to yielding, and vice versa. An example of this predicted relationship and the expected combined result of reception and yielding on opinion change is shown in Figure 8–2. Though McGuire suggests that very simple or very complex messages might produce linear relationships to the amount of opinion change, the curvilinear, inverted-U relationship between self-esteem and opinion change is the one which would be expected

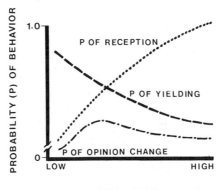

Figure 8-2 Predicted relationship of the personality variable of self-esteem to the mediating processes of reception and yielding and to the resulting amount of opinion change. (Adapted from McGuire, 1968b, p. 1151.)

to occur in the majority of situations, rather than the linear relationship sought by earlier investigators.

McGuire's hypotheses regarding personality and persuasibility do not constitute a precisely-stated theory, but rather a general outlook on the relationships to be expected. Nevertheless, there is a rather large body of research reporting interaction effects which are supportive of his viewpoint (e.g., Lehmann, 1970; Dinner, Lewkowicz, & Cooper, 1972). For example, Nisbett and Gordon (1967) showed that simple but poorly substantiated messages produced most attitude change in low self-esteem subjects, whereas complex but well substantiated messages were most effective in high self-esteem subjects.

Self-esteem is the personality variable most studied in relation to persuasibility, stemming from the early work of Janis and Field (1959). Other frequently studied personal characteristics have been anxiety, dogmatism, and intelligence. As with self-esteem, none of these characteristics should be expected to show uniform linear relationships to attitude change except in occasional unusual circumstances. Reviews of recent findings concerning personality and attitudes can be found in McGuire (1969, pp. 241–252), Sears and Abeles (1969), and Kiesler and Munson (1975).

Evaluation of Learning Approaches

As mentioned earlier, there is no single unified learning theory of attitude change, and each of the approaches we have discussed is at best a partial, incomplete theory. Some, like the Hovland group's approach, are not theories at all in the technical sense of the word. Despite their common characteristics, these approaches do not really build together toward a unified theory. They differ among themselves in many details, such as their procedures and operational definitions of their concepts; they apply most clearly to different types of situations; and they all fail to cover some other types of attitude change situations.

McGuire, who was a member of the Hovland group of researchers, has recently concluded that learning-theory approaches to attitude change may have been "a fertile error" (McGuire, 1969, p. 266). They were fertile in suggesting areas and procedures for research, but they have often been wrong in the details of their experimental predictions. Clearly, theories of conditioning and learning can explain many attitude change phenomena, and particularly also findings in the area of attitude formation. Yet even in this area of their greatest applicability, they are vulnerable to the criticism that subjects' *awareness* of the conditioning procedures may be responsible for much of the effect obtained (Kiesler et al., 1969). If so, then cognitive or perceptual theories would be more appropriate ways of understanding and explaining attitude changes.

In the following chapter we will examine cognitive and perceptual theories of attitude change in some detail.

SUMMARY

The topic of attitude change has generated much more research than other aspects of attitudes and has inspired a profusion of competing theories. The two most common settings for attitude change research are classroom studies, using large groups of subjects, and laboratory studies, which typically run subjects individually with more complex manipulation and control of variables. The multitude of topics studied in attitude change research can be organized into groups of variables concerning the source, message, audience, and medium of communication.

Methodological problems in attitude change research are numerous. There are many alternative research designs and attitude measurement methods which can be utilized in order to obtain more valid data. Demand characteristics and experimenter bias effects can contaminate research results unless careful precautions are taken to minimize them. Subject effects, such as those stemming from evaluation apprehension or the use of volunteer subjects, may also occasionally distort research findings. Finally, deception in experiments can cause subject suspicion, which in turn sometimes produces biased results. However, the use of simulated experiments (passive role-playing) as an alternative to deception generally appears to create more problems than it solves.

Though all current theories of attitude change have serious limitations and none has achieved general acceptance, they still have an important role to play. They guide our research efforts, provide a context for understanding observed facts, and help us to predict future events. Theories are always held tentatively and never considered proven in any final sense, though they may be disproved by contrary evidence. The many theories discussed in this and the following chapter are largely complementary—i.e., they often have different areas of applicability, and they rarely make directly opposing predictions.

Functional approaches emphasize that attitude change depends on the individual's personality needs and motivations. Attitudes which serve different functions will be aroused in different types of situations and changed by different types of influences. Though this approach seems plausible, it has not been widely accepted by researchers, and it has many poorly-defined aspects and methodological problems.

The many different *learning* approaches to attitude change have generated a great deal of research. They all stress stimulus-response connections, the importance of reinforcement or contiguity in learning, and extension or translation of concepts from animal learning experiments. Conditioning theories of attitude change have been proposed by many authors and supported by research on topics such as reward for advocating a position, and verbal reinforcement of opinions. Bem has presented an observational theory of self-perception, derived from Skinnerian behavioral notions, which emphasizes that attitude change often follows from behavior change rather than the commonly-postulated reverse sequence. Hovland's communication research program, though not presenting a systematic theory of attitude change, was extremely fruitful in generating research on the steps of the communication process: attention, comprehension, and acceptance.

Among the variables concerning the communication *source*, the clearest relationships to attitude change have been found for source credibility, defined as expertness. An expert source usually produces more attitude change, but there are a number of exceptions to this general rule. The intriguing notion of a "sleeper effect" by which low credibility sources could produce delayed attitude change has not been confirmed in recent research.

Message variables which have been extensively studied include order effects of primacy or recency, and fear appeals. Early studies found strong fear arousal less effective than weak fear appeals in producing attitude and behavior change, but most recent studies have found strong fear appeals more effective. Consequently, a curvilinear theory has become popular, positing an inverted-U relationship between fear arousal and attitude change, and also allowing for different effects of fear on attitudes, intentions, and behavior.

Personality characteristics have been among the most frequently studied *audience variables*. There seems to be a significant but small degree of general persuasibility across various topics and situations. However, current theories predict curvilinear relationships between personality traits and attitude change.

The various learning approaches to attitude change conflict with each other in many details and do not approach the status of a unified theory. Though they have been fertile in stimulating research on attitude change as well as attitude formation, many of their specific predictions have not been supported.

Suggested Readings

Karlins, M., & Abelson, H. I. *Persuasion: How Opinions and Attitudes Are Changed* (2nd ed.). New York: Springer, 1970.—A popularly-written little book stating practically-oriented principles which can be used by people who want to change others' opinions. Each principle is supported by simple descriptions of a few "specimen studies."

Kiesler, C. A., Collins, B. E., & Miller, N. *Attitude Change: A Critical Analysis of Theoretical Approaches.* New York: Wiley, 1969.—A thorough and readable description of the major theories of attitude change and the relevant research findings, including long chapters on learning theories and functional theories.

McGuire, W. J. The nature of attitudes and attitude change. In G. Lindzey & E. Aronson (Eds.), *The Handbook of Social Psychology* (2nd ed.). Vol. 3. Reading, Mass.: Addison-Wesley, 1969. Pp. 136–314.—Pages 172-265 of this monumental chapter contain a scholarly and often-cited review of research on the major variables involved in persuasive communication and attitude change.

Rosenthal, R., & Rosnow, R. L. (Eds.). *Artifact in Behavioral Research.* New York: Academic Press, 1969a.—A major volume containing extensive chapters on methodological problems in attitude change research, including demand characteristics, experimenter effects, volunteer subjects, evaluation apprehension, and suspiciousness.

chapter 9

Attitude Change
Theories and Research:
cognitive and
perceptual approaches

Americans have, more than any other people I know, a willingness to change their opinions. —Gunnar Myrdal.

Most of our so-called reasoning consists in finding arguments for going on believing as we already have. —James Harvey Robinson.

It requires ages to destroy a popular opinion. —Voltaire.

Attitudes can sometimes change very rapidly, whereas in other situations they may prove very resistant to change. It is the goal of theories of attitude change to define the conditions under which attitudes will change and the ways in which this will occur. It is unlikely that any single theory will ever provide all of these answers, and our current theories are merely first approximations to the answers we are seeking.

Before we become too disillusioned with the state of our current theoretical knowledge, it may be well to recall a statement by Thomas Edison: "I have constructed *three thousand* different theories in connection with the electric light. . . . Yet in only two cases did my experiments prove the truth of my theory."

In that spirit of continual searching for closer approximations of the truth, this chapter will discuss several types of attitude change theories—cognitive theories stressing consistency or dissonance as explanatory variables, and perceptual theories focusing on social judgment or attribution processes.

CONSISTENCY THEORIES

In recent years **consistency theories** of attitude change have drawn more attention and inspired more research than any other group of theories. These theories are, first of all, cognitive theories; that is, they emphasize the importance of people's beliefs and ideas. As their name implies, their key feature is the principle that people try to maintain consistency among their beliefs, attitudes, and behaviors. Awareness of one's own inconsistency is viewed as an uncomfortable situation which every person is motivated to escape. Thus attitude change should result if individuals receive new information which is inconsistent with their previous viewpoints or if existing inconsistencies in their beliefs and attitudes are pointed out to them.

Consistency theories view people as essentially thoughtful and rational, adjusting their attitudes and behavior in accordance with incoming information. However, they do not assume a strict logical consistency, but rather a value- and emotion-tinged "**psycho-logic**," to use Abelson and Rosenberg's (1958) clever term. For instance, strict mathematical logic does not lead to the conclusion that "My enemy's enemy is my friend," but psycho-logic does (McGuire, 1969). Also, consistency theories have room for such "illogical" ways of maintaining consistency as **denial** of the truth of new information which conflicts with a person's present viewpoints, or searching for supportive data to **bolster** present attitudes when they have been challenged by new information (Abelson, 1959).

The original idea of consistency theory is usually credited to Fritz Heider's (1946) short paper, which he followed with a major book twelve years later (Heider, 1958). In the meantime, Festinger (1957) had launched dissonance theory, which is a form of consistency theory, but which is sufficiently different so that we will discuss it separately in the following section. Soon many other variants of consistency notions arose, so that just as with learning theory, there sometimes seem to be as many different consistency theories as there are consistency theorists. The major ones which we will discuss in this section are Heider's balance theory, theories involving consistency between affective and cognitive elements, and Osgood and Tannenbaum's (1955) congruity theory. More detailed information on these and other consistency theories can be found in books by Insko (1967) and Kiesler, Collins, and Miller (1969).

Heider's Balance Theory

Heider's theory concerns the way in which people perceive other people, objects, and ideas in their environment. For simplicity, he limits his discussion to three elements: the perceiver, P; another person, O; and some object or idea, X. Between each pair of elements there can be two types of relationships: a liking

Photograph courtesy of Fritz Heider.
Reprinted by permission.

Box 9-1 FRITZ HEIDER, *Father of Consistency Theory*

Fritz Heider's career has been greatly influenced by the school of Gestalt psychology. Born in Vienna, Austria in 1896, he took a Ph.D. in psychology at the University of Graz in 1920. Later he attended lectures by Lewin, Köhler, and Wertheimer at the University of Berlin, translated one of Lewin's books, and wrote about Gestalt theory and Lewinian theory. After three years of teaching at the University of Hamburg, he came to America in 1930 to do research and teach with Koffka at Smith College. He remained there, doing much of his research on problems of deafness, until moving to the University of Kansas in 1947.

Heider is famous for his development of consistency theory. His major work, The Psychology of Interpersonal Relations *(1958), has much in common with Lewin's field theory, and the following year he was honored with the Lewin Memorial Award by the Society for the Psychological Study of Social Issues. Among his other honors is the American Psychological Association's Distinguished Scientific Contribution Award for his work on social perception. Retired in 1967, he lives in Lawrence, Kansas.*

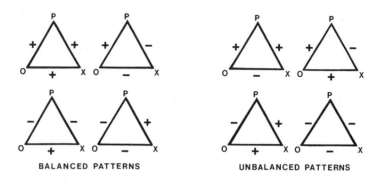

BALANCED PATTERNS   UNBALANCED PATTERNS

Figure 9-1 Balanced and unbalanced patterns according to Heider's theory. The lines between elements represent either liking or unit relationships. Positive relationships are shown by +; negative relationships are designated by −.

relationship, L (either positive or negative); or a unit relationship, U (also either positive or negative). The liking relationship is self-explanatory; the unit relationship refers to elements that are perceived as belonging together, for instance, due to ownership of one by the other, or similarity, or membership in the same group, etc.

With three elements in a system and either a positive or a negative relationship between each pair of elements, there are eight possible patterns. These eight patterns are shown in Figure 9-1. The characteristics of the relationships determine whether the pattern is balanced or unbalanced. A **balanced** state is one in which the relationships are in harmony so that there is no cognitive stress in the perceiver's view of the system, and consequently the system is stable and resists change. Conversely, an **unbalanced** system is unstable because it produces psychological tension in the perceiver which pushes toward change in the perceived relationships. Specifically, triadic systems are balanced when they have an odd number of positive relationships (either 3 or 1); otherwise they are unbalanced. As shown in Figure 9-1, the system is balanced if all three relationships are positive (P likes O, P likes X, O likes X) or if only one is positive (e.g., P likes O, P dislikes X, O dislikes X). However, when two relationships are positive and one negative (e.g., P likes O, P likes X, O dislikes X), the situation is cognitively uncomfortable and presses toward change. The definition of balance is less clear when all three relationships are negative (P dislikes O, P dislikes X, O dislikes X), but Heider states that this situation is unstable, so it is usually also considered as unbalanced.

Heider also discusses *dyadic* situations involving either two people or one person and one object. He states that balance exists if both the liking and the unit relationship have the same sign (e.g., P owns X, and P likes X). Also, with two people, balance requires that liking or disliking be reciprocated (that is, P likes O and O likes P is balanced; P likes O and O dislikes P is unbalanced). Again, unbalanced states "induce" or press for a change toward balance.

Heider's theory has been very influential in stimulating other cognitive consistency approaches. Its greatest limitation is its rather extreme degree of simplicity. It has no provision for degrees of liking or for degrees of balance. Systems with more than three elements are not considered. In the *triadic* system, only unidirectional relationships are discussed (e.g., from P to O, but not from O to P) and the possibility of having both liking and unit relationships between a single pair of elements is not considered. Also there is no specification of *which* changes will be made in order to restore balance in any given situation.

Some other theorists have modified Heider's basic formulation. Most notably, Cartwright and Harary (1956) applied mathematical graph theory to problems of cognitive balance and made many valuable revisions in Heider's theory. In particular, they extended it to any number of elements, allowed nonreciprocated relationships and different types of relationships simultaneously, and presented a way to determine degrees of balance. Feather (1967) used some of the same improvements suggested by Cartwright and Harary, and applied his more precise theory specifically to persuasive communication and resulting attitude change.

Despite the influential impact of Heider's thinking, his theory has not generated much research. In part this has been due to its roughness and lack of precision, the same factors that stimulated revisions and extensions of the theory. The most common form of research in this area has been to obtain ratings or other indications of the pleasantness or unpleasantness of hypothetical situations to test the theory's underlying postulate that balanced situations are more pleasant than unbalanced ones. What research has been done has not been consistently supportive, and it has suggested a number of needed revisions in the theory (e.g., Morrissette, 1958; Price, Harburg, & Newcomb, 1966). Perhaps most important, evidence has shown that people also have tendencies to prefer (a) positive, friendly personal relationships and (b) agreement of opinions rather than disagreement; and either of these two tendencies can often override the tendency to prefer balanced cognitive structures (Zajonc, 1968b; Sears & Whitney, 1973). That is, contrary to balance theory, people often disagree with their friends or like their opponents.

Affective-Cognitive Consistency Theories

Another kind of revision to Heider's theory has been proposed by Rosenberg and Abelson (1960; Rosenberg, 1960). We present this approach primarily because of its emphasis on consistency in the relationship of cognitive and affective elements (in other words, between beliefs and attitudes). In addition to this emphasis, the authors' several articles have presented a number of different improvements on the Heiderian balance theory model. For instance, they suggested that attitudes are influenced not only by the tendency toward balance, but also by a hedonic tendency to maximize one's gains and minimize one's costs. Perhaps most important, they gave a clear-cut classification of different ways of resolving imbalance and predicted the order in which these methods would be used. Their general principle is that the easiest ways of restoring balance will be tried first and used most frequently, and they presented experimental evidence supporting this principle (Rosenberg & Abelson, 1960).

In addition to these refinements of Heider's system, Rosenberg (1960) has emphasized the importance of consistency between the cognitive and the affective components of an attitude. Whenever these two components are not consistent, Rosenberg postulates, a homeostatic process will operate to bring them back into equilibrium. Several experiments have shown that a change in either the cognitive or affective component can produce a change in the other component. For instance, Carlson (1956) demonstrated that a change in cognitive elements could produce a change in affect toward racially desegregated housing, and a clever study by Rosenberg (1960) used hypnotic suggestion to show that a change in affect toward U.S. foreign economic aid could produce changes in beliefs about the importance and usefulness of such aid. Both of these experiments have been discussed in Chapter 3.

Though Rosenberg and Abelson's use of hypnotic suggestion in experimental research, and also their use of role-playing situations, raise methodological problems of their own, they should receive credit for creativity and persistence in suggesting improved approaches to consistency theory. Unfortunately, their revised theories have not stimulated much research except their own, so their validity and breadth of applicability are still largely untested.

Osgood and Tannenbaum's Congruity Theory

Among consistency theories, Osgood and Tannenbaum (1955) have been unique in the degree of quantification of their approach. They have measured attitudes by means of the evaluative dimension of the semantic differential (see Chapter 2), and they have made precise predictions about the direction and amount of attitude change. However, in compensation for its increased precision, the theory has a narrower scope than most other approaches. It deals solely with the results of communications in which a source (S) makes an evaluative assertion about some attitude object (O), and its predictions are based on the **congruity** of an individual's evaluation of the source, the object, and the message (M).

An example will help to clarify the details of this approach. Let us suppose that the U.S. President (S) said something favorable about Fidel Castro (O). The attitude toward each of these men which is held by a particular individual must have been previously measured, normally on a scale from +3 to −3. If the person's prior attitude toward the source is different from his attitude toward the object, the theory makes several predictions:

1. The person's attitudes toward both the source and the object will change (rather than only the attitude toward the object, as many theories would expect).
2. The amount of change in each attitude will be inversely related to the polarization (extremity) of the attitude. In other words, the more extreme attitude will change less than the milder attitude.
3. If S said something good about O, the person's final attitudes toward both S and O will be the same.
4. If S said something bad about O, the person's final attitudes toward S and O will be equidistant from zero (one positive and one negative).

In our example, if the person's prior attitude toward the President was $+1$ and toward Castro was -2, the final equilibrium point would be -1, with the rating of the President decreasing two points and the rating of Castro increasing one point. The same result would occur if Castro had said something good about the President. However, if one said something bad about the other, then their ratings would end up on opposite sides of zero, the President at $+1\frac{2}{3}$ and Castro at $-1\frac{2}{3}$. (The fact that, in the latter case, both ratings would increase following an unfavorable assertion is one of the most paradoxical consequences of the theory.)

Osgood's theory indicates that this amount of attitude change will occur as the result of a single communication, though it would not be expected to happen instantaneously. However, the theory also has some escape hatches. One is the *correction for incredulity*, which becomes necessary when a communication tries to bridge too large a discrepancy in attitudes (e.g., "U.S. President praises world Communist conspiracy," or "the Pope condemns official Catholic doctrine"). In such instances, an incredulous recipient of the message will just reject it as false. Another correction is the *assertion constant*, which is necessary because attitudes toward the object of a message have been found to change somewhat more than attitudes toward the source (about $\frac{1}{6}$ of a point more, according to the findings of Tannenbaum, 1953). Further details about the theory and formulas for computing the attitude change may be found in Insko (1967) or Kiesler et al. (1969).

How adequate is the theory? On one hand, with the corrections mentioned above, Tannenbaum (1953) found a correlation of $+.91$ between the predicted and observed attitude change in response to specially made-up newspaper stories—nearly perfect prediction. On the other hand, the extensive research literature on "prestige suggestion" has demonstrated many other factors, in addition to the prestige of the source, which can affect the amount of attitude change. For example, Rokeach and Rothman (1965) showed that considering the importance of S and O to the message recipient could markedly improve the predictions of attitude change. Similarly, Kerrick (1958) showed that the theory predicted better when the prestigeful source was relevant to the topic of the message than when the source wasn't relevant (e.g., a professional football star commenting on American foreign policy). The artificial simplicity of the theory in not allowing for degrees of positiveness or negativeness in the message is another major limitation.

In spite of these limitations, congruity theory seems to have performed quite well in its narrow goal of predicting attitude change in response to a persuasive communication (Tannenbaum, 1967).

Research on Consistency Principles

According to consistency principles, one's degree of liking for a person who is the source of a persuasive message should be positively related to the amount of one's resulting attitude change. In general, many studies have provided support for the theory by reporting such findings (e.g., Abelson & Miller, 1967). However, a number of exceptions have also been found which fit better into other theoretical frameworks.

Liking for the Source. One exception which follows an adaptation-level type of pattern is the "praise from a stranger" phenomenon. Praise from a stranger has more effect than praise from a family member or friend, probably because it is more novel and unexpected. Following the same principle, criticism has more impact when it comes from a friend than from a stranger (Harvey, 1962). Aronson and Linder (1965) have suggested a gain-loss miniature theory of interpersonal attraction, specifying that an *increase* in praise from another person will

Figure 9-2 Normally, source attractiveness and amount of attitude change are positively related.

produce greater liking for that person than will continuing high levels of praise, while a decrease in praise will lead to much lower liking.

Another exception to the normal relationship between liking and persuasiveness is the case of a disagreeable communicator delivering an unpopular message—a situation which follows dissonance-theory predictions (see next section). More acceptance of unpopular messages may be produced by a disliked source than by an attractive one (presumably because liking for the source cannot be used as a reason for listening and therefore dissonance is reduced by increasing the acceptance of the message). For example, Army reservists were persuaded to eat fried grasshoppers—definitely a counterattitudinal behavior—by an officer who behaved in an unpleasant, officious manner or a pleasant, friendly manner. Though equal numbers of men ate the disliked food in the two conditions, the men who did so for the unpleasant communicator showed more increase in liking for the grasshoppers than those who ate them for the pleasant communicator (Zimbardo, Weisenberg, Firestone, & Levy, 1965).

Similarity of the Source. Just as with liking, source-audience similarity does not always produce attitude change. Here we must distinguish between similarities which are relevant or irrelevant to the topic of the message. Relevant *attitudinal* similarities generally produce positive effects on attitude change, relevant dissimilarities produce negative effects, and irrelevant similarities have little or no effect. However, the effect of relevant *group-membership* similarities is determined by the relative status of the source and the audience. For instance, if the source is expert on the topic and the audience is not (e.g., T. S. Eliot giving his opinion on the merits of a poem), this *dis*similarity will produce more attitude change than a similar but nonexpert source (Simons et al., 1970).

Evaluation of Consistency Theories

The profusion of consistency approaches and their individual incompleteness have already been mentioned. Osgood and Tannenbaum's congruity theory is the most detailed and explicit in its predictions (and also one of the narrowest in its applications). Though it has had relatively good success in some experimental research, the *ad hoc* corrections which it requires and the many factors which it does not consider demonstrate its limitations and cast some doubt on the value of its quantifications. The many other consistency approaches, though less precise in their predictions, have generally had less empirical support when put to experimental tests, though they have been fruitful in suggesting many new and interesting areas of research. McGuire (1969, p. 270) concludes that consistency theories have been heuristically provocative but not distinguished for their empirical validity.

Whatever the value of consistency theories, it can reasonably be suggested that man does not live by consistency alone. Probably psychologists and other highly educated people are much more concerned with maintaining consistency in their thoughts, feelings, and actions than are the great majority of humankind. Bem (1970) has stated this viewpoint vividly:

> Inconsistency is probably our most enduring cognitive commonplace. . . . I suspect that for most of the people most of the time and for all the people some of the time inconsistency just sits there (p. 34).

In corroboration of this viewpoint, we have seen in Chapter 5 that most citizens tolerate a great deal of inconsistency in their political attitudes and opinions.

A theoretical viewpoint which helps to explain this widespread inconsistency has been suggested by Abelson (1968). He proposes that much of our knowledge and attitudees exist in isolated "opinion molecules," each of which contains one or a few facts, feelings, and sources of support. These opinion molecules serve us well in social conversation by giving us something to say on many topics (for instance, the sale of American wheat to Russia, or the dangers of nuclear energy). However, when not brought out for such use, they are generally kept in "logic-tight compartments" where we do not need to think about them in relation to other topics which might contain contradictory facts or feelings. Thus, most of us probably tolerate a great deal of inconsistency among our attitudes and beliefs all the time, and yet we are hardly ever even aware of it.

DISSONANCE THEORY

Our next major topic, cognitive dissonance theory, is a type of consistency theory. However, it has some unique aspects, and it has received so much attention and stimulated so much research that it deserves separate treatment. Conceived by Leon Festinger (1957), it has been modified by Brehm and Cohen (1962), Festinger (1964), and Aronson (1968), and studied experimentally by a whole generation of social psychologists. Without doubt, dissonance theory has aroused more controversy and received more praise and criticism than any other current theory in social psychology.

Nature of Dissonance Theory

The theory deals with the relations between "cognitive elements." These elements are items of knowledge, information, attitude, or belief that a person holds about himself or about his surroundings. Two elements can either be **consonant** with each other (that is, compatible or consistent), or dissonant, or irrelevant. The definition of a **dissonant** relationship is that *the opposite of one element would follow from the other element*—that is, x and y are dissonant if non-y follows from x. What "follows from" a cognitive element is determined

Photograph courtesy of Leon Festinger.
Reprinted by permission.

Box 9-2 LEON FESTINGER, *Eminent Theorist and Experimentalist*

Leon Festinger is probably the most famous of Kurt Lewin's many renowned students. Born in New York in 1919, he studied at CCNY and took his M.A. and Ph.D. with Lewin at Iowa. He taught briefly at the University of Rochester before rejoining Lewin at M.I.T. Following Lewin's death, he moved with the Research Center for Group Dynamics to the University of Michigan. At the age of 32 he became a full professor at Minnesota, subsequently moving to Stanford in 1955, and back to New York at the New School for Social Research in 1968.

Festinger's famous theoretical contributions include articles on social communication and social comparison processes, and his 1957 book, A Theory of Cognitive Dissonance, *which stimulated a prolific outpouring of research on attitude change. His fame as a clever experimentalist and a role model for productive students is also widespread. In addition to theoretical and experimental writings, his work includes field and observational research and statistical contributions. He has been elected to the National Academy of Sciences and received the American Psychological Association's Distinguished Scientific Contribution Award in 1959. In the early 1960s, he left social psychology and concentrated his research on the area of perception.*

by the person's expectations; thus dissonance can be the result of logical inconsistency, of the person's past experience concerning what things go together, or of cultural norms and values. The basic principles of the theory are that:

1. Dissonance, being psychologically uncomfortable, will motivate the person to try to reduce the dissonance and achieve consonance . . . [and to] avoid situations and information which would likely increase the dissonance.
2. The magnitude of the dissonance (or consonance) increases as the importance or value of the elements increases.
3. The strength of the pressure to reduce dissonance is a function of the magnitude of the dissonance (Festinger, 1957, pp. 3 & 18).

To use one of Festinger's examples, the cognition "I know I smoke" is consonant with the cognition "I know I enjoy smoking" but dissonant with "I believe smoking is bad for my health.'' (It would also be irrelevant to many other cognitions, such as ''I know that I live in the United States.'') Faced with such a dissonant situation, if the elements are important to him, the person will try to reduce the dissonance in one or more of the following ways: (1) He may change a cognition about his behavior, for instance by giving up smoking, or by deciding ''I only smoke a little.'' (2) He may change a cognition about the environment, for instance by deciding that smoking is not harmful, or that only heavy smoking is harmful. (3) He may add new cognitions to bolster one or the other of the dissonant elements: for instance, ''I know most of my friends smoke,'' or ''I believe the evidence linking smoking and cancer isn't conclusive,'' or ''I know the dangers from smoking are no greater than the dangers from driving a car,'' etc. (4) Since the amount of dissonance depends on the importance of the cognitions, he may reduce dissonance by deciding that one or more cognitions are less important, e.g., ''It really isn't very important that smoking is bad for my health. I'm going to live fast and die young.'' Though it is not always possible to reduce dissonance successfully, if the amount of dissonance is great enough, one or more cognitive elements will be changed. Moreover, cognitions are generally responsive to reality, so it is hard to change a cognition about one's behavior without also changing the behavior.

Areas of Application of the Theory

That is the basic skeleton of the theory, but it does not do justice to the richness of its applications. As Zajonc (1968b) has pointed out, the theory is basically an open one which can be applied to many different situations (in contrast, for instance, to congruity theory which only concerns communications in which a source makes an evaluative assertion about an object). Dissonance theory is stated in broad conceptual terms and does not make specific predictions about particular situations until additional assumptions are stated. For instance, in any situation it is necessary to specify the dissonant cognitions which are present and the feasible and infeasible ways of reducing the dissonance. When such additional assumptions are specified, the theory can be applied to countless situations, including many beyond the realm of attitude change research. It has even been applied to an understanding of partial reinforcement effects in rats as well as in human beings, and to participant observation studies of religious cultists!

In spite of the fact that it is a cognitive theory, dissonance theory has focused many hypotheses and experiments on people's overt behavior. It has been innovative in emphasizing that attitude change often *results from* a person's behavior rather than causing the behavior. In his original statement of the theory, Festinger suggested four major areas of its application. We will review each of those areas and very briefly summarize the relevant recent evidence on them.

The Consequences of Decisions.   The theory posits that dissonance is aroused by making a decision between two or more alternative objects or courses of action. The resulting dissonance is greater when: (a) the decision is an important one, (b) the unchosen alternative(s) is(are) nearly as attractive as the chosen one, and (c) there is low similarity between the various alternatives (e.g., choosing between going to an enjoyable sports event or reading an enjoyable book would create more dissonance than choosing which of two enjoyable books to read). Ways of reducing postdecision dissonance are decreasing the subjective attractiveness of the unchosen alternative, increasing the subjective attractiveness of the chosen alternative, or, occasionally, increasing the similarity of the alternatives in other ways (e.g., deciding that both sports events and reading are forms of recreation). In this area of postdecision dissonance, the experimental findings have generally supported the theory (e.g., Festinger, 1964) though there have been some contrary reports (e.g., Harris, 1969). An intriguing real-world study done at a race track showed that bettors' confidence in their chosen horse increased markedly immediately after they placed their bet—clear-cut support for the theory (Knox & Inkster, 1968).

In the course of these studies revisions were made to the theory, stressing the importance of **commitment** and **volition (choice)** as necessary conditions for dissonance arousal to occur (Brehm & Cohen, 1962). If people do not feel committed to (bound by) their decisions, there is no reason for them to experience dissonance, and the research findings show no evidence of dissonance reduction (Kiesler, 1968). Similarly, if they feel that they had little or no choice in their actions, then their dissonance is apt to be minimal (e.g., Linder, Cooper, & Jones, 1967), though evidence indicates that choice is not always necessary for the arousal of dissonance (Insko, 1967, pp. 269–270).

Voluntary and Involuntary Exposure to Information. Dissonance theory holds, in general, that dissonance-reducing information will be sought out and dissonance-increasing information will be avoided. However, it is often difficult or impossible to avoid contact with information which is being spread by the mass media or by one's acquaintances. If such new information were opposite to cognitions which one already held, then dissonance would result, and efforts would be made to reduce that dissonance. That might be accomplished by defensive misperception or misunderstanding, discrediting the information or its source, seeking other consonant information, or by changing one's attitude. There are studies which provide evidence for each of these processes occurring under some conditions. However, in general, dissonance theory has not been well supported in this area (Zajonc, 1968b; Kiesler et al., 1969). As we discussed in Chapter 7, there is little evidence for motivated selective exposure to information, which is a commonly mentioned dissonance-reducing mechanism.

Dissonance and Social Support. Disagreement with other people is another source of dissonance, and agreement with people can reduce dissonance. The theory posits that dissonance will be high if a disagreement is (a) extensive; on a topic which is (b) important and (c) difficult to verify through observation; and if the disagreeing persons are (d) many, (e) attractive, and/or (f) credible. In such situations dissonance can be reduced either by changing one's own opinion, or persuading the disagreeing person(s) to change their opinions, or by discrediting or derogating the other person(s). Alternatively, one may seek out others who agree with one's views, or try to obtain social support by communicating with and persuading others who are currently uninvolved in the issue. Festinger (1957) gave several examples of such group social support phenomena, including mild denial of reality ("it isn't really going to rain on our picnic"), spread of rumors, and mass proselyting for causes. The book *When Prophecy Fails* (Festinger, Riecken, & Schachter, 1956) illustrates how dissonance theory can explain the initiation of proselyting by a formerly secretive religious cult. However, Hardyck and Braden (1962) studied a somewhat similar group and pointed out additional conditions which were necessary in order for proselyting to occur. Because of the difficulties of such field studies (Thompson & Oskamp, 1974), and also because of the many ways in which dissonance can be resolved in social situations, there is little clear-cut evidence for or against this part of dissonance theory.

Effects of Forced Compliance. This area of research is the most controversial one and, in recent years, by far the most active one spawned by dissonance theory. It is also misleadingly named for, as the above comments concerning volition indicate, it is important for the creation of dissonance that subjects not feel "forced" to comply. A better name for this research area would be **counterattitudinal behavior**. The typical research procedure is to induce subjects to do or say something contrary to their opinions, using two or more levels of inducement for different subjects. The experimental prediction is that maximum dissonance (and dissonance reduction) will be created by the *minimum* successful inducement, whereas larger inducements will create less dissonance because their very size offers a reason for having performed the behavior. In the famous Festinger and Carlsmith (1959) study, subjects were paid either $1 or $20 to act briefly as assistants to the experimenter (and to be available for similar future assistance) by falsely telling another subject that a very dull experiment had been enjoyable and interesting. As predicted, the $1 group of subjects subsequently resolved their dissonance by changing their actual attitude toward the experiment to a more favorable level than did the $20 group. This is an effect of perceived amount of choice ("If I said that for only $1, I must really believe it" vs. "I said it because I was paid so much").

The controversy over this area of research is not primarily concerning the effects of perceived choice, but rather it stems from the role-playing task which the subject typically has to perform (Kiesler et al., 1969). One group of theorists has proposed and done experiments to show that the size of *incentive* for role-playing is positively related to the amount of attitude change—directly opposite to the dissonance prediction (e.g., Elms, 1967). However, it was soon pointed out that the occasional findings which supported incentive theory did not thereby disprove dissonance theory, and attention shifted to a search for *conditions* under which one or the other theory was upheld. Carlsmith, Collins, and Helmreich (1966) offered one resolution by showing a dissonance effect in interpersonal role-playing but an incentive effect in counterattitudinal essay-writing. However, Linder, Cooper, and Jones (1967) showed that even essay-writing could produce a dissonance effect under high-choice conditions. Freedman (1963) has supported dissonance theory in showing greater enjoyment of boring tasks when there was relatively little justification given for complying. However, Collins (1969) has failed to find dissonance effects in most of a long series of forced-compliance experiments.

Research findings in the forced-compliance area are still very confusing and complex, but there does seem to be some recent convergence of findings on the following conclusions. Dissonance effects are very likely to occur when counterattitudinal behavior is performed under conditions of (a) low incentive, (b) high perceived choice, with (c) unpleasant consequences of the behavior (for someone), and (d) awareness by the actor of personal responsibility for the consequences (Collins & Hoyt, 1972; Kiesler & Munson, 1975). A major recent reappraisal of the forced-compliance literature from a nondissonance perspective also seems to be quite consistent with these conclusions (Nuttin, 1975).

Bem's Critique of Dissonance Theory

Bem (1967) has suggested a different approach to the forced compliance area and to the post-decision attitude change area, based on his theory of self-perception. As we mentioned in Chapter 8, his theory postulates that one learns about one's own attitudes through **self-observation**. Thus, in the experimental situation with large vs. small rewards for counterattitudinal performance, Bem does not question the basic experimental predictions from dissonance theory, but rather gives a different theoretical explanation for them. He posits that subjects will observe the fact that they have said something unusual for them, and the size of the inducement, and interpret their true attitude in light of the size of reward (e.g., "I only said it because I was paid a lot; I don't really believe it").

Bem's method for studying his theory was to perform an "interpersonal replication," in which observer-subjects were simply told about the procedures experienced by a subject in one of the classic dissonance studies (e.g., Festinger & Carlsmith, 1959) and asked to estimate the original subject's true attitude. In general, these simulated replications have quite closely paralleled the results of the earlier experiments.

However, R. A. Jones et al. (1968) have pointed out that some crucial information about subjects' initial attitudes was not provided to Bem's observer-subjects; and when they did "interpersonal replications" incorporating that information, the results no longer paralleled the original experimental findings. Thus they concluded that observers and involved subjects were not always comparable and that "To explore the processes by which the attitudinal responses of involved subjects are determined it appears necessary to study involved subjects" (p. 267).

In his original theoretical statement, Bem (1967) had stated that involved participants in a behavioral episode and observers of the same episode are "isomorphic" (that is, identical) in their inference processes and conclusions about behavior. By 1970, Bem had retreated from this viewpoint and only claimed: "In identifying his own internal states, an individual *partially* relies on the same external cues that others use when they infer his internal states" (1970, p. 50, italics added). This is a much harder hypothesis to disprove—almost impossible, in fact—so the controversy has mostly been waged over Bem's earlier, more extreme formulation. Despite an occasional finding of actor-observer similarity, the research evidence is very conclusively opposed to Bem's hypothesis (E. E. Jones & Nisbett, 1971; Nisbett, Caputo, Legant, & Marecek, 1973; Storms, 1973).

Though Bem's theory of a passive process of self-perception has not been disproven by these results, it has also not been clearly supported. If passive observers can replicate experimental findings, it is quite possible that they are doing so because of their intuitive understanding of common ways of dissonance-reduction. As Zajonc (1968b, p. 375) comments: "Most subjects are also able to guess the trajectory of an apple falling from a tree, without doing serious damage to the laws of classical mechanics." Thus the two theories have not yet been successfully pitted against each other, and doing so may even be impossible.

Other Research Related to Dissonance Theory

According to dissonance-theory principles, two techniques which should have an effect on attitude change are: making a public commitment to a particular viewpoint, and active participation in stating persuasive arguments. Let us briefly examine some of the research on these topics.

Commitment. Interest in the topic of commitment goes back to the theory and research of Kurt Lewin (1947), who proposed that making a decision would "freeze" a person's beliefs and make them resistant to future counterpressures. Bennett (1955) confirmed that both private and public decisions had that effect, though most studies have found public commitment more effective (e.g. Hovland, Mandell, et al., 1957).

More complex effects of commitment have been studied by Kiesler (1971) and his colleagues, usually in situations involving commitment to consonant positions, but allowing subjects no choice about the commitment. Their results often parallel dissonance research findings for commitment to counterattitudinal positions. For instance, defense of one's beliefs for a small reward produces more resistance to later attacks than does defense of one's beliefs for a large reward.

When individuals have made a public commitment, they tend to become more extreme in their position and to avoid thinking about the implications of their behavior. Commitment also makes people more responsive to extreme but reputable messages which agree with them and more inclined to act on their beliefs if they are disputed (Kiesler & Munson, 1975).

Active Participation. Early studies by the Hovland group showed that active participation in improvising persuasive arguments produced more attitude change than did passive listening to the same arguments (King & Janis, 1956). Also, active participation produces longer-lasting attitude change (Watts, 1967).

An extension of this method is the technique of **role-playing**—that is, acting out the feelings and behavior that another person might display in a particular situation. This technique was shown to be effective in reducing the prejudice of whites who played the role of an advocate of peaceful racial integration (Culbertson, 1957). Another study had smokers play the part of a lung-cancer victim who had to undergo surgery. This dramatic emotional experience was found to reduce smoking significantly, an effect which lasted for at least 18 months (Mann & Janis, 1968). Undoubtedly the emotional impact of imagining, and in a sense experiencing, consequences which could happen to oneself is a powerful factor in producing attitude change through role-playing.

But why should active participation be so effective in the less-emotional situation where a person merely improvises or states arguments for a position which (s)he disagrees with? A variety of research studies have suggested several different explanations, any or all of which may apply in a particular situation. Preparing to argue against one's own position stimulates open-minded and unbiased evaluation of controversial information. Actually stating the arguments produces more attitude change than just preparing them, perhaps because greater effort is involved. People also remember their own improvisations better and judge them more favorably than others' improvisations.

Despite all the evidence for greater attitude change stemming from active participation, there are also situations where the opposite effect is found. Primarily this is true in the area of "cultural truisms" or beliefs which are so common that people have rarely ever heard them challenged. In such situations a person may be unmotivated or unable to improvise supportive arguments, and thus passive reception of someone else's arguments may have more effect than active participation (McGuire, 1964, 1969). Notice that these situations are generally ones where individuals are arguing for their own beliefs, which may later be attacked, whereas in situations where they are arguing *against* their own beliefs, active participation generally produces more attitude change.

Evaluation of Dissonance Theory

Dissonance theory must be given credit, first of all, for being exciting and influential enough to stimulate research by hundreds of followers and opponents.

This in itself is perhaps the most important function of a theory. It is also much broader in its applications than other consistency theories. Because of its unique way of defining inconsistency, it is particularly applicable to choice behavior in conflict situations, an arena which other consistency theories do not enter. Moreover, dissonance theory is particularly intriguing for its numerous "nonobvious" hypotheses—for instance, the inverse relationship of dissonance to incentive size in the $1 vs. $20 forced compliance situation. Dissonance experimenters have also become known for their ingenious experimental procedures, some of which require a high degree of theatrical talent and stage-setting, though they also raise the problems of believability and the ethics of deception.

Dissonance theory has also been severely criticized, most notably by Chapanis and Chapanis (1964), and defended just as stoutly by others (Silverman, 1964; Aronson, 1969). Many of the criticisms revolve around dubious methodological practices such as the discarding of some subjects or the citation of marginally significant findings—what Suedfeld (1971) has termed "inviting weaknesses" in the research. These criticisms are well-taken, but there are many supportive findings to which they don't apply. Another set of criticisms proposes alternative theoretical interpretations of the experimental findings (for instance, based on subject suspiciousness, or anxiety, or degree of reinforcement, or expectation of future unpleasant consequences, etc.). One or another of these explanations may seem plausible in any given experiment, but they are almost always after the fact interpretations. Moreover, they rarely have the parsimony, and never the broad range of applicability, of the dissonance predictions. Because of these kinds of criticisms the Chapanises concluded their critique by stating that, after five years of dissonance research, they must return "a verdict of NOT PROVEN" (1964, p. 21, capitals in original). However, these critics should be aware that no theory is ever proven! Theories can be disproved by contrary data, but at most they can only be supported by confirming data, never proven in any final or ultimate sense. As Aronson replied,

> Happily, after more than 10 years, it is still not proven; all the theory ever does is generate research (1969, p. 31).

Some more crucial criticisms of the theory can be made, however. Most important is the difficulty in making clear-cut predictions from the theory for a specific situation. This difficulty arises from two facts: that the same situation may create different amounts of dissonance in two individuals who have different prior cognitions, and especially that dissonance can be reduced in many different ways and even in several ways at once. These difficulties are usually overcome in experiments by contriving a situation in which the crucial cognitions are relatively clear-cut and in which most of the ways of reducing dissonance are blocked or are unlikely, so that clearcut predictions can be made and tested. But in everyday life situations, it is usually very difficult to tell what important cognitions a person has or what ways of reducing dissonance may be most likely.

Thus specific predictions are on shaky ground except in relatively rare or artificially controlled situations. This problem could be greatly reduced if an independent, quantitative measure of the amount of a person's dissonance could be developed (Suedfeld, 1971). However, we would still have to deal with the problem of individual differences in the tolerance for dissonance (or ambiguity).

Other criticisms and strengths of dissonance theory are presented at greater length by Insko (1967), Zajonc (1968b), and Kiesler et al. (1969). Despite the great impact of the theory and its domination of social psychological research in the 1960s, interest has recently shifted sharply to other approaches—particularly to attribution theory, which we shall discuss shortly. As a result, some observers expect that in the 1970s the theory may have to "be put on the endangered species list" (Kiesler & Munson, 1975, p. 425).

PERCEPTUAL APPROACHES TO ATTITUDE CHANGE

The final group of attitude theories which we shall discuss are those stemming from the study of perception—how people perceive and interpret other people and objects in their environment. In general, **perceptual approaches** view the process of attitude change as a change in the perception of the attitude object, rather than a change in beliefs or opinions about it. We will describe two theoretical approaches: Sherif and Hovland's (1961) social judgment theory, and recently developed attribution theories. Helson's (1964) adaptation-level theory is also a perceptual approach, but we have omitted it because it has not been very successfully applied to the area of social attitudes and behavior (Insko, 1967).

Sherif and Hovland's Social Judgment Theory

We have described the structural aspects of this theory at some length in Chapter 3. To recapitulate briefly, Sherif and his coworkers have presented the concept of three attitude latitudes—the latitudes of acceptance, rejection, and noncommitment. They have also concluded that the size of a person's latitude of rejection on an attitude issue is the best indicator of his(her) ego-involvement in that issue.

The attitude-change aspects of the theory, as presented in Sherif and Hovland's (1961) major theoretical statement, emphasize the principles of *assimilation* and of *contrast*. Most of their theory derives from research in experimental psychology, specifically from the classical area of psychophysics, which studies human perception and judgment of physical stimuli like weights, colors, sounds, etc. Just as these physical stimuli can be judged on scales of heaviness, brightness, or loudness, so can social stimuli like people or political viewpoints be judged and ranked on attitude scales. For instance, political candidates can be ranked (with some disagreement between judges, of course) on a scale of liberalism-conservatism, or they could be ranked on other more specific scales concerning their stands on civil rights, military spending, welfare programs, etc. The rater's own attitude on the particular issue serves as an important **anchor**, or reference point for judgment, in making such scale rankings.

The principle of **assimilation** states that social stimuli, such as persuasive messages, which are within a person's latitude of acceptance will be assimilated. This means that they: (a) will be seen as closer to the person's own attitude than they actually are, (b) will be favorably evaluated, and (c) will produce some change in the person's attitude in the direction advocated by the message. The principle of **contrast** states that when social stimuli are within a person's latitude of rejection, contrast will result. That is: (a) they will be seen as farther from the person's own attitude than they actually are, (b) they will be unfavorably evaluated, and (c) they will produce either no attitude change or, in some cases, attitude change opposite to the direction advocated (a "boomerang effect"). The relationship of amount of attitude change to the discrepancy between the person's attitude and the position advocated by the message will be positive in the latitude of acceptance and negative in the latitude of rejection—a curvilinear relationship (Freedman, 1964; cf. Insko, 1967, p. 68). Both assimilation and contrast effects on judgment will be greater for highly ego-involved individuals than for uninvolved ones, but their effects on attitude change will be smaller for involved individuals.

The nature of assimilation and contrast effects on judgment is dramatically illustrated in Figure 9-3. This graph is based on judgments of physical stimuli, in this case six weights ranging from 55 grams to 151 grams which were judged a total of 300 times by each experimental subject. In the top panel, without an anchor weight for comparison, the judgments of heaviness are spread out quite evenly. In the middle panel, the endpoint anchor can be likened to an attitude which is close to the stimuli to be judged, and it is clear that the judgments are assimilated toward the anchor. In the bottom panel, the extreme external anchor is similar to an attitude which is far distant from the positions advocated by persuasive messages (ones which are in the latitude of rejection), and accordingly the result is a contrast effect in which the stimuli are judged to be even farther from the anchor than they actually are.

Research Related to Social Judgment Theory

The theoretical topics which have received most research attention are the discrepancy of the message from the recipient's position and the ego-involvement of the recipient. We will briefly summarize the research in these two areas.

Message Discrepancy.   When a persuasive message is quite discrepant from the recipient's own attitude, (s)he may change the attitude, or (s)he may resolve

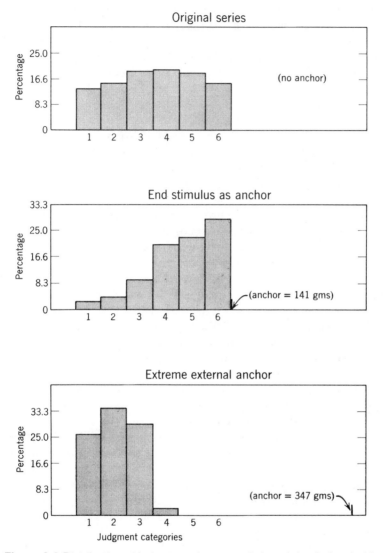

Figure 9-3 Distribution of judgments for a set of six weights judged without an anchor and with anchors at two different distances from the weights to be judged.

Source: Adopted from M. Sherif, D. Taub, and C. I. Hovland. Assimilation and contrast effects of anchoring stimuli on judgments, *Journal of Experimental Psychology,* 1958, *55*, p. 152. © 1958 by the American Psychological Association. Reprinted by permission. Figure reprinted from Kiesler, Collins, and Miller, 1969, p. 243, by permission of John Wiley and Sons, Inc.

the incongruity in one or more of several other ways: perceptual distortion of the message, derogation of the source, increased counterarguing, disparagement of the message, or under-recall of its contents. Several studies have shown the functional equivalence of these mechanisms, indicating that they may be used interchangeably as alternatives to attitude change, or they may be used in combination, depending on the situation (Johnson, 1966; Steiner, 1966; cf. McGuire, 1969; Sears & Abeles, 1969).

Two different relationships have been postulated to hold between message discrepancy and attitude change. Some researchers have predicted and found an approximately linear rising relationship (e.g., Zimbardo, 1960; Eagly, 1967). However, the more frequent finding is the inverted U-curve predicted by social judgment theory (e.g., Hovland, Harvey, & Sherif, 1957; Peterson & Koulack, 1969). Since the peak of the curve usually occurs at a high discrepancy level, the studies that obtained roughly linear findings may not have used messages which were extreme enough to produce a downturn in influence. With either linear or curvilinear findings, the amount of attitude change obtained is apt to be markedly less than the amount advocated by the message.

An interaction between message discrepancy and source credibility has often been found, as predicted by social judgment theory and consistency theories (e.g., Bochner & Insko, 1966). The rationale behind this interaction is that source derogation is less likely with a highly credible source, and therefore attitude change continues to increase up to higher levels of message discrepancy than it does with a less credible source who can be more easily disparaged.

The other interaction predicted by social judgment theory, between message discrepancy and ego-involvement, has had less clear-cut empirical support. The prediction is that with high ego-involvement in the issue, the peak of the attitude-change curve will occur at a lower discrepancy level (just as it does for a less-credible source). Some studies have found this effect (e.g., Freedman, 1964; Rhine & Severance, 1970); but many have failed to find it (Zimbardo, 1960; Rule & Renner, 1968).

Inconsistent findings such as these have been analyzed in detail by Fishbein and Ajzen (1975, pp. 474–488). They point out the great need in attitude change studies for more careful attention to the particular beliefs which are chosen as the dependent variables and to the many alternative processes by which these beliefs may be changed. For example, Eagly (1974) was unable to replicate Bochner and Insko's (1966) results, though using rather similar messages and procedures. However, neither study's dependent variable measure was exactly identical to the belief advocated in its persuasive message, and this difference may have been crucial to the obtained results.

Ego-Involvement.   As indicated in the preceding paragraphs, research on ego-involvement has had rather mixed results. Though some relationships to attitude change have been found, the specific details of Sherif's theory have not been well-supported, and many of the research results seem contradictory.

Zimbardo (1960) attempted to clarify this situation by distinguishing between *issue* involvement (interest and concern about the issue) and *response* involvement (concern about making a desirable response—appearing well-adjusted, acceptable to the experimenter, etc.). Zimbardo's results showed that high response involvement produced more attitude change. This finding is opposite to Sherif's theory, but it appears that the theory really concerns issue involvement rather than response involvement. Kiesler et al. (1969) have extended Zimbardo's distinction, concluding that people who are involved in their initial opinion will show less attitude change (Freedman, 1964; Miller, 1965). By contrast, when people's concern is raised about the importance of a new position that they might take, they will display more attitude change (King & Janis, 1956; Zimbardo, 1960; Miller & Levy, 1967). This resolution seems to make sense out of most of the apparently conflicting results.

Further research has indicated that when attitude change is decreased by the presence of issue involvement, the defense mechanism which is most likely to be used is message disparagement rather than derogation of the source (Eagly & Manis, 1966). Other recent research has helped to clarify additional effects of ego-involvement (Sherif, Kelly, Rodgers, Sarup, & Tittler, 1973).

The topic of ego-involvement is rather closely related to the concept of commitment, which we have discussed above in the section on dissonance theory (Rhine & Polowniak, 1971). Persons who are high in issue involvement are also high in commitment to their opinion on the issue (except for the small group of involved but undecided individuals). However, persons who are not ego-involved in an issue can become committed to a position on the issue either by making a private decision or by taking a public stand or some other relevant action.

Evaluation of Social Judgment Theory

Appraising this theory fairly is not easy. On one hand, it has stimulated quite a bit of research, though many studies were aimed at resolving controversies between it and dissonance theory. Also, much of the social judgment research has dealt with important real-world issues in a field setting (e.g., a referendum on prohibition in Oklahoma, and voter attitudes in a presidential election). On the other hand, the theory as it concerns attitude change is quite narrow in scope, dealing only with the variables of the person's ego-involvement and the message's discrepancy from the person's attitude. Also, the theory has been empirically derived from the results of experiments, so it has some gaps and inconsistencies and less logical coherence than would be desirable.

Partly because of these limitations of the theory, opinions differ as to how well research findings have supported it (Insko, 1967; Kiesler et al., 1969). Studies have shown that judges' own attitudes influence their judgments about the extremity of attitude items, but they have not supported many of the theory's more specific predictions (Zavalloni & Cook, 1965; Eiser & Stroebe, 1972). In predicting attitude change, the theory has been reasonably successful despite some negative evidence. However, dissonance theory has been equally or more successful, has much broader applicability, and takes into account additional variables like amount of incentive and degree of perceived choice. The relation found between attitude change and message discrepancy has most often been the curvilinear one predicted by social judgment theory, but there are many exceptions in the literature. In the area of ego-involvement the theory is somewhat confusing in predicting opposite effects of involvement on judgment and on attitude change, and predictions about involvement have suffered a number of set-backs in research studies. In applied research, Varela (1971) has claimed good success in using Sherif's notion of the latitude of acceptance to create a script by which salesmen could persuade resistant customers to buy more lavishly.

All in all, despite social judgment theory's intriguing aspects and the research that it has generated, it has not yet established a claim to a leading place in the attitude change area.

Attribution Theories

The final approach to attitude change which we shall discuss, attribution theory, has enjoyed a great wave of popularity in the 1970s, replacing dissonance theory as the most frequently cited approach in the social psychological research literature (Kiesler & Munson, 1975). Actually, there is not just one attribution theory but several parallel and partly overlapping approaches. In origin, they all stem from Heider's (1944) early paper on phenomenal causality, that is, on how people make inferences or attributions about the causes of events. Later Heider (1958) expanded his attribution principles in his book on interpersonal perception. He was interested primarily in the conditions under which attributions about the stable dispositions of people (e.g., their friendliness, honesty, likes and dislikes, etc.) would be made, based upon information about their actions. This is a question which we all try to answer for ourselves many times every day (e.g., ''I wonder why (s)he smiled at me''), so it has great practical as well as scientific interest. Depending upon the situation, attribution processes may result in attitude formation, attitude change, or support for one's existing attitudes.

Heider (1958) distinguished between internal attribution and external attribution. **Internal attribution** concludes that the cause of an individual's actions is a personal disposition—for example, ''she smiled because she is friendly.'' **External attribution** concludes that the cause of a person's actions is a factor outside the person—e.g., ''He succeeded because of good luck, or because the task was easy.'' Thus we may attribute the cause of a person's actions to his(her) own characteristics, to environmental factors, or to a combination of both. How do we arrive at this conclusion in any given instance? Heider says that we consider three factors: the person's ability, intention, and exertion. We evaluate ability in relation to the difficulty of the task, and we evaluate exertion by observation of the person's apparent effort. Intention is the hardest factor to evaluate because many actions have both intended and unintended consequences; therefore, it is difficult to determine the person's intentions from observing the consequences of his(her) actions. Nevertheless, Heider concluded that only when we perceive the person as intending the action's consequences do we infer **personal causality** and make internal attributions about the person's dispositions or traits.

Heider's discussion of attribution principles has been extended in many directions by several groups of researchers, of whom the most influential have been Jones and Davis (1965) and Kelley (1967). Bem's (1967) analysis of self-perception processes also should be included among attributional approaches, even though we have discussed it in the section on learning approaches in Chapter 8. Another major contribution to attribution theory was the volume by Jones, Kanouse, Kelley, Nisbett, Valins, and Weiner (1971). Due to space limitations, we will confine ourself here to brief presentations of the approaches of Jones and Davis and of Kelley.

Jones and Davis (1965) focus on the process of making inferences about personal causality. They propose that people first observe another person's actions and the effects of those actions, then use that information to infer the person's intentions, and finally make attributions about the person's traits or dispositions on the basis of their inferred intentions. They suggest four factors which will determine the strength and confidence of the resulting attributions: social desirability, common effects, hedonic relevance, and personalism. These variables have been described as follows (Oskamp, 1972c, p. 454):

1. The *social desirability* of the person's actions decreases the strength of attributions. We assume that the person intended the desirable effects of his actions rather than any undesirable ones. Since most people act in socially desirable ways most of the time, such behavior gives us little information about their real characteristics.
2. The *common effects* of two actions provide a basis for attributions about the actor's traits. For instance, the girl who acts warm and responsive toward her companion on an expensive dinner-and-theater evening *and* on a simple Coke date is seen as genuinely friendly rather than as a gold digger. The other side of this coin is that *noncommon effects* between a chosen action and a nonchosen one provide a basis for attributions. The boy who asks a girl only to a Coke date, when it is known that he has two tickets to the latest hit play and could have asked her to it, will probably be seen as not seriously interested in her.
3. The *hedonic relevance* of the person's actions (that is, the extent to which they are rewarding or costly to the perceiver) increases the strength of attributions. If your actions hurt me or help me materially, I am more likely to conclude that you are a harmful or helpful person than if your actions affected someone else rather than me.

4. The *personalism* of the other's actions (that is, the extent to which they are seen as being directed specifically at the perceiver) increases the strength of attributions. This principle represents a further extension of the hedonic relevance principle. If your actions hurt me and I perceive that they are directed specifically at me, I am even more likely to conclude that you are a hurtful person.

Kelley's (1967) contribution to attribution theory is complementary to Jones and Davis' approach. While Jones and Davis concentrate on internal attributions about personal causality, Kelley focuses largely on external attributions about impersonal environmental causes. For instance, if your friend Joe tells you he enjoyed a particular movie, this effect may be due to the movie's excellence (an external attribution) or to Joe's poor taste regarding movies (an internal attribution). Kelley suggests that an external attribution that the movie was a good one would be strengthened by three types of evidence: that Joe's response to the movie in question was *distinctive* rather than similar to his response to most movies; that Joe's response to the movie was *consistent* when he saw it at other times and under other conditions (e.g., with or without his girlfriend); and that Joe's response resembled the *consensus* of other observers.

Kelley has also applied these criteria of the validity of external attribution to an understanding of social influence effects. His basic point is that when a person's attributions about his(her) environment are stable and confident, (s)he will be less likely to need and want information from other people, and therefore also less susceptible to social influence. In contrast, when a person's prior attributions have been highly unstable, (s)he will be much more open to persuasion. Conditions which lead to attribution instability, according to Kelley's analysis, are: little social support, poor or ambiguous prior information, problems which are too difficult for the person's abilities, beliefs which have been disconfirmed, and other experiences which lower the person's self-confidence.

Research on Attribution Processes

A major research topic stemming from attribution theory concerns *actor-observer differences*. In part this issue has been discussed above in relation to Bem's critique of dissonance theory. One of the most important papers in this area concluded that actors tend to attribute their actions to situational factors, whereas observers of the same actions tend to attribute them to stable personal dispositions of the actor (Jones & Nisbett, 1971—see Figure 9-4). There is strong evidence for this conclusion, and Storms (1973) has shown that it results from the differing focus of attention of the two roles: the observer watching the actor's behavior, while the actor is alert to incoming situational stimuli. By a clever use of videotape, reversing the visual direction from which an actor and an observer watched a taped conversational episode which they had previously experienced, Storms was able to reverse the type of attributions that each of them made.

Figure 9-4 An example of actor-observer differences. Observers often attribute behavior to internal characteristics of the actor, whereas the actor often attributes it to situational pressures.

Evaluation of Attribution Theories

The first thing to be said about attribution theories is that there is not a single unified theory but a proliferation of related approaches dealing with causal inferences about oneself, other people, and the environment. The central figures in the field themselves state: "At present attribution theory is an amorphous collection of observations . . . [and lacks] a firm grasp of interrelated deductive principles" (Jones et al., 1971, p. x). Thus, whether it is really a theory is still in some doubt (Kiesler & Munson, 1975). Also, research studies have often neglected the central issues of the theory:

> few of the recently published studies seem to be direct extensions or tests of the underlying theory. Instead, most of these studies seem to be based on intuitive hypotheses, and their relationships to a systematic theory of attribution are usually left unstated, although there are some notable exceptions (Fishbein & Ajzen, 1972, p. 502).

Moreover, other reviewers question whether important theoretical details will ever be clearly stated because so many attribution proponents are preceeding inductively into new implications rather than trying to provide a clear deductive framework for the theory (Kiesler & Munson, 1975).

Nevertheless, the attribution approach has become extremely popular in recent years, and the large volume of research citing attribution viewpoints testifies to its heuristic value. The theory has potential implications for a wide variety of social phenomena, including the process of learning about oneself, the establishment of interpersonal trust, and the nature of incentive effects. Though there has been much use of attribution notions to explain data from other sources, there have also been experimental tests of theoretical predictions, and even a number of studies comparing attribution and dissonance predictions. However, on a number of important theoretical issues, dissonance theory seems to have been as well or better supported by the research evidence (Kiesler & Munson, 1975). Attribution proponents have modestly and wisely responded that their theories do not imperialistically assume an absence of other social motives, and they even grant that relatively logical attribution processes may be more typical among college undergraduates, the most commonly used research subjects, than among other people (Jones et al., 1971, p. xii).

Comparing evidence for the different "brands" of attribution theory, it appears that there is good research support for many of the points stated by Jones and Davis. Though Kelley's approach has broad implications, it has received less research attention, and it needs to develop a way of measuring a person's level of stable information about the world (Shaw & Costanzo, 1970). Bem's proposition that the inference processes of actors and observers are identical has been quite conclusively disproved. There is a good deal of inconsistency in some of the research findings, especially about attribution of responsibility for events (e.g., auto accidents). This particular problem is probably due to the many different ways in which responsibility can be interpreted (Heider, 1958; Shaw & Reitan, 1969). Undoubtedly the greatest problem with all attribution theories, from our present perspective, is that they have not been closely tied to the concept of attitude change nor applied to research in the traditional attitude-change areas (Kiesler & Munson, 1975).

A FINAL COMMENT ON THEORIES

It is obvious from our discussion in this chapter that all theories of attitude change have serious limitations. Some have greater problems than others, but all have rather crucial failings. Does that mean that we should abandon them, in effect saying "a plague on both your houses"? No, definitely not. Though that course might be emotionally satisfying, it would not be good science. The scientific reasons for developing and using theories have been presented earlier in

Chapter 8. As scientists, when we are faced with the inadequacies of our theories, our job is two-fold: first, to try to determine the range of conditions under which each theory holds, and second, to endeavor to construct better theories which will more fully explain the existing research evidence. This is an exciting and an urgent task.

We will close this chapter, as McGuire (1969) closed his landmark review of attitude change research, with a passage showing at once the weaknesses and the strengths of attitude change theories.

> In retrospect, these theories seem to have had a rather peculiar career. Each has an appreciable *a priori* plausibility; each has given rise to intriguing predictions; each has provoked admirable research. In short, each deserves to be true. Unfortunately, none seems to have any great deal of empirical validity. Nevertheless, it seems to us that, in any area to which one of these theoretical approaches has been applied with persistence, the result of the interaction between them and the data has been a clarification of the problem and an advance of the question (pp. 271–272).

SUMMARY

Cognitive *consistency* theories have generated a great deal of research, but they are fractionated into many partially conflicting mini-theories. The basic principle of all consistency theories is that awareness of inconsistency among one's ideas is an uncomfortable situation which will motivate cognitive changes, though not necessarily strictly logical ones. Heider, the father of consistency theory, proposed definitions of cognitive balance in both dyadic and triadic situations. Though very influential, this theory is overly simple and imprecise; consequently it has stimulated more revisions and extensions than research directed at its own provisions. Rosenberg and Abelson's version of consistency theory posits the importance of consistency between the cognitive and affective components of an attitude and also proposes a hierarchy of ways of resolving imbalance. Osgood and Tannenbaum's congruity theory is unique in its degree of quantification, but compensatingly narrow in its scope, which is limited to situations where a source makes an evaluative assertion about an attitude object. Within that arena, and with a number of empirical correction factors, it has often predicted attitude change quite well. In general, other consistency theories have been heuristically provocative but relatively low in the empirical validity of their research predictions. In part, this is probably due to the common and pervasive occurrence of cognitive *in*consistency in human psychological functioning.

Festinger's *dissonance* theory is a type of consistency theory but is unique in both its form and its ability to stimulate controversy and research. The theory deals with relations between cognitions (information, beliefs, attitudes, etc.), but it is stated in an open way which allows it to be applied to many diverse areas, from attitude change to partial reinforcement effects in rats. With later revisions that stressed the importance of volition and commitment as conditions for dissonance arousal, the theory has done quite well in predicting the consequences of making decisions. Its predictions regarding selective exposure to information have not been well-supported, and there is little clear-cut evidence concerning the role of social support in reducing dissonance. The area of "forced compliance," or counterattitudinal behavior, has been the most controversial of the theory's applications. There neither dissonance theorists nor incentive theorists have been consistently successful in pinpointing the conditions for their predicted types of attitude change. Bem's self-perception approach to this area, using uninvolved observer-subjects, has also stirred considerable interest, but further research has disproved some of Bem's basic assumptions. Dissonance theory and research have been subjected to many vitriolic criticisms, some justified and some ill-considered. All in all, it must be given credit for a good record in the postdecision area of research, for many intriguing "nonobvious" hypotheses, for ingenious experimental procedures, and above all for stimulating extensive research. However, major problems remain in the theory, and in recent years research interest has shifted sharply to other approaches—particularly to attribution theories.

In general, *perceptual* approaches consider attitude change as a change in the perception of the attitude object rather than a change in beliefs or opinions about it. Sherif and Hovland's social judgment theory is one example which derives its principles from perceptual research in experimental psychology. It considers the person's own attitude as an anchor and predicts assimilation of persuasive messages which are within the person's latitude of acceptance but contrast of messages in the latitude of rejection. The theory has been used to study some important real-world issues, but it is quite narrow in scope. It has generated a good deal of research on message discrepancy and ego-involvement, but enough of this research has been nonsupportive that the theory cannot be considered a primary one in the attitude change area.

Attribution theories, another type of perceptual approach, are currently very popular. They stem from Heider's writings about the conditions under which people make internal attributions (about other people's traits or dispositions, on the basis of their observed actions) or external attributions (about environmental conditions). Jones and Davis have extended Heider's ideas about personal causality (internal attribution), while Kelley has done the same for impersonal causality and has applied the resulting principles to an understanding of social influence processes. Bem's self-perception hypotheses can also be considered as a theory about attributions to the self. Though attribution approaches have great heuristic value and applicability to many different social phenomena, they are currently "an amorphous collection of observations" lacking in "interrelated deductive principles" (Jones et al., 1971, p. x). Jones and Davis' version has had relatively good research support whereas Bem's has not, but in general none of the attribution approaches have been applied extensively to traditional areas of attitude-change research.

Suggested Readings

Hastorf, A. H., Schneider, D. J., & Polefka, J. *Person Perception.* Reading, Mass.: Addison-Wesley, 1970.—A clearly written paperback volume containing a well-organized summary of research on attribution theory (pp. 70–89).

Insko, C. A. *Theories of Attitude Change.* Englewood Cliffs, N.J.: Prentice-Hall, 1967.—Contains a thorough and detailed summary and evaluation of research studies bearing on most of the major theories of attitude change, except for attribution theory.

Suedfeld, P. (Ed.). *Attitude Change: The Competing Views.* Chicago: Aldine Atherton, 1971.—Chapter 1 (pp. 1–62) presents a very readable and thoughtful summary of many theories of attitude change (but omitting attribution theory).

Zajonc, R. B. The concepts of balance, congruity, and dissonance. *Public Opinion Quarterly*, 1960, 24, 280–296.—An often-reprinted article which gives a clear and interesting summary and comparison of the three main consistency theories.

chapter 10

Problems and Prospects in the Attitude and Opinion Field

We have too many high sounding words, and too few actions that correspond with them.—Abigail Adams, 1774.

Attitude and action are linked in a continuing reciprocal process, each generating the other in an endless chain—Herbert C. Kelman.

What I want is to get done what the people desire to have done, and the question for me is how to find that out exactly.—Abraham Lincoln.

The politician who sways with the polls is not worth his pay.—Richard Nixon.

In this chapter we will first consider two long-standing questions that are still being debated—how are attitudes related to personality, and how are they related to behavior? Next we will explore some methodological problems and ethical issues—what differences are there between the findings of laboratory research and field research, and what ethical problems are raised in attitude and opinion research? Finally, we will examine the relationship of public opinion to public policy.

ATTITUDES AND PERSONALITY

The major issue here is whether or not attitudes have a systematic and close relationship to personality traits. Note that this is a different question than whether attitude *change* is related to personality, a topic discussed in Chapter 8 under the heading of Personality and Persuasibility.

Classical Studies of Attitudes and Personality

There are several classic studies that link attitudes and personality. One of the best known of all attitude studies—*The Authoritarian Personality* (Adorno et al., 1950)—began as a study of anti-Semitic attitudes. As the project developed, the focus broadened to include conservatism, ethnocentrism (a generalized attitude of prejudice toward many ethnic groups), and finally authoritarianism, which was conceptualized as a basic personality characteristic. Each of the major topics of the research, in turn, was studied through the development of a scale to measure it. The authors reported that the Anti-Semitism (A-S) Scale correlated +.53 with the first version of the F (for fascism) Scale, which was their measure of authoritarian personality tendencies. This relationship was at least partly due to the fact that each successive measurement scale was constructed by using the correlations of its items with the preceding scales as a basis for item selection. However, despite this methodological problem, the point here is that this highly influential research project both assumed and found a close relationship between personality characteristics and certain attitudes.

Some of the relationships that were reported, using methods of personality testing and intensive depth interviews, were as follows: Highly prejudiced individuals were found to have rigid personality characteristics; they were highly conventional in values and standards; they rejected any negative implications about themselves or their parents; and they projected socially unacceptable impulses or characteristics onto other people. As children, they typically reported having had parents who were concerned about status, who were cold and unloving, who used harsh physical punishment for infractions of family rules, and who gave love only for ''proper'' behavior.

Similar patterns of findings have occurred in other studies. For instance, Martin and Westie (1959) tested a representative sample of white adults in

Indianapolis with a short prejudice scale and then gave high- and low-scorers a battery of other tests and questionnaires. In comparison with tolerant individuals, they found highly prejudiced persons to be intolerant of ambiguity, superstitious, concerned about threat and competition, fundamentalistic in religious views, and high in F Scale scores. In addition, prejudiced people stressed obedience, severe discipline, and physical punishment as child-rearing methods.

A somewhat different approach was used by McClosky (1958), who began by constructing a scale measuring politically conservative attitudes. That scale and more than 50 other personality and attitude measures were given to a representative sample of over 1200 citizens in Minneapolis-St. Paul. Again strong relationships between attitudes and personality traits were found. The extreme conservatives scored highest by far in hostility, paranoid tendencies, rigidity, intolerance, and contempt for weakness. Despite (or because of) their criticalness of others, they were unusually defensive of their own imperfections. In sum, though McClosky started from a different point, his findings closely parallel those of Adorno et al.

Another classic study of attitudes and personality is the book by Smith, Bruner, and White (1956) which focused on international attitudes. In contrast to the previously-mentioned studies, the procedure used was an intensive case-study of 10 men who were chosen on the basis of their varied attitudes toward Russia—probably the most important topic in the field of foreign affairs in the early 1950s. The authors showed in detail how these men's attitudes toward Russia often paralleled and reflected their personality conflicts, defense mechanisms, and ways of relating to other people. (See Chapter 13 for a summary of other findings relating personality and international attitudes.)

Links between attitudes and personality have been further demonstrated by studies of prejudiced attitudes. One study showed that in both Greece and the United States insecure individuals were generally high in prejudice, though the typical target groups for prejudice differed in the two cultures (Triandis & Triandis, 1962).

Methodological Critiques

Individual Prejudice vs. Social Conformity. Though personality-based theories of prejudice have received some empirical support, they by no means account for all prejudice. Since they deal with *individual* prejudice, they are least applicable in situations where social norms prescribe prejudiced and discriminatory behavior from all members of the dominant group, as has been true in the American South. Despite the high degree of racial prejudice in the South, Southerners in general are no higher than Northerners on measures of authoritarian personality traits. Instead of personality being the source of most prejudiced attitudes, the evidence suggests that social conformity may be the more potent source of prejudice in those cultural settings where there are such clear-cut norms of discrimination (Pettigrew, 1959). (See Chapter 14 for more information on racial prejudice.)

The Authoritarian Personality. Methodological critiques of the authoritarian personality research have been extensive and varied (Christie & Jahoda, 1954; Kirscht & Dillehay, 1967). Here we can mention only a few of the points most relevant to our discussion of personality and attitudes. For a thorough review of the topic which reads almost like a mystery novel, see the chapter on authoritarianism by Brown (1965).

Four major criticisms of the authoritarian personality research are most important. First, the sampling procedures were far from representative since most subjects were obtained through organized groups such as labor unions, Kiwanis clubs, and university classes. However, Martin and Westie (1959) and McClosky (1958) studied representative samples of adults living in a major U.S. city, and their results also showed clear connections between attitudes and personality traits. Second, the interviewers, who were allowed wide discretion in their choice of questions, were shown the subjects' F-Scale scores before the interview, and thus they may have consciously or unconsciously tried to obtain interview responses consistent with the questionnaire data. However, again, this criticism is not applicable to Martin and Westie's and McClosky's similar findings because they used questionnaires for collecting their data.

A third methodological criticism of authoritarianism research is the problem of acquiescence response set (yea-saying), which occurred because all the items of the F-Scale were worded in the authoritarian direction (as discussed in Chapter 2). However, Martin and Westie's research methods did not suffer from this problem, and their results were highly similar to Adorno et al.'s. The fourth criticism of authoritarianism research is that demographic characteristics such as education and social class are quite strongly correlated with F-Scale scores, in a negative direction (Selznick & Steinberg, 1969). There is no escaping this fact, but it does not vitiate the relationship between personality and attitudes. It appears that underprivileged groups in the United States and many other countries are more likely to develop authoritarian personality structures and the typical pattern of accompanying attitudes than are middle- or upper-class groups.

Interaction Effects. A final methodological consideration relevant to all personality and attitude studies is one which moves beyond the **main effects** of a single personality or attitude variable considered in isolation. In addition to such main effects, studies are likely to find **interaction effects**, in which two or more stimulus situations differentially affect people who have different personality or attitude characteristics. For example, we might find that authoritarian individuals display more prejudice than do nonauthoritarians when dealing with a low-status minority person, but not when dealing with a high-status minority person. The pervasiveness and importance of such interaction effects have recently been stressed by Cronbach (1975) and Secord (1975), and greater attention to them is needed in research.

Recent Findings

Despite these criticisms of the methodology used in previous research relating attitudes and personality variables, some recent studies have continued to report clear-cut relationships. For instance, an integrated group of British, Australian, New Zealand, and U.S. studies, following-up Adorno et al. and later findings, have reinterpreted the attitudinal syndrome involved as one of conservatism versus liberalism (Wilson, 1973). Just as in the original authoritarian personality research, they reported significant correlations between conservative attitudes and personality characteristics such as introversion, anxiety, low self-esteem, and harsh and punitive child-rearing methods.

In the area of attitudes toward civil liberties, Zalkind, Gaugler, and Schwartz (1975) have also found linear relationships to several personality traits. In a large, fairly diverse sample of middle-class New York City adults, they found moderately strong positive relationships between attitudes favoring civil liberties and personality measures of flexibility, independence, and self-reliance. Moreover, these relationships remained significant even when the effects of age, education, and socioeconomic status were statistically controlled. Thus, recent studies continue to provide evidence that attitudes and personality are often linked in meaningful ways.

ATTITUDES AND BEHAVIOR

The topic of attitude-behavior consistency has been a subject of debate since the early days of social psychology (e.g., LaPiere, 1934), and in more recent years whole books have been written on the subject (e.g., Deutscher, 1973). In the few pages available here we will highlight the most important aspects of this issue.

The question of what relationships exist among the cognitive, affective, and behavioral components of attitudes (or between beliefs, attitudes, and behavioral intentions as separate concepts) was discussed in Chapters 3 and 9. Now our attention shifts from the components or aspects of attitudes to the link between attitudes and behavior (that is, overt responses).

Is what we say always consistent with what we do? Obviously not, for we can all think of cases of discrepancy between our own words and deeds, just as between the statements and actions of others. Since attitudes are usually measured through a person's verbal report, there is a likelihood that attitudes and actions often may not correspond. Let's suppose for a moment that we pushed this idea to its extreme and asserted that attitudes were completely unrelated to actions. If that were the case, what would be the value of having the concept of "attitude"? Upon reflection, it should be clear that there would be very little value to it, for as an intervening variable, "attitude" is only a useful concept if it conveniently summarizes, predicts, or is related to patterns of actual behavior. (For instance, recall Allport's definition that an attitude is a state of readiness which influences an individual's responses to objects and situations.)

Thus it can be seen that the verdict about the usefulness of the concept "attitude" depends largely on the empirical evidence regarding its relationship to behavior. What is the evidence? From the great mass of research in this area, we will mention a few studies which illustrate important points.

A Famous Early Study

In the early 1930s, when racial prejudice toward Negroes, Orientals, and most other foreigners was at a high level in the U.S., LaPiere (1934) traveled extensively around the country with a young, foreign-born Chinese couple. In a careful empirical manner he kept records on their acceptance and the quality of service they received in hotels, "auto camps," and restaurants. In addition, LaPiere attempted to vary the conditions experimentally by frequently having his Chinese friends enter restaurants first or do the negotiation for rooms. The results were dramatic: in about 10,000 miles of travel, the party was served (often with great hospitality) at 250 establishments and rejected at only one (a "rather inferior auto camp"). That was the behavioral measure.

To determine these establishments' attitudes toward Chinese as guests, LaPiere waited six months after the time of their visit and then sent each one a questionnaire asking, "Will you accept members of the Chinese race as guests in your establishment?" With persistence, he was able to get replies from 128, of which one auto-camp replied "Yes," nine respondents said it would depend on the circumstances, and 118 said "No." Identical questionnaires sent to 128 similar businesses which they had not visited produced exactly the same distribution of responses. As a result of this massive discrepancy between questionnaire responses and actual behavior, LaPiere concluded that in many social situations questionnaire data cannot be trusted, and that attitudes generally must be studied through observation of actual social behavior. Results highly similar to LaPiere's have also been obtained in other studies, such as one involving racially mixed parties of diners in New York restaurants (Kutner, Wilkins, & Yarrow, 1952).

Can we conclude from these findings that these businesspeople's attitudes and actions were inconsistent? No, we cannot! Though at first glance it would appear so, there are major methodological problems involved, which are causing what we may term "pseudo inconsistency."

Pseudo Inconsistency

One important point about the question of consistency has been made by Campbell (1963), who has emphasized the importance of **situational thresholds**. He stresses that often the verbal attitude statements and the overt behavioral measures have quite different thresholds, or levels of probability of occurrence. The reason for this discrepancy may be any of a number of factors which will be discussed a bit later in this section. As an example, take a political party member who doesn't contribute financially to his party. For convenience, let us say that about 50% of the adult registered voters belong to the party; yet we know that the number of financial contributors is never more than about 5%. Campbell points out that it would be grossly unfair to call the 45% who don't contribute "inconsistent." They are merely doing the easy (or common) thing and avoiding the difficult (or uncommon) behavior. The only true case of inconsistency would be a person who did the difficult, uncommon thing but failed to perform the easy, common action—in this example, one who contributed to the party but was not a member (e.g., a "Democrat for Nixon"). Such individuals are not only rare, but their behavior after the election is over often suggests that their attitude (stated party preference) was misclassified. For instance, consider the case of John Connally, who headed Democrats for Nixon in 1972 and then declared himself a Republican not too long after the election.

This analysis of **pseudo inconsistency** clearly applies to the LaPiere study of the Chinese couple's acceptance in restaurants and hotels. Its famous "inconsistency" was probably primarily a matter of differences in situational thresholds, for discrimination against members of another race is much harder in the face-to-face personal situation than in the abstract written-letter situation. Another example of this point is shown in Box 10-1.

Other methodological critiques of the famous "inconsistency" studies have also been made. Dillehay (1973) has pointed out that in phoning or sending questionnaires to a restaurant or hotel, there is no certainty that the attitude measure was provided by the *same person* whose behavior was earlier observed. Also, the base rate or commonness of the behavior can markedly affect the attitude-behavior correlation—where almost everyone chooses one response (as in the LaPiere study), a single inconsistent case can lower the correlation to nearly zero; whereas if the base rate is closer to 50%, one inconsistent case will have very little effect on the correlation (Fishbein & Ajzen, 1975, p. 373).

We can conclude that much (but by no means all) of the alleged inconsistency in the attitude-behavior research literature is actually pseudo inconsistency.

How Much Consistency?

But what about cases of real inconsistency between attitudes and behavior? How common are they, and what explanations can be found for them? Considerable attention has been directed to these questions in recent years. In one important review article, Wicker (1969) examined more than 30 studies bearing on the attitude-behavior relationship and concluded pessimistically that in most cases verbal measures of attitudes were only slightly related or were even unrelated to the expected behaviors. In only a minority of cases was the correlation coefficient between attitude and behavior higher than .30, and even this high a relationship indicates that the two measures have only about 10% of their variance in common; that is, they show only a small degree of overlap or similarity. Thus Wicker concluded that it is risky to conceptualize attitudes as a latent process underlying behavior and/or to try to predict behavioral responses from verbal attitude measures.

Box 10-1 *Pseudo Inconsistency of Attitude Measures: Differing Situational Thresholds*

Minard (1952) described a group of white and Negro coal miners who worked together in the same mines, but whose interaction patterns were very different in the mines than in the town where they lived. Campbell (1963) has clarified the misleading analyses which have been made of this supposed inconsistency, as follows:

> Minard's . . . comments on the Pocahontas coal miners involves two items which can be diagramed as [below]. His report clearly indicates that the settings of mine and town have markedly different situational thresholds for nondiscriminatory reactions of white miners, only 20 percent being friendly in town, 80 percent being friendly in the mines. He reports no instances of true inconsistency, i.e., being friendly in town and hostile in the mines. From this point of view, . . . [it is] clearly wrong to conclude that the middle 60 percent are persons "whose overt behavior provides no clue as to their attitudes." Their behavior clearly indicates that they have consistently middling attitudes. The two items, mine and town correlate perfectly.

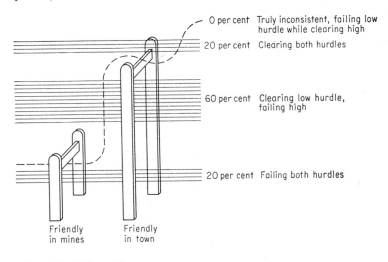

Source: Campbell, 1963, p. 161.

However, some of the articles reviewed by Wicker suffered from the pseudo-inconsistency problems which we have described above, while others did not really have a genuine measure of attitude or an actual behavioral criterion (Fishbein & Ajzen, 1975, pp. 359–361). Also, we may consider that correlations from .30 up to over .60, as found in the more successful studies, actually represent a high degree of accuracy in predicting a complex social behavior. Donald Campbell has pointed out that the correlation between two different *behaviors* (for instance, willingness to serve a minority group member, and sitting beside the same person on a bus) is probably lower still (cited in A. G. Miller, 1972). Indeed, Triandis (1964) has shown that behaviors involved in social distance and prejudice do not all cluster together with high positive correlations, but rather form five relatively distinct factors. Behaviors indicating general respect may be largely uncorrelated with acceptance into friendship relations, which in turn may be unrelated to marital acceptance. Similarly, low correlations might often be found between the same behavior in two different situations; for instance, Dutton (1971) found that enforcement of stated dress regulations in some Canadian restaurants was often different depending on whether a white couple or a black couple were the first ones to arrive informally dressed—interestingly, enforcement was often more lenient for black customers.

Despite some low correlations, there is much evidence of general attitude-behavior similarity. The election campaign opinion polls almost always show a close correspondence between *aggregate* public opinion and voting behavior, and Crespi (1971) has described other examples where polls have shown good ability to predict movie attendance and food brand preference. Another recent review of the research literature has concluded that attitudes and behavior are generally related (Calder & Ross, 1973).

There are several methodological refinements which have been shown to yield higher attitude-behavior relationships. Two are broader methods of measurement: a multi-item attitude scale instead of measurement by a single item (e.g. A. Campbell et al., 1960, p. 74), and a behavioral criterion scale made up of several actions instead of just one (Fishbein & Ajzen, 1975, pp. 359–363; Weigel & Newman, 1976). Two other methodological suggestions propose that we should measure attitudes toward situations (Rokeach, 1968) and/or attitudes toward a particular action rather than using the traditional measure of attitudes toward a person or class of persons (e.g., Schwartz & Tessler, 1972). For instance, in predicting how often students will cut a particular course, we should achieve better prediction by measuring the students' attitudes concerning the importance of the course and the act of cutting class than by measuring only the students' attitudes toward the instructor.

A final methodological requirement is that the attitude and the behavior should be measured at similar levels of specificity (e.g., Heberlein & Black, 1976). This was obviously a problem in LaPiere's (1934) study, where the attitude questionnaire asked about Chinese guests in general, but the behavioral decision was made regarding *a particular* Chinese couple, well-dressed, well-spoken, smiling, and accompanied by a white companion.

Reasons for Inconsistency

Despite any methodological improvements, there may still remain many instances of genuine and substantial inconsistency between attitudes and behavior. Wicker (1969) and Fishbein and Ajzen (1975) have suggested many factors which can help cause such inconsistency, among which are:

1. Instability of attitudes and intentions over time. Many studies have shown that attitudes and intentions shift over time, sometimes quite sharply (e.g., Schmiedeskamp & Cowan, 1972). Consequently, the longer the time between attitude measurement and behavioral observation, the greater the chances for inconsistency.
2. Other competing attitudes, motives, or values. A person might have a favorable attitude toward his political party but not contribute to it financially (the behavior measure) because he had a stronger favorable attitude to other organizations seeking his donations, or because he had a strong motive to save money (Audi, 1972). The same principle has been shown to apply regarding attitudes toward racial discrimination (Schuman, 1972) and toward smoking (Canon & Mathews, 1972).
3. Inadequate intellectual, verbal, or social skills. If a person lacks the intelligence or the information to recognize that his behavior does not match his attitude, inconsistency would not be surprising. This might happen, for instance, with a poorly informed voter backing a candidate whose views are actually contrary to his own.
4. Lack of volitional control over the behavior. Some behaviors, such as a mother's ability to breast-feed her newborn baby, are not completely under voluntary control. In one study about 25% of mothers with positive attitudes were nevertheless unsuccessful (Newton & Newton, 1950).
5. Unavailability of alternative behaviors. A good example is the person who regularly buys a daily newspaper even though he detests it, because it is the only one conveniently available in his city.
6. Situations involving normative prescriptions of "proper" behavior. A very familiar example is that we are taught to be polite to people even though we don't like them. Also, the norms held by other people present in the situation are important: a strong racist would be less likely to walk out of a racially mixed gathering if he knew that most of the others present supported social integration of the races.
7. Important expected consequences of the behavior. It has been well-established that many restaurant and hotel managers, despite strong anti-Negro attitudes, have nevertheless begun serving black patrons following the passage of antidiscrimination laws when they were faced with the prospect of legal punishment for racial discrimination. In a weaker form, this consideration of likely consequences is probably also involved in the preceding category (norms regarding proper behavior).
8. Unforeseen extraneous events. For instance, even a family with a strongly favorable attitude toward church attendance might miss Sunday service if they had a seriously ill child, or if their car wouldn't start, or if a heavy thunderstorm intervened.

We may conclude from this list that attitudes are by no means the only factors necessary in order to predict behavioral responses, and sometimes they are not even among the most important factors. Thus a certain amount of inconsistency between attitudes and behavior is to be expected, the amount depending on the particular situation. Wicker (1969) and Fishbein and Ajzen (1975) have concluded that, the more similar the situations are in which the two attitude and behavior measures are obtained, the greater will be the amount of consistency. This principle has been supported by some empirical studies, but in addition we need further information on which particular dimensions of similarity are most important in determining the attitude-behavior relationship.

Systems for Predicting Behavior

Fishbein was the first author to try to combine several of these factors systematically in predicting behavior. He suggested a mathematical formula which contains both attitudinal and normative factors. They include: (a) the person's beliefs about the consequences of performing a particular behavior, (b) his evaluation of those consequences, (c) his normative beliefs regarding the expectations of relevant others, and (d) his motivation to comply with those expectations. These two pairs of factors are combined mathematically, multiplying each pair together, weighting them appropriately, and then adding the two products. (See Fishbein & Ajzen, 1975, pp. 301–303 for more details.) This equation is used to predict behavioral intentions, rather than behavior, and in 13 studies the average multiple correlation found was a very high figure of $+.75$ (Fishbein & Ajzen, 1975, p. 310). Many studies have shown that behavioral intentions, in turn, are usually good predictors of overt behaviors (Kothandapani, 1971; Fishbein & Ajzen, 1975, pp. 373–374). For instance, a person's intention to attend church on Sunday morning is likely to be highly correlated with the behavior of actually attending.

Much more research on this and other prediction systems is needed in order to determine whether they are successful in improving the prediction of behavior from attitudinal data. As another example, several studies have shown improved prediction from use of the factor of extraneous events (Wicker, 1971; Brislin & Olmstead, 1973). For instance, prediction of a person's actual church attendance can be improved if we know what he would probably do if he were confronted by unexpected events, such as a heavy thunderstorm, or his car not starting.

Another prediction system has been developed by Sheth (1974), primarily for use in predicting consumer buying intentions and actual purchasing behavior. The system is complex; it includes measures of habits, evaluative beliefs, the general social environment, the anticipated situation, and unexpected events, in addition to affect, behavioral intentions, and behavior. Using this model to predict purchases of a newly introduced instant breakfast product by a sample of 954 housewives, Sheth found quite high relationships—multiple correlations of almost $+.70$ with behavioral intentions and almost $+.50$ with purchase behavior.

Taken together, these studies clearly show that in order to predict people's behavior it is not enough simply to know their attitudes. Though attitudes are one important determinant of behavior, there are many other important determinants as well—personal habits, social norms, the particular situation, unexpected events, and others.

Furthermore, much recent research has shown that people's behavior also has a reciprocal effect on their attitudes. For example, Lieberman (1956) showed that being promoted to (or demoted from) the positions of foreman or union shop steward had clear-cut effects on workers' job-related attitudes. Other prominent examples include the effects of "forced compliance" or counterattitudinal advocacy (discussed in Chapter 9 in relation to dissonance theory), effects of commitment and of active participation on attitude change (also discussed in Chapter 9), and the prointegration attitudinal changes that followed U.S. school desegregation (described in Chapter 14).

Thus we may conclude with Kelman (1974) that "attitudes are alive and well and gainfully employed in the sphere of action," for we have good evidence of

> the engagement of attitude and action in a continuing, reciprocal, circular process. Not only is attitude an integral part of action, but action is an integral part of the development, testing, and crystallization of attitudes (p. 324).

LABORATORY RESEARCH VS. FIELD RESEARCH

We turn next to a topic which has received increasing attention in recent years—what differences are there, if any, between the results of experimental, laboratory research and those of studies done in real-life field settings? One initial clarification may be needed: though most research in field settings uses survey methods and correlational (nonmanipulative) designs, these are not necessary characteristics of **field research**. Bickman and Henchy (1972) have presented a collection of field research studies, most of which are true experiments, with all of the advantages in manipulation, control, precision, and stronger causal inferences which the term "experiment" implies. (For a discussion of the advantages and disadvantages of different types of research methods, together with examples of each method, see Oskamp, 1972b.)

Many of the differences between laboratory and field studies of attitudes have been summarized by Hovland (1959) and McGuire (1969). In research on persuasion and attitude change it is usually found that laboratory studies show stronger effects than field studies. However, this contrast is probably due largely, if not entirely, to a number of methodological differences which are frequently *confounded* with the laboratory-field distinction. To clarify this point, here is a list of some of the typical methodological characteristics of laboratory studies—ways in which they are apt to differ from field studies (also see Figure 10-1):

1. An authoritative, prestigious situation. The experimenter or other communicator is in a position of power and authority, and demand characteristics encourage attitude change.

2. No distractions. In contrast, mass media communications often have to compete with many other distracting stimuli.
3. Less ego-involving or important topics. These are chosen so as to maximize attitude change, whereas field research has often studied more important issues such as political attitudes.
4. College students as subjects. Students are better informed, quicker to understand, and more responsive to rational persuasion than the average citizen.
5. Disguised persuasive intent. Often experiments cover up their true purpose, while commercial advertisers, politicians, and other real-world communicators usually make a direct persuasive appeal, thus allowing the recipients to evade the message if they are so inclined.
6. No counter-persuasion. In everyday life there are almost always messages from competing products, groups, or individuals, which tend to lessen the original message's effect.
7. Better measures of attitude. The laboratory situation allows more extensive and careful attitude measurement than most real-world situations.
8. Attitude change is usually measured immediately. By contrast, in field research the measurement of change may be many days or weeks after the message, thus showing a diminished effect due to the passage of time.

The Importance of Field Research

The issue of generalizability is one where field research usually has an advantage due to the real-world nature of the tasks and settings involved. When laboratory research uses highly unusual tasks and settings, and particularly when the participants are very aware of performing as subjects under the experimenter's scrutiny, its results may not be applicable to most situations in the world outside of the laboratory. However, Aronson and Carlsmith (1968) have emphasized that the supposed artificiality of experimental situations need not be an obstacle to the generalizability of results as long as the situation is convincingly constructed to have **experimental realism** (believability and impact) for the subjects.

The lab-vs.-field issue is by no means a one-sided one. Even dedicated laboratory researchers usually grant the importance and necessity of field research and recognize its relation to their own investigations. For instance, Leon Festinger, one of the most noted laboratory experimenters in social psychology, wrote:

> Laboratory experimentation, as a technique for the development of an empirical body of knowledge, cannot exist by itself. Experiments in the laboratory must derive their direction from studies of real-life situations, and results must continually be checked by studies of real-life situations (1953, pp. 169–170).

In recent years many behavioral scientists have issued calls for more field

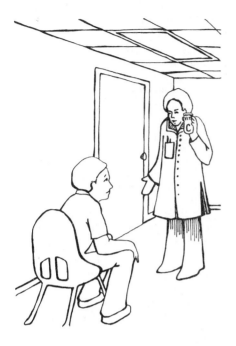

Left panel: Line drawing of young college student (male) in a small, bare-walled experimental room with no other furnishings, looking at speaker in a white lab coat who is saying "Take lots of Vitamin C."

Right panel: Line drawing of middle-aged man watching TV, which has message "Buy our Vitamin C." He is seated in a messy living room with a magazine in his hand, two children fighting on the floor, the telephone ringing, and his dog jumping up on his legs.

Figure 10-1 Some differences between laboratory and field research settings.

research and broader application of scientific theory and methods to a variety of social problems in the real world (e.g., McGuire, 1967, 1973). As a result of such clarion calls, there has been increased attention directed toward field research methods recently. The volume edited by Bickman and Henchy (1972) is just one indication of this trend. However, two studies of the contents of major social psychological journals show that, despite the talk about field research, very little of it is yet being reported in the scientific literature—well below 10% of all articles (Bickman & Henchy, 1972, p. 1; Fried, Gumpper, & Allen, 1973).

ETHICAL PROBLEMS IN ATTITUDE RESEARCH

Ethical questions arise in any kind of research activity, and attitude and opinion research is no exception. Psychologists and other attitude researchers have been attentive to ethical questions for many years, and they have developed thorough guidelines to protect the interests of research subjects and of society in general (American Psychological Association, 1953, 1967, 1973; Field, 1971). Though most attitude and opinion studies do not pose major ethical problems, the following important issues must be considered by any worker in this field.

Harmful Consequences.   This is the most serious ethical problem in research, but it arises mostly in medical research, or in behavioral research involving administration of drugs, emotional situations such as encounter groups, or use of painful stimuli like electric shock. Only rarely does the risk of harmful consequences occur in attitude and opinion research, as in the case of threats to subjects' self-esteem (e.g., Bramel, 1963; Walster, Berscheid, Abrahams, & Aronson, 1967). However, these few atypical cases have generated a great deal of comment and concern.

Deception.   Far more common in attitude and opinion research than the problem of harmful consequences is the issue of deception of research subjects by giving them false information. One survey of the social psychological literature showed that about 40% of studies used some deception (Seeman, 1969). Questions have been raised not only about the morality of deceiving subjects, but also about the effect this will have over the long run on public attitudes toward psychology and sociology as disciplines (Kelman, 1967; Bickman & Henchy, 1972, p. 3).

On the other hand, in order to obtain valid results in experimental studies, it is often essential that the research subjects not be aware of the hypotheses being tested. Thus some secrecy is usually necessary, and often this can only be accomplished by actively misleading the participants. In general, the currently accepted ethical principles prescribe that deception should only be used if there are no other legitimate ways to accomplish the same research goal and if the importance of the research warrants the amount of deception used. In actual practice, some surveys have shown that psychologists are more concerned about the use of deception than are research subjects (Sullivan & Deiker, 1973). And even when subjects have had previous experience with deception in research, it does not necessarily bias their responses in later studies (see the discussion of deception and suspicion in Chapter 8).

Informed Consent.   In recent years, it has become an essential ethical requirement of experiments that the subjects have consented to participate in an informed and knowledgeable way, after an explanation of any possible risks or unpleasant aspects of participation (American Psychological Association, 1973). If subjects agree to take part after a full and open explanation of the attendant risks and benefits, it is generally felt that they are doing so as free agents and that the researcher's ethical obligation in this area has been satisfied. However, this principle has not usually been extended to survey studies of public opinion, largely because the risks involved in participation are limited to minor inconvenience at most. And in observational studies of public behavior, such as marching in a demonstration or buying a particular product, the informed consent of participants is hardly ever obtained—largely because it would be very difficult or impossible to do so, and it might be more of a bother than a service to the subjects (see Bickman & Henchy, 1972, p. 5).

Invasion of Privacy. A related question concerns when and how subjects' privacy must be protected. Of course, anonymity and confidentiality of data are essential—participants' names or identification must never be linked with their behavior or opinions in reporting research results. But particularly in observational studies, the line where invasion of privacy begins is apt to be very fuzzy. Is concealed tape recording of an interview acceptable? What about listening to shoppers' conversations as they examine the merchandise? Or how about checking the number of liquor bottles in people's trash (Webb et al., 1966)? Probably the line which most researchers would draw is that public behavior or behavior in public places may legitimately be observed and/or recorded, whereas private behavior in private places must be protected from observation through techniques such as "bugging," high-powered microphones, etc.

Inconvenience to Participants. Though most attitude studies involve only minor inconvenience at most, researchers must be vigilant to avoid any unnecessary inconvenience. For example, in survey interviews, questions must be worded so that embarrassment is minimized, time requirements must be reasonable, and repeated calls or inconvenient hours should be avoided (Crossley, 1971). A deplorable example of respondent inconvenience is the misleading tactics of some salesmen who disguise their initial approach as a consumer survey; one study found that very recent experience with such a deceptive practice lowered response rates to a legitimate survey interview *by 75%* (Sheets, Radlinski, Kohne, & Brunner, 1974).

Debriefing of Participants. In experimental research it has been a traditional requirement that subjects are interviewed or informed at the end of the experimental session. This accomplishes several goals: the investigator usually thanks them and gives them information about the research topic in return for their cooperation; any deception is carefully explained, the need for it described in detail, and its effectiveness checked on; participants' questions are answered and any remaining anxiety which they may have is allayed; and appeals for secrecy about the research procedure are often made so that future subjects will not learn information which might invalidate the research results. If this debriefing is done thoroughly and sensitively, most investigators feel that subjects come to appreciate the value of the research, accept the need for any deception, and leave with a positive feeling about their experience (Aronson & Carlsmith, 1968, p. 32).

In field research, by contrast, it is rare and often impossible to debrief individuals after their participation in a study. Usually there is little or no deception which needs to be explained and no reason for participants to have been upset or anxious; so debriefing is less necessary. Particularly in observational research, such as a study of traffic violations, if individuals did not know they had been observed, informing them about it might only raise their concern rather than lowering it (Bickman & Henchy, 1972, pp. 96–97).

Reporting of Results.   In scientific publication, standards for reporting research results are carefully specified and overseen by journal editors. However, studies involving important social issues, particularly survey research findings, are often reported in the public press without the careful details and safeguards which reputable scientists would insist on. In fact, some unscrupulous pollsters have been known to slant their data collection or reporting for devious political ends (Roll & Cantril, 1972). To help eliminate these unfortunate instances, the American Association for Public Opinion Research (AAPOR) in 1968 made an important addition to its code of professional ethics and practices (Field, 1971). The new standards specify that any report of survey or poll results which is made public should contain information on the sponsor of the survey, the wording of questions, the method and dates of interviewing, the population sampled and sample size, and the likely amount of sampling error in the results. Adherence to these standards will not prevent all abuses of polls, but it will make their interpretation much more open to the scrutiny of other investigators and informed citizens.

The Obligation to Do Research.   Though researchers must give careful thought to all of the ethical problems discussed above, they cannot just throw up their hands in defeat and give up the research enterprise. The duty of the trained scientist to gather information and knowledge which can be put to public use is also an ethical imperative. To withdraw from that responsibility would be just as unethical as to do research in ways which ignored the rights of participants.

> Since research is the scientist's distinctive way to contribute to human welfare, he has an obligation to pursue it to the best of his ability (American Psychological Association, 1973, p. 8).

PUBLIC OPINION AND PUBLIC POLICY

Related to ethical issues in attitude research are the questions about uses and abuses of opinion polls in practical politics which we considered in Chapter 4. Now, as the final major topic in this chapter, we turn to broader policy questions concerning whether and how public opinion affects or is reflected in public policy. First, *should* public opinion affect public policy? Second, *does* it do so, and if it does, in what ways and under what circumstances? And finally, what uses are there for social science research in the public policy arena?

Should Public Opinion Affect Public Policy?

This is a question which has been asked by political philosophers for centuries. In general, we can distinguish three main types of answers which have been given. One position, which we may call the "will of the people" viewpoint, holds that legislators and political administrators should make their decisions entirely in accordance with the opinion of their constituents. This view was stated before the French Revolution by Jean Jacques Rousseau in his treatise *The Social Contract*, and it was strongly supported by Thomas Jefferson. Later Abraham Lincoln expressed it well in the quotation at the beginning of this chapter: "What I want is to get done what the people desire to have done, and the question for me is how to find that out exactly."

By contrast, another viewpoint holds that the calm, reasoned "judgment of the representative" should guide his vote rather than the popular clamor or the shifting winds of public opinion. This position was prominently espoused by the British parliamentarian Edmund Burke and by Alexander Hamilton in *The Federalist Papers*. A later and less elegant statement of the same principle is seen in Richard Nixon's admonition against "swaying with the polls."

A third viewpoint might be called the "party responsibility" approach. Becoming popular after the rise of strong national parties, it holds the representative responsible, not to his own local constituents, but to the program developed by his party, designed to satisfy the needs of the whole nation. Clearly in this

Figure 10-2 Should political leaders be guided by the "will of the people"?

approach, national public opinion is an important determinant of the party platform.

Another dimension of the question about the role of public opinion is: *which* public opinion? As we discussed in Chapter 5, mass public opinion may differ greatly from elite public opinion. On any given political issue, a large majority of the whole population is usually unconcerned and/or uninformed. Therefore, is it reasonable to guide policy by overall public opinion, with its weak preferences and shifting viewpoints? Or, on the other hand, should the "involved public," the minority who are concerned over a particular issue, be the ones who guide official policy? Some observers have suggested that, since organizations rather than individual citizens are the dominant force in our political system, opinion polls should measure the views of organizations instead of individuals (Goldner, 1971). But if that approach is followed, how can we avoid giving undue weight to vocal pressure groups and self-interested lobbyists?

These are difficult questions, and no final philosophical answers can be given to them. However, it is clear that, if public opinion is to be consulted, modern opinion polls give us a greatly improved method of doing so. Before the 1930s, political leaders had to seek the "will of the people" through newspaper editorials, through letters from the few involved citizens who took the trouble to write them, or through discussion with their highly selective circle of acquaintances. Now, with modern polling techniques, national leaders can learn with great accuracy the views of the total electorate *or* the opinions of the most concerned citizens, and they can balance these against the claims and demands of pressure groups and lobbyists (Gallup, 1965; Etzioni, 1969; Bogart, 1972a).

The types of issues on which public opinion should be consulted is also a question. Many authorities have concluded that the public should determine the decisions on broad, general questions having to do with the goals of public policy, rather than the specific means of achieving these goals. As Child (1965) expressed it, the public is most competent

> to determine the basic ends of public policy, to choose top policy makers, to appraise the results of public policy, and to say what, in the final analysis is fair, just, and moral. On the other hand, the general public is not competent to determine the best means for attaining specific goals, to answer technical questions, to prescribe remedies for political, social, and economic ills, and to deal with specialized issues far removed from the everyday experience and understanding of the people in general (p. 350).

Clearly, official policy cannot follow opinion poll results or specific questions in detail because the results are often unclear, shifting, uninformed, or ill-considered. For instance, in 1954 during the Korean War, over 60% of respondents to a Gallup Poll said they favored using atomic artillery shells against the Chinese army, and one-third advocated dropping hydrogen bombs on China (Bogart, 1972a, p. 19). Fortunately, such simplistic "ultimate solutions" were not adopted by the U.S. government. However, polls inherently have great difficulty in focusing on the more complex and varied alternative policies which have to be considered by diplomats and statesmen.

Though there are dangers in public opinion influencing national policy too greatly, there are also undesirable consequences when government has so much power that it can readily manipulate public opinion. An extreme example is the use of propaganda in Hitler's Germany, but a trend in the same direction seems to have occurred recently in the United States with the increase in presidential power and official secrecy (Childs, 1965, p. 351).

Though social scientists have studied public opinion extensively, they are only beginning to study what effects it actually has on government actions and the process by which it is or is not translated into public policy (Smith, 1971). We will look next at some studies which bear on these questions.

Does Public Opinion Affect Public Policy?

Research in this area has shown not one typical pattern, but many different ones, depending largely on the issue involved. Some issues have displayed a direct effect of public opinion on government policy, others no effect, and still others a reverse effect (policy influencing public opinion).

Direct Effects of Public Opinion. One of the issues where public opinion had its greatest effect on policy was the civil rights struggle of the 1950s and 1960s. A famous study of this topic by Miller and Stokes (1963) compared the attitudes, perceptions, and roll call votes of a sample of 116 Congressmen with the attitudes of their election opponents and of a sample of their constituents, district by district. The correspondence between constituents' attitudes and legislator's roll call votes on civil rights questions was shown by a correlation of almost +.6, much the highest of the three issues studied. Moreover, additional analyses indicated that Representatives by and large correctly perceived their constituents' attitudes and chose to vote accordingly, regardless of their own attitudes (Cnudde & McCrone, 1966). This pattern is quite different than the ones found on some other issues.

Other studies of U.S. legislators' attitudes have found them to correspond quite well to the general public's on the issues of aid to racial minorities, the missile program, and the Vietnam War (Backstrom, 1972). On a local level, Pettigrew and Riley (1972) showed that the average racial attitude in Texas counties was a strong determinant of the amount of school desegregation in the counties. Other indications of the power of public opinion can be seen in the competition for party nominations as the U.S. Presidential candidate. It was largely adverse public opinion which led Lyndon Johnson to withdraw from the 1968 Presidential race and similarly forced George Romney out of the Republican race even before the first state primary election.

Even where public opinion does not determine government policy, it may set limits on the policy options which leaders feel free to consider (Rosenberg, 1967; Roll & Cantril, 1972). This appears to have been true both in the Vietnam War and in the gradual U.S. mobilization before World War II. Starting in 1939, President Franklin D. Roosevelt was probably the first national leader to use poll results in a planned, programmatic way. He commissioned Hadley Cantril to do repeated public opinion polls, and endeavored very successfully to manage the buildup in aid to Britain so that a majority of citizens would continue to respond that the pace was "about right."

Lack of Effect of Public Opinion.   A common case where public opinion does not get translated into national policy is where one or both houses of Congress throws up roadblocks against a popularly endorsed proposal. This happened in the 1950s to Federal Aid to Education bills and a bit later to Medicare proposals (Childs, 1965). For nearly 40 years Congress has remained oblivious to strong national majorities who favor gun control legislation (Erskine, 1972b). In 1970, there were sharp discrepancies between public opinion and Congressional attitudes on treatment of suspected criminals, family income maintenance approaches to welfare programs, and wage and price controls (Backstrom, 1972).

Though the House of Representatives was planned as the branch of government which would be directly responsive to public opinion, that has often not been the case. In the Miller and Stokes (1963) study, it was shown that House roll call votes on social welfare issues were only slightly correlated with constituents' attitudes, and votes on foreign affairs were essentially unrelated to them. Further analyses led the authors to conclude that on social welfare issues legislators generally follow the "party responsibility" model, voting in accordance with their party platform, whereas in the realm of foreign affairs, they tend to yield their independent judgment to the expertise of the Administration.

Reverse Effects—Policy Influences on Public Opinion.   It is in the field of foreign affairs that public opinion most often follows rather than leads official policy (Rosenberg, 1967; Etzioni, 1969). This is probably because public ignorance of and indifference to policy issues tends to be proportional to their geographic distance from home, so most foreign affairs engage little citizen attention and develop public attitudes which are weakly held and rather easily changed (Rosenberg, 1967). A specific example can be seen in the many twists and turns of public opinion which followed changing Administration decisions regarding nuclear testing from 1954 to 1963 (unilateral suspension of tests, the international nuclear moratorium, resumption of testing, preparation for atmospheric tests, and finally the test-ban treaty with Russia). Through all these events public opinion rather faithfully followed official policies (Childs, 1965; Rosi, 1965). Other similar cases show continuing public approval for the steadily mounting U.S. military budget since 1945 and for President Kennedy's firm response in the

1962 Cuban missile crisis (Childs, 1965), but also for conciliatory actions such as President Nixon's easing of tensions with mainland China.

Despite public willingness to follow the Administration lead in foreign affairs, there are some limits to public acquiescence. The most clear-cut example is the Vietnam War. Early in the war it appeared that President Johnson could lead and influence popular opinion at will (Lipset, 1966); but as U.S. casualties, budgets, and impatience with the military stalemate increased, popular approval of the war gradually changed to disapproval and finally forced a change in administrations and a withdrawal from the war (Mueller, 1971).

The fact that political leaders can often sway public opinion may encourage abuses of democratic procedures. President Nixon's attempts to cover-up the Watergate deceptions are well-known examples. Ironically, political propagandists may often use slanted opinion polls in their attempts to mold public opinion in their favor. A particularly flagrant example is cited by Bogart (1972a, pp. 10–12) concerning the Congressional debate over President Nixon's antiballistic missile (ABM) proposals in 1969. At a time when less than half of the public favored development of an ABM system, a later-repudiated private poll was publicized in full-page newspaper ads by a pro-ABM "Citizens Committee," purporting to show that 84% of the nation backed the ABM system.

Continuing campaigns for political influence are conducted by the public information staffs of federal government agencies—a group totaling about 7000 employees in the 1950s (Childs, 1965, pp. 297–298). The fact that the Department of Defense had about 6,000 of this total may help to account for the continuing public approval of escalating U.S. military budgets over the years!

Uses for Social Science Research

In the public policy arena there are many uses for social science research. George Gallup (1965) and other pollers have long insisted that more attention to legitimate scientific opinion polls could improve the processes of government. A sad example was provided by the abortive Bay of Pigs Cuban invasion attempt in 1961, which was apparently based on the assumption that many Cubans were ready to rise up against the Castro regime. However, in 1960 Lloyd Free had conducted a careful opinion poll of 1,000 urban Cubans which showed that they backed Castro overwhelmingly, and attention to those findings could have avoided the Bay of Pigs debacle (Cantril, 1967, pp. 1–5). Somewhat similarly, Ralph White (1970) has suggested that a careful analysis of South Vietnamese public opinion toward the Viet Cong versus the Saigon government could have kept the United States from its disastrous military involvement in Vietnam.

An example where poll information was usefully employed occurred in Edward Brooke's first campaign for the U.S. Senate in 1966. Private polls showed him that his early lead in the campaign was dropping sharply, especially among the more prejudiced voters. Consequently, he decided to confront the racial issue directly on TV programs, condemning extremists on both sides of the civil rights struggle. Partly as a result, his support increased to a 61% landslide, and he became the first Negro popularly elected to the U.S. Senate (Becker & Heaton, 1967).

Specialized governmental agencies also have many uses for social science research. The U.S. decision to ban all over-land flights by the supersonic transport plane resulted from large-scale field studies in St. Louis and Oklahoma City which found a majority of residents reporting substantial annoyance with a continuing series of sonic booms (Borsky, 1969). The Canadian government recently has been making very extensive use of survey findings in policy formation (Schindeler & Lanphier, 1969), and Goodwin and Tu (1975) have presented some highly pertinent research on public approval, knowledge, and complaints concerning the U.S. Social Security system. At the local level Fiedler, Fiedler, and Campf (1971) have demonstrated the value of survey methods in identifying major community problems which the reputed community leaders are not aware of.

In general, many high-level Federal administrators are quite receptive to the use of social science research, according to a study by Nathan Caplan (*Behavior Today*, 1975b). However, the way in which they use it often leaves much to be desired. A majority of policy-relevant research data is gathered by each agency's own staff, with their obvious biases and vested interests in the outcome; and even when the research is done by an outside agency, it may be commissioned and used for its political impact rather than its objective value (Weiss, 1972). Also there are cases where good research is done but then largely ignored by the government. Prominent examples of this are the research done for the Surgeon General's Advisory Committee on Television and Social Behavior (Bogart, 1972b), and the President's Commission on Obscenity and Pornography. The latter commission's findings, gathered at a cost of $2 million, were not just ignored but were actively repudiated by many Congressmen and by President Nixon, who called them "morally bankrupt" (*Los Angeles Times*, 1970).

Obviously, this is not the sort of research utilization which one would hope for. By contrast, Campbell (1971) has advocated that we become an "experimenting society," in which new social and political programs will be tried out as planned scientific experiments with careful evaluation of their effects. Such an honest, nonpartisan, and accountable approach would be a great improvement over today's typical extremes of complete lack of evaluation of government programs or over-advocacy of programs whose value has not been established.

Other writers have also proposed an active role for social scientists in evaluating the performance of, and in prescribing needed changes in, not only government, but also business and the mass media (e.g., Lasswell, 1972). Since training for such roles is not usually included in most behavioral science curricula, there should be more attention to the need for such preparation. One useful example is Brayfield's (1976) description of a graduate training program which aims at preparing psychologists to play a responsible scientific role in the field of public affairs. However, in giving advice to policy makers, we should keep in mind the earlier section of this chapter on attitude-behavior discrepancies. We must agree with Deutscher (1965) that social scientists should be very cautious about giving such advice unless they have studied behavioral outcomes as well as people's attitudes and opinions.

SUMMARY

This concluding chapter of Part I has discussed five important continuing areas of controversy in the field of attitudes and opinions. A close link between personality and attitudes has been expected and found in many well-known research studies. Though major methodological critiques have been made of the research on prejudice and authoritarianism, recent studies have continued to report relatively clear-cut relationships between certain attitudes and personality variables.

The attitude-behavior relationship has been a question since the 1930s, when a famous early study apparently showed great inconsistency between people's verbal attitude statements and their actions. However, methodological critiques have pointed out several factors which can misleadingly produce an appearance of inconsistency. Though there is often real inconsistency between attitudes and actions, the typical pattern is one of a moderate positive relationship. We have listed eight factors which may lead to inconsistency, and thus it is clear that a person's attitudes are only one of many influences on his(her) behavior. Several systems have been suggested for predicting behavior from attitudes and other factors, but it has also been found that a person's actions can have a reciprocal effect in modifying his(her) attitudes.

Laboratory experimental studies of attitudes generally show stronger effects than field studies, largely because of a number of methodological differences which are frequently confounded with the laboratory-field distinction. However, field studies often have an advantage in the generalizability of their results, and the findings of laboratory studies must always be verified in real-life situations. Though field research is still in a distinct minority position, its popularity appears to be growing gradually.

Attitude researchers have been concerned about ethical questions for many years. Harmful consequences are rare in attitude research, but deception is a common and controversial practice. Researchers must avoid invasion of privacy, undue inconvenience to research participants, and misleading reporting of results; and they must carefully consider the pros and cons of obtaining informed consent and of debriefing participants after the study. Finally, the scientist's societal obligation to provide knowledge by continuing to do research is also an ethical imperative.

The relationship of public opinion to public policy has several aspects. Philosophers have debated for centuries whether a representative should vote in accordance with the will of the people, his own best judgment, or his party's platform. It appears that the public is most competent to determine broad questions of the goals of government policy rather than the means for achieving them. Modern survey methods provide a greatly improved way of determining both mass and elite public opinion, but there are dangers in political leaders either following public opinion too slavishly or leading it too manipulatively.

In U.S. political life there are several different typical patterns of the effect of public opinion. In the area of civil rights, legislators have been found to vote quite closely in accordance with their constituents' views; and on issues of war policy, public opinion has set limits on the options that leaders could consider. By contrast, on Federal Aid to Education, Medicare, and gun control legislation, Congress has thrown up continuing roadblocks which frustrated the public will. On social welfare issues legislators tend to follow their party's platform rather than public opinion, while in foreign affairs public opinion tends to follow, and even be manipulated by, official policy. Many uses for social science research in the public policy arena have been illustrated in this and preceding chapters.

Suggested Readings

Bickman, L., & Henchy, T. *Beyond the Laboratory: Field Research in Social Psychology.* New York: McGraw-Hill, 1972.—A highly readable collection of papers, emphasizing field experiments using nonreactive methods. Chapters 5,7, and 8 (on racial prejudice, attitudes and behavior, and consumer behavior) are especially relevant to attitudes.

Brown, R. *Social Psychology.* New York: Free Press, 1965.—Chapter 10 is a fascinating summary of research on the authoritarian personality.

Calder, B.J., & Ross, M. *Attitudes and Behavior.* Morristown, N. J.: General Learning Press, 1973.—A 34-page pamphlet which nicely summarizes theory and research in this area.

Roll, C. W., Jr., & Cantril, A. H. *Polls: Their Use and Misuse in Politics.* New York: Basic Books, 1972.—Chapter 7 contains much intriguing information about public opinion and public policy, while Chapters 2 and 3 describe desirable and undesirable uses of polls in politics.

part II

Public Opinion on Socially-Important Topics

This section discusses the content of public attitudes and opinions on a variety of important topics. Some of these are classical areas in the study of public opinion: political attitudes, international attitudes, and racial prejudice. Political attitudes and voting are given the most space due to the vast amount of scientific attention they have received over the years. The other topics are currently "hot" areas of study in the social sciences because of their importance to the future of humanity: sexism, ecology and pollution, and population problems.

As a supplement to these summary chapters, the reader is encouraged to delve into primary sources in the voluminous literature on public opinion. One indispensable journal in this area is *The Public Opinion Quarterly*, founded in 1937. Other very useful sources are articles that give particularly clear and interesting overviews of areas of public opinion. The four selections listed below are excellent examples of this sort and are highly recommended because they add a unique perspective to the topics considered in Part II.

Stuart Chase. American values: A generation of change. *Public Opinion Quarterly*, 1965, 29, 357–367.

William Watts & Lloyd A. Free. Worries and concerns. In W. Watts & L. A. Free, *State of the Nation 1974*. Washington, D. C.: Potomac Associates, 1974. Pp. 19–30.

Daniel Yankelovich. Turnabout. In D. Yankelovich, *The New Morality: A Profile of American Youth in the 70's*. New York: McGraw-Hill, 1974. Pp. 3–11.

Peter Goldman. Black America in the 1970's. In P. Goldman, *Report from Black America*. New York: Simon & Schuster, 1969. Pp. 200–211.

Political Attitudes I

---

*(The President) is the last person in the world to know what the people really want and think.—*James A. Garfield.

*Our government rests on public opinion. Whoever can change public opinion can change the government practically as such.—*Abraham Lincoln.

*Popular opinion is the greatest lie in the world.—*Thomas Carlyle.

Political attitudes and behavior have received far more attention than any other area of public opinion. As the quotes above show, they have been the subject of great controversy as well as great interest. Some authorities, like Abraham Lincoln, have claimed that government decisions were based firmly upon public opinion. Others, such as George Gallup (1965), have doubted that they were, but felt that they should be. Still others, like Thomas Carlyle, have scoffed at the concept of public opinion and the notion that it could or should affect governmental decisions.

The political attitude area is almost unique among areas of public opinion in having an easily measured behavioral concomitant, the vote. Therefore voting behavior is frequently used as the criterion in political attitude surveys, or as the dependent variable of greatest interest. However, voting only occurs periodically, and it is only rarely that a specific political issue is presented directly to the public for their vote, as in a referendum or constitutional amendment or bond issue, etc. Therefore, we cannot confine our interest to voting behavior alone, but we must also consider public attitudes on various important political issues.

This chapter and the next one will be organized in three major sections, based on the dependent variable being studied. In this chapter we will consider political attitudes per se, particularly attitudes on important issues which are not put to public vote. In the following chapter we will first consider factors influencing *individuals'* voting behavior and then shift the focus to **aggregate** voting as a dependent variable, adding together all the individual votes and studying the patterns which occur within an election and the changes from one election to the next.

PRESIDENTIAL POPULARITY

Probably the most familiar single index in all of political polling is the Presidential "popularity" rating or, more accurately, the rating of people's approval of the President's performance in office. For decades, stretching back to the administration of Franklin D. Roosevelt, the Gallup Poll has been asking a question such as "Do you approve or disapprove of the way Ford is handling his job as President?" More recently, the Harris Poll has also reported regular results of a similar question. It is widely known that fluctuations in these poll results can send shivers up and down the backs of White House staff members, or raise Presidential spirits (and campaign dollars) when the results are favorable.

What do these approval ratings demonstrate about Presidential popularity? Generally they start relatively high when a President comes into office and decline later as his actions or inaction displease various subgroups of the populace. President Truman began with a very high 87% approval rating in the difficult circumstances after FDR's death in the closing months of World War II, but the following year his rating hit a low of only 32%. Twice it rebounded briefly, but then it fell below 50% for the rest of his administration. President Eisenhower's rating was remarkable in that it stayed high for so long, fluctuating around 70% for four years. However, it fell as low as 50% in his second term and ended around 60%. John Kennedy entered office with about 70% approval, which climbed to the high 70s after a year in office, but then dropped to about 60% before he was assassinated in 1963. At that crisis point, President Johnson received initial approval ratings around 80%, which declined somewhat in spite of his early legislative successes; as the Vietnam War became more and more unpopular, his ratings fell steadily and hovered around 40% by the end of his administration.

Richard Nixon's approval rating as President began somewhat lower than his predecessors', around 60%, and stayed in that range for nearly two years before falling to about 50%. His rating returned to about 60% for a year during his trips to China and Russia, his successful reelection campaign, and the signing of the Vietnam cease-fire agreement. Subsequently, however, Nixon's popular approval dropped sharply as the shadow of Watergate scandals lengthened over his administration, reaching his all-time low of 24% shortly before his resignation. President Ford entered his new office with an approval rating of 71%, but within a few months the figure had dropped to 50% as he struggled to overcome the combined blows of inflation, recession, and negative public reaction to his pardon of former-President Nixon. During most of 1975 his rating remained in the 40s, except for a brief return to 50% after U.S. recovery of the freighter Mayaguez from the Cambodian forces who had captured it (*Gallup Opinion Index*, 1975d).

In addition to their general tendency to decline over a president's term in office, these approval ratings also show a marked tendency to rise briefly after a decisive presidential action in international affairs, such as the Mayaguez incident, sometimes even after an unsuccessful one. Mueller (1973) has dubbed this the "rally-round-the-flag phenomenon." For instance, Kennedy's popularity rose from 72% to 83% following the Bay of Pigs fiasco, and from 62% to 76% after his successful handling of the Cuban missile crisis. Similarly, Johnson's approval rating rose ten points after he ordered bombings of North Vietnamese targets near Hanoi which had formerly been off-limits to U.S. bombers. But it also rose markedly, from 36% to 49%, when he declared a moratorium on the North Vietnam bombings in 1968 (Gallup, 1972).

In contrast to these rally effects, Presidential popularity sags predictably during economic slumps but does not rebound noticeably during economic booms. In an intriguing series of careful studies, Mueller (1973) has shown that wars may also depress public approval of the President, but that the Vietnam War had much less of this effect than commonly thought. See Chapter 13 for more details.

Despite the eye-catching headline appeal of these Presidential approval ratings, they are at best a very crude indication of popular political attitudes. They cannot be relied on as a guide for governmental decisions because of their oversimplicity and the fact that they can be quickly changed by the impact of events. A particularly dramatic example of their rapid fluctuation is the fact that less than a year before his unexpected victory over Dewey in the 1948 election, President Truman's rating stood at a dismal figure of only 36%.

CONCERNS OF CITIZENS

A better indicator of political attitudes would focus on the *issues* and concerns that are uppermost in people's minds, for instance by asking a question such as "What do you feel are the most serious problems facing this country today?" Questions similar to this have been repeatedly asked of national samples by the Gallup Poll, the University of Michigan's Survey Research Center, and other polling organizations. It may surprise you to realize how much the answers have varied from time to time, depending on the course of national and international events. Some examples will illustrate the range of responses.

In 1973 such a question was asked by poller Louis Harris as part of the first public opinion poll ever to be commissioned by Congress (U.S. Senate, 1973; summarized in *Newsweek*, December 10, 1973). The 1600 respondents were asked what they felt were the country's two or three biggest problems, and a summary of their answers is shown in Table 11-1. It is clear that in that year two major problems overshadowed all others in people's minds—inflation, mentioned by 64%, and lack of integrity in government, mentioned by 43%. Many of the other problems listed, though less salient in late 1973, were high on the list of people's concerns in some other years. For instance, the oil and energy shortage was mentioned much more prominently a few months later, in early 1974. Corruption in government and the energy shortage are both very recent additions to the ranks of major public concerns. In nearly 40 years of Gallup's polling, the issue of corruption in government had never been spontaneously mentioned by more than 3% of respondents until mid-1973, when it suddenly jumped to 16% as a result of publicity concerning the Watergate scandals (Erskine, 1973c).

Looking back to the decade of the 1960s, between 1966 and 1970 the Vietnam War generally was at the forefront of public concern, and between 1963 and 1965 worries were centered on the civil rights struggle, including problems of racial strife and racial discrimination. At many times, economic problems have been a major public concern; but for most of the post-World-War-II period, the greatest worry has been foreign affairs and threats to world peace.

These trends in public concerns over a 29-year period since 1947 are clearly shown in Figure 11-1. The graph lumps together all mentions of war, peace, and foreign affairs as the nation's single most important problem, and it compares their level with that of racial problems and of all economic problems such as unemployment, cost of living, taxes, and government spending. The data are from the Gallup Poll (Gallup, 1972; *Gallup Opinion Index,* 1972b, 1974e,

TABLE 11-1   Responses of a National Sample to a Question on
Our Nation's Biggest Problems, September, 1973

Problem	% Mentioning
Inflation, cost of living	64%
Integrity in government	43
Crime	17
Drugs	14
Welfare, welfare reform	13
Federal spending	12
Taxes	11
Pollution, ecology, overpopulation	11
Energy shortage	10
Education, schools	9
Alienation, social breakdown	8
Older people, elderly	7
Race, discrimination	7
Unemployment	6
Foreign policy	4
Health care	3
Employment, work	2
Housing	2
	243%

Note.—The table adds to more than 100% because people were asked to mention
two or three problems.
Source: Adapted from U.S. Senate, 1973, pp. 225, 49.

1975a, 1976). This graph shows dramatically how briefly racial problems held
center stage as the greatest American concern and how quickly both racial and
international problems were forgotten when economic worries increased in the
early 1970s.

It is also interesting to remember back to other serious national problems
which have sporadically reared their ugly heads and then been displaced as new
problems came to the fore. For instance, in 1953, 54% of respondents mentioned
the Korean War as our worst problem; in 1954, 17% said it was internal Communism in the U.S.; and in 1963, 24% mentioned Cuba. More recently, after the
civil rights struggle of the 1960s, the nation's most important problem was seen
as crime and riots in 1968 and 1969 (by 17% of respondents), college demonstrations and unrest in 1970 (by 27%), and the energy crisis in early 1974 (by 46%).
However, in between these occasional unusual worries, the recurrent twin problems of foreign affairs and of economic conditions continued to occupy people's
attention.

In comparing research findings such as those just described, readers should be
alert to the fact that they are influenced by the type of response required, the
wording of the question, and the basis used in tabulating responses. Different

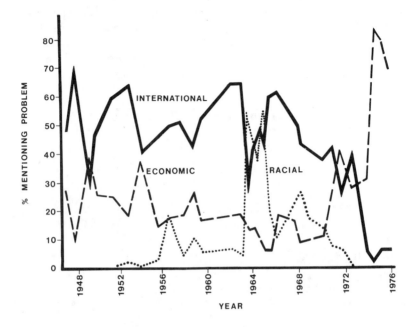

Figure 11-1 A 29-year summary of the public's view of our nation's most serious single problem, comparing international, economic, and racial problems from 1947 to 1976. (Data are from the Gallup Poll.)

findings may sometimes be obtained with free-response questions (e.g., "What are our biggest problems?") than with ones where a list of problems is read or handed to the respondent (e.g., "How worried are you about each of the following problems?"). For instance, using the latter format in a 1964 election study, Free and Cantril (1967) found considerably more concern for international problems than reported from the free-response items of the Survey Research Center study (RePass, 1971). Additionally, in comparing studies, it is important to note not only the question wording, but also the basis of tabulating responses. When several responses per person are allowed, as in Table 11-1, the resulting percentages of mentions are not comparable with studies which report only the first or most important response, such as those summarized in Figure 11-1.

TRUST IN GOVERNMENT

Another aspect of political attitudes is how much the citizens trust their government—not the current administration, but the government as a whole. The Survey Research Center has been measuring this topic since 1958, and its findings raise alarming doubts about the prospects for political stability in the United

States. The index of trust in government is based on five questions about the federal government's performance. Historically, many more citizens have shown a "high" level of trust than a "low" level—in 1958, the difference between these two percentages was about 50, and in 1964 it was over 40. However, by 1970 only 35% of citizens had a high level of trust while 37% had a low level, a difference of −2. By fall of 1973 this sharp downward trend had continued to the point where about twice as many Americans had low trust in their government as had high trust, and the index stood at about −25 (Institute for Social Research, 1972, 1974). Research by Bachman and Jennings (1975) suggests that the Vietnam war was partly responsible for this sharp decline. It remains to be seen whether the decline is a temporary effect of Vietnam and/or the Watergate scandals, or a more permanent phenomenon.

Trust in government can also be shown by examining citizens' ratings of how good a job various branches of the government are doing compared with their ratings of other institutions in our society. What would you guess to be the most-approved institutions in our country?

The results of such a comparison in the fall of 1973 are shown in Figure 11-2. Interestingly, the two most-approved institutions of the 15 included were the U.S. military and colleges and universities, both with scores around 5.5. Next came several private, nongovernmental institutions, and in seventh place stood the U.S. Supreme Court, which was the most-approved branch of the federal government with a score around 4.8. Congress was in ninth place, around 4.6; the federal government as a whole was in fourteenth place, below 3.9; and the President and administration took last place by a wide margin at 3.3. Again, it should be recognized that this negativism toward the federal government may be a relatively temporary result of Vietnam and/or Watergate. However, even if we discount some of the negativism toward the federal government, it is clear that many other organizations in our society are more widely admired and respected. The findings showed surprising approval of two recently much-maligned institutions, the military services and colleges and universities, as well as the similarly-criticized news media (Institute for Social Research, 1974).

Comparative data are available showing changes in public trust between 1966 and 1973 for a rather-similar list of ten major institutions (*Newsweek*, December 10, 1973). The relative ratings for this list are much the same as in the above study, with the addition of medicine and television news as highly-trusted institutions. With the exception of television news and the press, all eight other institutions *declined* in public trust since 1966, most of them quite markedly. Again the three branches of the federal government were low on the list, the Supreme Court in sixth place, Congress in seventh, and the Executive branch in last place (in 1966 it had been in seventh place, above organized religion, the press, and television news). Erskine's (1973b) summary of poll results over the years also confirms that there has generally been more public trust in Congress than in the President.

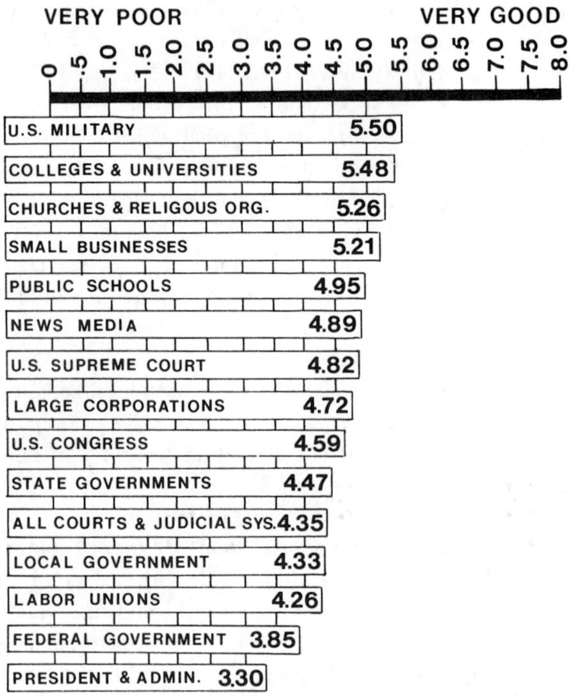

Figure 11-2 The public's average ratings of how good a job each of fifteen major institutions is doing for the country. (Data from Institute for Social Research, *ISR Newsletter*, Winter 1974, p. 8.)

THE QUALITY OF LIFE

A fascinating recent trend in measuring political attitudes is to develop standardized **social indicators** as indices of the quality of life in various spheres, analogous to the well-known economic indicators such as gross national product, unemployment rate, and the cost of living index. This development is part of a general trend toward increased consideration of human values and personal satisfactions in business and industry and in economic and political decision-making. A related proposal, long advocated by Senator Walter Mondale and others, is the creation of a Presidential Council of Social Advisors, parallel in function to the Council of Economic Advisors. Interest in social indicators was fostered by grants from the Russell Sage Foundation, the Social Science Research Council, and some government agencies (Bauer, 1966; Sheldon & Moore, 1968; U.S. Department of Health, Education, and Welfare, 1969), and more recently it has been sponsored financially by the National Science Foundation's program of Research Applied to National Needs.

The first large-scale national surveys in this area were conducted in 1971 and 1972 by several different research organizations. They have focused on a variety of areas which affect people's satisfaction with their lives, including marriage and family, health, satisfaction with job and income, leisure activities, race relations, civil liberties, women's rights, political alienation, and general happiness (Nicholls, 1972; Wilcox, Brooks, Beal, & Klonglan, 1972). The intent of such studies is to construct meaningful measures of the psychological and sociological aspects of our national life patterns (perhaps an index of Gross National Happiness, or Employment Satisfaction; or how about a Cost of Loving Index to measure marriage and family satisfaction?). Once developed, these indices would be measured at regular intervals to show trends and changes in our national quality of life.

Unfortunately, there are no reliable psychological survey data to tell us whether the "good old days" were really so good for most people as we often think they were in retrospect. Certainly today's assembly-line jobs, high divorce rate, urban crowding, and air pollution are factors which diminish general satisfaction. Yet the past century had problems of equal or greater impact, such as child labor, high death rates, slum tenements, and unpaved roads covered with horse manure.

Some clues about national worries and satisfactions can be obtained from the published polls during the 40 years since scientific sampling methods were introduced. Erskine (1973a) summarizes these reports concerning Americans' goals and problems as follows:

> First and foremost, over the period surveyed, Americans' chief aims in life turn out to be anything but materialistic. Most wish for peace of mind, family contentment, and, secondarily, health. Regrets are almost entirely that they did not get enough education. Conversely, however, worries and fears in the U.S. are overwhelmingly economic. Financial insecurity and not being able to make ends meet are almost universal bugaboos. Rarely is wealth *per se* given any priority among people's hopes for their lives (p. 132).

An example of recent survey findings on the quality of life comes from a Survey Research Center study (A. Campbell, Converse, & Rodgers, 1976). Interviews were conducted with a national sample of over 2,100 persons 18 years of age and older. In general, respondents were more likely to say that life was getting worse in this country than that it was getting better, a finding very similar to the ones cited above about citizens' trust in government. About half of the sample saw no change in the quality of life, about one-third felt it was deteriorating, and only about one-sixth saw it as improving. The most common complaints cited were increasing alienation, public protests and disorders, crime, drug usage, declining morality, behavior of young people, inflation, government policies, taxes, and ecological problems. These findings are quite consistent with those of the 1973 Harris poll conducted for a Senate subcommittee (*Newsweek*,

December 10, 1973). That survey found 45% of citizens saying that conditions had worsened in the last 10 years, compared to 35% who felt that life had improved. Overall, 53% of Harris' respondents agreed that "There is something deeply wrong in America today," whereas in 1968 at the height of the Vietnam War and protest only 39% had agreed with that statement.

Despite this prevailing pessimism, the absolute level of dissatisfaction with American life does not seem to be high. On most of the 15 different areas of life asked about in the SRC study, relatively small minorities of respondents placed themselves on the dissatisfied side of the scale. The greatest satisfaction was reported with marriage and family life (3% and 6% being dissatisfied), while the lowest satisfaction was found for standard of living, amount of education, and savings (14%, 28% and 36% being dissatisfied, respectively). On three other key items, 22% reported unfair treatment by public officials, 11% said they were not free enough to live the kind of life they wanted, and only 8% said they were dissatisfied with life in the United States today, "all things considered." A mere 2% of the sample were dissatisfied on all three items. These are the most deeply alienated members of the population, and the results showed that they were much more likely to be found among the young, well-educated, metropolitan residents, and blacks than among other population subgroups (Campbell, Converse, & Rodgers, 1976).

ATTITUDES OF POPULATION SUBGROUPS

This last finding brings us to another very important topic, the differing political attitudes of various subgroups in the population. In this area there is a great mass of demographic information, which we will only skim over quickly. Interested readers can find sources for further exploration in the Suggested Readings at the end of this chapter.

The "Traditional Wisdom"

The commonly-accepted beliefs about the relationship of demographic factors to political attitudes and behavior are partly a mythology and partly based on depression-era political alignments which have changed markedly in more recent elections. For instance, the Republican Party has traditionally been considered the party of older people, farmers and rural residents, the well-to-do, and upper educational and occupational groups; while the Democratic Party was supposed to be favored by the opposite groups, particularly by union members, blacks, and Catholics. Though many of these conclusions were correct during the great Depression and World War II, Miller (1960) has concluded that they largely lost their validity after the 1948 election, during the Eisenhower era. His findings show that urban-rural differences in voting were largely a myth; in overall nationwide results the Republicans did somewhat better in small cities and towns than in either rural or urban areas. Though older people had been more Republican, by 1956 age differences in voting were nearly eliminated; and the same was true of income differences (except for the few people in very high income categories). Upper educational and occupational groups, which had been strongly Republican earlier, were only a bit more conservative than other citizens in 1956. Voting differences between farmers and union members were completely eliminated by 1956, while blacks and Catholics, though still more Democratic than the total population, showed a marked decrease in their degree of Democratic preference.

Many of the above changes in voting patterns must be ascribed to Eisenhower's unique ability to appeal to all segments of the population, for in 1960 and later elections there was a partial return to earlier voting patterns (Pool, Abelson, & Popkin, 1964; Roper, 1965; Key & Cummings, 1966). In particular, union members, blacks, and Catholics returned to the Democratic fold in large numbers, giving Kennedy his razor-thin margin of victory. However, it is still true that in subsequent elections much of the "traditional wisdom" has proved inapplicable. As a result, many empirical studies have been done, and the recent scientific literature on subgroup differences in political attitudes has destroyed many former stereotypes.

Recent Research Findings

Urban-Suburban Residence. Zikmund (1967) compared urban and suburban residents of seven major metropolitan areas on a large number of measures of political attitudes, party identification, political interest, and party loyalty. He found major effects of residential area only in party identification: more city dwellers consider themselves Democrats, while suburbanites are more strongly independents and Republicans. All of the other ten political characteristics studied showed much greater differences between different metropolitan areas (e.g., New York vs. Chicago vs. Los Angeles) than between cities and suburbs in general. Thus we may conclude that in many political characteristics Boston suburban dwellers are more similar to Boston city dwellers than they are to suburbanites near San Francisco, for example.

Age. The "traditional wisdom" holds that as people get older, an increasing percentage of them tend to identify with the Republican Party, and there is some empirical evidence for the correctness of that conclusion during the 1950s (Crittenden, 1962, 1969). However, people's political attitudes are influenced not only by their age, but also by the specific political experiences of each successive generation, such as living through depressions, wars, etc. The effects of these differing experiences on different generations can be determined through a **cohort analysis**—an analysis which follows each generation, or cohort, longitudinally as they get older. (By contrast, the more-common age analysis lumps together the responses of 50-year-olds in 1950 with the responses of other 50-year-olds in 1960 and 1970, groups which were born 10 and 20 years later and so had quite different political experiences.) When cohort analyses are done on the variable of political identification, they tend to decrease some of the apparent linkage between conservatism and increasing age (Cutler, 1969). Moreover, for the period of the 1960s, there seems to be no clear relationship between party identification and either age or generational experiences (Klecka, 1971).

Geographic Region. Despite the "melting pot" notion of social homogenization in the United States, there is strong evidence that regional differences still exist and may even be increasing. Of the four major census regions, Northeast, North Central, South, and West, the South still persists as clearly the most conservative, with the West and Northeast being most liberal. These differences were found not only in political attitudes, but also in most items studied in the areas of religious and moral views, racial, and occupational attitudes (Glenn & Simmons, 1967). On the average the South was about 15 points above the other three regions in the percentage of respondents classified as conservative on all of these topics. A study of support for Goldwater before the 1964 election (Crespi, 1965) confirmed that the South was by far the most conservative region politically, though in this case the West was next in line rather than most liberal.

Social Class. Though upper-income and upper-occupational groups still tend to be more conservative politically than other subgroups, the 1964 Goldwater election provided a good example of the many exceptions to this rule (Crespi, 1965). Of the major occupational groups, only farmers were significantly above average in Goldwater support; and among income levels, only the $3000-$5000 annual income group were significantly more likely to prefer Goldwater.

In a careful examination of social-class trends between 1936 and 1969, Glenn (1973) found two interesting and conflicting patterns. He showed that class-based differences in *party identification* remained strong during that period, lower-class individuals tending to identify with the Democratic Party and upper-class ones with the Republican Party. However, class-based differences in actual *voting* have declined steadily during the 1950s and 1960s, except in the South where the recent emergence of a viable two-party system has led to an increase in class-based voting. Specifically, the difference in percentage of Republican voting between white-collar and blue-collar classes has dropped, outside the South, from about 20% in the pre-Eisenhower years to about 12% in the 1960s, whereas in the South the same figures have risen from about 10% to about 25%. Thus, in most of the country, social class is diminishing as a political determinant, but it is not completely dead by any means.

Status Inconsistency. It has been suggested by several authors that people having inconsistent social statuses (low occupational prestige but high income, high education but low income, etc.) are inclined to hold extreme political attitudes, either right-wing ones or left-wing ones (e.g., Geschwender, 1967). However, Eitzen (1970, 1972) has shown that people whose statuses are inconsistent on education, occupational prestige, and income are intermediate in the extremity of their political attitudes between consistently high-status and consistently low-status individuals. Using scales measuring liberalism-conservatism in three different content areas (social welfare, civil rights, and internationalism), he found 3½ times as many liberals as conservatives. Both liberals and conservatives were found disproportionately more among the high-status individuals, whereas status inconsistents were proportionately represented in both categories, and low-status respondents were hardly ever conservative in their overall political attitudes. These results, from a representative national sample, indicate that the findings are apt to be misleading if high-status and low-status individuals are grouped together as "status-consistents" for comparison with "status-inconsistents."

White Ethnic Groups. In recent years it has become common to think of American white ethnic groups (the second- and third-generation descendents of non-Anglo-Saxon European immigrants) as racists, hawks, and "hard hats." Greeley (1972) has examined this stereotype and found very little truth in it. Taking data from various national polls, he studied the attitudes of respondents who were Jewish, Polish, Irish, German, Italian, Scandinavian, and Slavic in relation to those of WASPs. In general he found that these white ethnic groups were more likely to be doves on the Vietnam War than the average respondent was, were more sympathetic to government welfare programs and to racial integration, were more concerned about pollution problems, and so on. Of course, there were differences between the various ethnic groups and the various issues examined, but in general the results showed very clearly that the "hard-hat" stereotype of white ethnics as bigots is inaccurate and dysfunctional for our society.

LIBERAL-CONSERVATIVE IDEOLOGY

One of the most basic aspects of people's political attitudes is their ideological viewpoint. We have discussed political ideology extensively in Chapter 5, but a few additional issues will be examined here. One issue of interest is to what extent adherents of the two major U.S. political parties hold different political ideologies. McClosky, Hoffman, and O'Hara (1960) compared self-reported Republican and Democratic identifiers, and found relatively little difference in their ideological stand on issues of public policy. However Ladd (1972; Ladd & Hadley, 1973) has proposed that these "citizenry parties" should be defined using behavioral criteria, based on regularity of voting support for the party's

262 Political Attitudes I

nominees. Using such a definition reduces the size of the group classified as adherents of each party, and these groups do show rather wide ideological differences, just as leaders of the two parties do.

Another issue is whether ideological thinking is a stable characteristic of the voter or is markedly influenced by the events of a particular election campaign. The approach of *The American Voter* (Campbell et al., 1960) and of Converse (1964), as reported in Chapter 5, led to the view that only a small minority of the population *ever* uses ideological concepts such as "liberal" and "conservative"in assessing political issues. However, their findings were based principally upon the 1956 election, which was not marked by any clear-cut ideological issues. Field and Anderson (1969) have compared the 1956, 1960, and 1964 elections, using the same SRC data on which Campbell et al. and Converse based their conclusions for 1956. Results showed conclusively that the 1956 election was lowest in respondents' ideological references, and the 1964 election between Goldwater and Johnson was the highest. Because of minor differences in scoring rules from the Campbell et al. procedures, 21% of the population were classified as ideologues in 1956, but the figure was 27% in 1960, and rose markedly to 35% in 1964. Moreover, almost all of the increase in 1964 was attributable to one candidate—Goldwater—rather than to the other candidate or to the two parties' platforms or activities; and a majority of the ideological references to Goldwater were negative even though the Republican Party was perceived very positively that year. Thus, the authors conclude that "the voters understood Goldwater only too well" (p. 385).

Since 1964, it appears that the ideological emphasis of elections has continued and even increased. In 1968 a marked ideological flavor was imparted to the campaign by George Wallace's third-party candidacy—a candidacy which was appealing enough, it has been estimated, to change the winner in eight states and cost Humphrey the election (Mitofsky, 1969). Even more clearly, in 1972, McGovern's candidacy led to an unprecedented emphasis on national policy issues and political ideologies (A. Miller, W. Miller, Raine, & Brown, 1973). Though McGovern's personal attractiveness as a candidate was also rated low by many voters, it seems to have been the ideological issues which cost him crucial support from normally-Democratic voters. On each of the issues which were most important to voters in the 1972 election—Vietnam, urban unrest, campus disorders, the rights of accused persons, and government aid to minority groups—there was a substantial group of Democrats who disagreed strongly with McGovern's policies and defected to vote Republican.

These authors conclude that three successive Presidential elections which have focused on national problems and policy issues have transformed the American electorate and introduced a new era of issue politics. Changes in other factors which have affected recent voting trends are discussed in Chapter 12.

Photograph courtesy of Princeton
University Archives. Reprinted by
permission.

Box 11-1 HADLEY CANTRIL, *Pioneer Survey Researcher*

Best known for his studies of public opinion, Hadley Cantril was also a researcher in perceptual psychology. Born in Utah in 1906, he attended Dartmouth College, and received his Ph.D. from Harvard. After a few years of teaching, he joined the faculty of Princeton in 1936, later becoming chairman of the psychology department. He founded Princeton's Office of Public Opinion Research but left in 1955 to form the Institute for International Social Research. He died of a stroke in 1969.

Before World War II, Cantril was asked by President Roosevelt to assess Americans' feelings about involvement in the war, and later he advised both Eisenhower and Kennedy. His text Gauging Public Opinion *is a classic, and he wrote 17 other books and over 100 articles, including* The Invasion from Mars, *a study of panic reactions to Orson Welles' famous radio drama. He directed the Tensions Project of UNESCO, edited* Tensions That Cause Wars, *and conducted survey research in at least 14 nations, from Nigeria to Poland to Brazil.*

Ideological Conservatism versus Operational Liberalism

An important point about ideological positions has been made by Free and Cantril (1967). In their study of a national sample of over 3000 respondents, they found that, ideologically, Americans tend to lean in a conservative direction. Using five questions on abstract, general views regarding federal interference in state and local matters, government regulation of business, local solutions of social problems, belief in economic opportunity in America, and belief in individual initiative, they constructed an index of **ideological** liberalism or conservatism. The results showed that the American public fell in the following categories:

Completely or predominantly liberal	16%
Middle of the road	34%
Completely or predominantly conservative	50%

However, the results were markedly different for an index of **operational** liberalism or conservatism, which involved attitudes toward five specific government programs—federal aid to education, Medicare, the federal low-rent housing program, urban renewal, and federal efforts to reduce unemployment and poverty. At this specific, or operational, level the public leaned strongly in the liberal direction, as follows:

Completely or predominantly liberal	65%
Middle of the road	21%
Completely or predominantly conservative	14%

Combining the findings of these two scales makes a fascinating picture, which is presented in Table 11-2. The table shows, in the upper-left-hand corner, that 90% of the ideological liberals were also liberals on the operational scale, a highly consistent picture. In the same column, it is clear that an overwhelming majority (78%) of ideological middle-of-the-roaders were actually liberals on operational questions. But most intriguing is the finding that nearly half (46%) of ideological conservatives were operational *liberals*! These results demonstrate that New Deal-type government programs aiming at the welfare of all citizens have gained very wide public support, even among professed conservatives. The authors describe the situation of these supposed conservatives as "schizoid" since in practice they favor exactly the sort of government programs which, in theory, they should oppose. The authors also conclude that the operational dimension is "the most significant (one) from any functional point of view" (p. 50), since it indicates the kind of specific government programs that people will support.

TABLE 11-2 Combination of Results from Ideological and Operational Scales of Liberalism-Conservativism

	Ideological scale		
Operational scale	Liberal	Middle of the road	Conservative
Liberal	90%	78%	46%
Middle of the road	9	18	28
Conservative	1	4	26
Total	100%	100%	100%

Source: Adapted from p. 37 of *The Political Beliefs of Americans:A Study of Public Opinion,* by Lloyd A. Free and Hadley Cantril. © 1968 by Rutgers State University. Reprinted by permission of the Rutgers University Press.

LEADING PUBLIC OPINION VERSUS FOLLOWING IT

We have mentioned at several points above that public attitudes change from time to time in response to events. The growing acceptance over the years of operationally liberal government programs is one example of such attitude change. Another example is the frequent fluctuations in presidential popularity, and particularly the typical increases in the President's ratings after he takes some decisive action in international affairs.

As these examples show, the public is usually more concerned with reaching a goal (stopping a war, ending a recession, etc.) than with the methods whereby the goal is reached. Thus, as far as the public is concerned, the President has a rather wide latitude in choosing specific programs, as long as they seem to be directed toward the important goal of that period. Because of most people's lack of information, low level of involvement in specific issues, and eagerness to believe that progress is being made, the public will usually give a favorable rating to any newly proposed presidential solution to national problems, even to programs which it had formerly rated unfavorably, such as greater recognition for Communist China, or imposition of price and wage controls.

These conclusions are doubly true in the unfamiliar and mysterious (to most Americans) area of foreign affairs. Lipset (1966) has illustrated this point with many examples from the Vietnam War era. During that period of national frustration and discontent, President Johnson was able to present clear-cut escalations of the conflict (e.g., extensions of U.S. bombing raids, mining of Haiphong harbor) as attempts to bring peace closer, and a majority of Americans accepted this rationale. In the long run, as American casualties climbed to painfully high levels, public opinion gradually shifted and produced pressures to end the war (Mueller, 1973). But in the short run at least, as Lipset stresses, the President can lead public opinion very effectively rather than following it:

> the opinion data indicate that national policy-makers, particularly the President, have an almost free hand to pursue any policy they think correct and get public support for it (1966, p. 20).

In domestic affairs also, George Gallup (1965) has emphasized, citizens are often ready to accept new and unfamiliar programs. In fact, because of their lower degree of ideological commitment, the public is often way ahead of the politicians in this regard. Charles Farnsley, a U.S. Congressman and former mayor of Louisville, Kentucky, agrees completely, as he states in this back-stage glimpse of political life:

> I found surveys particularly helpful, when I was Mayor, in overruling my advisors. Political advisors have a lot of stereotyped "don'ts": don't do thus and so; the

public's against it; it'll be fatal to you if you do. But my surveys would frequently show me that such timidity and caution were unwarranted. The public was not only willing to go along with unorthodox and presumably politically dangerous actions, they were ready and eager for them (Farnsley, 1965, p. 464).

DIRECTIONS FOR FUTURE RESEARCH

What questions are still unanswered in the field of political attitudes, and what are promising directions for future research? Hennessy (1970) has recommended major concentration on studying the attitudes of various elite groups, because of the research findings showing that most members of the mass public do not have consistent political belief systems nor meaningful political attitudes. Among his specific research suggestions are:

1. Development of techniques for screening out the responses of uninvolved and uninformed individuals (what Converse has called "nonattitudes").
2. Study of how political attitudes can be *created* in people who don't already have them (that is, political socialization and political education processes).
3. Research on the relation between political attitudes, political actions, and attitude change in leadership groups—with consideration of the processes of bargaining and compromise which are involved.
4. Study of the policy effects of elite groups' political attitudes, and the degree of independent initiative in policy choices which leaders can exercise.

Somewhat similar recommendations have been made by Goldner (1971) and by Rossi (1966). Goldner has stressed that the political process involves the interactions of competing and cooperating *groups*, and that the political attitudes of any individual are irrelevant except as they are expressed through group pressures. Consequently, he recommends the study of organizations rather than individuals. Similarly Rossi has urged adoption of a *systemic* analysis of voting behavior, concentrating on how reciprocal rewards and benefits are achieved by the various components of our political system: candidates, political leaders, local party workers, constituents, and affected organizations.

In the area of political polling, Field (1973) has emphasized the need for more information concerning the effects of polls on voters, on candidates, on the news media, and on the political process in general. Studies of the election campaigns of Senator Edward Brooke (Becker & Heaton, 1967) and of Goldwater in 1964 (Benham, 1965), among others, have clearly demonstrated the value to candidates of reliable polling information. Undoubtedly, the future will see many more candidates planning and modifying their campaigns in the light of poll information on their familiarity to voters, their popularity, the image which the public has of them, and the current importance of various issues to the voters in their area.

SUMMARY

Presidential approval ratings are the most familiar measure of public political attitudes. They tend to decline during a President's term in office, but often rise for a time after decisive presidential actions. Concerns of citizens about problems facing the country are a better index than presidential popularity because they help to identify the source of people's discontent or satisfaction. During the 1950s and early 1960s, issues of foreign affairs, war, and peace were generally mentioned as the nation's most serious problems. Starting in 1963 racial problems took first place, followed by the Vietnam War in 1965, and economic worries in 1971. In 1973 lack of integrity in government became a strong secondary public concern.

Another useful measure is the index of public trust in our government, which has been declining very sharply ever since the late 1960s. Among important American institutions, the military and colleges and universities were rated most favorably in 1973, while the Executive branch of the federal government was rated most unfavorably by far. An important recent trend in measuring political attitudes is the development of standard social indicators of the quality of life, analogous to the familiar economic indicators such as gross national product. Initial findings indicate a generally high level of satisfaction for most people in most areas of their lives, but a pessimistic feeling that life is getting worse for them rather than better.

Traditional patterns of political attitudes among population subgroups, based on Depression-era alignments, began to change rather markedly during the Eisenhower era of the 1950s. Urban-suburban, social class, and age differences in political attitudes are much smaller than has been commonly believed; and white ethnic groups in general are not the hawks and racists that they have often been portrayed to be. However, regional differences still persist, with the South being the most conservative region.

Liberal or conservative ideological views are not solely a stable characteristic of individuals, for they can also be influenced by events. The political campaigns of 1964 through 1972 have displayed a striking increase in ideological emphasis and introduced a new era of issue politics. Though most Americans tend toward a conservative position on ideological issues, on operational questions concerning specific government programs they are strongly liberal. The President can often lead public opinion very effectively rather than following it in his choice of specific programs and operational procedures.

Future research on political attitudes should concentrate heavily on the study of political elite groups and organizations which attempt to exert political influence. We also need more information concerning the effects of polls on voters, candidates, the media, and the political process in general.

Suggested Readings

Campbell, A., Converse, P. E., Miller, W. E., & Stokes, D. E. *The American Voter*. New York: Wiley, 1960.—A landmark study of political attitudes and voting behavior. Chapters 11–15 present a thorough summary of demographic influences on political attitudes. Also available in a paperback abridged version.

Campbell, A., Converse, P. E., & Rodgers, W. L. *The Quality of American Life: Perceptions, Evaluations, and Satisfactions.* New York: Russell Sage Foundation, 1976.—An extensive report on one of the first large-scale studies which has attempted to develop a set of social indicators.

Free, L. A., & Cantril, H. *The Political Beliefs of Americans: A Study of Public Opinion.* New Brunswick, N. J.: Rutgers University Press, 1967.—A careful national study of the liberal versus conservative beliefs and attitudes of Americans as of 1964.

Roll, C. W., Jr., & Cantril, A. H. *Polls: Their Use and Misuse in Politics.* New York: Basic Books, 1972.—A practically-oriented and interestingly-written little book. Chapter 3 describes ways in which polls can develop useful information on political attitudes.

Sears, D. O. Political behavior. In G. Lindzey & E. Aronson (Eds.), *The Handbook of Social Psychology* (2nd ed.). Vol. 5. Reading, Mass.: Addison-Wesley, 1969. Pp. 315–458.—A detailed and scholarly summary, including a discussion of U.S. citizens' attitudes toward government officials and institutions (pp. 414–431) and a summary of the political effect of demographic factors (pp. 382–399).

chapter 12

Political Attitudes II: Voting

Democracy substitutes selection by the incompetent many for appointment by the corrupt few. —George Bernard Shaw.

Our government is a government of political parties under the guiding influence of public opinion. There does not seem to be any other method by which a representative government can function. —Calvin Coolidge.

I always voted at my party's call,
And I never thought of thinking for myself at all. —W. S. Gilbert.

In this chapter we will discuss two aspects of voting behavior: *individual* voting decisions and *aggregate* voting patterns. Since many of the demographic factors that influence voting behavior as well as political attitudes per se were examined in the preceding chapter, those factors will not be repeated here. Instead, we will focus on several other major determinants of individual voting decisions that have been discovered in a series of major election studies.

SOME DETERMINANTS OF INDIVIDUAL VOTING DECISIONS

Cross-Pressures

Historically, the first such factor to be analyzed came from the first large-scale scientific election study (Lazarsfeld, Berelson & Gaudet, 1948). This research on the 1940 election, reported in a landmark volume called *The People's Choice*, was a **panel study** in which 600 residents of Erie County, Ohio, were each interviewed seven times between May and November to investigate factors involved in changing voting preferences. (Interestingly, and unexpectedly, nearly 70% of the respondents showed *no changes* in voting intentions from start to finish of the study.)

In this research, predictions of the respondents' voting patterns were made using a score called the Index of Political Predisposition (IPP), based on a combination of three demographic variables—religion, social class, and urban or rural residence. At the various levels of this index the proportion of respondents voting Democratic ranged from 26% at one extreme to 83% at the other, indicating a strong relationship of the index to voting decisions. (However, as mentioned in the preceding chapter, these demographic variables no longer relate as closely to voting behavior as they did in the 1930s and 1940s.)

In this study **cross-pressures** were defined as contradictory voting predispositions on the three variables (e.g., being a middle-class Catholic, or a working-class rural resident). Respondents who were under such conflicting pressures were also found to fluctuate in their voting intentions, to show less interest and attention to the campaign, to be more influenced by other persons' views, and to reach their voting decision later than other citizens. These results of political cross-pressures, however defined, seem generally to hold true up to the present day (Berelson & Steiner, 1964; Sears, 1969). However, in a pioneering simulation of factors involved in the 1960 election, Pool, Abelson, and Popkin (1964) found that cross-pressured voters did not display lower turnout than other voters.

Personal Influences

Following the Erie County study, a very similar panel study of the 1948 election was conducted by the same research group in Elmira, New York (Berelson, Lazarsfeld, & McPhee, 1954). Here a major variable of interest was the personal influence stemming from the voting intentions of the respondents' closest friends and family members. The investigators found this kind of influence to be strongly associated with the person's own voting intentions (Kitt & Gleicher, 1950). For instance, in this heavily Republican area the following relationships were found between the voting intentions of the respondent and those of his(her) three closest friends:

3 friends Republican	93% intended to vote Republican	
2 Republican, 1 Democratic	68% " " " "
2 Democratic, 1 Republican	50% " " " "
3 friends Democratic	19% " " " "

The same kind of pattern held for differences of voting intentions between the respondent and his(her) immediate family and changes in the respondent's voting intentions between June and August. In cases where all of the family agreed with the respondent, 80% to 90% held to their original voting intention in August. But where some but not all family members were in agreement, about 70% remained unchanged in August; and where all family members disagreed with the respondent's voting plans, nearly half changed their intentions by August.

Party Identification

Party identification as a determinant of voting decisions has been emphasized in the highly influential series of studies conducted by the University of Michigan's Survey Research Center (Campbell, Gurin, & Miller, 1954; Campbell et al., 1960). Measurement of the concept does not involve official party membership, registration, or campaign activity, but depends entirely on the respondent's self-classification as a strong or not-so-strong Republican or Democrat or as an Independent. Converse (1964) has shown that party identification, so measured, is quite a stable personal characteristic (tau-beta over $+.7$ for a two-year interval). Among major-party identifiers, 82% retained the same party identification in three interviews between 1956 and 1960; however, by contrast, only 40% of independents kept the same self-classification over the four-year period (Sears, 1969, p. 333).

In elections from 1956 to 1968, party identification was found to be more highly correlated with voting behavior than any other factor studied, such as attitudes toward campaign issues or toward the candidates (Declercq, Hurley, & Luttbeg, 1975). In 1952, party identification correlated nearly $+.6$ with Presidential choice, whereas the other attitude measures correlated only in the range of $+.2$ to $+.5$ (Campbell & Stokes, 1959). In both 1952 and 1956, about 83% of major-party identifiers ended up voting for their party's Presidential candidate, and those were years when Democratic defectors were relatively numerous (Campbell et al., 1960). In elections for Congress and other less important

Photograph courtesy of Angus Campbell.
Reprinted by permission.

Box 12-1 ANGUS CAMPBELL, *Noted Survey Researcher*

Director of the Survey Research Center at the University of Michigan for over 20 years, Angus Campbell has been a trail-blazer in attitude and opinion research. Born in Indiana in 1910, he attended the University of Oregon and took his Ph.D at Stanford in 1936. After teaching at Northwestern, he assisted Rensis Likert in the Division of Program Surveys of the U.S. Department of Agriculture during World War II, and moved with him to Michigan when the Survey Research Center was founded in 1946. In 1970 he succeeded Likert as Director of the Institute for Social Research.

Best known for his research on political attitudes and voting, Campbell has led survey studies of U.S. elections ever since 1948, resulting in pace-setting volumes such as The Voter Decides, The American Voter, *and* Elections and the Political Order. *More recently he has published influential work on racial attitudes (cited in Chapters 2 and 14) and on social indicators of the quality of life (described in Chapter 11). His many achievements have been honored by his election to the National Academy of Sciences and receipt of the Distinguished Contribution Awards from both AAPOR and APA.*

offices, party loyalty is usually even higher; it was over 88% in the 1958 Congressional election (Stokes & Miller, 1962).

However, in recent elections, particularly 1964 and 1972, there has been a marked decrease in the importance of party identification in determining voting behavior (Declercq et al., 1975). Since about 1966 there has been a large increase in the number of voters who consider themselves independents and who switch their vote at successive elections. This process has gone so far as to lead some analysts to refer to the "decomposition" of the party system (Burnham, 1970; Pomper, 1975). Ticket-splitting has also increased sharply, with an amazing 45% of all congressional districts electing a Congressman of the opposite party from their Presidential vote in 1972 (Pomper, 1975).

Candidate Images

Though party identification still remains an important factor in voting, the candidate's characteristics can also have a major impact, particularly in certain elections. In 1960, Kennedy's Catholic religion became the most crucial issue of the campaign, with large numbers of anti-Catholic votes going to Nixon and many Catholics switching to support Kennedy. Compared with the normal distribution of the vote, it has been estimated that Kennedy gained about 3 million Catholic votes, but lost about 4½ million Protestant votes (Converse, Campbell, Miller, & Stokes, 1961; Pool et al., 1964).

Stokes (1966b) has made a careful analysis of the relative impact of candidates and parties on U.S. political attitudes and voting between 1952 and 1964. He concluded that

> the emergence of new candidates for the Presidency . . . has in fact brought spectacular shifts in presidential voting despite the fact that over the same period there has been almost no perceptible shift in . . . the electorate's enduring party loyalties (p. 27).

The 1964 election between Goldwater and Johnson was a prime example, for contrary to the customary findings, in that year candidate image was the best predictor of Presidential vote (RePass, 1971). Field and Anderson (1969) have shown that Goldwater's image was much more negative than that of the other Presidential candidates of 1960 or 1964. The same problem of a negative image plagued McGovern in 1972 (A. Miller et al., 1973), and studies have shown that again that year candidate image was the best predictor of people's votes (Declercq et al., 1975; Kirkpatrick, Lyons, & Fitzgerald, 1975).

EFFECTS OF POLITICAL PERSUASION ON VOTING

The other major element influencing voting decisions is all of the persuasive communication which abounds during an election campaign—political propaganda, candidate oratory, editorials, personal appeals from acquaintances, and local "grass-roots" political activity. In Chapter 7 on Communication of Attitudes and Opinions we have discussed the general findings concerning persuasive communication. Here we will only consider a few of the most salient influences which affect political voting decisions.

Sears and Whitney (1973) have pointed out that most studies of political propaganda have showed relatively little resulting attitude change—often no change at all. However, this finding does not mean that propaganda is ineffective. In many cases the most important effect of political persuasion may be

reinforcement, that is, strengthening of people's already-existing attitudes. Also, it has been found that less than half of the change in partisan preference from one election to the next may actually occur during the campaign period (Blumler & McQuail, 1969). Thus a major function of campaign propaganda may be to support people's already-changed attitudes and to extend the amount of change where possible.

Problems in Political Persuasion

In order for persuasive arguments to have any effect on attitudes and/or behavior, they must be first received and then accepted, at least to some extent; and both of these processes pose problems for the political communicator.

Reception of persuasive arguments is a problem mainly because of low levels of public exposure and attention to political information. As we have pointed out in Chapter 5, many citizens are political "know-nothings," and most of the rest are relatively uninterested in political issues. As a result, most people simply do not "catch" the available political information, even when it is presented in a highly novel or dramatic way. For example, an unprecedented 20-hour-long telethon by Senator Knowland two days before the 1958 California gubernatorial election was viewed, even briefly, by less than 12% of adults in the area (Schramm & Carter, 1959). The 1960 Kennedy-Nixon debates were exceptional in reaching a huge audience (55% or more of the adult population), but this was partly because they were broadcast by all three television networks; in one city where an alternative TV program was also on the air the debate audience was reduced to 35%—still an exceptionally high figure (Katz & Feldman, 1962).

Another problem in the reception of political arguments is people's general tendency to expose themselves selectively to communicators and channels of information with whom they already tend to agree. As we have discussed in Chapter 7, this effect seems to be largely due to people following customary and convenient channels of information-exposure, rather than to any strongly motivated search for supportive ideas or avoidance of contradictory ideas (Sears & Freedman, 1967).

Acceptance of persuasive arguments, once they are received, is also a problem for the political communicator. Where people are committed to their party identification, or have strong loyalties to racial, religious, or ethnic groups, or see clear bases of economic self-interest, it is unlikely that contrary political arguments will be effective in changing their attitudes or votes. Longitudinal panel studies of both U.S. and British election campaigns have shown that a large majority of the public—as much as 80% in some elections—has made up their minds how to vote before the formal campaign even starts. In most elections no more than 10% of citizens change their voting preferences from one side to the other during the campaign—the other changers move from undecided to some candidate preference, or vice versa (Lazarsfeld et al., 1948; Benham, 1965;

Blumler & McQuail, 1969). However, it is also true, as Converse (1964) has stressed, that most people are not strongly committed to any position on most political issues. Thus, if a clear and effective argument can be presented to them on any given issue, it may be easy to sway their attitude—and even their vote if the issue is an important one.

The result of the above factors is that in elections where people's enduring commitments are relevant, political propaganda generally serves merely to reinforce their preexisting attitudes. But in elections where enduring commitments are not called into play, attitudes and votes are more labile, and political persuasion may have major effects. This is especially true in nonpartisan and primary elections where party identification does not provide a guide for voting. It is also applicable to partisan elections where economic, racial, or religious issues are not centrally involved because the candidates have taken "me-too" positions.

The greatest amount of attitude change in national election campaigns occurs in individuals who have relatively weak party identification (Sears, 1969). It also occurs among people with a relatively low level of interest in the campaign and a resulting low level of exposure to political propaganda. Thus, surprisingly, amount of attitude change is often negatively related to amount of exposure to the mass media (Converse, 1962; Dreyer, 1971).

Some interesting recent research findings on the effects of *particular kinds* of media exposure are presented in the following pages.

Television

One of the main effects of TV coverage of elections has been to make the candidates' personality and "image" more crucial factors in the campaign (Weiss, 1969). Since its first large-scale use in the 1952 Presidential election, television advertising has increased dramatically to an expenditure level of $34 million by major office-seekers in the 1970 election (Federal Communications Commission, 1971). This approach has proved to be the most efficient means of reaching a large proportion of the electorate, but there is still disagreement as to whether such contact changes many votes. Dawson and Zinser (1971) studied radio and TV advertising in the 1970 Congressional election and concluded that a candidate's proportion of the total expenditures for broadcasting in his race had a significant positive effect on his share of the total vote. However, this effect was only large enough to be crucial to the election outcome in the Senate races (where average expenditures were around $125,000 per candidate, as compared with only about $6,000 per candidate in House of Representatives contests), or in very close House races. In addition to this advertising effect, for both House and Senate contests there was also a significant advantage for incumbents and for candidates from the same party as the previous incumbent. In a study of a British election, where TV time was allocated equally to the parties, Blumler and McQuail (1969) found the effects of television campaigning not very dramatic.

Television exposure was most influential with viewers who had a low interest in the campaign but a high level of customary television usage.

Several studies have examined the process by which television influences voters. Atkin, Bowen, Nayman, and Sheinkopf (1973) found that a large number of TV ads for a candidate produced greater viewer *exposure*, apparently overcoming any tendencies toward selective exposure. However, the quantitative frequency of advertising did not influence viewer *attention* levels; instead, attention was related to the ads' qualitative characteristics, such as informative or entertainment value. These same qualitative factors influenced voting intentions also, particularly among undecided voters. More than half of them reported that the political ads for their chosen candidate helped them reach their decision, and many also mentioned the other candidates' ads as a factor weighing against them. Similarly, many of the already-decided partisans reported that their decision was reinforced by seeing the campaign advertisements—positively by their own candidate's ads and/or negatively by the opponent's. The authors concluded that

> a moderate number of high-quality, substantively informative advertisements may be more effective than a saturation presentation of superficial image-oriented spots (Bowen, Atkin, Sheinkopf, & Nayman, 1971, p. 458).

A panel study of television commercials in the 1972 election (Patterson & McClure, 1973) found that they had very pronounced effects on voters' *beliefs* about a candidate's issue position or personal traits (e.g., Nixon is against busing; McGovern is intellectual). However, they had very little effect on voters' *attitudes* toward issue positions or personal traits (e.g., busing is desirable; intellectuality is a good characteristic). As in other studies, the greatest belief change was found among low-interest voters. A study by Rothschild and Ray (1973), using a laboratory experiment setting, suggested that repetitive political advertising may be relatively successful in changing voting intentions in low-involvement elections such as state legislature races, but not at all effective in high-involvement elections such as Presidential campaigns.

Newspapers

Though newspapers were strongly preferred as a source of campaign information in earlier years (Milne & Mackenzie, 1958), the increasing trust in television and television news had eliminated newspapers' preference by 1972 (Kline, 1973). O'Keefe (1973) found that young first-time voters were much less likely to rely on newspapers for political information than were older adults. In the 1968 election Robinson (1972) found that a national cross-section ranked television as their most important source of campaign news; however, they were more likely to *vote* in accordance with their newspaper's election preference than with that of other media. Since 1968 was a very close election, and since about 80% of the nation's newspapers were pro-Nixon, this effect may have played an important role in the election outcome. Robinson found that, when other factors were held constant, voters exposed to pro-Nixon papers were about 6% less likely to vote for Humphrey than voters who read pro-Humphrey papers. As might be expected, this effect was strongest among Independents and undecided voters, where such differential voting reached levels of 35% to 40%. In total, Robinson concluded that the pro-Nixon newspaper endorsements had swayed about 3% of the overall vote to Nixon—enough to give him the election, since his winning margin was only 1% of the total vote.

Personal Contact

As we mentioned earlier in this chapter, personal contact has often been claimed to be the most effective influence on voting decisions, more powerful than any of the media (e.g., Katz & Lazarsfeld, 1955). However, there have also been researchers who disputed that claim (e.g., Pool, 1959). The original study of this topic (Lazarsfeld et al., 1948) found that less than half of their respondents mentioned personal contact as a campaign influence, and only one-fourth mentioned it as the most important factor. When personal contact was mentioned, wives most often mentioned their husbands as sources of influence, but men tended to mention business associates and neighbors. In a British study (Milne & Mackenzie, 1958) only about 12% of the respondents mentioned personal discussions as their most important source of election information, while over 80% mentioned one of the mass media. In the 1972 election O'Keefe (1973) found young first-time voters relied on personal sources of information much more than did older voters. However, Deutschmann (1962) has pointed out that discussions are very often held with like-minded individuals, and so they may serve more to reinforce existing voting intentions than to change them.

Several studies have shown clear-cut effects of personal contact. Rossi and Cutright (1961) found that contacts by political workers had only a slight effect on voting in Presidential elections, but they were absolutely crucial to the outcome of primary elections and very important in local partisan elections. Eldersveld (1956) conducted two field experiments which showed that **turnout** on election day was markedly higher for voters contacted by telephone or in person than for voters who received only a mailed appeal to vote or ones who were not contacted at all. Clausen (1968) concluded from the results of several national survey studies that just being interviewed about election issues and candidates is enough to increase respondents' turnout at the election. Kraut and McConahay (1973) put this conclusion to a careful experimental test and found it to be dramatically supported. Exposure to a short political-opinion interview, without any appeals to vote, more than doubled the voting turnout rate at a primary election held two weeks later. Even more surprising, the effect persisted strongly to another primary election four months after the interview, where turnout was still 60% above that of the uninterviewed control group. Perhaps these inves-

Figure 12-1 A new way to increase citizen involvement?

tigators have discovered a potent new method of increasing citizen involvement in politics!

Other Types of Public Exposure

An intriguing study of several other factors affecting election results was reported by Mueller (1970). His study dealt with a nonpartisan primary election for a newly created junior college board of trustees in Los Angeles in 1969, so it was unusual in that there were no incumbents and no partisan labels attached to the candidates. It was also unique in having 133 candidates, from which crowd each voter had to choose seven, probably with minimal information about their qualifications for the job. In this unusual situation, order on the ballot was found to have a strong effect on number of votes received, giving quite an advantage to candidates whose names began with A. Newspaper endorsements, particularly by the city's largest paper, also carried considerable weight, as did endorsement by a conservative campaign group which was also very active in the election through personal contacts. A ballot-listed occupation which was related to education gave a candidate a slight boost, and ethnic identification (having a Spanish surname or being a well-known Negro) conferred a clear advantage, probably again because of active campaigning by minority groups. Finally, having a familiar and famous name (particularly being the son and namesake of former governor Edmund G. Brown) produced a spectacular additional windfall of votes. These influences on voting results, which can be seen so clearly in this unusual election, are probably also operative to a lesser degree in many other elections.

FACTORS AFFECTING AGGREGATE VOTING

Before the development of public opinion surveys allowed us to study factors influencing individuals' voting decisions, the only way to analyze election outcomes was in terms of aggregate voting results for different geographic areas. This is still a useful analytic approach, and it has produced some interesting findings. Since about 1920 the Census Bureau has published data on the demographic and social characteristics of each small census tract in the United States, and these data can be very illuminating when linked with aggregate voting results for the same areas.

Other facts about our society can also be tied to aggregate voting trends; for instance Campbell (1962) has shown that the advent of radio as a nearly-universal household possession was accompanied by a dramatic rise in voter turnout for elections in the 1930s. Undoubtedly this was at least partly due to radio's ability to carry political information and appeals to the less-educated and less-involved portions of the populace who were unlikely to get the same type of information by reading. By contrast, the advent of nationwide television in the 1950s was not accompanied by any clear increase in voter turnout. Though television has replaced radio as a major source of information and has increased the importance of candidates' visual images, Campbell's data show that it has not produced any noticeable increase in the information level or political involvement of the electorate.

Typical Aggregate Voting Patterns

Some of the facts about aggregate voting patterns are relatively well-known. First, voter turnout in Presidential election years is markedly higher than in the intervening "off-year" Congressional elections. The percentage of the electorate voting in Presidential elections since World War II has ranged between approximately 50% and 65%, while it has been only about 38% to 45% in the off-year elections. The difference in turnout at successive elections has always been at least 10% of the electorate, so the dropoff in voting after each Presidential election ranges from one-fifth to one-third of the previous election's voters. It is also well-known that the party in power typically loses seats in the House of Representatives at the off-year election; this has happened at every off-year election in this century except 1934.

Two less-well-known facts about voting patterns are related to the above observations. In Presidential elections the variation in percentage of voters choosing a given party is about twice as great as in off-year elections (Stokes & Miller, 1962); that is, there are larger swings in party dominance of the vote in Presidential years. Also, when there are large increases in voter turnout, the added votes usually go very heavily to one party rather than being split more equally.

Campbell (1964) has offered an explanation for these facts of aggregate voting, based on two important characteristics of individual voters, their *party identification* and their degree of *interest in politics*. Survey Research Center panel studies have shown that these two attributes are both quite stable over time for most individuals. What's more, they are related; in general, people who are highly interested in politics are likely to have a strong party identification. Such people tend to vote regularly in every election whereas less interested individuals only vote when strong situational forces push them to do so. Thus voters in the lower-interest off-year elections tend to be the core group of politically interested citizens with strong party identifications. They are rather unlikely to shift parties, so the division of the vote is quite stable from election to election. By contrast, the greater ballyhoo and hullabaloo of Presidential elections bring many additional voters to the polls, most of whom are only marginally interested in politics.

Moreover, at any given time there are a variety of **short-term forces** which influence people's voting intentions—such factors as important recent events, the candidates' personal characteristics, the public images of the majority parties, and current issues developed in the campaign. When these short-term forces are approximately balanced in the degree to which they favor one party or the other, the division of the total vote will be determined mainly by the pattern of **long-term political characteristics** in the population, that is, by political interest and party identification. However, the short-term forces often build up and favor one candidate and party over the other ("they kept us out of war," "peace and prosperity," "end the mess in Washington," etc.). When that occurs, strongly committed voters may not shift their vote, but marginal voters are attracted to the favored party in droves.

Thus it sometimes happens that in high-interest Presidential elections which stimulate a high voter turnout there is a dramatic surge to the favored candidate. But in the next Congressional election, most of those off-and-on voters stay home, the division of the vote returns close to its normal level, and the party that is in the White House loses seats in Congress.

Two other aspects of voter turnout are also of interest here. Throughout this century there has been a gradual but steady increase in voter turnout in the United States, and also an increase in ticket-splitting by voters (Roper, 1965). These facts indicate a greater degree of political participation by the electorate and possibly also an increase in political sophistication and discriminating judgments about candidates. Also, though the all-time maximum turnout was only about

65% of the electorate, this figure is misleadingly low due to the multiplicity of state laws which prevent many citizens from voting if they are ill or disabled, traveling or living abroad, or have recently moved. Roper (1965) reports that in 1960 the election turnout of citizens who met all state voting requirements was actually 82%. The recent federal law which standardized and shortened the registration period in elections for President should diminish registration problems and help to increase voter turnout still further.

Switchers and Standpatters

One way of classifying groups of voters is to lump together all those who switched their party vote from one Presidential election to the next, the **switchers**, and compare them with those who voted for the same party at both elections, the **standpatters**. There is also a third group, whom we can call ''new voters,'' consisting of young adults who have reached voting age since the last election and of older individuals who did not vote then, for whatever reason. Key and Cummings (1966) have made a thorough analysis of these three groups, based on Gallup Poll and National Opinion Research Center (NORC) national survey findings for the period from 1936 to 1960.

The switchers are the group most responsible for changing patterns of party victory and defeat. How many such voters are there, and what are they like? First of all, they are much more numerous than you might think from an examination of changes in the division of the vote. For instance, in 1956 President Eisenhower got about 58% of the vote, an increase in his winning percentage of about 2% over the 1952 election results. However, this does not mean that only 2% of voters switched their preference that year. The 2% figure is a net change, made up of many individuals who switched their vote from Democratic to Republican and many others who switched from Republican to Democratic. Historically, the proportion of vote switchers has ranged from about 10% to about 20% in various elections, but in 1968 they jumped to an unprecedented 33% (Converse, Miller, Rusk, & Wolfe, 1969).

The standpatters are a much larger group, about 60% to 75% of total voters, making up the backbone of support of each party. However, standpatters alone would rarely ever be numerous enough to win an election, and the out-of-office party in particular is compelled to direct its appeals at potential switchers and new voters. The ''new voters'' (who include many older people with low political interest) generally number from 15% to 20% of the voters at each Presidential election.

Typically, switchers come more from the ranks of Democratic Party identifiers than from the Republican Party, partly due to the lower average interest in politics of Democrats, and partly because there are more registered Democrats. However, in elections following a major Republican victory such as Eisenhower's in 1952, there have been more defections from those who voted

Republican in the past election than from Democratic ranks. Of course, many of these "defectors" from the Republican ranks were actually Democratic party identifiers returning "home" after previously defecting to vote Republican in 1952. For the 1960 election, Key and Cummings (1966, p. 25) have estimated the following contribution of the three voter groups to each candidate's total vote:

Kennedy vote:	Standpatters	19.1 million
	Switchers	10.3 million
	New voters	4.8 million
	Total	34.2 million
Nixon vote:	Standpatters	26.6 million
	Switchers	2.7 million
	New voters	4.8 million
	Total	34.1 million

Let us look more closely at the 1960 election to determine some of the characteristics of the large group of switchers (over 20% that year). That election was the first one in over 30 years in which a Catholic was nominated for President, and the Catholic vote was widely thought to have been responsible for Kennedy's slim victory. However, statistics show other clean-cut and even stronger trends at work. One trend was a return toward New-Deal-era status polarization in voting, with lower status groups such as blue-collar workers, people without college educations, and Negroes shifting strongly toward the Democratic Party. The shift among Catholic voters was even more striking: nearly 60% of the Catholics who had voted Republican in 1956 switched to a Democratic vote in 1960. However, there was also an off-setting Protestant vote against Kennedy which involved a larger total number of votes. The most important factor of all in the election was the return of formerly defecting Democratic party identifiers to the fold. Nearly 80% of this group switched back to a Democratic vote in 1960, a proportion substantially larger than the shift of Catholics to Kennedy. Thus the results of the 1960 election can be seen as a reinstatement of the normal Democratic Party voting patterns of many subgroups in society, rather than primarily as a religious plebiscite (Key & Cummings, 1966, p. 123).

The "Normal" Vote

This analysis of the 1960 election leads us to another important question: what is the **"normal" vote**, that is, the most likely division of the popular vote? In 1960 the split was almost exactly 50-50. Since there are two major parties, and since they frequently succeed each other as election winners, you might assume that the normal state of affairs is a 50-50 division of party strength. However, that is not the case. Statistics show that since 1936 the "normal" Democratic Party proportion of the vote has been 54% (Campbell, Converse, Miller, &

Stokes, 1966). An even higher proportion of party identifiers are Democratic, but Republican party identifiers, on the average, are higher in political interest. Also there is an increasingly large group of Independents who tend to divide their votes, somewhat unevenly, between the two parties. The net result of these group loyalties and interests is that, in national elections where short-term forces do not favor either party, the Democrats can expect to receive about 54% of the votes cast.

In the preceding period of Republican Party ascendancy, from 1896 to 1928, the "normal" expected Republican proportion of the vote was also 54%. The fact that these two percentages are identical has led Sellers (1965) to speculate that this level of partisanship may represent a natural limit within our political system. He has concluded that

> there seems to be at work a constant tendency toward equilibrium that is built into the structure of the American two-party system. The persistent narrowness of the margin between the parties is one of the most striking characteristics of the system. . . . There is a tendency not only for a minority party to readjust its image so as to detach groups from the majority coalition, but also for a party with an oversized majority to force out groups in the process of deciding which part of its coalition its policies will favor (pp. 28, 30).

In their current status as a minority party, the Republicans have to seek issues and candidates that will appeal to the nonideological marginal voters (weakly committed Democrats and Independents) who can swing the election to them.

Figure 12-2 The "normal" division of the vote.

This was a fact which they forgot, to their ultimate distress, in nominating Goldwater in 1964. In post-Depression elections where there has been a surge of voters to the Republican Party, as in Eisenhower's victories in 1952 and 1956, this movement has occurred in all population subgroups, even among such traditionally Democratic groups as Negroes or union members (Campbell, 1964). Roper (1965) has attempted to explain this by suggesting that we are basically a moderate, middle-of-the-road nation, and that even formerly highly partisan subgroups are shifting toward the political middle. Glenn (1973) has confirmed this view in relation to socioeconomic status in his analysis of decreases in class-based voting between 1936 and 1968.

Cycles of Party Dominance

The historian Charles Sellers (1965) has analyzed changes in the electoral fortunes of U.S. political parties all the way back to the nation's first election in 1789. On the basis of his careful quantitative study, he concludes that

> oscillations from one party to the other do not occur in random fashion, from one election to another. Instead, the parties supplant each other by blocks of elections, both presidential and congressional, each block extending over a period of some years. Moreover, there is a tendency for a party's majorities within a block to rise and fall by regular, graded steps, rather than bouncing up and down in a random fashion (p. 19).

To explain this sequence of gradual voting changes, he proposed that there is an underlying gradual oscillation in the pattern of party identification in the electorate. A period of **ascendancy** of one party (typically 12 years or less) is followed by a period of **equilibrium** (sometimes as long as 16 years) in which the difference between the two parties' share of the Presidential and Congressional vote is small and shifting in direction. Then forces in the nation or the world lead to a period of **realignment** (ranging from 2 to 10 years in length) "in which the underlying pattern of party identifications is substantially and durably altered" (Sellers, 1965, p. 22). The realignment phase is usually accompanied by a third-party movement or even multiple parties, which provide a temporary home for many of the voters whose party identifications are shifting. Surprisingly, the end result of the pressures toward realignment may just as often be a renewed ascendancy of the previously dominant party as a shift to ascendancy of the former minority party. A rather similar analysis has been made by Burnham (1970).

Another historian, Arthur Schlesinger (1939) has also described cyclical "tides of American politics"; however, he ascribed them to alternating periods of liberal and conservative public sentiment. By contrast, Campbell (1964) has emphasized that most fluctuations of party electoral success in the U.S. have not been based on shifts in ideological stance among the electorate, but on a simple desire for change in leadership. The 1952 election was an excellent example, for Eisenhower's victory was not due to any conservative wave in the populace. Rather, Campbell says, "The voters were not asking for any specific platform of legislation; they just wanted a new bunch of fellows to run things better" (p. 755).

Classification of Elections

The three phases of the party voting cycle described by Sellers are paralleled by three basic types of Presidential elections. Campbell (1966) has termed these types maintaining, deviating, and realigning elections.

Maintaining Elections. These are elections in which the underlying pattern of party identifications is maintained and is reflected in the distribution of the vote. In other words, the majority party of that era retains power or is returned to power. Truman's reelection in 1948 is one example, as is Kennedy's victory in 1960, though the latter has also been termed a reinstating election since the majority party had previously been out of power. It is typical of maintaining elections that there are no overriding policy issues nor particularly attractive candidates impelling marginal voters disproportionately toward one party. It is also typical for voter turnout to be relatively low because of the lackluster campaign, though 1960 was an exception to that tendency.

Deviating Elections. These are campaigns in which the pattern of party identification remains unchanged, but short-term forces lead to the defeat of the majority party. These forces may be strong candidate personalities or important events or issues which impel many citizens to shift their vote temporarily away from their basic party allegiance. After these personalities or events have passed from the current political scene, the balance of the vote reverts back to an advantage for the current majority party. Examples of deviating elections occurred in 1952 and 1956, when Eisenhower's personality and reputation exerted a major effect on the vote, and in 1968, when controversies over the Vietnam War and George Wallace's third-party candidacy led to the defeat of Hubert Humphrey and the Democratic Party. Another example is the 1916 election, where Woodrow Wilson was elected during a period of Republican dominance as the majority party.

Stokes (1966a) has calculated that the chance of a deviating election occurring is slightly over one-quarter, given the current 54% normal Democratic advantage. That is, given favorable circumstances as in 1968 or an attractive candidate as in 1952, the Republican Party can expect to win every third or fourth election on the average, despite its disadvantage in numbers of party loyalists. In deviating elections the most important short-term influence on the vote is apt to be the candidate's image, rather than policy issues or events. In fact, Sellers (1965) has shown that in every election which displayed a particularly strong surge of voters to one candidate in a two-party race, the winners—

> Washington, Jackson, Harrison, Taylor, Grant, and Eisenhower—were "popular hero" candidates who were widely revered for their military achievements and personal characteristics before entering politics. . . . Apparently, only such candidates have the power to draw to the polls the previously apathetic citizens who mainly create the surge effect (p. 22).

Realigning Elections.   In a period of realignment, popular political feelings are so intense and issues and/or events have such an impact that there is a shifting of the basic party loyalties of part of the electorate. Such periods are rare, but very important to our political system. Since the emergence of the Republican Party in 1856–1860 in the conflict over slavery, there have been only two other periods of basic political realignment: the reascendance of the Republicans with McKinley's election in 1896, and the shift to Democratic dominance during the Depression with Roosevelt's victories in 1932-1936 (Campbell, 1964). The differences between these three periods and the deviating "surge" elections are fascinating:

> Neither Lincoln, McKinley nor Roosevelt, it may be noted, was a military figure and none of them possessed any extraordinary personal appeal at the time he first took office. The quality which did distinguish these elections was the presence of a great national issue and the association of the two major parties with relatively clearly contrasting programs for its solution. In some degree, national politics during these realigning periods did take on an ideological character. The flow of the vote was not a temporary reaction to a heroic figure or a passing embarrassment of the party in power; it reflected a reorientation of basic party attachments growing out of a conflict regarding governmental policies (Campbell, 1964, p. 753).

The issues which lead to major political realignment leave their effects, not just on individual citizens, but on the party loyalties of whole groups within society. In 1856 and 1896 the groups that changed their political views were mostly regional ones; in 1936 the Depression-induced issues led to political changes related to voters' social class status. During the Depression, and probably also in earlier realignments, it was largely the young, first-time voters who switched party identification permanently, whereas older voters who switched their votes tended to change back again in subsequent elections (Campbell et al., 1960).

Based on the above findings it is interesting to speculate on the nature of recent Presidential elections. 1964 was clearly a maintaining election, with an extra surge of votes related to candidate images and policy issues. Nixon's victory in 1968 is a bit harder to classify. It was probably a deviating election, but the presence of a viable third-party challenge and the importance of circumstances and issues rather than candidate images raise the possibility that 1968 may have been the beginning of a period of realignment. The 1972 election, with its landslide victory for the former minority party and the great importance of ideological issues in the campaign, was a further indication of strong realigning forces at work in the electorate (A. Miller et al., 1973). However, just as with Goldwater in 1964, the negative candidate image of McGovern in the 1972 election was a factor which suggests classifying it not as a realigning election, but as a deviating one.

If 1972 was indeed a realigning election, Seller's analysis of electoral cycles reminds us that we still cannot tell what the ultimate shape of the realignment will be. Though it began with a major Republican victory, it may end with either party in the ascendancy. Certainly the twin blows of Watergate and recession have greatly dimmed Republican hopes to build a new dynasty based on the "silent majority." Probably the shape of future events will be determined rather largely by the Democratic Party's action in the 1976 election and its aftermath. If Carter's narrow victory can be forged into an alliance of important emerging groups in society—an alliance which can replace the fading coalitions of the New Deal, Fair Deal, New Frontier, and Great Society—the Democratic Party may be the beneficiaries of the "realignment of the 1970s." If not, the Republican Party, under new leadership, may yet inherit the dominant position which has been held for 40 years by the Democrats. Either way, this is a fascinating era for the political observer.

Predicting the Vote

Is it possible to successfully predict electoral outcomes using polling methods? There are several ways to answer this question. First, we know that the major commercial polls have not "come a cropper" since their failure to predict the 1948 election, and that they correctly noted Humphrey's last-minute comeback in 1968, pronouncing the outcome "too close to call." In thirteen Congressional and Presidential elections from 1950 to 1974, The Gallup Poll's average error in predicting the outcome was only 1.4%, a figure well within the poll's expected margin of sampling error (*Gallup Opinion Index*, 1975d).

Studies of both the 1960 and 1964 elections have shown that about 80% of voters had their minds made up by August and did not change their voting intentions in the three months between then and election day (Benham, 1965). These findings on national samples are entirely consistent with the findings of the first major scientific election study, Lazarsfeld et al.'s (1948) study in the small area of Erie County, Ohio. The occurrence of similar results in elections 24 years apart, and in a landslide victory as well as a photo-finish, is remarkable and imparts considerable confidence in the finding. It also indicates a strong possibility of correct prediction of the election outcome, since for all but the closest contests,

> the campaign for the underdog becomes nothing more than running out a pop fly and hoping his opponent will drop the ball (Benham, 1965, p. 188).

In the 1960 election, Pool et al. (1964) developed some elaborate computer simulations of the electorate and reported a number of encouraging findings concerning their accuracy of prediction. For instance, the extent of the anti-Catholic vote was a major question, and their computer analysis of poll data enabled them to advise Kennedy that by August this issue had already had its full impact on voting intentions, so that "he had nothing to lose by calling further attention to his religion with an appeal to fair play" (Abelson, 1968, p. 22). The accuracy of the computer predictions also helped to demonstrate the fictitious nature of suspected "hidden feelings" which respondents were unwilling to divulge to interviewers. Neither prejudiced anti-Catholic voting in 1960, nor pro-Goldwater racial "white backlash" in 1964, exceeded the amount readily reported to interviewers. Again prediction from the polls was shown to be basically accurate.

Another demonstration of excellent prediction has been given by the recent television "projections" of election winners only minutes after the polls have closed in a given state. These predictions are made on the basis of the early returns from a few "key districts," which are chosen to be representative of the voting patterns of the state. In 1964 and 1966 the predictions made in this way by both NBC and CBS Television proved to be over 99% correct—a sensational batting average in any league (Skedgell, 1966; Abelson, 1968).

However, there are two kinds of election situations that have proved to be much harder to predict correctly—i.e., primary elections and referendum campaigns. This is true partly because the efforts of local political workers are very influential in primaries and local partisan elections, whereas voters' longstanding predispositions are much more important to the results of national campaigns (Rossi & Cutright, 1961). Since grass-roots political efforts are not usually measured in opinion polls, poll results in primary elections are often far off base. Also, the coalition of voters to whom a candidate must direct his appeals in a primary election may be quite different than those whose support will be vital in the following general election. A particularly clear example of this phenomenon was described by Jennings and Zeigler (1966a, 1966b) in a Congressional campaign in Atlanta where the winning candidate's vote totals, broken down by precinct areas, correlated less than +.2 in the primary and general elections.

Another reason that primaries and referenda are hard to predict is that the overarching factor of party identification is irrelevant to voters' decisions in these campaigns, so other less-stable voting determinants are called into play. One result is that there are often volatile swings in candidate strength late in the campaign when the voters finally begin to pay attention to the candidates and issues. In 1964, for example, there were three state primaries that were crucial in the Republican Presidential nomination race—New Hampshire, Oregon, and California—and the commercial polls predicted the wrong winner in all three, two of them because of last-minute trends. However, in 1968 and 1972, improved procedures helped the state polls to predict primary results quite accurately, particularly when the polling was done just a few days before the election (Felson & Sudman, 1975). Abelson (1968) has suggested that in dull primary campaigns any late trend toward changing candidate strength that is apparent a week before the election should be extrapolated and heavily weighted in predicting the final outcome. Also, he has shown that in referendum campaigns where an abstract principle (e.g., equality) is pitted against a concrete fear or desire (e.g., blacks moving into the neighborhood), the concrete side of the issue will gain heavily in the closing days of the campaign.

In spite of these obstacles to correct prediction, research indicates that high levels of predictive accuracy can often be reached using survey data. In most voting situations the issues that actually affect voters' decisions are few, and their effects generally combine in a simple additive way to determine the final outcome (Pool et al., 1964). Thus, if a few crucial issues can be identified and the major voter types who respond to them can be specified, simple arithmetical combinations of these data should produce predictions that are very close to the final vote results. The television election-night predictions use this rationale and demonstrate the validity of this approach to voting prediction.

SUMMARY

Individual voting decisions are affected by several major determinants. Personal influences from friends or family members often have an effect, and cross-pressures due to a person's noncongruent demographic characteristics generally produce lower interest and fluctuating voting intentions. An individual's party identification is a relatively stable personal characteristic and is often the most important determinant in voting. However, in some recent elections, the public's image of the candidates has become an even more important factor.

Political persuasion is generally much more likely to reinforce existing attitudes than to change contrary attitudes. Reception of political persuasion attempts is limited, and their acceptance is also unlikely if there are any contrary commitments or loyalties. However, in primaries and nonpartisan elections, attitudes and votes are more apt to be influenced by persuasion.

The advent of television in politics since 1950 has made the personality and "image" of a candidate more important in the campaign. Though television campaign advertising sometimes influences voting, its effects are complex and often unpredictable. Newspapers' political endorsements frequently have a noticeable effect on readers' voting—in fact, enough to decide a close race such as the 1968 Presidential election. Personal contact, often considered the most important single influence on voting, is particularly effective in local or primary elections. In low-interest elections, even factors such as order on the ballot or a familiar name can markedly affect vote totals.

Aggregate voting patterns in Presidential elections reflect the turnout of many marginally interested voters, who are more influenced than regular voters by the short-term forces favoring one party or the other at that time. Citizens who switch their vote at successive elections make up only 10% to 20% of the electorate, but they often determine the election outcome.

The "normal" or average division of the vote has been 54% Democratic since 1936, whereas between 1896 and 1928 it was 54% Republican. Historically, a period of ascendancy by one party is usually followed by a period of rough equilibrium, and then eventually by a period of realignment when the electorate's pattern of party identifications is markedly altered. A deviating election is one in which short-term forces produce a victory by the minority party without any basic realignment.

Since 1950 the major U.S. polling organizations have had a remarkably good record in predicting the division of the popular vote. Election-evening computer projections of campaign victors, based on early returns from a few "key districts," have had a sensational record of accuracy; and even the volatile primary elections have been predicted relatively well since 1968.

Suggested Readings

Campbell, A., Converse, P. E., Miller, W. E., & Stokes, D. E. *Elections and the Political Order.* New York: Wiley, 1966.—A detailed analysis of factors affecting the aggregate "flow of the vote" from one election to the next.

Key, V. O., Jr., & Cummings, M. C., Jr. *The Responsible Electorate: Rationality in Presidential Voting, 1936–1960.*—An interesting discussion of voting trends over 25 years, including the impact of political standpatters, switchers, and new voters.

Sears, D. O., & Whitney, R. E. *Political Persuasion.* Morristown, N. J.: General Learning Press, 1973.—This short pamphlet gives a theoretical and empirical summary of factors affecting reception and acceptance of political propaganda.

Sellers, C. The equilibrium cycle in two-party politics. *Public Opinion Quarterly,* 1965, 29, 16–38.—A fascinating presentation of the quantitative history of U.S. election campaigns since 1789, using concepts related to those of Campbell et al. (1966).

Weiss, W. Effects of the mass media of communication. In G. Lindzey & E. Aronson (Eds.), *The Handbook of Social Psychology* (2nd ed.). Vol. 5. Reading, Mass.: Addison-Wesley, 1969. Pp. 77–195.—A thorough and scholarly analysis. Pages 155–177 discuss mass media effects on voting behavior.

International Attitudes

Wars begin in the minds of men.—UNESCO Charter.

Our images of Italy, of Turkey, and of Austria are formed of biased history texts and loaded newspaper stories. . . . Similarly the legend of the crude, materialistic, uneducated American goes unchallenged in much of the world.—Ross Stagner.

O wad some Power the giftie gie us
To see oursel's as ithers see us!—Robert Burns.

This chapter discusses how people develop their attitudes toward other nations and their images of foreign peoples. To what extent are their sources of information limited and/or biased? As a result, are their international attitudes stereotyped, or are they sensitive to reality factors? What kinds of people tend to develop warlike attitudes, for instance, or isolationistic viewpoints? Finally, how can international attitudes be changed?

Much of what we have already learned about political attitudes applies directly to international affairs. However, there are some special ways in which international attitudes are unique. One characteristic feature is that many people's attitudes are formed despite their having little or no direct contact with other nations, foreigners, or issues of foreign affairs. As a result, the attitudes may be quite unrelated to the realities of world affairs. Of course all of our attitudes are based on our perception of the environment rather than on the actual, objective situation. But in the field of foreign affairs the gap between perception and reality is apt to be especially large.

Images. A number of authors from different disciplines have emphasized the gap between international attitudes and international reality by using the term **images** to describe our often-distorted views of other nations and peoples (e.g., Boulding, 1959; Kelman, 1965; Jervis, 1970). The following quotation clearly conveys that point of view:

> Americans do not know Russia; they know an image of Russia; subject to many errors and misconceptions. In fact, they do not know America, but only an image thereof; and it is sometimes amazing to find how we differ among ourselves as to the attributes of our nation. Certainly, the national image is not the same for Barry Goldwater and Lyndon Johnson (Stagner, 1967, p. 12).

THE IGNORANT PUBLIC

Even more than in the area of political attitudes, public information about world affairs is sharply limited. Some examples are provided in Patchen's (1964) study of American attitudes and information about the Far East. The 1429 subjects in that survey were a representative sample of the general adult public. In the spring of 1964, after two years of warfare in Vietnam involving U.S. troops, 25% of the respondents said they had not even heard of the war. Similarly, 28% did not know that the government of mainland China was communistic, and 29% were unaware of the existence of another Chinese government (on Taiwan, or Formosa). Only 54% of the respondents had read or heard about Mao Tse Tung.

Many other compilations of public ignorance have been made (e.g., Erskine, 1963c). The implications of this lack of public information are clear: many people in our society are "know-nothings," and if you ask their opinions, especially about world affairs, you will very likely be measuring what Converse has called "non-attitudes," based on a complete lack of information and understanding. Thus, it is important for attitude surveys to eliminate or isolate such respondents by the use of careful screening questions so that their "attitudes" are not lumped together with those of more knowledgeable citizens. The latter group, the "issue publics" in Converse's terminology, are the ones whose attitudes are more likely to be meaningful and stable.

The "Know-a-Lots." Just as there are many "know-nothings," there are also a small but important group of "know-a-lots" who tend to be well-informed on all aspects of a given issue area. In his study of foreign affairs information, Robinson (1967) showed that there was a cluster of citizens who got most or all of the items correct, in sharp contrast to a larger group who performed at or near a chance level of information.

Who are these "know-a-lots," and what are they like? Analysis of data from Patchen's (1964) survey of information about the Far East showed that their most important characteristic was having a college education, next was being in a white-collar job, and third was having an above-average income level.

Similar results were found by Free and Cantril (1967) in their national sample study. One additional predictor of a high level of international information was being a veteran (many of whom, of course, had served overseas). Some of the worst-informed groups were women, rural residents, Southerners, and people over 50 years old.

CHILDREN'S VIEWS OF FOREIGN PEOPLES

How do our international attitudes originate and develop? When do children begin to become aware of foreign nations and peoples, and how do their attitudes change with increasing age?

A pace-setting investigation of these questions was performed by Lambert and Klineberg (1967) as an outgrowth of research planning by the United Nations Educational, Social, and Cultural Organization (UNESCO). The study used a careful cross-cultural approach in eleven different areas of the world: the United States, Bantu children in South Africa, Brazil, English Canada, French Canada, France, Germany, Israel, Japan, Lebanon, and Turkey. In each area 300 children at three age levels (6, 10, and 14) were interviewed at length by native interviewers. The sample was carefully selected from among lower-class and middle-class urban children, but was not representative of the whole nation's child population.

The structured interviews with the children concentrated on their conceptions of their own national groups, on which foreign peoples were similar to or different from them, and on liked and disliked nationalities. Table 13-1 shows a sample of the findings, comparing children's descriptions of their own nationality with the most typical descriptions of their nations by other national groups.

TABLE 13-1 Most Typical Descriptions of Various National Groups as Seen by Children of Their Own and Other Nations

Nationality	*Self-description*	*Description by other nations*
American	good, wealthy, free	good, wealthy, intelligent, aggressive
Bantu	factual statements (e.g., dark-skinned) and similarity references (e.g., like us)	(description of "Negroes from Africa") good, uncultured, unintelligent, dominated, poor, bad, aggressive
Brazilian	good, intelligent, cultured, happy, unambitious	good (no other terms)
English-Canadian	good, wealthy, free, cultured	(not obtained)
French-Canadian	good, wealthy, peaceful patriotic	(not obtained)
French	good, intelligent, cultured, happy, bad	(not obtained)
German	good, ambitious, wealthy, intelligent	good, aggressive, intelligent, bad
Israeli	good, religious, peaceful, intelligent	(not obtained)
Japanese	poor, intelligent, bad	(not obtained)
Lebanese	similarity references (e.g., like us), good	(not obtained)
Turkish	good, peaceful, ambitious, religious, patriotic, clean	(not obtained)
Chinese	(not interviewed)	good, poor, aggressive, bad
Indians from India	(not interviewed)	good, poor
Russians	(not interviewed)	aggressive, good, intelligent, bad, dominated

Note.—Terms are listed in approximate order of their frequency of usage in each national description.

Source: Adapted from W. E. Lambert & O. Klineberg, *Children's Views of Foreign Peoples,* 1967, pp. 102, 143. Reprinted by permission of Irvington Publishers, Inc.

Of course, these national descriptions are stereotypes, frequently based on little information and having doubtful validity at best. Nevertheless, this glimpse of children's national images provides intriguing food for thought. For instance, nearly all nations' children regarded their own people as "good," but (in 1959, when the interviewing was conducted) the Bantu and the Japanese did not —perhaps the result of racial oppression and disastrous defeat in war, respectively. Similarly, positive evaluations were foremost in descriptions of almost all other nations, though Russians were seen as "good" less often than they were seen as "aggressive." (It is well to remember that this study was done during the cold-war period and almost entirely in nations allied to the United States rather than to Russia.) The other descriptive terms showed much greater differences —from wealthy and free, to intelligent, cultured, and happy. Whether any of these stereotypes have changed markedly since then with the flow of international events is an important but unanswered question.

Interestingly, of all the groups interviewed, the American children were most strongly inclined to express liking for foreign peoples, both those they viewed as similar and those they felt were dissimilar. To a lesser degree, the same was true of Canadian, Bantu, and French children. In contrast, the Japanese and Turkish children expressed least liking for foreign peoples.

Development of Children's Attitudes

The process of development and change in these attitudes toward foreign peoples is particularly important. At age 6 many of the children could give only very sparse responses about foreign peoples—mostly simple factual information and evaluations of "good" or "bad." At ages 10 and 14 there was a progressive increase in the range of evaluative categories used, such as intelligent, aggressive, poor, wealthy, peaceful, dominated, and ambitious. At the same time there was a change in the type of descriptive statements—from physical characteristics, clothing, and language, to a greater emphasis on personality traits, habits, political and religious characteristics, and material possessions. Interestingly, evaluative and descriptive statements about other nations tended to be related in opposite ways to liking for the nations: children describe well-liked nations with many factual, descriptive terms and with relatively few evaluative terms, whereas less-liked nations were characterized with many evaluative terms (often negative) and few factual descriptions.

Even at age 6, many children gave stereotyped evaluative descriptions of their own group, while they described foreign peoples in more objective, factual terms. The authors concluded that the stereotyping process gets its start in children's early conceptions of their own group, and that between 6 and 14 years children develop increasingly stereotyped views of foreign peoples.

ADULTS' VIEWS OF FOREIGN PEOPLES

A pioneering study of adult attitudes, quite similar to the one with children just described, was conducted by Buchanan and Cantril (1953). Entitled *How Nations See Each Other*, the study was sponsored by UNESCO and carried out in 1948 and 1949. At that time, shortly after World War II, only the more industrialized nations had public opinion polling organizations, so the study was carried out in nine relatively advanced nations: Australia, Britain, France, parts of West Germany, Italy, the Netherlands, Norway, Mexico (only in cities), and the United

States. In each country a quota sample of about 1000 adults was interviewed with a rather short interview schedule of 21 questions. Instead of using open-ended questions, as in the Lambert and Klineberg (1967) study with children, a list of 12 adjectives was presented for the respondent to choose from in describing two foreign peoples (Americans and Russians) and his own countrymen. Thus the sampling was more extensive and more representative than in the Lambert and Klineberg children's study, but the interview content was much less extensive.

Since this study is now outdated, only a few highlights of its results will be presented here. When the survey was taken in 1948, the United States was clearly the best-liked foreign country in the eight Western nations studied (an average of 33% of respondents so listed it), while Russia was least-liked (by an average of 36% of respondents). Of the countries surveyed, only France departed from this pattern, choosing the Swiss as the best-liked people and the Germans as least-liked. Britain was second best-liked, with an average mention of 12%, and the Scandinavian countries as a whole were third with 8%. In the least-liked category, Germany was second with 16% and Japan third with 7%. America was mentioned as least-liked by 3%, and the same number listed Russia as most-liked. In addition to the tensions of the U.S.-Russian competition, the authors point out that several other factors helped to determine feelings of friendliness toward the nations. About 18% of the mentions were made on the basis of alliances in the recently-concluded war, with enemies generally being disliked and allies liked. Nations which were neutral in the war were also quite well-liked (an average mention of about 10%). Nations which shared a common language and/or culture in most cases had strongly-friendly feelings for each other, but sharing a common boundary was slightly more likely to lead to disliking than to liking. Interestingly, the bordering countries which were well-liked were all smaller than the country which liked them, and thus unlikely to be a military or economic threat.

Table 13-2 shows the characteristics most commonly ascribed to foreign peoples. As with the Lambert and Klineberg study of children's attitudes, it must be remembered that the data all came from Western, noncommunist countries and represent very gross stereotypes of the peoples described. However, each nation's stereotype was relatively clear-cut. Russians were seen in mostly unflattering terms: domineering, cruel, hardworking, and backward. Americans (in that era of the Marshall Plan for aid to Europe) were generally viewed as practical, progressive, hard-working, and generous. The respondents' own country, no matter which one it happened to be, was usually seen in highly favorable terms: peace-loving, hardworking, intelligent, and brave.

Of course, these national stereotypes can sometimes change quite rapidly, as the Russian image had changed for the worse in the few years since the end of World War II (Klineberg, 1964). This fact led the authors to suggest that

> stereotypes are less likely to govern the likes and dislikes between nations than to adapt themselves to the positive or negative relationship based on matters unrelated

TABLE 13-2 Percentage of Countries Using Various Adjectives to Describe Themselves and Other Nations

Adjective	People described					
	Russians	*Americans*	*British*	*French*	*Chinese*	*Own countrymen*
	(8)[a]	*(7)*	*(3)*	*(3)*	*(3)*	*(8)*
Hardworking	69[b]	43	33	33	100	62
Intelligent		14	67	67	11	62
Practical		86	17			
Conceited		14	50	67		
Generous		43		33		38
Cruel	75				44	
Backward	62				100	
Brave			33	33	11	62
Self-controlled			67			
Domineering	94	14		17		
Progressive		86				
Peace-loving			33	50	33	75

Note.—The three most frequently used adjectives were tabulated for each combination of describing country and people described.

[a]The number in parentheses is the number of describing countries.

[b]Ties for third-place adjectives resulted in percentages not evenly divisible by the number of describing countries.

Source: Adapted from Buchanan & Cantril, 1953, p. 50.

to images of the people concerned. . . . they may follow and rationalize, rather than precede and determine, reaction to a certain nation (Buchanan & Cantril, 1953, pp. 56–57).

USIA Surveys of Western Europe

A major source of information on international attitudes is an extensive series of studies conducted in Western European countries for the United States Information Agency (USIA), reported on by Merritt and Puchala (1968). These surveys began in 1952 and continued at frequent intervals through 1965. In each survey a representative national sample in each of several countries was interviewed by a polling organization located in that country, and the results were analyzed and interpreted by the USIA research staff. These findings represent, in a sense, a long-term continuation and extension of Buchanan and Cantril's original UNESCO study, and thus they enable us to see changes in international attitudes over a period of years.

An important conclusion from the USIA surveys is presented in Figure 13-1, which shows changes in attitudes toward six different countries from October, 1954, to February, 1964. The attitudes plotted are those of a composite group made up of random samples of citizens from four Western European countries—France, West Germany, Italy, and Great Britain—who were asked their feelings about each of the other countries. The method of plotting used is one which emphasizes long-term underlying trends in attitude change and largely discounts short-term fluctuations. This method utilizes linear regression formulas which best fit the changing course of attitudes toward each country by citizens of the other three countries, over the ten-year time span. The starting and ending points based on these regression formulas are shown on the graph by linear arrows stretching from the 1954 position to the 1964 position. The coordinates of the graph represent the two most important dimensions of attitudes toward other nations, the degree of friendliness on the horizontal axis, and on the vertical axis the degree of importance or salience of the nation (based on the percentage of respondents having firm opinions about it). Though this plotting method is difficult to describe, it gives a clear and simple picture of changes in international attitudes.

The attitude changes between 1954 and 1964 shown in Figure 13-1 are remarkably parallel. First, all six countries registered gains in the friendliness toward them shown by the other three Western European nations. Second, all countries except Russia also displayed gains in their importance to the other nations. Third, all countries maintained their same relative position over the 10-year period, with the United States receiving most friendliness, Great Britain

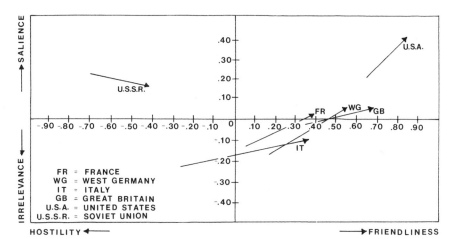

Figure 13-1 Changes from 1954 to 1964 in the composite attitudes of four Western European countries toward six nations. (From *Western European Perspectives on International Affairs: Public Opinion Studies and Evaluations*, Richard L. Merritt and Donald J. Puchala (Eds.), p. 133. Data in part II © 1968 by Frederick A. Praeger, Inc., New York. Reprinted by permission.

next most, and Russia least, while the United States and Russia remained first and second in importance to the others. Finally, all the countries except Italy ended up at least slightly above zero on the importance dimension, and Italy moved considerably in that direction. Thus, the graph reflects and quantifies the international trends of the early 1960s such as increased U.S.-Russian détente and growing integration of the European Economic Community (Merritt, 1968).

Several other findings of the USIA surveys provide fascinating information on international attitudes and beliefs about U.S. and Russian scientific progress. The sensitivity of such opinions to dramatic international events has been quite clearly demonstrated. For instance, the launching of Sputnik, the first Russian earth satellite, in November of 1957, was one of the most widely publicized events in history—public awareness of Sputnik shortly after its launching ranged as high as 97% in Norway and 96% in France. At that time, of the four Western European nations, only the West Germans, by a small margin, believed that the United States was ahead of Russia in science. However, a year later, after American satellite successes, all four nations showed large shifts toward belief in U.S. scientific superiority, and only the French still believed that Russia was ahead of the United States scientifically (Almond, 1968). Over this same time period, general attitudes toward the U.S.A. (in all of the four countries except Italy) showed a parallel pattern, with a small dip after Sputnik was launched and a rise by the following year (Merritt & Puchala, 1968, pp. 243–244).

COLD WAR ATTITUDES

Another important aspect of international attitudes is the views of each other's country held by Americans and Russians, the major Cold War protagonists. The attitudes of the Russian common man are rather hard to estimate for several reasons. Public opinion polling is very little used in the U.S.S.R., interviews with Russian citizens are often permeated with caution, and the views of Russian defectors are obviously biased. Nevertheless, several researchers investigating this area have reached remarkably similar conclusions.

A unique opportunity to study Russian attitudes came to Urie Bronfenbrenner, a social psychologist who was one of the first American scientists to visit Russia during a thaw in U.S.-Russian relations in 1960. He was allowed to travel quite freely without a guide in a number of cities, and since he spoke fluent Russian, he was able to converse with many of the common citizens. He held conversations with many people whom he chose in a semirandom manner and talked with systematically, and he returned with some fascinating observations and conclusions.

The Mirror Image

Bronfenbrenner's (1961) main conclusion was that Soviet citizens view the world almost exactly as American citizens do, but with a reversed evaluative direction—a **mirror image** in international perceptions. For instance, each nation sees itself as peace-loving and can give many reasons and arguments to support that view. Similarly, both Americans and Russians view the other nation as aggressive and threatening to foment a war at any moment, as evidenced by its huge expenditures for armed forces and military weapons. Consequently each nation feels that it must arm itself heavily for "defensive" purposes—to prevent the warlike other from carrying out its aggressive plans. In these respects the two countries hold exact mirror images of each other. The major common themes in the international viewpoints of Soviet and American citizens noted by Bronfenbrenner are listed and illustrated in Box 13-1.

Many other aspects of the mirror image have been described by Ralph White (1961, 1965) and documented by quotations from official statements or government leaders, and by interviews with foreigners who have visited each country. (In fact, Holsti, 1962, in a careful content analysis study, has shown that a prime example of mirror-image beliefs is contained in the public statements of John Foster Dulles, the U.S. Secretary of State during the Eisenhower administration.) White points out that most Americans and most Russians view the vast bulk of the other country's citizens as good, peace-loving individuals. But each country has a "black-top" image of the other—a belief that their leaders are evil, aggressive, and reckless. Though each country lives in constant fear of reckless aggressive actions by the other, neither is able to see that the other's actions are often motivated by fear rather than by hostile intent. Surprisingly enough, each side uses similar standards in judging themselves and the other side—truthfulness, strength, material advancement, courage, unselfishness, etc.—but since they do not see any given event from the same viewpoint, they apply these standards to an entirely different perception of world affairs. Finally, each side claims that the other's statements are propaganda, intended to deceive, and therefore it pays little attention to them.

In spite of these many similarities, U.S.-Russian perceptions are not a perfect reflection of each other. The mirror image has "flaws"—points where the reciprocal perceptions don't match exactly. One such wrinkle in the mirror is the Russians' strong feeling of warmth and friendliness for the American people, which is only feebly reciprocated by Americans. Another is the Russians' admiration for America's wealth and material progress, whereas Americans view Russia as poor, drab, and inefficient. Though both nations highly value "democracy," they hold quite different meanings of that term: Americans emphasize free elections and individual freedoms, whereas Russians stress citizens' responsibilities to serve the common good.

The Double Standard

Despite these and other small discrepancies, the mirror image in U.S. and Russian attitudes seems to be a well-established fact. If Russians and Americans observe the same world events and emerge with opposite conclusions, then it

Box 13-1 *Mirror Images of the U.S.A. and U.S.S.R.*

American Image of Russia

Russian Image of America

1. They are the aggressors.
They have imposed communist regimes on many countries by force.

They prevent disarmament by refusing to allow inspection.

1. They are the aggressors.
They have established American bases and troops on every border of the U.S.S.R.
They turn down our disarmament proposals and even send spy planes illegally over our country.

2. Their government exploits and deludes the people.
Communist party members, though a small part of the population, control the government.
Russian elections are a travesty since only one party is on the ballot.
The Russian radio and press are controlled by the government.

2. Their government exploits and deludes the people.
A capitalist-militarist clique controls the American government.

American voting is a farce since both parties' candidates are chosen by the same powerful interests.
The American radio and press are controlled by the capitalist-militarist interests.

3. Their people are not really sympathetic to the regime.
The Russian people distrust their government propaganda.
They praise communism only because they have to in order to avoid getting in trouble.
They would prefer to live under our system of government.

3. Their people are not really sympathetic to the regime.
The American people disapprove of their government's aggressive actions.
Most of them don't say anything controversial in order to avoid sanctions against liberal elements.
If they knew what communism is really like, they would choose it as their form of government.

4. Their leaders cannot be trusted.
Though they claim to favor disarmament, they are probably carrying on secret nuclear tests.
Everything they do is part of an aggressive communist plan.

4. Their leaders cannot be trusted.
Though they claim to favor disarmament, they insist on inspection only to discover our secrets.
They take advantage of our hospitality by sending in spies disguised as tourists.

5. Their policy verges on madness.
The Soviet position on such issues as Berlin and disarmament is completely unrealistic.
They carry their actions even to the brink of war.
Only Western restraint and coordinated reaction to the Russian provocations over Berlin avoided World War III.

5. Their policy verges on madness.
The American position on such issues as East Germany and disarmament is completely unrealistic.
They carry their actions even to the brink of war.
Only Soviet prudence and restraint in reacting to the American U-2 plane provocations avoided World War III.

Source: Extracts from Bronfenbrenner (1961, pp. 46–48).

follows that both sides are probably using a **double standard** for evaluating international affairs. Oskamp (1965; Oskamp & Hartry, 1968) demonstrated that a double standard of evaluation does indeed underlie the mirror image. He developed a list of 50 international actions which had been taken in substantially equivalent forms by both the United States and the U.S.S.R.—both countries had increased their military budgets, blockaded foreign areas, made disarmament proposals, signed joint treaties, sent great musicians to perform in the other country, etc. When American college students were asked to indicate how favorable they felt toward these identical actions by the two countries, they were markedly more favorable toward almost every one of the U.S. actions than to the comparable Russian action. Some of the differences were as large as 4 points on a 6-point scale; for instance, the students felt quite favorable to the U.S. blockading a nearby area but quite unfavorable toward Russia blockading an area near her.

This double standard in evaluating international events makes possible the mirror-image phenomenon. Americans generally see any action by their own country, either warlike or peaceful, in a much more favorable light than if the same action is taken by Russia. It can safely be assumed that Russian citizens also are generally more favorable to actions of their own country, though no questionnaire studies of the double standard have been conducted in Russia. More recent research (Oskamp, 1972a) has shown, as predicted, that students in Great Britain have much less of a double standard in evaluating U.S. and Russian actions. (Of course, they would be expected to show a clear-cut double standard in evaluating actions of their own country in relation to those of another nation, such as France. In fact, laboratory studies have shown that a mirror-image evaluative attitude toward two fictitious national groups can be easily created in an internation simulation experiment—Streufert & Sandler, 1971.)

Though the double standard in international affairs is pervasive, it is not impervious to events. The protest movement which developed in the United States during the Vietnam War at first had little effect on the size of subjects' preference for U.S. actions, but by 1971 the size of the double standard had decreased by more than half, at least among the small-college students with whom this research was conducted (Oskamp, 1972a). In particular, U.S. warlike or hostile actions and U.S. nonmilitary sanctions against other nations were evaluated less favorably in 1971 than in 1968 or 1963, while Russian peaceful statements were evaluated more favorably than earlier.

The Meaning of "Socialism" and "Capitalism"

Another aspect of cold-war attitudes, which has been demonstrated very persuasively by White (1966), is the differing meanings attached to the words "socialism" and "capitalism." White derived his data largely from the USIA surveys of public opinion in Great Britain, France, West Germany, and Italy. When representative samples in these four countries were asked to rate the

United States on a scale from completely capitalistic (0) to completely socialistic (10), an amazing 63% of them said the United States was completely capitalistic (0 on the scale) while 25% more put it at 1 or 2 on the scale. By contrast, in groups of Americans whom White has asked the same question, no one ever rated the United States at 0, and the typical response was usually about 5—roughly halfway between complete capitalism and complete socialism.

When the USIA surveys asked Western Europeans how much capitalism or socialism they wanted for their own countries, by far the most common answer was 5 on the 0-10 scale, given by 35% of the respondents; 65% chose answers in the range from 3 to 7, with 23% higher and 12% lower. White cites this and other evidence to show that in many countries "capitalism is on balance a slightly dirty word" and "that in most of the world the word socialism is more unequivocally positive than the word capitalism is negative" (p. 219).

How is it possible for Americans and Europeans to see the amount of socialism in the United States so differently? White makes a convincing case that the reason is largely that Europeans and Americans ascribe quite different meanings to the term. When Americans speak of socialism, they often refer to government ownership of industry, whereas in most other countries the term is used much more to refer to government responsibility for social welfare and government regulation of industry and labor. Similarly, to Americans capitalism primarily means private ownership of industry, whereas in most other countries it means excessive political power for rich men (capitalists) and lack of social welfare for poor people. In addition, most other peoples (outside of Russia, China, and Eastern Europe) dislike communism, which they associate with dictatorship and violence, and make a sharp distinction between it and socialism. (Indeed the dominant party in many countries is named Democratic Socialists or some variation thereof.) In contrast, many Americans use the words communist and socialist almost interchangeably as pejorative terms.

An important substantive lesson can be drawn from these semantic distinctions. White concludes that American social welfare programs and government regulative laws have given us an intermediate level of socialism (probably not far from the level preferred by many Europeans). However, there is a great ignorance of that fact overseas, and Americans compound that problem by often referring to our system as capitalistic and by "confusing socialism with Communism and condemning both in the same breath" (p. 228). White recommends, in the interest of clearer communication and understanding with other nations, that we should try

> to avoid needless emphasis on issues in the area of socialism that we and they may disagree on, and to emphasize instead the principles of democracy that we and they have in common. . . . We can then define what America stands for unambiguously as a maximum of democracy, a minimum of government ownership, and a medium-to-high amount of social welfare (White, 1966, p. 228).

AMERICAN ATTITUDES ON INTERNATIONAL ISSUES

On the topic of Americans' attitudes toward various international issues, some interesting results were obtained in a comprehensive study by Free and Cantril (1967).

Internationalism

Free and Cantril interviewed two national probability samples totaling over 3000 respondents during the fall of 1964. They developed a scale of five items to measure the degree of **internationalism**. A respondent was classified as "completely internationalist" if he agreed that the United States should cooperate fully with the United Nations and take into account the views of its Allies, and disagreed with the statements that the United States should go its own way in international matters, mind its own business internationally, and concentrate more on its own national problems. (The items were more complex than that but are abbreviated here for convenience.) A respondent who varied from the above pattern on only one item was classified as "predominantly internationalist." There were parallel categories on the isolationist side and an intermediate "mixed" category. The distribution of respondents was as follows:

Completely internationalist	30%
Predominantly internationalist	35
Mixed	27
Predominantly isolationist	5
Completely isolationist	3
	100%

This very heavy preponderance of internationalist views is a dramatic and important finding. It is even more striking when compared with the very high levels of isolationism that existed in the United States before World War II. For instance, a Gallup Poll in 1937 asked, "If another war like World War I developed in Europe, should America take part again?" and 95% of Americans said "No"! As late as 1939, 66% of Americans said the United States should not help either side if Germany and Italy went to war against England and France (Free & Cantril, 1967, p. 63). By contrast, in 1964, though there were group differences in degree of internationalism (which will be discussed in a later section), all population subgroups which were analyzed had at least a majority of members who were internationalistic.

The high degree of internationalism is also interesting to consider in relation to the parallel finding by Free and Cantril that most Americans were quite poorly informed about international affairs. Analyzing a question about U.S. prestige abroad, Free and Cantril reported:

the well informed held a jaundiced view, the moderately informed were sanguine, while the uninformed were positively euphoric. Similarly, the response of the majority of college-educated people was negative; of those with only a high school or grade school education, positive. Apparently, the more one knows about international affairs, the less well he thinks the United States is doing abroad (p. 78).

An important aspect of American international policy has been our foreign aid program. From the late 1950s through the middle 1960s, Americans generally reported favoring foreign aid programs by about a 3-to-2 margin. However, Free and Cantril found a plurality (44%) advocating a reduced level of foreign economic aid. This and other related findings led the authors to conclude that the position of most Americans could best be described as one of "qualified internationalism."

Relations with Other Nations

Americans also show some ambivalence in their attitudes toward specific other nations. For instance, in our most important national relationship, that with Russia, Americans have been found to favor firmness but also conciliation. Free and Cantril reported 61% agreement that "The United States should take a firmer stand against the Soviet Union than it has in recent years." In spite of this position, an overwhelming majority of respondents (85%) favored continuing negotiations with Russia in attempts to strengthen world peace, and 70% favored negotiations toward mutual arms reductions (Free & Cantril, 1967, pp. 83–85). Yet at the same time a majority of Americans agreed on the necessity of keeping the United States "as the world's most powerful nation at all costs, even going to the very brink of war, if necessary" (p. 93).

Attitudes toward mainland China were also notably mixed. In 1964 a pronounced majority of respondents indicated that Communist China would turn out to be a greater threat than Russia to the United States, and yet there was an almost even split as to whether it would be wise for the United States to establish diplomatic relations with China within the next five years. Also polls by Harris and Gallup in 1966 found that 55% of Americans were favorable toward admission of Communist China into the U.N. under certain specified conditions. As a result of these findings, Free and Cantril concluded that "American public opinion seems to be fairly malleable when it comes to the Chinese problem" (1967, p. 89). It should be kept in mind that this was written well before admission of mainland China into the U.N. in 1971 and President Nixon's subsequent dramatic trip to Peking.

Many other public opinion researchers have reached similar conclusions about Presidential latitude in leading public opinion (e.g., Lipset, 1966; Rosenberg, 1967; Mueller, 1971). Thus it is truly surprising to note the administrative and congressional disregard of such findings for many years before Nixon's initiatives toward détente with China.

Trends in International Attitudes

International attitudes, like other attitudes, are subject to change over time, and recent years have seen many international events which could have a marked impact on attitudes. The long buildup and gradual winding-down of the Vietnam War, growing normalization of relations with Russia, and the dramatic moves toward détente with China were all events of this crucial sort. So the question must be asked: Did these and other events actually produce any major changes in Americans' international attitudes?

A book entitled *State of the Nation 1974* by Watts and Free (1974) is one of the most important recent public opinion studies in this area, because it contains a number of comparisons of trends in international attitudes. Its findings are based on similar questions and research methodology used in 1974, in 1972, in 1968, and in some cases as far back as 1964 (Free & Cantril, 1967). Like the earlier books, it utilized a national probability sample, in which over 1800 Americans were interviewed during April, 1974. Results of some of its important trend comparisons are shown in Table 13-3.

Looking first at general internationalism, the table shows an increase in individuals on the isolationistic side of the spectrum only in 1974, but a continuing marked drop since 1964 in the number of "completely internationalistic" respondents and an increase in the "mixed" or middle-of-the-road category. The item about U.S. war brinksmanship shows a clear-cut reversal since 1964, with more respondents in 1972 and 1974 opposing such a course. However, surprisingly, in 1974 there was a decrease in the number of people opposing U.S. economic aid to foreign countries. Similarly, the last item in Table 13-3 shows some increase from 1972 to 1974 in support for military spending. Thus, as in the previous section of this chapter, there is a mixed picture—decreasing internationalism and brinksmanship in recent years, accompanied by increasing support for foreign aid and military spending.

Other findings of Watts and Free, not presented in the table, showed that almost two-thirds of respondents perceived a sharp drop in America's national situation in the last five years, since 1969. The nation's current international situation was rated somewhat more positively than its domestic situation, though in both cases a large plurality described the picture as "only fair." However, looking only at the last year or two, over two-thirds of respondents felt that the United States had made at least some progress in world affairs during that period, primarily because of improving relationships with China and with Russia, and reduced tensions in the Middle East and elsewhere in the world.

Despite that recent progress, three times as many respondents said U.S. prestige abroad was low as said it was high, whereas in 1964 a majority had seen U.S. prestige as high. Nevertheless, in 1972, 69% of the sample said that U.S. international actions had generally been a force for good in the world during recent years, indicating that the Vietnam War controversy had still not tarnished most people's "good-guy" image of their own country. However, a noticeable

TABLE 13-3 Some Trends in Americans' International Attitudes from 1964 to 1974

Scale or item	1964	1968	1972	1974
Internationalism-isolationism scale (5 items)				
Completely internationalist	30%	25%	18%	11%
Predominantly internationalist	35	34	38	30
Mixed	27	32	35	38
Predominantly isolationist	5	6	5	14
Completely isolationist	3	3	4	7
The U.S. should maintain its dominant position as the world's most powerful nation at all costs, even going to the brink of war, if necessary.				
Agree	56	50	39	42
Disagree	31	40	50	43
Don't know	13	10	11	15
Economic aid to foreign countries should be: (somewhat different items)				
Increased	} 32	—	7	9
Kept at present level		—	33	43
Reduced	44	—	42	33
Ended altogether	15	—	13	11
Don't know	9	—	5	4
U.S. spending for defense and military purposes should be:				
Increased	—	—	9	17
Kept at present level	—	—	40	40
Reduced	—	—	37	33
Ended altogether	—	—	5	4
Don't know	—	—	9	6

Source: Adapted from Table 7 on page 219, small unnumbered tables on pages 251 (top); 254, 259, from *STATE OF THE NATION 1974* by William Watts and Lloyd A. Free © 1974 by Potomac Associates, Basic Books, Inc., Publishers, New York; and from Free & Cantril (1967, p. 72).

weariness and decrease in internationalist enthusiasm was evident in the massive 87% agreement that "The U.S. should continue to play a major role internationally, but cut down on some of its responsibilities abroad" (Watts & Free, 1973, p. 204).

Public Opinion Regarding the Vietnam War

The Vietnam War has been called the most divisive and bitter American experience since the Civil War. To investigate that contention scientifically, let us look more systematically at public opinion data on American atittudes toward the war over the course of its development. Mueller (1971, 1973) has conveniently summarized these data, reported at various times by several national polling organizations, and compared them with the progression of similar attitudes during the course of American involvement in the Korean War of 1950–1953. His findings will probably surprise you.

Mueller derived his data from public responses to the following basic poll question, repeated with some slight variations many times during the Vietnam and Korean Wars: "Do you think the U.S. made a mistake sending troops to fight in Vietnam (Korea)?" The changing pattern of support over time for the Vietnam War is plotted graphically in Figure 13-2. In reading this graph, note that the figures shown can be below 50% and still be pluralities, since usually 10–18% of respondents were undecided. Since the Vietnam War had no clear starting point, and was initially given little attention by U.S. public opinion, Mueller arbitrarily chose as its beginning date mid-1965 when American troops and bombers were being committed to the war in large numbers. Figure 13-2 also shows, for comparison, the pattern of support over time for the Korean War in response to similar poll questions.

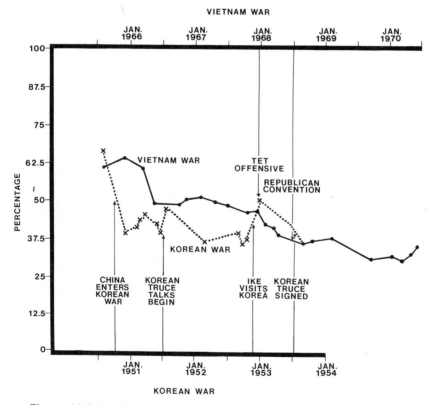

Figure 13-2 Public support for the Vietnam and Korean Wars. (Adapted from Mueller, 1971, pp. 362, 364.)

These data demonstrate several points. First, both wars began with high public support (over 60% pro and less than 25% con)—what Mueller calls a "rally-round-the-flag phenomenon." Then, fairly quickly, there was a marked drop in public enthusiasm, followed by a slow decline in support over a period of years. There were also fluctuations in attitudes related to a few highly dramatic events—particularly in the Korean War, when the Chinese entry into the war caused a huge early drop in support and President Eisenhower's visit to Korea to speed up the truce talks produced a clear increase in public support. However, in general, most events do not seem to have had much effect on the underlying trend of public support for the wars.

Comparing support for the two wars, it is clear that the Korean War was lower in public support for almost its whole course of time. This finding is sharply contrary to the many claims that the Vietnam War was "the most unpopular war in [U.S.] history" (Wise, 1968). However, Mueller points out that the Korean War started abruptly and involved much higher early casualties than the Vietnam War. Using the statistical technique of regression analysis, he was able to demonstrate that

> In each war, support . . . started at much the same level and then every time American casualties increased by a factor of 10 (i.e., from 100 to 1,000 or from 10,000 to 100,000) support for the war dropped by about 15 percentage points (1971, p. 366).

Thus, Mueller concludes that patterns of public support for the two wars were very similar. It is true, of course, that approval of the Vietnam War eventually dropped lower than the Korean War levels, but it only did so after the war had gone on longer and American casualties had climbed much higher than in Korea. Analysis of poll data from other kinds of questions also leads to the same final conclusion: contrary to popular belief, opposition to the Vietnam War, though louder and more vocal than during the Korean war, was definitely not more extensive.

What of the future—will the Vietnam War remain in the public memory as an ebb tide of national discord and controversy? That depends a great deal on later events in Vietnam and in U.S. foreign relations. Mueller found that, after the Korean War was terminated, its public popularity rose gradually over a period of years. However, World War II, from a high support rating during the war (around 75%), dropped somewhat in popularity in the immediate postwar years. And World War I's retrospective popularity dropped to only 28% in 1937—lower than any support levels found for the Korean or Vietnam wars. However, World War I's rating was markedly affected by world events and soared to higher levels after the German invasion of France and the Japanese attack on Pearl Harbor. This finding has led Mueller to urge caution in predicting the ultimate public attitude regarding the Vietnam War.

Events of the next ten years will not change the facts about Vietnam, but they may change how we recall and evaluate what happened there (1971, p. 373).

WHO HOLDS WHICH ATTITUDES?

Let us turn from discussion of various types of international attitudes, to consider the **correlates** of these attitudes. That is, we will ask the question: What kind of people hold specific types of international attitudes? Despite some differences in findings, there is a great deal of general agreement among research studies in this area.

Cold War Attitudes

Major reviews of studies on hard-line cold war attitudes versus conciliatory viewpoints have been made by Rosenberg (1965a, 1967) and Scott (1965). Their findings closely resemble those for isolationism, which are presented in the following section.

An important caution to keep in mind here is that significant differences found in this area usually represent at most a moderate degree of relationship—one which would allow for many exceptions in individual cases. Briefly stated, some of the frequently found correlates of hard-line, intransigent international attitudes have been found to be: male sex, Eastern European background, Midwest or Mountain States residency, general religiosity, a business background, conservative views, low information, authoritarian personality characteristics, personal insecurity, and hostility and aggressiveness.

Isolationism

Two major national survey studies of isolationist versus internationalist attitudes have reported findings which are largely complementary. One survey study, by Free and Cantril (1967), has been described previously in this chapter. The other study (McClosky, 1967), conducted in the late 1950s, was unique in that it used long paper-and-pencil questionnaires with large representative samples of respondents. Actually, McClosky studied three major samples: a national cross-section of about 1500 cases, a representative sample of about 1100 Minnesota residents, and a mail survey of over 3000 political leaders who had been delegates and alternates to the 1956 Democratic and Republican conventions. A key measure used by McClosky was a carefully constructed and validated 9-item scale of isolationism including items such as the following:

> Most of the countries which have gotten economic help from America end up resenting what we have done for them.

George Washington's advice to stay out of agreements with foreign powers is just as wise now as it was when he was alive.

McClosky concentrated his research primarily on personality correlates of isolationism, whereas Free and Cantril reported mostly **demographic** correlates. Their findings will be integrated and presented together here. Again it should be remembered that the relationships described range from weak to moderate in size, allowing for many individual exceptions.

Demographic Correlates of Isolationism. Both studies agreed that poorly informed individuals and those with little education were more likely to be isolationists, as were rural residents. Free and Cantril reported that persons age 50 and over, and non-labor-force-members (mostly retired people) tended toward isolationism. They also found Protestants more isolationistic than Catholics, and Jews clearly lowest. The Southern states which voted for Goldwater in 1964 were most isolationistic, while the East and Midwest were least so. Republican party members and the poor were quite isolationistic, while professionals and white-collar workers showed the opposite trend. McClosky's findings also showed the poor and culturally deprived as more isolationistic. He reported a similar trend for individuals who were politically inactive and those who were members of few organizations. Though there was no discernable difference between rank-and-file Democrats and Republicans, Republican party leaders were clearly more isolationistic than Democratic leaders.

Personality Correlates of Isolationism. McClosky reported findings on over 70 different scales, most of them measures of personality characteristics. His results can be briefly summarized as follows: Isolationists showed many of the characteristics of authoritarianism, such as ethnocentric and anti-Semitic beliefs, and tendencies to acquiesce to authority. They were also typified by intolerance of ambiguity, obsessive tendencies, rigidity, and inflexibility. Several scales showed isolationists to be low in democratic convictions and commitment (tolerance, faith in procedural rights, etc.) and high in elitism and willingness to "take the law into one's own hands." They were also high in political alienation (cynicism, suspiciousness, and a sense of political futility).

Another prime characteristic of isolationists, according to McClosky's findings, was misanthropy. They tended toward hostile and paranoid views of the world, including lack of faith in people, contempt for weakness, and intolerance of human frailty. Yet at the same time they were low in ego strength themselves, suffering from anxiety, guilt feelings, frustrations, and lack of satisfaction in life.

McClosky also found that general orientations of isolationism or internationalism tended to be carried over into beliefs about specific foreign policy issues such as foreign aid, immigration, tariffs, etc. On most such issues isolationists tended to hold attitudes markedly in the conservative direction. Not only that, but isolationism even carried over into conservative *domestic* policy positions for the political leaders, though there was no such clear relationship for the cross-section sample of average citizens.

As a final refinement, McClosky was able to divide isolationists empirically into two sub-types: peaceful, and aggressive (or jingoistic). The peaceful isolationist wants the nation to withdraw into its shell and avoid most contacts with other nations, including any threats or use of force. The jingoistic isolationist, on the other hand, relies on power and the threat of force to insure his nation's safety behind its impregnable defenses. McClosky has shown that peaceful isolationists are less driven by aversive psychological needs like hostility and alienation, and therefore are more like nonisolationists than are jingoistic isolationists.

Vietnam War Attitudes

Studies of attitudes on more specific foreign policy issues, such as Vietnam War policies, have generally found correlates similar to those discussed in the previous two sections. For instance, Cantril and Roll (1971) interviewed a national sample of over 1400 persons in 1971 about their preference for ending the Vietnam War through a compromise settlement versus fighting on to insure a noncommunist government there. Between 1968 and 1971 the hard-line response of continuing the war decreased dramatically in popularity, from 62% down to 36%. Categories of respondents who most frequently said "fight on" in 1972 were men, high school graduates, manual laborers, 30–49 year-olds, residents of the Midwest or South, and people with moderate incomes. By contrast, those most eager to end the war were more often the nonwhites, college graduates, 21–29 year-olds, and urban residents.

HOW DO INTERNATIONAL ATTITUDES CHANGE?

International attitudes, like many other attitudes, tend to be formed initially in the child's socialization process and are based on information and norms received from the family and the school. Though attitudes about other nations, foreigners, or international issues are sometimes developed through the child's or adolescent's personal experience, it is more common for them to be formed without any direct contact with the attitude object (Scott, 1965). In spite of that, once formed, international attitudes are usually quite resistant to major changes, even through relevant personal experience. What factors can produce changes in people's international attitudes?

Contact with Foreigners. Foreign travel is often thought to influence attitudes of both the traveler and those host country citizens with whom the visitor comes in contact. For instance, foreign student programs and cultural exchanges have often assumed that getting to know foreigners will lead to greater liking for them and increase international goodwill. However, review of empirical studies of such programs shows that these assumptions are much too simple and are frequently in error (Pool, 1965). The purpose of the travel (study, tourism, business trip, military assignment, etc.) must be considered, as well as the social and cultural situation which travelers meet in relation to their backgrounds and expectations. Foreign contact will usually increase detail and differentiation in attitudes, but it may cause either favorable or unfavorable changes, no change at all, or a change from either extreme toward a more moderate view. A common finding is a U-shaped curve of favorability toward the host country over the time period of the visit, and some research has shown a second U-shaped pattern of readjustment upon return to one's own country (Selltiz & Cook, 1962; Gullahorn & Gullahorn, 1963).

Personal Experiences.   Other than contact with foreigners, personal experiences of other sorts can sometimes affect international attitudes. A prime example is Rappoport and Cvetkovich's (1968) report on attitude changes in a group of Vietnam veterans. Though hardly any of them had felt negative toward the war before their own overseas duty, most of the veterans who had been in intense combat had become much more critical of the war; by contrast, a majority of the light-combat and rear echelon noncombat groups had become more positive toward the war while in Vietnam. These findings are particularly interesting because they run counter to predictions which would be made from the dissonance theory principle that one comes to like what one has suffered for.

Impact of Events.   A thorough review of this topic has been made by Deutsch and Merritt (1965). Attitude change can result from spectacular events, which receive much media coverage, or from "cumulative events" which take place gradually over a long time (e.g., increasing industrialization of a country). However, often even spectacular events have no effect on attitudes, or they may cause only a brief fluctuation followed by a return to the preexisting attitude. For instance, following the failure of the Cuban Bay of Pigs invasion attempt, the events of the Cuban missile crisis in 1962 did not change the level of public opposition to an American invasion of Cuba (about 65% opposed). By contrast, Russian suppression of the Hungarian uprising in 1956 led to an average 19% drop in favorability toward Russia in four Western European countries. However, six months later nearly half of this drop had dissipated, and following the launching of Sputnik in October 1957, there was another 8% increase in favorability toward Russia. The most dramatic changes in political alignments usually involve attitude changes by only 20% to 30% of the population, and such changes almost always involve a combination of spectacular events and cumulative events. Either type of event alone is apt to produce attitude changes of no more than 10%.

Education and Persuasion.   A review of research on education and persuasion attempts to influence international attitudes (Janis & Smith, 1965) indicates that there are many sources of resistance to such approaches. For instance, both group affiliations and personality needs are likely to reinforce a person for maintaining his current attitudes. For this reason, intended audiences often do not receive adequate exposure to the message, let alone take the further steps of attention, comprehension, and acceptance (e.g., Star & Hughes, 1950). Little research has been done specifically on persuasion regarding international attitudes, but a few studies have shown that significant attitude changes can be achieved under the right conditions (e.g., Putney & Middleton, 1962). The many laboratory studies on social influence processes can supply hypotheses for future work in this area.

Government Programs. Governments and the mass media manage much of the public presentation of information which is relevant to international attitudes. By giving special attention to (or withholding it from) certain events, developments, or programs, they are in a position of potential influence over public attitudes (Deutsch & Merritt, 1965). In the era of the Cold War between the United States and Russia, some proposals were advanced for ways to break the vicious circle of mutual distrust, suspicion, and hostility. For instance, Osgood (1962) suggested that one of the major powers should begin a preannounced program of small unilateral steps to reduce world tensions, which the other major power would be urged to reciprocate in ways which it felt would further reduce tension. This approach would reverse the upward spiral of the arms race and break the typical logjam of intransigence in negotiations which allows each nation to prevent any beneficial movement by the other. Etzioni (1969) has described the actions and statements of the U.S. government between June and November, 1963, as a partial test of this gradualist approach to détente, which he calls the "Kennedy experiment." He concludes that these actions did lead to a reduction of world tensions and to less hostile international attitudes.

RESEARCH ON INTERNATIONAL ATTITUDES

Most research on international attitudes is unsophisticated and descriptive in nature. Sometimes it only presents item responses for the whole sample of respondents (e.g., 72% feel that the United States should cooperate fully with the United Nations). More often such responses are cross-tabulated with one or more other variables, providing a breakdown by categories on the second variable (e.g., 47% of grade school graduates are isolationistic, but only 32% of high school graduates and 23% of college graduates are isolationistic). However, two-way or three-way "cross-tabs" are still descriptive in nature, and most studies provide data for only one point in time and one nation (or, frequently, for one subgroup within a nation, such as students).

Such descriptive surveys are valuable in aiding communication of public viewpoints and letting decision-makers know in some detail about public beliefs and feelings. However, there is a real need for more sophisticated studies comparing attitudes across several periods of time, and in several countries, and using statistical analyses to show the significance and stability of trends (Etzioni, 1969). The USIA surveys of Western European countries (Merritt & Puchala, 1968) provide some of the best examples of such comparative research, now unfortunately all but abandoned by the USIA under later presidents.

Finally, to achieve a causal understanding of factors in attitude change, experimental and quasi-experimental research designs are needed to test and verify hypotheses developed from anecdotal and descriptive studies. In the field of international attitudes, experimental research on attitude change has hardly begun.

SUMMARY

Our images of foreign nations and peoples are often incomplete and distorted. Particularly in the area of world affairs, public information is sharply limited. Children's views of foreign peoples begin to be formed as early as age 6 and usually start with simple factual and descriptive information and basic evaluations in terms of "good" and "bad." Children generally describe their own nation with stereotyped positive evaluations such as "good," or "peaceful." They tend to describe well-liked nations with many factual, descriptive terms and relatively few evaluative terms, but less-liked nations with more negative evaluative terms and fewer factual descriptions.

Adults' stereotypes of other nations seem to be based largely on national alliances or competition. Neutral nations and nations with a similar language or culture are typically well-liked, but large bordering nations are apt to be disliked. The USIA surveys of public opinion in many Western European countries between 1952 and 1965 provided valuable information on cross-national comparisons and on changes in international attitudes over time.

The cold war competition between the United States and Russia has developed mirror-image perceptions of world affairs in which each side sees itself as peace-loving and virtuous and sees the other side as aggressive and reckless, its power-less people unwillingly being controlled by their exploitive leaders. This mirror-image phenomenon is based upon a double standard of evaluation of international actions. Another source of international misunderstanding and confusion is the differing meanings which Americans and other nations ascribe to the terms "socialism" and "capitalism."

Research in the 1960s showed the American people to be strongly internationalistic, though that characteristic has diminished in recent years. Americans show considerable ambivalence in their attitudes toward Russia and China, favoring both increased firmness and conciliation—both the iron fist and the velvet glove. Most respondents see U.S. prestige abroad as much lower now than in the 1960s, and over the same period U.S. brinksmanship has become markedly less popular with Americans. Though the Vietnam War was marked by highly vocal opposition, its public support was higher than the Korean War's for several years, and public disapproval of both wars increased in close relationship with the logarithm of the number of U.S. war casualties.

In studies of isolationism, moderate-sized relationships with many other factors have been found. Demographic correlates include low information and education, lower social class, rural residence, and Protestant religion. Personality correlates include authoritarian characteristics, alienation, misanthropy, and conservatism. Rather similar patterns have been found for hard-line cold war and Vietnam War attitudes.

Though international attitudes are often formed during childhood without any direct contact with the attitude object, these attitudes are usually quite resistant to major changes, even through personal experience. The main factors which (on occasion) are effective in influencing international attitudes are: contact with foreigners, personal experiences such as combat participation, spectacular or cumulative world events, education and persuasion campaigns, and government programs combining international actions and public statements.

Suggested Readings

Etzioni, A. Social-psychological aspects of international relations. In G. Lindzey & E. Aronson (Eds.), *The Handbook of Social Psychology* (2nd ed.). Vol. 5. Reading, Mass.: Addison-Wesley, 1969. Pp. 538–601.—An erudite review of research, leaning toward a sociological and theoretical viewpoint.

Kelman, H. C. (Ed.). *International Behavior: A Social Psychological Analysis.* New York: Holt, Rinehart & Winston, 1965.—A collection of review articles written specially for this volume by many outstanding authorities. Part One, on national and international images, is particularly relevant to attitudes.

Osgood, C. E. *An Alternative to War or Surrender.* Urbana: University of Illinois Press, 1962.—An eminent psychologist's proposal for a practical approach to easing world tensions. This readable little book suggested the basic approach of the "Kennedy experiment."

Stagner, R. *Psychological Aspects of International Conflict.* Belmont, Calif.: Brooks/Cole, 1967.—A short, interesting introduction regarding the relevance of psychological theories and research to international affairs.

chapter 14

Racism and Prejudice

Theodore Weissbach

There is no more evil thing in this present world than race prejudice, none at all. . . . It justifies and holds together more baseness, cruelty, and abomination than any other sort of error in the world.—H. G. Wells.

No State shall make or enforce any law which shall abridge the privileges or immunities of citizens of the United States; nor shall any State deprive any person of life, liberty, or property, without due process of law; nor deny to any person within its jurisdiction the equal protection of the laws.—The Fourteenth Amendment to the U.S. Constitution.

Our nation is moving toward two societies, one black, one white—separate and unequal.—National Advisory Commission on Civil Disorders.

Despite our pledge of "one nation . . . with liberty and justice for all," the United States has been called a racist society by both foreign and domestic critics. Rather than being a "melting pot" where all peoples can blend into a harmonious, unified population, the United States can be characterized as exclusionary, hostile, condescending, and undemocratic in its race relations. It was only in 1954 that the Supreme Court struck down the doctrine of "separate-but-equal" and forced public schools in the South to abandon segregated dual school systems. Since then, access to public accommodations, voting rights, and equal employment opportunity for all Americans have been guaranteed in law. Though it is encouraging to view the record of civil rights legislation and court decisions of the past few decades, the necessity to legislate and to litigate demonstrates the pervasiveness of racism in our daily lives. When the United States celebrated its bicentennial in 1976, it could be proud of its real accomplishments in race relations. However, racism is still a fact of American life, so much work remains to be done.

WHAT IS RACISM?

Not everyone agrees about what constitutes racism or racist behavior. The term **racism** is a broader one than "racial prejudice," and it is generally used to include not only prejudice, but also "hostility, discrimination, segregation, and other negative *action* expressed toward an ethnic group" (Marx, 1970, p. 101, italics added). **Prejudice**, in turn, can be defined as an intolerant, unfair, or irrational unfavorable *attitude* toward another group of people (Harding et al., 1969). Most authorities agree that racism can be found at both the individual level and the institutional level. A person might be considered an individual racist if prejudiced attitudes and discriminatory behavior against another racial group were important and central parts of his life—for instance, if he frequently talked about them, acted upon them, or tried to persuade other people to share the same attitudes and behavior patterns.

Institutional racism is a new term in our language, but it describes an age-old pattern of behavior. It refers to formal and explicit laws and regulations which discriminate against certain ethnic groups, as well as to informal, but powerful, social norms which limit the opportunities and choices available to certain ethnic groups. Examples of formal institutional racism include the recent dual school systems in the South, housing covenants which formerly prohibited the sale of homes in certain areas to "undesirable" minority groups, and laws which prohibited interracial marriages. On the informal level, colleges and universities have had "gentlemen's agreements" and quotas to admit only a small percentage of minority applicants no matter how good their qualifications. Similarly, many business firms hire only the "right" sort of person—one who would be acceptable at the club. Real estate agents and lending institutions still try to "steer" minority group members away from purchasing homes in certain areas. On a subtler level, the use of certain standardized procedures like aptitude testing for job selection or college admission can be a form of institutional racism if it unfairly or invalidly discriminates against minority group members who could actually succeed on the job or in the college if given a chance (Jones, 1972).

Individual and institutional racism are not mutually exclusive. It is doubtful that institutional racism could develop or survive without support from many individual racists, nor is it likely that individual racism would thrive without strong social support. This chapter concentrates on individual racism and particularly on racial attitudes regarding black people. However, it is important to remember that the focus of the civil rights movement has been on combating institutional racism, and that racism often is directed against Chicanos, Orientals, Jews, and other ethnic minorities in addition to blacks.

CHILDREN'S RACIAL ATTITUDES

Bigots are made, not born. Social scientists believe, like Aristotle, that at birth the mind is a blank slate (at least with respect to social attitudes), and experience writes upon it. As described in Chapter 6, we learn not only through personal experience but through social interaction. In Gordon Allport's (1954) words, many of our attitudes and opinions toward groups of people are *adopted*, i.e., learned from our family and culture, rather than *developed*, i.e., learned through life experiences that lead us to fear or dislike minority groups.

Attitudes of Young Children

Attitudes cannot exist without awareness, and racial awareness seems to develop quite early. Children as young as three years old can identify their own race and the race of others. By seven years of age, almost 100% can accurately discriminate between their own and other racial groups (Clark & Clark, 1947; Goodman, 1964).

A number of ingenious methods have been used to elicit racial preferences and attitudes from very young children. The best known is the doll technique developed by Kenneth B. and Mamie P. Clark (1947). Children are shown two dolls (or sometimes more), one representing a black child, the other a white child, and asked to respond to a number of questions by choosing one of the dolls. The questions include: Which doll is most like you? Which is the black (white, Negro, colored) doll? Which is the good (bad) doll? Which is the doll you would like to play with? On the basis of the doll choices, it was established that white children had a strong preference for the white dolls. Further, white children tended to attribute good qualities to the white dolls and bad qualities to the black dolls (e.g., Clark & Clark, 1947; Asher & Allen, 1969). There has been little disagreement in the interpretation of the results of these studies for white chil-

Photograph courtesy of Kenneth B.
Clark. Reprinted by permission.

Box 14-1 KENNETH B. CLARK, *Pioneer Racial Attitude Researcher*

Recently retired as Distinguished Professor of Psychology Emeritus at the City College of New York, Kenneth B. Clark has had a real impact on the position of minority groups in the United States. Born in Panama in 1914, he grew up in Harlem, attended Howard University, and earned a Ph.D. at Columbia University in 1940. After brief periods of teaching and wartime research, he joined the faculty at CCNY, where he remained for the rest of his career. In recent years he also served as President of the Metropolitan Applied Research Center, and upon retirement he founded a consulting firm dealing with human relations and affirmative action issues.

The early research of Clark and his wife on the self-images of Negro children was cited in the 1954 U.S. Supreme Court decision regarding school desegregation, Brown vs. Board of Education. *Since then he has served as consultant to many organizations and written books such as* Prejudice and Your Child, Dark Ghetto, The Negro American, A Relevant War Against Poverty, *and* Pathos of Power. *He is a member of the New York State Board of Regents, and in 1971 he was elected President of the American Psychological Association.*

dren. White children appear to learn racial discrimination early in life. They have strong positive attitudes toward themselves and other members of their race, and they have negative reactions to blacks.

Black Pride

Until the late 1960s, the results for black children seemed equally unambiguous. They too preferred and identified with *white* dolls and rejected black dolls. These data, from the studies cited above and many others, were interpreted to mean that black children developed the same racial attitudes as white children (prowhite, antiblack). The result was a diminished self-concept coupled with an unrealistic and self-defeating wish to be white (Chethick, Fleming, Mayer, & McCoy, 1967; Coles, 1968).

In the late 1960s, new studies began to challenge the earlier findings. Greenwald and Oppenheim (1968) argued that black children may have misidentified themselves as white in earlier studies because experimenters failed to take account of the range of skin color of black Americans. From the light-skinned black child's point of view, the white doll may in fact have looked more like him(her) than the black doll. It was found that in earlier studies, the percentage of misidentification was much higher among light-skinned than dark-skinned blacks (80% vs. 23% in the Clarks' study).

In addition to concern with experimental artifacts, researchers had reason to believe that increased racial integration and black pride would be reflected in improved self-concepts among black children. Bunton and Weissbach (1974) found that after twelve weeks in all-black, community-controlled public schools in Washington, D.C., 5– and 6–year-olds became significantly more problack in their doll choices. Hraba and Grant (1970) found that black children in integrated schools in Lincoln, Nebraska were as problack in their doll choices as white children were prowhite. Similarly, Crooks (1970) reported that black children in Halifax, Nova Scotia, who had just completed an enriched, integrated, preschool program identified themselves as black and chose black dolls as the ones they preferred more frequently than a control group of black children who had not experienced the program. These results seemed to indicate that for some black children under some conditions racial preferences were changing. What is not yet clear is whether these changes in doll preferences truly represent a change in self-concept, and if there has been a change in self-concept, what the implications are for behavior. As Asher and Allen (1969) ask, "Are black people who express white preference less assertive, more likely to do well in school, less likely to participate in a civil rights demonstration?" (p. 165).

It seems apparent that both black children and white children learn prejudice early, largely from family members and other early socializing influences. Black children, who used to grow up to dislike themselves almost as much as whites seemed to dislike them, may have benefited most from the fairly recent emphasis on black pride. Their self-images reflect a better self-concept and hold promise of a positive view of their own race.

RACIAL AND ETHNIC STEREOTYPES

What are "they" like, anyway? Most of us, whether we care to admit it or not, hold many ethnic stereotypes: the "crafty" Jew, the "lazy" black, the "gentlemanly" Briton, the "drunken" Irishman, the "stupid" Pole. Even if we reject the accuracy or appropriateness of stereotypes, we can laugh when Archie Bunker uses them.

The noun **stereotype** originally referred to a metal printer's mold, which could exactly reproduce a printed page. Walter Lippman (1922) borrowed this term to describe "pictures in our heads"—perceptions of individual members of an ethnic group as all being identical copies of each other, all having similar traits. The use of stereotypes is unjustified when they do not correspond to the facts or when they are invoked to rationalize harmful discrimination and prejudice. We usually apply the term stereotype to someone else's generalizations, for we rarely perceive our own generalizations about people as distorted or unjustified (Brigham, 1971).

Just as with international attitudes (discussed in Chapter 13), the degree of stereotyping is usually measured by assessing the amount of consensus in people's choice of traits as typical of members of some ethnic group. If the percentage of agreement is high, a stereotype is said to exist. When measured in this way, the content of stereotypes seems to have remained fairly consistent over a period of about forty years (Katz & Braley, 1933; Brigham, 1971). The amount of consensus seems to have declined significantly, but 25% or more of a mid-1960s sample of college freshmen and sophomores still described blacks as lazy, superstitious, musical, ostentatious, and pleasure-loving (Karlins et al., 1969).

It is not clear at this time how racial stereotypes relate to racial attitudes. Bettelheim and Janowitz (1964) argue that even the most tolerant people occasionally engage in stereotyped thinking. Research with college students, however, shows that some of them are reluctant to participate in stereotyping studies (Gilbert, 1951; Karlins et al., 1969). Further, the kind of instructions given to subjects has a significant effect on the amount of consensus. There is much greater agreement when the instructions ask what traits *others* attribute to blacks than when they ask about the subjects' *own* perceptions (Brigham, 1972). And, when given the choice of attributing traits or not, many will choose not to attribute traits to groups (Redisch & Weissbach, 1974). The mere availability of stereotypes may contribute to prejudice and discrimination, but it is also possible that people can possess stereotypes without letting them affect their behavior and attitudes toward individuals.

WHITE RACIAL ATTITUDES

"This is our basic conclusion: Our nation is moving toward two societies, one black, one white—separate and unequal" (*Report of the National Advisory Commission on Civil Disorders*, 1968, p. 1). This prophetic statement, made in the wake of the racial disorders of the mid-1960s, summarized the despair of many about the future of race relations in the United States. Is there good reason for such despair, or were the members of the Commission simply overwhelmed by the events of the 1960s? There is no simple answer to this question.

It has become popular among white liberals and black militants to describe the United States as a racist society. Yet, the status of race relations in the United States is so complex that no simple summary statement, no catch phrase such as white racism, can do justice to the complexity.

Racial Attitude—Singular or Plural?

There are two important truisms about racial attitudes: (1) people vary in degree of racial prejudice, and (2) within the same person, race-related attitudes will differ depending on the domain of the attitude.

A helpful way of organizing a summary of racial attitudes is to use the dimension of social distance (Bogardus, 1925) and to recall the several different aspects of social distance found by Triandis (1964), which we discussed in Chapter 2. Various activities in our lives require different degrees of social distance (or intimacy) from other people who also engage in these activities. For example, we can share citizenship in a country with millions of people without ever personally contacting any of them. On the other hand, marriage requires great intimacy of contact, both physical and spiritual. Though the data are not absolutely consistent, in general, white Americans resist interracial relationships most vehemently when social distance is small (intimacy is greatest) and least when social distance is large. Thus, in one important study of white racial attitudes, only 12% of the respondents said they would mind a lot or a little if they had a qualified Negro supervisor on their job, while 44% would mind a lot or a little if a Negro family of the same income and education moved next door (Campbell, 1971). In a nationwide survey, 84% of respondents said they would object to a close friend or relative marrying a Negro, and 90% stated that they would object to their own teenage daughter dating a Negro (Brink & Harris, 1963, p. 148). In other words, there was relatively little resistance to equal employment, a fair amount of resistance to equal housing, and a great amount of resistance to interracial dating and marriage. As social distance decreases, prejudice increases. While some small proportion of the white population may be opposed to any kind of racial equality, most people are willing to accept equality in some spheres of their lives, if not in all of them.

Further, most of the comparative longitudinal data on race relations show that the proportion of white Americans that support increased equality has risen steadily over the last thirty to forty years. For example, the results of four surveys by the National Opinion Research Center (NORC) in the years 1942, 1956, 1963, and 1972 showed a steady liberalization of white racial attitudes (Hyman & Sheatsley, 1964; Greeley & Sheatsley, 1972). The percentage of white northerners who supported school integration rose from 40% to 61% to 73% to 84% (and of white southerners from 2% to 14% to 34% to 66%) over the 30 year period covered by the surveys. Similarly. the percentage of whites who would vote for a "generally well-qualified" black if nominated by their party for president increased from 38% to 67% between 1950 and 1969 (Gallup, 1972).

The data do not seem to support unequivocally the basic conclusion of the President's Commission on Civil Disorders quoted at the beginning of this section. At least in some areas (employment, politics, and schools are examples), most Americans favor equality. A closer look at some of the specifics of racial attitudes may help us to decide more intelligently what is the status of racial attitudes in America.

School Integration and Busing

If there is a single event in the last 30 years which stands out in the battle for equal rights, it is the 1954 decision of the Supreme Court of the United States in *Brown vs. Board of Education*. This decision, which held that separate educational facilities for blacks were inherently unequal, was the basis for new social policy which began to change the structure of race relations in this country. While desegregation efforts were concentrated on the dismantling of *de jure* (by law) dual school systems of the South, support in the North was high. Surprisingly to many, support for desegration also grew in the South as newly integrated school systems proved that they could function very satisfactorily (cf. Coleman et al., 1966). In the South, the amount of busing in school systems, particularly in rural areas, was often *reduced* as a result of the dismantling of dual school systems. It was no longer possible to bus black and white children past each other to reach segregated schools.

Nevertheless, two problems have hounded the school desegregation process. The first problem is "white flight." According to research by Stinchcombe, McDill, and Walker (1969), acceptance of desegregation decreases as the proportion of blacks in a school increases. Whites remove their children from desegregated schools and often move away to a neighborhood or suburban area where there are fewer blacks. While the proportion of parents objecting to *any* form of school desegregation was decreasing between 1965 and 1970, the proportion who objected to a student body which was more than one-half black increased slightly in both the North and the South (Knapp & Alston, 1972).

A second serious problem is busing. Even though more than 40% of American children were bused to school prior to court desegregation decisions which required busing to achieve racial balance in schools, and even though busing in the past has been viewed almost universally as a way to improve education (by consolidating resources and facilities), busing to achieve desegregation is favored by no known segment of white Americans (see Table 14-1). Ladd and Lipset (1975) report that only 18% of the American public supports busing to achieve school integration. Even among college professors, one of the most liberal groups of Americans to be found, a majority (53%) oppose busing to achieve integration. Can we conclude from this that we are all secret racists?

It seems clear that the busing issue may bring many values into painful conflict within individual citizens. On one hand, most people value equal opportunity and integration, and on the other hand, they value quality of education, local control of schools, monetary costs, children's time and safety, etc. Consistent with this analysis, Kelley (1974) found that opposition to busing is not related generally to racist attitudes. That is, a large proportion of the more than 80% of the populace which opposes busing does not object to school desegregation in general, to having blacks in their homes for dinner, to intermarriage between blacks and whites, and so on. And, while it is possible to predict with some accuracy attitudes toward neighborhood desegregation, for instance, from other racial attitudes, it is not usually possible to predict attitudes toward busing from other

TABLE 14-1   Opinions of Various Groups of White Respondents about Busing to Achieve School Integration

Group	% favoring busing
General public	18%
Faculty members	47
College graduates	24
Professionals	22
Managers	10
Clerical workers	14
Skilled wage workers	16
Semiskilled and unskilled	21

Note.—Percentages are based on those members of a national sample who expressed an opinion.
Source: Adapted from Ladd & Lipset, *The Chronicle of Higher Education*, Oct. 20, 1975, p. 2.

racial attitudes—they are not related among the general public. Only among highly educated elite groups is busing seen as related to issues of racial prejudice—a pattern very reminiscent of Converse's findings on political attitudes, discussed in Chapter 5.

What can be concluded from these data? American whites favor school desegregation to a point. Generally speaking, the smaller the proportion of racial minority children, the more favorable the attitude toward desegregation. However, most whites oppose busing to achieve racial balance. Unfortunately, though racism may not be the reason for opposition to busing, the consequence of opposition to busing where wide-scale segregation exists is to perpetuate racial segregation.

White Reactions to Racial Protest

During the 1960s, the nation was torn by urban riots. What effect did these disturbances have on the progress toward increasingly widespread support of integration noted by Sheatsley (1966)? Bellisfield (1972) reports that attitudes toward school and neighborhood desegregation continued to grow more favorable after the riots, even in riot areas. The increases were slower in riot areas than nonriot areas, but no evidence of a "white backlash" was observed in acceptance of integration.

But the effects of the riots were not all benevolent. The percentage of whites who felt uneasy and worried about racial violence increased from 43% to 52% between 1966 and 1970. A majority of whites reported that they felt more uneasy about violence after the riots than before, and increased percentages of whites reported that desegregation was proceeding too fast. A majority of respondents to a 1968 Harris poll agreed that blacks were "asking for more than they are ready for" and were "more violent than whites" (cited in Brigham & Weissbach, 1972).

The range of reactions to the urban riots was very wide indeed. Recall the interview responses quoted in Box 2-1. What was the main cause of the disturbances? One person said, "Nigger agitators;" another replied, "Dissatisfaction . . . with the way they are treated." How might disturbances be prevented? "Ship them all back to Africa." "Not only promise but actually improve conditions."

Campbell (1971) reports that a plurality of 46% of a sample of whites in 15 cities believed that the best way to prevent a Detroit-type riot in their own city was to strengthen police control, while 33% said that the best way was to improve Negro conditions. However, when the question was put in terms of a long time perspective (five to ten years), 54% advocated improving conditions while only 17% endorsed tighter police controls. Those that favored tighter police controls were usually less accepting of interracial contact, less sensitive to racial discrimination, and less sympathetic to black protest. Only 5% of the respondents (8% of men and 3% of women) condoned counterrioting by whites, while 93% said that dealing with riots should be left entirely to the authorities. It is important to note that opposition to violent protest does not automatically lead to active personal hostility. But hostility and brutality by martial authority (police and National Guard) was condoned by 58%—"Martial law is shoot now and ask questions later" (Brink & Harris, 1966).

In summary, the picture is somewhat contradictory. Whites stated that blacks deserved to have their rights, but they should not pursue them too vigorously. Discrimination and prejudice were recognized by whites (61% agreed in 1966 that blacks were discriminated against), but many of these same people also believed that there would be a personal price to pay if the desegregation process was too rapid. If blacks achieved their rights quickly, integration in housing and personal relationships was also likely to increase rapidly. Among whites living in areas where blacks would like to move, 76% opposed integrated housing (Brink & Harris, 1966). Campbell (1971) reported that 30% of his sample believed whites have a right to exclude blacks from their neighborhood, while an additional 21% opposed laws to prevent discrimination in housing.

When fear of black violence is added to fear of close personal relationships with blacks, it is not surprising that so many whites reacted negatively to the disturbances of the 1960s, It is encouraging that this fear did not reverse the trend toward acceptance of equal rights for blacks in education and employment.

WHICH WHITES HOLD WHICH ATTITUDES?

Personality

During the 1950s, the book called *The Authoritarian Personality* (Adorno et al., 1950) provided an explanation of prejudice based on psychoanalytic theory (see Chapter 10). The authors concluded that prejudiced individuals were the product of authoritarian child-rearing practices (strict physical punishment, reverence for parents and other authority figures, denial of sexuality, and so on). Among the consequences of these child-rearing practices was an inability to accept negative feelings about one's self or one's own group. Denial of self-blame led to the attribution of blame for bad thoughts and deeds to scapegoats —usually minority groups, who could not defend themselves and who occupied a low status in the community. Everything that could not be accepted in oneself was "projected" onto a weaker target. Thus prejudice was seen, in effect, as a personality disorder (see Brown, 1965, for an excellent discussion of authoritarianism and its relation to prejudice). Prejudice has also been found to be related to dogmatic opposition to women's liberation, opposition to civil liberties in general, and a rigidly punitive view of law enforcement (Maykovich, 1975).

While *The Authoritarian Personality* provided some important insights into the dynamics of prejudice, recent research has produced other explanations of prejudice in terms of social norms and educational level. These findings indicate that it is often more fruitful to look for understanding of prejudice at the level of the social context rather than at the personality level. Let us look at some of these demographic and group factors.

Demography

Generally, there are three important correlates of racial prejudice for whites: region of the country, education, and age (Maykovich, 1975). Southerners hold generally less favorable attitudes toward blacks than do northerners. It is now agreed that the regional difference is not a function of differences in personality between people in the North and South but a difference in social norms (Pettigrew, 1959). In the South, important social institutions like the churches and schools were (and still are) more likely to support segregation than similar institutions in the North. Therefore, racial prejudice in the South was a sign that a person was well integrated into his(her) community—conforming to its social norms—whereas in a more equalitarian social system racial prejudice might be a sign of personality disturbance, as proposed by Adorno et al. (1950).

People with a college education are less prejudiced on the average than people who have not attended college. This difference appears to be a relatively recent one. According to Campbell (1971), it is the person's *personal* experience with college in recent years that results in a more liberal racial attitude. Parents' education does not seem to matter; thus it is not the child's background that is responsible for the difference.

Younger people hold more positive racial attitudes than older people. However, this relationship seems to be explained by the steady increase in the proportion of young people who attend college. There are few differences in racial attitudes between young and old for those who have not attended college. It may be, as Campbell (1971) suggests, that the recent growth of social science disciplines which directly analyze the racial issue—social psychology, social anthropology, and sociology—has had a significant effect on the racial attitudes of college students.

White Ethnics

Archie Bunker is often considered as typical of the blue collar, white, Anglo-Saxon Protestant—the font of bigotry in the United States. It appears that this portrayal is fairly accurate. For example, Levine (1971) reports that blue collar whites do not favor housing integration, but that two-thirds say they would not themselves move if their neighborhood became integrated as long as whites remained in a substantial majority. Like Archie, they are not likely to form a neighborhood welcoming committee for new minority neighbors, but neither are they eager (or perhaps economically able) to move away as long as they remain in the majority.

On the other hand, recent racial strife in Boston over the busing issue has fueled the belief that "white ethnics" (particularly Irish, Italian, and Polish) are even more bigoted than the Archie Bunker WASP. In fact, however, recent research by Greeley (1972) indicates that white ethnic groups are significantly more liberal on racial issues than native-born, white Protestants. Greeley suggested three reasons for the inaccurate portrayal of the racial attitudes of white ethnics: (1) there is a snobbish tendency among middle-class, white liberals toward the group just below them, (2) white liberals need some justification for social policies which favor blacks at the expense of their closest competitors—the white ethnics, and (3) those who write about race relations know very little about American ethnic communities.

The actual findings for a national sample on a 7-item Guttman scale were as follows: Of seven white ethnic groups, Jews were by far most prointegration, scoring about 5.8. They were followed by Irish (5.0) and German Catholics (4.6). German Protestants, Scandinavians, Italians, and Slavs were tied at 4.4, but they were all considerably more favorable to integration than WASPs, who had an average score of 3.7 (Greeley, 1972).

RACIAL ATTITUDES OF BLACK AMERICANS

One of the more positive beliefs about race relations in America goes like this. Blacks and whites really are very much alike; they want the same things for themselves and for their children—a good income (and the comforts that brings), good schools, freedom from fear of repression and crime, opportunity to get ahead, and so on. In general, this belief seems correct; black and white Americans do share the same aspirations. But blacks and whites do not agree on how blacks might best achieve the goals of middle America, nor do they always agree on which goals are most important (Wilson, 1970).

Perhaps not surprisingly, blacks and whites seem to agree that the most important goals are legal, political, and economic equality; the least important goals are school, residential, and personal-social integration (Myrdal, 1944; Wilson, 1970). Note that both blacks and white believe that changes are most important (and perhaps most attainable) in areas where social distance is greatest, where racial interaction of a personal nature is least required. Wilson (1970) reports both races also prefer self-help methods of achieving equal opportunity (e.g., improvement of grade schools) over hand-out methods (e.g., more welfare funds). It would seem that blacks are not much more eager than whites for social integration.

Still, when blacks are asked whether they prefer integrated schools and/or housing to segregated facilities, large majorities respond in the affirmative. Approximately 60% in Detroit (Schuman & Hatchett, 1974) and 74% in a nation-wide sample (Goldman, 1970) preferred integrated neighborhoods, and 78% of the same nationwide sample (taken in 1969) would like to see their children go to school with white children.

There is no necessary inconsistency between assigning a low priority to neighborhood and housing integration on the one hand and endorsing them by a large majority on the other. Blacks do not support neighborhood and school integration primarily because they want more social intercourse with whites. Rather, integration is mostly viewed as a means in the struggle to achieve a better life. "I want to enjoy some of the good things they have, and this is the only way I can. . . . When you call the police in an all-Negro neighborhood, they won't come, but if you live in a mixed neighborhood, they will. . . . I believe I could really feel like a first-class citizen living in a mixed neighborhood" (Goldman, 1970, pp. 180–181).

School Integration and Busing

Blacks, like whites, support school integration, but for different reasons. Whites support school integration as long as the percentage of blacks is not too high. Blacks support school integration because they believe that whites get a better deal in the schools: more experienced teachers, more funds, newer schools and materials, expectations of success, and so on. It is perhaps for those reasons that a majority of blacks do not favor black principals, even in predominantly black schools, nor do they believe that black students are better taught by black teachers (Schuman & Hatchett, 1974).

A plurality of blacks (45%) favored school busing to achieve racial integration as late as 1969, but the percentage had dropped from 50% in 1963. The decline in the percentage of blacks who supported busing was accompanied by a similar decline in the percentage of blacks who believed that whites' attitudes toward blacks would improve (from 73% in 1963 to 61% in 1969). And a majority of blacks (53%) believed that whites in the North (where busing is now focused) care no more than whites in the South for giving blacks a better break (Goldman, 1970).

Employment

Affirmative action and equal-opportunity employment are phrases often seen in advertisements for employment. How do blacks feel about progress in eliminating job discrimination? Blacks in Detroit (Schuman & Hatchett, 1974) did not believe job discrimination had disappeared; 63% in 1971 believed that a white would be hired before a black even if qualifications were equal. Yet, more than two-thirds believed that a young black could get ahead if he worked hard enough, despite prejudice and discrimination. More than 80% preferred to work in racially mixed groups, and a majority believed the "work situation" was improving. A very great majority of blacks work with whites (in the Detroit survey, the figure was 91%). Of those who worked with whites, 69% reported that they got together with whites frequently for lunch while only 9% reported that they never did. Of those with white supervisors, 82% reported equal treatment of blacks and whites.

Thus, despite the belief that blacks are discriminated against in obtaining employment, most blacks do not report discrimination in their own job situation. Perhaps most encouraging, 64% of blacks (as compared to only 46% of whites) agreed that "children born today have a wonderful future to look forward to."

Alienation and Protest

Earlier in this section, evidence was presented that blacks shared many of the same goals as whites, suggesting that blacks are not alienated from white society. Schuman and Hatchett (1974) made one of the most careful and objective analyses of **alienation**. Eleven survey items, which tapped responses of Detroit blacks concerning perception of discrimination in various domains and willingness to take action or support policies to correct discrimination, formed an *alienation from white society index,* the results of which are shown in Table 14-2.

There are two extremely important conclusions to be drawn from these data. First, only two items out of 11 produced even a plurality of alienated responses (items 1 and 2 in Table 14-2). The second conclusion is that blacks were more alienated on eight of 11 items in 1971 (six significantly more) than they were in 1968. It is safe to say that there is still no monolithic black hostility toward whites, but apparently black alienation was increasing in the early 1970s. The two largest changes were in the percentage who believed that whites want to keep blacks down (23% to 41%) and the percentage who thought blacks ought to be ready to use violence if peaceful means failed (23% to 44%). At present we cannot determine whether these shifts in attitudes also signal a shift in action. There has been relatively little black racial protest activity since 1971 and no repetition of the wave of urban violence of the 1960s. On the other hand, whites have taken to the streets in Boston and Louisville to protest busing. It is understandable that these actions on the part of whites would increase the percentage of blacks who believe whites want to keep blacks down and who are disenchanted with peaceful protest as a means to achieve racial equality.

TABLE 14-2   Percentage of Detroit-Area Blacks Endorsing Items Concerning Alienation from White Society

Items	1968 (N=439)	1971 (N=214)
1. Many places will hire a white before a black with the same qualifications	57%	63%
2. Whites want to keep blacks down	23	41
3. Lot of progress in getting rid of racial discrimination	72	67
4. Can trust some white people	82	75
5. Black customers treated as politely as whites in big downtown stores	68	56
6. Black teachers do *not* take more interest than do whites in teaching black students	57	62
7. Prefer to live in racially mixed neighborhoods	56	62
8. Non-violent protest is best way to gain black rights	60	47
9. Do *not* support violence if non-violence doesn't work	77	56
10. Should *not* necessarily be black principals in predominantly black schools	57	56
11. The U.S. is worth fighting for if we got in another World War	86	91

Note.—Items have been shortened and paraphrased.

Source: Extracts from pp. 5–10 of H. Schuman & S. Hatchett, *Black Racial Attitudes: Trends and Complexities*. Ann Arbor, Mich.: Institute for Social Research. © 1974 The University of Michigan.

THE DISTRIBUTION OF BLACK RACIAL ATTITUDES

Like the racial attitudes of whites, black racial attitudes can be related to region of the country, education, and age. However, the findings are not always as clear as they are for whites. In general southern blacks are slightly more conservative (or less alienated or less radical) than northern blacks, but the differences are small (Goldman, 1970). The data do not support any notion that southern blacks are more passive, compliant, or docile than northern blacks.

Riot participants (self-reported) in northern urban centers were more often long-term residents of the city, relatively better educated than nonrioters, higher in their job aspirations, more likely to have voted, and more favorable in their self-perceptions and perceptions of their race. In short, these data sharply dispute the "riff-raff theory" of rioting and protest. To quote Caplan (1970, p. 71):

> The militant is a viable creature in search of practical responses to arbitrary institutional constraints and preemptions which deny him the same freedom and conventional opportunities as the white majority. He is the better educated but underem-

ployed, politically disaffected but not the politically alienated. He is willing to break laws for rights already guaranteed by law, but under ordinary circumstances he is no more likely to engage in crime than his nonmilitant neighbor.

For whites, a college education is apt to be linked to positive racial attitudes; but for blacks the opposite result is found. Well-educated blacks (with 16+ years of education) are the most alienated group of blacks (Schuman & Hatchett, 1974). Almost as alienated from white society are blacks without high school diplomas (if questioned by black interviewers). In one study of black college students (Banks, 1970), it was found that black students were becoming less authoritarian (perhaps less ready to accept society's view of them) and more negative in their attitudes toward the white majority. If education helps to create a critical awareness of our society, it is not surprising to find that, during college, blacks become more alienated toward white society while whites become more sympathetic toward black protest.

Young blacks are more radical than older blacks. They are more likely to support militant and separatist action (Caplan, 1970). Though younger whites are more tolerant of blacks, younger blacks are less tolerant of whites. However, it would be incorrect to infer that many blacks of any age group hate whites. As Marx (1967) concluded, "They don't hate (whites), but they don't like them either" (p. 179). In fact, those lowest in anti-white feeling are most militant in their support of civil rights actions (Marx, 1967; Caplan, 1970).

CHANGING RACIAL ATTITUDES

Over the past 30–40 years, whites' racial attitudes have generally become much more positive. This has been true in spite of the fact that many whites say that black civil rights leaders have been "pushing too hard" for equality, and in spite of the many inner-city riots of the 1960s. The years of civil rights marches, sit-ins, and protests have dramatized the issue of racial equality and reduced the prejudiced attitudes of many Americans.

In fact, it is clear that the changes in laws and segregation practices have often led to more favorable racial attitudes, rather than more favorable attitudes preceding the changes in laws and practices. Thus, though whites often complain about civil rights changes being too rapid, when a new law is passed or a new desegregation step is taken, people's attitudes soon adjust, and more and more people express favorable opinions toward the new practice. One clear example, discussed above, is the positive change in attitudes concerning school integration which followed the Supreme Court decision ordering school desegregation, and which has continued into the 1970s. Another example is the favorable racial attitude changes which often occur in suburban neighborhoods some months after the first black family moves into the neighborhood (Hamilton & Bishop, 1976).

Of course there have been occasional local setbacks, as in the violence and protest over school busing in Boston in 1975 and 1976. Usually these violent episodes have occurred when important community leaders publicly opposed the changes, as happened in Boston, thus making it easier for firebrands to whip up disorder and violence. On the other hand, when community leaders (whatever their private feelings) unite in advocating orderly and nonviolent procedures, even major social changes have usually been made with little public disturbance. These findings again show the greater importance of social norms, compared to the impact of private attitudes, in the area of race relations (Pettigrew, 1969).

Black racial attitudes have also shown marked changes, both up and down, in the course of the last 20 years. During the early 1960s blacks were generally more optimistic about progress toward racial equality and about whites' willingness to assist in that progress than they are currently. In general, it has been shown that U.S. attitudes toward integration, among both whites and blacks, are most positive in people who have experienced integration and much less favorable in people who have not had interracial contact (Pettigrew, 1969). Thus, the racial separatist movements among blacks, if long continued, would be likely to lead to less favorable racial attitudes among both blacks and whites.

The greatest contributions to racial attitude change have come from new laws motivated by the nonviolent militance of the 1950s and 1960s. Changes in behavior mandated by law appear to be responsible for making new kinds of interracial contact a reality (in housing, schools, public places of accommodation, and on the job). While not all contact has led to reduced interracial hostility, types of contact which were impossible yesterday *have* become commonplace today. Americans of all ethnic origins share public accommodations, work together, and, in many places, go to the same schools in relative peace and harmony. If the trend continues, the fear of many white Americans about interracial housing and perhaps even interracial marriage will also become a thing of the past.

Experimental Studies of Racial Attitude Change

In this section we will examine briefly some of the methods which social scientists have tried in experimental attempts to change prejudiced racial attitudes.

Interracial Contact. One of the prevailing hypotheses about race relations is that contact between groups who dislike each other, under favorable conditions, will lead to increased liking and decreased prejudice. Amir (1969) argued that the following conditions must be met: (a) the members of each group must be of equal status, *or* (b) the members of the minority group of a higher status than the majority group members; (c) there must be a favorable climate for intergroup contact, (d) the contact must be of an intimate rather than casual nature, (e) the contact must be rewarding and pleasant, and (f) the two groups should have a mutual goal which requires interdependent and cooperative action. Unfortunately, all of these conditions are seldom met completely in "real life."

Cook (1969) created contact conditions like those above in a laboratory study. Black and white college women met together over a one-month period to participate in a simulation exercise (a game which was supposedly being evaluated for use as a management training device). The black women and half of the white women were experimental confederates; the other white women were chosen for their highly negative attitudes toward blacks. The game required a high degree of cooperation, provided a basis for fairly close contact (two hours per day for 20 work days), equal-status contact (since the subject and the two confederates rotated jobs), and a superordinate goal (winning and earning a bonus). Also, during each two-hour session, breaks occurred which provided planned opportunities for pleasant interracial contact, discussion of race-related topics, and personal comments which allowed the black confederate to establish herself as an individual and to weaken racial stereotypes held by the subject.

A comparison of the subjects' racial attitudes before and after the contact experience showed a significant positive change in racial attitudes by about 40% of the women, whereas in an untreated control group of prejudiced women only 12% showed significant favorable attitude change. There was also some evidence that the change was generalized beyond the experimental situation. These results are encouraging, though the monetary cost to achieve this amount of attitude change was very great. However, the findings leave open the question of whether similar results could be obtained in a real-life field situation.

Sherif and his colleagues (1961) demonstrated that induced cooperation could weaken hostility among rival groups in a boys camp. Weigel, Wiser and Cook (1975) have built on this work and the study described above (Cook, 1969) to test in a real-life situation "the effects of interethnic contact on ethnic relations and attitudes in . . . newly desegregated junior and senior high schools" (p. 219). Students in small interdependent groups of mixed ethnic composition (black, Chicano, and white) who worked in experimental classrooms were more likely to engage in cross-ethnic helping behavior and to have greater relative respect for each other than students taught in regular classrooms where individual competition was stressed. These results provide support for the view that administrative arrangements and practices can affect racial attitudes in a positive way.

Experiencing Discrimination. Weiner and Wright (1973) demonstrated that white children who had a planned experience of arbitrary discrimination in their classrooms were more willing to interact with black children and showed decreased prejudice as compared to a control group who had not undergone the experience. Role-playing the part of a minority group member has become a regular part of many human relations training programs which attempt to increase the sensitivity of public officials (particularly police officers) to minority problems (e.g., Pfister, 1975; Sata, 1975).

Spotlighting Values.   Rokeach (1971) and his colleagues demonstrated that the exposure of value-attitude-behavior inconsistencies can produce changes in race-related attitudes and behaviors. Rokeach's typical experimental procedure highlights inconsistencies between ratings of two values (freedom and equality) and the relationship of these values to civil rights attitudes and behavior. Subjects are shown a table which indicates the relative importance of 18 values for Michigan State University students. The table shows that "freedom" is ranked first, "equality" eleventh; and the experimenter interprets this discrepancy for the subjects as follows: "Michigan State University students, in general, are much more interested in their own freedom than they are in freedom for other people" (p. 454). The subjects are given time to compare their own responses with those in the table, and later they are shown a second table which indicates that students who rank "equality" high are more likely to participate in or sympathize with civil rights demonstrations. The experimenter points out that people who are against civil rights value their own freedom, but not the freedom of others.

Rokeach (1971) found relatively long-lasting value and attitude changes as a result of this fairly simple experimental procedure, and he also found clear-cut changes in behavior. Experimental subjects were more likely than control subjects, who had not received information about inconsistencies within their value-attitude system, to respond favorably to a NAACP solicitation for memberships 15–17 months after the experimental treatment and to register for courses in ethnic relations 21 months after the treatment. Though the absolute number of subjects who responded in these ways was not large, these results are still very impressive for such a simple and straight-forward procedure.

Rokeach and McLellan (1972) extended this work in an important way; they tested whether information about others without comparable information about oneself can have a long-term impact on values, attitudes, and behaviors. Part of the subjects saw the two tables but did not rank the values for themselves nor compare their rankings with the tables. Both this procedure and Rokeach's original procedure resulted in significant positive changes in the rankings of the values "freedom" and "equality." In addition, these two procedures were significantly more effective than a control group in increasing willingness to support a campus civil rights group four months after the experiment. Though such value-change procedures could have ominous effects if they were extensively used by the mass media, a distinction must be drawn between results obtained with a captive audience of introductory psychology students and the mass media audience. As we have discussed in Chapters 7 and 10, the mass media audience can refuse to read, to watch, or to listen to appeals which might upset their sense of self-satisfaction. Also, in a democratic society, there are apt to be other powerful media presenting opposite appeals to the public.

Rokeach and Cochrane (1972) took an additional step, studying persuasion through face-to-face confrontation with the experimenter. They found that such confrontation by a significant other neither enhanced nor detracted from the amount or quality of lasting value change. In a further experiment, Rokeach (1975) tested whether values could be changed by interaction with a computer, rather than a human agent. This was done in a situation where there was no special emphasis on a few key values such as "freedom" and "equality." The procedure allowed subjects to compare their value rankings with those obtained for various reference groups such as college students, older people, etc. Statistically significant changes in rankings were found two months later, with the greatest changes occurring for those whose value rankings were most discrepant from the rankings of reference groups which they positively evaluated (such as other students). In sum, these studies by Rokeach and his colleagues are exciting and promising demonstrations of ways of making attitude change research relevant to socially-important issues. Readers with special interests in this area can consult Brigham and Weissbach (1972) and Katz (1975) for more extensive reviews of research on approaches to eliminating racial prejudice.

SUMMARY

Many have argued that racism is pervasive in the United States, as demonstrated by the necessity for sweeping court decisions and new civil rights laws. At the individual level, *racism* means a pattern of prejudiced attitudes and discriminatory behavior which is important and central in a person's life. *Institutional racism* refers to formal, explicit laws and regulations which discriminate against certain ethnic groups, and also to informal social norms which limit the opportunities and choices available to certain ethnic groups. Individual and institutional racism operate so as to support and bolster each other.

Children learn racial discriminations and preferences early in life from early socializers (parents, school, church) more often than from personal experience. The content of racial stereotypes has shown little change in the past 40 years, but the degree of consensus about stereotypes and willingness to stereotype have decreased.

Whites' racial attitudes appear to depend upon social distance. They are willing to grant equality to blacks (and other minority groups) in areas of interaction (such as employment) that do not require close personal contact, but most whites strongly resist more intimate contact—mixed housing, dating and marriage, and even school integration when the proportion of blacks in schools is more than a small minority. The violent racial protests of the late 1960s did not stop the progress toward more positive racial attitudes that has been well documented in the past 40 years, but whites fear black protest more now than previously. College educated, younger, and northern whites hold more positive racial attitudes than do other whites.

Blacks share with whites many basic goals in life, but they disagree somewhat about how to achieve those goals. In general, blacks support rapid desegration, apparently largely because they believe that whites control access to the good things in life rather than because they want social integration. While many blacks believe discrimination is still a powerful force in American life, relatively few are alienated from the system. However, the amount of alienation has been increasing.

Positive changes in racial attitudes since the 1950s have been caused largely by changes in the law and in public practices brought about through peaceful protest. Though whites often complain about civil rights changes being too rapid, they soon adjust and become increasingly favorable to new laws or practices. People who have experienced racial integration, both whites and blacks, are much more favorable to it than those who have not.

Experimental studies of racial attitude change have been carried out by social scientists in attempts to pinpoint the conditions which will facilitate positive attitude change. In particular, studies of interracial contact and of value inconsistencies have shown ways of making attitude change rescarch relevant to important social issues.

Suggested Readings

Brigham, J. C., & Weissbach, T. A. (Eds.). *Racial Attitudes in America: Analyses and Findings of Social Psychology.* New York: Harper & Row, 1972.—A collection of significant psychological research and theorizing in the area of black-white attitudes.

Campbell, A. *White Attitudes toward Black People.* Ann Arbor: Institute for Social Research, University of Michigan, 1971.—The results of a 15-city survey are thoroughly analyzed.

Katz, P. (Ed.). *Toward the Elimination of Racism.* Elmsford, New York: Pergamon, 1975.—Sponsored by the Society for the Psychological Study of Social Issues, this major handbook on race relations is relatively nontechnical in style.

Schuman, H., & Hatchett, S. *Black Racial Attitudes: Trends and Complexities.* Ann Arbor: Institute for Social Research, University of Michigan, 1974.—Especially good for its detailed examination of the problems of comparing and interpreting data from different surveys.

chapter 15

Sex-Role Attitudes

Catherine Cameron

Women are our property. . . . They belong to us, just as a tree that bears fruit belongs to a gardener.—Napoleon Bonaparte.

God put both sexes on earth and each has its own purpose. I'd hate like hell to wake up next to a pipefitter.—Barry Goldwater.

The only position for women in SNCC is prone.—Stokeley Carmichael.

Both men and women have one main role—that of a human being.—Edmund Dahlström.

The negative quotes above could be paralleled scores of times, but positive ones are rare. A predominant theme in reference to women throughout history is that women are different from, less than, and subordinate to men. A German proverb states: "A woman has the form of an angel, the heart of a serpent, and the mind of an ass." Because women have been viewed in these stereotyped ways, their "place" in society has been prescribed on the basis of their sex rather than individual characteristics. At the same time, the range of allowable behavior for men has also been limited by related stereotypes of appropriate masculine conduct.

SEXISM AND RACISM

The 1970s added a new word to the language of prejudice: **sexism**, a prejudicial attitude or discriminatory behavior based on the presumed inferiority or difference of women as a group. It is no semantic accident that this word is a first cousin to "racism." In the United States the link between the struggle, on the part of blacks and women, for equality and self-determination is historically rooted. In the nineteenth century, the abolitionist and feminist movements were closely interrelated; many suffragist leaders, both men and women, had honed their political skills in the slavery abolition movement (Myrdal, 1944).

The women's liberation movement of the twentieth century is also linked to black equality. In 1964, Title VII of the Civil Rights Act was passed prohibiting discrimination on the basis of race and sex. The "sex" provision was added as a stumbling block to the bill's passage, according to Bird (1968, pp. 4–10). Neglect of that provision by the Equal Employment Opportunities Commission led in 1966 to the formation of the National Organization for Women, which has since spearheaded the moderate wing of the women's liberation movement (Freeman, 1973).

The parallel between the struggle of blacks and that of women is not only historical, but based on a similar ideology and experience of subordination. Thomas made this point as early as 1907 in a penetrating analysis titled "The mind of woman and the lower races." Myrdal (1944) pointed out the paternalism basic to our society, which provides a rationale and arguments favoring inequality. Kirkpatrick (1963) discussed the analogous situation of blacks and women, listing 36 parallel items. These ranged from rationales for subordination (biological inferiority and religious prescriptions), to discriminatory practices in education, sexuality, and occupations, to the minimizing of individuality through stereotyping (as emotional, infantile, and sly). Similarly, Hacker (1951) described various accommodating attitudes (such as deference, concealment of feelings, and subtlety in getting one's way), which are defense mechanisms employed by both groups.

340

Two major differences can be traced in the subordination of women and that of blacks. First, blacks were separated out as a group, whereas women's lives have been individually and intimately intertwined with members of the dominant male group. Women have known far greater informal power through liaison with individual men, but little strength as a group. Second, blacks were literally owned and sold as property on the auction block, whereas women were "wards" by law. The influence of British common law in American history gave husbands custody of the wife's person, property, earnings and children; yet, ironically, one of the ways of "keeping woman in her place" was to put her on a pedestal. A Madonna view of womanhood, at its height in the nineteenth century, contrasted with a coarser image of men, supported the double sexual standard, and restricted women's activities. Man's "better half" was kept in the kitchen or nursery, unsullied by the evils of the labor market and the sordidness of politics. The "weaker sex" was protected from the physical strain of employment and the mental and emotional stress of higher education. Women found it hard to object to being venerated!

Sexism may be the most deeply rooted prejudice of the human race, since it is founded on the fundamental dichotomization of the human race into male and female, with "Adam's Rib" as the second sex. Like all prejudice it cuts two ways, and men's behavior is limited by the reverse of the stereotypes evolved for women. The study of sex roles will be incomplete until equal attention has been given to the problems involved for men.

The facts of discrimination against women in many realms of life have been very thoroughly documented by statistical data, gathered by sources such as the U.S. Department of Labor, Women's Bureau (e.g., 1974). Also, the literature of the feminist movement is now prolific and readily available, though its thrust tends to be more polemical than empirical. To complement these well-established bodies of literature, this chapter will attempt to fill a major gap by focusing on research into sex role attitudes and their origins.

ORIGINS OF SEX ROLES—BIOLOGICAL OR CULTURAL?

There is no question that the roles of men and women have differed throughout history, but it is important to clarify whether the differences are inevitable or optional. Two terms need to be distinguished here. A person's **gender** refers to innate physical identity as male or female. It is a biological fact, whereas **sex roles** are social expectations—learned cultural prescriptions for sex-appropriate personality and behavior. The traditional assumption has been that gender and sex roles are inevitably linked in human life. To examine this assumption, we will look at evidence from research on gender identity and from cross-cultural studies.

Gender Identity

Perhaps the most determining statement for one's future occurs in the delivery room when the nurse or doctor pronounces "It's a boy" or "It's a girl." The question of "how do they know?" seldom occurs—after all, it's obvious. However, it's not as simple as that, according to Money and Ehrhardt (1972), who have spent decades studying hermaphrodites—individuals whose sexual gender as male or female is ambiguous. As examples, occasionally a genuine penis may resemble a clitoris, or a child may appear to be male and yet test chromosomally as female. When such an anomaly is recognized early, a gender is assigned, usually on the basis of chromosomal sex. Hormonal treatments, operations, etc., may be performed so that the gender is clarified for the child and for society. The assigned gender greatly affects people's attitudes toward the child and the way that it is reared. If, on the other hand, a sexual anomaly goes unrecognized for a period of time, the psychological impact of an attempted change of sexual identity after age two can be devastating to the child.

Money maintains that research with hermaphrodites demonstrates that the gender assigned and accepted (gender identity) can have more impact than physical gender. Though Money believes that there are some inherent psychosexual differences between men and women, he says that there are only four biological imperatives: menstruation, gestation, and lactation for women; impregnation for men—all other behavior is possible for both sexes. In short, physical gender apparently determines some predispositions, but a person's behavior is extensively modifiable by learning and culture (Chafetz, 1974).

Cross-Cultural Studies

Another way of determining whether behavior is biologically linked is through cross-cultural examination of sex roles. Universality of such roles would argue for biological determinism; variability would demonstrate the power of learning. Stephens (1963) found definite regularities in the division of labor in several hundred societies, but there was no task which was exclusive to one sex in all of the cultures.

Margaret Mead (1935) startled the world with her early study of three New Guinea tribes which showed marked variation in role differentiation and expression. Mead found that Arapesh men and women were both typically "feminine" in Western terms: considerate, gentle, and cooperative. Mundugumor men and women both displayed "masculine" traits of aggressiveness and the absence of tenderness. The Tchambuli displayed differential personality traits, but they reversed the Western patterns: men were dependent and nurturant, while the women were impersonal and managerial. In 1957 Barry, Bacon, and Child (1972) studied 110 primitive societies and found information supportive of Mead's study. Sex roles matched, reversed, or blurred our typical dichotomous patterns.

Photograph courtesy of Margaret Mead.
Reprinted by permission.

Box 15-1 MARGARET MEADE, *Pioneer Researcher on Sex Roles*

Both by her research and her example, Margaret Mead has been uniquely influential in expanding the role of women in our society. Now retired as Curator Emeritus of Ethnology at the American Museum of Natural History in New York after 43 years of continuous service, she continues to lecture, go on anthropological expeditions, and work for causes she believes in.

Born in 1901 in Philadelphia, Mead attended Barnard College and earned her Ph.D. in anthropology at Columbia in 1929. By then she had already been on an expedition and written her first famous book, Coming of Age in Samoa. *It was quickly followed by* Growing Up in New Guinea, Sex and Temperament in Three Primitive Societies, *and eventually by 39 other books.*

In addition to her curator duties, Mead has held over 20 short-term lectureships at universities in five different countries, made 15 anthropological expeditions, accepted about 20 honorary degrees and 30 special awards, and served on innumerable boards, committees, and councils. Notable among her honors are membership in the National Academy of Sciences and election as President of the American Anthropological Association and the American Association for the Advancement of Science.

In explanation, D'Andrade (1966) theorized that the typical division of labor, and related personality traits, are extensions of primitive biological necessity. Women, by nature less strong than men and encumbered by pregnancy and lactation, tended to center their activities near their living area; men, stronger and not thus burdened, were freer to travel, hunt, and handle dangerous situations. Therefore, in most societies, men had the most important, strenuous, and dangerous tasks, and their appropriate temperaments were aggressive and dominant. Women were generally home-centered in their tasks, and their personalities accordingly became more passive and nurturant. This minimal division of labor was an aid to survival at first. However, maternal childcare, which was essential during lactation, was extended beyond the mandatory period; and hunters became the "obvious" persons to make tools. Such social roles have been further elaborated throughout history. Their original rationale long forgotten, sex roles became normative patterns. Strong attitudes supporting them were per-petuated in succeeding generations by culturally prescribed customs and child-rearing patterns.

The last quarter of the twentieth century should help untangle biological and cultural causation, at least for women. They have been freed by the population boom and the pill from the mandate of motherhood, and they can now choose whether to enter an automated work world where physical strength is no longer a prerequisite. Their handling of these options will powerfully affect sex-role attitudes in the future.

INFLUENCES ON SEX-ROLE ATTITUDES

A great deal of research has examined influences which may be responsible for current sex-role views. These socializing pressures are the "attitudes behind our attitudes." Among these sources of influence are clinicians who treat our minds and bodies, social scientists who describe our place in society, writers of children's literature who shape early attitudes, and the mass media which press value-laden messages upon us.

Psychotherapists

The writings of psychotherapists have had a profound impact on developing attitudes toward the personality and role of women. Freud's view of woman —that her anatomy was her destiny—assigned her firmly to her place in the home. Freud defined woman biologically and psychologically as an incomplete male, who envied the man's masculine appendage and superior creative capacities. Her sexuality was pronounced immature unless orgasm was achieved through vaginal penetration by the male penis. This view went relatively unchal-lenged until Masters and Johnson (1966) proved that the clitoris is the center of sexual stimulation and that an orgasm is an orgasm, however triggered.

Weisstein (1971) pointed out that other leaders in the psychiatric field (Bet-telheim, Erikson, and Rheingold) have described the well-adjusted woman as defining herself in terms of men—in the roles of wife, mother, and homemaker. Chesler (1972) believes that this kind of viewpoint among "healing" profession-als has contributed greatly to pathological diagnoses of women who do not fit the mold, and to the fact that twice as many women as men were hospitalized for emotional and mental disturbance between 1950 and 1968.

A frequently cited study suggests that clinicians still view women patients much as Freud did (Broverman, Broverman, Clarkson, Rosenkrantz, & Vogel, 1970). Male and female psychiatrists, psychologists, and social workers were asked to describe mentally healthy men, women, and adults on a list of be-havioral and personality traits. Results showed that a double standard of mental health was held by both male and female practitioners. Trait ratings of the healthy man and the healthy adult were highly similar, but ratings of the healthy woman differed from both. She was described as more dependent, submissive, easily influenced, emotional, and subjective, and less competitive, aggressive, and adventuresome—all characteristics otherwise attributed to unhealthy adults. If these clinicians practice what they preach, they encourage women patients to adjust to norms which are opposed to increasing maturity and individuality.

To counter this kind of treatment approach, the American Psychological Association has set up a task force on Sex Bias and Sex Role Stereotyping in Psychotherapeutic Practice, and new groups of "feminist therapists" have recently begun to offer clients more individualized treatment approaches.

Gynecologists

Scully and Bart (1973) examined 12 gynecology texts, published since Masters' and Johnson's research, to determine how experts on female physiology and sexuality are trained. They examined the texts for evidence of change away from two traditional stereotypes which have been disproved by the new research findings:

1. Man's sexual drive vs. woman's urge to procreate,
2. Vaginal vs. clitoral orgasm, the former being described as the "mature" response.

Analysis regarding the first stereotype revealed that 3 of the 12 texts did not even index female sexuality, three characterized women as generally nonorgasmic, six stressed her primary interest in sex for procreation, and 8 of the 12 emphasized the stronger male sex drive. None mentioned women's capacity for multiple orgasms. Concerning the second stereotype, vaginal vs. clitoral orgasm, the study found that 8 of the 12 texts did not even index orgasm. None mentioned that portions of the vagina have no nerve endings and therefore lack sensation. One specified that the clitoris is the focus of sensation, but two continued affirmation of vaginal orgasm as the only mature response.

Major breakthroughs have been made recently in understanding women's sexual physiology and functioning. However, gynecologists in training are apparently not being informed of them if their textbooks are any indication. Since gynecologists are the official experts on women, Scully and Bart ended their article with the thought, "With friends like that, who needs enemies?"

Historians and Sociologists

The writings of social scientists may be more influential on public opinion than literary writings because of people's faith in the objectivity and factuality of scientific findings. However, attitudes toward sex roles revealed by writers in the social sciences are characterized by androcentrism (a focus on men), stereotyping, and a bipolar view of sex roles. Research into history books has illustrated these biases.

> Sexism in historical writing is much like sexism in daily life. For the most part women are made invisible. When discussed at all, women . . . appear as part of the domestic scenery behind the real actors and action of national life (Rosen, 1971, p. 541).

Even writers who have tried to focus on women have found it difficult to examine their activities in history without reference to domestic roles. One author, for example, called the work and friends of suffragists "spouse surrogates," as if women were incomplete in themselves.

Sociology, often defined as the study of man in society, might be more accurately described as the study of *males* in society. An examination of 10 introductory sociology texts published between 1966 and 1971 revealed that only half of these books indexed any reference to women (Kirschner, 1973). Half mentioned the increasing equalitarianism of the American family, usually with scant reference to either the causes or consequences of this important phenomenon. Only 2 of the 10 texts mentioned the significantly lower wages earned by women, a factor which Kirschner regarded as the key to understanding women's place in the economy. The evidence demonstrates that introducing beginning students of sociology to information about women is not considered important.

Marriage and Family Textbooks

The textbooks used in marriage and family classes, above all sources, would be expected to present a realistic picture of sex roles as they are and as they may develop. However, they are shot through with unsubstantiated "facts" and prescriptive judgments. Ehrlich (1971) analyzed the content of six leading marriage and family texts on several important dimensions, and her findings are a serious indictment of family writers' scientific objectivity. Examining sexual attitudes, she found women typically described as asexual. The active, aggressive male was depicted as normal; the woman with a high sexual drive was a "nymphomaniac," needed "psychiatric attention," and/or "endangered her marriage" with her demands. Turning to sex roles, the male was "selector" in courtship and "status-bestower" in marriage. Traditional homemaker/breadwinner roles were upheld as natural, proper, and expedient; women should sacrifice "over-emancipation" if it threatened to weaken the institution of marriage. Concerning work roles, women who sought to combine marriage and career were said to threaten their femininity and maternal and marital relationships (no data were given in the texts to back these generalizations). The textbooks suggested that a woman might take a job (preferably part-time) to add to family income, *provided that her husband agreed and her work did not interfere with her household obligations.* (My own examination of some current revisions of these texts has found little shift in their basic viewpoint.)

Children's Literature

An important critique of books for children is contained in a small paperback called *Dick and Jane as Victims* (Women on Words and Images, 1975b). A content analysis of 134 elementary school readers, made in 1972 and carefully documented, revealed a consistent pattern of stereotypic messages to the nation's children. The differential treatment accorded boys and girls in the 2760 stories studied illustrates some assumptions underlying sex-role attitudes which may be learned in school. Boys in these school readers were more clever than girls by a four to one ratio. They were more heroic (ratio 4:1)—e.g., saving others from fires, stampedes, storms, and rampaging buffalo. They had far flung adventures (ratio 3:1) such as panning for gold, weathering tornados, and catching cattle rustlers. By contrast, girls stood passively, hands behind their backs, admiring the feats of their brothers. They carried out domestic work (ratio 3:1 compared to boys) and did so cheerfully while boys more grudgingly helped Mother with "her" chores. Father was the fun person, the problem-solver and adventure-promoter. Mother was colorless and unimaginative as she obsessively cleaned, cooked, and scolded. The following additional data on sex ratios compare the 1972 study of 134 readers with a 1975 analysis of 83 later readers (the two missing ratios were not reported by the authors).*

	1972	*1975*
Boy- to girl-centered stories	5:2	7:2
Man- to woman-centered stories	3:1	—
Male to female occupations	6:1	3:1
Male to female biographies	6:1	2:1
Male to female illustrations	—	2:1

The apparent trend toward greater sexual balance suggested in the 1975 study should be evaluated somewhat cautiously; several publishers who knew of the earlier research declined to submit their readers for analysis, and their absence might have skewed the findings. However, the researchers felt that the 1975 sample did reveal more realism. Females were permitted a wider range of individuality, and males were not held as much as before to impossible standards of heroism and emotional strength.

*Source: Adapted from pp. 10, 11, & 66 of *Dick and Jane as Victims: Sex Stereotyping in Children's Readers* by Women on Words and Images, P.O. Box 2163, Princeton, N.J., 08540, (1975b).

Another important research project (Weitzman, Eifler, Hokada, & Ross, 1972) examined the socialization of preschool children through prize-winning picture books. The Caldecott Medal is given yearly by the American Library Association to the best preschool book; it may mean 60,000 sales for the book, and it is influential in setting standards for other children's literature. The study analyzed 18 Caldecott winners and runners-up for the period 1967–1971. The sex roles portrayed were similar to those described in the previous study. There was an active/passive, outdoor/indoor, task-oriented/person-oriented dichotomy between males and females.

A prototypical example from an earlier preschool book titled *The Very Little Girl* is an illustration showing a fragile little girl being dragged along by a tiny dachshund on a leash. A companion book called *The Very Little Boy*, by the same author and illustrator, contains a parallel drawing of a boy of the same age successfully giving commands to and caring for a dog twice his size (Weitzman et al., 1972, pp. 1139–1140).

Perhaps the most flagrant fallacy in the Caldecott award books concerned the occupational picture presented. During a period when close to half of American women worked, the *only* occupational roles portrayed for women were wife and mother, *fairy, fairy godmother, and underwater maiden!* Hardly a realistic or challenging set of options!

The Mass Media

The mass media which pervade modern life generally present consistent stereotyped messages about sex roles. The extensiveness of bias may be demonstrated by analysis of television and of popular humor.

Women on Words and Images (1975a) described a content analysis of 16 prime-time, widely viewed TV shows aimed at family audiences. In situation comedy shows, 55% of the major and minor characters were men; in adventure shows 85% of the major characters and 65% of the minor characters were male. Both men and women displayed a high proportion of "negative" behaviors (59% and 66% respectively), but women displayed twice as much incompetence (20% vs. 9%). Analysis of commercials showed 55% of the speaking parts were female, but 96% of the authoritative voice-overs which summarized the products' assets were male! A study of news stories on television (Sacramento Branch, American Association of University Women, 1974) showed a 5½:1 male-female ratio of commercial announcers, though the number of advertised products intended for each sex was almost equal. Straight news stories (over 5,000 of them) were more often about men (ratio 6:1), and usually reported by men (10:1). Feature news stories (almost 2,000) concerned men more than women by a 3:1 ratio, and were mostly reported by men (6:1).

A study of humor in the *Reader's Digest* showed similar media bias (Zimbardo & Meadow, 1974). When sexism comes in the guise of humor, it can have stronger effects on attitudes because readers may be off-guard to any message other than the joke. In the study, over 1,000 jokes from the years 1947–48, 1957–58, and 1967–68 were analyzed. There was 6 times as much antiwomen as antimen humor, with over 30% of all the jokes analyzed being antiwomen. Incongruously, women were shown as being dumb and incompetent, yet dominating and exploitative of men. Though there has been a decline in these jokes and their female/male ratio, in the late 1960s 10% of "Cartoon Quips" still showed negative female stereotypes. Suggesting that other media would show the same general pattern, Zimbardo and Meadow comment:

> If the message transmitted across all of these diverse channels of communication is consistent, then there is no reason to question that it is a statement of *fact* and not of *opinion* or biased perspective. As evidence of reality it goes unchallenged, becoming part of an ideology which then selectively guides subsequent processing of relevant information to accommodate it to these established "truths" (1974, p. 2).

PAST TRENDS IN SEX-ROLE ATTITUDES

We have examined some of the influences which help to shape current sex-role attitudes. Now let's look back about 40 years and trace the historical pattern of attitudinal shifts on certain key topics: the idea of a woman President (as reflected in opinion poll data), views on women and work, and attitudes toward women's roles.

A Woman for President?

Public attitudes toward the employment capabilities of women are perhaps most stringently tested by the question: "If your party nominated a woman for President, would you vote for her if she were qualified for the job?" The Gallup Poll has posed this question, with slight variations in wording, to citizens since 1937 (Erskine, 1971; Gallup, 1972), as has NORC more recently (Ferree, 1974). Combining data for both sexes, public opinion changed between 1937 and 1975 from 33% positive to 73% positive. The changes over time are shown, separately for men and women respondents, in Figure 15-1. Over the years, there has been a roughly linear increase in positive attitudes. A sharp rise followed the end of World War II, possibly because of women's competency in war work; but there was a surprising decline in women's favorability to a woman President during the 1960s. This decline may have been related to the era of the "feminine mystique"—the idealization of the "wife-mother" role described by Friedan (1963). In the 1960s men for the first time became more favorable to a woman President than women were, but women caught up with them again in 1971. The issues of the women's liberation movement and the status of women did not

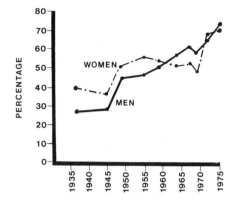

Figure 15-1 Historical trends in percentages of American men and women who are willing to vote for a woman for President. (Data from Erskine, 1971; Gallup, 1972; and *Los Angeles Times,* 1976)

receive public attention through major news media coverage until after 1969 (Morris, 1973), and this may have been an influential factor in women's 1971 increase.

Women and Work

Erskine (1971) reviewed public opinion, as revealed in polls over the years, toward working wives, equal pay, and the capability of women. Findings indicated that women were consistently more favorable than men toward working wives, the percentages ranging from 18% vs. 12% in 1936, to 47% vs. 40% in 1967. When the question asked only about young women working in their first few years of marriage, 81% of women and 77% of men favored it. Between 1942 and 1954, overall public opinion favoring equal pay for women shifted from 78% to 87%. However, when asked whether there was often good reason for unequal pay, nearly 70% agreed that there was. This indicates that expression of "liberal" views can be diminished by even the suggestion of a rationale for the status quo.

Shortly after World War II, men were credited with more ability than women by both sexes (Erskine, 1971). Forty percent of the sample believed men were more intelligent than women as compared to 20% favoring women; 35% saw no difference. Men were believed to possess more creativeness, decision-making ability, talent for handling people, and common sense. They were also considered more even-tempered and level-headed. (However, on all these qualities, fewer women than men believed that men were superior.) Women received better ratings from both sexes on handling details and, from women, on openness to new ideas. Though many women have wanted opportunities in the labor market, many have also held negative views of their own qualifications. As late as 1970, 49% of men and 40% of women believed that women could not run businesses as well as men.

A major problem with poll information, as is illustrated in the paragraphs above, lies in the fact that a given issue may be raised only once, it may be worded differently when repeated, or there may be many years when no information is available. Lack of comparable data and of information on many topics plagues opinion poll research on women's roles. On the other hand, questionnaire research seldom has sample breadth. It has tended to accumulate a mountain of scholarly knowledge about white, male, college sophomores! Until more systematic *and* representative data are available from both polls and questionnaires, our knowledge about sex-role attitudes will remain frustratingly incomplete.

Questionnaires on Women's Roles

Beginning in the 1930s, when Parsonian theory was reinforcing and even creating sex-role stereotypes, Kirkpatrick (1963, pp. 153–154) did remarkably bias-free research, recording shifts in sex-role attitudes over time. His Belief-Pattern Scale, containing 40 feminist and 40 antifeminist statements, was first administered during the depression to college students and their parents. The students were found to be more liberal, especially the girls. A gradual ensuing trend toward liberality in sex-role attitudes was interrupted by a sharp drop in the 1960s, similar to that for women respondents on the woman-for-President question discussed above.

Spence and Helmreich (1972) took up where Kirkpatrick left off, using similar questionnaire categories with updated content. They administered an Attitudes towards Women Scale (AWS) to a large sample of college students and their parents. Like Kirkpatrick, they found students significantly more liberal than the older generation and women significantly more liberal than men for both generations.

In summary, both poll data and questionnaire studies have indicated a trend over time toward liberalization of U.S. sex-role attitudes.

ASPECTS OF CURRENT SEX-ROLE ATTITUDES

Sex roles were defined earlier in this chapter as social prescriptions for sex-appropriate personality and behavior. Societal assumptions of differential personality traits for men and women are associated with different behavioral expectations as well. A famous early sociologist, Thomas (1923), recognized that what we expect often influences our view of "reality" more than objective facts do. If we define women as illogical and men as insensitive, we will "see" these traits in individual women or men, whether or not they are there. Furthermore, Merton

(1957) argued that expectation actually helps create the reality anticipated. Traits expected of men and women tend to develop in the manner of a ''self-fulfilling prophecy.''

Mednick and Weissman (1975), in reviewing studies of sex-role stereotypes, found they affected not only one's own behavior, but also expectations regarding the behavior of others. Personality and behavioral stereotypes provide a rationale for rigidly prescribing role behavior without allowing for individuality. They restrict societal options as well as personal flexibility.

Sex-Typed Personality Traits

Psychological sex-role stereotypes have typically been studied through the use of adjective check lists. Findings have shown remarkable consistency over time and differing samples, whether one examines the work of Smith (1939) on children, McKee and Sherriffs (1957) with college students, or Broverman et al. (1970) with a sample of clinicians. In 1972, Broverman et al., reviewed their own work with several other samples in addition to clinicians and reported sex-role stereotypic consensus across groups varying in sex, age, marital status, religion, and education. In research studies men are typically perceived as possessing competent-intellectual traits, whereas women's perceived traits cluster around warmth-expressiveness. Women are also viewed in negative terms as being more passive, dependent, and emotional than men.

Stereotyping has even occurred in the scientific measurement of personality. Constantinople's (1973) analysis of the problems involved in constructing measures of masculinity-femininity emphasized that the customary bi-polar organization of items along a single continuum is rooted in the assumption that femininity is the opposite, absence, or even the negative of masculinity.

Lately, researchers developing masculinity-femininity scales have broken with this stereotypic approach. In addition they have avoided another fallacy of early research, the labeling of persons not scoring in the ''appropriate'' masculine or feminine range on the scale as confused or ambivalent about their sexuality. Sandra Bem (1974) and Berzins (1975) and his colleagues have developed rather similar scales to measure psychological **androgyny**, meaning the balanced possession of both typically-masculine and typically-feminine characteristics. Within their systems, an individual who scores high on just the masculine or feminine scale can be referred to as **sex-typed** or **sex-reversed**, depending on the person's gender, while an individual who scores high on both scales is called androgynous.

These new instruments have encouraged improved research into the relationship between personality types and sex-role behavior. For instance, Bem (1975) compared the comfort and flexibility of sex-typed, sex-reversed, and androgynous individuals on some experimental tasks which required independence of judgment and other tasks which required nurturance and expressive behavior (such as interacting with a young baby). Both Bem (1975) and Berzins (1975) cite numerous studies besides their own which indicate that sex-typed persons are typically less flexible, creative, intellectual, and socially poised, and have greater anxiety and lower self-esteem than androgynous individuals. These findings suggest that stereotypic personalities are not as socially functional for men and women as our society has assumed.

Male and Female Roles

There are surprisingly few measures of attitudes toward sex-role behavior which are both well designed and carefully applied. Most scales and inventories have rarely, if ever, been empirically compared to other measures, and it is therefore difficult to interpret their findings. The only instruments which have been used with large and varied samples are Mason and Bumpass' (1973) Sex Roles Scale and Equal Opportunity Scale and the Maferr inventories (Steinmann, 1975). A few other scales found in the literature should be noted: Kirkpatrick's (1963) scale, which was developed in the 1930s; Kitay's (1940) scale including both personality and behavior variables; Gump's (1972) recent scale; my own Autonomy for Women Inventory (Arnott, 1972, 1973); Spence and Helmreich's (1972) scale on Attitudes towards Women; and Jacobson, Anderson, Berletich, and Berdahl's (1976) Beliefs about Equal Rights Scale (BAERS). These latter scales have been used almost exclusively on small samples of college students, so generalization of their findings is hazardous. The need for development of stronger instruments and their application to representative samples is evident. In spite of these weaknesses, the research findings are stimulating and provocative.

Sex-Role Ideals. The Maferr Foundation (Male-Female Role Research) of New York has focused for 20 years on the perceptions of both men and women regarding sex roles. Close to 30,000 persons (generally younger, better educated, and of higher socioeconomic status than average, permitting wider role choice), have been included in samples from 17 cultures (Steinmann & Fox, 1974). The Maferr male and female inventories contain 34 items, half of which emphasize family orientation and half, self-orientation. Respondents answer the questions three times—for perception of their own sex role, their own ideal, and their perception of the ideal held by the opposite sex.

Findings with this instrument were surprisingly consistent across time and culture until the late 1960s. Women saw themselves as having a balanced emphasis on family nurturance and self-realization, and their ideal woman was a little more domestic; however, they believed that men's ideal woman was *much* more passive, submissive, and family-centered. In a pattern partially mirroring that of women, men saw themselves as fairly balanced in orientation, giving self-achievement needs slight priority over the needs and desires of their families. Their ideal male was a bit more committed to achievement, but they perceived women as idealizing a strongly family-oriented male. In other words, both sexes saw a small gap between what they were and wanted to be, but a much larger gap between what they were and what the opposite sex wished of them.

Did this perceived gap really exist? The fascinating fact is that both sexes denied it! Men's "ideal woman" was almost identical to women's own ideal, with roughly equal nurturant and self-actualization components. Women's "ideal male" was even more aggressive and self-oriented than the men's ideal. Thus, neither sex was trying to force the other into the family-centered mold. At least, so they said!

Follow-up interviews showed that each sex doubted the sincerity of the other's apparent tolerance. When, specific situational behavior was examined, it was found to be easier for a man to support abstract "equality" than to accept diminished attention to his needs because of a working wife. (Tavris, 1973, and Komarovsky, 1973, have also documented this.) Similarly, a woman might want her husband to be successful, yet still resent the time and attention his work took from family activities.

In recent years, Steinmann (1975) reports that the extent of perceptual discrepancy has increased. Since 1968, women have been laying increasing stress on their own self-achievement rather than on the familial role (though emphasis on both remains). Data for six countries (United States, Czechoslovakia, Brazil, England, Greece, and Israel) have supported this finding cross-culturally. Except in Greece, men were giving at least token support to women's aspirations. However, in *every* country surveyed the women seriously distrusted male "liberalism," and the greater their education, the stronger was women's belief that men wanted them back in the home. Similarly, Parelius (1975) found a marked shift away from the traditional sex-role attitudes among college women between 1969 and 1973, but little change in their perception of men as relatively conservative in this area. Steinmann feels that both men and women must learn to balance family and achievement values in order to close the discrepancy gap and bring about the companionship which both sexes rate as the most desired trait in a spouse.

Sex Roles Among Married Women.   Data from a national study in 1970 were analyzed by Mason and Bumpass (1973) for a sample of almost 7,000 ever-married women under age 45. The findings showed that education was by far the most significant concomitant of liberal sex-role attitudes. Liberal scores were also obtained by women low in religiosity, black women, and those who were currently working.

On individual items, a good deal of ambivalence was evidenced by these women respondents. There was almost unanimous support for equal pay, three-quarters felt men should not refuse to work under women, and about two-thirds endorsed equal and prestigious job opportunities for women. On the other hand, about 80% believed it was better for all involved if men were the bread-winners, and women took care of child-rearing! About half of the respondents felt that children should not stand in the way of a desired career, yet concern for the welfare of children of working mothers was expressed. (These women sound much like the "moderates" in my study, who were uncomfortably riding the fence between commitment to career and commitment to home—Arnott, 1972).

Sex Roles and Adolescents.   Among adolescents, a surprising homogeneity of values concerning behavior appropriate to males and females was found by Berger, Gagnon, and Simon (1972). Results of their study warrant attention since the sample was a large and random one (nearly 3,200 cases), closely paralleling the 1970 census distribution of 14-18 year olds in Illinois. The authors summarized the adolescent viewpoint as follows:

> Women should have more opportunity; they don't always have to be agreeable; spouses should share duties and at the same time women really do want to be taken care of; and while opportunity is all right in the abstract, a female boss may be too much. In a sense this is the middle way of gender role expectations, a middle way that transcends class, race and gender inside of youth culture (p. 13).

The researchers believe their findings suggest that early socialization for gender roles (e.g., the sex-typed kind described by Weitzman et al., 1972) does not continue through adolescence and that this bodes well for sexual equality. However, the present author believes these findings instead suggest the same ambivalence found in the adult populations discussed earlier. Approximately two-thirds of these adolescents favored more leadership opportunities for women, and three-quarters favored shared bread-winning and child-rearing roles. Yet how can this equalitarian view be implemented when about 80% believe that women want to be "taken care of by men," half would not want a woman boss, and one-third of the males feel girls should be agreeable rather than speaking their minds?

Attitudes toward Women's Liberation

The women's liberation movement (WLM) has fought against personality and behavioral stereotyping and has spearheaded recent changes in the roles of women. In examining attitudes toward sex roles, therefore, it is especially informative to look at people's opinions of this movement.

A national survey of 1,312 adults was conducted in 1970 by the CBS News Poll (Chandler, 1972) to determine the impact of women's liberation. Four out of five persons had heard of the movement; of these, about half sympathized with overall objectives, and about one-third approved of the means used to achieve them. Three-quarters of those surveyed felt women could achieve the same goals without joining a liberation group; this was backed by the finding that 80% of women would not join such a group. Only about one-third of those surveyed held the stereotype of movement women as masculinized, maladjusted man-haters.

About 55% favored the Equal Rights Amendment. When the findings were broken down by sex, they showed men *more* approving than women of the Equal Rights Amendment and the goals and means of women's liberation. Men are more likely than women to take the movement seriously but, interestingly, *less* inclined to feel it will cause "real changes" in society. Chandler concluded:

> In general, the survey results indicate a climate of sympathy for some of the more realistic objectives of Women's Lib, but some difficulty in overcoming long-held values (p. 38).

An estimate of recent increases in public favorability toward women's liberation can be determined from this and other poll data. For 1970, Chandler found 55% of men and 41% of women sympathetic with "overall women's liberation objectives." For the same year, Roper found 44% of men and 40% of women favoring "efforts to strengthen women's status," but by 1974, Roper's percentages had increased nearly 20%—to 63% for men and 57% for women (*Senior Scholastic*, 1974). Staines and Jayaratne (Institute for Social Research, 1974) found 59% of men and 52% of women favored the liberation movement and its efforts to bring changes for women. However, when the term "liberation" was removed from questions, a far *more* liberal response was achieved.

Another large-scale study was conducted by Tavris (1973), using written questionnaires to survey readers of *Psychology Today*. It should be noted that this sample was younger, better educated, more liberal, and had a higher average income than the general public surveyed in most polls. From nearly 20,000 replies, a sample of 890 males and 616 females (none members of women's liberation groups) was drawn for analysis of responses. Results for the additional sample of 778 members of women's groups were not reported, since they were "obviously proliberation." (This omission had some drawbacks, as noted below.)

An important contribution of Tavris' research was her conclusion that the male sample was composed of three groups: (1) approximately 10% traditionalists, who were truly threatened by the WLM; (2) the same proportion of ideological equalitarians, who strongly supported their wives working and who shared household tasks and child rearing; and (3) an intermediate group which Tavris called the "unliberated liberals." She found that the latter "support women's liberation as long as it stays somewhere else" (p. 196). Their *attitudes* were equalitarian but their *behavior* was traditional. For example, 73% approved equality in household and childcare responsibilities, but only 15% of married men actually shared these tasks. They approved of the WLM, but few felt it had made their behavior more egalitarian. They approved of their wives working, but many would not let their wives' possible unhappiness influence their own career plans. Findings on these ideologically liberal, but behaviorally rigid, men may help explain the surprising amount of tolerance toward women's liberation claimed by Chandler's male sample.

Who Holds Which Attitudes?

The distribution of attitudes towards women's liberation in various population subgroups is intriguing.

Sex Differences. The single most interesting fact is that men present themselves consistently as more liberal than women. Roper's 1974 results showed men more liberal than women in every category except for persons who were single, widowed, or under 30 (*Senior Scholastic,* 1974). Chandler (1972) also reported greater tolerance among men. Tavris (1973) found women "much more cautious than men on matters of ideology" (p. 178)—though omission of liberation women from her sample undoubtedly skewed her findings. She emphasized that support of a liberal ideology is easier if it does not have to be lived out in the specifics of day to day life (see also Steinmann & Fox, 1974, and Morris, 1974).

Marital Status. Persons who were married or widowed (especially housewives who did not want to work) were far less supportive of liberation objectives than single or divorced persons, according to Roper and Chandler. Tavris did not find marital status as a factor, but her omitted group of feminists probably contained many unattached women.

Age and Education. According to Roper's and Tavris's findings, youth and education are powerful variables, especially for women, leading to favorable attitudes toward women's liberation. However, Chandler found education negatively correlated and concluded that better-educated women felt they had already "made it" on their own and didn't need the movement.

Race. Roper found black women to be strong supporters for change, though they are not usually active in the liberation movement (see also Morris, 1974).

Other Factors. Tavris noted that major variables contributing to support for women's liberation by both sexes were political radicalism, religious liberalism, approval of wives working, and perception of sex differences as cultural rather than biological. For men, a sense of sexual threat from "equal" women was an important negative factor; for women, experiences of occupational or sexual exploitation were prime factors in support for the WLM.

Analyzing the distribution of attitudes toward male and female roles in general is more complicated than studying attitudes toward the WLM because of the many and varied approaches used in research studies. Findings, however, generally parallel those above. In samples of the general public, men are more liberal in attitude than women; but among college samples, women are generally more liberal. Current employment for a woman, especially if strong commitment is involved, is also associated with flexible sex-role attitudes (Arnott, 1972; Mason & Bumpass, 1973). So too is past maternal employment (Vogel et al., 1970), particularly if one's mother found employment satisfying (Arnott, 1972).

Future Possibilities

The future is uncertain. However, changing legislation, expanding opportunities, and personal experiences are alerting men and women to previously unforeseen options. The extent to which their more open attitudes will be matched by commitment to social change remains to be seen.

Researchers and educators are beginning to treat former assumptions as areas for investigation and reform. Arnott (1972, 1973) noted a tendency for "traditional" couples to exhibit lack of communication, and "moderates" to display role tension; but individuality and respect were more common among "liberal" couples who had survived their confrontation with changing roles. Tavris (1973) believes truly nontraditional marriages to be rare, difficult to maintain, and yet the key to the future.

However, society in general and men in particular have a major stake in the status quo of family life. Until and unless widespread child care centers and shared household tasks become a reality, married women must carry dual roles of home and work. Moreover, attitude change and behavioral change are not always correlated. It is even possible that institutions and individuals, inoculated with a small dose of change, may never catch the real thing!

SUMMARY

In the United States, there has been a link between the struggles against racism and sexism in both the nineteenth and twentieth century. Women as well as blacks have faced parallel forms of stereotyping and discrimination which have prevented fulfillment of their individual potential. Both groups have had to demonstrate that cultural assumptions, rather than biological inferiority, have produced their limitations. The variability of sex-roles cross-culturally, and the initial maleability of infants' gender identity are strong arguments against the viewpoint that sex roles are biologically determined.

Some important influences on our sex-role attitudes include psychotherapists who uphold a double standard for the mental health of men and women, gynecology texts which have ignored new findings about women's sexuality, and historians and sociologists who have virtually ignored women in their writings. In marriage and family texts, women's "place" is often presented as asexual, self-sacrificing homemakers, who risk personal and marital failure if they try to combine home and career. Writers of children's literature, who influence the most impressionable age group, generally depict an unrealistic dichotomization of male-female personality and behavior. Finally, the mass media also feature the predominant presence, authority, and positive presentation of men as compared to women.

Over the past 40 years, a definite trend toward more liberal sex-role attitudes is evident, as seen both in national opinion poll responses and also in questionnaire research findings.

Attitudes concerning appropriate personality traits for men and women have been found to be heavily stereotyped, but new research instruments have identified a group of "androgynous" individuals who are more flexible in their behavioral repertoire than strongly sex-typed persons.

Studies of attitudes toward "appropriate" sex-role behavior have revealed large communication gaps between the sexes, and also much ambivalence—i.e., desire for more equalitarian relationships, but reluctance of both men and women to relinquish old attitudes and behavior patterns. Research on attitudes toward women's liberation has revealed rather widespread sympathy for the overall objective of strengthening women's status. In general, men express more liberal attitudes than women, but most do not appear committed to implementing change in their personal lives.

Factors most associated wtih liberal sex-role attitudes have been found to be: advanced education, unattached marital status, being young, and being black. These factors are especially powerful influences for women. In contrast, religious and political conservatism and a strong emphasis on women's home-maker role are negatively associated with liberal sex-role attitudes.

Suggested Readings

Farrell, W. *The Liberated Man: Beyond Masculinity: Freeing Men and Their Relationships with Women.* New York: Random House, 1974.—A mix of research and personal experiences concerning the limitations of stereotyped masculinity and its destructive consequences. Farrell also describes 21 ways in which men can benefit from women's liberation.

Gornick, V., & Moran, B. K. (Eds.). *Woman in Sexist Society: Studies in Power and Powerlessness.* New York: Basic Books, 1971.—This broad collection of contemporary feminist writings, though polemical in tone, is well-organized and includes convincing logic and research.

Huber, J. (Ed.). *Changing Women in a Changing Society.* Chicago: University of Chicago Press, 1973.—These articles, which also appeared as the January, 1973, issue of the *American Journal of Sociology,* present interesting research on current sex roles.

chapter 16

Attitudes Toward the Environment and Pollution

Mark W. Lipsey

We travel together, passengers in a little space ship, dependent upon its vulnerable resources of air and soil, . . . preserved from annihilation only by the care, the work and, I will say, the love we give our fragile craft.—Adlai Stevenson.

If pollution is unchecked, life in all the seas could be extinguished in 30 years.—Arthur Cooper.

We have met the enemy, and he is us.—Pogo Possum.

Within the last decade, environmental issues have burst upon American consciousness. Within a relatively short time environmental quality went from a nonissue to a major public concern. As recently as 1968, national opinion polls that asked respondents to name the most important problems facing the country rarely turned up an environmental complaint. Only a few years later environmental issues, particularly pollution, regularly appeared among the top ten problems cited by the public. Thus in recent years the problems of environment, pollution, and natural resources have ranked close to inflation, crime, Vietnam, and government corruption as major national issues in the opinion of most Americans (Erskine, 1972a; *Gallup Opinion Index*, 1972a, 1973). Between 1965 and 1970, the percentage of the U.S. population who felt air pollution was "serious" more than doubled, jumping from 28% to 69%, while similar responses regarding water pollution increased nearly as much, from 35% to 74% (Erskine, 1972a; Buttel & Flinn, 1974).

Paralleling the increased levels of public concern was greatly expanded coverage of environmental issues in the mass media. The number of environmentally oriented articles in one sample of U.S. periodicals showed nearly a 500% increase between 1953 and 1969 with the bulk of the expansion occuring after 1960 (McEvoy, 1972). This quantitative change has been accompanied by qualitative changes in the content of typical articles as well. Earlier articles were more likely to deal with such matters as natural history and environmental problems in rural areas. More recently, the emphasis has shifted to problems of the urban environment, especially those created by industrialization, e.g., lack of open space, air and water pollution, population density, and land use.

Perhaps even more striking than the expanded media coverage has been the explosion of membership in environmental organizations, shown in Figure 16-1. The Sierra Club, one of the most popular organizations, has experienced a dramatic increase from a scant 7,000 members in 1952 to over 100,000 in 1970, and it is still growing (Sewell & Foster, 1971). Other groups such as the Wilderness Society and the Audubon Society have also experienced skyrocketing membership increases. Since the early 1970s some leveling of growth rates has occurred but there is no evidence of a decline. In fact, during the energy shortage of 1974 the membership of the National Audubon Society took its biggest jump ever, a 30% increase.

Recent polls, depending on issue and wording, show that between 50% and 90% of the U.S. population purports to be seriously concerned about each of the major **environmental problems** (Erskine, 1972a). Despoliation of the natural surroundings, e.g., air pollution, water pollution, soil erosion, destruction of wildlife, and so forth, is the overarching issue which elicits the greatest public concern. One national survey found that 86% of the population was at least "somewhat" concerned about these matters and 51% were "deeply concerned" (National Wildlife Federation, 1969). Air and water pollution were generally

361

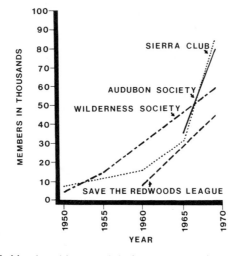

Figure 16-1 Membership growth in four conservation organizations. (Data supplied by the organizations--graph from McEvoy, 1972, p. 221.)

viewed as the most pressing problems, but other environmental issues such as the dangers of pesticides, preservation of open spaces, or wildlife preservation were top priority topics for 18% of the sample. In fact, three-fourths of the respondents were in favor of setting aside more public land for the conservation of wildlife and wilderness.

In addition to the types of environmental concern just mentioned, several other topics have received increasing attention recently. Noise pollution has become a prominent issue in many urban areas, particularly around major airports (e.g. Fiedler & Fiedler, 1975). The super-sonic transport (SST) and release of freon gas from aerosol cans have been cited as causing possible damage to the ozone layer above the earth's atmosphere, with resulting increases in skin cancer caused by ultraviolet radiation from the sun (*Not Man Apart*, 1975). On earth, radiation danger to millions of people could easily result from theft of nuclear materials or weapons, from accidents or sabotage at nuclear-fueled power plants, or from leakage of the wastes produced by such plants—wastes which remain deadly for thousands of years (*Newsweek*, 1975; Union of Concerned Scientists, 1975; *U.S. News & World Report*, 1976a). The organization called Friends of the Earth has been particularly active in warning against such dangers through its publication *Not Man Apart*. Partly as a result, California and six other states held state-wide elections in 1976 on the issue of postponing construction of nuclear power plants until their safety had been proven.

Sizeable majorities of the public also express concern over other issues with environmental implications. Since the "energy crisis" of 1973–74, for example, the potential problems of resource scarcity have received increased public attention (*Gallup Opinion Index*, 1974a; Curtin, 1976). In one poll, 60% to 73% of a national sample reported that they had conserved electricity, heating fuel, and/or gasoline as a result of the petroleum shortages (*Gallup Opinion Index*, 1974a). Another problem, one that may be an underlying factor in both resource scarcity and environmental deterioration, is population expansion. About two-thirds of an Illinois sample, for example, said they thought the U.S. population was growing too fast (Simon, 1971); and 77% of a national sample of youth aged 15–21 thought it was important that they limit their own family size in order to control future population growth (Harris & Associates, 1971, p. 393). Chapter 17 discusses population problems at length.

There is thus widespread public concern about environmental deterioration, pollution, resource scarcity, population growth, and so forth. Indeed, environment has become an apple pie and motherhood issue—hardly anyone is willing to admit publicly that they are not deeply concerned about it. However, we must raise questions about whether this concern will be carried into public action, and how long environmental issues will continue to hold center stage as a crucial social problem. Downs (1972) has presented a theory of the "issue-attention cycle" for social problems, tracing their development from the stage of serious problems which have not engaged public attention, to the crisis stage of alarmed discovery and action proposals. However, after that, disillusionment usually sets in as it becomes clear how costly solving the problem will be and how much its continuation may benefit some segments of the nation (e.g., the automobile industry). As a result, public interest usually declines and attention shifts elsewhere without any fundamental solutions to the problem having been found.

Will this be the fate of the environmental movement? That certainly seems possible, and between 1972 and 1974 the proportion of the U.S. population who reported concern over air and/or water pollution declined about 5% (Watts & Free, 1974). However, it is far too early to predict the decline and fall of environmentalism. To help us in understanding attitudes toward environmental issues, in the pages that follow we will explore the characteristics of those people who express the most concern about environmental quality, the factors that seem to influence people's opinion about environmental issues, and the public's potential for taking action to ameliorate the problems.

WHO IS MOST CONCERNED?

Though the general level of public concern with environmental problems is high, some subgroups in the population express more concern than others. For example, the degree of environmental concern reported in public opinion polls has shown rather regular relationships to such respondent characteristics as education, age, income, and occupation.

Education appears to be one of the most important of the variables that distinguish those highly concerned about environmental quality from those less concerned. Opinion polls typically find a spread of 25 percentage points or more between the proportion of the least educated and the proportion of the most educated who express high levels of environmental concern. Among college graduates, for instance, a majority of 50% to 70% or more typically gives the most extreme rating possible when asked their opinion of the seriousness of environmental problems. However, among those with a grade school education or less, it is rare to find more than 35% to 40% who express that level of concern (Harris & Associates, 1971, pp. 51–58; Dillman & Christenson, 1972; McEvoy, 1972).

Age shows a somewhat more complex relationship to opinion on environmental issues. When it is simply a matter of expressing concern verbally about environmental problems, a greater proportion of the youthful population generally responds positively. The differences between them and older cohorts, however, are not always large, and in some cases no age differences have been found at all (e.g., De Groot, Loring, Rihm, Samuels, & Winkelstein, 1966). When we consider actual behavior regarding environmental matters, those who act are not generally any younger than their less active counterparts. For example, those who participate in environmental organizations, attend environmental "teach-ins," or engage in household antipollution behavior have not been found to be any younger than people who are not involved in these activities (e.g., Peters, 1973).

The *socioeconomic status* of those who express the highest levels of environmental concern shows an especially interesting pattern. Though the poor people in urban slum areas are greatly affected by pollution, their concern about environmental quality is apt to receive a lower priority than more immediately pressing problems like employment and housing (Swan, 1970). Generally those with higher family incomes are more likely to be worried about environmental problems and to feel that something should be done about them. However, those with incomes over $20,000 a year typically express slightly less concern about environmental problems than those in the next highest income bracket. (Costantini & Hanf, 1972; Dillman & Christenson, 1972).

This relationship between income and concern about environmental quality can be understood more fully when people's occupations are also taken into account. The highest income strata are populated by persons from two rather different types of occupations who differ markedly in their perception of environmental problems. Business owners and executives in industrial and commercial organizations express less concern about environmental issues than do persons in the professions or officials in governmental agencies (Hine & Gerlach, 1970). It is this combination of high income and relatively modest environmental concern among business leaders that appears when the highest income brackets are examined.

Some studies have examined sex, race, religion, marital status, and other such variables in relation to environmental issues, but the results have generally been nonsignificant or inconsistent. One circumstance that does appear to be important, however, is the *region of the country* in which people reside. Though responses vary depending on the particular issue, Americans living in the West and Northeast typically express more concern over environmental problems than those in the Midwest or South. In part, of course, this may be because certain environmental problems are more severe in those areas. Another common finding which may have important implications for people's dedication to environmental action is that far fewer people see pollution as a serious problem in their *own* community than see it as a serious national problem (e.g., Murch, 1971). If the problem is generally seen as located far away, will people's determination to solve it remain high and persistent?

Some of the significant results from one national survey of public concern about environmental problems are shown in more detail in Table 16-1.

WHAT PROMPTS ENVIRONMENTAL CONCERN?

A number of factors seem to predispose people to be concerned about en-

TABLE 16-1   Public Concern about Environmental Problems

	Level of Environmental Concern				Number of inter- views
	Deeply con- cerned	*Some- what con- cerned*	*Not very con- cerned*	*No opin- ion*	
National results	51%	35%	13%	2%	1503
By sex					
Men	56	31	10	3	744
Women	46	38	14	2	759
By education					
College	62	32	6	0	395
High school	52	37	10	1	748
Grade school	39	34	20	7	352
By annual family income					
$10,000 and over	58	34	8	0	449
$7,000–$9,999	53	38	8	1	336
$5,000–$6,999	55	35	8	2	237
Under $5,000	41	34	20	5	463
By region of country					
East	46	38	12	4	425
Midwest	56	34	9	1	400
South	44	36	16	4	428
West	59	31	10	0	250

Source: Adapted from McEvoy, 1972, p. 225.

vironmental issues or, sometimes, provide a direct instigation to attitude change. Among the characteristics of people that make them more receptive to environmental issues are the extent of their knowledge or awareness about environmental issues, their personal values, and activities and experiences that bring them into contact with the environment. In addition, certain more striking circumstances often provide a direct stimulus to heightened environmental concern, for instance, exposure to pollution and environmental deterioration, experience with shortages caused by resource scarcity, or involvement in a community that suffers a dramatic environmental incident. These are examples of the effect of salient incidents on attitudes, which we discussed in Chapter 6.

Information and the Mass Media

We might suppose that the more a person knew about environmental issues, the more concerned they would be about the problems and, perhaps, the more they would favor activity designed to reduce the seriousness of those problems. The evidence on this point, however, is somewhat ambiguous. A few studies have reported that those people who were most knowledgeable about environmental matters showed higher levels of concern about environmental problems or were more likely to engage in such behavior as household antipollution activities. In other studies no such relation has appeared (e.g., Maloney, Ward, & Braucht, 1975).

The situation is more clear-cut when information is provided as part of an explicit program of environmental education. Though such programs are not always successful, under favorable circumstances they can affect both environmental attitudes and behavior. For example, a two-year-long elementary school program in Montreal had a visible influence on the participating students. When several classes from the school were taken on a field trip to a nature area, the children in the environmental program were much more respectful in their behavior toward the wildlife, plantlife, soil, and water than other young visitors (Asch & Shore, 1975).

Most people, of course, do not participate in formal programs of environmental education. They get their information about pollution and environmental problems from TV or the newspapers. It has yet to be demonstrated that such information has a direct and immediate effect on an individual's opinion about environmental issues, but there is little doubt that it has an indirect and cumulative effect. For instance, the communications media play a significant role in determining when an environmental "condition" becomes an environmental "problem" in the public's mind—an example of the agenda-setting function of the mass media, discussed in Chapter 7. Aircraft noise provides a case in point. "Noise pollution" has been evident around large urban airports for many years without being labeled an environmental problem. In one study conducted before the widespread attention attracted by the environmental movement, only 3% of respondents in Seattle mentioned aircraft noise as a problem; a few years later the identical question produced complaints from more than 15% of the respondents (Fiedler & Fiedler, 1975). Public perceptions of air pollution have shown a similar influence from media coverage. As long ago as 1959, sizeable proportions of the residents in some areas would report that they were bothered by air pollution *when they were asked a direct question*. It was not until after the greatly increased media coverage of environmental issues during the late 1960s, however, that pollution began to be cited spontaneously to public opinion pollsters as a community "problem" (Auliciems & Burton, 1971).

Values and Personal Activities

Evidence suggests that a person's value orientation, particularly with regard to nature, has a significant influence on the perception of environmental problems. In one representative study, public health officials and environmental engineers whose personal value orientation emphasized the subordination of nature to human control tended to feel that environmental problems were not matters for great concern and, moreover, that public involvement in such issues was not desirable. Officials who viewed nature as dominant over humans, on the other hand, were much more concerned about environmental problems and supportive of public involvement in the decision-making process (Sewell, 1971). A similar contrast differentiates members of antipollution organizations from nonmembers —members are much more likely to assert the desirability of human activity harmonizing with nature rather than triumphing over nature (Levenson, 1973).

One way in which a nonexploitive orientation to nature may be expressed is through recreational activities in natural settings. Among backpackers, for example, the aesthetic satisfaction of being close to nature ranks as a primary motive for the activity. Being close to nature may also produce heightened awareness and concern for environmental problems by providing firsthand experience with their significance. Even a common activity such as gardening may sensitize participants to the fragility of the ecosystem, the dangers of pesticides, problems of soil erosion, and so forth. Indeed, those with a sustained interest in gardening have been found to have more regard for nature, less favorable attitudes toward industrial development, and more concern about the issues of environmental deterioration and population growth than nongardeners (Kaplan, 1973). Of course, these results do not demonstrate that gardening *causes* these attitudes, but some mutual facilitation certainly seems possible.

Outdoor recreation conducted through organized groups can have even more impact on individuals' environmental attitudes and behavior than solitary activity. In a recreational organization, each individual is exposed to other people, some of whom may have provocative information or especially intense feelings about environmental issues. In addition, organized groups may take a special proprietary interest in the natural facilities they use and thus be moved to action if those facilities begin to deteriorate or are threatened by outside influences. Such organizations as the Sierra Club appear to have developed their activist tendencies in this way. Originally they were expressive organizations devoted to the recreational interests of their membership. As wilderness areas came under increasing threat from industrialization and development, however, they gradually became instrumental organizations attempting to wield political influence in the service of their environmental concerns (Faich & Gale, 1971).

Instigating Experiences

It may be that the development of deeply felt attitudes about the environment, particularly the kind that result in significant behavior change, is impelled only by an especially moving experience that precipitates the transformation. Hine and Gerlach (1970) report that intense "personal commitment" to the environmental movement generally has its source in a subjective "identity altering" experience or a "bridge burning" act in which the person takes palpable risks, such as physical injury, jail, or loss of job.

A dramatic environmental incident such as a major discharge of pollutants may provide transforming experiences and a context for bridge burning acts. Such a crisis can arouse concern about the environment from many people all at once and may leave permanently changed behavior, values, and perceptions in its wake. The oil discharge near Santa Barbara, California, that covered 25 miles of beaches with crude oil in 1969 illustrates the effect that a sufficiently outrageous environmental disaster can have on a community. Nearly the entire city was mobilized in the effort to clean up the damage and shut down the offending oil rigs. In the resulting political fracas there is little doubt that many Santa Barbara citizens, including some of its most prominent figures, became "radicalized" on environmental issues (Molotch, 1971).

Such incidents are becoming increasingly common, common enough to intrude on the lives of a very large number of people. For example, during one year (1973) in Illinois alone there were 514 pollution incidents of sufficient severity to produce property damage, livestock or fish kills, evacuation, interruptions in water supply, or hospitalization of some persons. The occurrence of such an incident frequently results in community mobilization in the political arena. Such incidents, for instance, are more predictive of community action than are actual pollution levels if those levels have accumulated gradually rather than precipitously (Bridgeland & Sofranko, in press). For participants in community action and for those who are educated by media coverage of the initial incident and the resulting community activity, concern about environmental issues can undergo considerable change. Those who had not given much thought to environmental problems before the incident may become much more sensitized to the dangers and feel obligated to act upon their new concerns.

Not everyone, of course, is likely to get involved in one of these public, political incidents. A different type of stimulus to altered attitudes and behavior toward environmental issues may be provided by experience with serious resource shortages, especially those that come with little forewarning. People who experience even temporary inconvenience or privation because of scarcity of a basic commodity which has always been available in abundance may be startled into modifying their views on environmental issues. The gasoline shortage of 1973–74 gave the U.S. public its first lesson on the finiteness of natural resources, and the skyrocketing prices of petroleum products since then may serve as a daily reminder of the message. Experiencing the gasoline shortage did increase the levels of conservationist behavior among a large majority of the population, and some of the detailed data are presented later in this chapter. Though most people appear to have responded to the "energy crisis" at a relatively superficial level, 10% to 25% reported that they cut down "very much" on their consumption (Curtin, 1976). Among these there may well have been some people who were perturbed enough by the shortage to alter their consumption substantially and permanently.

Exposure to Noxious Environmental Conditions

Though increased concern about environmental issues may occasionally be the product of particularly dramatic experiences, a more common formative influence is repeated exposure to a stimulus situation. Typical examples are daily exposure to pollution, noise, crowding, and other noxious effects of ecological irresponsibility (see Figure 16-2 for an example). It has been amply demonstrated, for example, that the people who experience the greatest concentrations of air pollution also express the highest levels of concern about the environment, or at least about the quality of the air (e.g., Smith, Schueneman, & Zeidberg, 1964). The same pattern seems to hold for exposure to water pollution; in fact, those whose exposure includes contact with the water, such as swimmers, express more concern than those who only come close, such as fishermen (Willeke, 1968). In many instances, however, the relationship between exposure to pollution and concern about environmental problems is diminished because the middle-class, whose education and socioeconomic status predisposes them to be more responsive to social problems, generally have the means to avoid living in the most polluted areas. Furthermore, some of those close to a source of pollution usually have a vested economic interest in that source. For example, they may be employed by the source and therefore be less inclined to complain about it. (This topic is discussed more fully later in this chapter.) Other things being equal, however, it appears that those who are recurrently exposed to noxious environmental conditions generally develop greater concern about the problems.

A somewhat similar but more complex relationship seems to hold between residency in urban areas, with the associated crowding, noise, and pollution, and individuals' general level of environmental concern and activity. Residents of

Figure 16-2 An example of big-city smog. Shockingly, these pictures were taken over twenty years ago, in 1955, on the same day in San Francisco. (Photographs reprinted by permission of the *San Francisco Chronicle.*)

larger cities typically report higher levels of concern about environmental problems, but the relationship is not linear—residents of the largest cities tend to voice somewhat less concern on the average than residents of the next-to-largest grouping of cities (Erskine, 1972a). Socioeconomic differences (the high percentages of very poor people in the largest cities) and other factors confounding the effects of exposure probably play a role in this result.

The effects of exposure to noxious environmental conditions may be due, in large part, to the physiological stress they cause for those who experience them. Wolpert (1966) has proposed that the cumulation of perceived environmental stress can eventually reach a threshold point at which it becomes capable of motivating changed attitudes and new behaviors. When pollution problems are considered, it may be the threat to physical health that is most stressful to those exposed to pollution on a daily basis. Air pollution definitely has an effect on health, particularly for those who are susceptible to respiratory ailments. Furthermore, many of the people who live in polluted areas are quite aware of its effects upon them—eye irritation, breathing difficulty, etc. As Wolpert's stress threshold notion suggests, the longer people are exposed to air pollution the more exasperated they seem to become with the problem—instead of habituating to it as some theories would lead us to expect. Moreover, those who have been exposed to the polluted conditions the longest are the ones most likely to favor "situation-altering" behavior—in particular, to press for effective regulation of pollution sources (Medalia, 1964). Perhaps other dimensions of environmental stress, e.g., noise, crowding, aesthetic revulsion, and so forth, also motivate concern and activity for environmental quality.

HOW WILLING ARE PEOPLE TO ACT?

Public concern about environmental problems will not in and of itself lessen those problems. Some actions may be required, individually and collectively, if pollution is to be significantly reduced, natural resources preserved, and population stabilized. We have seen that a large majority of the populace views environmental problems as serious and has generally favorable attitudes toward doing something about them. Moreover, many of the factors that prompt concern over environmental problems are such that the general level of concern can be expected to increase, rather than decrease, in the future. Awareness of environmental problems seems to be spreading beyond the middle class where it was concentrated in the late 1960s (Buttel & Flinn, 1974). Increasing numbers of people are engaging in outdoor recreational activities (Ferriss, 1970), and it is quite possible that the number of individuals who experience resource shortages, noxious environmental conditions, and local environmental incidents firsthand will also continue to grow.

The Technological "Fix"?

In spite of the relatively high and increasing level of environmental concern among the public at large, there is considerable evidence that most people are not willing to invest significant amounts of their own time, money, or effort in improving environmental conditions. Indeed, a sizeable proportion of the populace does not seem to feel that any particular effort will be required from them at all. They expect environmental problems to be solved through improved technology, such as pollution control devices, alternate energy sources, and so forth. In one Minnesota sample, 83% of the respondents agreed that "technology got us into the environmental crisis, and technology will get us out" (Tichenor, Donohue, Olien & Bowers, 1971). A few years later the percentage had declined somewhat but still included nearly three out of four people questioned (Donohue, Olien, & Tichenor, 1974).

Many analysts believe, however, that environmental problems will not be solved simply by applying the quick technological fix (e.g., Meadows, Meadows, Randers, & Behrens, 1972). They feel that at least some amount of change will be required in the behavior and lifestyle of the typical American, especially the broad middle class. For example, energy shortages may be reduced much more effectively, at least for the immediate future, if consumers practice strenuous conservation than if massive resources are poured into the development of alternative energy sources. Similarly, achieving a significant decrement in the amount of urban air pollution may require commuters to considerably reduce their dependence on the private automobile in favor of such alternatives as carpooling and mass transit.

Personal Sacrifices

If technological solutions do prove to be inadequate for solving many environmental problems, some support must come from the general public. However, when people are asked what sacrifices they would be willing to make for improving the environment, they typically report rather modest levels. The National Wildlife Poll (National Wildlife Federation, 1969) found that while 51% of the public purported to be deeply concerned about the environment and 86% at least somewhat concerned, only 4% were willing to pay as much as $100 *per year* in additional taxes to improve their surroundings, and only 22% were willing to pay as much as $50 per year. In a 1972 poll, however, the proportion of respondents willing to pay as much as $50 or $100 more each year to combat water pollution had risen to 31% and 18%, respectively; and 50% expressed willingness to pay $50 extra for antipollution equipment on a car (Watts & Free, 1973). Nevertheless, much higher proportions (up to 90% in some samples) have indicated to various pollsters that more money should be spent on environmental problems, in spite of their relatively low willingness to accept an increased tax burden.

This apparent contradiction can be resolved by examining public opinion regarding various sorts of governmental expenditures. Environmental matters, especially pollution, are one area in which many people feel the government should be spending more money, but there are other items on which they feel much less money should be spent. Thus the public apparently feels that the cost of increased spending for environmental problems should be borne by *reallocating* money from other projects, not by increasing taxes on the individual citizen. They would prefer to fund pollution control, for instance, by cutting back on such things as foreign aid, defense spending, and the space program (Harris & Associates, 1971, pp. 49–50; Dillman & Christenson, 1972). The following responses, from a 1971 Harris poll, illustrate these conclusions (Erskine, 1972a):

> Here is a list of various areas in which the federal government now is spending money. If you had to choose, on which two or three would you like to see spending cut first? From the same list, which two or three areas of government spending would you like to see cut least?

	Cut first	Cut least
Pollution control	3%	57%
Aid to education	4	66
Aid to cities	9	30
Poverty programs	13	34
Highway financing	14	19
Farm subsidies	20	17
Other defense spending	30	16
Welfare spending	37	21
Space program	50	13
Foreign aid	61	3
Vietnam spending	64	8

Not only is the public reluctant to shoulder an increased tax burden to improve environmental conditions, but they show a disinclination to endure personal inconveniences for environmental benefit. For example, after making relatively modest cutbacks in the use of fuel and electricity during the 1973–74 "energy crisis," a majority of a national sample felt that further reductions would be fairly difficult, and one-fourth to one-third thought they would be *very* difficult (Curtin, 1976). A Gallup poll taken during the height of the shortage did indeed find that most people reported driving less, turning thermostats down, and other such things. But a solid majority was opposed to any procedure that might result in more substantial inconvenience, e.g., rationing gasoline, closing service stations on Sunday, or ending TV broadcasts at 11:00 p.m. each night (*Gallup Opinion Index*, 1974a).

Conflicts of Interest

When inconvenience becomes economic privation, environmental concerns erode still further. In 1972, a substantial majority of the U.S. public (60%) opposed the idea of deliberately limiting economic and technical growth in this country for environmental reasons if it might result in fewer jobs and a lower standard of living (Watts & Free, 1973). However, in 1974, a similar question about regulating population and industrial growth *in the area where respondents lived* found 54% in favor and only 37% opposed (Watts & Free, 1974).

More clear-cut evidence comes from studies that have examined the environmental attitudes of people with a direct and personal economic stake in an environmentally damaging condition. Generally these studies have found that the individuals involved would rather suffer or deny the environmental problems than compromise their economic interest in its cause. Such "conflict of interest" circumstances were revealed in a small Utah community of about 7000 people in which 40% of the households had members who were employed by a nearby steel plant. The steel plant was the only major enterprise in the neighborhood that released smoke and exhausts into the atmosphere, so there was little doubt about the source of any air pollution that residents experienced. Eight out of ten residents said they were aware of air pollution, but only 19% of the steel plant employees reported being seriously "bothered" by it compared to 80% of the residents who were not employed in the factory (Creer, Gray, & Treshow, 1970). Clearly, the level of concern about the air pollution problem was inversely dependent upon the economic interest residents had in its source.

Similar results have appeared in studies of resort and vacation communities such as Lake Tahoe and the Vermont lakeshore communities where tourism is the major industry. Seasonal visitors to these areas have generally expressed more concern about deterioration of the environment than residents who live in the mess year round (Bevins, 1972; Costantini & Hanf, 1972).

Actual Behavioral Change

Another important way to examine public opinion regarding environmental problems is to look at what people actually do with regard to the environment in contrast to the attitudes they express when asked. Sufficiently concerned people, for example, might engage in a wide range of personal conservation behavior, participate in group activities such as clean-up campaigns, seek out information regarding environmental problems, involve themselves in political activity on environmental issues, or even move away from polluted areas. As might be expected given the relatively high levels of expressed concern for the environment, many people do participate in such behavior. Widespread participation, however, seems to be restricted to those activities that entail comparatively modest effort and inconvenience. Household conservation activities, for example, are fairly common. In an Illinois sample, 55% to 75% reported regular use of returnable bottles, saving newspapers for recycling, and/or buying low-phosphate detergents (Kronus & Van Es, in press). During the peak of the 1973–74 gasoline shortage, a Gallup poll found 7 of 10 respondents reporting that they lowered household temperatures, 6 in 10 who said they used less electricity, and 4 in 10 who indicated that they used their automobile less (*Gallup Opinion Index*, 1974a). On the other hand, only 8% had joined a carpool even though two or three times that number could share a ride based on commonality of origin and destination (Horowitz, 1975). Further details of responses during the 1973–74 gasoline shortage are presented in Table 16-2.

Even among people more responsive and concerned about environmental issues than the general public, participation in the more drastic forms of environmental behavior is relatively low. Among those who voluntarily attended one of the first "environmental teach-ins" at the University of Michigan in 1970, for instance, only a handful decided to change their behavior substantially. In fact, 60% of the Michigan participants did not plan any changes at all in their behavior as a result of what they learned at the teach-in even though one of the prime reasons people reported for coming was to find out what action they could take. Of those who did plan specific actions, most were intending to buy different kinds of products, write their Congressman, and so forth. Only 13% mentioned changes that involved a significant alteration of their lifestyle, for example, modifying occupational plans, having fewer or no children, or changing living habits (Lingwood, 1971).

One sobering study illustrates the difficulty that even highly motivated people have when attempting to modify their daily behavior for conservationist purposes (Kohlenberg, Phillips, & Proctor, 1975). During the course of this particular

TABLE 16-2   Percentage of Respondents Who Said They Conserved Energy during the Winter of 1973–74

	Heat	*Electricity*	*Gasoline*
Overall results	62%	64%	60%
By extent of conservation			
Very much	13	14	23
Somewhat	49	50	37
Not very much	18	20	19
Not at all	14	15	19
By region of country			
West	69	70	57
North Central	60	54	56
Northeast	61	71	65
South	61	64	61
By degree of urbanization			
Central city	42	63	68
Adjacent suburbs	67	70	59
Other cities	63	64	58
Rural areas	64	61	61

Source: Adapted from Tables 1 & 4 in R. T. Curtin, "Consumer adaptation to energy shortages," *Journal of Energy and Development*, 1976, 2(1).

project, three volunteer families struggled to change their habits of electrical power consumption. They were not attempting a radical cutback in the amount of electricity they consumed, but were merely trying to use it at different times to avoid increased "peak time" usage, the heavy use of electricity during mid-morning and early evening by most residential consumers. Provided with information about peaking and about the amount of electricity consumed by various household appliances, these families were able to reduce peaking by only a negligible amount. Even when a signal light was installed to give them immediate feedback on their consumption, the effect was relatively small. It was only with a signal light, continuous feedback from a chart recorder, and an opportunity to earn incentives of *up to twice the amount of the monthly utility bill* that much of a reduction in peaking was achieved, but even those conditions failed to eliminate increased usage entirely.

A more hopeful finding comes from an experimental study of Iowa City residents who were attempting voluntary energy conservation. Results showed reductions in natural gas usage by 10% (during the fall of 1973) and electricity usage by 20% (in the summer of 1974, after the energy crisis). These results were obtained only in a public commitment condition where families expected to have their names listed in the newspaper as participants in the conservation program. A self-monitoring condition, where anonymous residents kept regular records of their energy usage, achieved almost as great energy savings. However, a private commitment condition, where participants expected anonymity and did not keep energy usage records, was no better than a no-contact control condition (Pallak & Cummings, 1976). This study is particularly useful in that it begins to clarify the incentives and methods which can be effective in changing individuals' environmentally-related behavior. An analysis of incentives and sanctions which can increase compliance with environmental protection standards by corporations and local governments has been offered by Nagel (1975).

In general, it appears that when the level of effort or inconvenience is relatively low—e.g., product choices, recycling newspapers, or turning the thermostat down a few degrees—the public seems willing to take action for the sake of the environment. They show considerably less willingness to act, however, when effort and inconvenience are high or economic loss is threatened, as in driving less, joining a carpool, changing occupations, or substantially reducing consumption of power and fuel. Furthermore, even when they are willing to act, people sometimes find it difficult to make the sacrifices necessary to significantly alter their established patterns of behavior.

WHAT DO PEOPLE THINK SHOULD BE DONE?

Both the expressed opinions and the actual behavior of the general public indicate relatively little enthusiasm for investing personal, individual effort or expense to ameliorate environmental problems. Yet we know that public concern about environmental problems is high. What, then, do people think ought to be done about these problems? The weight of evidence clearly shows that most people prefer some form of governmental action rather than personal, individual efforts. Perhaps in some instances they see government action as being more effective than individual efforts—for instance, in 1972, 81% of a national sample favored a federal law against selling beverages in throw-away bottles or cans (Watts & Free, 1973). Since then, Oregon has had good success with such a law on a statewide level.

As noted earlier, a majority of the public feels that more governmental money should be spent on environmental problems, but most do not want those increased expenditures to be passed along to them in the form of increased taxes. They much prefer that the money be made available by cutting back on such items as foreign aid, national defense, and the space program. If still more funds were required for government programs, a large plurality of people prefer that the polluting industries themselves be required to bear the cost (Erskine, 1972a). Implicit in these views is the notion that the government would be able to do something about the quality of the environment if sufficient funds were available. Other evidence shows that most people feel that the government not only has the ability to improve environmental conditions, but has the primary responsibility for doing so. For instance, during the 1973–74 gasoline shortage, 39% of respondents to a national poll said they thought controls on the use of energy should be made more strict, 49% said they should be kept about the same, and only 6% said they should be made less strict. However, the more extreme step of a law requiring gas rationing was opposed by a majority of respondents (*Gallup Opinion Index*, 1974a).

Other studies show a similar stress on governmental action. In the Toronto area nearly three-fourths of poll respondents felt that the responsiblity for action against pollution belonged to some level of local, regional, or national government (Barker, 1971). In addition, local governments were viewed as having more responsibility in this matter than national government. In American communities, also, most people feel that pollution and environmental quality are matters for governmental action (Medalia, 1964; Schusky, 1966; Simon, 1971). Many surveys have shown that people want Congress to give a top priority to solving such problems. In particular, many people favor close regulation of industries to prevent discharge of pollutants (Erskine, 1972a).

The record of recent government actions on several environmental fronts has been admirably summarized by Watts and Free (1974, pp. 147–163). Private organizations have also been effective in influencing environmental policy in several ways. As one example, legal action by the Sierra Club led to a 1973 Supreme Court decision ''that industries may not degrade any [environmental] quality in any area which they move into'' (Milbrath & Inscho, 1975, p. 33). In the political arena, two small organizations called Environmental Action and the

League of Conservation Voters were outstandingly successful in 1972 and 1974 in defeating many congressmen on their list of the "Dirty Dozen" with bad environmental records, and in electing other candidates with proenvironmental records (Kelley, Stunkel, & Wescott, 1975). As of 1974, a majority of the U.S. population felt that the nation had made at least some progress in reducing air and water pollution, and about 90% wanted government spending in these areas to be increased or kept at its current level (Watts & Free, 1974).

In recent years, of course, government programs to improve environmental quality have become increasingly common. Perhaps the most notable example is the Environmental Protection Agency's (EPA) regulation of automobile emissions—an action resulting in the unfortunate by-products of reduced mileage, poor drivability, and increased expense. Whether public support for regulation of polluting industries will be reduced from its current high levels if it becomes clear to consumers that personal inconvenience and expense are its side effects remains to be seen. There appears to be great potential for conflict, however, in the public's desire to have government do something about environmental problems and their reluctance to get personally involved. As mentioned earlier, public concern about air pollution and water pollution, though still high, was somewhat lower in April of 1974, following the gasoline shortage, than it had been in 1972 (Watts & Free, 1974).

In short, most members of the public neither desire nor expect to lessen environmental problems through their own personal conservation and antipollution activities. Nor do they have any particular enthusiasm for enduring personal inconvenience in order to improve environmental quality. They feel that environmental problems are primarily the responsibility of the government, and they say they want greater activity on this front from Congress. One of the more interesting issues of the coming decade will be whether or not governmental regulation can significantly improve the quality of the environment and conserve scarce resources without requiring unpopular sacrifices from the general population. If not, the currently high levels of public support for improving environmental conditions may plummet precipitously.

SUMMARY

Beginning in the mid-1960s, public concern about environmental problems escalated dramatically. Increasing percentages of the respondents to public opinion polls described the problems as serious, mass media coverage soared, and environmental organizations enjoyed a membership boom that still continues.

The highest levels of environmental concern are generally found in the upper middle class, among people who have high education, income, and occupational status. This is less true of those in business fields, however. The young express more environmental concern than their elders, but do not generally engage in more environmentally-relevant behavior.

Among the factors which lead individuals to heightened concern about environmental issues are explicit environmental education, the mass media, and personal values or activities that emphasize harmony with nature. Other more dramatic circumstances such as an oil spill, personal experience with resource shortages, or recurrent exposure to noxious environmental conditions may sharply increase environmental concern among some affected individuals.

The high general level of environmental concern does not mean, however, that most people are willing to suffer considerable personal effort, expense, or inconvenience to improve environmental conditions. Many expect improvements to come through technological innovations, not changes in their way of life. People generally are willing to undertake small amounts of household conservation behavior, but relatively reluctant to accept an increased tax burden or other economic sacrifices to achieve environmental benefits.

The public plainly feels that reduction of environmental problems is one of the top-priority responsibilities of government. Most respondents suggest that governmental expenditures be reallocated from such areas as foreign aid and defense to environmental programs, and many also favor increased regulation of polluting industries. It remains to be seen whether government action can significantly improve the quality of the environment and conserve finite resources in coming years without requiring significant behavior changes from the general public.

Suggested Readings

Burch, W. R., Jr., Cheek, N. H., Jr., & Taylor, L. (Eds.). *Social Behavior, Natural Resources, and the Environment*. New York: Harper & Row, 1972.—A general reader on environment and human behavior, containing articles about consumption and use of the environment, public opinion, and social policy.

Erskine, H. The polls: Pollution and its costs. *Public Opinion Quarterly*, 1972a, 36, 120–135.—A compilation of results from various public opinion polls from the mid-1960s to the early 1970s regarding pollution and the environment.

Molotch, H. The radicalization of everyone? In P. Orleans & W. R. Ellis, Jr. (Eds.), *Race, Change, and Urban Society*. Beverly Hills, Calif.: Sage, 1971. Pp. 517–560.—An engaging discussion of the politicization of ordinary citizens, with examples from the Santa Barbara oil spill in 1969.

Maloney, M. P., & Ward, M. P. Ecology: Let's hear from the people. *American Psychologist*, 1973, 28, 583–586.—Stresses the importance of the behavioral aspects of ecological issues and pleads for more intensive study.

chapter 17

Attitudes Toward Population Issues*

Burton Mindick

No geological event in a billion years . . . has posed a threat to terrestrial life comparable to that of human overpopulation.—Paul R. Ehrlich and Anne H. Ehrlich.

Every day the equivalent of twenty divisions of Martians invade this planet without their field rations.—Lord Ritchie-Calder.

Your task is to ensure that there is enough bread on the tables of mankind, and not to encourage an artificial birth control, which would be irrational, in order to diminish the number of guests at the banquet of life.—Pope Paul VI.

*Grateful acknowledgement is made for partial support of work on this chapter by NICHD research grant HD 08074 to Stuart Oskamp, Principal Investigator.

As you can see from the preceding quotes, feelings run very strongly concerning the topic of population. Phrases such as "population bomb" and "doomsday" are used regularly by those who favor the limitation of population size; and charges of "racism" and "genocide" are leveled with equal frequency by those who oppose limitations.

This emotionality is understandable in view of the importance of the issues involved. If one sees overpopulation as a threat to all life on this earth, a threat worse than an ice age or the submergence of entire subcontinents (Ehrlich & Ehrlich, 1970), then the issue is crucial. Authors on the other side such as Colin Clark (1973) view the stabilization or decline of population size as leading to technological, economic, and cultural stagnation, great increase in the amount of government regulation, and consequent loss of basic human rights and freedoms by individuals. With such high stakes, it is not hard to understand why opinions in this area are so strongly held.

THE PRO AND CON OF POPULATION

There seems little doubt in anyone's mind that there are serious problems in getting the earth's life-giving resources to all needy members of the world's present and future populations. It is hard to argue with the realities of extreme poverty, famine, and death which already afflict large segments of the world's population. Those who would limit population size point out that largely because of modern medical practice, the death rate has been sharply lowered, and that this has dramatically increased rates of population growth (Ritchie-Calder, 1974). Increased rates of agricultural production simply cannot keep pace with runaway population growth. Opponents reply that the problem is not population size, but maldistribution of food and other vital resources. Some persons, groups, and countries have too much at the expense of others, who have too little. As Slater, Kitt, Widelock and Kangas have put it, "hunger is not a matter of too many people. It is a matter of too much theft" (1971, p. 419).

Pronatalists assert in addition that improved agricultural technology can take care of any future population increases if only we would devote ourselves earnestly to this goal. Pope Paul's (1965) statement about ensuring "enough bread on the tables of mankind" carries this implication. **Population limiters** reply that the "carrying capacity" of our earth is not infinite. Technology, for example the "miracle crops," may solve some hunger problems temporarily, but that will only lead to larger populations which will then exhaust the earth's resources all the sooner. Furthermore, they say that to define the problem in terms of food distribution alone is much too narrow an approach. Natural resources, open space, clean air, and pure water cannot be provided limitlessly to unlimited human populations.

A Historical (Not Hysterical) View

The problem of excessively large world population relative to available resources has not been an ever-present problem throughout human history. According to some estimates, world population size (now amounting to some four billion people) did not reach the one billion mark until as late as 1830 (Brown, 1974). Population growth has not been at all continuous. Throughout history, natural disasters, floods, droughts, insect plagues, etc., caused millions of deaths directly and millions more indirectly through decreases in agricultural production and consequent famine. Wars, for example the Hundred Years' War (1337–1453), and especially the Thirty Years' War (1618–1648) in Europe, have always made their gory contribution to population decline. Widespread disease, often as a result of warfare, has resulted in enormous loss of life. Langer (1964) has estimated that in the late fourteenth and early fifteenth centuries, bubonic plague struck down one-fourth to one-third of the inhabitants of Europe, and the black death struck Europe with similar dreadful effects in the seventeenth century.

Considering such drastic depopulations as these, it is easy to see why some societies have viewed themselves as essentially underpopulated. This resulted in high fertility norms for individual families, and at the societal level there were religious, cultural, ethical, and legal norms *for* increased fertility and *against* birth control, abortion, and other fertility-reducing practices. It was not, as some contemporary polemicists claim, that pronatalist norms were solely the result of sheer stupidity and blindness, or premeditated calculation to enslave men or women, or total disregard of individual rights. Increased numbers of births were seen as being in the economic, political, military, and moral interest of society, as well as of the family and the individual.

This may have been true until late in the eighteenth century, when the number of world inhabitants was approaching one billion and the rate of increase reached a point where the earth's population was doubling every 80 years. (The rate of population growth is often more important that the absolute population size.) Perhaps the critical moment in world population management was reached at this time, and gradually it began to be recognized, at least in the western world, that high rates of fertility were no longer in the interest of either the individual or the society. It is probably no accident that at just about this time (in 1798) Thomas Malthus published his famous *Essay on the Principle of Population* warning that population growth was likely to outstrip agricultural production. Fertility rates in Europe had already begun to decline (Coale, 1969), but death rates were declining even more sharply as a result of manifold improvements in agriculture, transportation, sanitation, and medicine (see Figure 17-1). During the latter nineteenth and early twentieth centuries, many European countries eased some of their burgeoning population problems by exporting large numbers of their citizens to the United States.

The U.S., expanding geographically and economically, generally welcomed

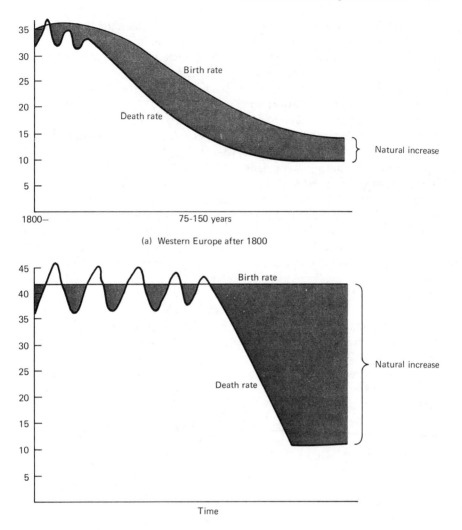

(a) Western Europe after 1800

(b) Less Developed Countries, Mid-20th Century
(The sharp drop in the death rate began between
1940 and 1960, depending upon the specific country)

Figure 17-1 Rough graph of approximate birth and death rates of two groups of nations over time. (From Shirley Foster Hatley, *Population Quantity vs. Quality,* © 1972, p. 49. Reprinted by permission of Prentice-Hall, Inc., Englewood Cliffs, N.J.)

both immigrants and births until about 1920. In Europe, drastic declines in fertility during World War I as well as the tremendous loss of life in that conflict seemed to make concern about overpopulation quite inappropriate. In the United

States, the Great Depression, which followed only a decade after the end of the war, exerted a very "depressive" effect on the U.S. birth rate. Thus, both in the United States and in Europe, during the 1930s there were marked feelings that Malthus' theory about population growth was simply wrong.

In a 1932 issue of the distinguished *Scientific Monthly,* S. J. Holmes asked, "Will birth control lead to extinction?" (Pohlman, 1973, p. 3). Similarly, U.S. economist J. J. Spengler inquired with more than a hint of alarm, "Will the birth rate continue to decline? Will the swarming peoples of Latin America, Africa, and the Orient crush the low birth-rate nations?" (Pohlman, 1973, p. 4). A 1938 report of the Committee on Population Problems, U.S. national resources committee, expressed apprehension about low birth rates and a consequent static and aging population. Members of this committee, demographers W. S. Thompson and P. K. Whelpton, stated that even with the highest rates that could be reasonably assumed, there would be a natural increase of less than 50 million from 1935 to 1980 (Pohlman, 1973, p. 7). As of 1975, five years before that period's end, there has actually been an increase in the U.S. population of nearly 90 million, or virtually twice the predicted increase, and we are still growing (U.S. Bureau of the Census, 1975).

With these facts in mind, it is easy to see why there was little concern about overpopulation in this country until quite recently, and why that concern seems to have come upon us with a rush. Now, however, the world population situation seems to be rapidly approaching a crisis stage. It is estimated that total world population reached 4 billion in 1976, and by the year 2000 it will nearly double to 7.5 billion people, about two-thirds of them in Asia (United Nations Association, 1969). Longer-range forecasts predict 11 billion people on this earth in 2050 if present birth rates continue, and it seem extremely unlikely that any agricultural or technological "miracles" can provide food and other needed resources for such hordes.

A Complex Issue

The problem of population control becomes even more complex when we consider the *who* and the *how* of limiting births. On the international scene, many leaders still believe that having a large population will bring major-power status and economic development (Clark, 1973). Developing countries are therefore often unwilling to accept the urgings of more developed nations to control population size.

At the national level there are problems regarding those whose religious or moral views are strongly pronatalist. There are also ethnic-political groupings who view attempts at population control as being directed specifically against *their* fertility levels and intended to reduce the size of their constituencies.

On a more personal level, there are parents who may be "all for" the regulation of population size, but do not see their adolescent son/daughter as sexually active, and may resent sex education, provision of contraception, or abortion services by public and private birth-planning agencies. Those who are sexually active, married or unmarried, often do not see a relationship between their gratification or their plans for family size, and the problems of world population, ecology, and pollution.

Then too, there are questions regarding the *how* of birth control. There are many safe and effective methods which can be used. But there are problems of the acceptability and the medical contraindications of certain methods for certain individuals. There are the side effects, the "hassle" and expense which is sometimes involved, and the simple fact that no birth control method is ideal for everyone.

Thus it is evident that relating birth control policies at the individual, national, and international levels to the overall needs of humanity involves a great many considerations, and at every level there may be conflicting attitudes and opinions. In recognition of this complexity, Gough (1975) has suggested five separate subscales to measure population attitudes. They are: **modernity, population management, family planning, birth control,** and **abortion.**

These five dimensions do not exhaust the areas of possible population concerns. Other factors, such as one called "general environmental concern," could be added to the list. Furthermore, some of Gough's five dimensions are partially overlapping. For example, family planning, the "belief in the desirability and rationality of planning for each child and for total family size" (p. 124) is very much dependent on the availability and judged efficacy of birth control methods, while abortion is regarded by many people as an important alternative to contraception and a form of family planning and population management. Modernity, however, is a dimension which applies most clearly to developing nations and to distinct cultural subgroups within industrial nations.

Despite the overlap among Gough's five dimensions, they do touch on some of the most salient and controversial aspects of population attitudes. Therefore, we will use the last four of them (omitting modernity) as an outline for the next four sections of this chapter and as a guide to help us in exploring the many aspects of population attitudes.

POPULATION MANAGEMENT ISSUES

The Gallup Poll apparently did not assess U.S. attitudes toward overpopulation until as late as 1959. During the period immediately following World War II, many western countries were seeking to increase their birth rates. In light of present circumstances, it is curious to read of a 1946 Gallup survey asking whether the U.S. government should, like the British government, pay new parents "baby bonuses." A baby bonus was a weekly allowance of two dollars for every child under 16, designed to help stimulate the birth rate. Though 61%

of those polled were opposed to the idea, the question itself reflects the birth-rate concerns of the postwar era (Gallup, 1972, p. 598).

By 1959, however, the question of a ''great increase in population which is predicted for the world during the next few decades'' was raised (Gallup, 1972, p. 1654—see Table 17-1). Three-quarters of those surveyed replied that they had heard about this issue. Only 21% of these, however, were worried about it.

TABLE 17-1   U.S. National Surveys of Concern about Population Growth (1959–1971)

Year	Source	Population asked about	Type of question asked	Response	
1959	Gallup Poll	World	Have you heard about the great population increase predicted?	Yes No	75% 25
			[a]Are you worried or not worried about it?	Worried Not Worried No Opinion	21% 69 10
1963	Gallup Poll	World	Are you worried about the population increase?	Worried Not Worried No Opinion	25% 66 9
		U.S.	[b]Same as above	Worried Not Worried No Opinion	30% 66 4
1965	*Look* Magazine Poll	World	Have you heard about the great population increase predicted?	Yes No Don't Know	82% 16 2
			Are you worried or not worried about this increase?	Worried Not Worried Don't Know	29% 65 6
1965	Population Council	World	Do you view this growth as a serious problem?	Serious Not Serious Don't Know	62% 28 10
		U.S.	Same as above	Serious Not Serious Don't Know	54% 39 7
1967	Population Council	World	Same as above	Serious Not Serious Don't Know	71% 21 8
		U.S.	Same as above	Serious Not Serious Don't Know	55% 39 6
1969	National Wildlife Federation	U.S.	Do you think it will be necessary to limit the human population or not?	Necessary Not Necessary Don't Know	44% 43 13
1971	U.S. Commission on Population Growth and America's Future	U.S.	Is U.S. population growth a serious problem?	Serious Not So Serious No Problem No Opinion	65% 26 7 2

Year	Source	Population asked about	Type of question asked	Response	
1971	Gallup Poll	U.S.	How concerned are you about the effect of population growth on the quality of life?	Concerned	54%
				Little Concerned	46
			How serious a problem is present U.S. population growth?	Major problem now	41%
				Not a problem now but will be in year 2000	46
				Not a problem now and not expected to be	13

aFor those who answered "Yes."

bPut to those who had heard about the population increase (70%).

Sources: Erskine (1967), Opinion Research Corporation (1971), Barnett (1972), Gallup (1972), Lipson & Wolman (1972).

Looking at the results for the first three polls shown in Table 17-1, it appears that during the 1960s U.S. public opinion with regard to world population was not overly concerned about the problem, with never more than one-third of those queried expressing worry. But in attitude research we need to look carefully at the wording of the questions. In 1965 about 65% of Americans were not "worried" about world population growth, but 62% saw this growth as a "serious problem" (Population Council survey). This concern about world population increase rose a bit further, and in 1971 *U.S.* population growth was viewed as serious by about 65% of Americans, with about half concerned about its effect on the quality of their lives. Thus, in describing recent U.S. attitudes toward population growth, perhaps the word "worry" is too extreme. But the words "serious concern" do seem appropriate.

Most individuals save their worrying for more immediately pressing concerns. Between 1965 and 1975 the most important problems worrying Americans included: race-relations, riots, the Vietnam War, student uprisings, inflation, recession, unemployment, the energy crisis, crime, and Watergate. Thus, we can understand why Americans have not been distraught over population problems. Apparently, though, they have been aware and concerned.

Table 17-1 also shows that Americans have a greater concern about world population expansion than that of the United States. This probably reflects the fact that our national resources are not so severely strained by population as those of a country like India, for example. But it is also a truism in this field that people tend to worry more about others' "excess fertility" than their own.

As to what U.S. citizens think ought to be done to help control population, unfortunately, there is little data. The 1965 *Look* Magazine poll is the only national survey asking about a range of actions (Erskine, 1967). Its respondents answered as follows:

Use of birth control methods	33%
Education and advice on birth control	25
Government aid and financial help on birth control	2
Reduce illegitimate births	2
Miscellaneous (sterilization, wars, abortions, other ways to keep people busy, etc.)	10
Do nothing, it's up to the individual	22
Don't know, no answer	19
(Some people gave more than one answer)	113%

Simon (1971), who polled Illinois residents, reported results virtually identical with those of the nationwide *Look* poll. More recently, in 1974, a heavy majority of respondents to a national poll (71%) said that they favored reducing U.S. population growth by encouraging birth control, and this figure was up from a bare plurality only two years before (Watts & Free, 1973, 1974). Thompson, Applebaum, and Allen (1974), questioning a North Carolina sample, found wide acceptance for such population control policies as informational and educational campaigns, good job opportunities for women, as well as free contraception and abortion. The latter investigators found strong resistance to ideas like passing laws restricting births, special permits for more children, and contraception in the water supply; but resistance to such sweeping government intervention is easily understandable. Furthermore, drastic measures are all the more inappropriate because U.S. citizens in recent years seem to have changed their minds (and their behavior) about their desired levels of fertility.

PLANNING A FAMILY

Recent birth rate fluctuations in the United States have included a marked trough between about 1927 and 1945, followed by the "baby boom" at the end of World War II, and another sharp decline since about 1964. Middleton (1960) has ingeniously traced U.S. "fertility values" as mirrored in American twentieth century magazine fiction. Analyzing the story content for desired family-size norms between 1916 and 1956, he showed that the U-shaped curve of actual fertility was reflected quite faithfully in the attitudes embodied in the popular fiction of the day. Interestingly, he also found a very consistent decline in fertility norms favoring the very large family of five or more children.

Turning to a more conventional (and precise) way of assessing attitudes toward desired family size, we may look at nearly four decades of Gallup polling in this area. Since 1936 this national survey has asked the question, "What do you think is the ideal number of children for a family to have?" As shown in Figure 17-2, the percentage of respondents favoring four or more children rose from 34% in 1936, to a high of 49% in 1945 (the end of World War II). The figure remained

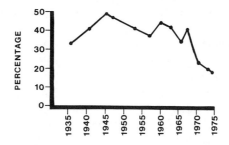

Figure 17-2 Percentage of Gallup Poll respondents favoring an ideal family size of 4 or more children. (Data from *Gallup Opinion Index,* 1974d.)

fairly high until 1960 (roughly the end of the baby boom years) and then declined sharply to a 1974 figure of 19%. If we compare this measure of **ideal family size** with a curve of actual live births during the same period, we find that the two graphs are quite similar. This seems to be a good example of attitude-behavior consistency in the population as a whole.

Gallup data gathered early in 1974 show nearly half of those questioned (49%) favored having two children or less, while 22% considered three children "ideal," and 10% had no opinion. The appeal of the "only child" family has not really increased over the last 30 years (only 2% wanted such families), and it is clear that the idea of the "no-child" family has not caught on, a bare 1% declaring this as their ideal. By far the most frequently expressed aim was having two children, reported by 46% of those surveyed. Significantly, the survey also indicated that 2.0 children was the median number of desired children, and this figure is below the **replacement level** fertility rate (the birth rate at which population size neither rises nor declines) of 2.1 births per woman (*Gallup Opinion Index,* 1974d).

The Costs and Benefits of Having Children

Another Gallup question which bears on the decline in the number of children desired is: "What is the smallest amount of money a family of four (husband, wife, and two children) needs each week to get along in this community?" (*Gallup Opinion Index,* 1974c). The following list shows the 37-year trend: 1937—$30; 1947—$43; 1957—$72; 1967—$101; and 1974—$152. Since this figure has shown a five-fold increase between 1937 and 1974, it seems likely that rising costs of living have contributed to declines in desired family size.

The relationship between economic conditions in this country and fertility rates is generally accepted today by both demographers and economists. Perhaps the most striking example of economics-related fertility changes occurred during the depression of the 1930s when the birth rate dropped to a then all-time low. It is well to remember, also, that this sharp decline occurred despite the lack of modern effective methods of birth control such as "the pill." Also, Simon and Simon (1975) have recently reported research suggesting that monetary incentives can be influential in either raising or lowering aspirations of family size. Both the benefits conferred and the costs imposed by having children affect what is called the **perceived value of children**. Pohlman (1969) has assembled a comprehensive list of the many costs involved—costs which go far beyond simple financial considerations. There are costs in terms of husband-wife relationships, sacrifices in parents' roles because of confinement to the home, loss of career opportunities for both husbands and wives, reduction in favorite recreational activities, and many others.

Over against these costs are arrayed what prospective parents regard as the value of children. Hoffman and Hoffman (1973) have presented a thorough classification system for the various benefits children are perceived as bringing to their parents. The scheme was derived from empirical analysis of survey responses in many countries and includes nine distinct areas of benefits which parenthood can confer:

1. Adult status and social identity
2. Expansion of the self, tie to a larger entity, "immortality"
3. Morality: religion; altruism; good of the group; norms regarding sexuality, impulsivity, virtue
4. Primary group ties, affiliation
5. Stimulation, novelty, fun
6. Creativity, accomplishment, competence
7. Power, influence, effectance
8. Social comparison, competence
9. Economic utility

Unfortunately, space does not permit further analysis of research on the value of children. The interested reader is referred to the Pohlman (1969) study, an excellent monograph by Fawcett (1970), and the Hoffman and Hoffman (1973) research mentioned above. We can conclude from current low levels of fertility and expressed attitudes favoring small families that most couples in the United States now feel it is possible to obtain the benefits of having children while having a smaller number of them. This parental deduction is not simply a selfish one, for there is a feeling that with smaller families one can give more attention, love, and material benefits to each child. Furthermore, societal interest also now seems to ask couples to limit the size of their families.

BIRTH CONTROL

Limitation of family size demands the availability and the use of effective methods of contraception. How does U.S. public opinion stand on the matter of birth control? The answer depends on whether the question asks about birth control generally, or whether it specifies to whom birth control is to be made available. The answer also depends on the age of the group being polled as well as the period of our recent history when the question was asked. We see once again that public opinion on any issue must be interpreted very carefully.

In a cautionary article, Blake (1969) has declared that it is highly misleading to conclude that public pressure had built up during the 1960s for the federal government to promote the availability of birth control. She suggests that the public has long been generally in favor of birth control, but that there has been no dramatic increase in pro-birth-control attitudes over recent years. Examining Gallup polls on this issue between 1937 and 1964, Blake points out that favorability toward birth control increased among men from 66% to 89%, and among women from 70% to 86%. To Blake this is not a dramatic increase in the acceptance of contraceptive practice. One might venture to reply that increases from around 68% to around 88% do constitute important changes in public opinion—from a strong majority to near unanimity. In a public opinion area involving a complex and important issue, having 90% of the populace in favor of something in as close to unanimity as one is likely to get. But that is not the only problem with Blake's conclusions.

In 1937 the question Gallup asked was, "Do you favor the birth control movement?" In 1938 through 1947 the question was far more specific. It asked respondents if they favored having a government agency give birth control information to married couples. In 1959 through 1964 the question asked whether or not birth control information should be supplied to anyone who wanted it. Notice how the questions have increased in specificity over the years. Notice also the change in the target of birth control information from married people to "anyone who wants it." Scholars who have studied this area have noted that there is a continuum of strength of opinion on different specific questions. More people say they favor the birth control movement in the abstract, than the number who approve of supplying birth control information, and somewhat fewer still endorse the distribution of birth control supplies. Thus, in the Commission on Population Growth survey (Lipson & Wolman, 1972), while 87% approved of government distribution of birth control information, only 74% approved of distribution of the necessary supplies.

There is another continuum ranging from providing information or supplies to no one, through supplying married couples, to supplying anyone (including unmarried teenagers) who may want birth control. The *Look* Magazine survey of 1965, for example, showed 80% approval for distribution of birth control information for anyone who wanted it, but when the questions became more specific, only 4% thought that the information was appropriate for unmarried people. By 1971, however, 69% of those surveyed approved specifically of birth control information for unmarried persons 18 years or older (Gallup, 1972)—a tremendous increase.

Thus, there has not just been an upswing over the last 30 years in U.S. public opinion favoring contraception. This favorability has increased along the dimensions just discussed: information vs. supplies, and only for married couples vs. anyone who desires it. Hence, the increase in pro-birth-control attitudes is much greater than that suggested by Blake's (1969) figures of a rise in favorability from 68% to 88%. Furthermore, Blake's figures are limited to respondents between the ages of 21 and 44. This group has historically reported the strongest pro-birth-control attitudes. As we will see later in this chapter, it is the 45 and over age group which has typically displayed less enthusiasm for birth control, and it is in this group (an important segment of the voting and public-policy-determining citizenry) that the most significant changes have occurred.

To sum up then, the evidence examined here (also see Jaffee, 1973) suggests that there is widespread support in this country for the availability of birth control. Over the last 40 years a majority of Americans have expressed opinions in favor of birth control. Recently this majority has grown to as near unanimity as one finds on any complex public policy issue. Support for birth control is not only high among adults of child-bearing age, but it has also sharply increased among the previously less-favorable older age groups. Finally, attitudes increasingly favor making birth control information and supplies available to the young and the unmarried and not just to older married adults.

Specific Contraceptive Methods

As for the practice of birth control, it has been estimated by the demographers Westoff and Ryder (1969) that among women in the fertile years, 97% have used some method of contraception or plan to use it. Westoff (1972), reporting on the 1970 National Fertility Survey, has provided data on couples aged 45 and under who were then living together and practicing contraception. Percentages of this group using various contraceptive methods were:

1.	Birth control pill	34.2%
2.	Surgical sterilization (husband or wife)	16.3
3.	Condom	14.2
4.	I.U.D.	7.4
5.	Rhythm	6.4
6.	Foam	6.1
7.	Diaphragm	5.7
8.	Douche	3.2
9.	Withdrawal	2.1
10.	Other	4.6
	Total	100.2%

Of the 3810 couples surveyed, 65% were at that time using one or more contraceptive methods, while 35% were not. Clearly, the oral contraceptive was the most popular single method by a wide margin, with surgical sterilization (for either husband or wife) in second place. Gough (1973) has noted that surgical methods seem to be increasing rapidly in popularity.

A valuable study which shows the relationship of birth control attitudes to beliefs and behavioral intentions was done by Jaccard and Davidson (1972). Using Fishbein's predictive system with a sample of 73 women, they showed that a woman's overall attitude toward using birth control pills was closely linked to 15 salient beliefs about the consequences of taking such pills. Furthermore, her attitude toward birth control pills and her normative beliefs (beliefs about the wishes of important other persons) in turn could be combined to give an excellent prediction of her behavioral intentions about using the pill ($r = +.84$). This study shows how the methodological procedures we have discussed in Chapters 2 and 10 can be used to understand and predict attitudes having important real-life consequences.

It is hard to keep track of public opinion with regard to specific contraceptive methods. A 1966 Gallup poll found that 61% of those questioned thought that the pill was safe; 7% thought it was not and, surprisingly, the "no opinion" group reached 32% (Gallup, 1972, p. 2044). Well over half said that they would recommend the pill to a woman who did not want any more children, but 31% said they would not. This study indicates generally positive attitudes toward the pill but a fair amount of uncertainty as well. This uncertainty continues. Rorvik (1971) has estimated that during the 1969–70 "pill scare" 1.5 million women abandoned oral contraception at least temporarily, leading to what Ziegler (1970) has called a "major epidemic of unwanted pregnancies." Furthermore, Gough (1973) has cited several studies of birth control practices showing that typically as much as 40% of the sample changes their contraceptive method over the course of only a relatively few months. More recently, problems with the Dalkon shield I.U.D. have affected attitudes toward and use of this contraceptive device. Thus, although we can get an idea about the relative popularity of various birth control methods both in opinion studies and surveys of use (the pill and surgical methods still remain highest), there can be relatively wide shifts in opinion based on scare headlines and changing medical reports. However, the continuing clear element in the situation is the very widespread use of birth control among fecund women.

ABORTION

Abortion remains a birth control method of last resort in some countries of the world where the more effective contraceptive methods are not accessible, e.g., Japan, where the pill and the I.U.D. are largely unavailable (Boffey, 1970). U.S. attitudes seem to favor contraception in the first instance rather than a retroactive solution such as abortion. There are strong moral and religious strictures in Western culture about postconception methods of limiting fertility. The Judaeo-

Christian ethic, respect for the individual, and reverence for human life all militate against abortion if it is considered as the taking of a human life. The big question is: when do we consider that separate, viable human life has come into being?

In January of 1973 the United States Supreme Court differentiated sharply between the three trimesters of normal pregnancy, striking down state laws prohibiting abortion during the first three months, allowing greater regulation during the second trimester and still more restrictions on abortion during the third three months. A 1975 Gallup poll asked, "Do you think abortions should be legal under any circumstances, legal under only certain circumstances, or illegal in all circumstances?" (*Gallup Opinion Index*, 1975b, p. 12). Three-quarters of those replying were for the legality of abortion under all or at least some circumstances. But when the question was asked about the legality of abortion in terms of the three trimesters, 70% favored abortion under at least some circumstances during the first three months, 46% during the second three, and only 37% during the final trimester. Clearly then the time factor is a key to the public's (as well as the Supreme Court's) approval or disapproval of abortion.

A second important element is the nature of the circumstances which impel the abortion. This element was omitted from a 1974 Gallup poll (*Gallup Opinion Index,* 1974b), which asked simply, "The U.S. Supreme Court has ruled that a woman may go to a doctor to end pregnancy at any time during the first three months of pregnancy. Do you favor or oppose this ruling?" This poll was taken in March, 1974, only a year before the survey cited just above (April, 1975). Yet, the margin of approval was extremely small, 47% for, and 44% against. A later 1974 poll (*Gallup Opinion Index,* 1974f) taken in October, asking about the legality of abortion, reflected the same kind of narrow margin. Yet only six months later, there was a 75% response in favor of abortion under at least some circumstances.

These data indicate that it is not only the time factor but the circumstances which determine opinions on abortion, pro or con. Just what these circumstances are has not been specified in recent national polls, but there are bits of evidence about them. During 1962 a Gallup survey found a majority of those polled expressed agreement with an Arizona woman who had obtained an abortion in Sweden because she had taken the drug thalidomide during her pregnancy. Due to the drug, the fetus was deformed, and public opinion was nearly two to one in favor of her action. A similar margin favoring abortion because of possible fetal deformity was obtained in a 1966 Gallup survey (Gallup, 1972, p. 1984). More significant still was the 77% support for abortion where the health of the mother is in doubt. The poll did not state whether "health" included psychological health as well as physical, but increasingly, legal interpretations of this term seem to include both aspects. Interestingly, only 18% in this 1966 poll felt that insufficient economic support for additional children justified the practice of abortion.

A recent poll of a representative sample of California citizens allows comparison of changes in abortion attitudes from 1969 to 1976 (Field, 1976). The proportion of respondents who approved abortion "if the baby might be born with a serious deformity" remained very high (77% in 1969, 81% in 1976). However, those approving "if the family can't afford another child" increased sharply (from 30% to 50%), as did approval "if the mother should desire it for any reason" (going from 15% to 42%).

Whatever the precise circumstances which the public feels might justify abortion, the findings cited above show widespread support for early abortion (during the first trimester), and for abortion under some special circumstances. This support, as we see in the next section, is found among almost all population subgroups—including those which have traditionally been opposed to abortion under any and all circumstances (even danger to the prospective mother's life). By comparison with the famous 1962 case cited above, when an Arizona woman had to go to Sweden for an abortion, we can see a great deal of change in the law, in public opinion, and in health-care practice over the past decade.

Yet in spite of these general changes in public opinion, 1976 saw a major spurt of activity by antiabortion, "pro-life" factions in the U.S. Many political efforts were made toward a constitutional amendment reversing the 1973 Supreme Court ruling on abortion, and a New York woman campaigned for the Presidency solely on a "pro-life" platform (she even managed to raise enough contributions to qualify for federal matching funds for her campaign). These developments can be understood, not as the last gasp of a dying cause, but as the intense activities of those who hold extreme views on the abortion issue. They are relatively few in number, but they are willing to invest considerable money and effort in their cause, and to threaten to vote solely on the abortion issue, ignoring candidates' stands on all other issues such as employment, foreign affairs, or inflation. A large-scale poll done for the Catholic Church showed that 13% of respondents said they would cast their ballot solely on the antiabortion issue, while 15% said they would vote solely on a proabortion basis (*U.S. News & World Report,* 1976b). It is in the wide middle ground between these two extremes where the recent changes toward more favorable abortion attitudes have occurred.

ATTITUDES OF VARIOUS POPULATION SUBGROUPS

Let us continue our breakdown of population attitudes by considering how various subgroups of the public view the four population topics which we have been discussing.

Age Differences

Age factors have often divided public opinion rather sharply. The 1965 *Look* Magazine survey (Erskine, 1967) showed only slightly greater worry about population among younger age groups, but a 1971 Gallup survey showed stronger results, a spread of nearly 20% between the oldest and youngest groups. Also, this gap was wider when the question concerned the effect of U.S. population growth on the quality of life (68% vs. 44%). Realistically, it does seem likely that population problems will become even more severe in the future and thus affect the now-young more than the older generation. But it is also clear that even the 50-plus age groups are not unconcerned about population problems. With regard to family size, older persons again show a slightly greater tendency to favor large families (*Gallup Opinion Index,* 1974d).

Support for birth control has been high among the young (e.g., the 21–24 year old age group) for 40 years now, registering 81% way back in 1936, as compared with 70% of the general populace (Gallup, 1972, p. 41; also see *Gallup Opinion Index,* 1975c). In 1965, *Look* Magazine found the 20-30 age group 87% in favor of dissemination of birth control information, while the 50 and over age group, gave 65% approval (a distinct rise over their 1947 level of 49%). This historical comparison illustrates a point mentioned earlier, that support for birth control among the young has remained consistently high, while it is the oldest age groups that have been increasing in approval.

With regard to abortion, both young and old agree that it should be permitted

Figure 17-3 An example of age differences in population attitudes.

in early months, and under some circumstances later on. It is only when the question concerns acceptance of abortion without any limiting circumstances that the older groups display a more traditional view (*Gallup Opinion Index,* 1975b).

Differences Between the Sexes

Probably the most remarkable aspect of male and female attitudes related to population is that differences seem virtually nonexistent (e.g., McCutcheon, 1974). There is an indication that some years ago, women were very slightly more proabortion than men, but most recent figures indicate, if anything, a reversal of this pattern (*Gallup Opinion Index,* 1974b, 1974f, 1975b). The greatest difference was found in March of 1974 when 51% of the men and 43% of the women favored abortion at any time during the first trimester of pregnancy. These data lend no support to the frequent recent claims that in these important attitude areas "male-chauvinists" have perpetuated a public policy in direct opposition to women's expressed attitudes and interests. Happily, this is one opinion area where American men and women can and do agree.

Race Differences

Where data on population growth attitudes have been broken down by race (Erskine, 1967), somewhat greater concern has been expressed by whites than nonwhites. However, Barnett (1972) found no significant differences between races on opinions expressed in the 1967 and the 1969 Population Council surveys.

Whites and nonwhites do differ on questions of ideal family size. In 1968, nonwhites showed a somewhat stronger preference for four or more children than whites (56% vs. 47% respectively—Gallup, 1972, p. 2169). These figures changed remarkably by 1974. Though both groups decreased, the disparity increased to 37% of nonwhites wanting four or more children versus only 15% of whites (*Gallup Opinion Index,* 1974d). However, though attitudes and actual fertility usually tend to be quite parallel, in this case they apparently are less so. Many demographers (e.g., Sweet, 1974) have pointed out that there is a great convergence in the fertility rates for blacks and for whites; and although fertility for black women still remains somewhat higher, there is a tendency for it to approach that of white women rather closely, especially in urban areas.

There are only minor differences between blacks and whites in attitudes concerning the availability of birth control supplies or information, with approval for both groups ranging from 73% to 88% (Erskine, 1967; Lipson & Wolman, 1972). Similarly, racial differences are small with regard to abortion attitudes. When the question concerns some specific circumstances, nonwhites tend to be somewhat less proabortion than whites; but the differences are small, and more than 60% of both whites and nonwhites approve of abortion under at least some circumstances (*Gallup Opinion Index,* 1974f, 1975b).

Religion

Official Papal pronouncements about "artificial" methods of birth control and opposition to abortion suggest that U.S. Catholics would disagree sharply with Protestants in these areas. It appears, however, that this traditional wisdom was only moderately correct in recent decades and is largely incorrect today. Attitudes were divergent throughout the early 1960s, but 1965 seems to have been the watershed. Today, although differences do exist, they tend to be rather small.

In 1962, the number of Protestants approving of abortion because of fetal deformity was nearly twice the number of Catholics, but by 1966, the gap narrowed to ten percentage points (Gallup, 1972). In 1975, a majority of both Protestants and Catholics approved abortion under some circumstances, and differences between the two groups tended to be less than 10%. Comparison of polls from the early 1960s with the 1971 Commission on Population Growth survey reveals a similar marked convergence of attitudes with regard to family size, birth control, and population concern generally (Lipson & Wolman, 1972; see also Westoff & Ryder, 1969; Barnett, 1972).

Although Jewish attitudes in the population area are too often not listed separately, in one important survey, Jewish attitudes were consistently even more in favor of birth control information or supplies, liberalized abortion laws, and limitation of population growth than were those of Protestants and Catholics (Lipson & Wolman, 1972). Overall, however, the most impressive aspect of population attitudes among religious subgroups is their great current consensus, whatever their past differences may have been.

Income

Support for government action to slow down population growth is greater among respondents with high income and educational level (Opinion Research Corporation, 1971). However, income and occupation are not significantly related to attitudes toward the population problem generally (Barnett, 1972), and Thompson et al. (1974) found income and education only moderately successful in predicting attitudes towards acceptance of policies to limit population. Persons at different economic and educational levels tend to prefer different kinds of population control policies, rather than being clearly for or against population control—except at the lowest end of the income scale, where there is greater pronatalism in several areas: population growth, family size, birth control, and abortion (Thompson et al., 1974). It is ironic that this group which is least able to support children is most favorable to having them!

Education

Education is positively correlated with concern about population problems (Barnett, 1972; Thompson et al., 1974). In the Commission on Population survey (Lipson & Wolman, 1972), college graduates were consistently much more concerned about population and had more liberal attitudes toward sex education than did persons who had not finished high school. In all of the four major content areas we have been discussing, there are consistent moderate to very large differences (10 to 40 percentage points) between groups having the least and the most education. As an example of very large differences, in 1974 71% of the college educated were proabortion, compared to only 30% of those with a grade school education (*Gallup Opinion Index,* 1974f). Thus, of all the demographic variables, education seems to make the greatest difference in population-related attitudes, though Westoff and Ryder (1969) suggest that education-related differences in natalist attitudes are now diminishing.

Summing Up Subgroup Differences

Perhaps surprisingly, region of the country and political affiliation have been found to make very little difference in support for government-provided birth control information or other population attitudes (Barnett, 1972; Lipson & Wolman, 1972). Barnett (1970) found Republicans slightly more favorable than Democrats toward government intervention to limit population growth (an interesting reversal of the usual reactions to government action), but the differences were not consistent across age groups.

In general, we may agree with Barnett (1972) that the most striking finding is the relatively low usefulness of demographic factors in explaining and predicting attitudes toward population issues. Of the many demographic variables examined by Barnett, only two—religion and education—sometimes (although by no means always) made a difference in attitudes. We have seen that education and income do make a difference in population attitudes, especially at the very low end of these two scales. Race and religion display smaller differences, and there is evidence of a marked convergence of the opinions of various racial and religious groups. The degree of consensus in population attitudes achieved over the last decade in U.S. history is remarkable.

POPULATION ATTITUDES IN OTHER NATIONS

We have noted earlier that U.S. citizens tend to regard world population problems with more concern than those of their own country and are quite willing to have birth control provided to various nations. That leads to the question: how do other nations themselves feel about the matter?

A great deal of information about indigenous attitudes for specific countries has been obtained by the so-called **KAP studies** (Knowledge, Attitudes, and Practices of birth control and family planning) and the Value of Children studies discussed earlier. Fawcett (1970) has reported that more than 400 KAP studies have been carried out in virtually all of the world's major geographic and cultural areas. These studies, however, have been increasingly criticized as being unreliable for many purposes (Cernada & Crawford, 1973) because of the lack of rapport between the (typically) western interviewers and the usually nonwestern respondents (Hoffman & Hoffman, 1973), and because "courteous" respondents have often been known to give answers they thought the interviewers wanted to hear (Poffenberger, 1975).

One element which frequently emerges in studies of other nations is the importance of modernity and higher levels of formal education (Fawcett & Bornstein, 1973). The modern industrialized nations tend to have lower birth rates, and their peoples generally express attitudes consistent with these same low fertility levels. Recently there have been marked declines in four or more children as an ideal family size for Canada, Australia, Spain, Great Britain, Uruguay, Sweden, and Greece (*Gallup Opinion Index,* 1974d); and Japanese leaders are so concerned about their nation's low birth-rate that they have recently stated their hopes of raising fertility levels in their country (Boffey, 1970). Soviet bloc leaders seem to be moving toward a position similar to Japan's. Chinese leaders, however, despite rhetoric to the contrary, have instituted rigid fertility limitation policies (Kellogg, Kline & Stepan, 1975). In most of the developing nations, birth rates remain high, and traditional attitudes favoring fertility persist. The most notable exception to this rule is found among the more westernized and better educated elements in these countries, among whom actual births as well as attitudes suggest that low fertility is more normative (Fawcett & Bornstein, 1973).

With regard to abortion, The Gallup Organization (*Gallup Opinion Index,* 1974c) polled seventy world leaders concerning the U.S. law permitting abortion during the first trimester of pregnancy. Only 36% said that their own laws permitted such abortions, although 57% stated that they themselves wanted such a ruling to be passed in their own lands. However, with this polling procedure, we have moved from the area of public opinion to the elite opinion of national leaders. And while in many instances these leaders do reflect the views of their peoples, clearly that is not always the case.

The Bucharest Conference

The attitudes of many national leaders were expressed in the 1974 Conference on World Population Problems held in Bucharest. Although some of the resolutions passed there were salutary, the conference was a disappointment to many Western observers who had hoped for more clear-cut commitments to reducing birth rates on the part of the countries with run-away fertility. Hill (1974) reported that great emphasis was placed on each country's sovereignty and its right to pursue whatever population policy it felt to be in its own best interest. Western countries were criticized for advocating population control for others instead of limiting their high levels of natural resource consumption. As one commentator observed: "distribution of wealth, not contraceptives, was the key issue" (Norris, 1975). Many speakers asserted that, following economic development of the poor nations, population problems would take care of themselves (just as fertility dropped after industrialization in many Western nations). The conference generally seemed to lean toward the view that population growth is an asset—indeed the host country, Rumania, had itself banned abortion in 1966 to increase its birth rate.

If the world leaders at this conference were really reflecting their peoples' attitudes and practices, then there is a great reason for concern about world population problems. U.S.- and U.N.-supported family planning programs are making progress in many parts of the world, but there is an increasing feeling among experts on international population growth that, even if people have only as many children as they want, the worldwide problem will still be acute.

LOOKING AHEAD

In the United States, the current picture seems much more optimistic. Birth rates are currently at the lowest levels in U.S. history—down 20% just between 1970 and 1975 (Sklar & Berkov, 1975; *Behavior Today,* 1976). There seems to be a broad and developing consensus in U.S. attitudes about population control as well as the areas of family size, birth control, and abortion. This same picture seems to typify most other Western industrialized countries, though the developing nations provide much greater cause for alarm. But even in the United States, complacency does not seem appropriate. Educators, toy manufacturers, baby food purveyors, etc., have all begun to feel the effects of the recent "birth dearth," and as this reduction of numbers moves up the age continuum, other suppliers of goods and services may begin to rethink support for population control. Furthermore, a recent report on California fertility by Sklar and Berkov (1975) shows that women in their later 20s may be starting to have previously postponed births before they reach their 30s. A large number of women are now in the 21–29 year-old age cohort, and Sklar and Berkov warn about a possible new "baby boom" for the United States as a whole, if incipient trends in California truly foretell future U.S. national patterns.

There is, of course, a risk in extrapolating from present trends to future events under the assumption that present base rates will not change. Still, though predictions can prove fallacious, we cannot afford to ignore present fertility trends; and careful evaluation of public attitudes and behavior will continue to be important. Hysterical headlines, on the other hand, though they may help to alert us to the dangers of overpopulation, often create as much resistance as they overcome. Although population control and reduced family size seem vitally important goals, their proponents need to be thoughtful about the effects of such policies on the strength of the family, the society, and reverence for human life, among other values.

On the other hand, the achievement of population control may be absolutely essential to many long-sought goals of humanity, such as peace and prosperity. Karl Menninger has pointed this out, writing that often "the unwanted child becomes the undesirable citizen, the willing cannon-fodder for wars of hate and prejudice." Consequently, Menninger views planned parenthood as "an essential element in any program for increased mental health and for human peace and happiness" (Menninger, 1942, pp. 222–224).

SUMMARY

Attitudes toward population growth, both pro and con, can be highly emotional ones because of the profound nature of the issues involved. Proponents of population growth say that the problem is essentially one of maldistribution of available resources. Opponents point out that the carrying capacity of the earth is limited and there is a likelihood of a global ecological catastrophe if present growth rates persist.

Although overpopulation has occasionally existed before in human history, it is most acutely felt today because of the reduction of death rates through modern medical science and technology—particularly dramatic in the non-Western countries. In the U.S., high fertility and possible overpopulation did not become matters of concern until the effects of the postwar baby-boom of the 1940s and 1950s became apparent. Today overpopulation in the United States is a serious concern for Americans, but not their greatest source of worry.

Since 1960, U.S. fertility rates have declined sharply to the lowest levels in our history, and standards of desired family size have decreased proportionately. Over the past four decades there has been a great liberalization of U.S. public attitudes toward the provision of birth control information, services, and supplies by government. The increase in favorability is especially noticeable in regard to subsidization of such services, and their distribution even to the young and unmarried. A similar liberalization of attitudes has occurred toward abortion, especially under certain specified circumstances and during the first three months of pregnancy. With regard to all four areas of population attitudes which we have discussed, there is now a fair amount of consensus among U.S. citizens—even including many traditionally divergent subgroups. Age, race, sex, religion, region, and political affiliation show, at most, small differences in population-related attitudes. Only income and education have a larger impact on attitudes, with pronatalist views being strongest at the very low end of these two scales.

On the international scene it is much more difficult to draw clear-cut conclusions. In the Western world the pattern is becoming very similar to that of the United States. However, among the Soviet bloc countries, and in Japan, attempts are being made to increase fertility in order to accomplish economic goals. Some of the "third world" countries have embraced some Western fertility goals and methods of contraception, but many have not, either for religious and cultural reasons or because they believe that large populations bring greater world power.

Though the U.S. population picture seems relatively bright, both in attitudes and practices, a new "baby boom" is not beyond the bounds of possibility. Continuing vigilance, an understanding of the consequences of both pronatalist and antinatalist views, and a long range concern for the ecological consequences of population are vital to the future welfare of both the U.S. and the world.

Suggested Readings

Fawcett, J. T. (Ed.). *Psychological Perspectives on Population.* New York: Basic Books, 1973.—A comprehensive, readable book containing chapters by leading psychologists in the population field.

Hart, H. H. (Ed.). *Population Control: For and Against.* New York: Hart Publishing, 1973.—A fascinating little volume containing arguments, pro and con, about population control. The authors include Max Lerner, Margaret Mead, Colin Clark, Amitai Etzioni, and Julian Huxley.

Pohlman, E. H. *Population: A Clash of Prophets.* New York: New American Library, 1973.—This delightful paperback contains vignettes concerning population from many historical and unusual sources.

Westoff, C. F., & Ryder, N. B. Recent trends in attitudes toward fertility control and in the practice of contraception in the U.S. In S. J. Behrman, L. Corsa, & R. Freedman (Eds.), *Fertility and Family Planning: A World View.* Ann Arbor: University of Michigan Press, 1969. Pp. 388–412.—A brief but authoritative historical perspective on U. S. contraceptive attitudes and practices.

References

Abelson, R. P. Modes of resolution of belief dilemmas. *Journal of Conflict Resolution,* 1959, 3, 343–352.

Abelson, R. P. Computers, polls, and public opinion—Some puzzles and paradoxes. *Trans-action,* 1968, 5(9), 20–27.

Abelson, R. P., & Miller, J. Negative persuasion via personal insult. *Journal of Experimental Social Psychology,* 1967, 3, 321–333.

Abelson, R. P., & Rosenberg, M. J. Symbolic psycho-logic: A model of attitudinal cognition. *Behavioral Science,* 1958, 3, 1–13.

Abrams, M. The opinion polls and the 1970 British general election. *Public Opinion Quarterly,* 1970, 34, 317–324.

Abramson, P. R. Political efficacy and political trust among black schoolchildren: Two explanations. *Journal of Politics,* 1972, 34, 1243–1269.

Adorno, T. W., Frenkel-Brunswik, E., Levinson, D. J., & Sanford, R. N. *The Authoritarian Personality.* New York: Harper, 1950.

Allport, G. W. Attitudes. In C. Murchison (Ed.), *A Handbook of Social Psychology.* Worcester, Mass.: Clark University Press, 1935. Pp. 798–844.

Allport, G. W. *The Nature of Prejudice.* Reading, Mass.: Addison-Wesley, 1954.

Almond, G. A. Public opinion and the development of space technology: 1957–60. In R. L. Merritt & D. J. Puchala (Eds.), *Western European Perspectives on International Affairs: Public Opinion Studies and Evaluations.* New York: Praeger, 1968. Pp. 86–110.

Almond, G. A., & Verba, S. *The Civic Culture.* Princeton, N.J.: Princeton University Press, 1963.

American Psychological Association. *Ethical Standards of Psychologists.* Washington, D.C.: American Psychological Association, 1953.

American Psychological Association. *Casebook on Ethical Standards of Psychologists.* Washington, D.C.: American Psychological Association, 1967.

American Psychological Association. *Ethical Principles in the Conduct of Research with Human Participants.* Washington, D.C.: American Psychological Association, 1973.

Amir, Y. Contact hypothesis in ethnic relations. *Psychological Bulletin,* 1969, 71, 319–342.

Anderson, N. H. Test of a model of opinion change. *Journal of Abnormal and Social Psychology,* 1959, 59, 371–381.

Anderson, N. H. Integration theory and attitude change. *Psychological Review,* 1971, 78, 171–206.

Arnott, C. C. Husbands' attitude and wives' commitment to employment. *Journal of Marriage and the Family,* 1972, 34, 673–684.

Arnott, C. C. Feminists and anti-feminists. *Sociology and Social Research,* 1973, 57, 300–306.

Aronson, E. Dissonance theory: Progress and problems. In R. P. Abelson, E. Aronson, W. J. McGuire, T. M. Newcomb, M. J. Rosenberg, & P. H. Tannenbaum (Eds.), *Theories of Cognitive Consistency: A Sourcebook.* Chicago: Rand McNally, 1968. Pp. 5–27.

Aronson, E. The theory of cognitive dissonance: A current perspective. In L. Berkowitz (Ed.), *Advances in Experimental Social Psychology* (Vol. 4). New York: Academic Press, 1969. Pp. 1–34.

Aronson, E., & Carlsmith, J. M. Experimentation in social psychology. In G. Lindzey & E. Aronson (Eds.), *The Handbook of Social Psychology* (2nd ed.). Vol. 2. Reading, Mass.: Addison-Wesley, 1968. Pp. 1–79.

Aronson, E., & Golden, B. W. The effect of relevant and irrelevant aspects of communicator credibility on attitude change. *Journal of Personality,* 1962, 30, 135–146.

Aronson, E., & Linder, D. Gain and loss of esteem as determinants of interpersonal attraction. *Journal of Experimental Social Psychology,* 1965, 1, 156–171.

Arterton, F. C. The impact of Watergate on children's attitudes toward political authority. *Political Science Quarterly,* 1974, 89, 269–288.

Asch, J., & Shore, B. M. Conservation behavior as the outcome of environmental education. *Journal of Environmental Education,* 1975, 6(4), 25–33.

Asch, S. E. Forming impressions of personality. *Journal of Abnormal and Social Psychology,* 1946, 41, 258–290.

Asher, S. R., & Allen, V. L. Racial preference and social comparison processes. *Journal of Social Issues,* 1969, 25(1), 157–166.

Atkin, C. K., Bowen, L., Nayman, O. B., & Sheinkopf, K. G. Quality versus quantity in televised political ads. *Public Opinion Quarterly,* 1973, 37, 209–224.

Atkin, C. K., Galloway, J., & Nayman, O. Mass communication and political socialization among college students. *Public Opinion Quarterly,* 1973, 37, 443–444.

Audi, R. On the conception and measurement of attitudes in contemporary Anglo-American psychology. *Journal for the Theory of Social Behaviour,* 1972, 2, 179–203.

Auliciems, A., & Burton, I. Air pollution in Toronto. In W. R. D. Sewell, & I. Burton (Eds.), *Perceptions and Attitudes in Resource Management*. Ottawa, Canada: Policy Research and Coordination Branch, Department of Energy, Mines, and Resources; Resource Paper No. 2, 1971, Pp. 71–80.

Axelrod, R. The structure of public opinion on policy issues. *Public Opinion Quarterly,* 1967, 31, 51–60.

Bachman, J. G., & Jennings, M. K. The impact of Vietnam on trust in government. *Journal of Social Issues,* 1975, 31 (4), 141–155.

Backstrom, C. H. Congress and the public: How representative is the one of the other? *Public Opinion Quarterly,* 1972, 36, 420–421.

Bagdikian, B. H. Bias in the weekly newsmagazines. In R. M. Christenson & R. O. McWilliams (Eds.), *Voice of the People: Readings in Public Opinion and Propaganda*. New York: McGraw-Hill, 1962. Pp. 148–164.

Bancroft, G., & Welch, E. H. Recent experience with problems of labor force measurement. *Journal of the American Statistical Association,* 1946, 41, 303–312.

Bandura, A. Vicarious processes: A case of no-trial learning. In L. Berkowitz (Ed.), *Advances in Experimental Social Psychology* (Vol. 2). New York: Academic Press, 1965, Pp. 3–55.

Banks, W. M. The changing attitudes of black students. *Personnel and Guidance Journal,* 1970, 48, 739–745.

Barber, T. X., & Silver, M. J. Fact, fiction, and the experimenter bias effect. *Psychological Bulletin Monograph Supplement,* 1968, 70 (6, Pt. 2), 1–29.

Barker, M. L. Beach pollution in the Toronto region. In W. R. D. Sewell, & I. Burton (Eds.), *Perceptions and Attitudes in Resource Management*. Ottawa, Canada: Policy Research and Coordination Branch, Department of Energy, Mines, and Resources; Resource Paper No. 2, 1971. Pp. 37–47.

Barnett, L. D. Political affiliation and attitudes toward population limitation. *Social Biology,* 1970, 17, 124–131.

Barnett, L. D. Demographic factors in attitudes towards population growth and control. *Journal of Biosocial Science,* 1972, 4, 9–23.

Barron, F. Review of the Edwards Personal Preference Schedule. In O. K. Buros (Ed.), *The Fifth Mental Measurements Yearbook*. Highland Park, N. J.: Gryphon Press, 1959. Pp. 114–117.

Barry, H., III, Bacon, M. K., & Child, I. L. A cross-cultural survey of some sex differences in socialization. In J. M. Bardwick (Ed.), *Readings on the Psychology of Women*. New York: Harper & Row, 1972. Pp. 205–209.

Bass, B. M. Authoritarianism or acquiescence? *Journal of Abnormal and Social Psychology,* 1955, 51, 616–623.

Bauer, R. A. The obstinate audience: The influence process from the point of view of social communication. *American Psychologist,* 1964, 19, 319–328.

Bauer, R. A. (Ed.). *Social Indicators*. Cambridge, Mass.: Massachusetts Institute of Technology Press, 1966.

Bauer, R. A., & Bauer, A. H. America, mass society, and mass media. *Journal of Social Issues,* 1960, 16(3), 3–66.

Bauer, R. A., & Greyser, S. A. *Advertising in America: The Consumer View.* Boston: Graduate School of Business Administration, Harvard University, 1968.

Becker, J. F., & Heaton, E. E., Jr. The election of Senator Edward W. Brooke. *Public Opinion Quarterly,* 1967, 31, 346–358.

Behavior Today. How the media affect elections. August 11, 1975, p. 532. (a)

Behavior Today. Using social science. August 18, 1975, p. 539. (b)

Behavior Today. Fertility rate hits record low in 1975. April 5, 1976, p. 6.

Bellisfield, G. White attitudes toward racial integration and the urban riots of the 1960's. *Public Opinion Quarterly,* 1972, 36, 579–584.

Bem, D. J. An experimental analysis of self-persuasion. *Journal of Experimental Social Psychology,* 1965, 1, 199–218.

Bem, D. J. Self-perception: An alternative interpretation of cognitive dissonance phenomena. *Psychological Review,* 1967, 74, 183–200.

Bem, D. J. *Beliefs, Attitudes, and Human Affairs.* Belmont, Calif.: Brooks/Cole, 1970.

Bem, S. L. The measurement of psychological androgyny. *Journal of Consulting and Clinical Psychology,* 1974, 42, 155–162.

Bem, S. L. Beyond androgyny: Some presumptuous prescriptions for a liberated sexual identity. Paper presented at American Psychological Association meeting, Chicago, September, 1975.

Bendiner, R. National Q-&-A game: The polls. *New York Times Magazine,* Aug. 23, 1953, pp. 13, 36, 38–39.

Benham, T. W. Polling for a presidential candidate: Some observations on the 1964 campaign. *Public Opinion Quarterly,* 1965, 29, 185–199.

Bennett, E. Discussion, decision, commitment and consensus in "group decisions." *Human Relations,* 1955, 8, 251–274.

Bennett, W. L. *The Political Mind and the Political Environment.* Lexington, Mass.: Heath, 1975.

Bentler, P. M., Jackson, D. N., & Messick, S. Identification of content and style: A two-dimensional interpretation of acquiescence. *Psychological Bulletin,* 1971, 76, 186–204.

Berelson, B. R., Lazarsfeld, P. F., & McPhee, W. N. *Voting: A Study of Opinion Formation in a Presidential Election.* Chicago: University of Chicago Press, 1954.

Berelson, B. R., & Steiner, G. A. *Human Behavior: An Inventory of Scientific Findings.* New York: Harcourt, Brace & World, 1964.

Berger, A. S., Gagnon, J. H., & Simon, W. Gender role expectations among adolescents. Paper presented at American Sociological Association meeting, New Orleans, July, 1972.

Berkowitz, L. Social norms, feelings, and other factors affecting helping and altruism. In L. Berkowitz (Ed.), *Advances in Experimental Social Psychology* (Vol. 6). New York: Academic Press, 1972, Pp. 63–108.

Berzins, J. I. New perspectives on sex roles and personality dimensions. Paper presented at American Psychological Association meeting, Chicago, September, 1975.

Bettelheim, B., & Janowitz, M. *Social Change and Prejudice.* New York: Free Press, 1964.

Bevins, M. I. Attitudes on environmental quality in six Vermont lakeshore communities. *Vermont Agricultural Experiment Station Bulletin,* June, 1972, No. 671.

Bickman, L., & Henchy, T. *Beyond the Laboratory: Field Research in Social Psychology.* New York: McGraw-Hill, 1972.

Bird, C. *Born Female: The High Cost of Keeping Women Down.* New York: David McKay, 1968.

Bird, C., Monachesi, E. D., & Burdick, H. Infiltration and the attitudes of white and Negro parents and children. *Journal of Abnormal and Social Psychology,* 1952, 47, 688–699.

Blake, J. Population policy for Americans: Is the government being misled? *Science,* 1969, 164, 522–529.

Blumler, J. G., & McQuail, D. *Television in Politics: Its Uses and Influence.* Chicago: University of Chicago Press, 1969.

Bochner, S., & Insko, C. A. Communicator discrepancy, source credibility, and opinion change. *Journal of Personality and Social Psychology,* 1966, 4, 614–621.

Boffey, P. M. Japan: A crowded nation wants to boost its birthrate. *Science,* 1970, 167, 960–962.

Bogardus, E. S. Measuring social distance. *Journal of Applied Sociology,* 1925, 9, 299–308.

Bogart, L. *Silent Politics: Polls and the Awareness of Public Opinion.* New York: Wiley-Interscience, 1972. (a)

Bogart, L. Warning: The Surgeon General has determined that TV violence is moderately dangerous to your child's mental health. *Public Opinion Quarterly,* 1972, 36, 491–521. (b)

Borsky, P. N. The use of social surveys in policy decisions on the sonic boom. *Public Opinion Quarterly,* 1969, 33, 467–468.

Boulding, K. E. National images and international systems. *Journal of Conflict Resolution,* 1959, 3, 120–131.

Bowen, L., Atkin, C. K., Sheinkopf, K. G., & Nayman, O. B. How voters react to electronic political advertising: An investigation of the 1970 election campaigns in Wisconsin and Colorado. *Public Opinion Quarterly,* 1971, 35, 457–458.

Bramel, D. Selection of a target for defensive projection. *Journal of Abnormal and Social Psychology,* 1963, 66, 318–324.

Brayfield, A. H. How to create a new profession: Issues and answers. *American Psychologist,* 1976, 31, 200–205.

Breed, W., & Ktsanes, T. Pluralistic ignorance in the process of opinion formation. *Public Opinion Quarterly,* 1961, 25, 382–392.

Brehm, J. W. A dissonance analysis of attitude-discrepant behavior. In M. J. Rosenberg, C. I. Hovland, W. J. McGuire, R. P. Abelson, & J. W. Brehm, *Attitude Organization and Change: An Analysis of Consistency among Attitude Components.* New Haven, Conn.: Yale University Press, 1960, Pp. 164–197.

Brehm, J. W., & Cohen, A. R. *Explorations in Cognitive Dissonance.* New York: Wiley, 1962.

Bridgeland, W. M., & Sofranko, A. J. Community structure and issue-specific influences on community mobilization over environmental quality. *Urban Affairs Quarterly,* in press.

Brigham, J. C. Ethnic stereotypes. *Psychological Bulletin,* 1971, 76, 15–38.

Brigham, J. C. Racial stereotypes: Measurement variables and the stereotype-attitude relationship. *Journal of Applied Social Psychology,* 1972, 2, 63–76.

Brigham, J. C., & Cook, S. W. The influence of attitude and judgments of plausibility: A replication and extension. *Educational and Psychological Measurement,* 1970, 30, 283–292.

Brigham, J. C., & Weissbach, T. A. (Eds.). *Racial Attitudes in America: Analyses and Findings of Social Psychology.* New York: Harper & Row, 1972.

Brink, W., & Harris, L. *The Negro Revolution in America.* New York: Simon & Schuster, 1963.

Brink, W., & Harris, L. *Black and White: A Study of U.S. Racial Attitudes Today.* New York: Simon & Schuster, 1966.

Brislin, R. W., & Olmstead, K. H. An examination of two models designed to predict behavior from attitude and other verbal measures. *Proceedings, 81st Annual Convention, APA,* 1973, 8, 259–260.

Bronfenbrenner, U. The mirror image in Soviet-American relations: A social psychologist's report. *Journal of Social Issues,* 1961, 17 (3), 45–56.

Broverman, I. K., Broverman, D. M., Clarkson, F. E., Rosenkrantz, P. S. & Vogel, S. R. Sex-role stereotypes and clinical judgments of mental health. *Journal of Consulting and Clinical Psychology,* 1970, 34, 1–7.

Broverman, I. K., Vogel, S. K., Broverman, D. M., Clarkson, F. E., & Rosenkrantz, P. S. Sex role stereotypes: A current appraisal. *Journal of Social Issues,* 1972, 28 (2), 59–78.

Brown, L. R. *In the Human Interest: A Strategy to Stabilize World Population.* New York: Norton, 1974.

Brown, R. *Social Psychology.* New York: Free Press, 1965.

Buchanan, W., & Cantril, H. *How Nations See Each Other: A Study in Public Opinion.* Urbana: University of Illinois Press, 1953.

Bunton, P. L., & Weissbach, T. A. Attitudes toward blackness of black preschool children attending community-controlled or public schools. *Journal of Social Psychology,* 1974, 92, 53–59.

Burch, W. R., Jr., Cheek, N. H., Jr., & Taylor, L. (Eds.). *Social Behavior, Natural Resources, and the Environment.* New York: Harper & Row, 1972.

Burnham, W. D. *Critical Elections and the Mainsprings of American Politics.* New York: Norton, 1970.

Buttel, F. H., & Flinn, W. L. The structure of support for the environmental movement, 1968–70. *Rural Sociology,* 1974, 39, 56–69.

Calder, B. J., & Ross, M. *Attitudes and Behavior.* Morristown, N.J.: General Learning Press, 1973.

Campbell, A. Has television reshaped politics? *Columbia Journalism Review,* 1962, 1(2), 10–13.

Campbell, A. Voters and elections: Past and present. *Journal of Politics,* 1964, 26, 745–757.

Campbell, A. A classification of presidential elections. In A. Campbell, P. E. Converse, W. E. Miller, & D. E. Stokes, *Elections and the Political Order.* New York: Wiley, 1966. Pp. 63–77.

Campbell, A. *White Attitudes toward Black People.* Ann Arbor: Institute for Social Research, University of Michigan, 1971.

Campbell, A., Converse, P. E., Miller, W. E., & Stokes, D. E. *The American Voter.* New York: Wiley, 1960.

Campbell, A., Converse, P. E., Miller, W. E. & Stokes, D. E. *Elections and the Political Order.* New York: Wiley, 1966.

Campbell, A., Converse, P. E., & Rodgers, W. L. *The Quality of American Life: Perceptions, Evaluations, and Satisfactions.* New York: Russell Sage Foundation, 1976.

Campbell, A., Gurin, G., & Miller, W. E. *The Voter Decides.* New York: Harper & Row, 1954.

Campbell, A., & Stokes, D. E. Partisan attitudes and the presidential vote. In E. Burdick & A. J. Brodbeck (Eds.), *American Voting Behavior.* Glencoe, Ill.: Free Press, 1959. Pp. 353–371.

Campbell, D. T. *The Generality of Social Attitudes.* Unpublished doctoral dissertation, University of California, Berkeley, 1947.

Campbell, D. T. Social attitudes and other acquired behavioral dispositions. In S. Koch (Ed.), *Psychology: A Study of a Science* (Vol. 6). New York: McGraw-Hill, 1963. Pp. 94–172.

Campbell, D. T. Stereotypes and the perception of group differences. *American Psychologist,* 1967, 22, 817–829.

Campbell, D. T. Methods for the experimenting society. Paper presented at American Psychological Association meeting, Washington, D.C., September 1971.

Campbell, D. T., & Stanley, J. C. *Experimental and Quasi-Experimental Designs for Research.* Chicago: Rand McNally, 1966.

Cannell, C. F., Fisher, G., & Bakker, T. Reporting of hospitalization in the health interview survey. *Health Statistics,* Series D, No. 4. Washington, D.C.: U.S. Department of Health, Education, and Welfare; Public Health Service, 1961.

Cannell, C. F., & Kahn, R. L. Interviewing. In G. Lindzey & E. Aronson (Eds.), *The Handbook of Social Psychology* (2nd ed.). Vol. 2. Reading, Mass.: Addison-Wesley, 1968. Pp. 526–595.

Canon, L. K., & Mathews, K. E., Jr. Concern over personal health and smoking-relevant beliefs and behavior. *Proceedings, 80th Annual Convention, APA,* 1972, 7, 271–272.

Cantril, A. H., & Roll, C. W., Jr. *Hopes and Fears of the American People.* New York: Universe Books, 1971.

Cantril, H. *The Invasion from Mars.* Princeton, N.J.: Princeton University Press, 1940.

Cantril, H. *Gauging Public Opinion.* Princeton, N.J.: Princeton University Press, 1944.

Cantril, H. *The Human Dimension: Experiences in Policy Research.* New Brunswick, N.J.: Rutgers University Press, 1967.

Cantril, H., & Allport, G. W. *The Psychology of Radio.* New York: Harper, 1935.

Caplan, N. The new ghetto man: A review of recent empirical studies. *Journal of Social Issues,* 1970, 26(1), 59–73.

Carlsmith, J. M., Collins, B. E., & Helmreich, R. L. Studies on forced compliance: I. The effect of pressure for compliance on attitude change produced by face-to-face role-playing and anonymous essay writing. *Journal of Personality and Social Psychology,* 1966, 4, 1–13.

Carlson, E. R. Attitude change through modification of attitude structure. *Journal of Abnormal and Social Psychology,* 1956, 52, 256–261.

Cartwright, D., & Harary, F. Structural balance: A generalization of Heider's theory. *Psychological Review,* 1956, 63, 277–293.

Cernada, G. P., & Crawford, T. J. Some practical applications of social psychology to family-planning programs. In J. T. Fawcett (Ed.), *Psychological Perspectives on Population.* New York: Basic Books, 1973. Pp. 428–449.

Chafetz, J. S. *Masculine/Feminine or Human? An Overview of the Sociology of Sex Roles.* Itasca, Ill.: F. E. Peacock Publishing, 1974.

Chandler, R. *Public Opinion: Changing Attitudes on Contemporary Political and Social Issues.* New York: Bowker, 1972.

Chapanis, N. P., & Chapanis, A. Cognitive dissonance: Five years later. *Psychological Bulletin,* 1964, 61, 1–22.

Chesler, P. *Women and Madness.* Garden City, N. Y.: Doubleday, 1972.

Chethick, M., Fleming, E., Meyer, M. F., & McCoy, J. N. Quest for identity. *American Journal of Orthopsychiatry,* 1967, 37, 71–77.

Childs, H. L. *Public Opinion: Nature, Formation, and Role.* Princeton, N.J.: Van Nostrand, 1965.

Christie, R., Havel, J., & Seidenberg, B. Is the F Scale irreversible? *Journal of Abnormal and Social Psychology,* 1958, 56, 143–159.

Christie, R., & Jahoda, M. (Eds.). *Studies in the Scope and Method of "The Authoritarian Personality."* New York: Free Press, 1954.

Clark, C. In H. H. Hart (Ed.), *Population Control: For and Against.* New York: Hart Publishing, 1973. Pp. 102–132.

Clark, K. B., & Clark, M. P. Racial identification and preference in Negro children. In T. M. Newcomb & E. L. Hartley (Eds.), *Readings in Social Psychology.* New York: Holt, Rinehart & Winston, 1947. Pp. 169–178.

Clausen, A. R. Response validity: Vote report. *Public Opinion Quarterly,* 1968, 32, 588–606.

Cnudde, C. F., & McCrone, D. J. The linkage between constituency attitudes and Congressional voting behavior: A causal model. *American Political Science Review,* 1966, 60, 66–72.

Coale, A. J. Fertility trends in the modern world. In S. J. Behrman, L. Corsa, & R. Freedman (Eds.), *Fertility and Family Planning: A World View.* Ann Arbor: University of Michigan Press, 1969. Pp. 3–24.

Cohen, B. C. *The Press and Foreign Policy.* Princeton, N.J.: Princeton University Press, 1963.

Coleman, J. *The Adolescent Society.* New York: Free Press, 1961.

Coleman J. S., Campbell, E. Q., Hobson, C. J., McPartland, J., Mood, A. M., Weinfeld, F. O., & York, R. L. *Equality of Educational Opportunity.* Washington, D.C.: U.S. Government Printing Office, 1966.

Coles, R. *Children of Crisis.* Boston: Faber, 1968.

Collins, B. E. The effect of monetary inducements on the amount of attitude change produced by forced compliance. In A. C. Elms (Ed.), *Role Playing, Reward, and Attitude Change.* New York: Van Nostrand Reinhold, 1969. Pp. 209–223.

Collins, B. E., Ellsworth, P. C., & Helmreich, R. L. Correlations between pupil size and the semantic differential: An experimental paradigm and pilot study. *Psychonomic Science,* 1967, 9, 627–628.

Collins, B. E., & Hoyt, M. F. Personal responsibility-for-consequences: An integration and extension of the forced compliance literature. *Journal of Experimental Social Psychology,* 1972, 8, 558–593.

Columbia Broadcasting System, Office of Social Research. *Bandwagon: A Review of the Literature.* New York: Columbia Broadcasting System, 1964.

Connell, R. W. Political socialization in the American family: The evidence re-examined. *Public Opinion Quarterly,* 1972, 36, 323–333.

Constantinople, A. Masculinity-femininity: An exception to the famous dictum? *Psychological Bulletin,* 1973, 80, 389–405.

Converse, P. E. Information flow and the stability of partisan attitudes. *Public Opinion Quarterly,* 1962, 26, 578–599.

Converse, P. E. The nature of belief systems in mass publics. In D. Apter (Ed.), *Ideology and Discontent.* New York: Free Press, 1964. Pp. 206–261.

Converse, P. E., Campbell, A., Miller, W. E., & Stokes, D. E. Stability and change in 1960: A reinstating election. *American Political Science Review,* 1961, 55, 269–280.

Converse, P. E., & Dupeux, G. Politicization of the electorate in France and the United States. *Public Opinion Quarterly,* 1962, 26, 1–23.

Converse, P. E., Miller, W. E., Rusk, J. G., & Wolfe, A. C. Continuity and change in American politics: Parties and issues in the 1968 election. *American Political Science Review,* 1969, 63, 1083–1105.

Cook, S. W. Motives in a conceptual analysis of attitude-related behavior. *Nebraska Symposium on Motivation,* 1969, 17, 179–231.

Cook, S. W., & Selltiz, C. A multiple-indicator approach to attitude measurement. *Psychological Bulletin,* 1964, 62, 36–55.

Cook, T. D., Bean, J. R., Calder, B. J., Frey, R., Krovetz, M. L., & Reisman, S. R. Demand characteristics and three conceptions of the frequently deceived subject. *Journal of Personality and Social Psychology,* 1970, 14, 185–194.

Cook, T., & Insko, C. Persistence of attitude change as a function of conclusion re-exposure: A laboratory-field experiment. *Journal of Personality and Social Psychology,* 1968, 9, 322–328.

Coombs, C. H. Psychological scaling without a unit of measurement. *Psychological Review*, 1950, 57, 145–158.

Costantini, E., & Hanf, K. Environmental concern and Lake Tahoe: A study of elite perceptions, backgrounds, and attitudes. *Environment and Behavior*, 1972, 4, 209–242.

Couch, A., & Keniston, K. Yeasayers and naysayers: Agreeing response set as a personality variable. *Journal of Abnormal and Social Psychology*, 1960, 60, 151–174.

Creer, R. N., Gray, R. M., & Treshow, M. Differential responses to air pollution as an environmental health problem. *Journal of the Air Pollution Control Association*, 1970, 20, 814–818.

Crespi, I. The structural basis for right-wing conservatism: The Goldwater case. *Public Opinion Quarterly*, 1965, 29, 523–543.

Crespi, I. What kinds of attitude measures are predictive of behavior? *Public Opinion Quarterly*, 1971, 35, 327–334.

Crittenden, J. Aging and party affiliation. *Public Opinion Quarterly*, 1962, 26, 648–657.

Crittenden, J. Reply to Cutler. *Public Opinion Quarterly*, 1969, 33, 589–591.

Cronbach, L. J. Beyond the two disciplines of scientific psychology. *American Psychologist*, 1975, 30, 116–127.

Cronbach, L. J., & Furby, L. How should we measure "change"—or should we? *Psychological Bulletin*, 1970, 74, 68–80.

Crooks, R. C. The effects of an interracial preschool program upon racial preference, knowledge of racial differences, and racial identification. *Journal of Social Issues*, 1970, 26(4), 137–144.

Crossley, H. M. Honesty with respondents and interviewers. *Public Opinion Quarterly*, 1971, 35, 476–478.

Crowne, D. P., & Marlowe, D. *The Approval Motive.* New York: Wiley, 1964.

Culbertson, F. M. Modification of an emotionally held attitude through role playing. *Journal of Abnormal and Social Psychology*, 1957, 54, 230–234.

Curtin, R. T. Consumer adaptation to energy shortages. *Journal of Energy and Development*, 1976, 2(1).

Cutler, N. E. Generation, maturation, and party affiliation: A cohort analysis. *Public Opinion Quarterly*, 1969, 33, 583–588.

Cutlip, S. C. Content and flow of AP news—From trunk to TTS to reader. *Journalism Quarterly*, 1954, 31, 434–446.

D'Andrade, R. G. Sex differences and cultural institutions. In E. E. Maccoby (Ed.), *The Development of Sex Differences.* Stanford, Calif.: Stanford University Press, 1966. Pp. 174–204.

Dawson, P. A., & Zinser, J. E. Broadcast expenditures and electoral outcomes in the 1970 congressional elections. *Public Opinion Quarterly*, 1971, 35, 398–402.

Declercq, E., Hurley, T. L., & Luttbeg, N. R. Voting in American presidential elections: 1956–1972. In S. A. Kirkpatrick (Ed.), *American Electoral Behavior: Change and Stability.* Beverly Hills, Calif.: Sage, 1975. Pp. 9–33.

DeFleur, M. L., & Westie, F. R. Verbal attitudes and overt acts: An experiment on the salience of attitudes. *American Sociological Review,* 1958, 23, 667–673.

DeFleur, M. L., & Westie, F. R. Attitude as a scientific concept. *Social Forces,* 1963, 42, 17–31.

DeGroot, I., Loring, W., Rihm, A., Jr., Samuels, S. W., & Winkelstein, W. J., Jr. People and air pollution: A study of attitudes in Buffalo, New York. *Air Pollution Control Association Journal,* 1966, 16, 245–247.

Dentler, R. A., & Monroe, L. J. The family and early adolescent conformity and deviance. *Marriage and Family Living,* 1961, 23, 241–247.

Deutsch, K. W., & Merritt, R. L. Effects of events on national and international images. In H. C. Kelman (Ed.), *International Behavior: A Social-Psychological Analysis.* New York: Holt, Rinehart & Winston, 1965. Pp. 132–187.

Deutsch, M., & Krauss, R. M. *Theories in Social Psychology.* New York: Basic Books, 1965.

Deutscher, I. Words and deeds: Social science and social policy. *Social Problems,* 1965, 13, 235–254.

Deutscher, I. *What We Say/What We Do: Sentiments and Acts.* Glenview, Ill.: Scott, Foresman, 1973.

Deutschmann, P. J. Viewing, conversation, and voting intentions. In S. Kraus (Ed.), *The Great Debates.* Bloomington: Indiana University Press, 1962. Pp. 232–252.

Dillehay, R. C. On the irrelevance of the classical negative evidence concerning the effect of attitudes on behavior. *American Psychologist,* 1973, 28, 887–891.

Dillman, D. A., & Christenson, J. A. The public value for pollution control. In W. R. Burch, Jr., N. H. Cheek, Jr., & L. Taylor (Eds.), *Social Behavior, Natural Resources, and the Environment,* New York: Harper & Row, 1972. Pp. 237–256.

Dinner, S. H., Lewkowicz, B. E., & Cooper, J. Anticipatory attitude change as a function of self-esteem and issue familiarity. *Journal of Personality and Social Psychology,* 1972, 24, 407–412.

Donohue, G. A., Olien, C. N., & Tichenor, P. J. Communities, pollution, and the fight for survival. *Journal of Environmental Education,* 1974, 6(1), 29–37.

Doob, L. W. The behavior of attitudes. *Psychological Review,* 1947, 54, 135–156.

Doob, L. W. Goebbels' principles of propaganda. *Public Opinion Quarterly,* 1950, 14, 419–442.

Downs, A. Up and down with ecology: The issue-attention cycle. *Public Interest,* 1972, 28 (Summer), 38–50.

Dreyer, E. C. Media use and electoral choices: Some political consequences of information exposure. *Public Opinion Quarterly,* 1971, 35, 544–553.

Dutton, D. G. Reactions of restaurateurs to blacks and whites violating restaurant dress requirements. *Canadian Journal of Behavioral Science,* 1971, 3, 298–302.

Eagly, A. H. Involvement as a determinant of response to favorable and unfavorable information. *Journal of Personality and Social Psychology Monograph Supplement,* 1967, 7, No. 643, 1–15.

Eagly, A. H. The comprehensibility of persuasive arguments as a determinant of opinion change. *Journal of Personality and Social Psychology*, 1974, 29, 758–773.

Eagly, A. H., & Manis, M. Evaluation of message and communication as a function of involvement. *Journal of Personality and Social Psychology*, 1966, 3, 483–485.

Easton, D., & Dennis, J. The child's image of government. *Annals of the American Academy of Political and Social Science*, 1965, 361, 40–57.

Easton, D., & Dennis, J. *Children in the Political System: Origins of Political Legitimacy.* New York: McGraw-Hill, 1969.

Edelman, M. *The Symbolic Uses of Politics.* Urbana, Ill.: University of Illinois Press, 1964.

Edwards, A. L. *Techniques of Attitude Scale Construction.* New York: Appleton-Century-Crofts, 1957.

Edwards, A. L. The assessment of human motives by means of personality scales. In D. Levine (Ed.), *Nebraska Symposium on Motivation* (Vol. 12). Lincoln: University of Nebraska Press, 1964. Pp. 135–162.

Edwards, A. L., & Kilpatrick, F. P. A technique for the construction of attitude scales. *Journal of Applied Psychology*, 1948, 32, 374–384.

Efron, E. *The News Twisters.* Los Angeles: Nash Publishing, 1971.

Ehrlich, C. The male sociologist's burden: The place of women in marriage and family texts. *Journal of Marriage and the Family*, 1971, 33, 421–430.

Ehrlich, J., & Riesman, D. Age and authority in the interview. *Public Opinion Quarterly*, 1961, 25, 39–56.

Ehrlich, P. R., & Ehrlich, A. H. *Population, Resources, Environment: Issues in Human Ecology.* San Francisco: Freeman, 1970.

Eiser, J. R., & Stroebe, W. *Categorization and Social Judgement.* London: Academic Press, 1972.

Eitzen, D. S. Social class, status inconsistency and political attitudes. *Social Science Quarterly*, 1970, 51, 602–609.

Eitzen, D. S. Status inconsistency and consistency of political beliefs. *Public Opinion Quarterly*, 1972, 36, 541–548.

Eldersveld, S. J. Experimental propaganda techniques and voting behavior. *American Political Science Review*, 1956, 50, 154–165.

Elms, A. C. Role playing, incentive, and dissonance. *Psychological Bulletin*, 1967, 68, 132–148.

Epstein, E. J. *News from Nowhere: Television and the News.* New York: Random House, 1973.

Epstein, R., & Komorita, S. Childhood prejudice as a function of parental ethnocentrism, punitiveness, and outgroup characteristics. *Journal of Personality and Social Psychology*, 1966, 3, 259–264.

Erskine, H. G. The polls: The informed public. *Public Opinion Quarterly*, 1962, 26, 669–677.

Erskine, H. G. The polls: Textbook knowledge. *Public Opinion Quarterly*, 1963, 27, 133–141. (a)

Erskine, H. G. The polls: Exposure to information. *Public Opinion Quarterly*, 1963, 27, 491–500. (b)

Erskine, H. G. The polls: Exposure to international information. *Public Opinion Quarterly*, 1963, 27, 658–662. (c)

Erskine, H. The polls: More on the population explosion and birth control. *Public Opinion Quarterly*, 1967, 31, 303–313.

Erskine, H. The polls: Women's role. *Public Opinion Quarterly*, 1971, 35, 275–290.

Erskine, H. The polls: Pollution and its costs. *Public Opinion Quarterly*, 1972, 36, 120–135. (a)

Erskine, H. The polls: Gun control. *Public Opinion Quarterly*, 1972, 36, 455–469. (b)

Erskine, H. The polls: Hopes, fears, and regrets. *Public Opinion Quarterly*, 1973, 37, 132–145. (a)

Erskine, H. The polls: Presidential power. *Public Opinion Quarterly*, 1973, 37, 488–503. (b)

Erskine, H. The polls: Corruption in government. *Public Opinion Quarterly*, 1973, 37, 628–644. (c)

Etzioni, A. Social-psychological aspects of international relations. In G. Lindzey & E. Aronson (Eds.), *The Handbook of Social Psychology* (2nd ed.). Vol. 5. Reading, Mass.: Addison-Wesley, 1969. Pp. 538–601.

Evans, R. I., Rozelle, R. M., Lasater, T. M., Dembroski, T. M., & Allen, B. P. Fear arousal, persuasion, and actual versus implied behavioral change: New perspective utilizing a real-life dental hygiene program. *Journal of Personality and Social Psychology*, 1970, 16, 220–227.

Faich, R. G., & Gale, R. P. The environmental movement: From recreation to politics. *Pacific Sociological Review*, 1971, 14, 270–287.

Farnsley, C. P. Polls as a tool of government. *Public Opinion Quarterly*, 1965, 29, 463–464.

Farrell, W. *The Liberated Man: Beyond Masculinity: Freeing Men and Their Relationships with Women.* New York: Random House, 1974.

Fawcett, J. T. *Psychology and Population: Behavioral Research Issues in Fertility and Family Planning.* New York: The Population Council, 1970.

Fawcett, J. T. (Ed.). *Psychological Perspectives on Population.* New York: Basic Books, 1973.

Fawcett, J. T., & Bornstein, M. H. Modernization, individual modernity, and fertility. In J. T. Fawcett (Ed.), *Psychological Perspectives on Population.* New York: Basic Books, 1973. Pp. 106–131.

Feather, N. T. Cigarette smoking and lung cancer: A study of cognitive dissonance. *Australian Journal of Psychology,* 1962, 14, 55–64.

Feather, N. T. A structural balance approach to the analysis of communication effects. In L. Berkowitz (Ed.), *Advances in Experimental Social Psychology* (Vol. 3). New York: Academic Press, 1967. Pp. 100–166.

Federal Communications Commission. *Survey of Political Broadcasting: Primary and*

General Election Campaigns of 1970. Washington, D. C.: Federal Communications Commission, 1971.

Felson, M., & Sudman, S. The accuracy of presidential-preference primary polls. *Public Opinion Quarterly*, 1975, 39, 232–236.

Ferree, M. M. A woman for President? Changing responses: 1958–1972. *Public Opinion Quarterly*, 1974, 38, 390–399.

Ferriss, A. L. The social and personality correlates of outdoor recreation. *Annals of the American Academy of Political and Social Science,* 1970, 389, 46–55.

Festinger, L. Laboratory experiments. In L. Festinger & D. Katz (Eds.), *Research Methods in the Behavioral Sciences.* New York: Dryden, 1953. Pp. 136–172.

Festinger, L. *A Theory of Cognitive Dissonance.* Stanford, Calif.: Stanford University Press, 1957.

Festinger, L. (Ed.). *Conflict, Decision, and Dissonance.* Stanford, Calif.: Stanford University Press, 1964.

Festinger, L., & Carlsmith, J. M. Cognitive consequences of forced compliance. *Journal of Abnormal and Social Psychology*, 1959, 58, 203–210.

Festinger, L., Riecken, H. W., & Schachter, S. *When Prophecy Fails: A Social and Psychological Study of a Modern Group that Predicted the Destruction of the World.* New York: Harper, 1956.

Fiedler, F. E., & Fiedler, J. Port noise complaints: Verbal and behavioral reactions to airport-related noise. *Journal of Applied Psychology*, 1975, 60, 498–506.

Fiedler, F. E., Fiedler, J., & Campf, S. Who speaks for the community? *Journal of Applied Social Psychology*, 1971, 1, 324–333.

Field, J. O., & Anderson, R. E. Ideology in the public's conceptualization of the 1964 election. *Public Opinion Quarterly*, 1969, 33, 380–398.

Field, M. D. The researcher's view. *Public Opinion Quarterly*, 1971, 35, 342–346.

Field, M. D. The political process and the research process. *Public Opinion Quarterly*, 1973, 37, 440.

Field, M. D. Abortion support growing, poll finds. *Los Angeles Times*, April 27, 1976, Part II, p. 5.

Fillenbaum, S., & Frey, R. More on the "faithful" behavior of suspicious subjects. *Journal of Personality*, 1970, 38, 43–51.

Fishbein, M. An investigation of the relationships between beliefs about an object and attitude towards that object. *Human Relations*, 1963, 16, 233–239.

Fishbein, M., & Ajzen, I. Attitudes and opinions. *Annual Review of Psychology,* 1972, 23, 487–544.

Fishbein, M., & Ajzen, I. Attitudes toward objects as predictors of single and multiple behavioral criteria. *Psychological Review*, 1974, 81, 59–74.

Fishbein, M., & Ajzen, I. *Belief, Attitude, Intention, and Behavior: An Introduction to Theory and Research.* Reading, Mass.: Addison-Wesley, 1975.

Fitzsimmons, S. J., & Osburn, H. G. The impact of social issues and public affairs television documentaries. *Public Opinion Quarterly*, 1968, 32, 379–397.

Free, L. A., & Cantril, H. *The Political Beliefs of Americans: A Study of Public Opinion.* New Brunswick, N. J.: Rutgers University Press, 1967.

Freedman, J. L. Attitudinal effects of inadequate justification. *Journal of Personality*, 1963, 31, 371–385.

Freedman, J. L. Involvement, discrepancy, and change. *Journal of Abnormal and Social Psychology*, 1964, 69, 290–295.

Freeman, J. The origins of the women's liberation movement. In J. Huber (Ed.), *Changing Women in a Changing Society*. Chicago: University of Chicago Press, 1973. Pp. 30–49.

Frenkel-Brunswik, E., & Havel, J. Prejudice in the interviews of children: Attitudes toward minority groups. *Journal of Genetic Psychology*, 1953, 82, 91–136.

Fried, S. B., Gumpper, D. C., & Allen, J. C. Ten years of social psychology: Is there a growing commitment to field research? *American Psychologist*, 1973, 28, 155–156.

Friedan, B. *The Feminine Mystique*. New York: Dell, 1963.

Friedrich, L. K., & Stein, A. H. Pro-social television and young children: The effects of verbal labeling and role playing on learning and behavior. *Child Development*, 1975, 46, 27–38.

Funkhouser, G. R. The issues of the sixties: An exploratory study in the dynamics of public opinion. *Public Opinion Quarterly*, 1973, 37, 62–75.

Gallup, G. *A Guide to Public Opinion Polls* (2nd ed.). Princeton, N. J.: Princeton University Press, 1948.

Gallup, G. Polls and the political process—Past, present, and future. *Public Opinion Quarterly*, 1965, 29, 544–549.

Gallup, G. H. *The Gallup Poll: Public Opinion 1935–1971*. New York: Random House, 1972.

Gallup Opinion Index. Most important problem. August, 1972, Report No. 86, p. 12. (a)

Gallup Opinion Index. Most important problem. October, 1972, Report No. 88, p. 9. (b)

Gallup Opinion Index. Most important problems. October, 1973, Report No. 100, p. 11.

Gallup Opinion Index. Few find energy controls too strict; wide compliance found. January, 1974, Report No. 103, p. 8. (a)

Gallup Opinion Index. Public attitudes are split over court abortion ruling. April, 1974, Report No. 106, pp. 22–24. (b)

Gallup Opinion Index. Income needs and food expenditures hit highs. April, 1974, Report No. 106, pp. 25–26. (c)

Gallup Opinion Index. Large families falling from favor here as well as abroad. May, 1974, Report No. 107, pp. 25–28. (d)

Gallup Opinion Index. Most important problem. October, 1974, Report No. 112, p. 15. (e)

Gallup Opinion Index. Public opinion referendum. November, 1974, Report No. 113, pp. 1–17. (f)

Gallup Opinion Index. The economy. Most important problem. April, 1975, Report No. 118, pp. 1–2. (a)

Gallup Opinion Index. Stage of pregnancy is key to public approval of abortion. July, 1975, Report No. 121, pp. 11–13. (b)

Gallup Opinion Index. Special section: College students. September, 1975, Report No. 123, pp. 12–24. (c)

Gallup Opinion Index. The presidency. November-December, 1975, Report No. 125. (d)

Gallup Opinion Index. Most important problem. February, 1976, Report No. 127, p. 3.

Geschwender, J. A. Continuities in theories of status consistency and cognitive dissonance. *Social Forces,* 1967, 46, 160–171.

Gilbert, G. M. Stereotype persistence and change among college students. *Journal of Abnormal and Social Psychology,* 1951, 46, 245–254.

Gillig, P. M., & Greenwald, A. G. Is it time to lay the sleeper effect to rest? *Journal of Personality and Social Psychology,* 1974, 29, 132–139.

Glenn, N. D. Class and party support in the United States: Recent and emerging trends. *Public Opinion Quarterly,* 1973, 37, 1–20.

Glenn, N. D., & Simmons, J. L. Are regional cultural differences diminishing? *Public Opinion Quarterly,* 1967, 31, 176–193.

Goldberg, M. E., & Gorn, G. J. Children's reactions to television advertising: An experimental approach. *Journal of Consumer Research,* 1974, 1, 69–75.

Goldman, P. *Report from Black America.* New York: Simon & Schuster, 1970.

Goldner, F. H. Public opinion and survey research: A poor mix. *Public Opinion Quarterly,* 1971, 35, 447–448.

Goodman, M. E. *Race Awareness in Young Children* (Rev. ed.). New York: Crowell Collier, 1964.

Goodwin, L., & Tu, J. The social psychological basis for public acceptance of the Social Security system: The role for social research in public policy formation. *American Psychologist,* 1975, 30, 875–883.

Gore, A. Political public opinion polls. *Congressional Record,* Aug, 22, 1960, 106, 16958–16965.

Gornick, V., & Moran, B. K. (Eds.). *Woman in Sexist Society: Studies in Power and Powerlessness.* New York: Basic Books, 1971.

Gough, H. G. A factor analysis of contraceptive preferences. *Journal of Psychology,* 1973, 84, 199–210.

Gough, H. G. An attitude profile for studies of population psychology. *Journal of Research in Personality,* 1975, 9, 122–135.

Graber, D. The press as opinion resource during the 1968 Presidential campaign. *Public Opinion Quarterly,* 1971, 35, 168–182.

Greeley, A. M. Political attitudes among American white ethnics. *Public Opinion Quarterly,* 1972, 36, 213–220.

Greeley, A. M., & Sheatsley, P. B. Changing attitudes of whites toward blacks. *Public Opinion Quarterly,* 1972, 36, 432–433.

Greenberg, B. S. Diffusion of news of the Kennedy assassination. *Public Opinion Quarterly,* 1964, 28, 225–232.

Greenberg, E. S. (Ed.). *Political Socialization.* New York: Atherton, 1970.

Greenstein, F. I. *Children and Politics.* New Haven, Conn.: Yale University Press, 1965.

Greenwald, A. G., Brock, T. C., & Ostrom, T. M. (Eds.). *Psychological Foundations of Attitudes.* New York: Academic Press, 1968.

Greenwald, H. J., & Oppenheim, D. B. Reported magnitude of self-misidentification among Negro children—Artifact? *Journal of Personality and Social Psychology,* 1968, 8, 49–52.

Griffith, W. R. Children's perceptions of the President during Watergate: Attitudes toward instrumental and expressive activities. Paper presented at meeting of Western Psychological Association, Sacramento, Calif., April 1975.

Gullahorn, J. T., & Gullahorn, J. E. An extension of the U-curve hypothesis. *Journal of Social Issues,* 1963, 19(3), 33–47.

Gump, J. P. Sex-role attitudes and psychological well-being. *Journal of Social Issues,* 1972, 28 (2), 79–92.

Guttman, L. A basis for scaling qualitative data. *American Sociological Review,* 1944, 9, 139–150.

Hacker, H. M. Women as a minority group. *Social Forces,* 1951, 30, 60–69.

Hamilton, D. L., & Bishop, G. D. Attitudinal and behavioral effects of initial integration of white suburban neighborhoods. *Journal of Social Issues,* 1976, 32, in press.

Hammond, K. R. Measuring attitudes by error-choice: An indirect method. *Journal of Abnormal and Social Psychology,* 1948, 43, 38–48.

Harding, J., Proshansky, H., Kutner, B., & Chein, I. Prejudice and ethnic relations. In G. Lindzey & E. Aronson (Eds.), *The Handbook of Social Psychology* (2nd ed.). Vol. 5. Reading, Mass.: Addison-Wesley, 1969, Pp. 1–76.

Hardyck, J. A., & Braden, M. Prophecy fails again: A report of a failure to replicate. *Journal of Abnormal and Social Psychology,* 1962, 65, 136–141.

Harris, L., & Associates. *The Harris Survey Yearbook of Public Opinion, 1970.* New York: Louis Harris and Associates, Inc., 1971.

Harris, R. J. Dissonance or sour grapes? Post-"decision" changes in ratings and choice frequencies. *Journal of Personality and Social Psychology,* 1969, 11, 334–344.

Hart, H. H. (Ed.). *Population Control: For and Against.* New York: Hart Publishing, 1973.

Hartley, S. F. *Population: Quantity vs. Quality.* Englewood Cliffs, N.J.: Prentice-Hall, 1972.

Harvey, O. J. Personality factors in resolution of conceptual incongruities. *Sociometry,* 1962, 25, 336–352.

Hastorf, A. H., Schneider, D. J., & Polefka, J. *Person Perception.* Reading, Mass.: Addison-Wesley, 1970.

Hatchett, S., & Schuman, H. White respondents and race-of-interviewer effects. *Public Opinion Quarterly,* 1975, 39, 523–528.

Heberlein, T. A., & Black, J. S. Attitudinal specificity and the prediction of behavior in a field setting. *Journal of Personality and Social Psychology,* 1976, 33, 474–479.

Heider, F. Social perception and phenomenal causality. *Psychological Review,* 1944, 51, 358–374.

Heider, F. Attitudes and cognitive organization. *Journal of Psychology,* 1946, 21, 107–112.

Heider, F. *The Psychology of Interpersonal Relations.* New York: Wiley, 1958.

Helson, H. *Adaptation-Level Theory.* New York: Harper & Row, 1964.

Hennessy, B. C. A headnote on the existence and study of political attitudes. *Social Science Quarterly,* 1970, 51, 463–476. (a)

Hennessy, B. C. *Public Opinion* (2nd ed.). Belmont, Calif.: Wadsworth, 1970. (b)

Hennessy, B. C., & Hennessy, E. R. The prediction of close elections: Comments on some 1960 polls. *Public Opinion Quarterly,* 1961, 25, 405–411.

Herz, M. F. Some psychological lessons from leaflet propaganda in World War II. *Public Opinion Quarterly,* 1949, 13, 471–486.

Hess, E. H. Attitude and pupil size. *Scientific American,* 1965, 212(4), 46–54.

Hess, R. D. The socialization of attitudes toward political authority: Some cross-national comparisons. *International Social Science Journal,* 1963, 25, 542–559.

Hess, R. D., & Torney, J. V. *The Development of Political Attitudes in Children.* Chicago: Aldine, 1967.

Hicks, R. A., & LePage, S. A pupillometric test of the bidirectional hypothesis. Paper presented at Western Psychological Association meeting, Los Angeles, April 1976.

Higbee, K. L. Fifteen years of fear arousal: Research on threat appeals: 1953–1968. *Psychological Bulletin,* 1969, 72, 426–444.

Hildum, D. C., & Brown, R. W. Verbal reinforcement and interviewer bias. *Journal of Abnormal and Social Psychology,* 1956, 53, 108–111.

Hilgard, E. R., & Payne, S. L. Those not at home: Riddle for pollsters. *Public Opinion Quarterly,* 1944, 8, 254–261.

Hill, G. 130 nations begin population talks. *New York Times,* August 20, 1974, p. 9.

Himmelweit, H. T., Oppenheim, A. N., & Vince, P. *Television and the Child.* London: Oxford University Press, 1958.

Hine, V. and Gerlach, L. P. Many concerned, few committed. *Natural History,* 1970, 79(10), 16–17 & ff.

Hoffman, L. W., & Hoffman, M. L. The value of children to parents. In J. T. Fawcett (Ed.), *Psychological Perspectives on Population.* New York: Basic Books, 1973. Pp. 19–76.

Hofstetter, C. R. Political disengagement and the death of Martin Luther King. *Public Opinion Quarterly,* 1969, 33, 174–179.

Hollander, S., Jr. Implications of the 1970 British fiasco. *Public Opinion Quarterly,* 1971, 35, 455.

Holmes, D. S., & Bennett, D. H. Experiments to answer questions raised by the use of deception in psychological research: I. Role playing as an alternative to deception; II. Effectiveness of debriefing after a deception; III. Effect of informed consent on deception. *Journal of Personality and Social Psychology,* 1974, 29, 358–367.

Holsti, O. R. The belief system and national images: A case study. *Journal of Conflict Resolution,* 1962, 6, 244–252.

Horowitz, A. D. An attitudinal model of carpooling behavior. Paper presented at American Psychological Association meeting, Chicago, August, 1975.

Horowitz, E. L., & Horowitz, R. E. Development of social attitudes in children. *Sociometry,* 1938, 1, 301–338.

Hovland, C. I. Reconciling conflicting results derived from experimental and survey studies of attitude change. *American Psychologist,* 1959, 14, 8–17.

Hovland, C. I., Harvey, O. J., & Sherif, M. Assimilation and contrast effects in communication and attitude change. *Journal of Abnormal and Social Psychology,* 1957, 55, 242–252.

Hovland, C. I., Janis, I. L., & Kelley, H. H. *Communication and Persuasion.* New Haven, Conn.: Yale University Press, 1953.

Hovland, C. I., Lumsdaine, A. A., & Sheffield, F. D. *Experiments on Mass Communication.* Princeton, N.J.: Princeton University Press, 1949.

Hovland, C. I., Mandell, W., Campbell, E. H., Brock, T., Luchins, A. S., Cohen, A. E., McGuire, W. J., Janis, I. L., Feierabend, R. L., & Anderson, N. H. *The Order of Presentation in Persuasion.* New Haven, Conn.: Yale University Press, 1957.

Hovland, C. I., & Sherif, M. Judgmental phenomena and scales of attitude measurement: Item displacement in Thurstone scales. *Journal of Abnormal and Social Psychology,* 1952, 47, 822–832.

Hraba, J., & Grant, G. Black is beautiful: A reexamination of racial preference and identification. *Journal of Personality and Social Psychology,* 1970, 16, 398–402.

Huber, J. (Ed.). *Changing Women in a Changing Society.* Chicago: University of Chicago Press, 1973.

Hyman, H. H. Do they tell the truth? *Public Opinion Quarterly,* 1944, 8, 557–559.

Hyman, H. H. *Survey Design and Analysis.* New York: Free Press, 1955.

Hyman, H. H. *Political Socialization.* Glencoe, Ill.: Free Press, 1959.

Hyman, H. H. *Secondary Analysis of Sample Surveys: Principles, Procedures, and Potentialities.* New York: Wiley, 1972.

Hyman, H. H., Cobb, W. J., Feldman, J. J., Hart, C. W., & Stember, C. H. *Interviewing in Social Research.* Chicago: University of Chicago Press, 1954.

Hyman, H. H., & Sheatsley, P. B. Some reasons why information campaigns fail. *Public Opinion Quarterly,* 1947, 11, 412–423.

Hyman, H. H., & Sheatsley, P. B. Attitudes toward desegregation. *Scientific American,* 1964, 211, 16–23.

Insko, C. A. Primacy versus recency in persuasion as a function of the timing of arguments and measures. *Journal of Abnormal and Social Psychology,* 1964, 69, 381–391.

Insko, C. A. Verbal reinforcement of attitude. *Journal of Personality and Social Psychology,* 1965, 2, 621–623.

Insko, C. A. *Theories of Attitude Change.* New York: Appleton-Century-Crofts, 1967.

Institute for Social Research. *ISR Newsletter,* Winter, 1972, 1(13).

Institute for Social Research. *ISR Newsletter,* Winter, 1974, 1(20).

Jaccard, J. J., & Davidson, A. R. Toward an understanding of family planning behaviors: An initial investigation. *Journal of Applied Social Psychology,* 1972, 2, 228–235.

Jacobson, L. I., Anderson, C. L., Berletich, M. S., & Berdahl, K. W. Construction and initial validation of a scale measuring beliefs about equal rights for men and women. *Educational and Psychological Measurement,* 1976, in press.

Jacoby, J. The construct validity of opinion leadership. *Public Opinion Quarterly,* 1974, 38, 81–89.

Jaffe, F. S. Public policy on fertility control. *Scientific American,* 1973, 229 (1), 17–23.

James, W. *Varieties of Religious Experience.* New York: Longmans, Green, 1902.

Janis, I. L., & Feshbach, S. Effects of fear-arousing communications. *Journal of Abnormal and Social Psychology,* 1953, 48, 78–92.

Janis, I. L., & Field, P. B. Sex differences and personality factors related to persuasibility. In I. L. Janis, C. I. Hovland, et al., *Personality and Persuasibility.* New Haven, Conn.: Yale University Press, 1959. Pp. 55–68.

Janis, I. L., Hovland, C. I., Field, P. B., Linton, H., Graham, E., Cohen, A. R., Rife, D., Abelson, R. P., Lesser, G. S., & King, B. T. *Personality and Persuasibility.* New Haven, Conn.: Yale University Press, 1959.

Janis, I. L., & Smith, M. B. Effects of education and persuasion on national and international images. In H. C. Kelman (Ed.), *International Behavior: A Social-Psychological Analysis.* New York: Holt, Rinehart & Winston, 1965. Pp. 190–235.

Jaros, D., Hirsch, H., & Fleron, F. J., Jr. The malevolent leader: Political socialization in an American sub-culture. *American Political Science Review,* 1968, 62, 564–575.

Jennings, M. K., & Niemi, R. G. The transmission of political values from parent to child. *American Political Science Review,* 1968, 62, 169–184.

Jennings, M. K., & Niemi, R. G. Continuity and change in political orientations: A longitudinal study of two generations. Paper presented at meeting of American Political Science Association, New Orleans, September 1973.

Jennings, M. K., & Zeigler, L. H. Class, party, and race in four types of elections: The case of Atlanta. *Journal of Politics,* 1966, 28, 391–407. (a)

Jennings, M. K., & Zeigler, L. H. Electoral strategies and voting patterns in a southern congressional district. In M. K. Jennings & L. H. Zeigler (Eds.), *The Electoral Process.* Englewood Cliffs, N.J.: Prentice-Hall, 1966. Pp. 122–138. (b)

Jervis, R. *The Logic of Images in International Relations.* Princeton, N. J.: Princeton University Press, 1970.

Johnson, H. H. Some effects of discrepancy level on responses to negative information about one's self. *Sociometry,* 1966, 29, 52–66.

Johnson, H. H., & Scileppi, J. A. Effects of ego-involvement conditions on attitude change to high and low credibility communicators. *Journal of Personality and Social Psychology,* 1969, 13, 31–36.

Jones, E. E., & Davis, K. E. From acts to dispositions: The attribution process in person perception. In L. Berkowitz (Ed.), *Advances in Experimental Social Psychology* (Vol. 2). New York: Academic Press, 1965. Pp. 219–266.

Jones, E. E. & Gerard, H. B. *Foundations of Social Psychology.* New York: Wiley, 1967.

Jones, E. E., Kanouse, D. E., Kelley, H. H., Nisbett, E. E., Valins, S., & Weiner, B. *Attribution: Perceiving the Causes of Behavior.* Morristown, N. J.: General Learning Press, 1971.

Jones, E. E., & Nisbett, R. E. The actor and the observer: Divergent perceptions of the causes of behavior. In E. E. Jones, D. E. Kanouse, H. H. Kelley, R. E. Nisbett, S. Valins, & B. Weiner, *Attribution: Perceiving the Causes of Behavior.* Morristown, N. J.: General Learning Press, 1971. Pp. 79–94.

Jones, E. E. & Sigall, H. The bogus pipeline: A new paradigm for measuring affect and attitude. *Psychological Bulletin*, 1971, 76, 349–364.

Jones, J. M. *Prejudice and Racism.* Reading, Mass.: Addison-Wesley, 1972.

Jones, R. A., Linder, D. E., Kiesler, C. A., Zanna, M., & Brehm, J. W. Internal states or external stimuli: Observers' attitude judgments and the dissonance-theory —self-persuasion controversy. *Journal of Experimental Social Psychology*, 1968, 4, 247–269.

Josephson, E., Haberman, P., & Zanes, A. High school drug behavior: A methodological report. *Public Opinion Quarterly*, 1971, 35, 462–463.

Kaplan, R. Some psychological benefits of gardening. *Environment and Behavior*, 1973, 5, 145–162.

Karlins, M., & Abelson, H. I. *Persuasion: How Opinions and Attitudes Are Changed* (2nd ed.). New York: Springer, 1970.

Karlins, M., Coffman, T. L., & Walters, G. On the fading of social stereotypes: Studies in three generations of college students. *Journal of Personality and Social Psychology*, 1969, 13, 1–16.

Katz, D. Do interviewers bias poll results? *Public Opinion Quarterly*, 1942, 6, 248–268.

Katz, D. The functional approach to the study of attitudes. *Public Opinion Quarterly*, 1960, 24, 163–204.

Katz, D., & Braly, K. Racial stereotypes of one hundred college students. *Journal of Abnormal and Social Psychology*, 1933, 28, 280–290.

Katz, D., & Stotland, E. A preliminary statement to a theory of attitude structure and change. In S. Koch (Ed.), *Psychology: A Study of a Science* (Vol. 3). New York: McGraw-Hill, 1959. Pp. 423–475.

Katz, E. The two-step flow of communication: An up-to-date report on an hypothesis. *Public Opinion Quarterly*, 1957, 21, 61–78.

Katz, E., & Feldman, J. J. The debates in the light of research: A survey of surveys. In S. Kraus (Ed.), *The Great Debates.* Bloomington: Indiana University Press, 1962. Pp. 173–223.

Katz, E., & Lazarsfeld, P. F. *Personal Influence.* Glencoe, Ill.: Free Press, 1955.

Katz, P. (Ed.). *Toward the Elimination of Racism.* Elmsford, New York: Pergamon, 1975.

Kelley, D. R., Stunkel, K. R., & Wescott, R. R. The politics of the environment: The United States, the USSR, and Japan. In L. W. Milbrath & F. R. Inscho (Eds.), *The Politics of Environmental Policy.* Beverly Hills, Calif.: Sage, 1975. Pp. 115–134.

Kelley, H. H. Attribution theory in social psychology. In D. Levine (Ed.), *Nebraska Symposium on Motivation* (Vol. 15). Lincoln: University of Nebraska Press, 1967. Pp. 192–238.

Kelley, J. The politics of school busing. *Public Opinion Quarterly*, 1974, 38, 23–39.

Kellogg, E. H., Kline, D. K., & Stepan, J. The world's laws and practices on population and sexuality education. Paper presented at Population Association of American meeting, Seattle, April, 1975.

Kelman, H. C. Compliance, identification, and internationalization: Three processes of attitude change. *Journal of Conflict Resolution*, 1958, 2, 51–60.

Kelman, H. C. (Ed.). *International Behavior: A Social-Psychological Analysis.* New York: Holt, Rinehart & Winston, 1965.

Kelman, H. C. Human use of human subjects: The problem of deception in social psychological experiments. *Psychological Bulletin*, 1967, 67, 1–11.

Kelman, H. C. Attitudes are alive and well and gainfully employed in the sphere of action. *American Psychologist*, 1974, 29, 310–324.

Kelman, H. C., & Hovland, C. I. "Reinstatement" of the communicator in delayed measurement of opinion change. *Journal of Abnormal and Social Psychology*, 1953, 48, 327–335.

Kerrick, J. S. The effect of relevant and non-relevant sources on attitude change. *Journal of Social Psychology*, 1958, 47, 15–20.

Kessel, J. H. Cognitive dimensions and political activity. *Public Opinion Quarterly*, 1965, 29, 377–389.

Kessel, J. H. *The Goldwater Coalition.* Indianapolis: Bobbs-Merrill, 1968.

Key, V. O., Jr., with Cummings, M. C., Jr. *The Responsible Electorate: Rationality in Presidential Voting.* Cambridge, Mass.: Harvard University Press, 1966.

Kidder, L. H., & Campbell, D. T. The indirect testing of social attitudes. In G. F. Summers (Ed.), *Attitude Measurement.* Chicago: Rand McNally, 1970. Pp. 333–385.

Kiesler, C. A. Commitment. In R. P. Abelson et al. (Eds.), *Theories of Cognitive Consistency: A Sourcebook.* Chicago: Rand McNally, 1968. Pp. 448–455.

Kiesler, C. A. *The Psychology of Commitment: Experiments Linking Behavior to Belief.* New York: Academic Press, 1971.

Kiesler, C. A., Collins, B. E., & Miller, N. *Attitude Change: A Critical Analysis of Theoretical Approaches.* New York: Wiley, 1969.

Kiesler, C. A. & Munson, P. A. Attitudes and opinions. *Annual Review of Psychology*, 1975, 26, 415–456.

King, B. T., & Janis, I. L. Comparison of the effectiveness of improvised vs. non-improvised role-playing in producing opinion changes. *Human Relations*, 1956, 9, 177–186.

King, R., & Schnitzer, M. Contemporary use of private political polling. *Public Opinion Quarterly*, 1968, 32, 431–436.

Kingdon, J. W. Opinion leaders in the electorate. *Public Opinion Quarterly*, 1970, 34, 256–261.

Kinsolving, C. Political polling in a primary: Sample attrition and turnout prediction. *Public Opinion Quarterly*, 1971, 35, 456–457.

Kirkpatrick, C. *The Family as Process and Institution* (2nd ed.). New York: Ronald, 1963.

Kirkpatrick, S. A. Political attitude structure and component change. *Public Opinion Quarterly*, 1970, 34, 403–407. (a)

Kirkpatrick, S. A. Political attitudes and behavior: Some consequences of attitudinal ordering. *Midwest Journal of Political Science*, 1970, 14, 1–24. (b)

Kirkpatrick, S. A., Lyons, W., & Fitzgerald, M. R. Candidates, parties, and issues in the American electorate: Two decades of change, In S. A. Kirkpatrick (Ed.), *American Electoral Behavior: Change and Stability.* Beverly Hills, Calif.: Sage, 1975. Pp. 35–71.

Kirschner, B. F. Introducing students to women's place in society. In J. Huber (Ed.), *Changing Women in a Changing Society.* Chicago: University of Chicago Press, 1973. Pp. 289–292.

Kirscht, J. P., & Dillehay, R. C. *Dimensions of Authoritarianism: A Review of Research and Theory.* Lexington: University of Kentucky Press, 1967.

Kitay, P. M. A comparison of the sexes in their attitudes and beliefs about women. *Sociometry*, 1940, 34, 399–407.

Kitt, A. S., & Gleicher, D. B. Determinants of voting behavior: A progress report on the Elmira election study. *Public Opinion Quarterly*, 1950, 14, 393–412.

Klapper, J. T. *The Effects of Mass Communication.* Glencoe, Ill.: Free Press, 1960.

Klapper, J. T. The social effects of mass communication. In W. Schramm (Ed.), *The Science of Human Communication.* New York: Basic Books, 1963. Pp. 65–76.

Klecka, W. E. Applying political generations to the study of political behavior: A cohort analysis. *Public Opinion Quarterly*, 1971, 35, 358–373.

Kline, F. G. Sources and impact of political information in the 1972 election. *Public Opinion Quarterly*, 1973, 37, 449–450.

Klineberg, O. *The Human Dimension in International Relations.* New York: Holt, Rinehart & Winston, 1964.

Knapp, M. J., & Alston, J. P. White parental acceptance of varying degrees of school desegregation: 1965 and 1970. *Public Opinion Quarterly*, 1972, 36, 585–591.

Knox, R. E., & Inkster, J. A. Postdecision dissonance at post time. *Journal of Personality and Social Psychology*, 1968, 8, 319–323.

Kohlenberg, R., Phillips, T., & Proctor, W. A behavioral analysis of peaking in residential electrical energy consumers. Paper presented at American Psychological Association meeting, Chicago, August, 1975.

Komarovsky, M. Cultural contradictions and sex roles: The masculine case. In J. Huber (Ed.), *Changing Women in a Changing Society.* Chicago: University of Chicago Press, 1973. Pp. 111–122.

Kothandapani, V. Validation of feeling, belief, and intention to act as three components of attitude and their contribution to prediction of contraceptive behavior. *Journal of Personality and Social Psychology*, 1971, 19, 321–333.

Kramer, G. H. The effects of precinct-level canvassing on voter behavior. *Public Opinion Quarterly*, 1970, 34, 560–572.

Kraus, S. Mass communication and political behavior: A reassessment of two decades of research. *Public Opinion Quarterly*, 1972, 36, 406.

Kraut, R. E., & McConahay, J. B. How being interviewed affects voting: An experiment. *Public Opinion Quarterly*, 1973, 37, 398–406.

Krech, D., Crutchfield, R., & Ballachey, E. *Individual in Society.* New York: McGraw-Hill, 1962.

Kronus, C. L., & Van Es, J. C. The practice of environmental quality behavior: Residential, life cycle, and attitudinal effects. *Journal of Environmental Education*, in press.

Kruglanski, A. W. The human subject in the psychology experiment: Fact and artifact. In L. Berkowitz (Ed.), *Advances in Experimental Social Psychology* (Vol. 8). New York: Academic Press, 1975. Pp. 101–147.

Kulik, J. A., Stein, K. B., & Sarbin, T. R. Disclosure of delinquent behavior under conditions of anonymity and non-anonymity. *American Psychologist*, 1966, 21, 651.

Kutner, B., Wilkins, C., & Yarrow, P. R. Verbal attitudes and overt behavior involving racial prejudice. *Journal of Abnormal and Social Psychology*, 1952, 47, 649–652.

Ladd, E. C., Jr. Political issues and differentiation of the citizenry parties. *Public Opinion Quarterly*, 1972, 36, 419–420.

Ladd, E. C., Jr., & Hadley, C. D. Party definition and party differentiation. *Public Opinion Quarterly*, 1973, 37, 21–34.

Ladd, E. C., Jr., & Lipset, S. M. Academics: America's most politically liberal stratum. *The Chronicle of Higher Education*, October 20, 1975, pp. 1–2.

Lambert, W. E., & Klineberg, O. *Children's Views of Foreign Peoples*. New York: Appleton-Century-Crofts, 1967.

Lane, R. E. *Political Ideology: Why the American Common Man Believes What He Does*. New York: Free Press, 1962.

Lane, R. E. Patterns of political belief. In J. N. Knutson (Ed.), *Handbook of Political Psychology*. San Francisco: Jossey-Bass, 1973. Pp. 83–116.

Lane, R. E., & Sears, D. O. *Public Opinion*. Englewood Cliffs, N. J.: Prentice-Hall, 1964.

Lang, K., & Lang, G. E. The mass media and voting. In E. Burdick & A. J. Brodbeck (Eds.), *American Voting Behavior*. Glencoe, Ill.: Free Press, 1959. Pp. 217–235.

Lang, K., & Lang, G. E. Reactions of viewers. In S. Kraus (Ed.), *The Great Debates*. Bloomington: Indiana University Press, 1962. Pp. 313–330.

Lang, K., & Lang, G. E. *Politics and Television*. Chicago: Quadrangle Books, 1968.

Langer, W. L. The black death. *Scientific American*, 1964, 210 (2), 114–121.

LaPiere, R. T. Attitudes vs. actions. *Social Forces*, 1934, 13, 230–237.

LaPiere, R. T. Type-rationalizations of group antipathy. *Social Forces*, 1936, 15, 232–237.

Lasswell, H. D. Communications research and public policy. *Public Opinion Quarterly*, 1972, 36, 301–310.

Lazarsfeld, P. F. *Radio and the Printed Page*. New York: Duell, Sloan, & Pearce, 1940.

Lazarsfeld, P. F. The controversy over detailed interviews—An offer for negotiation. *Public Opinion Quarterly*, 1944, 8, 38–60.

Lazarsfeld, P. F., Berelson, B., & Gaudet, H. *The People's Choice*. New York: Columbia University Press, 1948.

Lazarsfeld, P. F., & Merton, R. K. Mass communication, popular taste and organized social action. In L. Bryson (Ed.), *The Communication of Ideas*. New York: Harper, 1948, Pp. 95–118.

Lee, A. McC., & Lee, E. B. *The Fine Art of Propaganda: A Study of Father Coughlin's Speeches.* New York: Harcourt, Brace, 1939.

Lehmann, S. Personality and compliance: A study of anxiety and self-esteem in opinion and behavior change. *Journal of Personality and Social Psychology,* 1970, 15, 76–86.

Leiderman, P. H., & Shapiro, D. (Eds.). *Psychobiological Approaches to Social Behavior.* Stanford, Calif.: Stanford University Press, 1964.

Levenson, H. Perception of environmental modifiability and involvement in anti-pollution activities. *Journal of Psychology,* 1973, 84, 237–239.

Leventhal, H. Findings and theory in the study of fear communications. In L. Berkowitz (Ed.), *Advances in Experimental Social Psychology* (Vol. 5). New York: Academic Press, 1970. Pp. 119–186.

Levine, R. A. The silent majority: Neither simple nor simple-minded. *Public Opinion Quarterly,* 1971, 35, 571–577.

Levinson, D. J. Authoritarian personality and foreign policy. *Journal of Conflict Resolution,* 1957, 1, 37–47.

Lewin, K. Group decision and social change. In T. M. Newcomb & E. L. Hartley (Eds.), *Readings in Social Psychology.* New York: Holt, 1947. Pp. 330–344.

Lieberman, S. The effects of changes in roles on the attitudes of role occupants. *Human Relations,* 1956, 9, 385–402.

Lifton, R. J. *Thought Reform and the Psychology of Totalism.* New York: Norton, 1963.

Likert, R. A technique for the measurement of attitudes. *Archives of Psychology,* 1932, No. 140.

Linder, D. E., Cooper, J., & Jones, E. E. Decision freedom as a determinant of the role of incentive magnitude in attitude change. *Journal of Personality and Social Psychology,* 1967, 6, 245–254.

Lingwood, D. A. Environmental education through information-seeking: The case of an "environmental teach-in." *Environment and Behavior,* 1971, 3, 230–262.

Lippmann, W. *Public Opinion.* New York: Harcourt, Brace & World, 1922.

Lipset, S. M. The President, the polls, and Vietnam. *Trans-action,* 1966, 3(6), 19–24.

Lipson, G., & Wolman, D. Polling Americans on birth control and population. *Family Planning Perspectives,* 1972, 4, 39–42.

Litwak, E., Hooyman, N., & Warren, D. Ideological complexity and middle-American rationality. *Public Opinion Quarterly,* 1973, 37, 317–332.

London, P. The rescuers: Motivational hypotheses about Christians who saved Jews from the Nazis. In J. Macaulay & L. Berkowitz (Eds.), *Altruism and Helping Behavior: Social Psychological Studies of Some Antecedents and Consequences.* New York: Academic Press, 1970. Pp. 241–250.

Los Angeles Times. Nixon repudiates U.S. commission's obscenity report. October 16, 1970.

Los Angeles Times. Public opinion polls—An interference or a help in the electoral process? May 18, 1973, Part II, p. 11.

Los Angeles Times. Gallup Poll: Equality: The enemy is within. April, 22, 1976, Part IV, p. 5.

Luchins, A. S. Experimental attempts to minimize the impact of first impressions. In C. I. Hovland, W. Mandell, et al., *The Order of Presentation in Persuasion.* New Haven, Conn.: Yale University Press, 1957. Pp. 62–75.

Luchins, A. S., & Luchins, E. The effects of order of presentation of information and explanatory models. *Journal of Social Psychology,* 1970, 80, 63–70.

Lund, F. H. The psychology of belief: IV. The law of primacy in persuasion. *Journal of Abnormal and Social Psychology,* 1925, 20, 183–191.

Luttbeg, N. E. The structure of beliefs among leaders and the public. *Public Opinion Quarterly,* 1968, 32, 398–409.

Luttbeg, N. E. Attitude bias in community leader selection. *Social Science Quarterly,* 1970, 51, 750–754.

Lykken, D. T. The right way to use a lie detector. *Psychology Today,* March, 1975, pp. 56–60.

Maloney, M. P., & Ward, M. P. Ecology: Let's hear from the people. *American Psychologist,* 1973, 28, 583–586.

Maloney, M. P., Ward, M. P., & Braucht, G. N. A revised scale for the measurement of ecological attitudes and knowledge. *American Psychologist,* 1975, 30, 787–790.

Malthus, T. R. *Essay on the Principle of Population.* (G. Himmelfarb, Ed.). New York: Modern Library, 1960. (Originally published, 1798.)

Mann, J. H. The effect of inter-racial contact on sociometric choices and perceptions. *Journal of Social Psychology,* 1959, 50, 143–152.

Mann, L., & Janis, I. L. A follow-up study on the long-term effects of emotional role playing. *Journal of Personality and Social Psychology,* 1968, 8, 339–342.

Mann, L., Rosenthal, R., & Abeles, R. P. Early election returns and the voting behavior of adolescent voters. *Journal of Applied Social Psychology,* 1971, 1, 66–75.

Martin, J. G., & Westie, F. R. The tolerant personality. *American Sociological Review,* 1959, 24, 521–528.

Marx, G. T. *Protest and Prejudice: A Study of Belief in the Black Community.* New York: Harper & Row, 1967.

Marx, G. T. Racism and race relations. In M. Wertheimer (Ed.), *Confrontation: Psychology and the Problems of Today.* Glenview, Ill.: Scott, Foresman, 1970. Pp. 100–102.

Mason, K. O., & Bumpass, L. L. Women's sex-role attitudes in the United States, 1970. Paper presented at American Sociological Association meeting, New York, August, 1973.

Masters, W. H., & Johnson, V. E. *Human Sexual Response.* Boston: Little, Brown, 1966.

Maykovich, M. K. Correlates of racial prejudice. *Journal of Personality and Social Psychology,* 1975, 32, 1014–1020.

McArdle, J. B. *Positive and Negative Communications and Subsequent Attitude and Behavior Change in Alcoholics.* Unpublished doctoral dissertation, University of Illinois, 1972.

McClosky, H. Conservatism and personality. *American Political Science Review,* 1958, 42, 27–45.

McClosky, H. Consensus and ideology in American politics. *American Political Science Review,* 1964, 58, 361–382.

McClosky, H. Personality and attitude correlates of foreign policy orientation. In J. N. Rosenau (Ed.), *Domestic Sources of Foreign Policy.* New York: Free Press, 1967. Pp. 51–109.

McClosky, H., Hoffman, P. J., & O'Hara, R. Issue conflict and consensus among party leaders and followers. *American Political Science Review,* 1960, 54, 406–427.

McCombs, M. E., & Shaw, D. L. The agenda-setting function of mass media. *Public Opinion Quarterly,* 1972, 36, 176–187.

McCroskey, J. C. The effects of evidence as an inhibitor of counter persuasion. *Speech Monographs,* 1970, 37, 188–194.

McCutcheon, L. E. Development and validation of a scale to measure attitude toward population control. *Psychological Reports,* 1974, 34, 1235–1242.

McEvoy, J., III. The American concern with environment. In W. R. Burch, Jr., N. H. Cheek, Jr., & L. Taylor (Eds.), *Social Behavior, Natural Resources, and the Environment.* New York: Harper & Row, 1972. Pp. 214–236.

McGuire, W. J. A syllogistic analysis of cognitive relationships. In M. J. Rosenberg et al. (Eds.), *Attitude Organization and Change: An Analysis of Consistency among Attitude Components.* New Haven, Conn.: Yale University Press, 1960. Pp. 65–111.

McGuire, W. J. Inducing resistance to persuasion. In L. Berkowitz (Ed.), *Advances in Experimental Social Psychology* (Vol. 1). New York: Academic Press, 1964. Pp. 191–229.

McGuire, W. J. Attitudes and opinions. *Annual Review of Psychology,* 1966, 17, 475–514.

McGuire, W. J. Some impending reorientations in social psychology: Some thoughts provoked by Kenneth Ring. *Journal of Experimental Social Psychology,* 1967, 3, 124–139.

McGuire, W. J. Personality and attitude change: An information-processing theory. In A. G. Greenwald, T. C. Brock, & T. M. Ostrom (Eds.), *Psychological Foundations of Attitudes.* New York: Academic Press, 1968. Pp. 171–196. (a)

McGuire, W. J. Personality and susceptibility to social influence. In E. F. Borgatta & W. W. Lambert (Eds.), *Handbook of Personality Theory and Research.* Chicago: Rand McNally, 1968. Pp. 1130–1187. (b)

McGuire, W. J. The nature of attitudes and attitude change. In G. Lindzey & E. Aronson (Eds.), *The Handbook of Social Psychology* (2nd ed.). Vol. 3. Reading, Mass.: Addison-Wesley, 1969. Pp. 136–314.

McGuire, W. J. The yin and yang of progress in social psychology: Seven koan. *Journal of Personality and Social Psychology,* 1973, 26, 446–456.

McKee, J. P., & Sherriffs, A. C. The differential evaluation of males and females. *Journal of Personality,* 1957, 25, 356–371.

McNemar, Q. Opinion-attitude methodology. *Psychological Bulletin,* 1946, 43, 289–374.

Mead, M. *Sex and Temperament in Three Primitive Societies.* New York: Morrow, 1935.

Meadows, D. H., Meadows, D., Randers, J., & Behrens, W. W., III. *The Limits to Growth.* New York: Signet, 1972.

Medalia, N. Z. Air pollution as a socio-environmental health problem: A survey report. *Journal of Health and Human Behavior,* 1964, 5, 154–165.

Mednick, M. T. S., & Weissman, H. The psychology of women—Selected topics. *Annual Review of Psychology,* 1975, 26, 1–18.

Mendelsohn, H. Some reasons why information campaigns can succeed. *Public Opinion Quarterly,* 1973, 37, 50–61.

Mendelsohn, H., & Crespi, I. *Polls, Television, and the New Politics.* Scranton, Pa.: Chandler, 1970.

Menninger, K. *Love Against Hate.* New York: Harcourt, Brace, & World, 1942.

Merritt, R. L. Visual representation of mutual friendliness. In R. L. Merritt & D. J. Puchala (Eds.), *Western European Perspectives on International Affairs: Public Opinion Studies and Evaluations.* New York: Praeger, 1968. Pp. 111–141.

Merritt, R. L., & Puchala, D. J. (Eds.). *Western European Perspectives on International Affairs: Public Opinion Studies and Evaluations.* New York: Praeger, 1968.

Merton, R. *Social Theory and Social Structure.* Glencoe, Ill.: Free Press, 1957.

Middleton, R. Fertility values in American magazine fiction, 1916–1956. *Public Opinion Quarterly,* 1960, 24, 139–143.

Milbrath, L. W. Latent origins of liberalism-conservatism and party identification: A research note. *Journal of Politics,* 1962, 24, 679–688.

Milbrath, L. W., & Inscho, F. R. The environmental problem as a political problem: An agenda of environmental concerns for political scientists. In L. W. Milbrath & F. R. Inscho (Eds.), *The Politics of Environmental Policy.* Beverly Hills, Calif.: Sage, 1975. Pp. 7–34.

Miller, A. G. Role playing: An alternative to deception? A review of the evidence. *American Psychologist,* 1972, 27, 623–636.

Miller, A. H., Miller, W. E., Raine, A. S., & Brown, T. A. *A Majority Party in Disarray: Policy Polarization in the 1972 Election.* Ann Arbor, Mich.: Center for Political Studies, 1973.

Miller, N. Involvement and dogmatism as inhibitors of attitude change. *Journal of Experimental Social Psychology,* 1965, 1, 121–132.

Miller, N., & Campbell, D. T. Recency and primacy in persuasion as a function of the timing of speeches and measurement. *Journal of Abnormal and Social Psychology,* 1959, 59, 1–9.

Miller, N., & Levy, B. H. Defaming and agreeing with the communicator as a function of emotional arousal, communication extremity, and evaluative set. *Sociometry,* 1967, 30, 158–175.

Miller, W. E. The political behavior of the electorate. In E. Latham et al. (Eds.), *American Government Annual, 1960–1961.* New York: Holt, Rinehart & Winston, 1960. Pp. 40–48.

Miller, W. E., & Stokes, D. E. Constituency influence in Congress. *American Political Science Review,* 1963, 57, 45–56.

Mills, J., & Harvey, J. Opinion change as a function of when information about the communicator is received and whether he is attractive or expert. *Journal of Personality and Social Psychology,* 1972, 21, 52–55.

Milne, R. S., & Mackenzie, H. C. *Marginal Seat, 1955*. London: Hansard Society for Parliamentary Government, 1958.

Minard, R. D. Race relations in the Pocahontas Coal Field. *Journal of Social Issues,* 1952, 8(1), 29–44.

Mitofsky, W. J. Who voted for Wallace? *Public Opinion Quarterly,* 1969, 33, 444–445.

Molish, H. B. Projective methodologies. *Annual Review of Psychology,* 1972, 23, 577–614.

Molotch, H. The radicalization of everyone? In P. Orleans & W. R. Ellis, Jr. (Eds.), *Race, Change, and Urban Society.* Beverly Hills, Calif.: Sage, 1971. Pp. 517–560.

Money, J., & Ehrhardt, A. *Man and Woman, Boy and Girl.* Baltimore: Johns Hopkins University Press, 1972.

Morris, M. Newspapers and the new feminists: Blackout as social control? *Journalism Quarterly,* 1973, 50, 37–42.

Morris, M. I enjoy being a girl: The persistence of stereotypic views of sex roles. Paper presented at American Sociological Association meeting, Montreal, Canada, August, 1974.

Morrissette, J. O. An experimental study of the theory of structural balance. *Human Relations,* 1958, 11, 239–254.

Mosteller, F., Hyman, H., McCarthy, P. J., Marks, E. S., & Truman, D. B. *The Pre-Election Polls of 1948.* New York: Social Science Research Council, 1949.

Mueller, J. E. Choosing among 133 candidates. *Public Opinion Quarterly,* 1970, 34, 395–402.

Mueller, J. E. Trends in popular support for the wars in Korea and Vietnam. *American Political Science Review,* 1971, 65, 358–375.

Mueller, J. E. *War, Presidents and Public Opinion.* New York: Wiley, 1973.

Murch, A. W. Public concern for environmental pollution. *Public Opinion Quarterly,* 1971, 35, 100–106.

Murphy, G., & Likert, R. *Public Opinion and the Individual: A Psychological Study of Student Attitudes on Public Questions, with a Retest Five Years Later.* New York: Harper, 1938.

Myrdal, G. *An American Dilemma: The Negro Problem and Modern Democracy.* New York: Harper, 1944.

Nagel, S. S. Incentives for compliance with environmental law. In L. W. Milbrath & F. R. Inscho (Eds.), *The Politics of Environmental Policy.* Beverly Hills, Calif.: Sage, 1975. Pp. 74–94.

National Commission on the Causes and Prevention of Violence. *To Establish Justice, To Insure Domestic Tranquility.* New York: Award Books, 1969.

National Wildlife Federation. 33d annual meeting highlights Gallup. *National Wildlife,* 1969, 7, 18–19.

Nedzi, L. N. Public opinion polls: Will legislation help? *Public Opinion Quarterly,* 1971, 35, 336–341.

Newcomb, T. M. *Personality and Social Change.* New York: Dryden, 1943.

Newcomb, T. M., Koenig, K. E., Flacks, R., & Warwick, D. P. *Persistence and*

Change: Bennington College and Its Students after 25 Years. New York: Wiley, 1967.

Newsweek. Why the pollsters failed. July 6, 1970, p. 58.

Newsweek. Never again? April 5, 1971, pp. 22, 24.

Newsweek. What America thinks of itself. December 10, 1973, pp. 40–48.

Newsweek. Pulling the plug on A-power. February 24, 1975, pp. 23–24.

Newton, N., & Newton, M. Relationship of ability to breast feed and maternal attitudes toward breast feeding. *Pediatrics,* 1950, 5, 869–875.

Nicholls, W. L., II. Methodological problems with social indicators. *Public Opinion Quarterly,* 1972, 36, 448–449.

Niemi, R. G. Political socialization. In J. N. Knutson (Ed.), *Handbook of Political Psychology.* San Francisco: Jossey-Bass, 1973. Pp. 117–138.

Nisbett, R. E., Caputo, C., Legant, P., & Maracek, J. Behavior as seen by the actor and as seen by the observer. *Journal of Personality and Social Psychology*, 1973, 27, 154–164.

Nisbett, R. E., & Gordon, A. Self-esteem and susceptibility to social influence. *Journal of Personality and Social Psychology*, 1967, 5, 268–276.

Norris, P. S. World population problem. *American Psychologist*, 1975, 30, 935.

Not Man Apart. FAA plans to let Concorde fly into New York, Washington. Mid-April, 1975, p. 8.

Nuttin, J. M., Jr. *The Illusion of Attitude Change: Towards a Response Contagion Theory of Persuasion.* London: Academic Press, 1975.

O'Keefe, G. J. A developmental analysis of political communication behavior in the young voter. *Public Opinion Quarterly*, 1973, 37, 442–443.

Opinion Research Corporation. Study on population growth reveals concern among American public. *News from Opinion Research Corporation*, 1971. P. 1.

Orne, M. T. Demand characteristics and the concept of quasi-controls. In R. Rosenthal & R. L. Rosnow (Eds.), *Artifact in Behavioral Research.* New York: Academic Press, 1969. Pp. 143–179.

Osgood, C. E. *An Alternative to War or Surrender.* Urbana: University of Illinois Press, 1962.

Osgood, C. E. Cross cultural comparability of attitude measurement via multi-lingual semantic differentials. In I. S. Steiner & M. Fishbein (Eds.), *Recent Studies in Social Psychology.* New York: Holt, Rinehart & Winston, 1965. Pp. 95–107.

Osgood, C. E., Suci, G. J., & Tannenbaum, P. H. *The Measurement of Meaning.* Urbana: University of Illinois Press, 1957.

Osgood, C. E., & Tannenbaum, P. H. The principle of congruity in the prediction of attitude change. *Psychological Review*, 1955, 62, 42–55.

Oskamp, S. Attitudes toward U.S. and Russian actions: A double standard. *Psychological Reports*, 1965, 16, 43–46.

Oskamp, S. International attitudes of British and American students: A fading double standard. *Proceedings, 80th Annual Convention, APA,* 1972, 7, 295–296. (a)

Oskamp, S. Methods of studying human behavior. In L. S. Wrightsman, *Social Psychology in the Seventies.* Monterey, Calif.: Brooks/Cole, 1972. Pp. 30–67. (b)

Oskamp, S. Social perception. In L. S. Wrightsman, *Social Psychology in the Seventies.* Monterey, Calif.: Brooks/Cole, 1972. Pp. 430–457. (c)

Oskamp, S., & Hartry, A. A factor-analytic study of the double standard in attitudes toward U.S. and Russian actions. *Behavioral Science*, 1968, 13, 178–188.

Ostlund, L. E. Interpersonal communication following McGovern's Eagleton decision. *Public Opinion Quarterly*, 1973, 37, 601–610.

Ostrom, T. M. The emergence of attitude theory: 1930–1950. In A. G. Greenwald, T. C. Brock, & T. M. Ostrom (Eds.), *Psychological Foundations of Attitudes.* New York: Academic Press, 1968. Pp. 1–32.

Pallak, M. S., & Cummings, W. Commitment and voluntary energy conservation. *Personality and Social Psychology Bulletin*, 1976, 2, 27–30.

Parelius, A. P. Emerging sex-role attitudes, expectations and strains among college women. *Journal of Marriage and the Family*, 1975, 37, 146–153.

Parry, H. J., & Crossley, H. M. Validity of responses to survey questions. *Public Opinion Quarterly*, 1950, 14, 61–80.

Patchen, M. *The American Public's View of U.S. Policy Toward China.* New York: Council on Foreign Relations, 1964.

Patterson, T. E., & McClure, R. D. Political advertising: Voter reaction. *Public Opinion Quarterly*, 1973, 37, 447–448.

Payne, S. L. *The Art of Asking Questions.* Princeton, N. J.: Princeton University Press, 1951.

Perlman, D., & Oskamp, S. The effects of picture content and exposure frequency on evaluations of Negroes and whites. *Journal of Experimental Social Psychology*, 1971, 7, 503–514.

Perry, P. K. Election survey procedures of the Gallup Poll. *Public Opinion Quarterly*, 1960, 24, 531–542.

Perry, P. K. The turnout problem in election surveys. *Public Opinion Quarterly*, 1971, 35, 455.

Peters, W. H. Who cooperates in voluntary recycling efforts? In T.V. Greer (Ed.), *Increasing Market Productivity and Conceptual and Methodological Foundations of Marketing*, 1973 Combined Proceedings, Series No. 35. American Marketing Association, 1973.

Peterson, P. D., & Koulack, D. Attitude change as a function of latitudes of acceptance and rejection. *Journal of Personality and Social Psychology*, 1969, 11, 309–311.

Peterson, R. C., & Thurstone, L. L. *Motion Pictures and the Social Attitudes of Children.* New York: Macmillan, 1933.

Pettigrew, T. F. Regional differences in anti-Negro prejudice. *Journal of Abnormal and Social Psychology*, 1959, 59, 28–36.

Pettigrew, T. F. Racially separate or together? *Journal of Social Issues*, 1969, 25(1), 43–69.

Pettigrew, T. F. Race relations. In R. Merton & R. Nisbet (Eds.), *Contemporary Social Problems.* New York: Harcourt Brace Jovanovich, 1971. Pp. 407–466.

Pettigrew, T. F., & Riley, R. T. Contextual models of school desegregation. In B. T.

King & E. McGinnies (Eds.), *Attitudes, Conflict, and Social Change.* New York: Academic Press, 1972. Pp. 155–185.

Pfister, G. Outcomes of laboratory training for police officers. *Journal of Social Issues,* 1975, 31(1), 115–121.

Phillips, D. L., & Clancy, K. J. "Modeling effects" in survey research. *Public Opinion Quarterly,* 1972, 36, 246–253.

Poffenberger, T. Methodological problems in rural and village research in family planning. Paper presented at Western Psychological Association meeting, Sacramento, April, 1975.

Pohlman, E. H. *Psychology of Birth Planning.* Cambridge, Mass.: Schenkman, 1969.

Pohlman, E. H. *Population: A Clash of Prophets.* New York: New American Library, 1973.

Pomper, G. M. Impacts on the political system. In S. A. Kirkpatrick (Ed.), *American Electoral Behavior: Change and Stability.* Beverly Hills, Calif.: Sage, 1975. Pp. 137–143.

Pool, I. deS. TV: A new dimension in politics. In E. Burdick & A. J. Brodbeck (Eds.), *American Voting Behavior.* Glencoe, Ill.: Free Press, 1959. Pp. 197–208.

Pool, I. deS. Effects of cross-national contact on national and international images. In H. C. Kelman (Ed.), *International Behavior: A Social-Psychological Analysis.* New York: Holt, Rinehart & Winston, 1965. Pp. 106–129.

Pool, I. deS. Review of *Politics and Television* by K. Lang & G. E. Lang. *Public Opinion Quarterly,* 1969, 33, 287–289.

Pool, I. deS., Abelson, R. P., & Popkin, S. L. *Candidates, Issues, and Strategies: A Computer Simulation of the 1960 Presidential Election.* Cambridge: Massachusetts Institute of Technology Press, 1964.

Pope Paul VI. *Jamais plus guerre!* In Time-Life Books, *The Pope's Visit, 1965.* New York: Time, Inc., 1965.

Poppleton, P. K., & Pilkington, G. W. A comparison of four methods of scoring an attitude scale in relation to its reliability and validity. *British Journal of Social and Clinical Psychology,* 1964, 3, 36–39.

Price, K. O., Harburg, E., & Newcomb, T. M. Psychological balance in situations of negative interpersonal attitudes. *Journal of Personality and Social Psychology,* 1966, 3, 265–270.

Putney, S., & Middleton, R. Some factors associated with student acceptance or rejection of war. *American Sociological Review,* 1962, 27, 655–667.

Rankin, R. E., & Campbell, D. T. Galvanic skin response to Negro and white experimenters. *Journal of Abnormal and Social Psychology,* 1955, 51, 30–33.

Ranney, J. C. Do the polls serve democracy? *Public Opinion Quarterly,* 1946, 10, 349–360.

Rappoport, L., & Cvetkovich, G. Opinion on Vietnam: Some findings from three studies. *Proceedings, 76th Annual Convention, APA,* 1968, 3, 381–382.

Redisch, A., & Weissbach, T. A. Traits attributed by white students to black fellow students *versus* blacks in general. *Journal of Social Psychology,* 1974, 92, 147–148.

RePass, D. E. Issue salience and party choice. *American Political Science Review*, 1971, 65, 389–400.

Report of the National Advisory Commission on Civil Disorders. New York: Bantam, 1968.

Rettig, S. Relation of social systems to intergenerational changes in moral attitudes. *Journal of Personality and Social Psychology*, 1966, 4, 409–414.

Rhine, R. J., & Polowniak, W. A. Attitude change, commitment and ego involvement. *Journal of Personality and Social Psychology*, 1971, 19, 246–250.

Rhine, R. J., & Severance, L. J. Ego-involvement, discrepancy, source credibility, and attitude change. *Journal of Personality and Social Psychology*, 1970, 16, 175–190.

Richardson, S. A. *A Study of Selected Personality Characteristics of Social Science Field Workers.* Unpublished doctoral dissertation, Cornell University, 1954.

Riddleberger, A. B., & Motz, A. B. Prejudice and perception. *American Journal of Sociology*, 1957, 62, 498–503.

Ritchie-Calder, L. World health: An ethical-economic dilemma. *Center Report*, 1974, 7, 10–12.

Robinson, D., & Rohde, S. Two experiments with an anti-Semitism poll. *Journal of Abnormal and Social Psychology*, 1946, 41, 136–144.

Robinson, J. P. *Public Information about World Affairs.* Ann Arbor, Mich.: Survey Research Center, 1967.

Robinson, J. P. The audience for national TV news programs. *Public Opinion Quarterly*, 1971, 35, 403–405.

Robinson, J. P. Perceived media bias and the 1968 vote: Can the media affect behavior after all? *Journalism Quarterly*, 1972, 49, 239–246.

Robinson, J. P. Toward a more appropriate use of Guttman scaling. *Public Opinion Quarterly*, 1973, 37, 260–267.

Robinson, J. P. Public opinion during the Watergate crisis. *Communication Research*, 1974, 1, 391–405.

Robinson, J. P., & Swinehart, J. W. World affairs and the TV audience. *Television Quarterly*, 1968, 7, 40–59.

Rogers, E. M. *Diffusion of Innovations.* Glencoe, Ill.: Free Press, 1962.

Rogers, L. *The Pollsters.* New York: Knopf, 1949.

Rokeach, M. *The Open and Closed Mind.* New York: Basic Books, 1960.

Rokeach, M. Authoritarianism scales and response bias: Comment on Peabody's paper. *Psychological Bulletin*, 1967, 67, 349–355.

Rokeach, M. *Beliefs, Attitudes, and Values: A Theory of Organization and Change.* San Francisco: Jossey-Bass, 1968.

Rokeach, M. Long-range experimental modification of values, attitudes, and behavior. *American Psychologist*, 1971, 26, 453–459.

Rokeach, M. Long-term value change initiated by computer feedback. *Journal of Personality and Social Psychology*, 1975, 32, 467–476.

Rokeach, M., & Cochrane, R. Self-confrontation and confrontation with another as determinants of long-term value change. *Journal of Applied Social Psychology*, 1972, 2, 283–292.

Rokeach, M., & McLellan, D. D. Feedback of information about the values and attitudes of self and others as determinants of long-term cognitive and behavioral change. *Journal of Applied Social Psychology*, 1972, 2, 236–251.

Rokeach, M., & Rothman, G. The principle of belief congruence and the congruity principle as models of cognitive interaction. *Psychological Review*, 1965, 72, 128–142.

Roll, C. W., Jr., & Cantril, A. H. *Polls: Their Use and Misuse in Politics.* New York: Basic Books, 1972.

Roper, E. The politics of three decades. *Public Opinion Quarterly*, 1965, 29, 368–376.

Rorvik, D. M. Beyond the pill. *Look*, 1971, 35, 17–20.

Rosen, R. Sexism in history or, writing women's history is a tricky business. *Journal of Marriage and the Family*, 1971, 33, 541–544.

Rosenberg, M. J. Cognitive structure and attitudinal affect. *Journal of Abnormal and Social Psychology*, 1956, 53, 367–372.

Rosenberg, M. J. An analysis of affective-cognitive consistency. In M. J. Rosenberg, C. I. Hovland, W. J. McGuire, R. P. Abelson, & J. W. Brehm, *Attitude Organization and Change: An Analysis of Consistency among Attitude Components.* New Haven, Conn.: Yale University Press, 1960. Pp. 15–64.

Rosenberg, M. J. Images in relation to the policy process: American public opinion on cold-war issues. In H. C. Kelman (Ed.), *International Behavior: A Social-Psychological Analysis.* New York: Holt, Rinehart & Winston, 1965. Pp. 278–334.

Rosenberg, M. J. Attitude change and foreign policy in the cold war era. In J. N. Rosenau (Ed.), *Domestic Sources of Foreign Policy.* New York: Free Press, 1967. Pp. 111–159.

Rosenberg, M. J. The conditions and consequences of evaluation apprehension. In R. Rosenthal & R. L. Rosnow (Eds.), *Artifact in Behavioral Research.* New York: Academic Press, 1969. Pp. 279–349.

Rosenberg, M. J., & Abelson, R. P. An analysis of cognitive balancing. In M. J. Rosenberg et al., *Attitude Organization and Change: An Analysis of Consistency among Attitude Components.* New Haven, Conn.: Yale University Press, 1960. Pp. 112–163.

Rosenberg, M. J., Hovland, C. I., McGuire, W. J., Abelson, R. P., & Brehm, J. W. *Attitude Organization and Change: An Analysis of Consistency among Attitude Components.* New Haven, Conn.: Yale University Press, 1960.

Rosenthal, R. *Experimenter Effects in Behavioral Research.* New York: Naiburg, 1966.

Rosenthal, R. Interpersonal expectations: Effects of the experimenter's hypothesis. In R. Rosenthal & R. L. Rosnow (Eds.), *Artifact in Behavioral Research.* New York: Academic Press, 1969. Pp. 181–277.

Rosenthal, R., & Rosnow, R. L. (Eds.). *Artifact in Behavioral Research.* New York: Academic Press, 1969. (a)

Rosenthal, R., & Rosnow, R. L. The volunteer subject. In R. Rosenthal & R. L.

Rosnow (Eds.), *Artifact in Behavioral Research*. New York: Academic Press, 1969. Pp. 59–118. (b)

Rosi, E. J. Mass and attentive opinion on nuclear weapons tests and fallout, 1954–1963. *Public Opinion Quarterly*, 1965, 29, 280–297.

Rosnow, R. L. Whatever happened to the "Law of Primacy"? *Journal of Communication*, 1966, 16, 10–31.

Rosnow, R. L., Goodstadt, B. E., Suls, J. M., & Gitter, G. A. More on the social psychology of the experiment: When compliance turns to self-defense. *Journal of Personality and Social Psychology*, 1973, 27, 337–343.

Rosnow, R. L., & Suls, J. M. Reactive effects of pretesting in attitude research. *Journal of Personality and Social Psychology*, 1970, 15, 338–343.

Rossi, P. H. Trends in voting behavior research: 1933–1963. In E. C. Dreyer & W. A. Rosenbaum (Eds.), *Political Opinion and Electoral Behavior: Essays and Studies*. Belmont, Calif.: Wadsworth, 1966. Pp. 67–78.

Rossi, P. H., & Cutright, P. The impact of party organization in an industrial setting. In M. Janowitz (Ed.), *Community Political Systems*. Glencoe, Ill.: Free Press, 1961. Pp. 81–116.

Rothschild, M. L., & Ray, M. L. Involvement and political advertising effectiveness: A laboratory repetition experiment. *Public Opinion Quarterly*, 1973, 37, 448–449.

Rotter, J. B. Generalized expectancies for internal versus external control of reinforcement. *Psychological Monographs*, 1966, 80, No. 1, Whole No. 609.

Rubin, Z., & Moore, J. C., Jr. Assessment of subjects' suspicions. *Journal of Personality and Social Psychology*, 1971, 17, 163–170.

Rule, B. G., & Renner, J. Involvement and group effects on opinion change. *Journal of Social Psychology*, 1968, 76, 189–198.

Russo, F. D. A study of bias in TV coverage of the Vietnam War: 1969 and 1970. *Public Opinion Quarterly*, 1971, 35, 539–543.

Sacramento Branch, American Association of University Women. *The Image of Women in Television*. Sacramento, Calif.: American Association of University Women, 1974.

Sargant, W. *Battle for the Mind: A Physiology of Conversion and Brainwashing*. Garden City, N.Y.: Doubleday, 1957.

Sata, L. S. Laboratory training for police officers. *Journal of Social Issues*, 1975, 31(1), 107–114.

Sattler, J. M. Racial "experimenter effects" in experimentation, testing, interviewing, and psychotherapy. *Psychological Bulletin*, 1970, 73, 137–160.

Schaffner, P., & Wandersman, A. Familiarity breeds success: A field study of exposure and voting behavior. *Personality and Social Psychology Bulletin*, 1974, 1, 88–90.

Schindeler, F., & Lanphier, C. M. Participatory democracy in Canada: Paths for survey research. *Public Opinion Quarterly*, 1969, 33, 468–469.

Schlesinger, A. M. Tides of American politics. *Yale Review*, 1939, 29, 217–230.

Schmiedeskamp, J., & Cowan, C. D. The relationship between consumer attitudes and intentions to buy. *Public Opinion Quarterly*, 1972, 36, 429–430.

Schramm, W. *Mass Media and National Development.* Stanford, Calif.: Stanford University Press, 1964.

Schramm, W., & Carter, R. F. The effectiveness of a political telethon. *Public Opinion Quarterly,* 1959, 23, 121–127.

Schramm, W., Lyle, J., & Parker, E. B. *Television in the Lives of Our Children.* Stanford, Calif.: Stanford University Press, 1961.

Schuman, H. Attitudes vs. actions *versus* attitudes vs. attitudes. *Public Opinion Quarterly,* 1972, 36, 347–354.

Schuman, H., & Hatchett, S. *Black Racial Attitudes: Trends and Complexities.* Ann Arbor, Mich.: Institute for Social Research, University of Michigan, 1974.

Schusky, J. Public awareness and concern with air pollution in the St. Louis metropolitan area. *Journal of the Air Pollution Control Association,* 1966, 16, 72–76.

Schwartz, S. H., & Tessler, R. C. A test of a model for reducing measured attitude-behavior discrepancies. *Journal of Personality and Social Psychology,* 1972, 24, 225–236.

Scientific Advisory Committee on Television and Social Behavior. *Television and Growing Up: The Impact of Televised Violence.* Report to the Surgeon General, USPHS. Washington, D.C.: U.S. Department of Health, Education, & Welfare, 1972.

Scott, J. P., & Fuller, J. F. *Genetics and Social Behavior of the Dog.* Chicago: University of Chicago Press, 1965.

Scott, W. A. Attitude change by response reinforcement: Replication and extension. *Sociometry,* 1959, 22, 328–335.

Scott, W. A. Psychological and social correlates of international images. In H. C. Kelman (Ed.), *International Behavior: A Social-Psychological Analysis.* New York: Holt, Rinehart & Winston, 1965. Pp. 71–103.

Scott, W. A. Attitude measurement. In G. Lindzey & E. Aronson (Eds.), *The Handbook of Social Psychology* (2nd ed.). Vol. 2. Reading, Mass.: Addison-Wesley, 1968. Pp. 204–273.

Scully, D., & Bart, P. A funny thing happened on the way to the orifice: Women in gynecology textbooks. In J. Huber (Ed.), *Changing Women in a Changing Society.* Chicago: University of Chicago Press, 1973. Pp. 283–288.

Sears, D. O. Political behavior. In G. Lindzey & E. Aronson (Eds.), *The Handbook of Social Psychology* (2nd ed.). Vol. 5. Reading, Mass.: Addison-Wesley, 1969. Pp. 315–458.

Sears, D. O., & Abeles, R. P. Attitudes and opinions. *Annual Review of Psychology,* 1969, 20, 253–288.

Sears, D. O., & Freedman, J. L. Selective exposure to information: A critical review. *Public Opinion Quarterly,* 1967, 31, 194–213.

Sears, D. O., & Whitney, R. E. *Political Persuasion.* Morristown, N.J.: General Learning Press, 1973.

Secord, P. F. Social psychology in search of a paradigm. Paper presented to American Psychological Association meeting, Chicago, September, 1975.

Seeman, J. Deception in psychological research. *American Psychologist,* 1969, 24, 1025–1028.

Sellers, C. The equilibrium cycle in two-party politics. *Public Opinion Quarterly,* 1965, 29, 16–38.

Selltiz, C., & Cook, S. W. Factors influencing attitudes of foreign students toward the host country. *Journal of Social Issues,* 1962, 18(1), 7–23.

Selznick, G. J., & Steinberg, S. *The Tenacity of Prejudice: Anti-Semitism in Contemporary America.* New York: Harper & Row, 1969.

Senior Scholastic. Women's rights—How real the gains? November 21, 1974, pp. 11–13, 16.

Sewell, W. R. D. Environmental perceptions and attitudes of engineers and public health officials. *Environment and Behavior,* 1971, 3, 23–59.

Sewell, W. R. D., & Foster, H. D. Environmental revival: Promise and performance. *Environment and Behavior,* 1971, 3, 123–134.

Shaw, M. E., & Costanzo, P. R. *Theories of Social Psychology.* New York: McGraw-Hill, 1970.

Shaw, M. E., & Reitan, H. T. Attribution of responsibility as a basis for sanctioning behavior. *British Journal of Social and Clinical Psychology,* 1969, 8, 217–226.

Shaw, M. E., & Wright, J. M. *Scales for the Measurement of Attitudes.* New York: McGraw-Hill, 1967.

Sheatsley, P. B. White attitudes toward the Negro. *Daedalus,* 1966, 95, 217–238.

Sheatsley, P. B., & Feldman, J. J. A national survey on public reactions and behavior. In B. S. Greenberg & E. B. Parker (Eds.), *The Kennedy Assassination and the American Public.* Stanford, Calif.: Stanford University Press, 1965. Pp. 149–177.

Sheets, T., Radlinski, A., Kohne, J., & Brunner, G. A. Deceived respondents: Once bitten, twice shy. *Public Opinion Quarterly,* 1974, 38, 261–263.

Sheldon, E. H., & Moore, W. E. (Eds.). *Indicators of Social Change: Concepts and Measurement.* New York: Russell Sage Foundation, 1968.

Sherif, C. W., Kelly, M., Rodgers, H. L., Sarup, G., & Tittler, B. I. Personal involvement, social judgment, and action. *Journal of Personality and Social Psychology,* 1973, 27, 311–327.

Sherif, C. W., Sherif, M., & Nebergall, R. E. *Attitude and Attitude Change: The Social Judgment-Involvement Approach.* Philadelphia: Saunders, 1965.

Sherif, M. Some needed concepts in the study of social attitudes. In J. G. Peatman & E. L. Hartley (Eds.) *Festschrift for Gardner Murphy.* New York: Harper, 1960. Pp. 194–213.

Sherif, M., Harvey, O. J., White, B. J., Hood, W. E., & Sherif, C. W. *Intergroup Conflict and Cooperation: The Robber's Cave Experiment.* Norman: University of Oklahoma Book Exchange, 1961.

Sherif, M., & Hovland, C. I. *Social Judgment: Assimilation and Contrast Effects in Communication and Attitude Change.* New Haven, Conn.: Yale University Press, 1961.

Sherif, M., Taub, D., & Hovland, C. I. Assimilation and contrast effects of anchoring stimuli on judgments. *Journal of Experimental Psychology,* 1958, 55, 150–155.

Sheth, J. N. A field study of attitude structure and the attitude-behavior relationship. In

J. N. Sheth (Ed.), *Models of Buyer Behavior: Conceptual, Quantitative, and Empirical*. New York: Harper & Row, 1974, Pp. 242–268.

Shively, W. P. A reinterpretation of the New Deal realignment. *Public Opinion Quarterly*, 1971, 35, 621–624.

Siegel, A. E., & Siegel, S. Reference groups, membership groups and attitude change. *Journal of Abnormal and Social Psychology*, 1957, 55, 360–364.

Silverman, I. In defense of dissonance theory: Reply to Chapanis and Chapanis. *Psychological Bulletin*, 1964, 62, 205–209.

Simon, R. J. Public attitudes toward population and pollution. *Public Opinion Quarterly*, 1971, 35, 93–99.

Simon, R. J., & Simon, J. L. Money incentives and family size: A hypothetical-question study. *Public Opinion Quarterly*, 1975, 38, 585–595.

Simons, H. W., Berkowitz, N. N., & Moyer, R. J. Similarity, credibility, and attitude change: A review and a theory. *Psychological Bulletin*, 1970, 73, 1–16.

Skedgell, R. A. How computers pick an election winner. *Trans-action*, 1966, 4(1), 42–46.

Sklar, J., & Berkov, B. The American birth rate: Evidences of a coming rise. *Science*, 1975, 189, 693–700.

Slater, R. G., Kitt, D., Widelock, D., & Kangas, P. The earth belongs to the people: Ecology and power. In R. Buckhout et al. (Eds.), *Toward Social Change: A Handbook for Those Who Will*. New York: Harper & Row, 1971. Pp. 416–419.

Smith, A. J., & Clark, R. D., III. The relationship between attitudes and beliefs. *Journal of Personality and Social Psychology*, 1973, 26, 321–326.

Smith, D. D. Cognitive consistency and the perception of others' opinions. *Public Opinion Quarterly*, 1968, 32, 1–15.

Smith, H. L., & Hyman, H. The biasing effect of interviewer expectations on survey results. *Public Opinion Quarterly*, 1950, 14, 491–506.

Smith, M. B. A psychologist's perspective on public opinion theory. *Public Opinion Quarterly*, 1971, 35, 36–43.

Smith, M. B., Bruner, J. S., & White, R. W. *Opinions and Personality*. New York: Wiley, 1956.

Smith, S. Age and sex differences in children's opinions concerning sex differences. *Journal of Genetic Psychology*, 1939, 54, 17–25.

Smith, W. S., Schueneman, J. J., & Zeidberg, L. D. Public reactions to air pollution in Nashville, Tennessee. *Journal of the Air Pollution Control Association*, 1964, 14, 418–423.

Sorrentino, R. M., & Vidmar, N. Impact of events: Short- vs. long-term effects of a crisis. *Public Opinion Quarterly*, 1974, 38, 271–279.

Spence, J. T., & Helmreich, R. The Attitudes towards Women Scale: An objective instrument to measure attitudes toward the rights and roles of women in contemporary society. *JSAS Catalog of Selected Documents in Psychology*, 1972, 2, 66.

Staats, A. W. Social behaviorism and human motivation: Principles of the attitude-reinforcer-discriminative system. In A. G. Greenwald, T. C. Brock, & T. M. Ostrom (Eds.), *Psychological Foundations of Attitudes*. New York: Academic Press, 1968. Pp. 33–66.

Stagner, R. *Psychological Aspects of International Conflict.* Belmont, Calif.: Brooks/Cole, 1967.

Stanton, H., Back, K. W., & Litwak, E. Role-playing in survey research. *American Journal of Sociology,* 1956, 62, 172–176.

Star, S. A., & Hughes, H. McG. Report of an educational campaign: The Cincinnati plan for the United Nations. *American Journal of Sociology,* 1950, 55, 389–400.

Steiner, I. D. Personality and the resolution of interpersonal disagreements. In B. A. Maher (Ed.), *Progress in Experimental Personality Research* (Vol. 3). New York: Academic Press, 1966. Pp. 195–239.

Steinmann, A. Sex roles: Twenty years of cross-cultural research. Paper presented at American Psychological Association meeting, Chicago, September, 1975.

Steinmann, A., & Fox, D. *The Male Dilemma.* New York: Jason Aronson, 1974.

Stephens, W. N. *The Family in Cross-Cultural Perspective.* New York: Holt, Rinehart & Winston, 1963.

Stinchcombe, A. L., McDill, M., & Walker, D. Is there a racial tipping point in changing schools? *Journal of Social Issues,* 1969, 25(1), 127–136.

Stokes, D. E. Party loyalty and the likelihood of deviating elections. In A. Campbell, P. E. Converse, W. E. Miller, & D. E. Stokes, *Elections and the Political Order.* New York: Wiley, 1966. Pp. 125–135. (a)

Stokes, D. E. Some dynamic elements of contests for the presidency. *American Political Science Review,* 1966, 60, 19–28. (b)

Stokes, D. E., & Miller, W. E. Party government and the saliency of Congress. *Public Opinion Quarterly,* 1962, 26, 531–546.

Storms, M. D. Videotape and the attribution process: Reversing actor's and observer's points of view. *Journal of Personality and Social Psychology,* 1973, 27, 165–175.

Streufert, S., & Sandler, S. I. A laboratory test of the mirror image hypothesis. *Journal of Applied Social Psychology,* 1971, 1, 378–397.

Stricker, L. J. The true deceiver. *Psychological Bulletin,* 1967, 68, 13–20.

Stricker, L. J., Messick, S., & Jackson, D. N. Evaluating deception in psychological research. *Psychological Bulletin,* 1969, 71, 343–351.

Sudman, S. *Reducing the Cost of Surveys.* Chicago: Aldine, 1967.

Suedfeld, P. Models of attitude change: Theories that pass in the night. In P. Suedfeld (Ed.), *Attitude Change: The Competing Views.* Chicago: Aldine Atherton, 1971. Pp. 1–62.

Suinn, R. M., & Oskamp, S. *The Predictive Validity of Projective Measures: A Fifteen-Year Evaluative Review of Research.* Springfield, Ill.: Charles C Thomas, 1969.

Sullivan, D. S., & Deiker, T. E. Subject-experimenter perceptions of ethical issues in human research. *American Psychologist,* 1973, 28, 587–591.

Swan, J. Response to air pollution: A study of attitudes and coping strategies of high school youth. *Environment and Behavior,* 1970, 2, 127–152.

Swanson, C. E., Jenkins, J., & Jones, R. L. President Truman speaks: A study of ideas vs. media. *Journalism Quarterly,* 1950, 27, 251–267.

Sweet, J. A. Differentials in the rate of fertility decline: 1960–1970. *Family Planning Perspectives,* 1974, 6, 103–107.

Tannenbaum, P. H. *Attitude toward Source and Concept as Factors in Attitude Change through Communications.* Unpublished doctoral dissertation, University of Illinois. 1953.

Tannenbaum, P. H. The congruity principal revisited: Studies in the reduction, induction, and generalization of persuasion. In L. Berkowitz (Ed.), *Advances in Experimental Social Psychology* (Vol. 3). New York: Academic Press, 1967. Pp. 270–320.

Tavris, C. Who likes women's liberation—and why: The case of the unliberated liberals. *Journal of Social Issues,* 1973, 29 (4), 175–198.

Taylor, J. B., & Parker, H. A. Graphic ratings and attitude measurement: A comparison of research tactics. *Journal of Applied Psychology,* 1964, 48, 37–42.

Thistlethwaite, D. L. Impact of disruptive external events on student attitudes. *Journal of Personality and Social Psychology,* 1974, 30, 228–242.

Thomas, W. I. The mind of woman and the lower races. *American Journal of Sociology,* 1907, 12, 435–569.

Thomas, W. I. *The Unadjusted Girl.* Boston: Little, Brown, 1923.

Thompson, K. S., & Oskamp, S. Difficulties in replicating the proselyting effect in doomsday groups. *Psychological Reports,* 1974, 35, 971–978.

Thompson, V. D., Appelbaum, M. R., & Allen, J. E. *Population Policy Acceptance: Psychological Determinants.* Chapel Hill, N. C.: Carolina Population Center, 1974.

Thurstone, L. L. Attitudes can be measured. *American Journal of Sociology,* 1928, 33, 529–554.

Thurstone, L. L., & Chave, E. J. *The Measurement of Attitude.* Chicago: University of Chicago Press, 1929.

Tichenor, P. J., Donohue, G. A., & Olien, C. N. Mass media flow and differential growth in knowledge. *Public Opinion Quarterly,* 1970, 34, 159–170.

Tichenor, P. J., Donohue, C. N., Olien, C. N., & Bowers, J. K. Environment and public opinion. *Journal of Environmental Education,* 1971, 2(4), 38–42.

Tittle, C. R., & Hill, R. J. Attitude measurement and prediction of behavior: An evaluation of conditions and measurement techniques. *Sociometry,* 1967, 30, 199–213.

Tolley, H., Jr. *Children and War: Political Socialization to International Conflict.* New York: Teachers College Press, Columbia University, 1973.

Trager, H. G., & Yarrow, M. R. *They Learn What They Live: Prejudice in Young Children.* New York: Harper, 1952.

Treiman, D. J. Status discrepancy and prejudice. *American Journal of Sociology,* 1966, 71, 651–664.

Trenaman, J., & McQuail, D. *Television and the Political Image.* London: Methuen, 1961.

Triandis, H. C. Exploratory factor analyses of the behavioral component of social attitudes. *Journal of Abnormal and Social Psychology,* 1964, 68, 420–430.

Triandis, H. C. *Attitude and Attitude Change.* New York: Wiley, 1971.

Triandis, H. C., & Triandis, L. M. A cross-cultural study of social distance. *Psychological Monographs,* 1962, 76, No. 21 (Whole No. 540).

Troldahl, V. C., & Van Dam, R. Face-to-face communication about major topics in the news. *Public Opinion Quarterly*, 1965, 29, 626–634.

Tuchman, S., & Coffin, T. E. The influence of election night television broadcasts in a close election. *Public Opinion Quarterly*, 1971, 35, 315–326.

UNESCO. *Rural Television in Japan.* Paris: UNESCO, 1960.

Union of Concerned Scientists. *The Nuclear Fuel Cycle: A Survey of the Public Health, Environmental, and National Security Effects of Nuclear Power* (Rev. ed.). Cambridge: Massachusetts Institute of Technology Press, 1975.

United Nations Association of the U.S.A. *World Population.* New York: UNA-USA National Policy Panel, 1969.

U.S. Bureau of the Census. *1970 Census of Population: Subject Reports: Educational Attainment. Final Report PC(2)–5B.* Washington, D. C.: U.S. Government Printing Office, 1973.

U.S. Bureau of the Census. *Statistical Abstract of the United States: 1975* (96th ed.). Washington, D. C.: U.S. Government Printing Office, 1975.

U.S. Department of Health, Education, and Welfare. *Toward a Social Report.* Washington, D. C.: U.S. Government Printing Office, 1969.

U.S. Department of Labor, Women's Bureau. *The Myth and the Reality* (Pamphlet No. 2916–00015). Washington, D.C.: U.S. Government Printing Office, 1974.

U.S. News & World Report. Rip-offs from U.S. arms stockpiles. March 1, 1976, pp. 22–23. (a)

U.S. News & World Report. Why new uproar over abortions. March 1, 1976, pp. 14–15. (b)

U.S. Senate, Government Operations Committee. *Confidence and Concern: Citizens View American Government, A Survey of Public Attitudes.* Washington, D.C.: U.S. Government Printing Office, 1973.

Varela, J. A. *Psychological Solutions to Social Problems: An Introduction to Social Technology.* New York: Academic Press, 1971.

Vogel, S. R., Broverman, I. K., Broverman, D. M., Clarkson, F. E., & Rosenkrantz, P. S. Maternal employment and perception of sex roles among college students. *Developmental Psychology*, 1970, 3, 384–391.

Wade, S., & Schramm, W. The mass media as sources of public affairs, science, and health knowledge. *Public Opinion Quarterly*, 1969, 33, 197–209.

Walster, E., Aronson, E., & Abrahams, D. On increasing the persuasiveness of a low prestige communicator. *Journal of Experimental Social Psychology*, 1966, 2, 325–342.

Walster, E., Berscheid, E., Abrahams, D., & Aronson, V. Effectiveness of debriefing following deception experiments. *Journal of Personality and Social Psychology*, 1967, 6, 371–380.

Wang, C. K. A. Suggested criteria for writing attitude statements. *Journal of Social Psychology*, 1932, 3, 367–373.

Watts, W., & Free, L. A. *State of the Nation.* New York: Universe Books, 1973.

Watts, W., & Free, L. A. *State of the Nation 1974.* Washington, D.C.: Potomac Associates, 1974.

Watts, W. A. Relative persistence of opinion change induced by active compared to passive participation. *Journal of Personality and Social Psychology*, 1967, 5, 4–15.

Watts, W. A., & McGuire, W. J. Persistence of induced opinion change and retention of inducing message content. *Journal of Abnormal and Social Psychology*, 1964, 68, 233–241.

Webb, E. J., Campbell, D. T., Schwartz, R. D., & Sechrest, L. *Unobtrusive Measures: Nonreactive Research in the Social Sciences.* Chicago: Rand McNally, 1966.

Weber, S. J., & Cook, T. D. Subject effects in laboratory research: An examination of subject roles, demand characteristics, and valid inference. *Psychological Bulletin*, 1972, 77, 273–295.

Weigel, R. H., & Newman, L. S. Increasing attitude-behavior correspondence by broadening the scope of the behavioral measure. *Journal of Personality and Social Psychology*, 1976, 33, 793–802.

Weigel, R. H., Wiser, P. L., & Cook, S. W. The impact of cooperative learning experiences on cross-ethnic relations and attitudes. *Journal of Social Issues*, 1975, 31(1), 219–244.

Weiner, M. J., & Wright, F. E. Effects of undergoing arbitrary discrimination upon subsequent attitudes toward a minority group. *Journal of Applied Social Psychology*, 1973, 3, 94–102.

Weiss, C. H. Do research results affect policymaking—and how? *Public Opinion Quarterly*, 1972, 36, 451–452.

Weiss, R. F. An extension of Hullian learning theory to persuasive communication. In A. G. Greenwald, T. C. Brock, & T. M. Ostrom (Eds.), *Psychological Foundations of Attitudes.* New York: Academic Press, 1968. Pp. 109–145.

Weiss, W. Effects of the mass media of communication. In G. Lindzey & E. Aronson (Eds.), *The Handbook of Social Psychology* (2nd ed.). Vol. 5. Reading, Mass.: Addison-Wesley, 1969. Pp. 77–195.

Weisstein, N. Psychology constructs the female. In V. Gornick and B. K. Moran (Eds.), *Woman in Sexist Society: Studies in Power and Powerlessness.* New York: Basic Books, 1971. Pp. 207–224.

Weitzman, L. G., Eifler, D., Hokada, E., & Ross, C. Sex-role socialization in picture books for preschool children. *American Journal of Sociology*, 1972, 77, 1125–1149.

Westie, F. R., & DeFleur, M. L. Autonomic responses and their relationship to race attitudes. *Journal of Abnormal and Social Psychology*, 1959, 58, 340–347.

Westoff, C. F. The modernization of U.S. contraceptive practice. *Family Planning Perspectives*, 1972, 4, 9–12.

Westoff, C. F., & Ryder, N. B. Recent trends in attitudes toward fertility control and in the practice of contraception in the United States. In S. J. Behrman, L. Corsa, & R. Freedman (Eds.), *Fertility and Family Planning: A World View.* Ann Arbor: University of Michigan Press, 1969. Pp. 388–412.

White, R. K. Misconceptions in Soviet and American images. Paper presented at American Psychological Association meeting, New York, September, 1961.

White, R. K. Images in the context of international conflict: Soviet perceptions of the

U.S. and the U.S.S.R. In H. C. Kelman (Ed.), *International Behavior: A Social-Psychological Analysis*. New York: Holt, Rinehart & Winston, 1965. Pp. 238–276.

White, R. K. "Socialism" and "capitalism": An international misunderstanding. *Foreign Affairs*, 1966, 44, 216–228.

White, R. K. *Nobody Wanted War: Misperception in Vietnam and Other Wars* (Rev. ed.). Garden City, N. Y.: Doubleday, 1970.

Wicker, A. W. Attitudes versus actions: The relationship of verbal and overt behavioral responses to attitude objects. *Journal of Social Issues*, 1969, 25(4), 41–78.

Wicker, A. W. An examination of the "other variables" explanation of attitude-behavior inconsistency. *Journal of Personality and Social Psychology*, 1971, 19, 18–30.

Wilcox, L. D., Brooks, R. M., Beal, G. M., & Klonglan, G. E. *Social Indicators and Societal Monitoring: An Annotated Bibliography*. San Francisco: Jossey-Bass, 1972.

Wilcox, W. The congressional poll—and non-poll. In E. C. Dreyer & W. A. Rosenbaum (Eds.), *Political Opinion and Electoral Behavior: Essays and Studies*. Belmont, Calif.: Wadsworth, 1966. Pp. 390–400.

Wilker, H. R., & Milbrath, L. W. Political belief systems and political behavior. *Social Science Quarterly*, 1970, 51, 477–493.

Willeke, G. E. Effects of water pollution in San Francisco Bay. Report EEP-29, Project on Engineering-Economic Planning, Stanford University, October, 1968.

Wilson, G. D. (Ed.). *The Psychology of Conservatism*. London: Academic Press, 1973.

Wilson, W. Rank order of discrimination and its relevance to civil rights priorities. *Journal of Personality and Social Psychology*, 1970, 15, 118–124.

Wilson, W., & Miller, H. Repetition, order of presentation, and timing of arguments and measures as determinants of opinion change. *Journal of Personality and Social Psychology*, 1968, 9, 184–188.

Wise, D. The twilight of a president. *New York Times Magazine*, November 3, 1968, p. 27.

Withey, S. *Consistency of Immediate and Delayed Report of Financial Data*. Unpublished doctoral dissertation, University of Michigan, 1952.

Wolpert, J. Migration as an adjustment to environmental stress. *Journal of Social Issues*, 1966, 22(4), 92–102.

Women on Words and Images. *Channeling Children: Sex Stereotyping on Prime Time TV*. Princeton, N.J.: Women on Words and Images, 1975. (a)

Women on Words and Images. *Dick and Jane as Victims: Sex Stereotyping in Children's Readers*. Princeton, N.J.: Women on Words and Images, 1975. (b)

Woodmansee, J. J. The pupil response as a measure of social attitudes. In G. F. Summers (Ed.), *Attitude Measurement*. Chicago: Rand McNally, 1970. Pp. 514–533.

Wrightsman, L. S. Wallace supporters and adherence to "law and order." *Journal of Personality and Social Psychology*, 1969, 13, 17–22.

Wrightsman, L. S. *Social Psychology in the Seventies*. Monterey, Calif.: Brooks/Cole, 1972.

Zajonc, R. B. The concepts of balance, congruity, and dissonance. *Public Opinion Quarterly*, 1960, 24, 280–296.

Zajonc, R. B. Attitudinal effects of mere exposure. *Journal of Personality and Social Psychology*, 1968, 9(2, Pt. 2), 1–27. (a)

Zajonc, R. B. Cognitive theories in social psychology. In G. Lindzey & E. Aronson (Eds.), *The Handbook of Social Psychology* (2nd ed.). Vol. 1. Reading, Mass.: Addison-Wesley, 1968. Pp. 320–411. (b)

Zajonc, R. B. Brainwash: Familiarity breeds comfort. *Psychology Today,* 1970, 3(9), 33–35 & 60–64.

Zalkind, S. S., Gaugler, E. A., & Schwartz, R. M. Civil liberties attitudes and personality measures: Some exploratory research. *Journal of Social Issues*, 1975, 31(2), 77–91.

Zanna, M. P., Kiesler, C. A., & Pilkonis, P. A. Positive and negative attitudinal affect established by classical conditioning. *Journal of Personality and Social Psychology*, 1970, 14, 321–328.

Zavalloni, M., & Cook, S. W. Influence of judges' attitudes on ratings of favorableness of statements about a social group. *Journal of Personality and Social Psychology*, 1965, 1, 43–54.

Ziegler, F. J. Vasectomy and adverse psychological reactions. *The Annual of Internal Medicine*, 1970, 73, 853.

Zikmund, J. A comparison of political attitude and activity patterns in central cities and suburbs. *Public Opinion Quarterly*, 1967, 31, 69–75.

Zimbardo, P. G. Involvement and communication discrepancy as determinants of opinion conformity. *Journal of Abnormal and Social Psychology*, 1960, 60, 86–94.

Zimbardo, P. G., & Meadow, W. Sexism springs eternal—in *The Reader's Digest*. Paper presented at Western Psychological Association meeting, San Francisco, April, 1974.

Zimbardo, P. G., Weisenberg, M., Firestone, I., & Levy, B. Communicator effectiveness in producing public conformity and private attitude change. *Journal of Personality*, 1965, 33, 233–255.

Name Index

Subject Index